MW01625530

Also in the Variorum Collected Studies Series

COLIN HEYWOOD
Writing Ottoman History: Documents and Interpretations

FEDWA MALTI-DOUGLAS
Power, Marginality, and the Body in Medieval Islam

ANDRÉ RAYMOND
Arab Cities in the Ottoman Period: Cairo, Syria and the Maghreb

MICHAEL BRETT
Ibn Khaldun and the Medieval Maghrib

WAEL B. HALLAQ
Law and Legal Theory in Classical and Medieval Islam

MICHAEL LECKER
Jews and Arabs in Pre-and Early Islamic Arabia

G.H.A. JUYNBOLL
Studies on the Origins and Uses of Islamic Hadith

NEHEMIA LEVTZION
Islam in West Africa: Religion, Society and Politics to 1800

NICHOLAS LOWICK edited by JOE CRIBB
Coinage and History of the Islamic World

NICHOLAS LOWICK edited by JOE CRIBB
Islamic Coins and Trade in the Medieval World

R. B. SERJEANT edited by G. REX SMITH
Farmers and Fishermen in Arabia: Studies in Customary Law and Practice

SHAUL SHAKED
From Zoroastrian Iran to Islam: Studies in Religious History and Intercultural Contacts

GEORGE MAKDISI
Religion, Law and Learning in Classical Islam

WILFERD MADELUNG
Religious Schools and Sects in Medieval Islam

VARIORUM COLLECTED STUDIES SERIES

The Qur'an and its Interpretative Tradition

Professor Andrew Rippin

Andrew Rippin

The Qur'an and its Interpretative Tradition

Aldershot · Burlington USA · Singapore · Sydney

Published in the Variorum Collected Studies Series by

Ashgate Publishing Limited
Gower House, Croft Road,
Aldershot, Hampshire GU11 3HR
Great Britain

Ashgate Publishing Company
131 Main Street,
Burlington, Vermont 05401–5600
USA

Ashgate website: http://www.ashgate.com

ISBN 0–86078–848–2

British Library Cataloguing-in-Publication Data
Rippin, Andrew
The Qur'an and its Interpretative Tradition. (Variorum Collected Studies Series: CS715).
1. Koran – Criticism, Interpretation, etc.
I. Title.
297.1'226

US Library of Congress Cataloging-in-Publication Data
Rippin, Andrew.
The Qur'an and its Interpretative Tradition. / Andrew Rippin.
p. cm. (Variorum Collected Studies Series: CS715).
Includes bibliograhical references and indexes.
1. Koran – Commentaries – History and Criticism. 2. Koran – Criticism, Interpretation, etc. I. Title. II. Collected Studies: CS715.
BP130.45.R56 2001
297.1'226–dc21 2001022820

The paper used in this publication meets the minimum requirements of the American National Standard for Information Sciences – Permanence of Paper for Printed Library Materials, ANSI Z39.48–1984. ∞ ™

Printed by St Edmundsbury Press, Bury St Edmunds, Suffolk

VARIORUM COLLECTED STUDIES SERIES CS715

CONTENTS

This volume consists of xx + 336 pages

PUBLISHER'S NOTE

The articles in this volume, as in all others in the Collected Studies Series, have not been given a new, continuous pagination. In order to avoid confusion, and to facilitate their use where these same studies have been referred to elsewhere, the original pagination has been maintained wherever possible.

Each article has been given a Roman numeral in order of appearance, as listed in the Contents. This number is repeated on each page and quoted in the index entries.

INTRODUCTION

At the beginning of 1999[1] an article was published in the American popular magazine *The Atlantic Monthly* entitled "What is the Koran?" written by Toby Lester.[2] This was the first occasion, at least in recent decades, that the academic study of the Qur'ān had been brought to the attention of the general reading public. Suddenly, I had colleagues in far-flung disciplines who saw my field of study as one of importance and controversy. Not everyone in the field was happy with the attention, however. Some specialists especially complained about the journalistic, even sensationalistic approach taken by the author. That is, of course, an odd charge, suggesting a rather naïve view of the popular media. That a journalistic piece of writing should appear in a journalistic magazine is surely to be expected. It is likely, however, that the real objection stemmed from a different concern, that of the fear of letting the broader Muslim public know what scholars theorize about the foundations of Islam. Indeed, the reaction of many Muslims, both academics and the more general English-reading Muslim public, was one of disbelief that historiographical issues related to the rise of Islam should evoke such concern on the part of scholars. The dogmas of the divine origins of the Qur'ān and the inimitable character of its language are firmly embedded in the Muslim faith such that challenging them seriously enters the range of the "unthinkable".

The article "What is the Koran?" speaks of the recent tendency in some scholarly works to postulate a different account of Islam's origins than that which the faith community itself puts forth. Such works either

[1] Parts of this paper were previously presented in different forms at the University of Bologna, the University of Alberta and the University of British Columbia.

[2] Toby Lester, "What is the Koran?" *The Atlantic Monthly*, 283, i (January 1999), 43-56. The text of the article is available on the Web in *The Atlantic Monthly* archives (http://www.theatlantic.com/issues/99jan/koran.htm). The article provoked a number of other discussions of the Koran in the popular media; see, for example, Abul Taher, "Querying the Koran", *The Guardian*, August 8, 2000 (available online at http://www.guardianunlimited.co.uk//Archive/Article/0,4273,4048586,00.html). Readers who need further basic information on some of the subtleties which the issues raise in relationship to the Qur'ān will be well served by reading Michael Cook, *The Koran: a very short introduction*, Oxford, 2000, which is without a doubt the most lucid presentation available which also takes advantage of extensive current research. Cook is especially lucid in explaining the significance of variant readings and the writing of the text.

claim that Islam had its founding moment outside the Arabian peninsula or argue that so little is known of the formative period of Islam, other than the accounts provided by hagiographies of Muḥammad, that any reconstruction is necessarily no better than the tendentious sources upon which it is based. A key part of this approach to Islam, and the element which has undoubtedly created the greatest amount of controversy, relates to ideas about the formation of the Qurʾān.

Lester's article expresses interest in these theories especially in so far as historical evidence might support them. The stimulus for this discussion is a significant group of Qurʾān manuscripts found at Sana'a in the Yemen. This treasure trove of ancient manuscripts was discovered in 1972 during renovations to the Great Mosque. In 1979 a German team of scholars started working through some 12,000 fragments of parchment and paper, some of which (22 groups of fragments) have been dated to the eighth century primarily on the basis of their use of the early Arabic script of the *Ḥijāzī* style. This discovery has excited a good deal of scholarly and popular interest. The existence of early copies of the text of the Qurʾān might well be thought to help answer some of the riddles about its composition. So far, however, that has not been the outcome and only very tentative conclusions have been put forth.

Certainly, the existence of manuscripts of the Qurʾān from this early time indicates that the text – or, at the very least, substantial parts of it – existed in some sort of collected form by the eighth century. That, of course, does not tell us anything about the status of the text itself within the community of believers. Some discrepancies in the order of the *sūra*s found in a few manuscripts may indicate some variability in the overall form of the text. More interesting, though, is the fact that the text contains variant readings of a minor nature that suggest to some scholars that the idea of an oral tradition running parallel to the written one cannot be given full historical credence. What we may have evidence of in these manuscripts is the interpretative nature of the detailed notations in the Arabic script which were added to the text later; that is, the current accepted text might be viewed as the product of reflection upon a primitive written text and not upon the parallel transmission of an oral text as the Muslim tradition has suggested.

This, of course, is a very controversial notion. While the Muslim tradition has paid a good deal of attention to accounting for the physical collection of the Qurʾān, it has always done so in a somewhat unresolved manner by placing the collection stories alongside a parallel oral transmission of the text. Generally, Muḥammad himself is excluded from any role in the collection of the text, although it is possible to find some accounts which talk of him going over the whole text with ᶜAlī, his cousin, son-in-law and figurehead of the later Shīᶜa. Zayd ibn Thābit, a companion of Muḥammad, is generally credited with an early collection of the scripture, and the pages of that assembled text are said to have been entrusted to Ḥafṣa, one of Muḥammad's wives. Under the instructions of ᶜUthmān, the third ruler of the empire after the death of Muḥammad, the major collection of the text "as we now have it" (as traditional Muslim claims express it) is said to have taken place. Working on the basis of pieces of text written "on palm leaves or flat stones or in the hearts of men", the complete text (deemed to have survived in full) was written out and distributed to the major centres of the early empire. Thus, within thirty years of the death of Muḥammad, it is understood that the Qurʾān existed in its fixed, if skeletal form; theologically, it is held that the form in which the text existed at that point was an image of the "heavenly tablet", suggesting that its structure and content were precisely that which God desired for it.[3] From this skeleton text, which marked only the consonants of the Arabic script in a rudimentary form, the final text of the Qurʾān was developed over the next two centuries, such that all the subtleties of the language and the script were indicated. Most important from the Muslim perspective, it is held that an oral tradition preserved the full text from the time of its revelation, the written form serving only as a mnemonic device for the memorization of the text. Within Muslim tradition there are, thus, two ways of dealing with the Qurʾān: the oral, the tradition about which stems from Muḥammad, and the written, the tradition stemming from the caliph ᶜUthmān.

However, the evidence of some of the early manuscripts, it has been suggested, seems to indicate otherwise. Rather, it appears that there was a stage at which the written text of the Qurʾān was analyzed and determined as to its meaning and pronunciation on the basis of a skeleton consonantal text with no reference to a living oral tradition.

[3] See John Burton, *The Collection of the Qurʾān*, Cambridge, 1977, for a treatment of these various accounts and their potential significance.

That, at least, is the implication of the studies of some of those who have looked at the early manuscript evidence closely.

European scholarship since the nineteenth century has paid a great deal of attention to the accounts of the physical collection of the Qurʾān, attempting to resolve what have been perceived to be the internal inconsistencies in the various Muslim stories and to construct one scenario which would really "make sense". While recognition has been given to the oral tradition of transmission, no scholar has ever seriously worked that into the consideration. Scholarship has always worked on the supposition of a written transmission as being most important in the overall picture of the emergence of Islam. Consider Arthur Jeffery, writing in 1946 on the textual history of the Qurʾān:

> Faced with a bare consonantal text the reader obviously had to interpret it. He had to decide whether a certain sign was a *shīn* or a *sīn*, a *ṣād* or a *ḍād,* a *fā* or a *qāf*, and so on; and when he had settled that he had further to decide whether to read a verbal form as an active or a passive, whether to treat a certain word as a verb or a noun, since it might be either, and so on. In the first generation this problem would not have been so serious for the Qurrāʾ, for memory of what the text should be would in many passages decide the matter of how it was to be pointed and vowelled, and where the pauses that governed the meaning should be. Theoretically, one could suppose that this oral tradition as to how the text should be read could be transmitted carefully from generation to generation, as was the case with the old poetry, but actually the enormous body of variant readings that has been recorded proves that there was no consistent tradition on this matter transmitted.[4]

So, Jeffery argued from the existence of the variants that no consistent oral tradition was significant and thus that the written text must have been taken as primary by Muslims in finalizing the Qurʾānic text as we

[4] Arthur Jeffery, "A textual history of the Qurʾan", *Journal of the Middle East* Society, 1 (1947) reprinted in his *The Qurʾān as scripture*, New York, 1952, 97.

know it. Some have certainly argued that this is a cultural bias on the part of western scholarship with its overall preference for the written over the oral and its failure to understand oral transmission.[5]

It is instructive to compare this treatment of the oral and written versions to the more traditional presentation of Muhammad Abdel Haleem published in the *Islamic Quarterly*. Speaking of the earliest written form of the Qurʾān, he states,

> There was no distinction between letters of the alphabet of similar shape and there were no vowel marks. This may now give the impression that such a system must have given rise to great confusion in reading. This was not actually the case because the morphological patterns of words in Arabic enable readers to read even very unfamiliar material without the short vowels being marked. More important, however, as far as the Qurʾān was concerned, was the fact that learning and reading relied above all on oral transmission. In the Islamic tradition, writing remained a secondary aid... .[6]

It should be noted how the problem of similarly shaped characters is glossed over in Abdel Haleem's position. In essence, the appeal is directly to the oral tradition. Abdel Haleem suggests that the text needs no dots or dashes. When one puts this alongside G. R. Puin's charge, as quoted in *The Atlantic Monthly* article, that one-fifth of the Qurʾān is unintelligible as it stands, it is clear that Abdel Haleem and Puin are simply not discussing the issue from a common set of presuppositions, given that the former says that morphological patterns solve all the problems of Arabic.

As a further example, and a more extreme one, a series of articles written by James Bellamy is illustrative.[7] Bellamy argues that the very

[5] See William Graham, *Beyond the written word: Oral aspects of scripture in the history of religion*, Cambridge, 1987.

[6] Muhammad Abdel Haleem, "Qurʾānic orthography: the written representation of the recited text of the Qurʾān", *Islamic Quarterly*, 38 (1994), 172 (available on the Web at http://www. Islamic-awareness.org/Quran/Text/Scribal/haleem.html

[7] James A. Bellamy, "The mysterious letters of the Koran: Old abbreviations of the Basmalah", *Journal of the American Oriental Society*, 93 (1973), 267-85; "Fa-ummuhu hāwiyah: A note on surah 101:9", *Journal of the American Oriental Society* 112 (1992), 485-7; "Al-Raqīm

shape of the letters in the primitive Arabic script has led to numerous problematic passages in the Qur'an that can be solved by assuming a fairly consistent pattern of mis-readings (combined with slips of the pen and the like). Bellamy certainly represents most starkly the view that the textual tradition of the Qurʾān is the "real" one and that the oral tradition has played little or no part in its preservation. Bellamy's arguments are based on the suppositions of the discipline of textual criticism, which looks to solve textual problems through a series of set explanations: preferring a more difficult text over a correction which produces a simpler one, for example. He does not introduce into the argument any particular evidence for the presupposition about the transmission of the text and simply ignores any consideration of the oral tradition.

As Jeffery's writings suggest, the evidence for the irrelevance of the oral tradition was, in earlier scholarship, sought in the mass of variant readings to the Qurʾānic text which the Muslim tradition has preserved. This approach provoked more scholarly frustration than historical evidence. Some of my own earlier studies which are included in this volume illustrate why this is so. Through studies concerned with variant readings related to words in Qurʾān 7/40, 21/95, and 78/24 (articles VII, VIII, IX), it is possible to see that the variant reading traditions are tendentious, but it is impossible to determine the "original" reading on any firm basis. (Such issues are also illustrated by studies of lexicography[8] which show a willingness to manipulate meaning, often in tandem with variant readings; see articles XX, XXI). In the context of the article in *The Atlantic Monthly*, observations about the existence of variant readings also provoked the correct response that Muslims have always understood that there are variants to the text of the Qurʾān and that this is the "orthodox" position. There is no problem with variants, regardless of how their existence may be explained. Of course, it is a fact that popular Muslim opinion, which I often hear from students these days, is that the Qurʾān is the same down to the smallest dot in every

or al Ruqūd? A Note on Surah 18:9", *Journal of the American Oriental Society* 111 (1991), 115-17; "Some proposed emendations to the text of the Koran", *Journal of the American Oriental Society* 113 (1993), 562-73.

[8] Also see my "The designation of 'foreign' languages in the exegesis of the Qurʾān", in J. McAuliffe, B. Walfish, J. Goering (eds), *With reverence for the word. Medieval scriptural exegesis in Judaism, Christianity and Islam*, Oxford, forthcoming, and my essay "Foreign vocabulary", in Jane D. McAuliffe (ed.), *Encyclopaedia of the Qurʾān,* Leiden, forthcoming.

copy you consult; that "common wisdom" is simply wrong. In fact, the underlying point in this popular view always returns to a defense of the integrity of the text of the Qurʾān on the basis of the oral tradition and not the written text.

The material which was highlighted in *The Atlantic Monthly* article, however, suggests that, with early manuscripts of the Qurʾān especially those from the Yemen (but a significant number of other such texts exist, for example in London, Paris, the Vatican and St. Petersburg[9]), we have found different grounds for an understanding of the formation of the text. By means of the evidence provided in these early manuscripts examples can be given of instances in which words, because of the way they were written in the primitive script of the time, were likely mispronounced as a result of a misunderstanding of the script. This argues for the absence of a firm oral tradition. The relevance of this may be seen in some examples of proper names, the philological origin of which has remained somewhat of mystery to scholarship.[10] These include the name Ibrāhīm, more easily and better understood in a version closer to the Hebrew if read Abrāhām, and Shayṭān, once again closer to the Hebrew if read Sāṭān. Both of these developed readings depend upon the misunderstanding of the early writing of the long "a" sound in the middle of the word. In these early manuscripts, this sound is sometimes represented by a *yāʾ*. Over time, that tradition of writing was forgotten and its remnants are seen in the developed text of the Qurʾān only at the end of words with the writing of a long "a" as an *alif maqṣūra*. At some point, this *yāʾ* was read according to the rules of classical Arabic orthography and pronounced as a long "i" or the diphthong "ay" rather than the long "a" which it represented originally.[11]

[9] See Efim A. Rezvan, "Yet another "Uthmānic Qurʾān"", *Manuscripta Orientalia*, 6 (2000), 49-68 and the bibliography cited therein; also see E. A. Rezvan, *The Qurʾān and its world*, forthcoming.

[10] See, for example, Arthur Jeffery, *The foreign vocabulary of the Quran*, Baroda, 1938, 44-6 on Ibrāhīm ("the form would thus seem to be due to Muḥammad himself but the immediate source is not easy to determine"); 187-90 on Shayṭān.

[11] Gerd-R. Puin, "Neue Wege der Koranforschung: II. Über die Bedeutung der ältesten Koranfragmente aus Sanaa (Jemen) für die Orthographiegeschichte des Korans", *Universität des Saarlandes Magazin Forschung*, 1 (1999), 37-40, esp. 40 (available on the Web at http://www.uni-saarland.de/verwalt/kwt/f-magazin/1-99/Neue_Wege.pdf). Christoph Luxenberg, *Die syro-aramäische Lesart des Koran. Ein Beitrag zur Entschlüsselung der Koransprache*, Berlin, 2000, has recently argued that Syriac may prove to the background against which many other "difficult" readings in the Qurʾān may be profitably read. While many of the suggested textual

One response to these observations has arisen[12] which suggests that the manuscripts with such readings are, in fact, flawed and this is why they were discarded in the trash pile in Sana'a. Scholars have been deceived into thinking that, because the texts have survived, they have some historical value; that may not be the case, it is said. Indeed, in the history of manuscript studies, this is a familiar argument. It is, or at least was, one way of dealing with the Dead Sea Scrolls in relationship to the text of the Bible. Of course, the claim cannot be denied outright, but the existence of a consistent pattern of the writing of Arabic as in this case of using the internal *yāʾ* to represent a long "a" seems to suggest otherwise because of the very consistency of the usage in the manuscripts.

It is fair to say, then, that the manuscript tradition may have a significant implications for our understanding of the early history of the text of the Qurʾān. The study of these manuscripts is in its infancy, however, and the impact of these texts has yet really to be felt. The value and the point of the stories about the collection of the Qurʾān remain under debate among scholars. Regardless of the final outcome of all the discussions, one thing remains quite clear. The Qurʾān is, and has been from the beginning of the emergence of Islam as a firmly established religion, the primary point to which reference must always be made in order to define something as "Islamic". The Qurʾān is the defining point of Islamic identity. The emergence of the Muslim community is intimately connected with the emergence of the Qurʾān as an authoritative text in making decisions on matters of law and theology. What research has revealed is that scripture's status and authority was debated in early times, especially between the various religious communities of the Near East and also within the newly-emerging Islamic community itself. Elements of the process by which the Qurʾān emerged as the authoritative source, side-by-side with the emergence of the community of Islam itself, can be traced in the writing of various texts of Qurʾānic interpretation (*tafsīr*) in the early centuries of Islam,[13] in early works of law, and in several documents of inter-

emendations found in the book are arbitrary, the attention to orthographic matters on the basis of observations about the early Arabic script are especially welcome.

[12] Ali Mazrui, in *Islamic Horizons*, September-October 1999, 30.

[13] A point which originates with John Wansbrough, *Quranic studies: sources and methods of scriptural interpretation*, Oxford, 1977, part 4, on which see articles II and VI herein. Also see

religious polemic. The ultimate enshrinement of the text of the Qurʾān as we now know it, understood to be literally the word of God, miraculous, inimitable, linked to an illiterate prophet, which thereby gained its authority within the community, was the result of two to three centuries of vigorous debate as reflected in these texts of interpretation as well as in the evolution of the actual text of scripture.

A majority of the studies included in this volume are attempts to explain and show the implications of that position as they are displayed in early writing of *tafsīr*. The methodological point is made explicit in articles V and VI, both of which suggest that the debate which is witnessed in the early texts must be understood in the context of a very fluid system of Islam and as a part of the process of Islam reaching its self-definition. Detailed studies of texts ascribed to Ibn ʿAbbās (articles XIII, XIV, and XV) and al-Zuhrī (article XVI) attempt to make this point at least implicitly. Likewise, the material on the *asbāb al-nuzūl* in articles XVII, XVIII, and XIX emphasize the construction of a narrative framework for understanding the Qurʾān as an act which was exegetical in intent and by no means an "objective" reading of the text in light of history as might have naïvely been thought; such a history had to be created in order to substantiate and fix both scripture and Islam itself.[14]

It has always been my aspiration in these studies of the *tafsīr* tradition to demonstrate that a greater appreciation of the historical development of the attitude towards scripture could be attained by studying the progression of the evidence of what Muslims themselves said about the text. Variants, for example, become a part of the evidence for Muslim attempts to extract a meaning which coheres with that which is needed by the Muslim community. To put it in other words, demands which are "external" to the text required that the text be "brought into alignment" with those demands. In a series of essays reprinted here I attempt to argue variations on that theme, sometimes more successfully than others. Perhaps it is a measure both of the lack of reflection upon the process of studying *tafsīr* within the discipline of Islamic studies but

Herbert Berg, *The development of exegesis in Islam. The authenticity of Muslim literature from the formative period*, Richmond, 2000.

[14] For a somewhat different view of the *asbāb al-nuzūl* see Uri Rubin, *The eye of the beholder: the life of Muḥammad as viewed by the early Muslims*, Princeton, 1995, chapter 14.

also the very youthfulness of the field of study itself[15] that my early attempt in article I, "The Qur'an as literature: perils, pitfalls and prospects" continues to draw some interest along with some more recent but less direct attempts included in articles III and IV. Recent works by Daniel Madigan[16] and David Marshall[17] have rejected my attempt in preference to a more traditional approach of reading the text within the context of a (supposed) life of Muḥammad. There is clearly still a lot of work to do in pursuing the approach to Islam suggested in some of my articles. There remains a great need for understanding the texts of *tafsīr* themselves within their own historical contexts, a task which the encyclopaedia article on *tafsīr*, article X, broaches and which has been provided with more detail not only in my *Encyclopaedia of Islam* article on *tafsīr* but also by the significant work of scholars such as Claude Gilliot.[18] But, too, my own work has now led me to argue that when we do wish to speak of the Qurʾān itself and its world, then we must do so within the context of a broadly conceived Near Eastern monotheism.[19] The significance of this I ultimately see as unfolding into an overall theme that is due to be worked out in along-delayed book: that Muslim *tafsīr* has taken a work – the Qurʾān – that is the product of the Mediterranean religious mind and transformed it into the Muslim text we know. This role of the interpretation – which can be witnessed in other religious traditions as well[20] – can be better understood when it is viewed in light of a Qurʾān which has been liberated from the shackles of the exegetical tradition which makes certain presumptions about the

[15] I have emphasized this in the introduction to my edited volume *The Qur'an: formative interpretation*, Aldershot, 1999, xi-xii, and in the bibliographical article XI included here.

[16] Daniel Madigan, "Reflections on some current directions in Qurʾanic studies", *The Muslim World*, 85 (1995), 345-62.

[17] David Marshall, *God, Muhammad the unbelievers: a Qurʾanic study*, Richmond, 1999, especially section 1.1.c.

[18] A major statement in that direction is in his article on Central Asian *tafsīr:* Claude Gilliot "L'exégèse du Coran en Asie Centrale et au Khorasan", *Studia Islamica*, 89 (1999), 129-64.

[19] See my studies "The poetics of Qur'anic punning," *Bulletin of the School of Oriental and African Studies*, 57 (1994), 193-207; "The commerce of eschatology", in S. Wild (ed.), *The Koran as text*, Leiden, 1996, 125-35; "'Desiring the face of God': the Qur'anic symbolism of personal responsibility", in Issa J. Boullata (ed.), *Literary aspects of religious meaning in the Qurʾān*, Richmond, 2000, 117-24; "Muhammad in the Qurʾān: reading scripture in the 21st century", in Harald Motzki (ed.), *The Biography of the Prophet Muhammad: the Issue of the Sources*, Leiden, 2000, 298-309.

[20] See Frances Young, *Biblical exegesis and the formation of Christian culture*, Cambridge, 1997.

text seem "natural" or matters of "common sense" to the reader. This has been accomplished precisely because the interpretative tradition has been so successful in its approach to the text. To appreciate this accomplishment, we must first be able to read the Qurʾān within a background freed of the Muslim construct. Then, in returning to the works of *tafsīr*, we can achieve a better measure of the incredible creativity and accomplishment of the past masters of the exegetical imagination.

ACKNOWLEDGEMENTS

Grateful acknowledgement is made to the following persons, editors publishers and institutions for their kind permission to reprint the articles included in this volume: British Society for Middle East Studies, Durham (I); The University of Arizona Press, Tucson (II); E.J. Brill NV, Leiden (III, VI, VIII); the American Oriental Society, Ann Arbor (IV); Walter de Gruyter GmbH & Co. KG, Berlin (V); Oxford University Press (VII, IX, XIII, XIV, XVI, XVII, XIX, XX); the Gale Group, Farmington Hill (X); *The Muslim World*, Hartford (XI); Taylor & Francis, Andover (XII); the Institute of Asian and African Studies, Jerusalem (XV, XXII); *Islamic Culture*, Hyderabad (XVIII).

I

THE QUR'AN AS LITERATURE: PERILS, PITFALLS AND PROSPECTS

This paper is a revised version of a lecture given on January 19, 1982 in the Faculty of Humanities, University of Calgary. I would like to thank Dr Barbara Belyea, Department of English, University of Calgary for her kind invitation to present a paper in her lecture series 'Theories of Literature'. My thanks are also due, as always, to Dr J.Wansbrough of SOAS, London (A.R.).

i

The discipline of religious studies still seems to be very much afraid for its existence as a legitimate enterprise as distinct from theology, philosophy, history or even literature. As a result, its practitioners generally prefer to go about their business without letting other disciplines know precisely what it is they are doing. To suggest in the title of this paper, therefore, that literature and the Qur'ān may in some ways be brought together is to run the risk of attracting a certain amount of unaccustomed attention from certain other disciplines. Yet it is precisely this kind of attention and resultant fresh input which our discipline needs so badly in order to bring it out of its shell and into the dynamics of modern scholarly interaction.

At the same time, I am well aware of the potential pitfalls in any discussion of a topic such as the Qur'ān and literature; the dangers of dabbling in a field that is outside one's own true domain are very real -- one's dabbling is likely to be uncovered rather quickly by those who know better. So, rather than be over bold in this paper and enunciate a specific approach or set of assumptions with regard to literature -- a task which is certainly valuable -- I will simply do something which seems equally important, given the state of our discipline, and urge at least some degree of methodological awareness. It is important that we all know to some extent in what kind of assumptions we are involved when we sit down and study our texts and what the limits are concerning precisely what one can say as a result of our theoretical assumptions. What I hope to do in this paper, then, is to sketch out some of the issues that are at stake when it is suggested that we may take the Qur'ān as literature and then to suggest some of the positive and negative results and implications of adopting that approach.

For the benefit of non-Arabists and others unacquainted with the Qur'ān, a word or two about the latter are called for. The Qur'ān is a shortish book, generally said to be roughly the same length as the New Testament, and is divided up into 114 chapters of various lengths. The book could be described as a structuralist's dream text, one in which the Barthesian 'power of the text' will take some work to extract. (I should point out at once that structuralist analyses of the Qur'ān have not

I

progressed very far at all[1]). The text of the Qur'ān has little logical arrangement over and above a mechanical criterion of the length of the chapter, and that is only loosely employed: the text is arranged with the longest chapter towards the beginning and the shortest at the end; the only major exception to that rule is the first chapter, a short prayer which opens the book. Even within many of the chapters themselves there would appear to be, in a surface reading, no particular thematic, historical, literary or didactic unity. A given chapter of the Qur'ān will talk of salvation in general, then turn abruptly to the ancient Hebrew prophets, then discuss points of law for the Muslim community, and, finally, summarize polemical discussions taking place in the Near Eastern sectarian religious milieu. In literary form, then, the Qur'ān is nothing like the Bible, for example.[2]

Arabic literary theory -- and there has been an extensive history of it -- appears to have evolved out of a dogmatic need to prove the superlative literary merits of the Qur'ān. The Qur'ān was believed to be the literal rendering of the Word of God, and, naturally enough, God's speech could hardly be less than superb; the actual doctrine which emerged in Islam described the Qur'ān as an inimitable production. Some thinkers argued that the Qur'ān was inimitable because God prevented man from producing anything like it. For the most part, however, Muslims argued that the Qur'ān was inimitable on the basis of the content of the Qur'ān, the illiterate character of Muḥammad as a person and the actual literary merits of the book. Some thinkers saw the Qur'ān's literary merits as the proof of the inimitability itself, while other, more subtle, theorists argued that, although it was possible to demonstrate the superiority of the Qur'ān to all other literature in its actual literary merits, this alone could never actually prove the inimitability of the Qur'ān.[3]

One early writer on this topic was Abū'l-Ḥasan ʻAlī ibn ʻĪsā al-Rummānī who died in the year 996 of the Christian era.[4] Rummānī argued for the inimitability of the Qur'ān at least partially on the grounds of what may be translated as the 'aesthetic effectiveness [of the Qur'ān] on the verbal level,' the Arabic word being *balāgha*; this could also be translated perhaps more loosely as the rhetorical success of the Qur'ān. This aesthetic effectiveness, then, is analysed by Rummānī into ten categories: the use of metaphor; the use of simile; the use of hyperbole, including synecdoche; the use of paranomasia; the use of rhyme endings; the use of pleasing expression, by which he intends employment of various ways of expressing meaning either by direct reference, by context, by allusion or by use of an indicator; the use of words and letters in a harmonious way, meaning, perhaps, the absence of tongue-twisters; the use of alteration of individual words, a feature of Semitic languages whereby, for example, in the Arabic of the Qur'ān *mālik, malik, malīk* can all be used to mean 'king'; the use of concision, either ellipsis or brevity; and, finally, the use of implication, the notion, once again built within the structure of Semitic languages, that, for example, for every 'known' there is necessarily a 'knower' implied. Now, in order to demonstrate the Qur'ān's literary merits, it was, of course, necessary for Rummānī to compare the Qur'ān with something and, for him, that was usually profane speech. As an example of concision Rummānī cites the phrase 'Ask the town' as found in the Qur'ān;[5] this is then to be compared with normal speech, where concision would not be used, and the phrase would be rendered 'Ask *the people of* the town.' It is interesting to note that while Rummani treats this as an example of concision, other writers treat it as a metaphor. Other theorists who also wanted to demonstrate the superiority of the Qur'ān compared the text with poetry of both the pre-Islamic and Islamic periods.[6] Poetry was, and is, considered the finest literary production of the Arabs. Of course -- necessarily one might want to say -- the Qur'ān was always demonstrated to be superior in expression to whatever it was compared with.

So, while it could be said that Muslims themselves have treated the Qur'ān as literature in the sense that they have compared it with other literary productions, their very approach to it has always involved setting the Qur'ān apart, indeed above, all other literary creations due to its understood divine origins. It is this assumption which some students of the Qur'ān, including myself, have not been prepared to work under. To take the Qur'ān as literature from this alternative point of view is to take it on the same plane as all other literary productions. To those who may object and say that the Qur'ān is 'more' than other literature, I would reply, with Northrop Frye,[7] that this simply suggests to me that other methods of approach, or other sets of assumptions, are possible in the study of the book. But in contemplating the implications of saying that, we enter into the 'perils' part of this paper.

If, in discussions of English literature, one portrays Shakespeare not as the apogée of the English literary tradition, but rather as a boring and dry playwright from the irrelevant past and see, say, the writings of Charles Bukowski as the true exemplum of how English prose and poetry should be written, it is likely that such a position would be tossed aside by English scholars with a laugh. Now, while the analogy is not totally apt, I would suggest that the parallel of trying to remove the Qur'ān from its presupposed literary pedestal and to treat it without the necessary prerequisite of literary superiority -- which is not to say that its literary merits could not necessarily be demonstrated -- will involve one in far more than simple rebuke by laughter. I speak from experience.[8]

The problem involved is, of course, much like that faced in the study of the Bible perhaps a century ago, although in some circles it is still very much a hot issue. The most learned Dean of my university faculty, Peter Craigie, published a work a few years ago entitled 'The Influence of Spinoza in the Higher Criticism of the Old Testament.'[9] In that paper the argument is made for seeing the seventeenth-century philosopher Baruch

Spinoza as one of the crucial figures in the evolution of the critical method in the approach to the Bible. As Craigie points out, Spinoza's prime means of developing his critical method was by the very questioning of the traditional 'God-hypothesis' underlying the assumed composition of the Bible. Craigie also points to the final implication this change of assumption in the approach to the Bible has produced; the very authority of the Bible has been questioned by this change, he suggests. At the same time, this change in assumption has led to a dilemma, in Craigie's opinion, for scholars of religion: 'Whether the object of study be the Old Testament or the Qur'ān, a method which by definition excludes a 'God-hypothesis' is failing to account in some fashion for a central belief in the religion under examination.'[10]

Now this is neither the appropriate time nor forum for me to argue with my Dean about this matter, but I will quite brazenly admit that I am quite guilty of ignoring this specific 'God-hypothesis', at least in the way that I understand Craigie to mean it, in my studies of the Bible and the Qur'ān. But the interesting point here, and the reason for which I even bother raising the figure of Spinoza is that there was, and there is, a perceived difference on the part of some between Spinoza's approach to the Bible and those of similar methods with regard to the Qur'ān. The perception of many Muslims towards a critical approach to the Qur'ān is of an attack from the outside. Spinoza, on the other hand, worked from within his quasi-Jewish background and was dealt with in the appropriate manner by his community; he was placed under *ḥerem:* he was excommunicated. The method of censuring by excommunication, however, is not effective for Muslims, who perceive the source of the offensive studies as *outside* the community; rather, the only way such works can be censured is by situating them within the general adversary position: East versus West, Islam versus the West, good versus bad. Critical studies are condemned as representing the 'other side'. There often seems to be little middle ground for genuine intellectual interchange. Islam does not seem to have had or to have at the present time a Spinoza-figure for itself; when likely-looking figures have arisen they have generally been quickly subdued either through such means as being removed from their academic post or more commonly by having their publications removed from circulation. This is not to say that recent publications by some Muslims do not illustrate changed approaches to the Qur'ān; the philological method, for one, has found several very intelligent protagonists, but someone prepared to look at, for example, the mythic background and structure of the text is seemingly not to be found.[11]

The response of many Muslims to critical approaches to the Qur'ān, as expressed in this tendency to reduce things to Islam versus the West, has achieved new and rather interesting explications in works by the Columbia University professor of English, Edward Said. In the last few years, Said has written a trilogy on this general topic: *Orientalism*, *The Question of*

Palestine and *Covering Islam*.[12] Said's ultimate point is to argue for the PLO as the legitimate representative of Palestinian aspirations and to argue that Western perceptions of the Arabs are such as to debase any Arab rights to Palestine. One way this has been done, for example, is through the employment of the colonialist myth of bringing the advanced West to the helpless East. Now, that actual argument is not of particular interest to me here except for the support Said finds for his position in his analysis of what he calls 'orientalism'. Orientalism, Said argues, has fostered and furthered the helpless image of the Orient: it is necessary, for example, for Western orientalists to study the Qur'ān, Said represents them as implying, because orientalists assume that the Orient is incapable of truly explaining the Book even to itself, let alone to outsiders. The colonialist myth is thereby re-inforced by the orientalist approach; the orientalists are pawns, if not, in fact, active participants, in the political subjugation of the East, and most especially in legitimization of Israel over against the Palestinians.

What we have in the argument put forward by Said is a radical politicization of the task of the Islamicist, something which is, I believe, fairly unique within the field of religious studies. It is not of course unique in literary fields with the whole notion of the 'committed critic', which Said certainly represents. This demand for commitment leads to the position, in perhaps less subtle minds than those of Said's, of not wanting *anything* to be said about Islam unless it is positive in attitude. As has been expressed to me on a number of occasions, there is enough misunderstanding about Islam in the West without Islamicists always talking about how Muslims have failed to agree on so many important aspects of their faith, for example. Present what Islam 'ideally' stands for, they argue, and do not insult Islam more than it already has been insulted. Intellectual integrity, I would suggest -- being able to sleep nights -- is on dangerous grounds if it is compromised by such demands.

Said also argues that orientalists have reified Islam into an unchanging, even unchangeable substance; Islam emerges as a major force for conservatism and traditionalism alone, without the power to change or liberate or revolt. Said is, I feel, fairly accurate here. During the so-called crisis in Iran, an article appeared in the *Los Angeles Times*[13] which reported interviews with various specialists on Islam on the question of whether or not the Qur'ān permitted the seizure of diplomatic offices. The responses tried to answer the question in various typical academic fashions. But in the very posing of the question, and in the answers given, there is the interesting assumption that, if the Qur'ān did not say that it was possible to take over embassies, then there must be something wrong with Muslims doing so. If, on the other hand, the answer produced by the question had been that the Qur'ān did permit the seizure of embassies, then an immediate air of moral superiority would have been the appropriate response on the part of the audience. In either case, Islam, the article was suggesting, was an unchanging, unchangeable substance which should underpin all Muslim activities.

It is interesting to note, however, that at a recent academic meeting, Said was attacked for his 'revisionist' view of Islam and his denial of a true abstractable core of Islam. That core does indeed exist, some Muslims would argue. Such disagreements -- and the tone of the statement was definitely vituperative -- serve only to make the whole enterprise of Islamic studies even more difficult.[14]

ii

Still, Said's point leads me on to the next section of my paper and that is the 'pitfalls' of the Qur'ān as literature. These pitfalls are perhaps less severe than the perils, yet no less troublesome, for, in a sense, they are directly connected with the latter. Islamic studies in general and the study of the Qur'ān in particular are still oriented in a very historical-positivist manner, a position which leads directly to this reified notion of Islam, as Said has argued. For most scholars, the Qur'ān has an 'original meaning', a meaning it held for its utterer, that is Muḥammad, and/or a meaning held by its first hearers. This meaning can be determined or, at least in the view of more careful scholars, approximated, through historical analysis, a process rarely stated more subtly than 'what makes sense' to our historical perceptions. There is, therefore, a true, unchanging essence of Islam which can be determined and either implicitly or explicitly compared with various historical aberrations of Islam.

One of the arguments which I often seem to hear in defence of this approach to the Qur'ān is that, when studying the Qur'ān as literature, we must use a method which is 'appropriate to the text itself', that usually being one which involves the basic historical (but not theological, note!) assumptions of Muslims themselves or at least historical assumptions which the tradition of Islam itself suggests. Now, I must admit that I am at a loss to understand these statements and why they should be so adamantly held and expressed. The suggestion is made, for example, that we cannot simply take a method of literary analysis developed in the context of Biblical studies -- form criticism, say -- and impose it upon the Qur'ān.[15] I have been accused of 'methodological imperialism' (the terminology is interesting) for suggesting the possibility of doing so. But...*are* the assumptions with which one should approach *any* text in any sense dictated by the text itself? Take, for example, works of different genres: Is it possible or is it not possible to approach a play in the same way as a novel? Now, agreed, certain dimensions of a text may well be lost or glossed or even exaggerated by using certain methods or realms of assumptions, but does that make certain assumptions intrinsically less valid or useful than others for certain texts? If one wishes to argue that that *is* so, then how can one actually determine the so-called appropriate method or assumptions? Is the claim *really* being made that there is a one-to-one correspondence between text and method?

The pitfalls in approaching the Qur'ān as literature, then, I see perhaps most of all related to the failure of researchers to embrace the possibility of a plurality of methods or even a pluralistic attitude towards method. As far as I am concerned, if people wish to spend their lives looking for the author's intention or speculating over the meaning of the text to the first hearers, then so be it. The results produced by such investigations are indeed interesting, even valuable, but I fail to see them as anything more than one more link in the historical chain of reader-response to the Qur'ān, a response to be situated not back in the seventh-century origins of Islam, as many of those who champion the approach would like to have it, but rather to be situated in terms of the twentieth-century response developed by this community of historical scholarship. And this then brings me to what I see as the prospects of studying the Qur'ān as literature: I see the attempt at reconstructing the history of the reception of the text as the most valuable and most interesting approach. Now, I am quite aware that attempts are certainly made to justify the employment of this approach hermeneutically and to prove it as superior to all other approaches. I, myself, have on another occasion even attempted to treat the matter theoretically: to question the possibility of true historical knowledge due to the hermeneutical circle, to question the special claim to validity for the author's intention or original meaning.[16] This I do not, however, wish to do now but rather I would like to raise some aspects of and questions about the approach of the 'history of reception' or reader-response'.

A theory of the 'history of reception' always presupposes most centrally that any work needs a reader to create meaning and that each reader will extract meaning appropriate to his own time, presuppositions and expectations. But the theory also emphasizes, especially when explicated by someone such as Hans Robert Jauss, for example,[17] that any literary work is not created in a vacuum; that it stands in a context. Any given text stands within a continuum of literary experience; any given text is a part of an overall historical chain of literature and is therefore, in a sense, evidence of a response, in either posing a question or providing an answer, to previous literary works. This brings to my mind an interesting and perhaps rather obvious example in the case of the Qur'ān. The Qur'ān is quite clearly a reading -- with the full implications of that word intended -- of the Biblical tradition among the other strands of thought and literature. It stands as one point in the historical continuum of response to the Bible. Interestingly, it is quite easy to demonstrate that the Qur'ān is not simply a response to the Bible as a text, but, rather, it is a response within the framework of the continual Jewish and Christian responses to the Bible. The Qur'ān illustrates rather nicely the cumulative nature of reader-response. But the problem arises that, if we wish to study the Qur'ān within this historical continuum, just where do we 'cut into the universe of literary artifacts'?[18] Just where and how do we draw the appropriate limits to our study? It seems to me that ultimately the decision remains an arbitrary one: the researcher decides where he will cut into the literary pie, as it were, for his own peculiar reasons. If we then select any given work, the task before us seems to be to place that work within its overall context both backwards and forwards in time. As far as the Qur'ān goes, it simply exhausts me even to contemplate such a project! Yet such a point seems essential because the pitfalls in ignoring such an approach are quite astounding. One example from the Qur'ān will suffice. The Qur'ān speaks of Gabriel as the 'spirit of revelation', the means by which revelation was brought to Muḥammad. Now, it has been argued recently, by those who still search for the meaning taken by the first hearers,[19] that Gabriel is not an angel in the Qur'ān because the text does not say that he is; rather, Gabriel was understood, and presumably was intended to be understood, as some sort of spirit. Such a reading is fascinating; that certainly is what the text 'says', yet the reading seems to assume that the Qur'ān emerged in some sort of literary vacuum. It would seem to imply to me, although obviously not to those who argue the case, that the Qur'ān must have been virtually unintelligible to its contemporary hearers unless they happened to be fully acquainted with the modern methods of semantic analysis. In this case, to understand the Qur'ān outside of the Biblical tradition, in which Gabriel is one of the four major angelic figures, would seem in the end to place the researcher in a rather ridiculous position.

So, a full study of the Qur'ān in the framework of literary history will require the text to be put within its overall literary context, that then requiring a study of the overall Near Eastern religious milieu which preceded the emergence of Islam. It will also entail studying the reader-reaction to the Qur'ān; this aspect of the study is facilitated by a large body of information known technically as *tafsīr*, or, simply, exegesis. These works, which number in the thousands, were written, and continue to be written, as attempts to explicate the meaning of the Qur'ān. Each attempt to state that meaning is done, of course, within the social, economic, political and religious framework of each individual commentator. This is true, even if the commentator makes the attempt to base himself or herself upon traditional material written down in earlier centuries which, indeed, many commentators do. The editorial function of the later collator of the material still acts to impose a new interpretational construct upon the material.[20] And new interpretational constructs are the very material by which we may reconstruct the historical pattern of reader-response to the Qur'ān.

Whether or not this kind of approach necessarily avoids all the perils and pitfalls in the study of the Qur'ān as literature as outlined previously, I am not certain. One rather obvious peril, and one which I experience in a reaction to another paper of mine, is that in the very failure to provide the 'real' meaning of the text is perceived on the part of some, perhaps even many,as an irrelevance of the research itself.Much education is needed to convince people of the value and merits of literary history.

Finally, I would recapitulate the prospects in studying the Qur'ān as literature. Those prospects I see as located most profitably in a two-fold task: that of situating the Qur'ān in its literary tradition and that of situating the Qur'ān at the focal point of a reader-response study. The two combined will certainly produce studies which would, all at one time, emphasize the production of the Qur'ān as a literary artifact and emphasize the role of the Qur'ān and the impact of the Qur'an on Muslim life.

NOTES

1. The most successful studies are undoubtedly those by Mohammed Arkoun (see especially his 'Lecture de la sourate 18', in *Annales: Economies, Societes, Civilisations* 35 (1980), pp.418-435); Richard C.Martin, 'Structural Analysis and the Qur'ān: Newer Approaches to the Study of Islamic Texts', in *Journal of the American Academy of Religion: Thematic Issue,* 47 (1979), pp.665-683.
2. See John Wansbrough, *Quranic Studies: Sources and Methods of Scriptural Interpretation* (Oxford, 1977), Chapters 1 and 2, for the best available treatment of the literary form of the Qur'ān as compared with the Bible.
3. On the topic of inimitability see *Encyclopaedia of Islam, New Edition* (Leiden, 1955-) s.v., *iʿdjāz* and *op.cit.,* pp.79-83 and 231-232.
4. See his *'Al-nukat fī iʿjāz al-Qur'ān',* in Muḥammad Khalaf Allāh and Muḥammad Zaghlūl Sallām (eds.), *Thalāth Rasā'il fī iʿjāz al-Qur'ān* (Cairo, 1968), pp.75-113.
5. Qur'ān, xii:82; see al-Rummānī, *Nukat,* p.76.
6. See, for example, Gustave E.von Grunebaum (ed. and trans.), *A Tenth-Century Document of Arab Literary Theory and Criticism: The Sections on Poetry of al-Baqillānī's* Iʿjāz al-Qur'ān (Chicago, 1950).
7. Northrop Frye, *Anatomy of Criticism: Four Essays* (Princeton, 1957), p.315.
8. See, for example, my contribution (and the implicit responses to it) to Richard C.Martin (ed.), *Islam and the History of Religions: Essays in Methodology* (Berkeley, forthcoming 1983).
9. P.C.Craigie, 'The Influence of Spinoza in the Higher Criticism of the Old Testament', *Evangelical Quarterly* 50 (1978), pp.23-32.
10. Craigie, *op.cit.,* pp. 31-32.
11. Whether the works of a person such as Arkoun (see Note 1) will eventually require a statement such as this to be changed, only time will tell; such figures are generally lumped, regardless, into the 'other side' by their intellectual position.
12. Edward W.Said, *Orientalism* (New York, 1978; *The Question of Palestine* (New York, 1979); *Covering Islam: How the Media and*

the Experts Determine How We See the Rest of the World (New York, 1981).

13. *Los Angeles Times*, Wednesday, December 12, 1979, Section VIII, pp.1-2.
14. Hamid Algar, Plenary Session: 'The Rise of Islam as a Force in Recent International Affairs', American Academy of Religion Annual Meeting, San Francisco, December 19, 1981. Professor Algar was not present at the meeting and his paper was read for him; the 'vituperative' tone was in the style and content of the writing and not (necessarily) in the actual oral presentation.
15. Most revealing in this respect are the various reactions to the works by Wansbrough, especially his *Quranic Studies,* but also his *The Sectarian Milieu: Content and Composition of Islamic Sacred History* (Oxford, 1978).
16. A.Rippin, 'Methodological Considerations in the Study of *tafsīr'*, paper read at the American Oriental Society Annual Meeting, Boston, March 15, 1981.
17. See especially H.R.Jauss, 'Literary History as a Challenge to Literary Theory', in *New Literary History* 2 (1970), pp.7-37. Basic to any consideration of Literary History is Rene Wellek and Austin Warren, *Theory of Literature* (3rd edn; New York, London, 1977), Chapters 4 and 19.
18. Hayden White, 'Literary History: The Point of it All', in *New Literary History* 2 (1970), pp.173-185.
19. Fazlur Rahman, *Major Themes of the Qur'ān* (Minneapolis, Chicago, 1980), pp.97 and 131. See my review of this book, in *BSOAS* 44 (1981), pp.360-363. On Gabriel also see A.T. Welch, 'al-Ḳur'ān', *Encyclopaedia of Islam,* V, p.403, for a remarkably positivist statement.
20. See Wansbrough, op.cit., 120; Arkoun, op.cit., p.421.

II

Literary Analysis of *Qur'ān*, *Tafsīr*, and *Sīra*

The Methodologies of John Wansbrough

That Judaism and Christianity are religions "in history" seems to be a commonly accepted notion among many people today. The view is that history is the "proving ground" of these religions, that the intervention of God in the historical sequence of events is the most significant truth attested by these religions. Whether or not this is theologically valid is a question that must be left for those who pursue such questions; what is of interest here are the implications which this view has had for "secular" historical studies and, most importantly here, for the historical study of religion. The idea that these are religions "in history" has led to an emphasis on the desire to discover "what really happened," ultimately, because of the underlying belief that this discovery would demonstrate the ultimate truth or falsity of the individual religion. Now that may or may not be an appropriate task depending on the particular view of history taken by the historian, but it has led to one important problem in the study of religion—the supposition that the sources available to us to describe the historical foundations of a given religion, most specifically the scriptures, contain within them discernible historical data which can be used to provide positive historical results. In other words, the approach assumes that the motivations of the writers of such sources were the same as the motivations of present-day historians, namely, to record "what really happened."

Whether out of theological conviction or merely unconsciously, modern scholarship has approached Islam in the same way that it has traditionally treated Judaism and Christianity—as a religion of history, that is, as a religion that has a stake in history. Whether this approach is valid or invalid is not the point here. What is relevant is that this view has led to the same sort of attitude toward the sources available in the study of early Islam as that which characterizes the attitude in the study of Judaism and Christianity, namely, that these sources purport to record (and thus provide us with) an account of "what really happened." The desire to know what happened in the past is certainly not unreasonable, nor is it, theoretically, an impossible task; Islam most definitely has a history that needs to be recovered. But the desire to achieve positive results must not lead us to ignore the literary qualities of the sources available to us.

Very little material of "neutral" testimonial quality is available for the study of early Islam; sizable quantities of archeological data, numismatic evidence, even datable documents are all very much wanting. Evidence from sources external to the community itself are not plentiful either and the reconstruction of such material into a historical framework is fraught with difficulties. In *Hagarism*, Patricia Crone and Michael Cook have attempted such a reconstruction and, although they successfully draw attention to the problems involved in the study of Islam, they have not been able to get beyond the limitations inherent in the sources, for they are all of questionable historical authenticity and, more importantly, all are treatises based in polemic. No one has yet expressed the problem better than John Wansbrough: "[C]an a vocabulary of motives be freely extrapolated from a discrete collection of literary stereotypes composed by alien and mostly hostile observers, and thereupon employed to describe, even interpret, not merely the overt behaviour but also the intellectual and spiritual development of helpless and almost innocent actors?"[1] The other sources available to us—the Arabic texts internal to the Muslim community—consist of a limited mass of literature originating at least two centuries after the fact. Such information as this literature contains was written in light of the passage of those two centuries and would, indeed, seem to have a stake in that very history being recounted. These internal sources intended, after all, to document the basis of faith, the validity of the sacred book, and its evidence of God's plan for humankind. These sources recorded "Salvation History."

One brief example may help to clarify the exact dimensions of the problem. Nowhere has the attitude toward the historical character of the sources about the foundation of Islam proved to be more resilient than in the interpretation of the Qur'ān. Muslim exegetes have a category of information available to them called *asbāb al-nuzūl*, commonly translated as the "occasions of revelation," which have been thought by Western students of the Qur'ān to record the historical events concerning the revelation of individual verses of the Qur'ān. Careful analysis of the individual uses of these *asbāb* in exegesis reveals that their actual significance in individual cases of trying to understand the Qur'ān is limited: the anecdotes are adduced, and thus recorded and transmitted, in order to provide a narrative situation in which an interpretation of the Qur'ān can be embodied. The material has been recorded within exegesis not for its historical value but for its exegetical value. Yet such basic literary facts about the material are frequently ignored within the study of Islam in the desire to find positive historical results. A good example of what I mean is found in a recent article on Muḥammad's boycott of Mecca; a *sabab* (occasion) recorded in al-Ṭabarī's *tafsīr*[2] is used to defend and elaborate upon a complicated historical reconstruction about the life of Muḥammad.[3] The desire for historical results has led to an entire glossing of the problems and limitations of the sources.

The Nature of the Sources

John Wansbrough of the School of Oriental and African Studies at the University of London has made a systematic attempt to get beyond the problems involved in trying to understand the beginnings of Islam. In two recent books Wansbrough argues for a critical assessment of the value of the sources from a literary point of view, in order to escape the inherent theological view of the history in the account of Islamic origins. The two works, *Quranic Studies: Sources and Methods of Scriptural Interpretation* (hereafter *QS*)[4] and *The Sectarian Milieu: Content and Composition of Islamic Salvation History* (hereafter *SM*)[5] fit together quite logically, although it should be noted that there is some progression of thought between the two works on some specific topics. *QS* was written between 1968 and 1972 although it was published in 1977; *SM* was written between 1973 and 1977, but published in 1978. Those following Wansbrough's numerous reviews will appreciate that his thought has not stopped there either.[6] Wansbrough emphasizes that the ideas he has put forth in his books are a tentative working out of the problems involved. *QS* deals primarily with the formation of the Qur'ān along with the witness of exegetical writings (*tafsīr*) to that formation; *SM* develops the theme of the evolution of Islam further, through the traditional biographies of Muḥammad (*sīra* and *maghāzī*), and then works through the process of the theological elaboration of Islam as a religious community, examining the questions of authority, identity, and epistemology.

The basic methodological point of Wansbrough's works is to ask the prime question not usually posed in the study of Islam: What is the evidence? Do we have witnesses to the Muslim accounts of the formation of their own community in any early, disinterested sources? The Qur'ān (in the form collected "between two covers" as we know it today) is a good example: What evidence is there for the historical accuracy of the traditional accounts of the compilation of that book shortly after the death of Muḥammad? The earliest non-Islamic source testifying to the existence of the Qur'ān appears to stem from the second/eighth century.[7] Indeed, early Islamic sources, at least those which do not seem to have as their prime purpose the defense of the integrity of the canon,[8] would seem to witness that the text of the Qur'ān may not have been totally fixed until the early part of the third/ninth century.[9] Manuscript evidence does not allow for substantially earlier dating either.[10]

A question for many people still remains, however (and the answer to it evidences Wansbrough's most basic and radical point): Why should we *not* trust the Muslim sources? Wansbrough's answer to this is substantially different from other expressions of similar skepticism, for example as argued by John Burton in *The Collection of the Qur'ān*, where internal contradiction within the Muslim sources is emphasized and then that fact is combined with a postulated explanation of how such contradiction came about.[11] No, Wansbrough's point of departure is more radical: the entire corpus of early Islamic documentation must be viewed as "Salvation History." What the Qur'ān is trying to evidence, what *tafsīr*, *sīra*, and theological writings are trying to explicate, is how the sequence of worldly events centered on the time of Muḥammad was directed by God. All the components of Islamic salvation history are meant to witness the same point of faith, namely, an understanding of history that sees God's role in directing the affairs of humankind. And the difference that makes is substantial. To quote from a work that deals with the same problem, but from the biblical perspective, "Salvation history is not an historical account of saving events open to the study of the historian. Salvation history did not happen; it is a literary form which has its own historical context."[12] Salvation history comes down to us in a literary form and must be approached by means appropriate to such: literary analysis.

At the outset it may be appropriate to pay attention to the use of the term "salvation history" in connection with Islam, especially in light of questions raised about its use outside the Christian context in general. Most recently H. W. F. Saggs has pointed to the fact that although the term "salvation" has a clear meaning in Christian thought—"it is the saving of the individual soul from destruction or damnation by sin, for eternal life"—its application within Judaism would seem to mean "no more than that God maintained a particular religio-ethnic group in existence, when the operation of normal political and social factors might have been expected to result in its extermination."[13] The term "salvation" is ambiguous at best and perhaps only rightfully applied in the Christian case. So that may lead to the question: Are we straitjacketing Islam into a Christian framework by using such a term as "salvation history?" Wansbrough has attempted to make reasonably clear what he means by the term, and what it implies to him (e.g., *SM* ix, 31), making it evident that "salvation," as such, is not the defining characteristic of this history. Indeed, Wansbrough suggests (*SM* 147) that Islamic salvation history may perhaps be more accurately described as "election history" because of the very absence within its early formulation of an eschatological concern. Clearly Wansbrough does not conceive of "salvation" in the term "salvation history" as necessarily laden with its Christian connotations. But further, "salvation history" may be taken on a different level, simply as a technical term referring to literature involved in documenting what could just as easily be called "sacred history," that is, the "history" of man's relationship with God and vice versa. The intellectual baggage of *Heilsgeschichte* may simply be left behind in favor of reference to the literary genre.

Literary analysis of salvation history has been fully developed within biblical and Mishnaic studies; the works of Bultmann and Neusner are obvious prime examples.[14] All such works start from the proposition that the literary records of salvation history, although presenting themselves as being contemporary with the events they describe, actually belong to a period well after such events, which suggests that they have been written according to later points of view in order to fit the purposes of that later time. The actual "history" in the sense of "what really happened" has become totally subsumed within later interpretation and is virtually, if not totally, inextricable from it. The question of whether or not there is an underlying "grain of historical truth" may be thought to be of some concern here, namely, whether or not there must have been some sort of historical event or impetus out of which traditions grew and which, therefore, forms the kernel of the narrative. But the real problem here is that even if one admits the existence of such a "kernel" of history, is it ever possible to identify and extract that information? Wansbrough implies in his work that he feels that it is not, at least for the most part.[15] The records we have are the existential records of the thought and faith of later generations.

This basic insight into the nature of the sources is not totally new to the study of Islam. Goldziher, and Schacht even more so, understood that traditional sayings attributed to Muḥammad and used to support a given legal or doctrinal position within Islam actually derived from a much later period, from times when these legal or doctrinal positions were searching for support with the body of material called the *sunna*. It has become characteristic of Islamic studies after Joseph Schacht, however, either to water down or to ignore totally the implications of such insights. This was clear to Schacht himself toward the end of his life.

> One thing disturbs me, however. That is the danger that the results achieved by the Islamic scholars, at a great effort, in the present generation, instead of being developed and being made the starting point for new scholarly progress might, by a kind of intellectual laziness, be gradually whittled down and deprived of their real significance, or even be turned inside out by those who themselves had taken no part in achieving them. This has happened in the past to the work of Goldziher . . . and it has happened again, recently, with regard to the conclusions of the history of Islamic law achieved by critical scholarship.[16]

The "intellectual laziness" is, it seems to me, a counterpart to the desire to produce positive historical results—to satisfy that internal yearning to assert "what really happened."[17] The works of three people can be cited as the most obvious examples of the latter trend: in "The materials used by Ibn Isḥāq," W. M. Watt distorts the work of Schacht and attempts to use Schacht's results against the latter's own position,[18] and in the works of Sezgin[19] and Abbott[20] elaborate schemes are set forth to contradict the insights of Schacht, but are based on no *tangible* evidence. Sezgin especially displays an overt tendency to date works to the earliest possible historical period, with no apparent justification thereof, for example, in the case of the works of Ibn ʿAbbās.[21]

Wansbrough's argument, however, is that we do *not* know and probably never can know what really happened; all we can know is what later people *believed* happened, as has been recorded in salvation history. Literary analysis of such sources will reveal to us the components with which those people worked in order to produce their accounts and define exactly what it was that they were arguing, but literary analysis will not tell us *what* happened (although the *possibility* of historical implications of such studies cannot be, and certainly are not within Wansbrough's work, totally ignored).

The point of Islamic salvation history as it has come down to us today, Wansbrough argues, is more specific than merely to evidence the belief in the reality of the theophany; it is to formulate, by adopting and adapting from a well-established pool of Judeo-Christian religious themes, a specifically Arabian religious identity, the inception of which could be placed in seventh-century Arabia. At the beginning of *QS* Wansbrough brings forth a multitude of evidences from the Qur'ān which point to the idea that the very notions in that book demand that they be put within the total Judeo-Christian context, for example, the prophetic line ending in the Seal of the Prophets, the sequence of scriptures, the notion of the destroyed communities, and the common narrative motifs. This notion of extrapolation is, in a sense, the methodological presupposition that Wansbrough sets out to prove within his books by posing the question: If we assume this, does the data fit? At the same time he asks: What additional evidence appears in the process of the analysis to corroborate the presupposition and to define it more clearly?[22] This kind of approach to the material is similar to that of Harry A. Wolfson in his use of the scientific method of "conjecture and verification."[23] So the question raised by some critics concerning whether it is accurate to view Islam as an extension of the Judeo-Christian tradition cannot be considered valid until the evidence and the conclusions put forth in Wansbrough's works have been weighed. The point must always be: Is the presupposition supported by the analysis of the data? To attack the presupposition as invalid is to miss the entire point. To evaluate the work one must participate within its methodological presuppositions and evaluate the final results.

Wansbrough's Approach to the Sources

Charles Adams has summed up the common feeling of many students of the Qur'ān in the following words: "Such matters as the formation of the Qur'ān text, the chronology of the materials assembled in the text, the history of the text, variant readings, the relation of the Qur'ān to prior literature, and a host of other issues of this kind have been investigated thoroughly."[24] Wansbrough, however, has made it clear that we have really only scratched the surface of these studies. All previous studies, he states, have involved an acquiescence to the normative data of the tradition and are characterized by "a distinctly positivist method: serious concern to discover and to describe the state of affairs after the appearance of Islam among the Arabs . . ." (*SM* 2). What Wansbrough has done has been to bring to the study of Islam and the Qur'ān the same healthy skepticism developed within modern biblical studies (and modern historical studies in general) in order to supplant such positivism. At this point it is worth noting that the highly praised work of Richard Bell,[25] although supposedly using the biblical methodology consequent on the Documentary Hypothesis, has, in fact, progressed not one iota beyond implicit notions in the traditional accounts of the revelation and the collection of the Qur'ān; he took the ideas of serial revelation and the collection after the death of Muḥammad (the common notions accepted by most Westerns students of the Qur'ān) and applied them literally to the text of the Qur'ān. However, the primary purpose of employing modern biblical methodologies must be to free oneself from age-old presuppositions and to apply new ones. This Bell did not do; in fact, he worked wholly within the presuppositions of the Islamic tradition. Wansbrough's claim that "as a document susceptible of analysis by the instruments and techniques of Biblical criticism [the Qur'ān] is virtually unknown" (*QS* ix) can certainly not be questioned, least of all by adducing the work of Bell.[26]

Wansbrough has also tried to show a way to free the study of the Qur'ān from the uniquely fundamentalist[27] trend of the vast majority of modern treatments of the book in which the idea of an "original" meaning or intention is pursued relentlessly but ultimately meaninglessly. Such a position in scholarship has been reached especially because of two factors inherent in previous methodologies in the study of Islam. One, the basic historico-philological approach to Islam has become trapped by the consequence of narrow specialization on the part of its proponents. For the most part, there are few scholars active today who can move with equal agility throughout the entire Western religious framework and its necessary languages.[28] Scholars have come to feel that competent knowledge of Arabic and of seventh-century Arabia are sufficient in and of themselves to understand the rise of Islam.[29] No different are the views of such people as Serjeant, who attempt to champion the notion of the influence of pre-Islamic southern Arabia on Islam, but do so to the virtual exclusion of the Jewish element in the population there.[30]

The philological method has been affected also by a second method which within itself has produced the stagnation of Islamic studies within its fundamentalist framework. The irenic approach, which according to Charles Adams aims toward "the greater appreciation of Islamic religiousness and the fostering of a new attitude toward it,"[31] has led to the unfortunate result of a reluctance on the part of many scholars to follow all the way through with their insights and results. The basic problem of an approach to Islam that is concerned "to understand the faith of other men"[32] is confronted when that approach tries to come to grips with the historical dimensions of a faith that conceives itself as having a stake in that very history.[33] The irenic approach to Islam, it would seem, in order to remain true to the "faith of other men," is doomed most of all to avoid asking the basic question: How do we know?

Wansbrough's analysis of the basic character of the Qur'ān reveals his assessment of the extent of the problem involved in the use of these two approaches to the Qur'ān. Wansbrough isolates four major motifs of the Qur'ānic message, all from the "traditional stock of monotheistic imagery" (*QS* 1): divine retribution, sign, exile, and covenant. These motifs, Wansbrough notes, are "repeatedly signalled but seldom developed" (*QS* 1), a fact which leads him to emphasize throughout his works one of his major insights concerning the Qur'ān: its "referential" style.[34] The audience of the Qur'ān is presumed able to fill in the missing details of the narrative, much as is true of a work such as the Talmud, where knowledge of the appropriate biblical citation is assumed or supplied by only a few words. Only later, when

"Islam" as an entity with a fixed and stable identity (based on a political structure) comes into being after the Arabs' expansion out of their original home, does the Qur'ānic material become detached from its original intellectual environment and need written explication—explication that is provided in *tafsīr* and *sīra*.

Two of the examples discussed by Wansbrough will clarify his notion of the referential character of the Qur'ān. Most evident is the example of Joseph and the mention of the "other brother" in S. 12:59 (see *QS* 134, *SM* 24–25), parallel to the biblical account in Genesis 42:3–13; knowledge of this latter story is assumed on the part of the Qur'ānic audience, for within the Qur'ān no previous mention has been made of Benjamin and his being left at home due to Jacob's fears for his safety. Joseph's statement in the Qur'ān, "Bring me a brother of yours from your father," comes out of nowhere within the context of the Qur'ān, although not if one comes first with a knowledge of the biblical story. The second example is one which deals with Abraham's willingness to sacrifice his son and the removal within the Qur'ān of the dramatic impact contained in the biblical story, where the son does not know that he is the one to be offered (see *SM* 24). The question is far more complex because the Jewish exegetical tradition may play a role here; the study of Geza Vermes[35] makes it clear that many Jewish (and Christian) traditions adjust the story to let Isaac know he is to be sacrificed well before the actual event in order to emphasize the willingness of Isaac to offer himself. The Jewish exegetical tradition is referential as well; it already assumes that the basic story of the sacrifice is clear to its audience and that the significance of Abraham in the story will be evident to all who read the Bible; thus, the emphasis is on Isaac but certainly not to the exclusion of the role of Abraham. The position of the Qur'ān is similar. The knowledge of the biblical story is assumed; reference is made to developed traditions concerning the sacrifice. The referential character of the Qur'ān should make clear the insufficiency of an approach to the Qur'ān which looks at the so-called "exclusively Arabian" (whatever that may be!) character of the book and tries to ignore the total Judeo-Christian background.[36]

The notion of the referential style of the Qur'ān also leads Wansbrough to the supposition that what we are dealing with in Islam is a sectarian movement fully within the Judeo-Christian "Sectarian Milieu" (*QS* 20, also *SM* 45). The parallels between Qur'ānic and Qumranic literature, while not necessarily displaying an interdependency, *do* demonstrate a similar process of biblical-textual elaboration and adaptation to sectarian purposes.[37] The inner workings of the sectarian milieu are to be seen in both literary traditions.

The Qur'ān as a document, according to Wansbrough, then, is composed of such referential passages developed within the framework of Judeo-Christian sectarian polemics, put together by means of literary convention (for example, the use of *qul* ["say"] (*QS* 12 ff., also 47–48), narrative conventions (*QS* 18 ff.), and the conjunction of parallel versions of stories called by Wansbrough "variant traditions" (*QS* 20 ff.), which were perhaps produced from a single original tradition by means of variation through oral transmission within the context of liturgical usage (*QS* 27). Here, clearly enough, a variety of individual methods (e.g., form analysis, oral formulaic analysis) which have been worked out in fields outside Islam, primarily the Bible, are used by Wansbrough in his analysis of the nature of the Muslim scripture.

Significantly, Wansbrough's analysis reveals that the Qur'ān is not merely "a calque of earlier fixed forms" (*QS* 33), that is, it does not merely seek to reproduce the Bible in Arabic, adapted to Arabia. For one thing, the Qur'ān does not follow the fulfillment motif set as a precedent by the New Testament and its use of the Hebrew Bible. Rather, and, indeed, because of the situation of polemic from which the Qur'ān derives, there is a clear attempt made to separate the Qur'ān from the Mosaic revelation through such means as the mode of the revelation and the emphasis on the Arabian language of the Qur'ān.

Canonization and stabilization of the text of the Qur'ān goes hand in hand with the formation of the community, according to Wansbrough (*QS* 51). A final, fixed text of the scripture was not required, nor was it totally feasible, before political power was firmly controlled; thus the end of the second/eighth century becomes a likely historical moment for the gathering together of oral tradition and liturgical elements leading to the emergence of the fixed canon of scripture and the emergence of the actual concept, "Islam."[38] This time period, Wansbrough several times points out, coincides with the recorded rise of literary Arabic.[39] Further evidence for this position is derived in *QS* from a "typological analysis" of *tafsīr* (see *QS* 44 and ch. 4). The basic inspiration and thrust of Wansbrough's approach may once again perhaps be traced to modern biblical studies; such people as Geza Vermes and Raphael Loewe have been drawing attention to the need to stop plundering exegetical works, Greek and Aramaic translations of the Bible, and so forth, in order to find support, somewhere, for one's own argument. Rather, they suggest, such works must be studied as a whole with attention given to the historical context of their writing and to their literary context.[40] The analysis of Qur'ānic *tafsīr* literature into five genres—haggadic, halakhic, masoretic, rhetorical, and allegorical—once again sets the basic insight. The genres display an approximate chronological development in the above sequence and display a historically growing concern with the textual integrity of scripture and then with the community function of scripture.[41]

The *sīra*, while partly exegetical as Wansbrough explains in *QS*, has a much greater role in Islam: it is the narrative witness to the Islamic version of salvation history. Most significant here is Wansbrough's analysis (*SM* ch. 1) of much of the contents of the *sīra* into elaborations of twenty-three polemical motifs traditional to the Near Eastern sectarian milieu—items such as the prognosis of Muḥammad in Jewish scripture, the Jewish rejection of that prognosis, the role of Abraham and Jesus in sectarian soteriology, and resurrection. All these themes are elaborated within a narrative framework set in seventh-century Arabia but yet all are themes that had been argued so many times before among sectarian groups in the Near East. The analysis of the *sīra* underlines Wansbrough's main contention in both of his books that "by its own express testimony, the Islamic kerygma [is] an articulation . . . of the Biblical dispensation, and can only thus be assessed" (*SM* 45).

It will be clear to any attentive reader of *QS* and *SM* that Wansbrough's work still leaves much to be done with the basic data in order to work out fully the implications of his kind of study. Close and detailed analyses of the many texts involved are still needed in order to demonstrate and, indeed, to assess the validity of his approach. What Wansbrough has accomplished, it seems to me, is to point to a new direction that Islamic studies could take in order to revitalize itself; Wansbrough has marked a path in broad outlines, but the road must still be cleared.[42]

Several reviewers have seized upon (and, indeed, Wansbrough himself has emphasized the point)[43] various statements in *QS* with regard to methods determining one's results. I. J. Boullata, in his review of *QS*, put the matter this way: "To quote him from page 91 'Results are, after all, as much conditioned by method as by material.' If this is true and his material is given credence in spite of its selectivity, there remains a big question about his method and the extent to which it conditioned his results."[44] Fazlur Rahman in his book *Major Themes of the Qur'ān* makes a similar point about method.

> My disagreements with Wansbrough are so numerous that they are probably best understood only by reading both this book and his. (I do, however, concur with at least one of his points: "The kind of analysis undertaken will in no small measure determine the results!" [p. 21]) I do believe that this kind of study [i.e., the comparison with Judaism and/or Christianity] can be enormously useful, though we have to return to Geiger and Hirschfeld [! not Speyer?!] to see just how useful it can be when done properly.[45]

What does Rahman mean here concerning method? Does he mean to imply: Well, Wansbrough has a method and that has been his downfall; I have no method so I have imposed nothing upon the material? I doubt that Rahman wants to urge methodological naiveté. More likely, perhaps, Rahman means: Wansbrough has his method and I have mine, but mine is right. That the methods which Rahman (and virtually every other student in the field) imposes upon his study happen to be, for the most part, the traditional theologico-historical methods is a fact that needs to be recognized, just as does the fact that Wansbrough imposes literary methods. If the study of Islam is to remain a scholarly endeavor and retain some sense of intellectual integrity, then it must, first, become methodologically aware and, second, be prepared to consider the validity of other methods of approach to the subject. This means that Islamic studies must differentiate between the truth claims of the religion itself and the intellectual claims of various methods, for ultimate "truth" is not susceptible to methodological procedures. To remain within the search for the "true" meaning of Islam and not to be prepared to free oneself from, for example, the priority of history[46] within the study of Islam, will surely sound the death-knell for a potentially vital and vibrant endeavor of human intellectual activity.

Literary Analysis of Qur'ān, Tafsīr, *and* Sīra

1. John Wansbrough, *The Sectarian Milieu: Content and Composition of Islamic Salvation History* (Oxford: Oxford University Press, 1978), pp. 116–17; also see his review of Patricia Crone and Michael Cook, *Hagarism: the Making of the Islamic World* (Cambridge: Cambridge University Press, 1977) in *Bulletin of the School of Oriental and African Studies* [hereafter, *BSOAS*] 41 (1978):155–56. Other interesting reviews of *Hagarism* are J. van Ess in *The Times Literary Supplement* Sept. 8, 1978, pp. 997–98 and N. Daniels in *Journal of Semitic Studies* [hereafter, *JSS*] 24 (1979):296–304. Cf. M. A. Cook, "The Origins of *Kalam*," *BSOAS* 43 (1980):32–43 for a good example of what *can* be demonstrated by external sources. Also see Patricia Crone, *Slaves on Horses: The Evolution of the Islamic Polity* (Cambridge: Cambridge University Press, 1980) especially ch. 1; Michael Cook, *Early Muslim Dogma: A source-critical study* (Cambridge: Cambridge University Press, 1981), and his *Muhammad* (Oxford: Oxford University Press, 1983).

2. This *sabab*, the author admits (see note 3 below), is not found in al-Ṭabarī's *Ta'rīkh;* this fact should have raised the curiosity of the author about the literary qualities of the material with which he was dealing. It should be noted in this regard that al-Ṭabarī indeed recognized the difference between exegesis and history.

3. Fred McGraw Donner, "Mecca's Food Supply and Muhammad's Boycott," *Journal of the Economic and Social History of the Orient* 20 (1977):249–66; another, slightly different example is found in Uri Rubin, "Abū Lahab and Sūra CXI," *BSOAS* 42

(1979):13–28, esp. pp. 13–15. On the *asbāb al-nuzūl* see A. Rippin, "The exegetical genre *asbāb al-nuzūl*: a bibliographical and terminological survey," *BSOAS* 48/1 (1985).

4. *Quranic Studies: Sources and Methods of Scriptural Interpretation* (Oxford: Oxford University Press, 1977). Reviews of *QS* are as follows: *Bibliotheca Orientalis* [hereafter *BO*] 35 (1978):349–53 (van Ess); *BSOAS* 40 (1977):609–612 (Ullendorf); *Der Islam* 55 (1978):354–56 (Paret); *Journal of the American Oriental Society* [*JAOS*] 100 (1980):137–41 (Graham); *Jewish Quarterly Review* [*JQR*] 68 (1978):182–84 (Nemoy); *Journal of the Royal Asiatic Society* [*JRAS*] (1978):76–78 (Serjeant); *JSS* 24 (1979):293–96 (Juynboll); *Muslim World* [*MW*] 47 (1977):306–307 (Boullata); *Zeitschrift der deutschen morganländischen Gesellschaft* [*ZDMG*] 128 (1978):411 (Wagner); *Theologische Literaturzeitung* 105 (1980):1–19 (Rudolph).

5. Major reviews of *SM* are as follows: *BSOAS* 43 (1980):137–39 (van Ess); *Journal of the American Academy of Religion* [*JAAR*] 47 (1979): 459–60 (Martin); *JSS* 26 (1980): 121–23 (Rippin); *Der Islam* 57 (1980): 354–55 (Madelung); *BO* 37 (1981):97–98 (Juynboll); *JRAS* (1980):180–82 (Cook); *ZDMG* 130 (1980):178 (Nagel).

6. See esp. his review of Josef van Ess, *Anfänge muslimischer Theologie*, *BSOAS* 43 (1980):361–63.

7. See *SM* 58–59; Crone and Cook, *Hagarism*, pp. 17–18.

8. An example would be the *tafsīrs* ascribed to al-Kalbī and Muqātil; for a variety of reasons which he outlines in *QS*, Wansbrough concludes that the form in which the texts are found today probably stems from a period later than the date of the supposed authors.

9. Examples would be *Fiqh Akbar I*, and the *Risāla* of al-Ḥasan al-Baṣrī; see *QS*, 160–63.

10. See Wansbrough's review of Nabia Abbott, *Studies in Arabic Literary Papyri, II, Qur'ānic Commentary and Tradition*, in *BSOAS* 31 (1968):613–16; cf. A. Grohmann, "The Problem of Dating Early Qur'āns," *Der Islam* 33 (1957):213–31; Grohmann's whole point, of course, is to emphasize the difficulty involved in dating Qur'ānic manuscripts.

11. John Burton, *The Collection of the Qur'ān* (Cambridge: Cambridge University Press, 1977). See Wansbrough's review in *BSOAS* 41 (1978):370–71.

12. Thomas L. Thompson, *The Historicity of the Patriarchal Narratives: The Quest for the Historical Abraham* (Berlin and New York: Walter de Gruyter, 1974), p. 328.

13. H. W. F. Saggs, *The Encounter with the Divine in Mesopotamia and Israel* (London: Athlone Press, 1978), pp. 65–66.

14. See Wansbrough's review of Neusner's work *BSOAS* 39 (1976):438–39 and 43 (1980):591–92 and of Neusner's students, *BSOAS* 41 (1978):368–69 (Zahavy); 42 (1979):140–41 (Green); 43 (1980):592–93 (Gereboff). The most important work of Rudolf Bultmann is *The History of the Synoptic Tradition*, trans. John Marsh, 2d ed. (Oxford: Blackwell, 1968). Neusner has published so much it is virtually impossible to select any one writing; his paper, "The Study of Religion as the Study of Tradition in Judaism," in *Methodological Issues in Religious Studies*, ed. Robert D. Baird (Chico, Calif.: New Horizons Press, 1975), pp. 31–48, is most useful.

15. Neusner's work, on the other hand, seems to imply that a certain amount of historical information is extricable. Implicitly the debate is over basic concerns of interpretational theory, e.g., H. G. Gadamer, *Truth and Method* (New York: Seabury,

1978) *vs.* E. D. Hirsch, Jr., *Validity in Interpretation* (New Haven: Yale University Press, 1967).

16. Joseph Schacht, "The Present State of Studies in Islamic Law," *Atti del terzo Congresso di Studi Arabi e Islamici* (Naples: Instituto Universitario Orientale, 1967), p. 622. Schacht concludes: "I have too strong a confidence in the scholarly competence of the workers in the field of Islamic law, both lawyers and orientalists, to regard this as anything but a passing aberration." If only that were true!

17. Also out of the common desire (need?) to provide "endings," i.e., to eliminate ambiguity; see F. Kermode, *The Genesis of Secrecy* (Cambridge, Mass.: Harvard University Press, 1979), chapter 3; idem, *The Sense of an Ending* (New York: Oxford University Press, 1967).

18. W. M. Watt, "The Materials Used by Ibn Isḥāq," in *Historians of the Middle East*, ed. Bernard Lewis and P. M. Holt (London and New York: Oxford University Press, 1962), pp. 23–24. Watt quotes C. H. Becker (agreeing with Lammens), ". . . the *Sīra* is not an independent historical source. It is merely *ḥadīth*—material arranged in biographical order," (p. 23) to which Watt retorts: "Since Becker wrote, there has been the important work of Joseph Schacht on legal *ḥadīth*. . . . Professor Schacht holds that it was not until the time of al-Shāfiʿī (d. 820) that it became the regular practice for legal rules to be justified by a *ḥadīth* reporting a saying or action of Muḥammad. . . . If this theory is correct . . . then *ḥadīth* as they are found in the canonical collections were not in existence in the time of Ibn Isḥāq (d. 768)" (pp. 23–24). Thus, for Watt, the historical validity of Ibn Isḥāq's material is proven since it was written before the fabrication of legal *ḥadīth!* Cf. P. Crone, *Slaves on Horses*, p. 211, nt. 88: "Watt disposes of Schacht by casuistry."

19. Fuat Sezgin, *Geschichte des arabischen Schriftums*, (Leiden: E. J. Brill, 1967), vol. 1.

20. Nabia Abbott, *Studies in Arabic Literary Papyri*, II, *Qur'ānic Commentary and Tradition* (Chicago: University of Chicago Press, 1967); cf. Wansbrough's review (nt. 10 above).

21. See Sezgin, *GAS* 1:32; cf. A. Rippin, "Ibn ʿAbbās's *Al-Lughāt fi'l-Qur'ān*," *BSOAS* 44 (1981):15–25; also "Al-Zuhrī, *naskh al-Qur'ān* and the problem of early *tafsir* texts," *BSOAS* 47 (1984):22–43, and Wansbrough, *QS*, chapter 4.

22. An example of such "additional evidence" appears in *QS* and *SM* in the notion of "terminological transfer."

23. Harry Austryn Wolfson, *The Philosophy of the Kalam* (Cambridge, Mass.: Harvard University Press, 1976), p. 72; see Wansbrough's review of the work, *BSOAS* 41 (1978):156–57.

24. "Islamic Religious Tradition" in *The Study of the Middle East*, ed. L. Binder (New York: Wiley, 1976), p. 61.

25. Specifically *The Qur'ān, Translated*, 2 vols. (Edinburgh: T. & T. Clark, 1937–39), and *Introduction to the Qur'ān* (Edinburgh: University Press, 1963 [1953]).

26. Cf. Serjeant's review of *QS* in *JRAS* (1978):78, and also van Ess's review in *BO* 35 (1978):349.

27. The term is not meant as one of derision but rather as one descriptive of textual method; see James Barr, *Fundamentalism* (Philadelphia: Westminster Press, 1978), esp. pp. 11–89. Modern scholarship on the Qur'ān treats that book as textually (if not

theologically) inerrant and, more basically, lacking in contradiction. The latter point is nowhere more clearly illustrated than in attempts to understand prayer and almsgiving in the Qur'ān in terms of a (reconstructable!) historical progression; the alternative view that the various passages on these topics represent variant traditions of different localized communities which have been brought into conjunction seems far more plausible in light of our knowledge of Judeo-Christian tradition and its establishment. But to assert this is to contradict the typical Western approach to the Qur'ān.

28. See the well-phrased statements of Franz Rosenthal in the introduction to the reprint of Charles C. Torrey, *The Jewish Foundation of Islam* (New York: KTAV, 1967 [1933]).

29. M. Hodgson's emphasis on the Irano-Semitic background of Islamic culture may prove an honorable exception to this general statement; see Marshall G. S. Hodgson, *The Venture of Islam*, 3 vols. (Chicago: University of Chicago Press, 1974), esp. vol. 1.

30. For modern studies of South Arabia, see, for example, the following recent works: Jacques Ryckmans, *Les inscriptions anciennes de l'Arabie du Sud: Points de vue et problèmes actuels* (Leiden: E. J. Brill, 1973); and J. Pirenne, "La religion des Arabes préislamiques d'après trois sites rupestres et leurs inscriptions" in *Al-Bahit: Festschrift Joseph Henninger zum 70. Geburtstag am 12. Mai 1976* (St. Augustin bei Bonn: Anthropos-Instituts, 1976), pp. 177–217 and cf. the use Serjeant makes of such works in his review of *QS*, *JRAS* (1978):76–77.

31. Adams, "Islamic Religious Tradition," in *The Study of the Middle East* (see nt. 24 above), p. 38.

32. Adams, p. 40, in reference to the "irenic" approach to Islamic studies advocated by W. C. Smith.

33. Jane Smith, in "Islamic Understanding of the Afterlife" [paper presented at the symposium on Islam and the History of Religions (see preface to the present volume)], points directly to the problem very explicitly but seems not to see the solution: "Does the asking of 'wrong' questions necessarily mean that answers will be unrelated to the truths about actual Muslim faith and practice?" If the study of Islam continues to be confronted in terms of "actual Muslim faith and practice" then the problem will continue to exist. The question must be asked: "Is that what we are after?" "Are we studying sociology or intellectual history?" We can do either, and both are without a doubt important, but one cannot ask intellectual-historical questions of sociological data.

34. See *SM* 24–25; *QS* 1, 40–43, 47–48, 51–52, 57–58 as well as the analysis of haggadic *tafsīr* in chapter 4 of *QS* which Wansbrough conceives of as illustrating the point (see *SM* 24).

35. Geza Vermes, "Redemption and Genesis xxii—The Binding of Isaac and the Sacrifice of Jesus," in his *Scripture and Tradition in Judaism: Haggadic Studies*, 2d rev. ed. (Leiden: E. J. Brill, 1973), pp. 193–227. Also see P. R. Davies and B. D. Chilton, "The Aqedah: A Revised Tradition History," *Catholic Biblical Quarterly* 40 (1978): 514–46.

36. And this would include those who attempt to postulate some sort of aberrant Judaism and/or Christianity known specifically to Arabia.

37. This procedure within Qumran is perhaps most clearly enunciated in Bleddyn J. Roberts, "Biblical Exegesis and Fulfillment in Qumran," in *Words and Meaning:*

Essays Presented to David Winton Thomas, ed. Peter R. Akroyd and Barnabas Lindars (Cambridge: Cambridge University Press, 1968), pp. 195–207, although such an interpretation goes against the mainstream of Qumranic scholarship where the trend to try to identify characters such as the Wicked Priest and Teacher of Righteousness predominate as in, e.g., Vermes (see nt. 35 above). Also see *SM* esp. 52–54.

38. See *QS* 49; *SM* 58, 139, where the notion of the lack of eschatology in the *Sīra* indicates a secure political position.

39. "An historical circumstance so public [as the emergence of the Qur'ān] cannot have been invented": see Serjeant's review of *QS* in *JRAS* (1978):77. The notion that a "conspiracy" (!) is involved in such a historical reconstruction becomes a rallying point for many objections; see N. Daniel's review of *Hagarism* in *JSS* 24 (1979):296–304. Contrary to Daniel (p. 298), one could claim that one hundred years *is* a long time, especially when one is dealing not with newspaper headlines and printing presses but the gradual emergence of a text at first within a select circle, then into ever widening circles. One could point to similar instances of "conspiracies" in the canonization of other scriptures, for example the identification of John the disciple with the Gospel of John in well less than a century after the emergence of the text. Besides, as in so many things, it all depends on which conspiracies one likes or does not like; Serjeant says of John Burton [*The Collection of the Qur'ān* (Cambridge: Cambridge University Press, 1977)] that he "argues vastly more cogently than Wansbrough's unsubstantiable assertions, that the consonantal text of the Qur'ān before us is the Prophet's own recension," but involved in Burton's book—if one bothers to read it carefully and not get carried away by its conclusion—is a "conspiracy" to which Serjeant's objection to Wansbrough's theory should apply as well. But obviously the conclusions are what count for Serjeant, not the method by which they are reached. (See his review of *QS*, *JRAS* [1978]:76). Cf. also Angelika Neuwirth, *Studien zur Komposition der mekkanischen Suren* (Berlin and New York: Walter de Gruyter, 1981) and my review *BSOAS* 45 (1982):149–50.

40. See, for example, Raphael Loewe, "Divine Frustration Exegetically Frustrated—Numbers 14:34 *tenū'ātī*," in *Words and Meanings*, ed. Lindars and Akroyd, esp. pp. 137–38; G. Vermes, *Scripture and Tradition*, introduction.

41. The historical appearance of exegetical "lists" of scriptural passages, whether of (apparent) scriptural contradiction, semantic aspects, or legal rulings (see *QS*, chapter 4 for these types of lists) indicate the emergence of a fixed text of scripture. Note M. R. Waldman's observation in Chapter 6 of this book: "As the Qur'ān itself became 'listed,' i.e., arranged in fixed order according to some fixed criteria of listing, further listing of the contents of the Qur'ān according to other principles of listing followed naturally." Precisely, Wansbrough would perhaps say; the earliest evidence of "listing" according to other criteria indicates the likely historical moment of the emergence of the fixed Qur'ānic canon.

42. See my review of *SM*, *JSS* 26 (1981):121–23.

43. See his review of van Ess, *Anfänge muslimischer Theologie*, in *BSOAS* 43 (1980): 361–63.

44. *MW* 67 (1977):307; the quote from *QS* is somewhat out of context, although cf. Wansbrough's review of van Ess, *Anfänge* in *BSOAS* 43 (1980):361.

45. Fazlur Rahman, *Major Themes of the Qur'ān* (Chicago: Bibliotheca Islamica, 1980), p. xiv; see my review in *BSOAS* 44 (1981):360–63. Rahman incorrectly quotes

QS; it should read ". . . the kind . . ."; there is also no explanation point (!) in Wansbrough's text. The possibility that there could be a difference of opinion over the value of literary analysis *per se* cannot be overlooked but Rahman's statements hardly are sufficient to urge such a position; cf. however, van Ess's review of *SM*, *BSOAS* 43 (1980):137–39, where precisely that argument is attempted; one needs to look no further than, for example, Frank Kermode, *The Genesis of Secrecy* (see nt. 17 above) to see the continued vitality of literary analysis, however.

46. G. H. A. Juynboll, in his review of *QS* in *JSS* 24 (1979):293–96, expresses this inability perfectly: "What makes W.'s theories so hard to swallow is the obvious disparity in style and contents of Meccan and Medinan *sūras*" (p. 294). Similar to this are Rahman's comments in Chapter 12, and in *Major Themes*, p. xvi, about chronological "necessity" due to the doctrine of *naskh* (which he conceives of as "removal" of verses alone, not as legal abrogation). The possibility that *naskh* refers to replaced Jewish practices (Burton) or to abrogated earlier dispensation (Wansbrough) is not even entertained by Rahman; both these alternate solutions obviate the chronological "necessity."

III

RḤMNN AND THE ḤANĪFS[1]

1. *Introduction: Interpreting the Qur'ān*

The extent to which a work of literature provides interpretative keys within itself for the use of its readers is variable. Some texts appear to be totally self-referential, using only a shared linguistic basis by which to communicate to their audiences (it would of course be possible to conceive of a text which denies even that linguistic stratum; the text would then have to be considered a kind of code which could then be subject to interpretation). Other texts make greater attempts at providing tags by which interpretation may take place. Frequently, such tags are to the world outside the text; these, of course, may well be "fictional" but that is of no concern to the actual process of interpretation as performed by the reader. The tags still provide a framework for interpretation.

The Qur'ān comes close to being an example of the first type of text, one which is self-referential. That is, it is a work which provides very little information to its readers for interpretative strategies. For example, the narrative structure of the text is one of the first things which communicates the fact that this is not a text which is attempting to mirror the external world on a referential basis. The basic linguistic level of the text communicates to its readers certainly, but even there the status of the Qur'ān as the grounding of the Arab civilization means that the Arabic linguistic resources used by the text's readers have been filtered beforehand through the Qur'ānic material; the evidence of contemporary or pre-Qur'ānic linguistic material is slight at the best and highly debatable in value.

The reading of a text must take place within a "pre-figured system of co-ordinates."[2] This means that, in the specific case of the Qur'ān, we must bring some sort of conceptual framework to the text within

---

[1] This paper was presented to the Oxford Colloquium on *ḥadīth* and historiography in September, 1988. My thanks especially to Uri Rubin, Lawrence Conrad and Patricia Crone for their useful comments on the text. Funds allowing me to attend the Oxford colloquium were provided by SSHRCC.

[2] John E. Wansbrough, *Res Ipsa Loquitur: History and Mimesis* (Jerusalem, 1987), 16.

which interpretation may take place. We must put the text within a shared perspective by which we can have the text make sense. The common Orientalist approach with regard to the Qur'ān has been to follow the Muslim community's internal framework, one most clearly embodied in the *Sīra*: that is, the Qur'ān is primarily to be interpreted in light of biography, specifically the stages in the career of Muḥammad. This method works quite well within the limits of its own presuppositions but getting outside the circle produced by the interaction of the Qur'ān and the *Sīra* is, it seems to me, impossible; Wansbrough's analysis of the *Sīra* has displayed the extent to which that text has actually been structured around explaining the Qur'ān: "In the *Sīra* . . . history is itself generated by scriptural imagery or enhanced by scriptural reference."[3] The two sources confirm each other in the interpretative process in a manner which appears deceptively natural. An excellent example of the Orientalist approach is provided in an article by Alford Welch on Muḥammad in the Qur'ān.[4] Saying that he is using "only" the Qur'ān as a source, Welch attempts to provide as much information about Muḥammad as is possible. The entire enterprise is marked by a presupposed framework of what "prophetic experience" is (that is clearly the "pre-figured system of co-ordinates" here) in combination with a chronological (i.e., historical) framework provided by the *Sīra* (for example, the division between the "Meccan" and the "Medinan" contexts).

As an alternative framework, Wansbrough has employed the Biblical text to provide a paradigmatic view of salvation history, viewing the Qur'ān in terms of motifs developed within the Judeo-Christian sectarian milieu. Others have attempted to see the Qur'ānic text in literary terms—Neuwirth, for example,[5] who uses structural patterns in combination with literary themes as the basis of an understanding of how the text works and conveys meaning, at least in the "Meccan" *sūras*.[6]

One conceptual framework which, for a variety of reasons, has not proven very fruitful in the interpretation of the Qur'ān is the use of the basic resources of archaeology and epigraphy. Philological

---

[3] John Wansbrough, *The Sectarian Milieu: Content and Composition of Islamic Salvation History* (Oxford, 1978), 7.

[4] Alford T. Welch, "Muhammad's Understanding of Himself: the Koranic Data," R.G. Hovannisian and S. Vryonis Jr. eds., *Islam's Understanding of Itself* (Malibu, 1983), 15–52.

[5] Angelika Neuwirth, *Studien zur Komposition der mekkanischen Suren* (Berlin, 1981).

[6] See my review in *BSOAS*, 45(1982), 149–150.

material certainly has been employed (Jeffery's *Foreign Vocabulary*[7] being the major and most successful example), but this has not provided a sufficiently comprehensive framework in which to place the whole text; one reason for this, given the evidence, is that the Qur᾽ān is extremely eclectic in its linguistic gathering. The lack of extensive material based upon archaeological findings in Central Arabia has meant that situating the Qur᾽ān in that context has not proven possible (I will leave open for now whether or not, if such material were available, it would in fact prove applicable). Onc area which has proven somewhat more successful has been the material provided by Southern Arabia, both inscriptional and archaeological. Of course, these data have not yet provided an overall framework for interpretation of the Qur᾽ān either, but they have proven functional in a number of instances where certain clarifications of the relevance (or not) of South Arabia in understanding the Qur᾽ān have taken place. I have explored one such instance in a previous article on the supposed reference to the Mārib dam in the Qur᾽ān;[8] in that instance, it was discovered that the archaeological and inscriptional evidence was being interpreted in light of a doubtful Qur᾽ānic interpretation and provided no independent basis in itself for such reconstructions. Another instance where inscriptional material has been brought into conjunction with Islamic tradition was investigated by Lawrence Conrad[9] regarding the traditions about Muḥammad's birth, which although not directly related to the Qur᾽ān is certainly relevant to the general understanding of certain passages of it.

I do not wish to argue for a privileged position of archaeological material in the interpretation of texts. In fact, my overall point here is to urge extreme care in the use of the material all together. Disciplines such as archaeology, epigraphy and philology are not "neutral" sources of information but require, like texts, a system of "pre-figured co-ordinates" within which they may be interpreted. That is not to say that the attempt should not be made to interpret the data, but the claims which underlie such interpretations must be examined very carefully before the results of those interpretations are built upon even

---

[7] Arthur Jeffery, *The Foreign Vocabulary of the Quran* (Boroda, 1938).

[8] A. Rippin, "Epigraphical South Arabian and Qur᾽ānic Exegesis," forthcoming in *Jerusalem Studies in Arabic and Islam*.

[9] Lawrence I. Conrad, "Abraha and Muḥammad: Some Observations apropos of Chronology and Literary *topoi* in the Early Arabic Historical Tradition," *BSOAS*, 50(1950), 225–240. Another, more speculative attempt is Maxime Rodinson, "Une phrase de style coranique dans une inscription sudarabique?" *Comptes rendus du groupe linguistique d'études chamito-Sémitiques*, 12–13(1967–69), 102–105.

further. The example of Biblical archaeology must always serve as a sober reminder to those of us in Islamic studies of the dangers of rampant searching for parallelisms.[10] While archaeological data are, of course, valuable in the reconstruction of history, they are no more "objective" or "neutral" than other evidence, for all such data must be placed within an interpretation framework, be that constructed, as Fredric Brandfon has recently argued so cogently, according to the "correspondence theory" which sees historical facts as emerging "self-evidently" from the data, or the "coherence theory" which judges historical facts on the basis of their relationship to an overall historical context.[11]

2. *Epigraphical South Arabian and the Qurʾānic* ḥanīfs

An ongoing and significant problem in the interpretation of the Qurʾān revolves around the word *ḥanīf* and its possible relationship to the epigraphical data provided by ancient South Arabian inscriptions. Here we have a situation of some importance: the argument has been made that Epigraphical South Arabian material may provide a context by which we can understand the spiritual background to Islam, the development of monotheism in Arabia and thus the whole polemic which is carried on in the Qurʾān between the monotheists and the polytheists. A specifically Arabian context by which the Qurʾān should be understood is being argued for at the same time.

The basic argument, most recently presented by Beeston,[12] is as follows. A monotheistic period is evidenced in the South Arabian

[10] The best exposé of such practices is found in Thomas L. Thompson, *The Historicity of the Patriarchal Narratives: the Quest for the Historical Abraham* (Berlin, 1974), especially chapter 12, "Summary and conclusions," 317: "this argument . . . has been developed almost entirely on the basis of a harmonization of historical hypotheses that have been drawn from several distinct bodies of material . . . Historical reconstructions which would appear extremely hypothetical or even totally untenable on their own merits and within their own field of discipline, achieve, nevertheless, the appearance of plausibility when they are interpreted in light of similar reconstructions of possibly related materials, where reconstructions themselves first appear plausible in the projection of the total synthesis."

[11] Frederic Brandfon, "The Limits of Evidence: Archeology and Objectivity," *Maarav*, 4(1987), 5–43.

[12] A.F.L. Beeston, "Himyarite Monotheism," in *Studies in the History of Arabia*, II, *Pre-Islamic Arabia* (Riyad, 1984), 149–154. See also his "The Religions of pre-Islamic Yemen" and "Judaism and Christianity in pre-Islamic Yemen," Joseph Chelhod, ed., *L'Arabie du Sud: Histoire et civilisation*, I, *Le peuple yéménite et ses racines* (Paris, 1984), 259–269, 271–278. The suggestion has a long history in scholarly writings; see the references in F. Buhl, "Ḥanīf," *EI*, II, 258–260.

inscriptions, starting around the end of the fourth century C.E.[13] This is marked first by the emergence of what are clearly Jewish inscriptions and then, later, Christian ones. Many of these employ RḤMNN as the name of God. A substantial proportion of these monotheistic inscriptions, however, is neither Jewish nor Christian in terms of their explicit terminology. These inscriptions may be taken as representing some sort of native monotheist tendency worshipping God under the name RḤMNN (=al-Raḥmān), which may then be identified with the *ḥanīfī* movement spoken of in the Qur'ān.

This argument rests on two propositions: one, that the inscriptions eivdence a monotheism which is neither Jewish nor Christian, and two, that the Qur'ān and early Islamic sources provide a historical witness to a pre-Islamic monotheistic movement known as the *ḥanīfiyya*. Both of these propositions are tenuous and, to some extent, rest on the assumption of the assured nature of the other.

Do we have evidence that may be taken as historically firm that a group of monotheists, known as the *ḥanīfiyya*, existed in pre-Islamic times? If so, it may then be possible to interpret the inscriptions in light of that evidence. Or, approaching the issue the other way around, does the Epigraphical South Arabian material demand an interpretation of a non-Jewish, non-Christian monotheism? If that is the case, then it may be possible to interpret the Islamic literary evidence in light of the inscriptions. The problem here is a methodological one, involving the assessment of the nature of historical evidence and its interpretation.

3. *The Qur'ān*

Although the topic has been scrutinized in the scholarly literature many times (on very few subjects dealing with the Qur'ān is there so much bibliography[14]), it is necessary to rehearse the Qur'ānic material involving the word *ḥanīf* and its plural *ḥunafā'* once again in order to present the overall argument on the topic from the very beginning.[15]

---

[13] The dating of eras in South Arabian history remains uncertain and subject to scholarly dispute.

[14] Older bibliography on the subject is in Y. Moubarac, *Abraham dans le Coran* (Paris, 1958), 161, and updated in Frederick Mathewson Denny, "Some Religio-communal Terms and Concepts in the Qur'ān," *Numen*, 24(1977), 27–36.

[15] The significance of the widely cited Ibn Mas'ūd "variant" to Q.III:319, reading *ḥanīfiyya* rather than *islām* is unlikely to be more than exegetical and thus has no impact on the argument here.

II:135 They say, become Jews (*hūd*^{an}) or Christians (*naṣārā*), if you wish to be guided. Say, no, rather the *milla* of Abraham, a *ḥanīf* way, he was not of the polytheists.

III:67 Abraham was not a Jew (*yahūdiyy*^{an}) nor a Christian (*naṣrāniyy*^{an}); rather he was a *ḥanīf*, a *muslim*, he was not of the polytheists.

III:95 God speaks the truth. Follow the *milla* of Abraham, a *ḥanīf* way, he was not of the polytheists.

IV:125 Who is better religiously (*dīn*^{an}) than whoever submits (*aslama*) his face to God, who acts righteously (*muḥsin*), who follows the *milla* of Abraham, a *ḥanīf* way. God took Abraham as a friend.

VI:79 [Abraham said] Indeed, I have set my face in a *ḥanīf* way towards Him who created the heavens and the earth and I am not of the polytheists.

VI:161 Say, my Lord has guided me to a straight path, a right (*qiyam*) religion (*dīn*) the *milla* of Abraham, a *ḥanīf* way, he was not of the polytheists.

X:105 So set your face towards the religion, in a *ḥanīf* way, and do not be of the polytheists.

XVI:120 Indeed, Abraham was an *umma*, obedient to God, a *ḥanīf*, and he was not of the polytheists.

XVI:123 So We have revealed to you, "Follow the *milla* of Abraham, a *ḥanīf* way, he was not of the polytheists."

XXII:31 [Honouring the sacred rites of God and the food laws], being *ḥunafāʾ* to God, not polytheists.

XXX:30 Set your face towards the religion (*dīn*), in a *ḥanīf* way, the *fiṭra* of God in which people were created (*faṭara*) . . . that is the *qayyim*[16] religion.

XCVIII:5 They have been ordered only to worship, being *mukhliṣ* towards Him in religion (*dīn*), *ḥunafāʾ*, establishing prayer and practising charity; that is the religion (*dīn*) of the true (*qayyim*).

Ḥanif is sometimes translated as "upright religion," a rendering which is said to include overtones from the Arabic root sense of *ḥ-n-f* meaning "to incline" (to incline away from the polytheistic standards of the day towards Islam and thus become upright),[17] even though

16 Compare Q.IX:36, XII:40, XXX:43.

17 See, e.g., Jeffery, *Foreign Vocabulary*, 114, and Denny, "Religio-communal Terms," 33.

etymologically the word *ḥanīf* is generally thought to be derived from Syriac.[18] This attitude of "uprightness" is clearly associated in these Qurʾānic passages with Abraham, who, in his rejection of polytheism (see also Q. XXXVII:83–98 etc.), displays this "upright" attitude.[19] The Arab commentators on the Qurʾān, however, displayed some differences of opinion over whether, in the refrain *millat Ibrāhīma ḥanīf*[an], the word *ḥanīf* was supposed to qualify *milla* or Ibrāhīm. Al-Bayḍāwī, for example, suggests that *ḥanīf* may be either a *ḥāl* (an adverbial accusative of stage or condition) to the *muḍāf*, i.e., *milla*, or to the *muḍāf ilayhi*, i.e., Ibrāhīm.[20] Wright explains the situation by suggesting that *ḥanīf* is grammatically dependent upon Ibrāhīm,[21] *milla* being "virtually a part of" the latter, an opinion also found in *Tafsīr al-Jalālayn*;[22] this explanation strikes me as prejudging the situation somewhat, using grammar arbitrarily to support a conclusion reached by other (dogmatic) means. *Milla* in itself is a difficult word, frequently being taken as the equivalent of *dīn*, "religion", but also sometimes seen as more limited: "religious beliefs of a person" fits nicely and agrees with a suggested Aramaic/late Hebrew derivation, although Syriac is seen as a more likely source for the word, in which language is said to be employed as a technical term for "religion." The Qurʾānic usage may reflect the adoption of the Syriac term, modified by the sense connected to the Arabic root meaning of "way."[23] So, if *ḥanīf* is taken as a description of *milla*, then the sense is one of "upright religious beliefs" which were being followed by Abraham. One passage, Q.XVI:120, seems to suggest, however, that Abraham himself is the one displaying the *ḥanīfī* attitude and that sense may then be seen as applying in all instances: Abraham was "upright" in the upholding of his religious beliefs. A third possibility, that a passage such as Q.II:135 should be taken to mean "follow, in an upright manner, the religious belief system of Abraham" (the statement being directed towards the hearers of the Qurʾān) is

---

[18] A. Jeffery, *Foreign Vocabulary*, pp. 112–115; N.A. Faris and Harold W. Glidden, "The Development of the Meaning of Koranic Ḥanīf," *Journal of the Palestine Oriental Society*, 19 (1939/40), 1–13. Also see below, section 5 of this paper.

[19] See Moubarac, *Abraham*, especially chapter 2.

[20] Al-Bayḍāwī, *Anwār al-tanzīl wa-asrār al-taʾwīl* (Cairo, 1344/1225–26), 33.

[21] W. Wright, *A Grammar of the Arabic Language*, third edition (Cambridge, 1896–8), II, 119–120. Also see H. Reckendorf, *Arabische Syntax* (reprint Heidelberg, 1977), 114–115 (section 60/1).

[22] Al-Maḥallī and al-Suyūṭī, *Tafsīr al-Jalālayn* (Cairo, n.d.), I, 19.

[23] See Jeffery, *Foreign Vocabulary*, 268–269, and Denny, "Religio-communal Terms," 34–36.

entertained by some commentators,[24] but it does not fit into all the required contexts quite as smoothly as one may wish and thus has little to commend it.

The sense of the word *ḥanīf* in all the Qurʾānic passages is clearly to be opposed to the attitudes portrayed in Judaism and Christianity as well as, most emphatically, in polytheism. The *ḥanīfī* attitude is described as a counterpart of being *muslim* and *mukhliṣ*. The meaning of the first of these terms is, on one level, easy to understand: it means being a member of the religious community called "Islam." However, the term also presents a certain ambivalence in the sense that it also may be taken as descriptive of a person's religious attitude. This religious attitude has been subject to intensive scholarly investigation, and many would seem to agree that it conveys the sense of "total exclusive surrender" to the one God.[25] *Mukhliṣ*, on the other hand, is generally seen to convey a meaning of "purity," especially in terms of dedication to the one God, once again as the "exclusive" object of faith.[26]

The quality of being a *ḥanīf* is also conveyed as a part of the character of the "natural" religious impulse of humanity, *fiṭra*, and is used as a quality of a religion (*dīn*) which has a character described three times with the root *q-y-m*, generally taken in the sense of "true" or "established." The association of the *ḥanīfī* attitude in Q.XXII:31 and XCVIII:5 with religious ritual is to be noted also; having a *ḥanīfī* attitude would seem to involve community membership and obligations at least to some extent, as reflected perhaps in the term *milla* also.[27]

Finally, the use of the work *umma* in Q.XVI:120 is significant although problematic. The difficulty in making sense of calling Abraham an *umma* in that word's common meaning of "community" has led both classical Muslims commentators and some modern interpreters to understand the word as "paragon of virtue" or the like.[28]

---

[24] E.g., al-Naḥḥās, *Iʿrāb al-Qurʾān* (Cairo, 1985), I, 266, as his third opinion.

[25] Helmer Ringgren, *Islam ʾaslama and muslim* (Uppsala, 1949); D.Z.H. Baneth, "What did Muḥammad Mean When He Called his Religion 'Islam'? The Original Meaning of aslama and its Derivatives," *IOS*, 1(1971), 183–190; Denny, "Religio-communal Terms," 36–42.

[26] Helmer Ringgren, "The Pure Religion," *Oriens*, 15(1962), 93–96.

[27] Note the conclusions of Denny, "Religio-communal Terms," 35–36, in this regard.

[28] Toshihiko Izutsu, *Ethico-religious Concepts in the Qurʾān* (Montreal, 1966), 191–192, n. 6; Frederick Denny, "The Meaning of *ummah* in the Qurʾān," *History of Religions*, XV(1975–6), 38–39, nn. 14–15, with references to al-Ṭabarī, al-Rāzī, and *Tafsīr al-Jalālayn*.

As a number of other people have argued,[29] it is doubtful that one can make much out of these passages with regards to a historical referent; the term *ḥanīf* in the Qur᾽ān speaks of a spiritual attitude and to go beyond that is a shaky proposition at best. *Ḥanīf* reflects a notion of a basic religious impulse in humanity towards dedication to the one God. This is part of an overall social and ritual religious context, for sure, but more importantly, it is the basis of the Qur᾽ānic ideology of belief which is embodied in the myth of Abraham[30] and captured in the word *muslim*.

4. *Evidence from outside the Qur᾽ān*

It is, of course, possible to make the argument that we should interpret the work *ḥanīf* when used in the Qur᾽ān in light of the *Sīra* and other "early" sources, using the evidence which emerges from there concerning the *ḥanīfiyya*. The use of early poetry in a lexicographical approach has proven frustrating, however, because of the difficulty in interpreting the poetical texts themselves; Moubarac's survey of the relevant passages throws little light on the meaning of the term itself and certainly provides little help concerning the basic historical question of the existence of the *ḥanīfiyya* as a movement.[31]

There is another material, however, which some have suggested may provide independent evidence of the existence of the *ḥanīfiyya* and which may prove valuable in the interpretation of the epigraphical South Arabian material as well as the Qur᾽ān. Narratives in works such as the *Sīra* and other books of history contain references to individuals before and during the lifetime of Muḥammad who are spoken of as *ḥanīfs*. On the basis of information from such sources, some scholars have developed their historical reconstructions of the *ḥanīfiyya* to an impressive extent:

> [Muḥammad] now moved toward identifying his movement completely with the religion of Ibrāhīm, the *millat Ibrāhīm*, the *ḥanīfiyya*. . . Significantly, the movement took the name of the Ḥanīfiyya now, before becoming known as 'Islam' . . . . The old name of the movement, the *ḥanīfiyya*, suggests, besides the originally Meccan religious purification movement against polytheism, a kind of 'reform movement' with regards to the *ahl al-kitāb*.[32]

---

[29] E.g., W.M. Watt, "Ḥanīf," *EI*², III, 165–66; Fazlur Rahman, *Major Themes of the Qur᾽ān* (Chicago, 1980), 143–144.
[30] See Moubarac, *Abraham*, chapters 6 and 7.
[31] *Ibid.*, 153–159.
[32] Jacques Waardenburg, "Towards a Periodization of Earliest Islam According to its Relations with Other Religions," Rudolph Peters, ed., *Proceedings of the Ninth Congress of the Union Européenne des Arabisants et Islamisants* (Leiden, 1981), 311, 313.

It is clear from looking at stories told of the *ḥanīfs* in the *Sīra*, for example, that the Muslims of the second *hijrī* century and later thought in terms of a pre-Islamic religious movement known as the *ḥanīfiyya* (it is only at this time that the use of the abstract noun in this form emerges; it is not used in the Qurʾān). A central account tells of four people described as *ḥanīfs*: Zayd Ibn ʿAmr, Waraqa Ibn Nawfal, ʿUbayd Allāh Ibn Jaḥsh and ʿUthmān Ibn al-Huwayrith. Other sources speak of Umayya Ibn Abī al-Ṣalt, Quss Ibn Sāʿida, Abū Qays Ṣirma, Khālid b. Sinān Ibn Ghayth, Abū ʿĀmir ʿAbd ʿAmr Ibn Ṣayfī, and Abū Qays Ibn al-Aslat.[33] Wansbrough has suggested that the narrative in the *Sīra* dealing with the first four people serves, along with the story of Salmān al-Fārisī, in the mode of *praeparatio evangelica* and it represents "in the sense defined by Jolles, a myth . . . devised to interpret the spiritual, intellectual, and social transformation brought about by the mission . . . of an Arabian prophet."[34] For the Muslims after the time of Muḥammad, these stories function to sketch out the period of the *jāhiliyya* which serves as the point of comparison for all things Islamic. Rubin has objected to this interpretation of the *ḥanīfī* tradition, however, because of the existence of reports concerning three people called *ḥanīfs* who are also portrayed as being antagonistic towards Muḥammad and "no Muslim could have had an interest in characterizing these opponents of the prophet as *ḥunafāʾ*."[35] This suggests therefore that there must be some historical significance to the accounts—a kernel of historical memory must be contained within the narratives—and they are not simply back projections constructed on the basis of an imaginative vision of the pre-Islamic period. The people cited and treated in some detail by Rubin are Abū ʿĀmir ʿAbd ʿAmr ibn Ṣayfī, Abū Qays Ibn al-Aslat, and Umayya Ibn Abī al-Ṣalt. Rubin isolates what he terms an inter-*ḥanīfī* conflict or rivalry to account for this conflict between monotheists.

Putting all the accounts of these *ḥanīfs* together, however, suggests another interpretation to me. Christianity plays a significant role in

---

[33] See J.S. Trimingham, *Christianity Among the Arabs in pre-Islamic Times* (London, 1979), 263–264; Uri Rubin, "Ḥanīfiyya and Kaʿba. An Inquiry into the Arabian pre-Islamic Background of *dīn Ibrāhīm*," forthcoming in *Jerusalem Studies in Arabic and Islam*. Also see W.M. Watt, *Muhammad at Mecca* (Oxford, 1953), Excursus C, 162–164; T. Izutzu, *God and Man in the Koran: Semantics of the Koranic Weltanschauung* (Tokyo, 1964), 112–118.

[34] Wansbrough, *Sectarian Milieu*, 7; also quoted in Rubin, "Ḥanīfiyya," typescript note 1.

[35] Rubin, "Ḥanīfiyya," typescript 2.

the *Sīra* accounts of the *ḥanīfs*, with three of the four people converting to Christianity, and the fourth, Zayd ibn ʿAmr, searching in Syria among Christians but being told to return to Arabia. I wonder if, underlying these reports, and having an influence on all the accounts speaking of *ḥanīfs*, is a polemical motif of Christian rejection of the Islamic messenger. That is, these stories are functioning not only a *praeparatio evangelica* but also as stereotypical narratives of Christian rejection, thus forming the Christian counterpart to the rabbinic pericopes which play such a great role in the *Sīra*. The motifs of conflict with Muḥammad by certain *ḥanīfs* along with the association of other *ḥanīfs* with Christianity, I am suggesting, are all parts, rather indistinctly transmitted, of a building block of the *Sīra* which did not solidify in the same way as did the rabbinic pericopes: the Christian rejection of Muḥammad. They are, therefore, literary elements whose basic use was to elaborate and embellish the story of the life of Muḥammad; the historicity of such elements must remain unknown.

Now I do not wish necessarily to argue against the presence of a non-Christian or non-Jewish monotheistic trend in Arabia in the pre-Islamic period. Rather, what I am urging is methodological caution in the use of the sources in the desire to produce historical "facts." It seems to me quite possible to interpret traditions about the *ḥanīfiyya* as transmitted in later Muslim sources *not* as evidence of an organized monotheistic movement in pre-Islamic Arabia: these traditions are too coloured by the Islamic tradition to serve as independent historical witnesses to pre-Islamic times. What we have is evidence of the creative activity of later Muslim writers in the development of mythic narratives.

Likewise, it might well be suggested that the monotheistic trend spoken of by Sozomen,[36] in terms of an Abrahamic mythology apparently embraced by the Arabs, is not necessarily to be identified with a historical *ḥanīfiyya*. Furthermore, the clear echo of the Biblical understanding of place of the Arabs found in these three isolated lines of Sozomen's text (an echo which continues in later Muslim presentations also, for example in *Kitāb al-aṣnām* of Ibn al-Kalbī [d. 204/819][37]) raises justifiable doubts regarding the attribution of much serious historical weight to this source.

---

[36] See *ibid.*, typescript note 68; Michael Cook, *Muhammad* (Oxford, 1983), 81, 92; Patricia Crone, *Meccan Trade and the Rise of Islam* (Princeton, 1987), 190–191, note 104.

[37] Translated by N.A. Faris, *The Book of Idols, Being a Translation from the Arabic of the Kitāb al-aṣnām of Hishām ibn al-Kalbī* (Princeton, 1953).

I do not think that the *Sīra* material, or other texts of the same ilk, give us the grounds to support the existence of an organized *ḥanīfiyya* in pre-Islamic Arabia. The entire Abraham myth, of picturing him as a *muslim*, has been taken literally rather than "spiritually" by succeeding generations of followers of Islam (as a result of what may well be a human drive towards historicization), just as the term *ḥanīf* has been transformed from one of description of spiritual qualities to a historical phenomenon.[38] The *Sīra* is the text which performed a good measure of this transformation, putting in narrative form the mythic structures built into the Qurʾān, making them tangible and available for mass consumption.

5. *Epigraphy*

Do the inscriptions written in Epigraphical South Arabian provide any evidence of the existence of a monotheistic tendency, not identifiable as Judaism or Christianity which could then be associated with a movement known as the *ḥanīfiyya* in central Arabia? Among the thousands of inscriptions which have been discovered in the Sabian dialect of Epigraphical South Arabian, a relatively small number witness religious monotheism being practiced by at least some strata of society from late in the fourth century onwards. These inscriptions have been gathered in an excellent article by Christian Robin.[39] Seven inscriptions are seen to be explicitly Jewish. God has the title "Lord of the Jews" in two instances;[40] another invokes the "people of Israel."[41] There are four major inscriptions plus a number of lesser ones which are explicitly Christian. One inscription makes reference to the "Holy Spirit" and pronounces an invocation "in the name of

---

[38] For further thoughts on the role of the Abraham myth in Islam, see my "The Function of *asbāb al-nuzūl* in Qurʾānic Exegesis," *BSOAS*, 51 (1988), 1–20, and my forthcoming *Muslims, Their Religious Beliefs and Practices*: I. *The Formative Period* (London, 1989), chapter 1.

[39] "Judaisme et Christianisme en Arabie du Sud d'après les sources épigraphiques et archéologiques," *Proceedings of the Seminar for Arabian Studies*, X (1980), 85–96. Older articles on the same subject are still valuable for their discussion of the material: G. Ryckmans, "Les inscriptions monothéistes sabéennes," in *Miscellanea historica in honorem Alberti di Meyer* (Louvain, 1946), 194–205; J. Ryckmans, "Le christianisme en Arabie du Sud préislamique," *L'Oriente cristiano nella storia della civiltà* (Rome, 1964), 413–453.

[40] Ja 1028 (see A. Jamme, *Sabaean and Hasaean Inscriptions from Saudi Arabia* [Rome, 1966], 39*ff*.) and Ry 515 (see G. Ryckmans, "Inscriptions sud-arabes, 10e sér," *Le Muséon*, 66[1953], 314–315).

[41] Bayt al-Ashwal 1 (see G. Garbini, "Una bilingue sabeo-ebraica da Ẓafar," *Annali dell'Istituto Orientale di Napoli*, 30[1970], 154ff.)

RḤMNN, and His son Christ the Victorious."[42] Three inscriptions come from the time of Abraha, of which one starts with the invocation "By the might and aid and mercy of RḤMNN and of His Messiah and of the Holy Spirit."[43]

There remains, however, another group of monotheistic inscriptions which are not explicitly Jewish or Christian. Robin counts some fourteen inscriptions which invoke the one God, sometimes with the name RḤMNN, but the phraseology of the texts does not allow an immediate decision as to whether they are Jewish or Christian.[44] Phrases employed in these inscriptions include "RḤMNN, Lord of heaven" and "RḤMNN, Lord of heaven and earth.[45] Theories abound and this is one case where corroboration by other material is needed in order to provide a convincing argument. Robin, for example, builds a terminological and historical[46] argument for seeing the inscriptions as Jewish. This has been the common scholarly view in the past, constructed with help from apparent evidence for Jewish proselytizing activity in fifth-century Yemen.[47] In the absence of what he considers overwhelming evidence either way, Beeston opts for a native monotheistic tendency, non-Jewish and non-Christian, parallel to the *ḥanīfiyya*:

> If the main body of Raḥmānists before the 6th century was monotheistic without being committed Jews or Christians, they can only have been what a Muslim would call *ḥunafa*ᵓ. The late H.A.R. Gibb, with his usual perceptiveness, has expressed the opinion that there must have been *ḥunafā*ᵓ in Arabia in the few centuries before Islam; and the epigraphic evidence surveyed above seems to me to support this.[48]

---

[42] Istanbul 7608 bis; also see J. Ryckmans, "L'inscription sabéenne chrétienne Istanbul 7608 bis," *JRAS* (1976), 96–99.

[43] CIH 541; also see Sidney Smith, "Events in Arabia in the Sixth Century A.D.," *BSOAS*, 16(1954), 437.

[44] See the chart in Robin, "Judaisme et Christianisme," 92–93.

[45] See G. Ryckmans, "Heaven and Earth in the South Arabian Inscriptions," *JSS*, 3(1958), 225–236, for the overall context of such inscriptions.

[46] Some of the argument revolves around the beginning of the period of Christianity in South Arabia; see J. Ryckmans, "Le christianisme en Arabe," 413–453; A.F.L. Beeston, "Himyarite Monotheism," 149–150; Irfan Shahid, *Byzantium and the Arabs in the Fourth Century* (Washington, D.C., 1984), appendix 1, "Christianity in South Arabia," 100–104.

[47] See Edward Ullendorff, "Hebraic-Jewish Elements in Abyssinian (Monophysite) Christianity," *JSS*, 1(1956), 216–256, especially 223.

[48] Beeston, "Himyarite Monotheism," 151; the reference is to H.A.R. Gibb, "Pre-Islamic Monotheism in Arabia," *Harvard Theological Review*, 55 (1962), 269–280. In his articles in Chelhod, *L'Arabie du Sud*, Beeston is a bit more cautious. He makes his argument somewhat wider by appealing to the existence of other non-Jewish/non-Christian monotheistic tendencies in the Mediterranean and speaking of connections

The evidence for the existence of this tendency is not to be found in the inscriptions, however, except through the voice of silence: in no way is the existence of this tendency to a non-Jewish, non-Christian monotheism supported by other archaeological data. The appeal to the *ḥanīfiyya* is, in fact, an attempt to find a context for the inscriptions on the basis of other material. Beeston is interpreting the inscriptions within the "pre-figured system of co-ordinates" provided by the Islamic literary tradition.

Beeston's argument does not rest solely on this flimsy basis, however. The use of the name for God RḤMNN may be seen as another element in a contextual connection between the *ḥanīfiyya* and these monotheistic inscriptions. RḤMNN is directly equivalent to al-Raḥmān, the name of God used in the Qurʾān some 170 times (including the *basmala*).[49] RḤMNN is used in some South Arabian inscriptions to designate God in Jewish texts and the Father in Christian texts as well as being present in a number (eight according to Robin's listing) of the unspecific inscriptions. The connection seems obvious: the non-Jewish, non-Christian monotheism of South Arabia used RḤMNN as the name of God, and Muḥammad's *ḥanīfiyya* employed that name also. The association of the name al-Raḥmān in Muslim tradition with the Yemen, leading to its rejection by the Meccans on the grounds of its foreign-ness, would seem to confirm this picture.

However, it has often been pointed out that the use of RḤMNN is of Jewish origin and that the word itself was used by both Jews and Christians in South Arabia and elsewhere.[50] A path of transmission into the Qurʾān from either of those communities is likely, and thus the evidence, once again, does not necessarily provide any support for the existence of a South Arabian or Central Arabian native monotheism.

To bolster his argument even further and to make it more specific,

---

between that area and South Arabia whence the introduction of the tendency; this is, he says, what is called in Arabic "the faith of the *hunafāʾ*" (268). This argument raises the notion of the "evolution" of monotheism in Arabia through the emergence of the "High God" out of a pantheon of lesser entities. The evidence for this, in terms of the general history of religions, is slight however, and as a theory appears to be based more on evolutionary models of social behaviour than on detailed evidence. For arguments concerning the Qurʾānic data see W.M. Watt, "Belief in a 'High God' in pre-Islamic Mecca," *JSS*, 16(1971), 35–40; *idem*, "The Qurʾān and Belief in a 'High God'," *Der Islam*, 56: (1979), 205–211; Uri Rubin, "*Al-Ṣamad* and the High God: An Interpretation," *Der Islam*, 61(1984), 197–217.

[49] See Jacques Jomier, "Le nom divin 'al-Raḥmān' dans le Coran," in *Mélanges Louis Massignon* (Damascus, 1957), II, 361–381.

[50] See Jeffery, *Foreign Vocabulary*, 140–141.

Beeston locates a vehicle for this spread of Arabian monotheism. The evidence of the etymology of the word *ḥanīf*, which is certainly problematic in itself, is employed. The controversy which lies behind this claim is easily stated: virtually everyone agrees the Arabic word is derived from the Syriac *ḥanpe*, but the Syriac word means "heathen." How was the word transformed from a term of rebuke to one of eminent spiritual development? Nabataean is often seen as the place of transformation where the cognate is held to have meant "a follower of some branch of their Hellenized Syro-Arabian religion";[51] this view of the word's origin concurs in its general tendencies with a large proportion of the loan words found in the Qurʾān. Beeston, however, replaces this view by picturing a South Arabian context. That is, he suggests that the transformation of the term took place in the general South Arabian environment during the monotheistic period and that the term thereby became a part of the lingua franca of the Ḥijāz in pre-Muḥammadan times (Beeston does not actually say that the *ḥanīfiyya* movement itself spread from South Arabia to the Ḥijāz but that may well be taken as an implication).

> The difficulty [of the shift in the meaning of the term] is however largely obviated if we assume that the term *ḥanīf* entered the Arabic language not directly from Syria, but by way of Najrān. The Najrānites must have been well aware that the Syrian missionaries called all non-Christians, whether polytheistic or monotheistic, *ḥanpe*, and have taken the word into their own vocabulary. Makkans of the 5th century, with their strong trading connections with Yaman, must have been aware that the wealthier classes there were almost overwhelmingly monotheistic, and it would thus have been easy for them to adopt the term *ḥanīf* (used by the Najrānites to designate their neighbours on the south) in the specific sense of monotheist, excluding the other applications which the term had in Syriac.[52]

The basis for this etymological argument would seem to be lacking, constructed as it is upon the suggestion that things "must have" been this way. Of course, the argument is *plausible* but it provides no *evidence* by which the interpretation of either the inscriptions or the Qurʾān may be supported.

6. *Conclusion: the emergence of "facts"*

The conclusion to be reached by this study must be that the inscriptions provide no *independent* evidence of the history of the

---

[51] Faris and Glidden, "Development of the Meaning," 267.
[52] Beeston, "Himyarite Monotheism," 151.

ḥanīfiyya. Only by taking the Qur᾿ānic and later Arabic literary data as evidence for the existence of this group can the Epigraphical South Arabian inscriptions be interpreted to suggest actual evidence of this non-Jewish, non-Christian monotheism. But the evidence of the Qur᾿ān *vis-à-vis* a historical reality of the monotheistic tendency is in need of support in itself, support which it might be thought is to be found in this monotheistic period in the inscriptions. But such is pure circular reasoning.

Wansbrough has spoken of the "easy metamorphosis of the philologist's hypothesis into the historian's 'act' ";[53] subsequent building upon the emergent "fact" obscures the origins of such hypotheses and leads to an accumulation of tenuous interpretations. In the specific case of the relationship between South Arabia and the Qur᾿ān, Wansbrough's felicitous prose once again hits the mark: "the literary account of the Hijaz has gradually assumed the status of an archaeological site" while the South Arabian inscriptions, like the Ugaritic ones of which Wansbrough speaks, have been "translated into a narrative pattern of events."[54] This does not mean that a connection between South Arabia and the Qur᾿ān should not be pursued; rather, careful consideration is needed in the assessment of the data which are available to us, both on the Islamic and the South Arabian sides, before conclusions are reached. It is too easy—and far too tempting—to produce tenuous interpretations of data and see them as confirming one another without considering the weaknesses of the initial arguments. Two weak historical interpretations do not necessarily combine to make one strong "fact," despite strenuous efforts on the part of many historians to justify that procedure.

---

[53] Wansbrough, *History and Mimesis*, 18.
[54] *Ibid.*, 22.

IV

READING THE QURʾĀN WITH RICHARD BELL*

The publication of the mammoth work by Richard Bell, *A Commentary on the Qurʾān*, provides a welcome opportunity for reflection upon Qurʾānic studies and its future in the academic environment. The work, which was prepared over 40 years ago in order to accompany Bell's *The Qurʾān, Translated*, reveals Bell's attempts to discern the meaning of the Qurʾānic text in order to fit it into the life of Muḥammad. As a principle of history and textual interpretation, this approach has an honorable pedigree in Biblical and Qurʾānic scholarship; it has provided the prime reading strategy for scholars until recently. Whether it is still sufficient today is doubtful. Bell's work reveals its age.

Born in Scotland in 1876 and educated at Edinburgh, receiving degrees in both Semitic studies and divinity, Richard Bell[1] came to some prominence in the field of the study of the Qurʾan and early Islam with the publication in expanded form of his 1925 Edinburgh University Gunning Lectures, under the title *The Origin of Islam in its Christian Environment*.[2] A little over a decade later he published the work for which he has become most famous (and infamous), *The Qurʾān, Translated, with a Critical Re-arrangement of the Surahs*.[3] In the preface to that work, Bell mentioned that "owing to the cost of printing, the mass of notes which have been accumulated in the course of the work have had to be suppressed" (p. viii). In the decades surrounding the appearance of his translation, he also published a series of 15 articles on Muḥammad and the Qurʾān dedicated to explaining the ideas and principles lying behind his work.[4] Finally, just before his death in 1952, he was able to bring together some class lectures which provided a full explanation of his views on the Qurʾān,

* A review article of: *A Commentary on the Qurʾān*. By Richard Bell. Edited by C. Edmund Bosworth and M. E. J. Richardson. Two volumes. Journal of Semitic Studies Monograph 14. Manchester: University of Manchester, 1991. Pp. xxii + 608; [iv] + 603. £60.

[1] Biographical details on Bell are scant; see the editors' introduction to the work under review (1:xiii–xiv). Among additional obituaries is A. S. Tritton, *Journal of the Royal Asiatic Society* 1952–53: 180, who notes that Bell first worked on Arabic mathematical manuscripts but then gave that up for the Qurʾān; otherwise, Tritton comments, "his life was uneventful." Also see *University of Edinburgh Journal* 16.ii (1952): 107, which clarifies that Bell received an M.A. in 1897 and a D.D.

[2] First published, London: Macmillan, 1926; reprint, London: Frank Cass, 1968. Hereafter cited as *Origin*.

[3] Edinburgh: T. & T. Clark, 1937 (vol. 1); 1939 (vol. 2). Hereafter cited as *Qurʾān*.

[4] See the bibliography in W. M. Watt, *Bell's Introduction to the Qurʾān*, Islamic Surveys 8 (Edinburgh: Edinburgh Univ. Press, 1970), 179–80, for the list of the articles, all of which were published between 1928 and 1948; three of them were reprinted in *Der Koran*, ed. Rudi Paret, Wege der Forschung CCCXXVI (Darmstadt: Wissenschaftliche Buchgesellschaft, 1975): "Muhammed's Call," pp. 86–92; "Muhammad's Visions," pp. 93–102; "Muhammad and Divorce in the Qurʾān," pp. 103–10. Assembling all of the articles in one volume would be a worthwhile task. Six other articles are listed in *Index Islamicus* as written by Bell: "Critical Observations on the mistakes of Philologers, by Ali ibn Hamza al-Basri, part V: Observations on the Mistakes in the Book Called Ikhtiyar Fasih al-Kalam, composed by Abuʾl-ʿAbbas Ahmad ibn Yahya Thaʿlab, translated from a ms in the British Museum," *JRAS* 1904: 95–118; "List of the Arabic Manuscripts in the Baillie Collection in the Library of Edinburgh University," *JRAS* 1905: 513–20; "John of Damascus and the controversy with Islam," *Transactions of the Glasgow University Oriental Society* 4 (1913–22): 37–38; "Notes on Moslem traditions," *TGUOS* 4 (1913–22): 78–79; "Some early literary contacts between Moslem Spain and the East," *TGUOS* 13 (1947–49): 48–51; "A Moslem thinker on the teaching of religion: Al-Ghazzali A.D. 1058–1111," *Hibbert Journal* 42 (1943): 31–36. Some of these articles appear to be no more than summaries of oral presentations. Another note

something which he felt was desirable because they "have not always been understood"; these lectures appeared as *Introduction to the Qurʾan*.[5] In a publisher's note to the *Introduction*, mention was made once again of Bell's notes to his translation, which, it was clarified, were not the same as this text; the notes, it was said, "may be published if circumstances permit" (p. vi). In 1991, circumstances appear to have prevailed and the massive, two-volume *A Commentary on the Qurʾān*[6] has appeared. Having apparently lingered in microfilm form (the original typescript is reported to have gone missing) in a cupboard of Edmund Bosworth for some twenty years, these are Bell's notes to his translation which he had been revising for publication in the years before his death.

Assessments of Bell's scholarship have varied radically over the years. A recent attempt to rehabilitate the theories of Bell (whose analysis of the Qurʾān, it is stated, "has often been misunderstood or ignored by later writers. . . . But it must be remembered that Bell was a pioneer in this field . . . "[7]) is matched by strident condemnations of the work of this "Scottish crackpot."[8] Indeed, for some people, Bell seems to have become a prime representative of Christian-Orientalist bias; looking at some of his works in the library recently, I discovered that someone had written at the end of the preface to *Origin*, under the name Richard Bell, "F*** you son-of-an-infidel whore!" and his *Introduction* was defaced throughout, although in more reasoned language. These sorts of comments do not, of course, reflect an understanding of Richard Bell's principles of scholarship, only a reaction to his most infamous act, reordering the text of the Qurʾān by cutting it up into little bits.

Bell's approach to the Qurʾān developed, according to his own statements, while he was preparing his lectures which were published as *Origin*.[9] When asking the question, "what was the role of Christianity in the rise of Islam?" he saw a unifying development of that theme at work in the text of the Qurʾān. He came to rely on this insight because of the untrustworthy nature of Muslim tradition, especially as related to the first part of Muḥammad's life, and because of the confusion which he sensed in the text of the Qurʾān. Bell saw evidence of Muḥammad's own revisions in the Qurʾān and he argued that all of the *sūras*, even the shortest ones, were of a composite nature. Viewing Muḥammad's career in relation to his increasing knowledge of and contact with Christianity was Bell's overall insight. "The key to a great deal both in the Qurʾān and in the career of Muḥammad lies, as I hope to show just in his gradual acquisition of knowledge of what the Bible contained and of what Jews and Christians believed" (*Origin*, 68–69). Much of this reconstruction depended upon a psychological reconstruction of Muḥammad. "Muhammad was a visionary, no doubt, but he was not a crack-brained enthusiast. He was a very practical character. . . . He had the mystic quality of a seeker after truth but that did not destroy his practical bent. . . . His enterprise was, in my opinion, from the very start quite a rational and practical one . . . " (*Origin*, 71–72). This attempt to reconstruct the inner workings of Muḥammad's experiences and aims provided Bell with a principle by which the order of the Qurʾān could be understood. That the Qurʾān could be seen to *confirm* that reconstruction—that is, that a coherent whole emerged out of a perceived jumble—added validity to the initial reconstruction. Regarding the circularity in such a process, using the Qurʾān especially in the Meccan period to deduce historical progression in order to be able to reformulate the Qurʾān into a historical order, Bell simply urges that this "calls for careful consideration and prolonged discussion" (*Qurʾān*, 690).

Certain central themes are mentioned by Bell as providing the details that go along with the overall reconstruction; these themes have been isolated by J. E Merrill and W. M. Watt in earlier studies of Bell's work and there is no need to repeat those details here.[10] No

written by Bell is "Survey of Oriental Studies, *Der Islam*, 1920–1926," *TGUOS* 5 (1923–28): 42–43. A quick survey of some likely specialist journals has not uncovered any book reviews written by Bell. I am grateful to Dr. B. T. Lawson of the University of Toronto for helping me locate copies of some of Bell's publications.

[5] Edinburgh University Publications, Language & Literature, no. 6 (Edinburgh: Edinburgh Univ. Press, 1953); hereafter cited as *Introduction*. W. M. Watt's *Bell's Introduction* is a revised edition of this book.

[6] Hereafter cited as *Commentary*.

[7] A. T. Welch, *EI*[2] 5: 418a, s.v. "Ḳurʾān."

[8] S. Parvez Manzoor, "Method against Truth: Orientalism and Qurʾānic Studies," *Muslim World Book Review* 7.iv (1987): 35.

[9] How Bell came to be invited to give these lectures I have not been able to determine.

[10] John E. Merrill, "Dr. Bell's Critical Analysis of the Qurʾan," *The Muslim World* 37 (1947): 134–48, reprinted in *Der Koran*, ed. Paret, 11–24; W. M. Watt, "The Dating of the Qurʾān: A Review of Richard Bell's Theories," *JRAS* 1957 46–56, reprinted in William Montgomery Watt, *Early Islam Collected Articles* (Edinburgh: Edinburgh Univ. Press, 1990)

bly however, progressive change in emotion as linked the style of the Qur'ān was not considered by Bell to a major basis for analyzing the text, as it had been by öldeke. Emotion, Bell suggests, may reoccur and yle can be varied according to the dictates of the tuation. Those factors, therefore, cannot be reliable uides in chronology. Matters such as relations with the ews and Christians, use of certain elements of vocab- ary and details of ritual performance all provided Bell ith what he considered more credible criteria.

The Qur'ān, for Bell, was revealed in short passages hich may be distinguished through two means: form d content, and linguistic and rhythmic patterns. brupt change in rhyme patterns, repetition of rhyme ords, rupture in grammatical structure, sudden varia- on in verse length, and unwarranted shift in personal ronouns all point to revisions undertaken by Muḥam- ad due to a change in purpose sometime during his areer. Bell suggests that three periods may be sepa- ted in Muḥammad's career: the early period in which signs" and praise of God play the predominant role; ext, the Qur'ān period which covers the later Meccan d Medinan era up to the year 2 A.H.; and finally the ook period which is from the year 2 A.H. on.[11] Bell eaks of this in the following terms: "[Muḥammad] egan as the advocate of a renewed religion of gratitude the one supreme God, that faced with unbelief and jection, he enforced his message by the threat of pun- hment, first in the form of calamity falling upon spe- al unbelieving peoples, and that then as he acquired ore knowledge of Christianity and Judaism, he substi- ted for, or combined with this, the eschatological eas of Judgment to come and the punishments and re- ards of the future life . . . " (*Qur'ān*, 690).

The demands of these changed situations and plans in uḥammad's life meant that it was necessary to change rtain passages of the Qur'ān to fit into the new con- xt. The resulting unevenness was aggravated by the later collection of the text. Disjunctions in the Qur'ān, which cannot be attributed to Muḥammad's deliberate attempts to change the import of certain passages, are accounted for by speaking of documents being put together in a mechanical way; material written on the "back" of a "page" was placed following on from what was on the front by compilers who were faced with a stack of material and who did not know where it all belonged. Along with the deliberate reorganization of the material by Muḥammad himself, this resulted in frequent duplication and unevenness throughout the text.

* * *

Bell's theories do not appear in a scholarly vacuum and some contextualization of his work helps elucidate its underlying principles and its significance. Biblical studies may well be suggested as a likely context, especially since some might wish to argue that Bell's accomplishment was to apply certain methods developed in Biblical studies to the Qur'ān. Notably, Bell's books carry few references to contemporary Biblical scholarship other than occasional mention of editions of the Bible and Apocrypha.[12] But in terms of the general intellectual climate in turn-of-the-century Scotland, there is little doubt that ideas of *Tendenzkritik* and an increasingly prominent Form Criticism may be seen to be playing a role in every intellectual endeavor in religious studies of the era.

The Wellhausen documentary hypothesis of the Bible was fully entrenched in certain intellectual circles of England and Scotland by the 1890s and was widespread by the 1920s.[13] It is worth remembering what the accomplishment of Wellhausen was:

> Wellhausen did not invent critical methods; he merely applied them very skillfully. His own particular contribution was to link together the results of literary criticism with an entirely fresh conception of the history of Israel (and of early Christianity), completely rejecting

–33. Bell's *Introduction* gave several people pause to pon- r his approach: most significant is S. Vahiduddin, "Richard ell's Study of the Qur'an: (A Critical Analysis)," *Islamic ulture* 30 (1956): 263–72. Also see the reviews by Arthur ffery in *The Muslim World* 44 (1954): 254–58; Rudi Paret *Zeitschrift der Deutschen Morgenländischen Gesellschaft* 5 (1954): 497–501; Joseph Schacht in *Oriens* 7 (1954): 9–62; A. J. Arberry in *Bulletin of the School of Oriental d African Studies* 17 (1955): 380–81.

[11] For a reconsideration of Bell's ideas on this point, see lman Nagel, "Vom 'Qur'ān' zur 'Schrift': Bells Hypothese s religionsgeschichtlicher Sicht," *Der Islam* 60 (1983): 3–65.

[12] In *Commentary* works by F. C. Burkitt, R. H. Charles, E. Hennecke, W. R. Smith, and F. Weber are cited; none of these is significant in methodological terms. *Origin* refers to a number of books on the history of the Christian church.

[13] See Brevard S. Childs, "Wellhausen in English," *Semeia* 25 (1983): 85; also see John Rogerson, *Old Testament Criticism in the Nineteenth Century: England and Germany* (Philadelphia: Fortress Press, 1985), 266, and passim for the influence of Wellhausen in general. Wellhausen's most significant work, *Prolegomena zur Geschichte Israels*, was published in 1878.

> the church's traditional view of biblical history. His method was to turn directly from the chronological or geographical placing of a written source or a redactor to the outward events of that particular period, for the biblical writers were much influenced by the national or religious political life of their day, and did not consider the old traditions merely as such. They intended their work to have some effect upon contemporary conditions. This *direct connection between determining sources and historical events* is the main characteristic of Wellhausen's treatment to different historical fields.[14]

The viewing of scripture in relation to historical development (and of scripture having been reformulated in light of that history) is the fundamental argument here and only a few words need to be changed in the preceding quotation in order to make it applicable to the core motives and assumptions of Qurʾānic scholarship at the beginning of the twentieth century. The scholarly position has always been that, with a clear understanding of the development of Muḥammad's life, the Qurʾān may be rearranged so that it "makes sense" in terms of history (or, paraphrasing Wellhausen, this is to be done by "constructing history well"). In the case of the Qurʾān, furthermore, it has been observed that the traditional Muslim sources themselves support, if not in fact encourage, the basic principles lying behind work of scholars such as Wellhausen, Nöldeke, and Bell. That is, the ideas of form criticism (in the most general understanding of that method) may be put in conjunction with the material of Muslim tradition such that the latter is pushed to the (logical) extreme of its implications. Muslims speak of the Qurʾān as being written prior to its collection on "stones, palm leaves and the hearts of men"; a literary hypothesis for the origins of the text, one which would account for the text's apparent disjointedness, virtually jumps out at the scholar familiar with form criticism when faced with such Muslim testimony. If the distinction between the "J" and the "E" strands of Genesis suggested, to some people, two literary texts being woven together, then, on the evidence of the Muslim tradition itself, the same could be envisioned for the Qurʾān: a weaving together of a text, involving duplications and abrupt breaks, just as in the Bible.

[14] Klaus Koch, *The Growth of the Biblical Tradition: The Form-Critical Method* (New York: Charles Scribner's Sons, 1969), 70, emphasis in the original. A useful summary of Wellhausen's work is Douglas A. Knight, "Wellhausen and the Interpretation of Israel's Literature," *Semeia* 25 (1983): 21–36.

Of course, Wellhausen's work emerges in a contex of intellectual activity also and may be seen to have become so influential in its time because of its author' ability to synthesize the tendencies of German Biblic scholarship up to that point.[15] The same may be said fo Bell in terms of Qurʾānic studies. It is in fact difficult t argue that Bell's work is a matter of taking methods developed in Biblical studies and applying them freshl to the Qurʾān.[16] Rather, he worked within a line o Western scholarship on Muḥammad and the Qurʾā and responded to various issues within that contex reflecting upon the sources with which he was familia Studies of the Qurʾān and early Islam, especially thos appearing from the pens of German scholars in the decades on either side of the turn of the century (many o whom were deeply involved in Biblical studies als Wellhausen himself being the obvious example), provided the impetus and inspiration for the work of Bel In fact, the presuppositions of such studies may well b said to have informed virtually all of Qurʾānic scholarship, up to the time of Wansbrough and Arkoun, wh have presented the only real challenges to the domina paradigm of discussion.[17] A quick survey of scholarship on the Qurʾān reveals Bell's place. Abraham Geiger's 1833 study, which really must stand as th foundational work in the critical study of the Qurʾān

[15] See Knight, "Wellhausen," 21–25.

[16] It would certainly be misleading to view Bell's wor specifically in light of the ideas of form criticism, for Bell' work reveals a privileging of history over literary form suc that the *Sitz im Leben* of Qurʾānic passages is highlighted bu the idea of prophetic forms (which is central to all Biblic form-critical discussion) is downplayed, if not ignored. Be may be said, therefore, to follow more closely in the line o Wellhausen's *Tendenzkritik* with its concern for determinin the intention behind a given literary passage in light of a historical ordering of concerns. Form criticism per se was certainly making inroads at the time Bell was working on hi Qurʾān translation, with Gunkel's work appearing around th turn of the century and becoming more influential in th 1920s. See my general comments on this issue in "Literar Analysis of Qurʾān, *tafsīr*, and *sīra*: The Methodologies o John Wansbrough," in *Approaches to Islam in Religiou Studies*, ed. Richard C. Martin (Tucson: Univ. of Arizon Press, 1985), 158.

[17] John Wansbrough, *Quranic Studies: Sources and Methods of Scriptural Interpretation* (Oxford: Oxford Univ. Pres 1977); see my "Literary Analysis of Qurʾān," 151–6 Mohammed Arkoun, *Lectures du Coran* (Paris: Maisonneuv et Larose, 1982); see my *Muslims, their Religious Beliefs an Practices*, vol. 2: *The Contemporary Period* (London: Routledge, forthcoming), part 4, ch. 2.

hed to contextualize Muḥammad but Geiger does emphasize the movement of history in the development of Qur'ānic themes.[18] The fact of Jewish parallels s sufficient as an explanatory device for Geiger. stav Weil, in 1844, provided the first attempt[19] at a tematic chronological ordering of the *sūras* of the r'ān by tying an understanding of the history of Munmad to the text and arriving at what is now the olarly standard of three Meccan periods and one dinan. Most of his insights were based on stylistic nsiderations and, as Welch has pointed out,[20] a genl acceptance of the Muslim lists of *sūra* ordering. nificant refinements were added to this approach by eodor Nöldeke in 1860[21] and Hartwig Hirschfeld in 36 and 1902.[22] Bell worked within this trend but he v the interlocking of text and history as far more nplex than previous scholarship had suggested. Bell s quite extensively influenced in this direction, as he nself acknowledges (*Commentary*, 1:xx, and referes throughout), by Jacob Barth's posthumous arti-, "Studien zur Kritik und Exegese des Qorāns."[23] rth was the first to suggest that the Qur'ān had suffered extensively from disruptive editing. In his article he speaks of the need to rearrange sections of the text such that they "make sense." This he puts in opposition to Nöldeke's assumption of the fundamental structural coherence of major units of the text as it is now organized, such that, with a limited number of exceptions, entire *sūras* may be taken as blocks and dated as such.[24] Barth did not develop a theory as to how or why these reformulations took place except to speak of the vagaries of the collection process; it was Bell's contribution to provide a more extensive explanation and to apply the principles throughout the Qur'ānic text. Whether the final result of Bell's study has been the virtual dissolution of chronological pursuits in the study of the Qur'ān in the West, as Parvez Manzoor claims, seems unlikely.[25] On the other hand, the editors' referring in the preface to the *Commentary*, to the works of Neuwirth and Wansbrough as being impossible without the insights of Bell seems equally excessive.[26]

* * *

With this background in mind, it is possible to look more closely at Bell's *Commentary*. This requires that his *Qur'ān* be close at hand, although it is notable that, on many occasions, the two do not coincide exactly in the suggested meanings for given words (see, for example, references to Q. 4:76 and 78). One thing which struck me while reading these two works together is the extent to which Bell's Qur'ān translation is a distillation of this man's insights and can only justify its existence as a scholarly tool for displaying the implications of his theories. The text of the translation is extremely difficult just to "read," for Bell makes little effort to convey directly the sense of the text. English-language readers should be glad that they have the literary efforts of A. J. Arberry[27] especially, for it would be difficult to convince students or the public at large to read the Qur'ān if they had to contend with Bell's approach to the translation as their prime source. Compare, for example, a mundane case, the rendering of Q. 2:2 by

[18] Abraham Geiger, *Was hat Mohammed aus dem Juthume aufgenommen?* (Baden, 1833); notice the appendix, atements in the Qurán hostile to Judaism," which, while ertaining a historical transition and a new strategy on the t of Muḥammad after the change of the *qibla*, still speaks his in quite general terms.

[19] *Historisch-kritische Einleitung in den Koran* (Bielefeld, 44; 2nd ed., 1878). To suggest that this be recognized as first attempt at chronology is to argue a significant point. I have asserted elsewhere, Muslim attempts at ordering the *as* of the Qur'ān are in fact based upon principles quite erent from European historical concerns and are done with te different aims in mind: they do not entail "chronology" that word is used by modern historians. See my "The func-n of *asbāb al-nuzūl* in Qur'ānic exegesis," *BSOAS* 51 88): 1–20.

[20] *EI*[2] 5: 417a, s.v. "Ḳur'ān."

[21] *Geschichte des Qorāns* (Göttingen, 1860).

[22] *Beiträge zur Erklärung des Koran* (Leipzig, 1886); *New searches into the Composition and Exegesis of the Qoran* ndon, 1902). An excellent presentation of German scholarp of this period on Islam in light of Romanticism and storicism is to be found in Baber Johansen, "Politics and nolarship: the Development of Islamic Studies in the Fedl Republic of Germany," in *Middle East Studies: International Perspectives on the State of the Art*, ed. Tareq Y. nael (New York: Praeger, 1990), esp. pp. 75–90.

[23] *Der Islam* 6 (1916): 113–48. Barth (1851–1914) was a dent of H. L. Fleischer and T. Nöldeke; see the obituary by H. Becker in *Der Islam* 6 (1916): 200–202.

[24] Nöldeke does occasionally see displacement in the text, but clearly prefers not to privilege such a reconstructive method; see, for example, his treatment of Q. 29:18–22 in *Geschichte des Qorāns*, ed. F. Schwally (Leipzig: Dieterich'sche Verlagsbuchhandlung, 1909), 1:157, and other observations in "Zur Sprache des Korans" in his *Neue Beiträge zur semitischen Sprachwissenschaft* (Strassbourg: Trübner, 1910), 1–30.

[25] Manzoor, "Method against Truth," 35.

[26] *Commentary*, 1:xvi.

[27] *The Koran Interpreted* (London: Allen and Unwin, 1955).

Bell,[28] "Who believe in the Unseen, observe the Prayer, and of what We have provided them with give freely," and Arberry, "who believe in the Unseen, and perform the prayer, and expend of that We have provided them." Or Q. 3:145 in Bell: "Allah made good His promise to you when ye were sweeping them away by His permission, until when ye flinched and vied in withdrawing from the affair, and disobeyed after He had shown you what ye love." Arberry: "God has been true in His promise towards you when you blasted them by His leave; until you lost heart, and quarrelled about the matter, and were rebellious, after He had shown you that you longed for." The difficult syntax which abounds in the Qur'ān is aggravated by Bell's stilted approach to translation; the final result of his work is only further obscured by his attempt to restructure the text through typographical means.

Given Bell's interests and concerns regarding the Qur'ān and history as outlined above, it should come as no surprise that the main focus of attention in his *Commentary* lies in explaining the meaning of the text. This is crucial to Bell's enterprise of trying to make sense of the text in historical terms. That is, a "clear understanding" of what is being said enables him to situate the passage within the life of Muḥammad, which then confirms the interpretation of the text, provides some sense of chronology and furnishes evidence of disjunction in Qur'ānic passages. The *Commentary*, therefore, is primarily the elucidation of Bell's perception of the meaning of sections of the text, with a special emphasis on how they fit into Muḥammad's life. Bell's principle of splitting the text into fragments is prominent in the *Commentary* but what is significant is the emphasis that falls upon meaning in determining the extent of a given fragment. Certainly other formal characteristics come into play—rhyme, change of pronoun, length of verse—but Bell's analysis of the structure of the Qur'ān is based far more upon a careful (and frequently imaginative) reading of the text than other attempts, such as those of Neuwirth and de Caprona who privilege structure over those factors.[29] An illustration will help clarify this point. When Bell finds two verses close proximity which may be thought to have me ings that are related, then frequently he takes one ve to be a "substitution" for the other; this substitut works to reformulate the overall intent of a given p sage in order to make it fit a different historical sit tion. Arguing the evidence for such a reformulati then, depends on being able to fit the verse into one the major themes which Bell sees as having been aff ted by Muḥammad's change of strategy during his li A typical example may be found in the treatment Q. 4:27–32 where we see Bell segment the text on basis of meaning.[30] This passage, on prohibited degr of marriage, has been revised as "is evident fr vv. 31–32." Verse 31 "applies to" verse 27 because implies" (i.e., in its meaning) that the law is the sa as that of the Jews and Christians, which Bell judges be what verse 27 is speaking about. This then belor to the beginning of the Medinan period when "the re gion was being assimilated to that of previous mo theists" (one of Bell's major themes which he tra in the Qur'ān). Verse 32a ("Allah desireth to rel towards you, but those who follow lusts desire that should fall mightily away") suggests relaxation and t fits with the statements of verses 29–30. Finally, "[t considerable relaxation of v. 28 would correspond the conclusion, v. 32b, which is a separate verse. The comments which follow these observations in *Commentary* then explain the precise dimensions this progressive "relaxation." Bell does not appeal length of written documents or rhyme in order to arg his case; in this and most other instances, the obser tions are based upon his perception of the meaning the text.

The *Commentary* is structured to follow the text the Qur'ān in its so-called ʿUthmānic recension,[32] p

[28] Verse numbers throughout this review article are from the Flügel edition of the Qur'ān, which is the basis of all of Bell's work as well as Arberry's translation. Textually, it is worthy of note that Bell was generally loath to alter the received text; on several occasions in the *Commentary*, he argues against Jacob Barth's suggested emendations.

[29] See Angelika Neuwirth, *Studien zur Komposition der Mekkanischen Suren* (Berlin: Walter de Gruyter, 1981); on this book, see my review, *BSOAS* 45 (1982): 149–50, and Claude Gilliot, "Deux études sur le Coran," *Arabica* 30 (1983): 1–37. Pierre Crapon de Caprona, *Le Coran: Aux sources de la role oraculaire, structures rythmiques des sourates m quoises* (Paris: Publications Orientalistes de France, 1981).

[30] *Commentary*, 1:113–15.

[31] As indeed it is in the Egyptian Royal Edition of Qur'ān, with Flügel's verse 32 appearing as verses 27 and

[32] Both Nabih Amin Faris, *The Muslim World* 28 (19 409, and Arthur Jeffery, *JRAS*, 1938: 623, in reviewing Be *Qur'ān*, vol. 1, regretted that Bell did not attempt to print text in the order of composition; Jeffery recognized that, fr a practical point of view, this was not really possible, hc ever. Given the form of the *Commentary*, it is safe to say Bell himself saw no merit in the suggestion. Other interest reviews of Bell's *Qur'ān* include A. S. T[ritton], *BSOA* (1937–39): 1084–85 (on vol. 1), 10 (1939–42): 511 (on vol.

ding comments on overall thematic units and single rses. Its closest model in scholarship is Rudi Paret's r *Koran: Kommentar und Konkordanz*,[33] a work with ich comparison is inevitable, and unflattering to ll. Contrasting the principles and aims underlying th works is worthwhile. Paret manifests an overrid- concern with linguistic phraseology, Bell with se- ntic theme. Paret is interested in Biblical parallels, ll less so, perhaps reflecting different assumptions on part of the two authors regarding the depth of Bib- al knowledge available in seventh-century Arabia. th are concerned with etymology, Paret to a some- at greater extent. Paret wishes to distill the over- hing scholarly vision, Bell to concentrate on his own nstruct. An interesting example of overall difference approach is found in the treatment of parallel phras- in disparate passages. For Paret, parallels are cited what they accomplish in elucidating meaning and oviding further grammatical illustration. For Bell, a rallel passage can provide an indication of where a ision has taken place or where editing has combined ginally separate passages; sometimes he attempts to ablish which of two parallels is the "original" ver- n. An example may be seen in Bell's treatment of 2:60–61a, which he argues must be seen to follow from Q. 2:50 because of the way in which the paral- passage Q. 7:170 is structured narratively.[34] Among ll's positive traits is his willingness to admit that ngs are "unclear" (a word used very infrequently in ret's work) but this also argues that a reading which hlights the historical background in its approach to text may not be as self-confirming or as natural as it netimes appears.

* * *

There can be little doubt that in terms of information ovided—Bell's efforts at determining meaning in the r'ānic text—the *Commentary* is a valuable piece of rk and it is a happy event that it has seen the light of day. In terms of providing a reading strategy for the Qur'ān, however, the work reveals its age. The idea that history provides an explanation of textual phenomena still holds great sway in intellectual circles (it may be said to provide the basis for the above attempt to contextualize Bell, for example) but severe difficulties are involved in the case of Muḥammad and the Qur'ān within that process. Some of these are the result of problems experienced in devising a psychology of Muḥammad which may be projected onto a sequence of historical events.[35] In a rather condescending review of *Origin*, D. B. Macdonald[36] provides an excellent elucidation of such principles and a nice example of their problematic status: " . . . before we can hope with any success to read order into the chaos of the Koran and to re-arrange its fragments historically—as far as that is at all possible—we must from the Koran, read broadly, have acquired some idea of the psychology of Mohammed, of what inspiration and prophecy meant for him and for the Meccans to whom he preached." "What kind of memory and mind did Mohammed have?" Macdonald asks. "A very rag-bag of a mind he had, and to think of him as making orderly investigations is to misunderstand his whole psychological makeup." Bell needs to read the Qur'ān itself more closely, rather than Sale or Rodwell, if he is to discover "what kind of man is behind it," says Macdonald. There is no debate with Bell here over the required task—an understanding of Muḥammad—only on how that person is to be perceived psychologically.

But it is worth asking why there is this emphasis on the psychology of Muḥammad to begin with. It is not sufficient to suggest in response simply that Orientalists have assumed that the Qur'ān is Muḥammad's book and thus the text of scripture must be explained in terms of his life.[37] Rather, it needs to be recognized

hur Jeffery, *JRAS* 1941: 81–82 (on vol. 2); Rudi Paret, *entalistische Literaturzeitung*, 1939: 305–9 (on vol. 1), 41: 238–41 (on vol. 2).

3 Stuttgart, Kohlhammer, 1971; 2nd ed. 1977.

4 *Commentary*, 1:13. There is a discrepancy here between way Bell has structured his translation and the way the sage is presented in the *Commentary*. When writing *r'ān*, Bell felt verses 60 through 62 continued verses 44– and then verses 51 through 58a should come before 63ff. *Commentary* (a later work, it is to be remembered) he en- ains the possibility that verses 51 through 58a should come r verse 61a.

35 For some discussion of how to conceive a psychology of Muḥammad, see Régis Blachère, *Le Problème de Mahomet: Essai de biographie critique du fondateur de l'Islam* (Paris: Presses Universitaires de France, 1952); G. Bousquet, "Observations sociologiques sur les origines de l'Islam," *Studia Islamica* 2 (1952): 61–87.

36 *The Moslem World* 16 (1926): 309–10. Also see the review of *Origin* by R. Strothmann, *Der Islam* 16 (1927): 285–87.

37 Manzoor, "Method against Truth," 36, certainly perceives this issue and quite rightly points to the general epistemological assumptions of the "Western" approach. He is absolutely correct that the question of the historicity of knowledge is the basis of the dispute, but this of course is not a debate unique to "Muslim versus Western" approaches to

that what is involved here is an entire theory of history and of the interpretation of texts in which motivation is to be sought in order to explain events. The reader's task, this assumption suggests, is *to make sense* of a text. "Making sense" here means that a text becomes intelligible to its reader as some sort of representation of reality (in the sense that the text "coheres" with a pattern of life as we understand ourselves to have experienced it). The aim in reading the Qur'ān from this viewpoint then is to make it into a coherent whole. The means by which this is done are by positing sequences of events understood to have taken place externally to the text. By fitting the text into this sequence of events, coherence and intelligibility are produced. Psychology provides the overall patterning and the justifying bridge between the external events in which the author is involved and the text itself.[38]

The contemporary scholarly world, which lives in the light of James Joyce and deconstruction, has raised doubts about this construction of the reading experience, although it must be admitted that, sadly, the repercussions of this in Qur'ānic studies have barely been felt as yet. Those who attempt to see with the aid of this light urge the need to re-problematize all texts, including, in this case, the Qur'ān. The experience of disruptions within the text of scripture, it may be gued, is a significant factor in the reading (and listen and looking) event, and the desire to eliminate s surface ripples through the agency of historical rec struction impoverishes the significance of reading self. The challenge of the Qur'ānic text to scholarsl therefore, is not to reduce it to a coherent wh through the vehicle of history, but to celebrate the w in which the text disturbs the reader's sense of coh ence. This is not a matter of opposing an assumed se of textual coherence,[39] as the goal of the scholarly deavor, with a notion of incoherency, which seems be the fear of those who see newer methods of proaching literature as destroying any standards for terpretation. Contemporary literary approaches wish subvert that oppositional assumption from the very ginning. They wish to privilege the reader's experie and to pose a whole new set of questions and to sp of things such as the poetics, rhetoric and ideology the Qur'ān[40] and to situate the text within a my context of the Near Eastern religious milieu.[41] Only this way, it is suggested, will (post-) modern read sensibilities be satisfied. The works of Wansbrough Arkoun have already been mentioned as forerunn

the Qur'ān. Few people can discuss the related implications and positions with such lucidity as Stanley Fish; see, for example, "Anti-foundationalism, Theory, Hope, and the Teaching of Composition," in his *Doing What Comes Naturally: Change, Rhetoric, and the Practice of Theory in Literary and Legal Studies* (Durham: Duke Univ. Press, 1989), 342–55. Manzoor's own answer to this basic issue wishes to remove the problem from rational discussion by speaking of the time of revelation as a period distinct from all others. In my perception, that remains a position which reflects the certainty of faith and excludes all others from the discussion. See further, S. Parvez Manzoor, "Politics without Truth, Metaphysics, or Epistemology: Postmodernism—De(con)structed for the Muslim Believer," *Muslim World Book Review* 10.iv (1990): 3–12.

[38] Some valuable reflections on the use of coherence in interpretation may be found in F. Gerald Downing, "Criteria," in *A Dictionary of Biblical Interpretation*, ed. R. J. Coggins and J. L. Houlden (London: SCM Press, 1990), 151–53; John B. Henderson, *Scripture, Canon and Commentary: A Comparison of Confucian and Western Exegesis* (Princeton: Princeton Univ. Press, 1991), especially chap. 4. A valuable, lucid, introductory discussion of the basic interpretative issues is found in Catherine Belsey, *Critical Practice* (London: Routledge, 1980).

[39] Mustansir Mir, *Coherence in the Qur'ān* (Indianap American Trust Publications, 1986), presents arguments parallels to New Critical ideas about texts but still does provide a substantially different vision than earlier works urges a notion of thematic unity in order to overcome perception of structural discontinuity. For some interes reflections on the desire to render the Biblical text hist cally coherent see John Russiano Miles, "Radical Edit *Redaktionsgeschichte* and the Aesthetic of Willed Co sion," in *The Creation of Sacred Literature: Composition Redaction of the Biblical Text*, ed. Richard Elliot Fried (Berkeley and Los Angeles: Univ. of California Press, 19 85–99.

[40] See the way these ideas are used, for example, in Sternberg, *The Poetics of Biblical Narrative: Ideological erature and the Drama of Reading* (Bloomington: Ind Univ. Press, 1985); also see *The Bible as Rhetoric: Studie Biblical Persuasion and Credibility*, ed. Martin Warner (L don: Routledge, 1990); *"Not in Heaven": Coherence Complexity in Biblical Narrative*, ed. Jason P. Rosenblatt Joseph C. Sitterson Jr. (Bloomington: Indiana Univ. P 1991).

[41] A matter especially emphasized by Arkoun citing studies of Geo Widengren; see, for example, Mohammed oun, "The Notion of Revelation from Ahl al-Kitāb to Societies of the Book," *Die Welt des Islams* 28 (1988): 62-

f this tendency. Michael Zwettler's approach, in "A Mantic Manifesto,"[42] illustrates aspects of literary appreciation as a reading strategy. Michael Sells' essay, "Sound, Spirit, and Gender in *Sūrat al-Qadr*,"[43] provides a fine example of awareness of the "multidimensionality of meaning" available to the reader. Far more ambitious is the work of Michael Fischer and Mahdi Abedi in *Debating Muslims*.[44] The focus there—explicitly within the terminology of post-modern discourse, much to the disgust of some reviewers—on "Qurʾanic Dialogics" makes the point, "Can the polysemic and nomadic meanings of a text such as the Qurʾān overcome the unbewised efforts to reduce it to a monologic decree?"[45] Scholarship can—indeed, must, Arkoun has argued—do its part in this process and work to subvert those approaches which dictate monological readings.

Certainly the publication of such a mammoth work as Bell's *Commentary* provides a welcome opportunity for reflection upon Qurʾānic studies and its future in the academic environment. The fact that it was judged worthwhile to undertake the task of publishing a work which had been neglected for over 40 years, however, indicates the extent to which the discipline is still struggling to conceptualize an approach to this central topic within the study of Islam. What merit there is in this work lies in its emphasis on discerning the meaning of the text; we will be able to consider the appearance of the book worthwhile if, as a result of its circulation, it helps move scholarship away from a preoccupation with theories about the Qurʾānic text and turn attention to the actual text itself.

[42] "A Mantic Manifesto: The Sūra of 'The Poets' and the Qurʾānic Foundations of Prophetic Authority," in *Poetry and Prophecy: The Beginnings of a Literary Tradition*, ed. James L. Kugel (Ithaca: Cornell Univ. Press, 1990), 75–119.

[43] *JAOS* 111 (1991): 239–59.

[44] *Debating Muslims: Cultural Dialogues in Tradition and Postmodernity* (Madison: Univ. of Wisconsin Press, 1990), chap. 2; the chapter also appears in slightly different form as "Qurʾanic Dialogics: Islamic Poetics and Politics for Muslims and for Us," in *The Interpretation of Dialogue*, ed. Tullio Maranhão (Chicago: Univ. of Chicago Press, 1990), 120–53.

[45] Fischer and Abedi, "Qurʾanic Dialogics," 151; "unbewised" is an allusion to the passage from James Joyce quoted in the beginning of their chapter.

V

Studying early *tafsīr* texts[1])

Establishing the likely path of Muslim and Arab intellectual development during the first two *hijrī* centuries presents a major challenge for the historian. While the historian desires to employ the earliest possible sources in order to come ever closer to a better sense of the facts, the paucity of such sources and the questionable authenticity of those which do exist render the exercise fraught with substantial pitfalls.

The historiographical problems are present no matter which area of historical reconstruction one wishes to pursue. In Kees Versteegh's new book, *Arabic Grammar and Qur'ānic exegesis in early Islam,* a fairly simple question is posed: what is the historical background to the rise of Arabic grammatical studies? The masterful tome of Sībawayh (d. 177/793), *al-Kitāb,* presents us with a substantially developed picture of grammatical analysis. Versteegh reasons that there must have been some work which went on before this book could have been produced; it did not fall from the sky. Yet, it would seem that we have no existing precursors to it, and thus no historical picture within which to place it.

One of the merits of John Wansbrough's *Quranic studies: sources and methods of scriptural interpretation*[2]), which even his most ardent critics are forced to admit, is that he draws attention to (and provides some extremely acute analysis of) a quantity of Qur'ānic exegetical matter which stems from (perhaps) the second and third *hijrī* centuries. Most of the works which he studied had been listed in the histories of Arabic literature by Brockelmann and especially Sezgin,[3]) but few had ever been cri-

---

[1]) A review article of C. H. M. Versteegh, *Arabic grammar and Qur'ānic exegesis in early Islam.* Studies in Semitic Languages and Linguistics, edited by J. H. Hospers and C. H. M. Versteegh, XIX. Leiden, New York, Köln: E. J. Brill, 1993. xi, 230pp.; Miklos Muranyi (ed.), *'Abd Allāh b. Wahb (125/743-197/812). Al-Ǧāmi'. Die Koranwissenschaft.* Quellenstudien zur Ḥadīṯ- und Rechtliteratur in Nordafrika. Wiesbaden: Otto Harrassowitz, 1993. xiv, 292 pp; Miklos Muranyi (ed.), *'Abd Allāh b. Wahb (125/743-197/812). Al-Ǧāmi'. Tafsīr al Qur'ān (Die Koranexegese).* Quellenstudien zur Ḥadīṯ- und Rechtliteratur in Nordafrika. Wiesbaden: Otto Harrassowitz, 1993. xiv, 274 pp.

[2]) Oxford: Oxford University Press, 1977.

[3]) Sezgin's theories over the existence of books in early Islam colour his bibliographical presentations, however: see my "The present status of tafsīr studies", *The Muslim World,* 72(1982), 224–38.

tically analyzed before, least of all on the basis of their actual content.[4]) It is worth remarking that Wansbrough's interest in his study was not in reconstructing the history of *tafsīr* as such; rather, his aim was to look at the earliest texts for what they could tell us about the rise to canonical status of the Qur'ān itself. A model of the establishment of authority within religious communities suggests an overall chronology of *tafsīr* material: the move from haggadic, to halakhic, to masoretic is a development through time reflecting the emerging community's need and desire for the establishment of an authoritative text. This then leads to an overall insight into the nature and development of *tafsīr* as a discipline which is of some significance.[5])

Versteegh's reading of Wansbrough has led him to study these same early *tafsīr* texts with an eye to what they might tell us about the rise of the Arabic grammatical tradition before Sībawayh. From the perspective of Wansbrough's work, this is rather problematic since Wansbrough argues that grammatical analysis was a later stage in the development of *tafsīr*. Wansbrough sees nothing as "natural" or "obvious": in order to apply grammar or the testimony of poetry for lexicographical purposes to the Qur'ān, an argument had first to be mounted; what we read in some early texts, therefore, are arguments, back and forth, about the legitimacy of such processes. Versteegh's position does not coincide with this: it is only "natural" for him that early Muslims would have looked at the Qur'ān grammatically. As a result, Versteegh has a number of challenges in front of him concerning his use of the texts which Wansbrough has analyzed before he can proceed too far. First and foremost, he must argue for the historical reliability of the texts as a whole, thereby overriding concerns about later interpolations, editorial reformulations and other assorted tendencies which Wansbrough suggested could account for what he considered the anachronistic elements in some of the texts.

Versteegh's scholarly conversation is not with Wansbrough alone and other theories provide some of the challenges which he must confront in developing his theory on the rise of grammatical studies. There are some substantial areas of vigorous disagreement within the specialized study of the history of Arabic grammar. The most famous of these, which still polarizes much critical study, is the notion of

---

[4] Nabia Abbott, *Studies in Arabic literary papyri*, II, *Qur'ānic commentary and tradition*. Chicago: University of Chicago Press, 1967, pp. 92–113, reproduces a fragment of the text by Muqātil ibn Sulaymān (d. 150/765), *al-Wujūh wa'l-naẓā'ir* (on which, see further below), but Abbott's discussion does not grapple with the approach of the text to the Qur'ān, only with the various theories regarding the emergence of *tafsīr*. On Muqātil, also see Paul Nywia, *Exégèse coranique et langage mystique: nouvel essai sur le lexique technique des mystiques musulmans*. Beirut: Dar el-Machreq, 1970 and M. M. Sawwaf, "Early *tafsīr*: a survey of Qur'anic commentary up to 150 AH", in K. Ahmad, Z. I. Ansari (eds), *Islamic perspectives: studies in honour of Mawlānā Sayyid Abul A'lā Mawdūdī*. Leicester: The Islamic Foundation, 1979, 135–45.

[5]) See my "Literary analysis of Qur'ān, *tafsīr*, and *sīra*: the methodologies of John Wansbrough", in Richard C. Martin (ed.), *Approaches to Islam in religious studies*. Tucson: University of Arizona Press, 1985, 151–63.

the existence of Kufan and Basran schools of grammar, but there are many other issues which are raised and disposed of in this book in one manner or another. Versteegh's position on virtually all of the contentious points, whether raised by Wansbrough or M. G. Carter,[6]) is quite conservative. He wishes to trust the texts to be authentic, at least where there is no overt reason to doubt them. He wishes to continue to think in terms of schools of grammar, even if the distinction between them can become quite blurred. For him, the *tafsīr* texts he analyzes "bring us back to the dawn of Islam, to a period when there were still people around who had spoken to the Prophet personally, and who could still remember his words" (p.ix) although the concession is made that this may not be true in *every* case.

Clearly there will be a lot of gray areas in such a study and many points will arise on which some readers will want to register disagreement. But, despite that, Versteegh's analysis of the material at hand is illuminating and thorough. Everyone who is interested in *tafsīr* or grammar will profit greatly by the book.

Through his analysis of the early *tafsīr* texts for their use of grammatical terminology, Versteegh attempts to argue for a "natural" development of at least some of the terminology. Words started out being used in a "non-technical, general" sense but can eventually be seen, in some instances, to emerge with a particular technical employment.

An initial definition of "technical" terminology is needed, but it is not tackled as extensively as one might have wished within a book which makes these kinds of arguments. Versteegh (pp. 1–2) cites Jonathan Owens[7]) for his definition: "When a term is consistently used to represent a constant extensional class or a fixed process it can be taken as a technical term." As will be seen, one main problem here is the lack of evidence: when terms are only used several times within a book of 1000 pages which does not have grammar as its main focus, how does one assess their status as "technical"?

To provide the background to the material being studied, Versteegh starts off by presenting the state of the question by looking at the technical grammatical terminology of Sībawayh. Troupeau's *Lexique-index*[8]) facilitates the task and an initial assessment of the terms used has been undertaken by Ulrike Mosel.[9]) Notably,

---

[6]) See M. G. Carter, "Les origines de la grammaire arabe", *Revue des études islamiques,* 40(1972), 69–97; "Arabic grammar" in M. J. L. Young, J. D. Latham and R. B. Serjeant, *Religion, learning and science in the ʿAbbasid period.* Cambridge: Cambridge University Press, 1990, 118–38; and his impressive study, "Language control as people control in Medieval Islam: the aims of the grammarians in their cultural context", in R. Baalbaki (ed.), *Arab language and culture.* Beirut: American University of Beirut, 1983, 65–84 [= *al-Abḥāth,* 31(1983)].

[7]) Jonathan Owens, *Early Arabic grammatical theory: heterogenity and standardization.* Studies in the history of the language sciences, 53. Amsterdam/Philadelphia: John Benjamins Pub. Co, 1990, 11–2.

[8]) Gérard Troupeau, *Lexique-index du Kitāb de Sībawayhi.* Études arabes et islamiques, 3, VII. Paris: Éditions Klincksieck, 1976.

[9]) U. Mosel, *Die syntaktische Terminologie bei Sībawayh.* Dissertation, Universität München, 1975.

Sībawayh cannot be forced into Owens' definition of "technical terminology" for he appears to use different terms for the same phenomenon and the same term for apparently different ones. This, for Versteegh, ultimately points to the fact that Sībawayh must have inherited a number of traditions of analysis which he incorporated into his book alongside his own terminology, creating a certain level of inconsistency. The issue is further confused by later grammarians who sometimes maintain Sībawayh's terminology but change its meaning.

Having sketched the specific background to the historical question, the issue becomes one of where these earlier traditions of terminology came from. Versteegh looks first at the Kufan and Basran "schools" of grammar which are associated with different sets of terminology and different assumptions in the analysis of grammar. In very broad terms, Sībawayh's terminology is said to fall into the Basran category, al-Farrā' (d. 207/822; al-Farrā' is the only other significant early grammarian from whom we have a text) is associated with the Kufan school. Later grammatical tradition adopted the Basran scheme. But, as Versteegh admits, the issue is nowhere near as clear cut as this might suggest, for much overlap is to be found between the terminological sets. Carter has argued (following a strong tradition in the study of Arabic grammar starting with Gustav Weil, whose position is disposed of as "exaggerated distrust" by Versteegh, p. 16) for the fictive nature of the separation of the two schools, preferring to see a difference between the two thinkers, certainly, but avoiding the systematization suggested by "school" formation.[10])

Versteegh also pays attention to other theories on the background of the grammatical terminology. All such theories presume that Sībawayh did not invent the terminology himself, and that it must have had a historical background. Versteegh himself has written extensively about the Greek background,[11]) having argued that "terms were taken from the living practice of grammar teaching in the schools in the Byzantine provinces." (p. 26) In the present book, he wishes to back away from this position because of what he considers evidence for semantic shifts (in, for example, the word *iʿrāb*) which indicate a "semantic development" internal to the Arab community itself but, on occasion, parallel in terms of the semantic shift which took place in Greek technical terminology in its own emergence.

Syriac has been another suggested background. Here we have a culture which had already absorbed the Greek system of grammatical analysis and also the culture which gave Arabic many features of its writing system. It seems "reasonable" then, that aspects of terminology may have been taken over. The problem here is source material: we lack detailed knowledge of the earliest stages of Syriac grammar. What we do know comes from later writers and they have perhaps been influenced by the (later) Arab tradition.

---

[10]) Also see Claude Gilliot, *Exégèse, langue, et théologie en Islam*. Paris: Vrin, 1990, pp. 165–203; for an overall assessment of Gilliot's book within the context of the contemporary study of *tafsīr*, see my review in *Journal of Semitic Studies*, 36(1991), 358–61.

[11]) Kees Versteegh, *Greek elements in Arabic linguistic thinking*. Leiden: E. J. Brill, 1977.

Yet another theory revolves around legal terminology as argued by Carter especially. This suggests that grammatical terminology developed internally to the Arab community but that it was closely connected to other intellectual disciplines. Ultimately, Versteegh argues that none of these theories can be considered conclusive since we have so little evidence for the early stages of any Arab intellectual discipline; it all remains highly speculative.

A fundamental question in the argument looms at this point. Was Sībawayh, in fact, the first person to develop something we can technically call grammatical discussion? If so, then the search for "roots" is rather pointless. Carter has argued that prior to Sībawayh, there were only amateur dabblers in the field of grammar. Versteegh takes a more traditional view: there were technical grammatical experts (who are called the *naḥwīyūn* in Sībawayh) before Sībawayh "whose main preoccupation was to defend the language of the *Qur'ān* against corruption." (p. 37) In order to prove his point and develop it further Versteegh draws on a series of early Qur'ānic exegetical texts and mines them for evidence of grammatical discussion as well as evidence for the actual evolution of the terminology.

Versteegh is not unaware that the use of these texts is problematic and controversial. Some people, myself included, have argued that these texts are late renditions at best, which have been filtered through several generations of editors, compilers and copyists. Theoretically, there may well be a "historical kernel" of material that could be ascribed to a given person within these texts, but determining just what that kernel consists of is no longer possible. What is more, arbitrary and mythical ascriptions abound, rendering the entire ascription framework suspect. Versteegh will have none of this. He is convinced that "after the death of the Prophet the main preoccupation of the believers was with the text of the *Qur'ān*. This determined all their efforts to get a grip on the phenomenon of language, and it is, therefore, in the earliest commentaries on the *Qur'ān* that we shall have to start looking for the original form of language study in Islam." (p. 41)

Furthermore, while Versteegh admits that, in some cases, the best one can hope for is that the "content" of the text may be safely ascribed to its supposed author, in fact, given that his aim is the analysis of terminology, he has to rely on the accurate transmission of precise words within these texts as being from their authors. For the general authenticity and reliability of early works, appeal is made to Fuat Sezgin, Nabia Abbott and Harold Motzki.[12]) As well, Goldfeld's ideas regarding Ibn ʿAbbās's books[13]) are cited in general, if cautious agreement. It is unfortunate that

---

[12]) See especially Harold Motzki, "The *Muṣannaf of* ʿAbd al-Razzāq aṣ-Ṣanʿānī as a source of authentic *aḥādīth* of the first century A. H.", *Journal of Near Eastern Studies*, 50 (1991), 1–21.

[13]) Isaiah Goldfeld, "The *Tafsīr* of Ibn ʿAbbās", *Der Islam*, 58 (1981), 125–35; also see his "The development of theory in Qur'ānic exegesis in Islamic scholarship", *Studia Islamica*, 67 (1988), 5–27.

Norman Calder's *Studies in early Muslim jurisprudence*[14]) was published too late for Versteegh to consider in his arguments. It is Calder who provides the most stimulating counter models to much of Versteegh's discussion on issues regarding the composition and social situation of these "early texts".

To continue his argument, Versteegh next looks at the development of *tafsīr* as a technical enterprise. It is clearly necessary for him to do this, for Wansbrough's investigation of the material argued for a chronological ordering of exegetical types and, if this is accepted, many of the elements of the works which Versteegh wants to tap would need to be declared later editorial intrusions.

Overall, Versteegh does not see much chronological development in the elements of *tafsīr* at all. For him, reflection on the text from the beginning was based upon a need to derive matters from the text and virtually every tool available will have been used from the very beginning. He sees exegesis as consisting of a number of fundamental elements: *asbāb al-nuzūl,* anaphoric references, historical details, etymologies, comparisons of verses, abrogated passages, variant readings, lexical glosses, paraphrases, legal precepts, metaphorical interpretations, theological problems. Not all of these are present in one author but, contrary to Wansbrough, none are mutually exclusive (even in a chronological sense). (p. 92) The lack of later "intermediate scholarship" (e.g., that of lexicographers, jurisconsults, etc.) in these early texts Versteegh thus takes as a part of the evidence for their true ascriptions.

Versteegh feels that *tafsīr* arose in order to "investigate [the Qur'ān's] applicability to religious and social practices". (p. 63) This is where he fundamentally disagrees with Wansbrough who sees a need to create a coherent text of scripture which will be accepted as authoritative by the community as the first task of any religious society. Within this framework, coherence is first created through "haggadic" exegesis: that is, coherence is created on a narrative and popular level. For Versteegh, this cannot be the case, for even Ibn ʿAbbās is protrayed as worrying about the specifics of the language of the Qur'ān along with its laws only a few decades after the death of Muḥammad. "Occasions of revelation", *asbāb al-nuzūl,* therefore, are seen to be related directly to the applicability of a verse rather than being, as I have argued elsewhere,[15]) a narrative device within which interpretation is embedded. All this means that Versteegh has a substantially different view of the nature of *tafsīr* as a discipline than others in the field.

One of the ramifications of Versteegh's position is seen in his suggestion that we should understand that there are two approaches at work in early exegetical texts: "explanation of the text" – a rather simple process in his view – and sophisticated juridical discussions.[16]) This kind of distinction obscures the fact that narra-

[14]) Oxford: Oxford University Press, 1993; see my review in *Journal of Semitic Studies,* 39 (1994), 346–9.

[15]) See my "The function of *asbāb al-nuzūl* in Qur'ānic exegesis", *Bulletin of the School of Oriental and African Studies,* 51(1988), 1–20.

[16]) Versteegh's theories may be profitably compared with the carefully considered work of Claude Gilliot, for example his "Les débuts de l'exégèse coranique", in *Les premières écritures islamiques.* Revue du Monde Musulman et de la Méditerranée, 58. Aix-en-Provence: Édisud, 1991, pp. 82–100.

tive exegesis is itself a technically sophisticated procedure (so technical, I am tempted to add, that some people don't see its point) that has nothing naive about it. What it reflects is a different set of concerns than those of a jurist. Trying to fit these different modes of interpretation into the differentiation between *quṣṣāṣ* and *qurrā'*, as Versteegh suggests, is far too conjectural to be useful: we know no more about the social structure of the first century Muslim community than we do about the evolution of grammatical technical terminology. More likely is that we must look to factors such as literary genre as primary: only in this way can one understand the different character of ʿAbd al-Razzāq's *Muṣannaf* and *Tafsīr* for example.[17])

It is variant readings which Versteegh sees as the most important element in early *tafsīr* for his purposes. In the discussions of the issues related to the readings one might well expect to find grammatical terminology employed. The status of these discussions as taking place early on in Islamic history is crucial to the book's arguments, therefore. Versteegh notes that all the variants discussed in the early texts are "non-canonical" [thus suggesting (at best) a pre-4th hijrī century dating]. He disagrees with Wansbrough who declared such elements to be "intrusive" in haggadic works. However, statistically they clearly are: Versteegh is able to count 22 citations of variants in Muqātil, not a very impressive number in a work of that size. In two instances, Muqātil's textual gloss is of the variant and not the "canonical" text (see Q. 11/14 and 19/55). This suggests to me evidence for the intrusive character of the readings themselves: a later editor/compiler simply recognized the need to align the *Tafsīr* with the generally accepted understanding of the "ʿUthmānic" version of the Qur'ān and thus adduced a variant to serve the purpose. (cf. Versteegh's explanation, p. 79). In dealing with the variants, Versteegh cites ʿAbd al-Razzāq from his *Muṣannaf* and not his *Tafsīr*. That all these instances of cited variants should attach to points of law or ritual, then, is not surprising and can hardly be the basis for the implications Versteegh sees in them. ʿAbd al-Razzāq's *Tafsīr* does contain references to variants, although the terminology used to adduce them is not "technical" (e.g., *Tafsīr*, I, 176, ad. Q. 5/23, spoken of as *ḥurūf*; see Versteegh, p. 81. Also cf. the use of *qara'a* as "understand", *Tafsir*, I, 175. On this text, see further below).

In dealing with the practice of lexical glossing, Versteegh ignores, without explaining why, the works ascribed to Ibn ʿAbbās. That he has accepted my arguments concerning these texts seems unlikely.[18]) He is very interested in the ascription of words to foreign languages and dialects but is puzzled as to what they suggest. It seems to me that enumerating the languages which the Qur'ān included was a part of the general tendency towards "listing", an ancient practice characteristic of a

[17]) Versteegh has a tendency to adduce the *Muṣannaf* in order to show that the Qur'ān and the *sunna* were intertwined in early sophisticated discussions (pp. 76–7); but this is a function of the genre, not of the nature of all discussions – ʿAbd al-Razzāq was precisely arguing the point in the *Muṣannaf*.

[18]) See my "Ibn ʿAbbās's al-Lughāt fi'l-Qur'ān", *Bulletin of the School of Oriental and African Studies*, 44 (1981), 15–25 and "Ibn ʿAbbās's Gharīb al-Qur'ān", *Bulletin of the School of Oriental and African Studies*, 46 (1983), 332–3.

"cultured" society.[19]) But, as Wansbrough has also argued, listing provides a canonizing function: it unifies a text and suggests that it is whole; establishing that fact for the Qur'ān was of central concern to the Muslim community.

The heart of Versteegh's book lies in chapter 4, "Grammatical terminology in early *tafsīr*". Here, despite questions which the rest of the book might raise in its historical reconstructions, we find a treasure of close analysis of the texts, highlighting grammatical terminology and its meaning. Everyone who tackles the reading of the early *tafsīr*s will be indebted to Versteegh for having shone further light on the material in such a systematic fashion. Each of the major works (Mujāhid [d. 104/722], Sufyān al-Thawrī [d. 161/778], al-Kalbī [d. 146/763], Muqātil [d. 150/765], ʿAbd al-Razzāq [d. 211/827]; I will return to some discussion of these texts below) is examined and the terminology extracted and sometimes compared. As well, attention is paid to general treatments of the words referring to the meaning of words (especially *yaʿnī*), units of speech (e.g., *kalām, ḥarf*), and text types (as in the introduction to Muqātil's *Tafsīr*).

After this analysis, the problem which remains for Versteegh is to try to prove that there must have been a link between grammarians, Qur'ān readers and exegetes so that the lines of transmission from these texts to people such as Sībawayh were indeed possible. Biographical material and *isnād* structures are employed to demonstrate this. It is among the early reciters of the Qur'ān that Versteegh finds significant elements of contact. However, accounts of learning the Qur'ān with esteemed teachers who are also teachers of later grammarians such as are found in biographical notices are rather difficult to assess: they are best seen as attempts to convey the piety of the subject of the biography by later generations who would have expected that such meetings and teaching *must* have happened, although one would not want to deny that there may well have been a social reality reflected in some instances as well. In dealing with the biographical connections, Versteegh argues for a distinction between the enterprises of *tafsīr* and studying the readings; he then suggests that the sources quoted by the grammarians are not the exegetes but the readers. This puts a lot of weight on the matter of ascription, however. The observation is made that al-Farrā' is much more interested in reader authorities than grammarians, Sībawayh vice-versa. Versteegh wants to assign the reason for this to the difference between the Kufan and Basran schools, the latter disregarding readers, the former embracing them. (A Wansbroughian theory might suggest that, rather, al-Farrā' is the one who is arguing the point for the relevance and authority of the readings.) Evidence of this lies in works comparable to al-Farrā''s by Basrans al-Akhfash (d. 215/830) and Abū ʿUbayda (d. 210/824) in which quotations from grammarians significantly outweigh named Qur'ān readers. The readers became unacceptable to the Basran tradition because of "their use of non-technical vocabulary and their *ad hoc* reasoning with regard to grammatical problems in the text of the Qur'ān" (p. 182) The later grammarians do not quote the *tafsīr* sources which Versteegh has studied because (according to Versteegh) those writers were just

[19]) See my "Lexicographical texts and the Qur'ān" in *Approaches to the history of the interpretation of the Qur'ān*, A Rippin (ed.). Oxford: Oxford University Press, 1988, pp. 158–74.

incompetent in grammar and were interested in elucidating the meaning of the text only (!), whereas the grammarians were interested in the structure of language. For Versteegh, "the approach of the commentators did not allow for any intrinsic interest in the structure of language, since they were solely interested in explaining the text." (p. 195) On one level, it is hard to disagree with such an obvious statement: grammar is one discipline, exegesis another. But that explaining the meaning of the text depends upon the structure of the language is, to me, a clear assumption of every exegetical text: every gloss which is provided suggests that language conveys more than it says, in ways which depend upon a basic understanding, only implied certainly, about language. The presence of "non-technical" vocabulary, therefore, is unsurprising also. These texts were not designed for an audience of grammarians. Unfortunately, contrary to Versteegh, I do not see that this means necessarily that these works must precede the works of the grammarians, or even reflect necessarily a stage in discussing the text which comes before Sībawayh, for example.

Versteegh's final conclusion is that while the Kufan tradition (al-Farrā') is directly influenced by the exegetical writers, the Basran is not. This means that Sībawayh "broke with tradition by publishing his book as an independent publication, but he also devised a wholly new way of analyzing language." (p. 198) He was, in fact, far more innovative than he is normally given credit for. He transformed the study of grammar into a discipline of its own, with the aim of elucidating the Qur'ān no longer the primary goal. He introduced new terms, although not with total consistency. The Kufan tradition predates Sībawayh as indicated by the earlier exegetical works. Greek through Syriac was the vehicle for transmission of the remaining "obscure" points but, even here, it is on Kufa that the influence was more pronounced, due to the interest of that school in meaning rather than syntax as found in both the Greek and the exegetical traditions.

These conclusions are stimulating and, in arriving at them, Versteegh has produced some extremely valuable analysis. However, beyond some of the questionable historical deductions already pointed out, the bases on which the overall conclusions have been erected are extremely slender. Some comments on the texts involved in this study are required.

The books ascribed to Mujāhid and Sufyān al-Thawrī have been studied elsewhere[20]) and are, many would feel, collations made well after the fact from later sour-

---

[20]) G. Stauth, *Die Überlieferung des Korankommentars Muǧāhid b. Ǧabrs. Zur Frage der Rekonstruktion der in den Sammelwerken des 3. Jh. d. H. benutzten frühislamischen Quellenwerke.* Dissertation, Giessen, Justus-Liebig-Universität, 1969; F. Leemhuis, "Ms. 1075 *tafsīr* of the Cairene Dār al-Kutub and Muǧāhid's *Tafsīr*", in *Proceedings of the Ninth Congress of the Union Européenne des Arabisants et Islamisants, Amsterdam, 1st to 7th September 1978,* Rudolph Peters (ed.). Publications of the Netherland Institute of Archaeology and Arabic Studies in Cairo, 4. Leiden: E. J. Brill, 1981, pp. 169–80; Fred Leemhuis, "Origins and early development of the *tafsīr* tradition", in *Approaches,* pp. 13–30; Wansbrough, *Quranic studies,* pp. 140–5; Josef van Ess, *Theologie und Gesellschaft im 2. und 3. Jahrhundert Hidschra. Eine Geschichte des religiösen Denkens im frühen Islam.* Berlin: Walter de Gruyter, 1991 continuing, I, 227–8; Gilliot, "Les débuts", pp. 88–9.

ces. These works are therefore no different than the recently published *Tafsīr Ibn ʿAbbās* in the transmission of Ibn abī Ṭalḥa as reconstructed by its modern editor, al-Rajjāl (a text noted but not analyzed by Versteegh).[21]) The works of Mujāhid and al-Thawrī may be older in manuscript form but there is no reason to feel they are any more authentic. That the two books provide very little material for Versteegh's analysis renders their status as tenuous as ever and the claims made on their behalf quite doubtful.

Versteegh has studied the *tafsīr* of Muqātil quite extensively,[22]) as has Gilliot[23]) and, of course, Wansbrough.[24]) As a work, it is fascinating and it provides a great deal of material for analysis. While it has been subject to editorial intrusion and reformulation, its unique qualities mark it as undoubtedly quite early in the development of Islamic exegesis. A few marginal comments arising from Versteegh's use of the work will illustrate both the potential of the work for further study and the complexity of trying to fit the evidence into the overall picture of early Islamic exegesis. Consider the term *naẓīr*. Muqātil uses it to mean words with one meaning used in different contexts (although the sense of what is intended by "context" is quite variable). As Versteegh details, in early grammar this term became used to indicate words with the same syntactic status because of a resemblance in form. The delineation of words according to their *naẓāʾir* is one feature of Muqātil's *Tafsīr*, but it was also the subject of an entire book by him.[25]) The counterpart of *naẓīr* is commonly called *wajh*, indicating the different meanings given to one word; the two modes of analyzing vocabulary and structure become constants of the later exegetical tradition. Versteegh confuses some of this discussion by first referring to Muqātil's book devoted to the subject as *al-Ashbāh waʾl-naẓāʾir* (p. 70) and then later as *al-Wujūh waʾl-naẓāʾir* (p. 87) without ever clarifying the difference (if any) between the two words. In this discussion, account needs to be taken of the evidence provided in the text ascribed to al-Kisāʾī (d. 189/804: he was a grammarian, after all) variously called *Mushtabihāt al-Qurʾān* or *Mutashābih al-Qurʾān*, who uses the terms to indicate something of the same quality as *wajh*, and thus fitting in with the alternate title to Maqātil's works on words.[26])

---

[21]) Another similar text is the *Tafsīr* of Sufyān ibn ʿUyayna (d. 194/811); see C. Gilliot, "Les débuts", p. 89.

[22]) Kees Versteegh, "Grammar and Exegesis: the origins of Kufan grammar and the Tafsīr Muqātil", *Der Islam*, 67(1990), 206–42. Also see Isaiah Goldfeld, "Muqātil Ibn Sulaymān", *Bar-Ilan Arabic and Islamic Studies*, 2(1978), 13–30.

[23]) Claude Gilliot, "Muqātil, grand exégète, traditionniste et théologien maudit", *Journal asiatique*, 279(1991), 39–92.

[24]) Wansbrough, *Quranic studies*, pp. 122–36. Also see van Ess, *Theologie und Gesellschaft*, II, 516–32.

[25]) See Versteegh, pp. 70–1, 87; also see my "Lexicographical texts", pp. 167–71; Abbott, *Studies*, pp. 92–106; Wansbrough, *Quranic studies*, pp. 208–12; Muhammad Abdus Sattar, "Wujūh al-Qurʾān: a branch of tafsir literature", *Islamic Studies*, 17(1978), 137–52.

[26]) See Wansbrough, *Quranic studies*, pp. 212–5; also my "Lexicographical texts", pp. 171–3.

A second illustration of the significance of Muqātil's *Tafsīr* may be seen in the idea of *naskh*. This is a term of major importance and it is central to the development of both exegesis and technical terminology, but it hardly provides the evidence for an early emphasis within exegesis for "application" of the text that Versteegh wishes to see in it.[27]) Its earliest application may well be thought to be that as illustrated in Muqātil as replacement of a practice from before Islam, and is purely haggadic in character; such exegesis answers the question of the curious auditor of why did God say such-and-such (e.g., "enter houses through their doors" as in Q. 2/189) and it provides a means of a moral valuation consequent to the implementation of Islam. Such exegesis says nothing about the application of the text but asserts only that the statement in question was indeed revealed by God.

The work ascribed to al-Kalbī is the focus of a paper of mine presented at the "From Jahiliyya to Islam" colloquium in 1987 and recently published in *Jerusalem Studies in Arabic and Islam.*[28]) This paper is listed in Versteegh's bibliography, although it is doubtful that he has read it, and he probably just borrowed the summary of it which is available in an article of central importance to the overall topic of early *tafsīr* by Claude Gilliot.[29]) Versteegh continues Wansbrough's nomenclature of calling this work *Tafsīr al-Kalbī,* although there seem to me to be very few grounds on which to do so. The text reached its present form in the late 3rd or early 4th century. I have argued that the ascription of this very same text to al-Dīnawarī (d. 308/920) indicates this. Versteegh made his own job and the task of his readers more difficult by taking all his references to the text from a Chester Beatty manuscript copy of the text. While that copy (Chester Beatty 4224[30]) is extremely attractive and well preserved, the text has, in fact, been printed a great many times, usually under the title *Tafsīr Ibn ʿAbbās* (and Versteegh could easily have checked the Leiden manuscript copy [ms. 1651] of al-Dīnawarī, *al-Wāḍiḥ fī tafsīr al-Qurʾān* to verify all these facts).

The difference the dating of this text makes to Versteegh's argument is substantial. In fact, the role of the text in this entire enterprise must be questioned closely. Citation of variant readings to the Qurʾān abound in the "al-Kalbī" text and many of

---

[27]) On this point also see my "Al-Zuhrī, *naskh al-Qurʾān* and the problem of early *tafsīr* texts", *Bulletin of the School of Oriental and African Studies,* 47 (1984), 22–43.

[28]) A. Rippin, "*Tafsīr Ibn ʿAbbās* and criteria for dating early *tafsīr* texts", *Jerusalem studies in Arabic and Islam,* 18 (1994), 38–83.

[29]) Gilliot, "Les débuts", pp. 87–8. On al-Kalbī's *tafsīr,* also see Josef van Ess, *Ungenützte Texte zur Karrāmiya. Eine Materialsammlung.* Heidelberg: Carl Winter Universitätsverlag, 1980, pp. 50–3; idem, *Theologie und Gesellschaft,* I, 298–301; Etan Kohlberg, *A medieval Muslim scholar at work. Ibn Ṭāwūs and his library.* Leiden: E. J. Brill, 1992, p. 343. I have not had an opportunity to compare the passages which Kohlberg cites from Ibn Ṭāwūs, *Saʿd al-suʿūd,* with the printed text of "al-Kalbī"; Kohlberg does not seem to be aware that the text is published.

[30]) In my above cited article on *Tafsīr Ibn ʿAbbās,* this is text #14; see footnote 101 of that article for a comparison of this text with Chester Beatty 5465 copied in the previous year by the same scribe.

them are ones which fit within canonical schemes. It is clearly this characteristic which led Wansbrough to some rightfully cautious remarks about the text, suggesting that it shows evidence of massive editorial reformulation and that it presupposes the work of al-Farrā'.[31]) My own study of the text suggests that the ascription to al-Kalbī is quite arbitrary and is simply an appeal to authority, and the work is from a time well past al-Farrā'. Versteegh, on the other hand, considers Wansbrough's conclusions "unfair" on the basis that the argument is circular. Whatever the merits of Wansbrough's argument, Versteegh's own is very tenuous. He wishes to see al-Kalbī simply as an "exception" to a general tendency, reflecting this person's own individual bent in exegesis. It seems much more plausible to assert that the *tafsīr* reflects historically later concerns, especially in light of the textual evidence which points to a late date also. Versteegh's treatment of al-Kalbī's *tafsīr* does provide an extremely useful and extensive treatment of the names of the vowels which are used frequently in the text in order to clarify variant readings (pp. 125–30) but this becomes a part of his argument for the authenticity of the text. The problem may be that Versteegh thinks of al-Kalbī as a grammarian and then posits that variation in terminology means non-standardized, rather than late non-technical, usage.

The *Tafsīr* of ʿAbd al-Razzāq is a very interesting text. Unfortunately, Versteegh made hard work of his task once again by using the rather difficult manuscript from Cairo, Dār al-kutub 242 (Versteegh describes this manuscript on p. 156 as "very hard to read, and we have managed to analyze only parts of it."). The text was published, however, in 1986.[32]) For the reader of Versteegh's book, there are substantial difficulties as a result. The recent edition of the *Tafsīr* does not include the folio numbers of the manuscript (the editor also used the Ankara manuscript 4216, a text which likewise does not look very pleasant to read) and Versteegh frequently cites only the manuscript folio number for reference. Sometimes Versteegh provides the Qur'ānic reference which helps, but the editor of ʿAbd al-Razzāq only provides the verse numbers for the Qur'ānic citations in an index and not in the text itself, a minor inconvenience to be sure. Furthermore and more annoying to me personally, my microfilm copy of the Dār al-kutub manuscript (a copy made under Arab League auspices) is paginated and not foliated for approximately the first half of the manuscript. Versteegh could have helped those of us who wish to retrace his research steps by clarifying his references to the manuscript and its foliation.

ʿAbd al-Razzāq does not use much grammatical terminology in his *tafsīr*. This does not mean that it is not a book full of conventions and standard modes of discourse, however, as Versteegh suggests. Certainly the text does not contain many linguistic statements; rather, it abounds in other ways of expounding upon the text: paraphrase, gloss and, under-emphasized by Versteegh, completion. Changing the text, whether it be on the level of a particle (which Versteegh notes, pp. 158–9) or on

[31]) Wansbrough, *Quranic Studies*, p. 133, cited by Versteegh, p. 81.

[32]) The existence of this edition would seem not to be well known generally. I only learned of its existence recently through its citation in Claude Gilliot, "Une leçon magistrale d'orientalisme: L'*opus magnum* de J. van Ess," *Arabica*, 40(1993), 365, n. 63. I would like to thank Leah Kinberg, Tel Aviv, for obtaining a copy of the text for me.

the larger narrative and lexical level, is prominent. This is a highly sophisticated *tafsīr* with its own methodological parameters, one which needs further attention in order to place it within, and assess its contribution to, the overall discipline of *tafsīr*.

One unmentioned text which might have provided some additional light on the subject of early grammar is Abū ʿUbayd (d. 224/838), *Faḍāʾil al-Qurʾān* (Beirut, 1991, but also easily available in manuscript form, Berlin Ms. 451). While somewhat later than al-Farrāʾ, Abū ʿUbayd is usually described as attached to the Baghdad school. The work contains an extensive section devoted to Qurʾān readings[33]) but there are other references to grammar-related concerns throughout the work. The vocabulary of *iʿrāb* and internal vowelling is to be found scattered throughout the text, for example, *naṣab* re: Q. 4/66, p. 197; *rafʿ*, p. 199; *fatḥa*, p. 123. However, the book covers a large variety of topics, the unity of which is still unclear, and a detailed study of the text may well reveal a clearer picture of Abū ʿUbayd's contribution to the development of Qurʾānic studies and Islamic religious thinking, especially given the broad range of the works ascribed to him.[34])

The *tafsīr* text of ʿAbd Allāh ibn Wahb (d. 197/812) has just been edited and published by Miklos Muranyi in two volumes (with another volume expected to appear shortly). Every early work of *tafsīr* must be considered essential to the overall task of understanding the character and aims of formative Muslim exegesis, and thus it is unfortunate that this work was not available to Versteegh for consideration in his book.

Ibn Wahb's *Tafsīr* is another example of the early periphrastic type of exegesis, although its organization of the material appears to be related to the *musnad* category rather than following the text of the Qurʾān. The work contains much of the technical vocabulary of early *tafsīr* without any emphasis on variant readings or elements of grammar: *nazalat fī* (f. 7a), *fa-anzala* (f. 10a), *tafsīr* (f. 11a, 18a), *kull shayʾ fīʾl-Qurʾān* (f. 10b), *yurīdu* (f. 9b); lack of connection between scripture and comment in this text leads to a number of difficult readings (e.g., f. 2a)

Ibn Wahb's companion text on *ʿulūm al-Qurʾān* ("Koranwissenschaft") is even more interesting from a technical point of view for the development of certain aspects related to the place of the Qurʾān in Muslim learning in the 2nd–3rd centuries and the development of Islam, and, in places, is far more significant in terms of Versteegh's search for grammar and its terminology. The work is much like Abū ʿUbayd's *Faḍāʾil al-Qurʾan* in the sense that it is a somewhat disparate collection

---

[33]) Previously edited by A. Spitaler, "Ein Kapitel aus den *Faḍāʾil al-Qurʾān* von Abū ʿUbaid al-Qāsim ibn Sallām", in *Documenta islamica inedita. Festschrift für Richard Hartmann*, J.W. Fück (ed.). Berlin: Akademie Verlag, 1952, pp. 1–24.

[34]) Two other works of Abū ʿUbayd are clearly pivotal: *Kitāb al-nāsikh waʾl-mansūkh*. J. Burton (ed.). Cambridge: E. J. W. Gibb Memorial, 1987; and *al-Khuṭab waʾ-mawāʿiẓ*, Ramaḍān ʿAbd al-Tawwāb (ed.). Cairo, 1986. Both of these works are (almost) unique compared to later works in the same or similar genres. See the review of Burton's edition by M. Muranyi, *Die Welt des Islam*, 31 (1991), 264–9, and my own review in *Bulletin of the School of Oriental and African Studies*, 52 (1989), 346–7, and my follow-up note, "Abū ʿUbaid's *Kitāb al-nāsikh waʾl-mansūkh*", *Bulletin of the School of Oriental and African Studies*, 53 (1990), 319–20.

of ideas about the Qur'ān: *targhīb, i'rāb, ikhtilāf al-ḥurūf, naskh,* and *sujūd* are its (approximate) chapter headings. Some vocabulary of vowelling is to be noted e.g., *naṣab* (f. 9b), but, for the most part, variant readings are presented with little comment and no explanation and, in many instances, depend upon vowel marks written in the text (e.g., to distinguish *ghalabat* and *ghulibat* in the discussion of Q, 30/2, f. 11a) which might suggest that this text exists either as a transcript or memory aid of an oral presentation, or that the readings which are being presented are well enough known to need no explanation. (In a few places, letters are named in order to clarify matters: f. 12a, e.g.) The chapter on *al-nāsikh wa'l-mansūkh* is a fairly simple listing, similar to texts recently publishing ascribed to Qatāda (d. 118/736)[35]) and a detailed analysis and comparison of those texts (and that ascribed to al-Zuhrī) on the level of both contents and method may well be worthwhile (see Muranyi's comments, pp. 11–5).

It must also be remarked that Muranyi has produced lavish editions of these valuable texts. The actual pages of the *tafsīr* parchment manuscript (27 folios) are reproduced photographically and opposite each is the editor's transcription (the *'ulūm al-Qur'ān* volume, which was published first, separates the two elements into distinct sections of the book and consists of 27 folios also). A full scholarly apparatus is also provided, indicating parallel sources and identifying names. A short introduction preceeds each volume; an earlier volume provided a greater amount of narrative concerning Ibn Wahb and his life, times and works.[36]) *Isnād* charts and an index of Qur'ān verses are also provided.

The works by Versteegh and Muranyi display two different aspects to the development of the study of early *tafsīr*: Versteegh provides the synthesis, Muranyi supplies the detailed texual work upon which all later syntheses must proceed. Muranyi wishes to see his works as positioning our knowledge of early Islam within the early 2nd *hijrī* century; while it is certainly possible to argue against such an early date (based, as it is, on suppositions about and trust in *isnād* structures), there can be little doubt about the late 3rd century date of the manuscript itself, and thus there is absolute certainty of the comparatively early nature of the material. Versteegh's work is far more speculative and tenuous, but none the less stimulating for being so. The problem always comes back to one of the questionable character of the source material which makes reconstructing history so hazardous, and where a work such as Muranyi's textual edition puts us on substantially firmer ground.

---

[35]) Qatāda ibn Di'āma, *Kitāb al-nāsikh wa'l-mansūkh,* Ḥ.Ṣ. al-Ḍāmin (ed.). Beirut, 1984. See Claude Gilliot, "Exégèse et sémantique institutionnelle dans le commentaire de Tabari", *Studia Islamica,* 77 (1993), esp. 42–50.

[36]) M. Muranyi, *'Abd Allāh b. Wahb: Leben und Werk.* Wiesbaden: Harrassowitz, 92. Also see Sezgin, *GAS,* I, 466.

VI

Quranic Studies, part IV: Some methodological notes

1. Introduction

Of all the insights offered by John Wansbrough's *Quranic Studies* (1977), the theories proffered about the origins of the Qur'ān have tended to overshadow the others. It would seem that some people, knowing that the book contains these suggestions which run counter to accepted theories, have disregarded the entire work and cite it merely as an example of "Orientalist" misguidedness. As a result perhaps, the extensive treatment of the formative Muslim interpretative tradition, *tafsīr*, contained in part IV of *Quranic Studies* has not received the detailed attention that it has deserved among scholars.

Having said that, however, it must be clarified immediately that the analysis of the *tafsīr* texts conducted by Wansbrough does not stand apart from his overall theory on the Qur'ān. Indeed, part of the proof for the idea of the gradual emergence of the Qur'ān as an authoritative text within the Muslim community is based upon the evidence of the *tafsīr* texts. The implicit arguments which these texts contain for the definition of a canon of scripture and for the general development of notions of authority of scripture (such that reference to scripture on legal issues comes subsequent to the acceptance of the text as a whole as supported and promulgated through haggadic exegesis) all point in this direction for Wansbrough.

Putting aside the purposes to which Wansbrough used his analysis within his book, however, the significance of his work on the *tafsīr* texts remains. It is to this significance in terms of its impact upon the discipline and some of the challenges which the work has prompted that this essay will pay attention. This will be facilitated by looking at two recent works which typify some of the reactions to Wansbrough's work.

2. The significance of Wansbrough's work

One initial point is worth emphasizing. Wansbrough's analysis contained in part IV of *Quranic Studies* constitutes the first time many of the texts had been looked at with a scholarly eye. Most of the texts were in manuscript form when he looked at them; some were misidentified in manuscript catalogues. Since the publication of his book, all but one or two (as far as I can determine) of the significant early texts have been published. Whether one can say that in every instance this is a direct result of Wansbrough's work and his creating interest in the texts is doubtful but it may well be partially true in some cases. The foundational nature of Wansbrough's work may be appreciated by the references to it in recent works such as Josef van Ess, *Theologie und Gesellschaft im 2. und 3. Jahrhundert Hidschra*, volumes 1 and 2.[1]

Further scholarly studies have also built upon Wansbrough's work, in terms of adding clarification to the nature of some of the texts themselves, extending his scheme of analysis, or applying certain of his principles to the analysis of other texts. For example, I have pursued detailed studies of various texts ascribed to Ibn ʿAbbās (on which, see further below) (Rippin 1981; 1983), edited and analyzed a text on abrogation (*naskh*) which Wansbrough mentioned but had been unable to examine (1984), as well as attempted to apply some of the methods of analysis to a detailed re-examination of one text ascribed by Wansbrough to al-Kalbī (1994). As well, I have re-examined the role of one of the exegetical tools which Wansbrough isolated, the "occasions of revelation" (*asbāb al-nuzūl*), and reassessed its use within a broader framework of exegesis (1985; 1988). Norman Calder, in an impressive article "Tafsīr from Ṭabarī to Ibn Kathīr" (1993), has extended Wansbrough's analy-

1. See, for example, the treatment of Sufyān al-Thawrī (Ess 1990: 1.227-228) and Muqātil b. Sulaymān (Ess 1992: 2.516-528).

sis beyond the formative period of *tafsīr* and analyzed the procedural devices in the main exegetical works from the classical Islamic period. As a final example, Christopher Buck has used Wansbrough's isolation of exegetical procedural devices as a starting point for the analysis of the nineteenth century work of exegesis by Bahā'u'llāh, the *Kitāb-i Īqān* (1995).

But Wansbrough's work in this part of the book has also brought forth various challenges. Here I wish to focus not upon those works which may have suggested corrections of a factual or even an interpretative nature, but rather, those works which have suggested basic methodological challenges to the assumptions of his approach. There have not been many such works which have paid direct attention to part IV of *Quranic Studies* (in whole or in part) in this way and those that do tend to share a common methodological objection which has come forth in other contexts also in dealing with Wansbrough's work. This issue revolves around Wansbrough's insistence upon having textual evidence for historical claims and, what is more, seeing those texts which do provide evidence as complex expressions of several generations of editors. The claims put forth by mechanisms such as *isnād*s (chains of authorities) cannot be trusted to provide a good historical basis for discussion. However, other methodological issues do arise as well, as we shall see.

3. Ibn ʿAbbās

Perhaps the best example of the issue which is at stake revolves around the person of Ibn ʿAbbās. The fame and significance of this cousin of Muḥammad as the source of a great deal of exegetical material has been the focus of much attention in scholarly discussions of *tafsīr*, at least since the time of Goldziher (1920; compare, however, Gilliot 1985). Wansbrough drew attention to a series of texts ascribed specifically to Ibn ʿAbbās, all of them of a lexicographical nature. One of the roles of the figure of Ibn ʿAbbās within the development of *tafsīr*, according to Wansbrough's argument, was bringing the language of the Qur'ān into alignment with the language of the "Arabs" (variously defined, sometimes Bedouin, sometimes urban dwellers, sometimes the Ḥijāz as a whole). Identity of the people as solidified through language became a major ideological stance promulgated in such texts.

Such an argument, however, depended upon a number of preceding factors, including the emergence of the Qur'ān as authoritative, before it could be mounted. Such an argument could not have been contemporary with Ibn ʿAbbās, who died in 687 C.E., but must stem from several centuries later. The ascription to Ibn ʿAbbās was an appeal to authority in the past, to the family of the Prophet and to a name which was gathering an association with exegetical activity in general.

In an article on one of those texts ascribed to Ibn ʿAbbās, Issa Boullata (1991) challenges Wansbrough's basic assumption. By examining a manuscript of the text ascribed to Ibn ʿAbbās entitled *Masāʾil Nāfiʿ ibn al-Azraq* that likely dates from the eleventh century (also see Neuwirth 1993), Boullata argues that the tradition which aligns Ibn ʿAbbās with lexicographical matters related to the Qurʾān is early, although it was clearly subject to elaboration as time went on (the number of lexicographical items grows as do the details of the situation in which the lexicographical discussions took place). But Boullata raises the crucial issue: "J. Wansbrough believes that the reference of rare or unknown Qurʾānic words to the great corpus of early Arabic poetry is an exegetical method which is considerably posterior to the activity of Ibn ʿAbbās." (1991: 38) While the activity may have been limited, Boullata admits, "If there was anybody who could have dared to do it (or have such activity ascribed to him) it was Ibn ʿAbbās, the Prophet's cousin and Companion, because of his family relationship and authoritative position." (1991: 38) "Oral tradition" would have been the means by which these traditions from Ibn ʿAbbās were transmitted down to later exegetical writers. Just because poetical citations are not found in early texts (as Wansbrough had pointed out) does not mean, for Boullata, that such an exegetical practice did not exist. "One cannot determine what of these materials is authentic and what is not, but everything points to the possibility that there existed a smaller core of materials which was most likely preserved in a tradition of oral transmission for several generations before it was put down in writing with enlargements." (1991: 40)

"Possibility" and "most likely" are the key methodological assumptions of this historical approach, and certainly all historical investigations proceed on the basis of analogy of processes which underlie these assumptions. But Boullata underestimates the overall significance of what Wansbrough has argued. The debate is not over whether a core of the material is authentic or not (for even if it should be, if one cannot determine what is and what is not authentic, then nothing has been gained whatsoever and there is no significance to the claim). By underemphasizing issues of the establishment of authority of scripture and the bringing into comparison profane texts with scripture, Boullata avoids the central crux. Ultimately, the assertion is that it would have been "only natural" for the Arabs to have followed this procedure within exegesis. Boullata asserts that there is an "Arab proclivity to cite proverbs or poetic verses orally to corroborate ideas in certain circumstances. This is a very old Arab trait which Ibn ʿAbbās ... could possibly have had." (1991: 38) For Wansbrough, nothing is "natural" in the development of exegetical tools. The tools reflect ideological needs and have a history behind them.

Substantial evidence in favour of the overall point which Wansbrough makes in this regard stems from Claude Gilliot's (1990) extensive analysis of the *tafsīr* of al-Ṭabarī (d. 923 C.E.). It is surely significant that al-Ṭabarī would still be arguing in the tenth century about the role and value of the Arabic language in its relationship to the Qur'ān, and that his own extensive *tafsīr* work is founded upon an argument to make just that case for language. The relationship of the sacred to the profane in language was not an issue which allowed itself to be simply assumed within the culture. It was subject to vigorous debate and back-and-forth between scholars.

4. The development of *tafsīr*

Boullata's work is significant for picking up on this one important point in clarification of what is at stake in Wansbrough's arguments, but another recent work has presented a more comprehensive challenge to Wansbrough's account of the development of *tafsīr*. Some of the argument remains on the level of detail and interpretation, but other aspects of it are directed to the heart of Wansbrough's assumptions.

I have recently published an extensive review article (1996) of C.H.M. Versteegh's *Arabic Grammar and Qur'ānic Exegesis in Early Islam* (1993), so I will not repeat here the discussion of the undoubted merits and problems of this book. The key element is that Versteegh has gone to some of the same major texts that Wansbrough used in his study, but, for the purposes of his own work, he has found it necessary to assume that the texts represent the opinion of the authors to whom they are ascribed (or at least close to that). Where Wansbrough saw evidence of editorial reformulation in these texts, of later intrusions, reflecting the development of exegetical tools through time, Versteegh sees exegetical tools as being present from the earliest times because, like Boullata, he feels that it is "only natural" that materials of all sorts – and in this case he is most concerned with grammatically oriented analysis – would have been employed by the earliest exegetes. In order to assert that he can reliably use these early *tafsīr* texts as sources for grammatical terminology for authors prior to and contemporary with Sībawayh (d. 793 C.E.), Versteegh has to argue for the historical reliability of the texts as a whole and their ascription, and must discount the problem of later interpolation, editorial reformulation, and any other issues which might account for what Wansbrough saw as "anachronistic" elements in these early texts.

Versteegh's position nicely captures the historiographical dilemma of the study of early Islam. He is convinced that "after the death of the Prophet the main preoccupation of the believers was with the text of the *Qur'ān*. This determined all their efforts to get a grip on the phenomenon of language, and it is, therefore, in the earliest commentaries on the *Qur'ān* that we shall have to start looking for the original form of language study in Islam." (1993: 41) The vision of the rise of Islam which underlies this position is one that is significantly at odds with Wansbrough's and with others who have argued that "Islam" as we know it took a number of centuries to come into being and did not spring from the desert as a mature, self-reflective, defined entity. The idea that Muḥammad provided the community with its scripture and that after his death all focus immediately turned to coming to an understanding of that scripture and founding a society based upon it simply does not match the evidence which we have before us in Wansbrough's interpretation. Nor does it match the model by which we have come to understand the emergence of complex social systems, be they motivated by religion or other ideologies.

Within the field of *tafsīr* and its study, one of the critical factors underlying this significant difference of conception and approach lies in the actual understanding of what "interpretation" (that is, Muslim interpretation of scripture in this case) is all about. Versteegh conceives *tafsīr* as having the purpose of investigating the Qur'ān's "applicability to religious and social practices" (1993: 63). His conception, a common one within a certain traditional view of scholarship, sees interpretation as a process that goes on somewhat abstracted from society as a whole, an activity motivated by piety and a dispassionate (within the limits of pre-modern society) concern for the religious ethos and which took place right at the historical beginnings of Islam. This is, of course, a view which is reflected in classical Muslim understandings of *tafsīr* also, as enunciated by Ibn Taymiyya, for example, in whose *Muqaddima fī 'uṣūl al-tafsīr* we find the best expression of this approach (e.g., in the idea of ranking the generations following Muḥammad as being progressively less trustworthy as a source of interpretation). Wansbrough, on the other hand, along with what may best be termed the "post-modern" ethos, sees interpretation as a far more interactive and active participant within the society in which it takes place. No longer is there a picture of scholars sitting in their enclaves, carefully considering the text of the Qur'ān and its implications in light of the resources available to them, the results of which consideration are then published for public-scholarly consumption. Rather, a far more amorphous picture emerges. The pressures of the time and the needs of the society provide the impetus and the desired results of the interpretative efforts. The context for the results of the interpretative strategies is provided by the society in which it takes place. What is more, all interpretation becomes significant. For Versteegh, there are two kinds of interpretation: that which provides meaningful application of the text and that which is "simple explanation". For Versteegh, matters such as grammar are sophisticated while narrative techniques such as paraphrase, gloss, and completion are so "obvious" as to not be worthy of attention because they are "simple explanation". Wansbrough, on the other hand, argues that all such devices have significance and play a key role in the development of authority and of a canon. One cannot subject a work to detailed grammatical analysis prior to that work being demonstrated to be unified and coherent; nor can one undertake grammatical analysis until grammar has established itself as a legitimate tool for analysis.

Even within a field seemingly as specialized as the study of *tafsīr*, Wansbrough's work has serious implications for the overall conception of the discipline. At stake is more than simply a scepticism about texts. The ultimate point of dispute becomes one of understanding movements in human history, how they emerge and evolve. This may also be viewed in terms of the interpretative nature of human existence as mediated through language, a standpoint within the discussion of Islam that not many scholars have pursued despite its overwhelming presence within cultural studies as a whole.

References

Boullata, Issa J. (1991). Poetry citation as interpretive illustration in Qur'ān exegesis: Masā'il Nāfi' Ibn al-Azraq. In Wael B. Hallaq and Donald P. Little (eds.), *Islamic Studies Presented to Charles J. Adams*, 27-40. Leiden: E.J. Brill.

Buck, Christopher (1995). *Symbol and Secret: Qur'an Commentary in Baha'u'llah's Kitab-i Iqan*. Los Angeles: Kalimat Press.

Calder, Norman (1993). Tafsīr from Ṭabarī to Ibn Kathīr: Problems in the description of a genre, illustrated with reference to the story of Abraham. In G.R. Hawting and Abdul-Kader A. Shareef (eds.), *Approaches to the Qur'ān*, 101-140. London: Routledge.

Ess, Josef van (1990-1992). *Theologie und Gesellschaft im 2. und 3. Jahrhundert Hidschra*. Volumes 1 and 2. Berlin: Walter de Gruyter.

Gilliot, Claude (1985). Portrait "mythique" d'Ibn 'Abbās. *Arabica* 33: 127-184.

— (1990). *Exégèse, langue et théologie en Islam. L'exégèse coranique de Tabari (m. 311-923)*. Paris: Vrin.

Goldziher, Ignaz (1920). *Die Richtungen der islamischen Koranauslegung*. Leiden: E.J. Brill.

Neuwirth, Angelika (1993). Die Masā'il Nāfi' b. al-Azraq-Elemente des "Portrait mythique d'Ibn 'Abbās" oder ein Stück realer Literatur? Rückschüsse aus einer unbeachteten Handschrift. *Zeitschrift für Arabische Linguistik* 25: 233-250.

Rippin, Andrew (1981). Ibn 'Abbās's al-Lughāt fī'l-Qur'ān. *Bulletin of the School of Oriental and African Studies* 44: 15-25.

— (1983). Ibn 'Abbās's Gharīb al-Qur'ān. *Bulletin of the School of Oriental and African Studies* 46: 332-333.

— (1984). Al-Zuhrī, naskh al-Qur'ān and the problem of early tafsīr texts. *Bulletin of the School of Oriental and African Studies* 47: 22-43.
— (1985). The exegetical genre asbāb al-nuzūl: A bibliographical and terminological survey. *Bulletin of the School of Oriental and African Studies* 48: 1-15.
— (1988). The function of asbāb al-nuzūl in Qur'ānic exegesis. *Bulletin of the School of Oriental and African Studies* 51: 1-20.
— (1994). *Tafsīr Ibn 'Abbās* and criteria for dating early *tafsīr* texts. *Jerusalem Studies in Arabic and Islam* 18: 38-83.
— (1996). Studying early *tafsīr* texts. *Der Islam* 72: 310-323.
Versteegh, C.H.M. (1993). *Arabic Grammar and Qur'ānic Exegesis in Early Islam*. Leiden: E.J. Brill.
Wansbrough, John (1977). *Quranic Studies: Sources and Methods of Scriptural Interpretation*. Oxford: Oxford University Press.

VII

QUR'AN 21:95: "A BAN IS UPON ANY TOWN"

The Qur'ānic passage Sūra 21, verses 95–104, describes the two opposing aspects of the judgment day. The unbelievers' fate is foretold in verses 95–100 while, in contrast to that, the promise of avoidance of the catastrophes is given to the believers in verses 101–4. Introducing the former section is verse 95:

wa-ḥarāmun 'alā qaryatin ahlaknāhā annahum lā yarji'ūna

This may provisionally be translated,[1] following Bell,[2] as

A ban is upon any town which we have destroyed that they should not return.

Following this verse comes the condition that the inhabitants shall not return until Gog and Magog sweep over the hills, indicating the beginning of the apocalypse.

A number of interesting exegetical problems are to be found in this verse, and it is into these that the following discussion delves. They are, first, the meaning of *ḥarām* and its relationship to some variant readings; second, the question of *annahum* versus the variant *innahum*; third, the matter of the seeming redundant *lā* preceding *yarji'ūna*.[3] All three of these matters are interrelated, the answer to one often being dependent upon the presupposed position taken on the others. What they exhibit, also, is the use to which variant readings were put in order to

[1] The Arabic Qur'ān text is quoted from the standard Egyptian edition; verse numbers are given Egyptian/Flügel where there is a discrepancy.

[2] R. Bell, *The Qur'ān translated*, Edinburgh 1937.

[3] A fourth topic, of interest to the classical exegetes, relates to the verb *raja'a* and whether it necessarily refers to the unbelievers' physical return at the apocalypse (e.g. al-Bayḍāwī (d. 716/1316), *Anwār al-tanzīl*, Cairo 1330, IV, 46 and al-Shawkānī (d. 1250/1834–5), *Fatḥ al-qadīr*, Cairo 1350, III, 412), or whether it refers to their non-repentance and non-Muslim status from which they do not return (e.g. Sufyān al-Thawrī (d. 161/777–8), *Tafsīr al-Qur'ān al-Karīm*, Rampur 1965, 163, and al-Zamakhsharī (d. 538/1143–4), *al-Kashshāf*, Beirut 1947, III, 134–5, with an appropriate Mu'tazilī twist). This does not, however, relate directly to the matter of interest and is therefore left aside.

solve, or in some cases to complicate, the questions. As will be seen, most of the variant readings on this verse represent what would appear to be conscious attempts to come to grips with an obscure passage by alternative grammatical constructions and lexical variations; it seems unlikely that all the variants represent equally probable original readings.[1]

The basic assumption of most exegetes seems to be that *ḥarām* here means "forbidden", as it does so often in the Qur'ān.[2] It was sometimes given the lexical equivalent of *mumtani'*,[3] thus giving a literal rendering of the verse: "It is forbidden to a town which We have destroyed that they not return..." It was obvious to the commentators, however, that this gave a sense to the verse the opposite of what was intended, owing to the *lā* preceding *yarji'ūna*.

A number of solutions were then proposed for this problem. The easiest and the most obvious was to say that *lā* was semantically redundant. In many ways, this would seem to be an attractive solution, given the oral basis of the revelation and the possible desirability of emphasis within such a context.[4] Furthermore,

[1] Opinion on the value of variant readings varies: compare two recent views, R. Paret, "Textkritisch verwertbare Koranvarianten", in R. Gramlich (ed.), *Islamwissenschaftliche Abhandlungen: Fritz Meier zum sechzigsten Geburtstag*, Wiesbaden 1974, 198–204, and J. Wansbrough, *Quranic studies: sources and methods of scriptural interpretation*, Oxford 1977, 202–7.

[2] On *ḥarām* in the Qur'ān, see especially T. Izutsu, *Ethico-religious concepts in the Qur'ān*, Montreal 1965, 237–41. E. Gräf's *Jagdbeute und Schlachttier im islamischen Recht*, Bonn 1959, 15–25, is so concerned with the "taboo" nature of *ḥarām* that the interpretations must be handled carefully. A similar *caveat* applies to J. Chelhod's threefold division of *ḥarām* in *Les structures du sacré chez les Arabes*, Paris 1964, 50–1, an exegesis for which there is little justification in the Qur'ān itself.

[3] al-Zamakhsharī, III, 134; al-Bayḍāwī, IV, 46; al-Shawkānī, III, 412. Al-Farrā' (d. 207/822–3), *Ma'ānī al-Qur'ān*, Cairo 1955–72, III, 137–8 (on S. 57: 29), states in reference to S. 21: 95 *wa-fī al-ḥarām ma'nā al-jaḥd wal-man'*; the "forbidding" nature of *ḥarām* is only implicit in his actual commentary on the verse (II, 211). See additionally E. Beck, "Die b. Mas'ūdvarianten bei al-Farrā'. I", *Orientalia*, N.S. XXV (1956), 359–60.

[4] The matter of the oral origin of the Qur'ān has not received the attention it deserves; it will, I believe, prove a profitable direction of research. Wansbrough's comments (*Quranic studies*, 47–9) open up the discussion in a stimulating way. Regardless of whether one accepts Wansbrough's notion of pericopes, the original oral delivery of the Qur'ān (whether in the form we now know or in an abbreviated structure) seems certain. See now also R. C. Culley, *Studies in the structure of Hebrew narrative*, Philadelphia-Missoula 1976, for a discussion of the topic in relation to the Bible.

such a redundant *lā* has intra-Qur'ānic justification, for example, after the verb *manaʿa*, "to forbid", in SS. 6: 109, 7: 12 and 9: 54.[1] Not cited by any classical authorities consulted, but noted by Bergsträsser,[2] is 6: 151/152, where the verb *ḥarrama* exhibits a redundant *lā*:

Say: Come, I will recite what your Lord has forbidden you: that you associate not [!] anything with Him, and to be good to your parents, and not to slay your children because of poverty...[3]

The phrase here *ḥarrama rabbuka ʿalaykum allā tushrikū bihi shay'an* fits perfectly[4] within the rule formulated by grammarians for such a situation: "When verbs signifying to forbid, fear and the like are followed by أَنْ with the subjunctive, لَا is sometimes inserted after أَنْ ... without affecting the meaning."[5] The fact that this rule did not fully apply in S. 21: 95 was of no concern to early exegetes who did not have to contend with the binding nature of grammarians' rules during the early stage of Islam. Still, they did feel the compulsion to explain further the idea of a redundant *lā*; al-Farrā' in interpreting S. 7: 12, and citing 21: 95 as a parallel, effectively states that "two negatives make a positive".[6] Ibn Qutayba, in an example typical of his method,[7] states that the *lā* in 21: 95 was there to emphasise the fact that while the people would return, they had not done so at that time.

[1] Al-Farrā', I, 350 (on S. 6: 109); Ibn Qutayba (d. 276/889), *Ta'wīl mushkil al-Qur'ān*, Cairo 1373, 189–90; *idem*, *Tafsīr gharīb al-Qur'ān*, Cairo 1378, 288. Also see G. Bergsträsser, *Verneinungs- und Fragepartikeln und Verwandtes im Koran*, Leipzig 1914, 47, 58–9; T. Nöldeke, *Neue Beiträge zur semitischen Sprachwissenschaft*, Strassburg 1910, 20. Abū ʿUbayda (d. 210/825–6), *Majāz al-Qur'ān*, somewhat surprisingly, does not mention this passage.

[2] *Op. cit.*, pp. 53, 59.

[3] As translated by A. J. Arberry, *The Koran interpreted*, London 1955, a rendition closer to the Arabic than that of Bell's in this instance.

[4] The possibility exists, however, that S. 6: 151/152 is influenced by parallel phrasing in passages not introduced by a negative verb: 17: 23/24 introduced by *wa qaḍā rabbuka*; 2: 83/77, *akhadhnā mīthāq banī Isrā'īl*, and 4: 36/40 with no introduction, all use the same phraseology for these prohibitions. See R. Paret, *Der Koran, Kommentar und Konkordanz*, Stuttgart 1971, on 6: 151 for further parallels.

[5] W. Wright, *A grammar of the Arabic language*, 3rd edn, Cambridge 1896–8, II, 304–5.

[6] I, 374: referring to a line of poetry which starts *mā in ra'ayna* he states "*mā*" *jaḥd wa-*"*in*" *jaḥd, fa-jammaʿatā lil-tawkīd; wa-mithlahu*...[*21: 95*].

[7] *Ta'wīl*, 190. On Ibn Qutayba, see Wansbrough, *Quranic studies*, 221 n. 1, 222–4, 228–31.

QUR'AN 21: 95: "A BAN IS UPON ANY TOWN"

Even though the idea of a redundant *lā* would appear to be a part of the Qur'ānic idiom, simplistic grammatical answers such as those provided by al-Farrā' and Ibn Qutayba could not be accepted by the later exegetes, who strove in their work under the fully elaborated dogma of *i'jāz al-Qur'ān*, where the idea of a redundant *lā* would not prove methodologically satisfactory.[1] Thus we enter into the realm of fully grammatical explanations of the verse.

The most straightforward explanation is provided by Ibn al-Anbārī (d. 577/1181–2); after giving the explanation that *lā* is redundant, he states that the preferred version (preferred by al-Fārisī, it is claimed) is that *ḥarām* is the subject of a nominal sentence (*mubtada'*) whose predicate (*khabar*) is unexpressed.[2] Thus the verse can be reconstructed (*taqdīr*) as "A *ḥarām* on a town which we have destroyed, that they will not return, is existent or has been given", the latter part of the sentence being understood. The reason that this is the preferred version, according to Ibn al-Anbārī, is that an omitted predicate is more common in the Qur'ān than a redundant *lā*. This statement is certainly true, given the number of times phrases such as *matā'un fī al-dunyā* and *matā'un qalīlun* and isolated individual words occur in the Qur'ān. That these phrases cannot, according to the rules of grammar, be considered as sentences is clear enough.[3] However, the numerous exceptions of this type which occur in the Qur'ān, as collected for example by Nöldeke,[4] leave room for reflection on the development of Arabic grammar and, once again, the oral nature of the presentation of the Qur'ān, with which the rules of literary grammar cannot in every instance

[1] On the two-way play between exegesis and the *i'jāz* doctrine, see the introduction to G. E. von Grunebaum, *A tenth-century document of Arabic literary criticism*, Chicago 1950, esp. p. xvii, and Wansbrough, *Quranic studies*, 79–83.

[2] Ibn al-Anbārī, *al-Bayān fī gharīb i'rāb al-Qur'ān*, Cairo 1390, II, 165. Within the terms of reference of Ibn al-Anbārī, it would be of little advantage to state that *lā* was redundant since he would still be left with an incomplete sentence at the beginning. Note that this did not appear to be a problem for the early exegetes, i.e. before the strict application of the rules of grammar was widespread. Al-Farrā' on S. 10: 70/71 (I, 472), *matā'un fi al-dunyā*, which is not a sentence, cites the parallels 16: 117/118 and 43: 35 and suggests that a pronoun, either *huwa* or *dhāka*, has been omitted before them. He does not make this suggestion, however, in regard to 21: 95.

[3] Wright, *Grammar*, II, 253–4, 260–4. An indefinite subject of a nominal sentence cannot precede its predicate.

[4] *Neue Beiträge*, 15.

cope. Be that as it may, whether we assume a missing predicate or, indeed, consider *ḥarāmun ʿalā qaryatin* as a full sentence, as do most translations, actually changes the meaning very little. Yet the exegetes were always willing to uphold the rules of grammar; al-Zamakhsharī and al-Bayḍāwī exhibit this fully by giving a wide range of other grammatical explanations, for example, making *ḥarām* the predicate of *lā yarjiʿūna*, thus having an inverted word order but not an indefinite preceding subject.[1]

Another attempt by al-Zamakhsharī was to adduce a variant reading in order clearly to separate the two parts of the verse. Without mentioning any authority, although it seems unlikely that a scholar of the stature of al-Zamakhsharī would actually invent a variant for himself in such a matter, he suggests the reading *innahum* rather than *annahum*; thus the phrase *ḥarāmun ʿalā qaryatin ahlaknāhā* would have to be considered as totally separate from *innahum lā yarjiʿūna*, leaving no possibility of an ambiguous or redundant *lā*. So once again, *ḥarām* is considered to have an omitted *khabar*, which al-Zamakhsharī suggests is to be found in the previous verse; that is, the town is forbidden to reap the benefits of good works and meritorious endeavours. This has the disadvantage of destroying the parallelism of the two apocalyptic passages, verses 95–100 and 101–4,[2] but beyond that, the use of an unsupported variant in order to alleviate a grammatical problem leaves little confidence in the status of such variants in the first place and renders the whole interpretation suspect. The fact that the variant is adduced by al-Bayḍāwī, although in a most obscure manner so as to make it ambiguous what he is referring to, and Ibn Hishām (d. 731/1330–1),[3] who at least makes it clear that *annahum* is the intended recipient of the *kasra*, creates no more confidence in the variant. Both of these writers argue the point backwards, that is, by making the conjecture of a missing *khabar* of *ḥarām* which is supplied by the previous verse, and then saying that this proposed reconstruction would support the reading *innahum*. In this way, perhaps, an attempt is made to make it less obvious that the variant is brought forth for exegetical convenience rather than for the explanation of its actual existence.

[1] Al-Zamakhsharī, III, 135; al-Bayḍāwī, IV, 46. Presumably, in such a case *ḥarām* would mean "that which is forbidden".

[2] While Arberry and Bell in their translations preserve this parallelism, note that A. Yusuf Ali, *The Holy Qur'ān*, Lahore 1934 etc., separates the section beginning with verse 94.

[3] Al-Bayḍāwī, IV, 46; Ibn Hishām, *Mughnī al-labīb*, Damascus 1964, I, 279.

QUR'AN 21: 95: "A BAN IS UPON ANY TOWN"

The use of variants to solve the problems of this verse was not limited to *annahum/innahum*; indeed, a mass of variants has come down to us for the word *ḥarām*. While only one of these variants finds support among the prominent exegetes (that is, the reading *ḥirm*), the rest merely gathering passing mention at the most, each of the variants, it would seem, indicates another solution to the problems, one put forth at a certain moment during the process of the evolution of the Qur'ān into its present state. Within the system of canonical readings established by Ibn Mujāhid (663[1]) who died in 324/936, Abū Bakr (1321) (transmitter of a *riwāya* from 'Āṣim), Hamza (1190) and al-Kisā'ī (2212), all read *ḥirm* as opposed to *ḥarām*, the latter written with an *alif*.[2] Al-Farrā', who, of course, dates from prior to the establishment of the readings, reports that the *ahl al-madīna* and Ḥasan al-Baṣrī (1074) read the word as *ḥarām* with an *alif*, whereas Ibn 'Abbās (1891), 'Āmir (1000), Sa'īd b. Jubayr (1340), Yaḥyā b. Waththāb (3871) and Ibrāhīm al-Nakha'ī (125), all of whom were associated with the Kūfan School of Qur'ān reading, read *ḥirm*.[3] Within the later collections of *shawādhdh* readings, the following are among those noted by Ibn Jinnī:[4]

ḥarima, so read by Ibn 'Abbās, Sa'īd b. al-Musayyab (1354) 'Ikrima (2132) and Qatāda (2611); al-Shawkānī, III, 412, adds Sa'īd b. Jubayr to this list.
ḥaruma, so read by Ibn 'Abbās, Abū al-'Āliya (1272) and 'Ikrima
ḥarama, so read by Qatāda
ḥarim, so read by 'Ikrima
ḥarm, so read by Ibn 'Abbās

Further additions are given by Ibn Khālawayh:[5]

ḥurrima, so read by al-Yamānī (3106)
ḥarma, so read by 'Ikrima, a strange reading indeed

[1] For identification purposes, the number corresponding to the entry in Ibn al-Jazarī, *Ghayāt al-nihāya fī ṭabaqāt al-Qurrā'*, Cairo–Leipzig, 1932–5, is cited for each authority.

[2] Ibn al-Jazarī, *al-Nashr fī al-qirā'āt al-'ashr*, Cairo n.d., II, 324 (on S. 21: 95).

[3] Al-Farrā', II, 211. E. Beck's "Studien zur Geschichte der Kufischen Koranlesung. II", *Orientalia*, N.S. XIX (1950), 348, and "Der 'uṯmānische Kodex in der Koranlesung", *ibid.* N.S. XIV (1945), 366–7, put these readings within the context of the whole work of al-Farrā'.

[4] In Bergsträsser, *Nichtkanonische Koranlesarten im Muḥtasab des ibn Ginnī*, Munich 1933, 50.

[5] *Mukhtaṣar fī shawādhdh al-Qur'ān*, Cairo–Leipzig 1934, 93. A. Jeffery, *Materials for the history of the text of the Qur'ān*, Leiden 1937, has no additional

The first observation that can be made from this list, over and above noting the sheer quantity of variants, is the fact that all of the readings with the exception of *ḥarām* are minus the *alif*. In this connection, an interesting fact comes to light in al-Dānī's *Muqni'*, where the orthographic variant *ḥarām* with the *alif* written defectively حرم is transmitted on the authority of Nāfi'.[1] The only way to interpret this, it would seem, is to see it as a compromise solution between the variants حرم and حرام, for in no other instance, even according to Nāfi', is the word *ḥarām* ever written this way. Of the twenty-five additional times the word *ḥarām* appears in the Qur'ān, in all but two cases as a definite adjective, it is always written in full form. In the two instances in addition to S. 21: 95 where *ḥarām* occurs as an indefinite substantive, the phrases are: (S. 16: 116) *wa-hādhā ḥalālun wa-hādhā ḥarāmun*; and (10: 59) *ja'altum minhu ḥarāman wa-ḥalālan*. Both of these cases are especially interesting for, although *ḥarām* is written in full, *ḥalāl* in both instances is shortened to حلل according to the rule of an *alif* after a middle (or between a double) *lām*.[2] Thus the fact that *ḥarām* was not reduced in these two situations suggests that, in fact, such a reduction would be a peculiar occurrence. Since it is well known that *alif*s were probably the last long vowel to be added in the development of the Arabic script, as far as the "original" text of the Qur'ān goes, Nāfi''s variant is thus of little significance. It would seem from this evidence, however, that by Nāfi''s time two different orthographic traditions were associated with S. 21: 95: one tradition assimilated the reading to the rest of the occurrences of *ḥarām*; others maintained either a nominal or verbal reading without an *alif*. Nāfi', it would appear, attempted to reconcile what was obviously a very popular orthography with what became the most popular vowelling.

The verbal variant readings also would appear to be, in part,

readings although he does add a few unverifiable authorities; but in actual fact more of the important authorities and readings are omitted than are included.

[1] Al-Dānī, *al-Muqni' fī ma'rifa marsūm maṣāḥif ahl al-anṣār*, Damascus 1359, p. 12; see also Nöldeke–Bergsträsser–Pretzl, *Geschichte des Qorans*, Leipzig 1938, III, 21. Note that the Indian tradition of Qur'ānic calligraphy would appear to follow this school, e.g. A. Yusuf Ali, *The Holy Qur'ān*. The official Egyptian edition does not, however.

[2] Al-Dānī, *Muqni'*, 18; also see E. Sell, *The faith of Islam*, 3rd edn, London 1907, Appendix A, "'Ilmu't-Tajwīd" especially pp. 392–6 for a translated list of orthographic peculiarities, probably derived from Suyūṭī's *Itqān*.

a method of assimilating the orthography to Qur'ānic linguistic usage; this is especially true of the reading *ḥurrima*, for the second form passive of this verb occurs an additional six times in the Qur'ān, whereas the first form, whether vowelled *ḥarima*, *ḥaruma* or *ḥarama*, does not occur at all. Underlying all these verbal readings would also appear to be an attempt to make clear the meaning of the sentence; regardless of the vowelling, all were probably intended to give the meaning "It is forbidden to any town...". Significantly, as a result of the verbal reading, some of the grammatical problems were solved, e.g. the incomplete sentence and/or the preceding indefinite subject; of course, the *lā* would still prove inconvenient. Whether such grammatical niceties would have been of concern to the early authorities to whom these readings are attributed is unlikely; that they are, in fact, later ideas, given authority by being attached to reputable ancestors, seems probable, although a much fuller study of variants would have to be undertaken to prove that point.

As for the variant *ḥirm* versus *ḥarām*, it is no longer totally evident precisely what purpose this change could hope to serve; however, perhaps a trace of its character can still be seen. As early as al-Farrā' and Ibn Qutayba, the lexical equivalency of *ḥirm* and *ḥarām* was being promulgated, as in the statement of al-Farrā', *wa-huwa bi-manzila qawlika: ḥill wa-ḥalāl wa-ḥirm wa-ḥarām.*[1] This idea was continued through the centuries by, for example, al-Ṭabarī (d. 310) and al-Shawkānī.[2] However, the contrived nature of this equivalency and its lexicographical irrelevancy is brought to light in al-Ṭabarī's explanation of the enigmatic *ḥill* in S. 90: 2, where he states: *yuqālu minhu huwa ḥill wa-huwa ḥalāl wa-huwa ḥirm wa-huwa harām.*[3] The tautology thus created is of little assistance in the understanding of the words in question. Rather, the assertion of the lack of lexical differentiation in the readings probably arose out of a need to explain those variants which were becoming widespread, as compared, for example, to the verbal readings for this verse which probably only maintained a small group of adherents. The common notion of "dialectic variances" as an explanation of Qur'ānic variants

[1] Al-Farrā', II, 211; see also Ibn Qutayba, *Tafsīr*, 288.

[2] Al-Ṭabarī, *Jāmi' al-bayān fī tafsīr al-Qur'ān*, Cairo 1328, XVII, 68; al-Shawkānī, III, 412.

[3] S. 90: 2: *lā uqsimu bi hādhā-l-baladi/wa-anta ḥillun bi hādhā-l-baladi.* See al-Ṭabarī, XXX, 124.

may in many cases, be another example of this tendency to eradicate any significance in variant readings.[1]

However, if the exegete opted for the lexical equivalency of the two words, accepting the normal rendering of "forbidden" for *ḥarām/ḥirm*, he was still left with the problematic double negative. Thus it is not surprising to see put forth changes in lexical meaning of the words. In a report traced back to Ibn 'Abbās, al-Ṭabarī suggests that *ḥirm* means *'azm*, "it is decided or resolved". The fact that this meaning is given for *ḥirm* and not *ḥarām* at this relatively early stage of exegesis suggests the background of the reading *ḥirm*; that is, in order to get away from the commonly accepted notion of *ḥarām* as forbidden, another word with the same consonantal pattern and with no possible Qur'ānic parallel was put forth and defined by the requirements of the context. That is not to suggest, however, that *ḥarām* was necessarily the "original" reading; the possibility that the entire process operated in the reverse direction of this postulate must always be entertained. Either way, the statement of al-Ṭabarī contains the same implication. However, regardless of that fact, by the time of al-Zamakhsharī and al-Bayḍāwī the meaning *'azm* had been connected to *ḥarām* itself as well, although lexical changes were, for both of these exegetes, less attractive solutions to various problems than were grammatical explanations. Al-Bayḍāwī introduces this meaning at the end of his discussion with the non-committal *wa-qīla*.[2]

A closely related and somewhat more popular lexical variation was introduced by saying that *ḥirm* and *ḥarām* in S. 21: 95 meant *wājib*, "it is necessary". Ibn Qutayba and al-Shawkānī, along with other sources, all quote the same line of poetry in defence of this meaning:

fa-inna ḥarāman lā arā al-dhar bākiyan/'alā sajwihi illā bakaytu 'alā 'Amr

Indeed "it is necessary" that I should not see ever again someone crying/in his sorrow without that I weep for 'Amr.[3]

[1] The suggestion that *ḥarām* is the dialect of Quraysh and that *ḥirm* is from Hudhayl is made for S. 21: 95 in Ibn Ḥasnūn (d. 386/996), *al-Lughāt fī al-Qur'ān*, Beirut 1972, p. 35; this entire book is traced to Ibn 'Abbās (see *GAS*, I, 28). However, the fact that this explanation is not proffered in any other source consulted makes its status suspect. Regardless of that, the tendentious nature of the suggestion is obvious. See C. Rabin, *Ancient West Arabian*, London 1951, 6–16, esp. para. i, and note 2 on p. 211.

[2] Al-Ṭabarī, XVII, 68; al-Zamakhsharī, III, 134; al-Bayḍāwī, IV, 46.

[3] See Ibn Qutayba, *Tafsīr*, 288 and the note there for further references; al-Shawkānī, III, 412. Note that al-Māturīdī (d. 333), *Ta'wīlāt ahl al-sunna*,

As Aḥmad Ṣaqr, the editor of Ibn Qutayba's *tafṣīr* works, states in his note to this quotation, the source of the line is uncertain; some attribute it to al-Muḥāribī, a Jāhilī poet, others to al-Khansā' (see the article on her in *EI*[2]), in whose *Dīwān* it is not found. Thus the doubtful authority inherent in this line of poetry renders it almost unnecessary to comment that this line, even if genuine, adds little clarification to the matter at hand. All the other possible solutions put forth for the problems in S. 21: 95 could equally as well be suggested for this line of poetry. It puts us absolutely no further ahead.

Given the range of possibilities presented by the exegetes it may seem somewhat redundant to put forth yet another suggestion concerning this verse. Yet it seems necessary to state that the biblical notion of *ḥērem* may provide a clue to the interpretation of the apparent double negative in S. 21: 95. The idea of *ḥērem* makes it clear that the presumed negative sense of *ḥarām* in this verse is not necessarily to be accepted. *Ḥērem* as "ban" or, more specifically, "devoted to God" can be regarded as the positive aspect of the two-way relationship man $\lesseqgtr$ God inherent in the root notion of *ḥrm*, in which "forbidden to man" is the negative aspect. It is not proposed to enter into a full discussion of *ḥērem* here, for the literature on that concept is extensive.[1] Rather, a reminder that *ḥērem* as "devoted" can involve God's action on unbelievers by which they are totally destroyed and that the apocalyptic context of *ḥērem* plays its role in the Bible, for example, in Malachi iii. 24 and Isaiah xxxiv. 2–5, would seem sufficient. That these two factors are present in the context of S. 21: 95 with its use of the term *ḥarām* argues forcefully for a

MS. Hâlet Efendi 22, fol. 500a; Nuru Osmaniye 97/123, fol. 438b, states that, while according to the *ahl al-lisān wa al-lugha*, *ḥarām* and *ḥirm* have the same meaning just as do *ḥalāl* and *ḥill*, the *ahl al-ta'wīl* differentiate between them, giving *ḥirm* the meaning of *ḥatm wa-wājib* and *ḥarām* its obvious meaning of forbidden. This perhaps represents an intermediate stage in lexicographical identification of both *ḥirm* and *ḥarām* as *wājib*. Al-Zabīdī (d. 1205/1790–1), *Tāj al-'arūs*, Cairo 1306–7, VIII, 240, also gives the same suggestion on the authority of Ibn 'Abbās. This information is then repeated in E. W. Lane, *An Arabic-English lexicon*, London 1863–93, II, 554.

[1] See Koehler–Baumgartner, *Hebräisches und aramäisches Lexicon zum Alten Testament*, Leiden 1967, I, 339–41; H. Ringgren, *The prophetical conception of holiness*, Uppsala–Leipzig 1948, 3, 11–13, and bibliography there; J. Milgrom, "The concept of *ma'al* in the Bible and the Ancient Near East", *JAOS* XCVI (1976), 236–47, contains some relevant comments on *ḥērem*.

translation of the verse which reflects the biblical notion of *ḥērem*.[1] Freely rendered, the verse may run:

A city, which we destroyed, has been devoted to God, (resulting in the fact) that they may not return (to it)...

If the use of *ḥarām* in this verse does reflect the Hebrew *ḥērem*, and it would seem probable that it does, the confusion of the later exegetes and the use of variants to try to explain the problem can be understood. Whether the commentators' attempt to explain *ḥarām* by words with a positive sense such as *wājib* and *'azm* demonstrates a vague notion of the "devoting" aspect of the term remains an open question. What is clear is that several other solutions were attempted in order to make sense of the passage, most of which employed variant readings. The idea of using variants to support differing interpretations must have produced, at a certain stage in the development of Qur'ānic studies (probably prior to 200 A.H.), a rash of alternatives from which those which were more likely or better authenticated (i.e. with the power of *ijmā'* on their side) were selected as "canonical". That later exegetes could then use these variants along with employing more and more sophisticated grammatical explanations, under the pressures of the *i'jāz al-Qur'ān* doctrine, has been pointed out above. Even within those contexts, the variants still show traces of their original intention: to explain away grammatical and lexical difficulties. While obviously this is not true of all variant readings in the Qur'ān, many variants being too slight to alleviate any problem, in S. 21: 95 and in many others the exegetical nature of Qur'ānic variants is apparent.

[1] This may already be implicit in some English translations of the Qur'ān (e.g. Arberry, Bell, Yusuf Ali) by their use of the nondescript "ban"; cf. however the French and German versions of Blachère and Paret respectively. I have found no mention of S. 21: 95 in any of the "Jewish influence on the Qur'ān" literature.

VIII

QUR'ĀN 7.40: «UNTIL THE CAMEL PASSES THROUGH THE EYE OF THE NEEDLE»

THE brief note by M. B. Schub in *Arabica*, tome 23, fasc. 3, drew attention to the alternate readings and interpretations of the word *ǧamal* in Surah 7.40 Egyptian/38 Flügel[1]. This is not the first occasion, however, that this fact has been published; W. M. Watt, several years previously, delved into the same subject but more extensively and, I think it must be added, more accurately as far as the interpretation of al-Zamaḫšarī is concerned than the contribution of Schub[2]. Further information can still be added even to Watt's article however, in order to demonstrate a historical progression in the interpretation of this verse which puts the note by Schub in its proper perspective and, in some ways, corrects it.

The single word *ǧamal* in this verse has over the centuries produced a disproportionate amount of exegesis in relation to its seeming importance. As Watt has pointed out in his article, Sufyān al-Ṯawrī (d. 161) gave the interpretation of «a ship's rope» to the consonantal pattern *ǧīm-mīm-lām* without any indication of the vocalization. Attributed to Ibn 'Abbās (not totally *isnād*-less as Watt claimed), one may well doubt the historical value of this report, given the problem of the sources and date of compilation of the work as is pointed out in the introduction to the *tafsīr*[3]. We are on firmer ground with

---

[1] M. B. SCHUB, «It is easier for a cable to go through the eye of a needle than for a rich man to enter God's kingdom», *Arabica*, XXIII (1976), 311-312. Schub gives the verse number in note 1 as 41.

[2] W. MONTGOMERY WATT, *The camel and the needle's eye*, in C. J. BLEEKER, *et.al.* (eds.), *Ex Orbe Religionum, Studia Geo Widengren* (Leiden: Brill, 1972), pars altera, pp. 155-158. Also see A. S. TRITTON, *The Camel and the Needle's Eye*, *BSOAS*, XXXIV (1971), 139, who suggests a misreading at one time of *ǧ-m-l* as *ḥ-b-l* which was then perpetuated by «those of literal mind». That interpretation, of course, ignores the significance of the Christian exegesis of the New Testament parallel; see further below.

[3] Sufyān AL-ṮAWRĪ, *Tafsīr al-Qur'ān al-Karīm* (Rampur, 1965), p. 70. See Watt, p. 157 note 1. On Sufyān's *tafsīr* also see J. WANSBROUGH, *Quranic Studies: Sources and Methods of Scriptural Interpretation* (Oxford: University Press, 1977), esp. p. 137.

al-Farrā' (d. 207) and his brief but nevertheless, interesting comments on the verse. He clearly states his opinion that *ğamal* is the prevalent reading, and gives its meaning as *zawğ al-nāqa*, the mate of a female camel more than six years old. He then adduces a variant on the authority of Ibn 'Abbās, *ğummal*, with the meaning *al-ḥibāl al-mağmū'a*, a collection of ropes[4]. Abu 'Ubayda (d. 209) meanwhile makes no comment on the word *ğamal*, confining his comments to *samm al-ḫiyāṭ*, «the eye of the needle». Abū 'Ubayd (d. 223/4) mentions in the few brief notes of his work that have been published that Ibn 'Abbās read *ğummal* in this verse, to which he ascribed the meaning «a type of nautical rope», *al-qals min qulūs al-baḥr*. Ibn Qutayba (d. 286) on the other hand, gives the simple equivalency *ğamal* = *ba'īr*, a camel, with no further comment[5].

Such are the meagre pickings available on this word in early *tafsīr* works. It comes then somewhat as a surprise to see the extent to which the exegesis connected to *ğamal* explodes in al-ṬAbarī (d. 310). Over six pages in the latest printed edition of his *tafsīr* are devoted to just this one word, its reading and interpretation. Basically, al-Ṭabarī favours the reading *ğamal* meaning camel, defined as *zawğ al-nāqa*, *ba'īr* or several other possibilities. However, he also transmits through a number of reports two other readings attributed ultimately to Ibn 'Abbās and Sa'īd ibn Ğubayr, *ğummal* and *ğumal*. These are variously defined as different types of rope or collections thereof[6].

The rise in documentation makes it clear that this variant interpretation gained much currency in the century between al-Farrā' and al-Ṭabarī. That this is a late rise in importance is witnessed also by the fact that even though the variants are well documented in al-Ṭabarī, they did not gain «canonical» status within the systematizations of the *qirā'āt*, or variant readings, which were collected as a result of

---

4 AL-FARRĀ', *Ma'ānī al-Qur'ān* (Cairo, 1955), I, 379. On the meaning of *nāqa* see E. W. LANE, *An English-Arabic Lexicon* (London: Williams and Norgate, 1863-1893) under *ba'īr* and *ğamal*.

5 ABŪ 'UBAYDA, *Mağāz al-Qur'ān* (Cairo, 1954), I, 214 (under verse 39). For ABŪ 'UBAYD, see A. SPITALER, «Ein Kapitel aus den *Faḍā'il al-Qur'ān* von Abū 'Ubaid al-Qāsim ibn Sallām», in J. W. FÜCK (ed.), *Documenta Islamica Inedita* (Berlin: Akademie Verlag, 1952), p. 7 (report number 46) and p. 19. IBN QUTAYBA, *Tafsīr ġarīb al-Qur'ān* (Cairo, 1958), p. 167.

6 AL-ṬABARĪ, *Tafsīr al-Ṭabarī: Jāmi' al-bayān 'an ta'wīl āy il-Qur'ān* (Cairo, 1374), XII, 428-434. See WATT p. 156, for a further summary of al-Ṭabarī's comments. Some of the definitions suggested are: *qals al-safīna*, rope of boats; *al-ḥabl al-ġalīẓ*, thick or rough rope, and so forth.

the canonization process occurring early in the fourth century[7]. It is only within later collections of *šawāḏḏ* (isolated) readings that variants such as these were gathered and gained some sort of status. It is not without interest that within these books a further blossoming of the number of variants also takes place. Ibn Ǧinnī (d. 392) amassed the following readings and authorities:

ğummal: Ibn 'Abbās, Sa'īd ibn Ǧubayr, Muǧāhid, al-Ša'bī, Abū al-'Alā' ibn al-Šiḫḫīr, Abū Raǧā'.
ğumal: Ibn 'Abbās, Sa'īd ibn Ǧubayr, 'Abd al-Karīm, Ḥanẓala, Muǧāhid.
ğuml: Ibn 'Abbās, Sa'īd ibn Ǧubayr.
ğumul: Ibn 'Abbās.
ğaml: Abū al-Sammāl.

In Ibn Ḫālawayh (d. 370), the authorities have not proliferated to such a great extent and there are a few contradictions in the attribution when compared with Ibn Ǧinnī, but the readings themselves are the same[8].

In order to explain these variants and their interpretation, the far-fetched suggestion for *ğummal* as «polyglot nautical slang of the Eastern Mediterranean»[9] in origin is neither attractive nor necessary. Goldziher has noted the results of Christian-Muslim interaction and polemic on the *ḥadīṯ* literature and has even noted one instance in exegesis: the influence of the Christian concept of martyr on the exegesis of the Qur'ānic word *šahīd*[10]. The same process of influence can be envisaged for Surah 7.40, especially during the comparatively «cosmopolitan» era of al-Ṭabarī, although the roots of such are obviously earlier. Faced with a Christian interpretation of Matthew

[7] See, for example, AL-DĀNĪ, *al-Taysīr fī al-qirā'āt al-sab'* (Istanbul, 1930); IBN AL-ǦAZARĪ, *al-Našr fī al-qirā'āt al-'ašr* (Damascus, 1927). See A. JEFFERY, *Materials for the history of the text of the Qur'ān* (Leiden: Brill, 1937), pp. 1-18, for a history of the canonization process.

[8] See IBN ǦINNĪ, *al-Muḥtasab fī tabyīn wuğūh šawāḏḏ al-qirā't wa al-iḍāḥ 'anhā* (Cairo, 1386), I, 249 also G. BERGSTRÄSSER, *Nichtkanonische Koranlesarten im Muḥtasab des Ibn Ǧinnī* (Munich, 1933), p. 34. IBN ḪĀLAWAYH, *Muḫtaṣar fī šawāḏḏ al-Qur'ān* (Cairo, 1934), p. 43. JEFFERY, *Materials*, p. 43, 132, as is so often the case, has only a partial listing of readings and authorities.

[9] WATT, pp. 157-158.

[10] I. GOLDZIHER, *The Ḥadīth and the New Testament* in *Muslim Studies* (London: George Allen and Unwin, 1971), II, 346-362 (= *Muhammedanische Studien*, II, 382-400). See also p. 349, note 1, for *ḥadīṯ* use of the saying contained in Surah 7.40.

19.24, Mark 10.25 and Luke 18.25 which allowed a dual sense of the work *kamēlos* (an interpretation which existed well before Islam), Muslim polemicists/exegetes, ever willing to find every possible interpretation in the Qur'ān in order to prove its superiority to all other scriptures, responded in the only way open to them at that time — a variation of the vocalization and lexical identification of the consonantal pattern of the word *ğamal.* All of the variants to the word should probably be viewed as equal attempts to accomplish the same thing, that is, to create an alternative vowelling for the word to which could be attached the meaning «rope». That there was previously any basis in fact for such a meaning of the word, regardless of its vowel pattern, is doubtful. One thing that is totally clear, however, is that no alternative meaning could be attached to such a common word as *ğamal* and thus alternative vocalization had to be used as an exegetical method[11]. The attachment of the names of various authorities to these variants probably represents an attempt to give some historical basis to the various vocalizations. Of Watt's claim that «the word *jummal* must have existed previously, and cannot be something invented by a commentator» there is absolutely no proof. Even if *ḥisāb al-ğummal* did exist at that time with the meaning of «the use of a chronogram», there would not seem to be any connection between that and the notion of «rope», or even of a nautical context. Consequently, the idea of *ğummal*'s foreign origin cannot really be considered of any importance even if it is true, which is doubtful[12].

By the time of al-Zamaẖšarī (d. 538) such variants had clearly gained substantial authority. In his commentary to this passage, he adduces all of the *šawāḏḏ* readings[13]. Schub's quote from the text of al-Zamaẖšarī unfortunately omitted (with ellipsis points) most of these variants, leaving the false impression that the only variant suggested by him is *ğaml* (and also that this variant is attributed to Ibn ʿAbbās which it is not). The beginning of al-Zamaẖšarī's comments runs:

wa-qaraʾa ibn ʿAbbās al-ğummal bi-wazn al-qummal
wa-Saʿīd ibn Ğubayr al-ğumal bi-wazn al-nuğar

---

[11] My article *Qurʾān 21.95: 'A ban is upon any town'*, in *Journal of Semitic Studies*, XXIV 1979, 43-53, has attempted to show evidence of a similar, although somewhat more complex and not polemically-based, procedure for the word *ḥarām* in Surah 21.95. There, lexical variation is given both to *ḥarām* and the various variants, above all *ḥirm*, in order to solve syntactical and exegetical problems.

[12] See WATT, p. 157 and *EI*², «ḥisāb al-djummal».

[13] AL-ZAMAẖŠARĪ, *al-Kaššāf ʿan ḥaqāʾiq al-tanzīl* (Calcutta, 1856) I, 446-447.

wa-quri'a al-ǧuml bi-wazn al-qufl
wa al-ǧumul bi-wazn al-nuṣub
wa al-ǧaml bi-wazn al-ḥabl.

Thus, in fact, al-Zamaḫšarī adduces all five *šawāḏḏ* variants attributing only the first to Ibn ʿAbbās.

Nor can it be maintained, as does Schub, that al-Zamaḫšarī considers these variants (or just *ǧaml* alone) along with the meaning of cable or rope as the «original» and the more proper reading. Rather al-Zamaḫšarī goes on to state, after the quote given by Schub, that the reading *ǧamal* is the most frequent one because the eye of a needle is a simile for (*maṯṯala fī*) a narrow path (and a proverbial expression in Arabic) and the camel is a simile for a large object. Thus it is implied that «camel» is quite appropriate and applicable to the whole figure of speech and sense of the passage. As Watt states, all this «is part of his [Z's] defense of the obvious interpretation of the verse»[14], that is *ǧamal* = camel. Nowhere does al-Zamaḫšarī state his preference for a variant with the meaning «rope».

The other aspect of al-Zamaḫšarī's commentary given by Schub is the statement of Ibn ʿAbbās that «God made the more beautiful metaphor with 'cable' because ropes are related to threads which go through the eye of a needle»[15]. Of course the word *tašbīh*, translated by Schub as metaphor, is normally equivalent to «simile». Regardless, the use is anachronistic, to put it mildly, when put in the mouth of Ibn ʿAbbās. To classify this verse as *tašbīh* represents a sophisticated view of that figure, more appropriate to the fifth or sixth century. Most early theorists depend in their characterization of *tašbīh* on the use of the device of comparison (*adāh*). This is implicit in the examples given by such people as Qudāma ibn Ǧaʿfar (d. 310) and Ibn al-Muʿtazz (d. 296) and made explicit in al-Rummānī (d. 386)[16]. However, in this Qur'ānic verse the comparison can at best only be understood by implication, indicating a refinement in the definitional idea of *tašbīh*. Other theorists have classified the verse as hyperbole, for example al-Rummānī, using the term *mubālaġa*, and Ibn Abī al-Iṣbaʿ

---

[14] Watt, p. 156.

[15] Cf. Abū Hayyān (d. 754), *al-Baḥr al-Muḥīṭ* (Cairo, 1910-11) IV, 297, who quotes virtually identical words from Ibn ʿAbbās but prefaces it by saying *laʿallahu lā yaṣiḥḥu* «perhaps it is not a correct report».

[16] Qudāma ibn Ǧaʿfar, *Kitāb Naqd al-šiʿr* (Leiden: Brill, 1956) Arabic pp. 55-62; Ibn al-Muʿtazz, *Kitab al-Badīʿ* (London: Luzac, 1935) pp. 68-74; al-Rummānī, *al-Nukat fī iʿǧāz al-Qur'ān* in M. Ḫalafallāh and M. Zaġlūl Salām (eds.) *Ṯalāṯ rasā'il fī iʿǧāz al-Qur'ān* (Cairo, n.d.) esp. pp. 74-75.

(d. 654), who although greatly influenced by al-Rummānī, uses the terminology of Ibn al-Muʿtazz in this instance, *al-ifrāt fī al-ṣifa*; this is perhaps a simpler but ultimately unsatisfactory classification[17]. For none of these authors can this verse be a question of metaphor however; *istiʿāra* for most people (except perhaps al-Ǧurǧānī [d. 471]) was defined as the transfer of the sense of one word to another, a feature clearly not found in this verse[18]. Regardless of that, whether the verse be classified as simile or hyperbole, such an analysis is clearly a late phenomenon, hardly to be attributed to Ibn ʿAbbās. That al-Zamaḫšarī bothered to mention this report at all is a fact which must be given consideration but it does not necessarily mean, as Schub would have it, that al-Zamaḫšarī had a preference for the variant and its interpretation. Since al-Zamaḫšarī appears to feel that the word *ǧamal*, camel, is used appropriately as a simile also, it is unlikely he would want to concede one simile being «more beautiful» than another as the statement of Ibn ʿAbbās would imply. Such an idea could well destroy the framework the author builds in order to demonstrate the *iʿǧāz* of the Qur'ān; I think it must be granted that al-Zamaḫšarī is far too subtle a thinker to fall into such a trap. Rather, it is his attitude toward these variants which would seem to require that he treat them all as equals and thus treat them fully in exegesis. That he actually preferred one variant to another is doubtful.

After al-Zamaḫšarī, there is a decided trend away from placing any importance on the variants and their interpretation, as the pressure of polemics wanes and exegesis becomes more restrictive. In the *tafsīr* of al-Rāzī (d. 606), a work which defends orthodoxy over against the Muʿtazili stance of al-Zamaḫšarī, an unequivocable statement is made concerning Surah 7.40: *al-ǧamal mašhūr*, «the meaning of *al-ǧamal* is well-known», implying that *ǧamal* can stand only its obvious interpretation of «camel»[19]. al-Rāzī also provides much Arabic proverbial material to demonstrate how *à propos* the simile is. He then goes on, however, to quote al-Zamaḫšarī's statement on the variants and Ibn ʿAbbās' comments, but ends up by refuting the entire statement by suggesting that there is sufficient merit (*fā'ida*) in the normal and obvious interpretation and its simile without resorting to variant readings.

---

[17] AL-RUMMĀNĪ, p. 97; IBN ABĪ AL-ISBAʿ, *Badīʿ al-Qur'ān* (Cairo, 1957) p. 56; cf. IBN AL-MUʿTAZZ, pp. 65-68.

[18] See S. A. BONEBAKKER, *istiʿāra*, *EI²*, IV, 248-252.

[19] AL-RĀZĪ, *al-Tafsīr al-Kabīr : Mafātīḥ al-ġayb* (Cairo, 1938), XIV, 76-77.

For al-Bayḍāwī (d. 691), the variants and their interpretation clearly take second place. While all the variants are adduced, they are simply introduced by *quri'a* «it was read» with no ascription and no literary interpretation[20]. By the time of Ǧalālayn (al-Maḥallī [d. 864]; al-Suyūṭī, [d. 911]) variants have become an antiquarian interest; the word *ǧamal* is glossed over, obviously with the presumption that such a common word can give no difficulty[21].

Of course later encyclopaedist exegetes such as al-Šawkānī (d. 1250) resurrect these *šawāḏḏ* variants[22]. By that time, however, any reason for such variants and interpretations had been totally forgotten. Variants such as those for Surah 7.40 were created when polemically-based pressures on the exegetes were the strongest and the attitudes towards the Qur'ānic text less confining; it would, of course, be rash to suggest that all Qur'ānic variants have this origin or that they all demonstrate such a rise and fall in popularity (although most do exhibit this latter), but it would seem to be the case in Surah 7.40, as this survey of exegetes has shown[23].

---

20 AL-BAYḌĀWĪ, *Anwār al-tanzīl wa asrār al-ta'wīl* (Cairo: Ḥalabī, n.d.), III, 9.

21 AL-ǦALĀLAYN, *Tafsīr* (Cairo: Ḥalabī, 1934), p. 180.

22 AL-ŠAWKĀNĪ, *Tatḥ al-qadīr* (Cairo: Ḥalabī, 1350), II, 195-196.

23 For further discussion of this entire topic see now Samir KHALIL, *Note sur le fonds sémitique commun de l'expression 'Un chameau passant par le trou d'une aiguille'*, *Arabica*, XXV (1978), 89-94 and his references to which may be added E. F. F. BISHOP, *The Eye of the Needle*, *MW*, XXXI (1941), 354-359.

IX

QUR'ĀN 78/24: A STUDY IN ARABIC LEXICOGRAPHY

In James Barr's landmark study, *Comparative philology and the text of the Old Testament*, the problems involved in the use of Arabic dictionaries, especially in their application to the study of Semitic philology, are partially summed up by the following statement:

> ... the medieval Arabic lexicography did not act very critically or discriminatingly towards the material which it assembled. Quite secondary applications of words are found quoted alongside normal and frequent usages, and metaphorical applications may receive the same kind of treatment as normal ones.[1]

In the work of Lothar Kopf,[2] as Barr gratefully acknowledges, are found the most significant efforts toward bringing these problems to light and the explanation that the basis of the problems is often to be traced to religious influences and constraints, especially from the lexicographical tradition associated with the Qur'ān.

It has become too common and too easy, however, just to treat some of the definitions found in Arabic dictionaries as preposterous or as misunderstandings without ever appreciating the centuries of discussion that lie behind such meanings and the amazing variety of constraints that brought forth the

[1] James Barr, *Comparative philology and the text of the Old Testament*, Oxford 1968, 117.

[2] See especially his "Religious influences on medieval Arabic philology", *Studia Islamica*, V (1956), 33-59 (esp. 40-5); also "The treatment of foreign words in medieval Arabic lexicology", in Uriel Heyd (ed.), *Studies in islamic history and civilization*, Scripta Hierosolymitana IX, Jerusalem 1969, 191-205; also see the extracts from his "Arabic lexicography – its origin, development, sources and problems" [in Hebrew] in his *Studies in Arabic and Hebrew lexicography*, ed. M. Goshen-Gottstein, Jerusalem 1976, 13-114; the above two articles are reprinted in this latter volume, 19-45 and 247-61 respectively.

definitions in the first place. This is not to suggest that such meanings should be seen to have any greater intrinsic value within the study of language because of that fact, of course, but rather to suggest that the full dimension of Arabic lexicography have not been fully understood until the processes through which such "preposterous" meanings evolved have been carefully examined.

Barr cites the example, quoted from Stefan Wild,[3] of the root ḌḤK "to laugh" meaning "to menstruate" through its association with Qur'ān, sūra 11/71, the Qur'ānic version of the aetiological narrative of Sarah and the annunciation of Isaac's birth; Barr calls this one of the "more extravagant cases" of misleading Arabic lexicography.[4] Significant, however, I would claim, is the fact that the definition is probably a reflex of the understanding of the laughing statement of Sarah in the Bible, "After I am waxed old shall I have *'ednah*!" (Gen. xviii.12) where *'ednah* was often traditionally understood as "menstruation" rather than "[sexual] pleasure".[5] Such a conception of course makes no difference to the value of the Arabic lexicographical tradition nor it is intended to suggest doubts concerning traditional Jewish understanding of the Bible, but it does demonstrate that Arab lexicographers did not merely pull meanings out of thin air to put into their dictionaries; rather, they distilled a whole cultural milieu within them.

A further example of a different nature than the above may well indicate the range of influences at work and also some of the complexities of the issues which are glossed over in dictionaries such as Lane.[6] The example revolves around the word *bard*, related to the general Semitic root for "cold", as it is used in the Qur'ān at sūra 78/24. This verse, *prima facie*, seems to be describing hell (*jahannam* in Q. 78/21) as the place of the all-consuming fire in which the hapless inhabitants are consigned to exist forever: *lā yadhūqūna fīhā bard^an wa lā sharāb^an* "They will experience [lit. "taste"] in it neither cold nor drink". Now what is odd about this passage is that, when dealing with it, a large number of exegetes (and thus virtually

[3] *Das Kitāb al-'Ain und die Arabische Lexikographie*, Wiesbaden 1965, 50, n. 137.

[4] *Comparative philology*, 117, n. 2.

[5] See e.g., Genesis Rabba, XLVIII, 17 (also Rashi, *ad loc.*).

[6] *An Arabic-English lexicon*, London 1863-93.

the entire consequent lexicographical tradition) puts forth the suggestion that the use here of the common word for "cold", *bard*, signifies *nawm*, "sleep". This definition is the only one given, for example, by Abū 'Ubayda (d. 210/825),[7] al-Sijistānī (d. 330/942)[8] and Ibn Ḥasnūn (d. 386/996),[9] in whose work the word *bard* used in the meaning of *nawm* is suggested to be attribuable to the dialect of the tribe of Hudhayl.

Al-Sijistānī gives the proverb (*mathal*) *mana'a al-bard[u] al-bard[a]*, "cold prevents sleep", as proof of this meaning.[10] This is then also cited in al-Baghawī (d. 516/1122),[11] al-Zamakhsharī (d. 538/1144)[12] and al-Qurṭubī (d. 671/1273);[13] Lane, quoting from al-Zamakhsharī, vocalises and translates *al-barad[u]*, "cold".[14]

Abū 'Ubayda cites the following piece of poetry as his support, ascribing the (incomplete) line to al-Kindī: *fa-ṣaddanī 'anhā wa 'an qublatihā al-bard* "Sleep kept me from her and from her kiss"[15]. This is then also cited by al-Ṭabarī (d. 310/923)[16] and al-Qurṭubī,[17] although the latter reads *taqbīlihā* rather than *qublatihā*.

Ibn Qutayba (d. 276/889), on the other hand, cites as one of his suggestions for this verse the following line of poetry, being followed in this by al-Zamakhsharī[18] and al-Qurṭubī,[19] although Lane[20] quotes the line as also being used to demonstrate *bard* meaning "saliva": *fa-law shi'tu ḥarramtu al-nisā'a siwākum / wa-in shi'tu lam aṭ'am nuqākh[an] wa-lā bard[an]* "If I wished, I would declare forbidden all women except you. And if I wished, I

[7] *Majāz al-Qur'ān*, Cairo 1962, II, 282.
[8] *Gharīb al-Qur'ān*, Cairo n.d., 39.
[9] *al-Lughāt fī 'l-Qur'ān*, Beirut 1972, 50; for the attribution, dating and contents of this text see my "Ibn 'Abbās's *Al-lughāt fī 'l-Qur'ān*", *BSOAS*, XLIV (1981), 15-25. In editing the text, Ṣalāḥ al-Dīn al-Munajjid appears to have thought that *nawm* was being suggested as the meaning of *sharāb*; see his index to the text, 64.
[10] *Gharīb*, 39.
[11] *Ma'ālim al-tanzīl*, Bombay 1878, 954.
[12] *al-Kashshāf 'an ḥaqā'iq al-tanzīl*, Calcutta 1856, II, 1571.
[13] *al-Jāmi' li-aḥkām al-Qur'ān*, Cairo 1968, XIX, 178.
[14] *Lexicon*, I, 184.
[15] *Majāz*, II, 282.
[16] *Jāmi' al-bayān fī tafsīr al-Qur'ān*, Cairo 1323-9, XXX, 9.
[17] *al-Jāmi'*, XIX, 178.
[18] *Kashshāf*, II, 1571.
[19] *al-Jāmi'*, XIX, 178.
[20] *Lexicon*, I, 184.

would not taste sweet water nor sleep".[21] Note also that Lane vocalises *in shi'ti*, "If you wished", which would seem to make better sense of this line, although it is to be remembered that it is out of context from the original poem; on the other hand, such a reading is contradicted by the editions both of al-Zamakhsharī and al-Qurṭubī.

It may well be doubted that any of these *shawāhid*, or "witnesses", actually prove anything; the problems of ascription and transmission are slight when compared with the existence of opportunities for plain forgery in such matters. The invention of such "witnesses" to Qur'ānic vocabulary usages can easily be conceived, given the overwhelming pressure to produce such evidence, once the study of the Qur'ān had reached the stage of being compared to profane poetry.[22] Even the exegetes must have felt the ridiculousness of the situation, for a number of them seem to feel constrained to add an explanation of how *bard* could ever have evolved from its normal meaning of "cold" into "sleep"; Ibn Qutayba is typical when he states "[cold] is called because [sleep] cools [*yabradu*] the thirst of man during it".[23] Al-Farrā' (d. 207/822) does likewise.[24]

To determine how such a seeming linguistic oddity could have come about, it may be revealing to examine other Qur'ānic usages of the same term. The root BRD is not frequent in the Qur'ān, being limited to five instances including Q. 78/24. Once the word *barad* is found, in Q. 23/43. While the syntax of the passage is, and was for classical exegetes as well, somewhat problematic,[25] there seems to be little doubt about the meaning of the word: it would appear to be cognate to the Hebrew (and Aramaic) *bārād*, meaning "hail". Twice the participle form *bārid* is used, in both cases normally being understood as "that which cools". Q 56/44 is an after-life picture where there is no *bārid* to relieve the *ḥamīm*, generally

21 Ibn Qutayba, *Tafsīr gharīb al-Qur'ān*, Beirut 1978, 509.

22 See John Wansbrough, *Quranic studies: sources and methods of scriptural interpretation*, Oxford 1977, 97-102, 142-3, 216-18.

23 In the work *al-Qurtayn li-Ibn Muṭarrif al-Kinānī aw kitābay mushkil al-Qur'ān wa gharīb li-Ibn Qutayba*, Cairo 1355, II, 201; the statement is not to be found in his *Tafsīr gharīb al-Qur'ān* nor have I located it in his *Ta'wīl mushkil al-Qur'ān*, Cairo 1973.

24 *Ma'anī al-Qur'ān*, Cairo 1966-72, III, 228.

25 See e.g. al-Farrā', *Ma'ānī*, II, 256-7.

"boiling water" (see further below), and the *samūm*, "blast of fire". Q. 38/42 is notable for its conjunction of *bārid* and *sharāb*, as in Q. 78/24; Job is told to strike the group and ease his misery, for "Here is water to purify (*mughtasal*), cool (*bārid*) and drink (*sharāb*)". Finally, the word *bard* itself is found again at Q. 21/69. Here, Abraham is preaching to his fellow countrymen who respond by threatening to burn him. God comes to the rescue: *qulnā yā nār kūnī bard*[an] *wa-salm*[an] *'alā Ibrāhīm* "We said, 'Oh fire, be cool and safe for Abraham'". Once again, *bard* appears to act as the opposing force to fire and heat; the translation as "cool" or "cold" seems logical by both the context of the passages and by the general understanding of the root BRD.

The explanation for how *bard* could come to mean "sleep" rather than "cold" in Q. 78/24, then, would appear to lie elsewhere than in intra-Qur'ānic usage. It would seem that the ultimate reason, at least to begin with, lies in the understanding of the relationship between Q. 78/24 and the verse which follows it: 24 *lā yadhūqūna fīhā bard*[an] *wa lā sharāb*[an] 25. *illā ḥamīm*[an] *wa-ghassāq*[an].

The first problem to be faced in the interpretation of the verse concerns the meaning of the terms *ḥamīm* and *ghassāq*.

Ḥamīm does not seem to have created a large problem in its definition for the exegetical tradition, being found twenty times in the Qur'ān, a sufficient number to allow easy definition by context. A typical analysis of the word and its usage in the Qur'ān is found in a work by Muqātil b. Sulaymān (d. 150/767), where three instances of *ḥamīm* meaning "a close relative" are cited; otherwise the word means, he suggests, *ḥārr*, "hot water", especially that which has reached its boiling point.[26] The definitions, however, were not always quite so specific: Abū 'Ubayda, for example, simply defined it as "water".[27]

Ghassāq, on the other hand, was problematic; the root itself has only four instances of use in the Qur'ān and two of these, *ghasaq* at Q. 17/78 and *ghāsiq* at Q. 113/3 are generally rendered by "darkness" although even that is not without its problems,

[26] *al-Ashbāh wa 'l-naẓā'ir fi 'l-Qur'ān al-Karīm*, Cairo 1975, 320; on this text see Wansbrough, *Quranic studies*, 208-12, and Paul Nwyia, *Exégèse coranique et langage mystique*, Beirut 1970, 35-61.

[27] *Majāz*, II, 282.

probably as a result of the legal implications at Q. 17/78.[28] Thus other than Q. 78/24, the only other Qur'ānic use of *ghassāq* is at Q. 38/57, which parallels the former verse closely. Q. 38/56 introduces the picture of the inhabitants of hell burning; verse 57 then goes on to say: *hādhā falyadhūqūhu ḥamīm*[an] *wa ghassāq*[an] "This: they will certainly experience it: *ḥamīm* and *ghassāq*"

It is clear that the context of neither of these verses provides sufficient information to allow a close definition of the term. The exegetes thus had the opportunity of using their imaginations to provide an appropriate meaning; witness al-Qurṭubī's list of eleven different and possible meanings.[29] The point here, however, is not to determine the "true" or "original" meaning of the word[30] but rather to examine the popular proposed meanings and discover their background. There are three meanings that require detailed attention.

The first and most popular meaning is given by Lane as "thick purulent matter that will flow and drip from the skins of the inmates of hell".[31] This meaning is mentioned by al-Farrā',[32] Ibn Qutayba,[33] al-Ṭabarī[34] and al-Zamakhsharī[35] among many. The meaning is concistently related to the idea that *ghasaqa* as a verb means to "flow" (*sāla*) like a well. Second, *ghassāq* could mean a "cold wind", *zamharīr*; this is found in al-Ṭabarī, for example.[36] Third, as a modification of the second, *ghassāq* is "cold which burns due to its coldness". Al-Farrā'[37] and al-Baghawī[38] are among those who mention this possibility.

It is now possible to turn to a consideration of the relationship between Q. 78/24 and Q. 78/25. While the word *illā* in v. 25 may appear to be a normal "exceptive", the exegetes have over

[28] See e.g., Lane, *Lexicon*, VI, 2258; the problem revolves around the exact time of darkness with regard to the time of prayer.

[29] *al-Jāmi'*, XV, 221-2.

[30] Cf. Stefan Schreiner, "Zwei Miszellen zum koranischen Wörterbuch", *Der Islam*, LIV (1977), 109-11, where the attempt is made, rather pointlessly in my opinion, to determine the "original meaning".

[31] *Lexicon*, VI, 2258.

[32] *Ma'ānī*, II, 410.

[33] *Gharīb*, 509.

[34] *Jāmi' al-bayān*, XXX, 9-10.

[35] *Kashshāf*, II, 1571.

[36] *Jāmi' al-bayān*, XXX, 10.

[37] *Ma'anī*, II, 410.

[38] *Ma'ālim*, 954.

the centuries put forth as many as five different understandings of the function of *illā* in this verse; they can be illustrated graphically in the following ways:

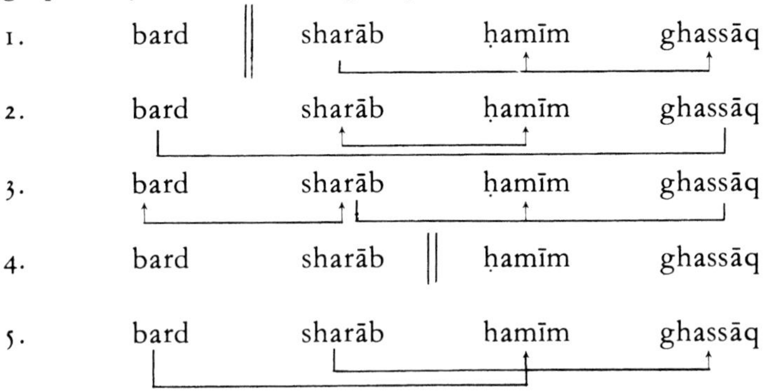

1. bard ‖ sharāb ḥamīm ghassāq
2. bard sharāb ḥamīm ghassāq
3. bard sharāb ḥamīm ghassāq
4. bard sharāb ‖ ḥamīm ghassāq
5. bard sharāb ḥamīm ghassāq

In number one, *ḥamīm* and *ghassāq* are conceived of as types of drink, *sharāb*, and thus *bard* remains alone, taking the meaning of either "cold" or "sleep". *Ghassāq* takes on the meaning of something that flows, such as suggested above, but never something that is cold. Makkī al-Qaysī (d. 437/1046) gives this as a reconstruction of the verse.[39]

Number two, on the other hand, is based on the understanding that *ḥamīm* is some kind of drink (e.g. water) and thus must be the exceptive of *sharāb* and therefore *ghassāq* must correspond to *bard*. *Bard* here never corresponds to "sleep" but always to "cold", presumably because *ghassāq* was never conceived of as some kind of unimaginably horrendous state of sleep, that perhaps being too far-fetched for most conscientious exegetes. *Ghassāq* in this case could take on either of the meanings related to "cold". Al-Ṭabarī mentions this possibility.[40]

Number threee was more imaginative, with *bard* and *sharāb* being taken together, almost as a hendiadys, meaning, simply enough, a cool drink; the net result was identical to that proposed in number one, except that *bard* always retained its meaning of "cold". Al-Farrā' [41] and Ibn Qutayba [42] suggest this possibility.

[39] *Kashf 'an wujūh al-qirā'āt al-sab'*, Damascus, 1974, II, 232.
[40] *Jāmi' al-bayān*, XXX, 9.
[41] *Ma'ānī*, III, 228.
[42] *al-Qurtayn*, II, 201.

Number four was the pattern which took advantage of a grammatical nicety: *illā* ("except") as *istithnā' munqaṭi'*, an exception "severed" from the preceeding term.[43] Al-Suyūṭī (d. 911/1505) develops this idea the furthest and the clearest by stating that *illā* here means *lākin*, "but".[44] *Ghassāq* and *bard* are thus both freed to take on whether meaning is chosen by the exegetes in this understanding, but as stated by al-Qurṭubī, this is the prime solution associated with *bard = nawm*.[45]

Finally, the fifth solution, a minority opinion at the best, seems to concentrate on the comparison of opposites: the coldest thing (*bard*) will be boiling water; the only drink (*sharāb*), a putrid effluent. Only Ibn Kathīr (d. 774/1373) mentions this, attributing the opinion to Abu 'l-'Āliya.[46]

Now the question of why *bard* would not be allowed to mean "cold" in possibilities one and four above can be approached. To explain it requires the suggestion of a tentative reconstruction of the process of the early exegetical understanding of the passage and thus is not without its difficulties; but, overall, it seems to be least plausible if not, in fact, totally probable. It seems likely that the initial perception of a problem in this verse came to the exegetes through the solution proposed in number two above: with *ḥamīm* always being understood as something to drink (*sharāb*), the desire for parallelism urged that *ghassāq* correspond to *bard* and thus that *ghassāq* be defined as something very cold, i.e. *zamharīr*. The problem with such an understanding should be apparent: hell is a place of unrelenting fire, by the Qur'ānic evidence (e.g. Q. 56/44 with its use of *bārid*) and in the traditional picture of hell produced by such people as Abu 'l-Layth al-Samarqandī (d. 373/983).[47] Two possible solutions seem to have been proposed. First, to keep *bard* as cold but redefine *ghassāq* as something so cold that it burns – this indeed was a popular answer. Second, to destroy the parallelism by changing the workings of *illā* (i.e. choosing possibility one or

[43] See William Wright, *A grammar of the Arabic language*, 3rd edn., Cambridge 1896-8, II, 336.

[44] *Tafsīr al-Jalālayn*, Beirut n.d., 780.

[45] *al-Jāmi'* XIX, 178.

[46] *Tafsīr al-Qur'ān al-'Aẓīm*, Cairo n.d., IV, 464.

[47] *Tanbīh al-ghāfilīn*, Cairo 1324, esp. 21, tr. in Arthur Jeffery, *A reader on Islam*, The Hague 1962, 232; also see T. O'Shaughnessy, "The seven names for Hell in the Qur'ān", *BSOAS*, XXIV (1961), 444-69, esp. the name *al-nār*, "the fire"; also Ṣoubḥi el-Ṣaliḥ, *La vie future selon le Coran*, Paris 1971.

four), a step which may well have followed from an initial suggestion that here *bard* did not mean "cold" but rather "sleep"; *ghassāq* then became free to mean whatever the exegete chose.

Support for this reconstruction, it seems to me, comes from the existence of a variant reading for the word *ghassāq*. Actually, the variant *ghasāq* is the most popular reading, a fact distorted by the modern acceptance of the Ḥafṣ version as the "official" text. In the system of the "seven readers", only Ḥafṣ, Ḥamza and al-Kisā'ī read *ghassāq*.[48] The attachment of the name of al-Kisā'ī to this reading may be significant, since one should note that al-Baghawī, one of the few exegetes to name authorities in this matter, states that Ibn 'Abbās (d. 68/687), al-Kisā'ī (d. 184/804) and Abū 'Ubayda all understood *bard* to mean "sleep" in this passage.[49] While this coincidence of al-Kisā'ī in both items may well be the result of arbitrary ascription of facts, the notion that *ghassāq* is connected to *bard* meaning "sleep" while *ghasāq* is connected to *bard* meaning "cold" receives further important support in later lexical writings; al-Zabīdī (d. 1205/ 1790) states that, according to some people, *ghasāq* has the meaning "intensely cold" and *ghassāq* means "that which flows from the bodies of the inhabitants of hell".[50] Thus the variant readings and the meanings of *ghassāq/ghasāq* and *bard* all fit together within the patterns outlined above. This would indicate, to me at least, a flurry of exegetical activity designed to solve the problems of the verse; the use of variants in such a situation is, of course, well known.[51] The attempted reconstruction of the exegetical evolution as sketched above receives a high degree of plausibility when combined with such evidence of exegetical activity through variants, I would contend.

The final question to be tackled revolves around why *nawm*, "sleep", would be chosen as the meaning of *bard* rather than something else (assuming, of course, that such a lexical identity had, originally, no basis in actual usage of the Arabic language, which seems a fairly safe assertion). One can only make

[48] See al-Dānī, *al-Taysīr fī 'l-qirā'āt al-sab'*, Istanbul 1930, 188.

[49] *Ma'ālim*, 954.

[50] *Tāj al-'arūs*, Cairo 1889-90, VII, 36, quoted in Lane, *Lexicon*, VI, 2258.

[51] See e.g., my "Qur'ān 21:95: 'A ban is upon any town", *JSS*, XXIV (1979), 43-53; also cf. my "Qur'ān 7.40: 'Until the camel passes through the eye of the needle'", *Arabica*, XXVII (1980), 276-82, for another purpose of variants (response to polemic).

conjectures on such matters, but the selection of "sleep" would seem to be a logical one, sleep being one of those essential elements of earthly existence, the continual deprivation of which would spell a certain end to this worldly life but would indicate a state of eternal agony in the hereafter.[52] Additionally, al-Qurṭubī manages to cite a prophetic tradition in support of his arguments with regards to this passage: Muḥammad was asked "Will there be sleep in paradise?", to which he replied "No! Sleep is the brother of death and there is no death in paradise".[53] I would hesitate to suggest which of the prophetic traditions or the explanation of *bard* = *nawm* came first, but, either way, a consistent picture was evolved for the use of the exegetes.

Thus we may conclude that the definition of *bard* as "sleep", is of course arbitrary and results from a desire to solve intra-Qur'ānic and Qur'ān versus dogma[54] conflict. The definition has had much influence, finding its way into most exegetical works and, from these, into lexical collections. Many generations of Muslim scholars studied the Qur'ān with a freedom and a resultant unleasing of creativity which has been obscured by the unhistorical nature of the Arabic lexicons. An examination of Qur'ānic exegetical sources reveals the story behind some of the more preposterous meanings recorded in those works.

[52] See Jane I. Smith, "Concourse between the living and the dead in Islamic eschatological literature", *History of Religions*, XIX (1980), 224-36, on the interesting development of the analogy between "sleep" and "death".

[53] *al-Jāmi'*, XIX, 178.

[54] That is, a pre-existent (probably common to the Near Eastern milieu) dogma on the nature of hell to be reconciled with the Qur'ānic data as exposed by the exegetical tradition.

X

TAFSĪR is an Arabic word meaning "interpretation"; it is, more specifically, the general term used in reference to all genres of literature which are commentaries upon the Qur'ān.

Tafsīr and Related Terms. The word *tafsīr* is used only once in the Qur'ān (25:33), but this is not overly surprising, for most technical terms involved in Muslim exegesis have been derived and adapted either from the field of rhetoric or from the legal tradition. In the case of *tafsīr* the word appears to have evolved from a description of a poetic figure in which one hemistich contains an explanation of the preceding one.

There is much discussion in various Arabic sources concerning the precise meaning of the term *tafsīr* and its relationship to other technical words such as *ma'ānī, ta'wīl,* and *sharḥ,* all of which connote "interpretation" in some way. Historically, *ma'ānī,* literally "meanings," appears to have been the earliest major term used for the title of works of interpretation; *ta'wīl,* literally related to the notion of "returning to the beginning," was introduced perhaps late in the third century AH (early tenth century CE) as the general term for works of Qur'anic interpretation, only to have been supplanted in the eleventh century CE by *tafsīr. Sharḥ* seems to have been reserved primarily for profane purposes such as commentaries on poetry, but it was also employed for Qur'anic super-commentaries. The prime focus of a dispute which took place probably in the early tenth century and which involved such central figures of early exegesis as Abū Ja'far al-Ṭabarī (d. 923 CE) and al-Māturīdī (d. 944) was the differentiation of *tafsīr* from *ta'wīl.* Both of these major exegetes, note, used the word *ta'wīl* in the title of their commentaries upon the Qur'ān: *Jāmi' al-bayān 'an ta'wīl āy al-Qur'ān* (The Gathering of the Explanation of the Interpretation of the Verses of the Qur'ān) and *Ta'wīlāt al-Qur'ān* (The Interpretations of the Qur'ān), respectively. The basic question at stake concerned the ways in which traditional material could be employed to provide exegetical data. *Ta'wīl,* in the understanding of some scholars, was interpretation which dispensed with tradition and was founded upon reason, personal opinion, individual research, or expertise, whereas *tafsīr* was based upon material *(ḥadīth)* transmitted through a chain of authorities from the earliest period of Islam, preferably from Muḥammad himself or at least from one of his companions. However, the point was certainly never clear, because other proposed differentiations between *ta'wīl* and *tafsīr* glossed those simple edges. Muqātil ibn Sulaymān, an early exegete (d. 767), for example, implies a distinction between *tafsīr* as what is known on the human level and *ta'wīl* as what is known to God alone. According to a similar notion, *tafsīr* applies to passages with one interpretation and *ta'wīl* to those with multiple aspects. And, of course, a further complication is indicated by the very title of al-Ṭabarī's *tafsīr:* that is, *ta'wīl* could be used for a work that was quite tradition-oriented, at least in basic form. A further suggestion is that the dispute over *tafsīr* and *ta'wīl* is to be traced back to the earliest sectarian disputes in Islam, between the general community and the followers of Muḥammad's son-in-law and cousin, ʿAlī ibn Abī Ṭālib (d. 661), known as the Shīʿah, who wished to appropriate the word *ta'wīl* for reference to interpretation of "concealed" (i.e., esoteric) parts of the Qur'ān as demanded by Shīʿī doctrine.

It should also be noted that the terms *tafsīr* and *ta'wīl* were not in fact the exclusive property or concern of Muslims; Jews and Christians writing commentaries on the Bible in Arabic used both words. The Jewish theologian Saʿadyah Gaon (d. 942) titled his Arabic translation of the Pentateuch *Tafsīr basīṭ naṣṣ al-Tūrāh* (The Simple Interpretation of the Text of the Torah), and the Copt Buṭrus al-Sadamantī in about the year 1260 wrote

Al-muqaddimah fī al-tafsīr (Introduction to Interpretation), which formed a part of his overall work on the interpretation of the New Testament Passion narratives. These are only two examples of use of the word *tafsīr* for scriptural interpretation outside Islam; many other similar instances could be cited.

Purpose of Tafsīr. Interpretation aims to clarify a text. *Tafsīr* takes as its beginning point the text of the Qur'ān, paying full attention to the text itself in order to make its meaning clear. It also functions simultaneously to adapt the text to the present situation of the interpreter. In other words, most interpretation is not purely theoretical; it has a very practical aspect of making the text applicable to the faith and the way of life of the believers. The first of these two interpretive aspects is generally provoked by insoluble problems in meaning, by insufficient detail, by intratextual contradiction, or by unacceptable meanings. Interpretation that fits the text to the situation serves to align it with established social custom, legal positions, and doctrinal assertions.

Other practical reasons can also be cited for the initial creation of *tafsīr* as an entity. As Islam expanded, it was embraced by a large number of people who did not know Arabic; interpretation, sometimes in the form of translations (although this was officially frowned upon) and other times in a simple Arabic which did not contain the ambiguities and difficulties of the original scriptural text, fulfilled the purpose of allowing easier access to the book. In addition, there was the basic problem of the text itself and how it was to be read. The early Arabic script was defective in its differentiation of letters of the alphabet and in the vocalization of the text; although eventually there arose an official system of readings *(qirā'āt)* which gave sanction to a basic seven sets of vocalizations of the text (with further set variations still possible to some extent), in the earliest period a greater freedom with regard to the text seems to have been enjoyed. This freedom extended to the consonantal structure of the text and was legitimized through the notion of the early existence of various codices of the Qur'ān, each with its own textual peculiarities. Differences between these versions and the later, official 'Uthmanic text (as far as theses could be cited by the exegetes), as well as the variations created by the different official vocalization systems, then demanded explanation and justification in order to establish claims that a particular reading provided the best textual sense. The end result was that *tafsīr* acted to establish a firm text of scripture within what became the set limits of the *qirā'āt*.

Origins of Tafsīr. Traditionally it has been held that *tafsīr* arose as a natural practice, originating with Muḥammad and then continuing organically from that point forward; the earliest material has thus become known as *tafsīr al-nabī* ("the interpretation of the Prophet"). Various companions of Muḥammad and some early believers are also seen as the major figures who started interpreting the Qur'ān and teaching people exactly what their understanding of the text was; central among them was 'Abd Allāh ibn 'Abbās (d. 687?), who gained the title *tarjumān al-Qur'ān*, "the interpreter of the Qur'ān."

A debate rages in the scholarly literature on the nature of early *tafsīr*, most especially over the idea of opposition to the activity itself in the early Islamic period. This notion was first isolated by Ignácz Goldziher in *Die Richtungen der islamischen Koranauslegung* (Leiden, 1920); on the basis of traditional Muslim reports concerning the caliph 'Umar (d. 644) and his punishment of a certain person (variously identified) for interpreting unclear passages of the Qur'ān, Goldziher concluded that interpretation of Qur'anic verses dealing with historical legends and eschatology was illegitimate. Harris

Birkeland in *Old Muslim Opposition against Interpretation of the Koran* (Oslo, 1955) rejected this contention on the basis of his own evaluation of the traditional reports, which suggested to him certain contradictions, especially over the identity of the flogging victim and over whether such punishment was in keeping with 'Umar's character. Birkeland has argued that, rather than general opposition to *tafsīr,* there was no opposition at all in the first Muslim century, that strong opposition arose in the second century, and that thereafter the activity of *tafsīr* was brought into and under the sphere of orthodox doctrine and requirements. In particular, strict methods were introduced for the transmission of the information, which formed the core of interpretational procedure, and in this way, *tafsīr* gained total acceptance. Nabia Abbott, in an excursus to her *Studies in Arabic Literary Papyri II: Qur'ānic Commentary and Tradition* (Chicago, 1967), reasserted Goldziher's isolation of early opposition on the basis of traditional information that the person in question certainly existed and that flogging was in keeping with the character of 'Umar. For Abbott, however, the opposition was limited to the interpretation of a specific category of unclear verses *(mutashābihāt),* a claim that she based on the traditional biographical material, which indicates that those people who are mentioned as opponents of *tafsīr* in fact transmitted much material themselves. Therefore, for Abbott, the only opposition to *tafsīr* that ever existed was that connected with the ambiguous or unclear verses. Precisely what is to be understood by the "unclear verses," however, is glossed over in this argument. Exegetes never have agreed and never will agree on which verses are unclear, or even on what that expression means. Some things are unclear to one person while they are perfectly clear to another, often because of a different (especially religious) perspective on the material.

The major problem with all of these discussions is the lack of substantial evidence, with the result that the entire argument remains speculative. Manuscript evidence for *tafsīr* barely reaches back to the third century AH (ninth century CE), at which point several genres of commentary had already emerged. Much of the material found in these texts seems to have originated in a popular worship context (such as semiliturgical usage or sermons) or in the storyteller environment provided by wandering preachers *(quṣṣāṣ)* and their didactic, homiletic sermonizing, which aimed to improve the religious sentiments of the uneducated majority of people. In other words, producing entertaining tales was a key to the development of *tafsīr*. From this point of view, the whole discussion of the origins of *tafsīr* as conducted by Goldziher, Birkeland, and Abbott is rendered rather redundant.

Legitimation of Tafsīr in the Qur'ān. While the Qur'ān does not explicitly state that it should be interpreted, commentators have been able to justify their profession over the centuries by reference to the text itself. The most famous and the most problematic passage applied in this way is surah 3:5–6, the terminology of which has been referred to several times in the preceding sections:

> It is He who has sent down to you the book in which are clear verses [*muḥkamāt*] that are the essence of the book and others that are unclear [*mutashābihāt*]. As for those in whose hearts is a perversion, they follow the unclear part, desiring dissension and desiring its interpretation [*ta'wīl*]. But no one knows its interpretation [*ta'wīl*] except God. And those firm in knowledge say: "We believe in it; all is from our Lord." Yet none remember except men who understand.

This passage establishes two categories of interpretation, perhaps most easily viewed as "clear" *(muḥkam)* versus "unclear" *(mutashābih)*. Many different translations and identifications have been put forth for the latter, some of which render the category hermeneutically trivial (e.g., identification of the "mysterious letters" which precede various surahs as the *mutashābihāt*), while others prove more valuable (e.g., identification of all verses with more that one interpretive aspect as *mutashābihāt*). Even more crucial, however, was the punctuation of the verse. The original Arabic text provides no indication of where stops and pauses should be taken; as a result, it was also possible to render the latter part of the pericope:

> But no one knows its interpretation except God and those firm in knowledge who say: "We believe in it; all is from our Lord."

With such a reading, the interpretive task was not limited to the rather trite exercise of making totally plain the already clear verses; the unclear verses, too, became targets for the commentators, and with that concept defined in some appropriate manner, the way was opened for the creation of a *tafsīr* on every verse of the Qur'ān.

Emergence of Tafsīr Literature. It seems fairly certain that written *tafsīr* works began to emerge in the second century AH at the latest. Documentation starts to proliferate toward the end of that period, and various modes of analysis (e.g., attention to the convergent lines of transmission of a text) also suggest this as the earliest verifiable period. The emergent literature itself can be analyzed into various categories which not only display the distinctive literary qualities and differences of the texts but also suggest an overall relative historical ordering of them. The five sequential categories suggested by John Wansbrough in his *Quranic Studies: Sources and Methods of Scriptural Interpretation* (Oxford, 1977) are narrative (aggadic), legal (halakhic), textual (masoretic), rhetorical, and allegorical. While the historical sequence itself may be open to some debate, the categorization itself is, in true scientific fashion, functional, unified, and revealing.

Narrative tafsīr. Narrative *tafsīr* is exemplified in the text by Muqātil ibn Sulaymān, which has subsequently been given the title *Tafsīr al-Qur'ān* (Interpretation of the Qur'ān), although that is unlikely to have been the original name, and is also embodied in various sections of the work by Ibn Isḥāq (d. 768), *Sīrat Rasūl Allāh* (The Life of the Messenger of God). The creation of an edifying narrative, generally enhanced by folklore from the entire Near Eastern world (including the heritages of Byzantium, Persia, and Egypt, but most especially that of the Judeo-Christian milieu) is the main feature of such commentaries. Adding detail to otherwise sketchy scripture and answering the rather mundane questions which the curious mind will raise when confronted by a contextless scriptural passage are the central concerns of this genre. In fact, the actual narrative seems to be of prime importance; the text of scripture remains underneath the story itself, often subordinated in order to construct a smoothly flowing narrative.

For the first part of surah 2:189 ("They are asking you about the new moons. Say: 'They are appointed times for the people and the pilgrimage'"), Muqātil tries to provide the answers for the curious reader. Just who is asking? Why did they ask? Precisely what did they ask? This type of approach is the essence of aggadic *tafsīr*. Muqātil provides the following comment on the verse:

> Mu'ādh ibn Jabl and Tha'labah ibn Ghanamah said: "O Messenger! Why is it that the new moon is just visible, then it appears small like a needle, then brightens until it is strong, then levels off and becomes a circle, only to start to decrease and get smaller, until it returns just as it was? Why does it not remain at a single level?" So God revealed the verse about the new moons.

The identification of the participants and the precise

question being asked (provided in a marvelously naive and therefore entertaining manner) are specified. The overall interpretation of the verse becomes clear through this supplying of contextual material.

Legal tafsīr. Muqātil ibn Sulaymān once again is a focal point in the development of legal interpretation. Here, the arrangement of the material becomes the prime indicator of the genre; whereas in narrative interpretation the order of scripture for the most part serves as the basic framework, for the legal material a topical arrangement is the definitive criterion. The fact that the actual content of Muqātil's legal *tafsīr*, entitled *Tafsīr khams mī'ah āyah min al-Qur'ān* (The Interpretation of Five Hundred Verses of the Qur'ān), is probably derived from his narrative *tafsīr* reveals that the prime criterion is indeed the form of the work.

Muqātil's text covers the following topics: faith, prayer, charity, fasting, pilgrimage, retaliation, inheritance, usury, wine, marriage, divorce, adultery, theft, debts, contracts, and holy war. This range of topics gives a fair indication of the nature of much of the material in the Qur'ān which was found to be of legal value.

Textual tafsīr. Activities centered on explanations of the lexicon of scripture, along with its grammar and variant readings, are the focus of textual commentaries. One of the earliest texts devoted to this type of analysis is that of the philologist al-Farrā' (d. 822) entitled *Ma'ānī al-Qur'ān* (The Meanings of the Qur'ān), a fairly technical work which primarily explains the difficult points of grammar and textual variants. The work of Abū 'Ubayd (d. 838), *Faḍā'il al-Qur'ān* (The Merits of the Qur'ān), is similar, although it is divided by topic rather than following the Qur'anic order, as does the work of al-Farrā'. Earlier simple texts also exist, including that by Muqātil ibn Sulaymān, *Kitāb al-wujūh wa-al-naẓā'ir* (The Book of [Word] Senses and Parallels), and al-Kisā'ī (d. 804), *Mushtabihāt al-Qur'ān* (The Resemblances of the Qur'ān), both of which are devoted to semantic analysis of the text. Muqātil's text compiles lists of word usages according to the number of senses of meaning *(wujūh)* of a given word; al-Kisā'ī's work is similar but deals with phrases rather than individual words.

Rhetorical tafsīr. Concern for the literary excellencies of scripture is the focal point of works such as that by Abū 'Ubaydah (d. 824), *Majāz al-Qur'ān* (The Literary Expression of the Qur'ān), although the origin of this type of analysis may well be in textual exegesis (with a grammatical focus) rather than in a purely literary type. The impetus for its development as a separate genre, however, was the nascent notion of the miraculous character of the Qur'ān and the literary evidence for it. While this became a full doctrine only in the fourth century AH, its exegetical roots are to be found here. The work *Ta'wīl mushkil al-Qur'ān* (The Interpretation of the Difficulties in the Qur'ān), by Ibn Qutaybah (d. 889), proves to be an important transition point between this earliest rhetorical analysis based upon grammatical and exegetical niceties and that of the later doctrine of the miraculous character or inimitability of the Qur'ān *(i'jāz)*. [*For further discussion, see* I'jāz.] In these texts attention is paid to the literary qualities of the Qur'ān which place it outside the norm of Arabic prose and poetry; various poetical figures are isolated, for example, are subjected to analysis for meaning, and, in many cases, are then compared with older Arabic poetry.

Allegorical tafsīr. Support for dissident opinion in Islam was generally found *ex post facto* through the expediency of allegorical interpretation. Supported through a terminological differentiation of the *ẓāhir* as *historia,* "literal," and the *bāṭin* as *allegoria,* "symbolic," the Ṣūfī *tafsīr* of Sahl al-Tustarī (d. 896) exemplifies this trend in the earliest period. No attempt is made in this work, however, to provide an overall allegorical interpretation; rather, it takes isolated passages from the text of scripture and views them in light of mystical experience. The order of scripture is followed in al-Tustarī's text as it now exists, although the initial compilation may not have followed any such order. About one thousand verses (out of some sixty-two hundred) in the Qur'ān are covered in this manner.

The commentary itself, which is structured piecemeal and reads in a disjointed fashion, contains much more than straightforward allegorical interpretation: legends of the ancient prophets, stories about Muḥammad, and even some about the author of the work himself also find their place. Nor is any overall pursuit of mystical themes to be found; indeed, its general nature is fragmentary. The esoteric portions of the text are formed around typically Ṣūfī meditations on the Qur'ān, each taking a key word from the text. Allegorical interpretation in this case becomes as much a process of thematic association as one of textual commentary.

Consolidation of Classical Tafsīr. It is with the fourth century AH (tenth century CE) that true works of *tafsīr* emerge, combining in various ways the five formative elements I have described above. The first landmark of this type of *tafsīr* is that of al-Ṭabarī, *Jāmiʻ al-bayān ʻan taʼwīl āy al-Qurʼān*, which gathers together in a compendium reports from earlier authorities dealing with most aspects of the Qur'ān. Verse-by-verse analysis is provided, each detailed with virtually every major interpretational trend (except sectarian). The material supplied in this manner is given in its full form, complete with the chains of transmitters for each item of information to lend the weight of tradition to each statement. This type of work is classically called *tafsīr bi-al-maʼthūr* ("interpretation by tradition"), as opposed to *tafsīr bi-al-raʼy* ("interpretation by opinion"), but the categories are misleading. Al-Ṭabarī provides his own personal interpretation, both implicitly by his editorial selection of material and explicitly by stating his opinion where different trends of interpretation exist, sometimes even going against the entire thrust of tradition and providing his own point of view; in this sense, this work, too, is *tafsīr bi-al-ra'y*.

In the centuries after al-Ṭabarī, *tafsīr* as an activity increased and became more and more sophisticated and, in some cases, reached voluminous quantities. Al-Māturīdī, Abū al-Layth al-Samarqandī (d. 983?), al-Tha'labī (d. 1035), and al-Wāḥidī (d. 1075) are all prominent people who in the fourth and fifth centuries AH produced volumes of *tafsīr,* sometimes, as in the case of al-Wāḥidī, in multiple editions.

Theological concerns begin to make a greater impact upon *tafsīr* in this period; it is a trend which culminates in the production of the most famous Qur'ān commentaries in the Muslim world, those of the rationalist Mu'tazilī al-Zamakhsharī (d. 1144), the philosopher Fakhr al-Dīn al-Rāzī (d. 1209), and the Sunnī traditionalist al-Bayḍāwī (d. sometime between 1286 and 1316). Debates rage among these authors, and many others, over the central questions of Islamic theology and the various positions to be found in the Qur'ān. Topics covered include free will and predestination, the attributes of God, the nature of the Qur'ān, the imposition of the tasks of the law, the nature and extent of the hereafter, and so forth. The Mu'tazilī al-Zamakhsharī opts for interpretation based upon reason in his commentary *Al-kashshāf 'an ḥaqā'iq ghawāmiḍ al-tanzīl* (The Unveiler of the Realities of the Secrets of the Revelation). Apparent contradiction between verses of the Qur'ān are resolved in favor of the Mu'tazilī doctrines of the unity and justice of God. Al-Bayḍāwī produced an edited version of the text by al-Zamakhsharī in his *Anwār al-tanzīl wa-asrār al-ta'wīl* (The Lights of the Revelation and the

Secrets of the Interpretation), removing in the process most of the Muʿtazilī tendencies and compressing the material into an even more concise form. Al-Rāzī's unfinished *tafsīr, Mafātīḥ al-ghayb* (The Keys of the Unknown), discusses the Qur'ān in terms of a rationalist philosophy which for the most part involved a rejection of the Muʿtazilī position and argued in support of orthodoxy. Humans, for al-Rāzī, are predetermined, and God's freedom and power cannot be confined by human rationality.

Encyclopedist *tafsīr* works in the tradition of al-Ṭabarī also continue with writers such as Ibn Kathīr (d. 1373), al-Shawkānī (d. 1839), and al-Ālūsī (d. 1854). The opposite trend toward distillation reaches its peak, in popular terms, with the *Tafsīr al-Jalālayn* of Jalāl al-Dīn al-Suyūṭī (d. 1505) and Jalāl al-Dīn al Maḥallī (d. 1459).

Specializations within Classical Tafsīr. While the all-encompassing commentary marks the highlight of exegetical activity in the classical period, the field of specialized Qur'anic sciences was emerging at the same time, providing a number of subdisciplines within *tafsīr*. Some of these are continuations of the earliest developments; others arise under new impetuses. General compendia of information on these sciences arise in the discipline known as *ʿulūm al-Qur'ān* ("the sciences of the Qur'ān"), represented by such works as *Nukat al-intiṣār li-naql al-Qur'ān* (Gems of Assistance in the Transmission of the Qur'ān), by al-Bāqillānī (d. 1012); *Al-burhān fī ʿulūm al-Qur'ān* (The Criterion for the Sciences of the Qur'ān), by al-Zarkashī (d. 1391); and *Al-itqān fī ʿulūm al-Qur'ān* (The Perfection about the Sciences of the Qur'ān), by al-Suyūṭī. The topics gathered in these books are also subjects of separate monographs by a wide variety of writers; these topics include *naskh,* abrogation of legal passages of the Qur'ān; *asbāb al-nuzūl,* the occasions of revelation of individual verses and surahs of the Qur'ān; *tajwīd,* recitation of the Qur'ān;

al-waqf wa-al-ibtidā', pauses and starts in recitation of the Qur'ān; *qirā'āt*, variants to the text of the Qur'ān; *marsūm al-khaṭṭ*, the writing of the Qur'ān; *aḥkām*, the laws of the Qur'ān; *gharīb*, the strange or difficult words in the Qur'ān; *i'rāb*, the grammar of the Qur'ān; *qiṣaṣ al-anbiyā'*, the stories of the prophets; and *i'jāz*, the inimitability of the Qur'ān. As these topics indicate, it is indeed difficult to separate developed *tafsīr* from both legal concerns *(fiqh)* and grammar *(naḥw)*.

Sectarian Tafsīr. Parallel to the development of mainstream Sunnī Muslim *tafsīr* in the classical period, works arose from various other Muslim groups, each pursuing its own particular sectarian aim and, once again, attempting to make the Qur'ān relevant to its own particular point of view and situation.

Shiism. For the Shī'ah in general, the authority of the imams who descended from 'Alī ibn Abī Ṭālib was ultimate in matters of interpretation of the Qur'ān. While *ḥadīth* traditions circulated in Sunnī circles were generally accepted, this material was often supplemented or corrected on the authority of the imams. The category of the *mutashābihāt* was particularly useful to the Shī'ah, for a number of appropriate "unclear" verses could be understood as referring to 'Alī and his family. Such verses were also useful for "discovering" stridently critical comments concerning the early leaders of the Muslim community, namely Abū Bakr (d. 634), 'Umar, and 'Uthmān.

The earliest Ithnā 'Asharīyah or Twelver Shī'ī *tafsīr* in existence today appears to be the somewhat fragmentary commentary of 'Alī ibn Ibrāhīm al-Qummī (d. tenth century) with the ascribed title *Tafsīr al-Qur'ān;* other prominent works include *Al-tibyān fī tafsīr al-Qur'ān* (The Explanation in Interpretation of the Qur'ān), by Muḥammad ibn al-Ḥasan al-Ṭūsī (d. 1067), and a major commentary which is a compendium of information comparable to that of al-Ṭabarī, *Majma' al-*

bayān li-'ulūm al-Qur'ān (The Collection of the Explanation of the Sciences of the Qur'ān), by Abū 'Alī al-Ṭabarsī (d. 1153 or later).

Allegorical interpretation is favored in Shī'ī *tafsīr* as a process of looking for the "inner" meaning in many passages. The special way of applying this method is to find references to 'Alī and his family, which, of course, serves to promote Shī'ī claims to power and legitimacy. For example, in al-Qummī's *tafsīr*, the notion of Islam itself is defined not simply as submission to God but also as submission to the authority of the line of imams. The use of textual variation is also present in some works, although whenever the Shī'ah have been powerful in political affairs and fully institutionalized, such notions have generally been rejected as anti–status quo. This was already true to some extent in the eleventh century but became even more so with the rise of the Safavids in the sixteenth century. The specific argument occurred over whether some of the Qur'ān had been changed, or even omitted by 'Uthmān when he ordered its compilation, in order to undermine Shī'ī claims. Passages referring directly to 'Alī had been erased, it was suggested. Al-Qummī argues, for example, that there are verses in the Qur'ān where "letters have been replaced by other letters," and he says that there are places where "verses contradict what God has sent down" (that is, they contradict or at least do not support Shī'ī beliefs). Al-Ṭabarsī argues, however, that the only change that has occurred in the Qur'ān concerns the overall order of the text itself and not its contents. One common textual variant which does receive wide acceptance among Shī'ī commentators concerns the word *ummah* ("community"), which is believed to be properly read *a'immah* ("leaders") or imams *(a'immah* being the plural of *imām* and having the same basic consonantal structure as *ummah).*

The Shī'ah, like the Mu'tazilah, looked to the Qur'ān

for support of the rationalist theological doctrines that were a key element of their belief system: free will and the created Qur'ān. Their interpretational method, therefore, is similar to that employed by al-Zamakhsharī. The Ismā'īlīyah likewise employed the Qur'ān as a reference point for their theologizing; the group's esoteric leanings, often characterized as extreme, are not witnessed in many texts but are found, for example, in the fragmentary *Mizāj al-tasnīm* (The Condition of *Tasnīm*) by Ismā'īl ibn Hibat Allāh (d. 1760). In general, the Ismā'īlī movement sees the outer meaning of the Qur'ān as only the symbol of the true inner meaning. The imam of the age, who has in him the true, full revelation, adapts the Qur'ān to the spiritual and mental condition of humanity through interpretation; eventually, people will be brought to the true and full meaning of the text, which is essentially the knowledge of the unity of God. Such is the presupposition with which all Ismā'īlī *tafsīr* approaches the text.

The more recent Bahā'ī movement establishes its clear Islamic heritage through the existence of works of *tafsīr* written in Arabic by Sayyid 'Alī Muḥammad al-Shīrāzī (1819–1850). Known as the Bāb, or "gate," he claimed to have initiated a new prophetic cycle and became the focal point of the movement which developed later as the Bahā'ī. Among his works are commentaries on surahs 12, 108, and 113 of the Qur'ān. In general these are marked by a spiritualistic interpretation of eschatology, including the notions of paradise, hell, death, and resurrection, all of which are taken to refer to the end of the prophetic cycle as well as the end of the physical world (although the latter is re-created by God in each prophetic cycle).

Sufism. Directly related to Shī'ī *tafsīr* in general is Ṣūfī interpretation, which provides a mystical speculation upon the Qur'ān. This interpretation usually justifies itself through reference to mystical activities believed to have been practiced and supported by Muḥammad. Sahl al-Tustarī, mentioned above, probably represents the earliest example of this tendency. Abū ʿAbd al-Raḥmān al-Sulamī (d. 1012) compiled his *Ḥaqā'iq al-tafsīr* (The Truths of Interpretation) from various Ṣūfī authorities and other important personalities. All of the material can be considered allegorical, since it is devoted to finding the inner meaning of each passage as it relates to the mystical quest. A typical example is found in the interpretation of surah 17:1, the classical reference to Muḥammad's "night journey" to heaven, which is taken as a reference to each mystic's ascent to the higher levels of consciousness. Another prominent Ṣūfī, Abū Ḥamīd al-Ghazālī (d. 1111), did not write a commentary on the Qur'ān as such but found many occasions on which to record his approach to the text of scripture from the point of view of the intellectual Ṣūfī. For al-Ghazālī as for most other mystics, the Qur'ān works on two levels: the practical and the cognitive. The former applies to the inner self and its purification without neglect of the outer activities, while the latter is a meaning found through inner experience in light of mystical thought, and it can be reached only through firm knowledge of the practical or outer aspects. ʿAbd al-Razzāq al-Kāshānī (d. 1330?) compiled perhaps the most widely known Ṣūfī *tafsīr*, although it has often been mistakenly attributed directly to his teacher, the famous Muḥyī al-Dīn ibn al-ʿArabī (d. 1240), and thus is usually known under the title of *Tafsīr Ibn al-ʿArabī* (The Interpretation of Ibn al-ʿArabī). As with al-Ghazālī, the outer principles of religion are not to be forgotten, although within the context of the *tafsīr* they certainly become submerged under allegorical interpretation, here seen in terms of the esoteric inner meaning as well as the symbolism of real events in the world.

Emergence of Modern Tafsīr. The rise of colonialism

and the impact of Western thought in the eighteenth and nineteenth centuries certainly did not spell the end of *tafsīr* activity; in fact, at various times, the modern world has provoked more and more voluminous commentary upon the Qur'ān. Modern *tafsīr* is no different in basic impetus from its classical counterpart; it, too, desires to fit the text of scripture to the conditions of the era contemporary with the interpreter.

The impact of science has perhaps been the major factor in creating new demands and also the element of contemporary life to which much early modern *tafsīr* made its response. Muslims had not understood the true message of the Qur'ān, most modernists argued, and had therefore lost touch with the true scientific, rational spirit of the text. Out of this basic point several elements have emerged that unite all modernist interpretations: (1) the attempt is made to interpret the Qur'ān in the light of reason ("to interpret the Qur'ān by the Qur'ān," as it is frequently phrased) rather than with all the extraneous material provided by tradition in the form of *ḥadīth* reports and earlier commentaries; "Back to the source" often becomes the motto of such approaches; (2) the attempt is made, through the expediency of interpretation, to strip the Qur'ān of all legendary traits, primitive ideas, fantastic stories, magic, fables, and superstition; symbolic interpretation is the primary means for such resolutions; (3) the attempt is made to rationalize doctrine as found in or as justified by reference to the Qur'ān.

The earliest focal point of modernist *tafsīr* activity arose in India. Shāh Walī Allāh (1703–1762) is often seen as the precursor of the Indian reformist movement, but that trend reached its true blossoming with the Indian civil servant and educator Sayyid Ahmad Khan (1817–1898), who wrote the first major explicitly modernist *tafsīr*, entitled simply *Tafsīr al-Qur'ān*. His commentary was directed toward making all Muslims aware of the fact that Western influence in the world required a new vision of Islam, for Islam as it was actually practiced and believed in by most of its adherents would be seriously threatened by modern advances in thought and science. Where, therefore, was the true core of Islam to be found? How was its center to be defined? For Ahmad Khan, these questions were to be answered through reference to the Qur'ān, which, if it were properly understood through the use of the powers of reason, would provide the necessary answers. The basis of the required social and educational reforms, for example, were to be found in the Qur'ān. By returning to the source of Islam, the religion would be revitalized and the future would be secure.

In the Arab world, Muḥammad 'Abduh (1849–1905), a vigorous champion of educational reform, also wrote a commentary on the Qur'ān, commonly called *Tafsīr al-Manār* (The Interpretation of al-Manār), which was completed after his death by his pupil Rashīd Riḍā (1865–1935). Not overly modernistic in outlook, 'Abduh's *tafsīr* does, however, urge the moderate use of rationality in matters of theology and tries to demonstrate that the Qur'ān is to be read primarily as a source of moral guidance applicable to the modern situation. The spiritual aspect of the Qur'ān was most important to 'Abduh, and he, like many commentators in the past, was quite prepared to leave certain matters in the Qur'ān unexplained and to concentrate on their mysteriousness rather than to suggest resolutions for interpretational difficulties.

This type of interpretation continues more recently in the Arab world, represented, for example, by the intellectual spokesman for the Egyptian Muslim Brotherhood, Sayyid Quṭb (1906–1959), who in his work *Fī ẓilāl al-Qur'ān* (In the Shade of the Qur'ān) interprets the text according to his own particular ideological leanings. India, too, has produced many such commentaries; examples are Abū al-Kalām Āzād (1888–1959), whose Urdu work *Tarjumān al-Qur'ān* (The Interpretation [or Translation] of the Qur'ān) emphasized the notion of the unity of man while its author faced the rising tide favoring the formation of Pakistan, and Abū al-A'lā Mawdūdī (1903–1979), the author of *Tafhīm al-Qur'ān* (The Meaning of the Qur'ān), who uses the Qur'ān to establish a blueprint for a future Islamic society in Pakistan to be formed through his political party, Jamā'at-i Islāmī.

The impact of Western science is perhaps the most notable aspect of modern commentaries. Both Ahmad Khan and 'Abduh were intent on encouraging their compatriots to embrace the scientific outlook of the West in order to share in the progress of the modern world. Often this effort involved little more than simply stating that the Qur'ān enjoins its readers to seek and use rational knowledge, but at other times it also involved the historical claim that Islam had developed science in the first place and had then passed it on to Europe, so that in embracing the scientific outlook in the present situation Muslims were only reclaiming what was truly Islamic. A more distinctive trend in *tafsīr* emerges also, however, primarily in the person of Ṭanṭāwī Jawharī (1870–1940) and his twenty-six-volume work, *Al-jawāhir fī tafsīr al-Qur'ān* (Jewels in the Interpretation of the Qur'ān). God would not have revealed the Qur'ān, so the argument goes, had he not included in it everything that people needed to know; science is obviously necessary in the modern world, so it should not be surprising to find all of science in the Qur'ān when that scripture is properly understood. Jawharī also makes reference to the classical notion of the miraculous character or inimitability of the Qur'ān *(i'jāz),* which he takes to refer primarily to the content of the text in terms of its knowledge concerning matters which are only now becoming clear to mankind. Since the scientific knowledge contained in the text is proof of its miraculous character, references are found in the Qur'ān for numerous modern inventions (electricity, for example) and scientific discoveries (the fact that the earth revolves around the sun).

Western thought has also influenced *tafsīr* in another way, although perhaps not so dramatically in terms of its popular acceptance as has "scientific" exegesis; the emergence of modern literary-philological-historical criticism has, thus far, played a fairly minor role but most certainly has found its supporters. 'Ā'ishah 'Abd al-Raḥmān, a university professor in Morocco who writes under the name Bint al-Shāṭi', represents a development of this line. This modern interpretation is not a resurrection of the philological type of commentary associated with al-Zamakhsharī, for example, who, although he wrote with great critical acumen, is for most modernists too full of unnecessary material which is seen to be a hindrance to understanding in the modern world; rather, 'Abd al-Raḥmān pursues a straightforward approach, searching for the "original meaning" of a given Arabic word or phrase in order to understand the Qur'ān in its totality. This process does not involve the use of material extraneous to the Qur'ān itself, except perhaps for the use of a small amount of ancient poetry, but rather it uses the context of a given textual passage to define a word in as many overall contexts as it occurs. Neither the history of the Arabs nor that of the biblical prophets nor scientific topics are to be found in the Qur'ān because providing such material is not seen to be the task of the text. The purpose of the narrative elements of the Qur'ān is to provide moral and spiritual guidance to the believers, not to provide history or "facts." Within the Muslim world, the attempt to demythologize scripture—as in this approach—marks the beginnings of an incorporation of a type of modern critical scholarship developed in the context of biblical studies; its future at this point, however, remains uncertain.

[*See also* Qur'ān *and the biographies of the principal scholars mentioned herein. For discussion of interpretation in other traditions, see* Biblical Exegesis *and* Scripture.]

BIBLIOGRAPHY

On the principles of interpretation there is little material available specifically for the Muslim context; works on Jewish *midrash* are, however, most useful. Reference should be made to Géza Vermès's "Bible and Midrash," in volume 1 of *The Cambridge History of the Bible,* edited by Peter R. Ackroyd and C. F. Evans (Cambridge, 1970); this essay has been reprinted in Vermès's *Post-Biblical Jewish Studies* (Leiden, 1975). Also see Renée Bloch's "Midrash," in volume 5 of the *Supplement au dictionnaire de la Bible,* edited by Louis Pirot and others (Paris, 1957); an English translation by Mary Howard Callaway has been published in *Approaches to Ancient Judaism,* edited by William S. Green (Missoula, Mont., 1978).

Four books are fundamental to the modern study of *tafsīr: Die Richtungen der islamischen Koranauslegung* (Leiden, 1920), a collection of Ignácz Goldziher's lectures delivered in 1913, has yet to be replaced as a general overview of the subject; Theodor Nöldeke's *Geschichte des Qorāns,* vol. 2, *Die Sammlung des Qorāns,* 2d ed. (Leipzig, 1919), contains, especially on pages 123–192, much valuable and basic material; John Wansbrough's *Quranic Studies: Sources and Methods of Scriptural Interpretation* (Oxford, 1977) is essential to the study of the formation and early development of *tafsīr* and to all discussions of terminology and genres of exegetical literature; volume 1 of Fuat Sezgin's *Geschichte des arabischen Schrifttums* (Leiden, 1967) records most of the known Arabic works of *tafsīr* up to the fifth century AH.

Jane I. Smith's *An Historical and Semantic Study of the Term "Islām" as Seen in a Sequence of Qur'ān Commentaries* (Missoula, Mont., 1975), discusses the works of seventeen exegetes on specific verses of the Qur'ān and at the same time provides useful introductions to the lives and works of the individuals.

On Ṣūfī *tafsīr* two excellent works exist: Paul Nwyia's *Exégèse coranique et langage mystique* (Beirut, 1970) and Gerhard Böwering's *The Mystical Vision of Existence in Classical Islam: The Qur'ānic Hermeneutics of the Ṣūfī Sahl al-Tustarī, d. 283/896* (New York, 1980). The latter discusses both textual and thematic matters in exemplary fashion.

Modern *tafsīr* has been analyzed by J. M. S. Baljon in *Modern Muslim Koran Interpretation, 1880–1960* (Leiden, 1961) and by J. J. G. Jansen in *The Interpretation of the Koran in Modern Egypt* (Leiden, 1974); both works provide basic yet informative overviews of the subject and bring Goldziher's work up to the present day.

Not many works of *tafsīr* have been translated, primarily because of their overly technical nature. Helmut Gätje has compiled extracts from various exegetes and arranged them thematically for the use of students in his *Koran und Koranexegese* (Zurich, 1971), translated by Alford T. Welch as *The Qur'ān and Its Exegesis* (Berkeley, 1976). Full works of *tafsīr* which have been translated are very few: *The Tales of the Prophets of al Kisā'ī*, translated by Wheeler M. Thackston (Boston, 1978), a book of the *qiṣaṣ al-anbiyā'* genre, and *The Recitation and Interpretation of the Qur'ān: Al-Ghazālī's Theory*, translated by Muhammad A. Quasem (London, 1982), are two worthwhile texts. Attention should be paid to *The Life of Muhammad: A Translation of Ishaq's "Sīrat Rasūl Allāh"* (1955; reprint, Lahore, 1967), by Alfred Guillaume for the passages of early *tafsīr* which are contained in it; reference to these is, however, unfortunately not facilitated by an index of Qur'anic verses in the translation. Translations of two chapters from the *Tafsīr* of al-Bayḍāwī are available. These are primarily intended for students of Arabic, since the discussion frequently tends to revolve around the sense of a given Arabic word or grammatical construction; *Bayḍāwī's Commentary on Sūrah 12 of the Qur'ān*, edited by A. F. L. Beeston (Oxford, 1963), is the most accessible of such texts. Modern *tafsīr* has not been served well by translation either, although the following are available: *The Meaning of the Qur'ān*, 8 vols., translated by A. A. Maududi (Lahore, 1967–1979); Abū al-Kalām Āzād's *Tarjumān al-Qur'ān*, 2 vols., translated and edited by Syed Abdul Latif (New York, 1962–

1967), and Sayyid Quṭb's *In the Shade of the Qur'ān,* translated by M. A. Salahi and A. A. Shamis (London, 1979).

Further bibliography on *tafsīr* will be found in my article "The Present Status of *Tafsīr* Studies," *Muslim World* 72 (July–December 1982): 224–238.

XI

THE PRESENT STATUS OF *TAFSĪR* STUDIES*

In the bibliographical text *The Study of the Middle East*, published in 1976, Charles Adams commented: "Qur'anic study is also badly neglected in another of its aspects, that which deals with the traditional interpretation of the Scripture of the Islamic community itself."[1] In comparing the situation of where we now stand in *tafsīr* studies with that of Arthur Jeffery's position in 1957 when he wrote "The Present Status of Qur'anic Studies,"[2] however, one may consider Adams' statement as somewhat overly strident, for there certainly have been some major steps made in the last twenty-five years. Large gaps certainly do still exist in even preliminary studies in the field but this indicates simply how far there is still to go in this immense topic.

When Jeffery wrote his article, one of his major interests, and that of a number of other people at the time, was to construct a printed text of the Qur'ān complete with a critical apparatus of textual and orthographic variants and so forth.[3] This project did not come to fruition, nor does it seem today very likely that it will, although the need for and the desirability of such is still there. Interest in these matters just does not seem to be present any longer. Jeffery's article paid attention especially to the appearance of original Arabic texts which were going to provide him with his raw material for the edition of the Qur'ān: a large number of them had appeared at that time and, interestingly enough, a substantial number have continued to be edited and printed. Among the numerous examples of works appearing recently are Ibn Mujāhid, *Kitāb al-Sabʿa fī 'l-Qirā'āt;*[4] Makkī al-Qaysī, *al-Kashf ʿan Wujūh al-Qirā'āt al-Sabʿ*;[5] al-Anbarī, *Kitāb Marsūm al-*

*This is a revised version of a paper prepared for the Second International Qur'ān Congress, New Delhi, December 1982. Research for this paper, travel to India and participation in the conference is made possible by grants from the Social Sciences and Humanities Research Council of Canada. Thanks are due to Alford Welch, Michigan State University, for suggesting the topic and agreeing to have my paper complement his own, "The Present Status of Qur'ān Studies."

[1] Charles Adams, "Islamic Religious Tradition," in L. Binder, ed., *The Study of the Middle East* (New York: John Wiley, 1976), pp. 64–65.

[2] *Middle East Institute: Report on Current Research*, Spring 1957, pp. 1–16.

[3] See, for example, A. Jeffery, "Progress in the Study of the Qur'ān text," *M.W.*, XXIV (1934), 4–16.

[4] Cairo, 1980.

[5] Damascus, 1974.

Khaṭṭ[6] and *Kitāb al-Maqṭūʿ wa 'l-Mawṣūl*,[7] both of the latter being of major interest because they push back the limits of the discussion of these orthographic topics to a century prior to al-Dānī,[8] the best source previously.

This material, and there really is much more of it that has become available in recent years than that just listed, when combined with the texts prepared in connection with the Qurʾān text project of Jeffery, Gotthelf Bergsträsser and Otto Pretzl,[9] amounts to a substantial body of material. But, if we are no longer concerned with constructing a critical text of the Qurʾān with variant apparatus, then of what use is all this data on the *qirāʾa* and textual scripts? To what other purposes may it be put, over and above basic studies in the texts and topics themselves which are, indeed, still wanting? One direction of research which seems rewarding and which has been developed by me in some recent articles is to try to reconstruct trends and motivations in exegesis as revealed by the use and invention of textual and orthographic variants to the Qurʾān.[10] That the very proliferation of these variants is evidence of repeated, differing attempts at interpreting difficult passages is easily ascertainable and has, in fact, been the position held on these issues by most critical scholarship in recent years. This does not, by any means, render the material useless, for hidden below the surface are the exegetical insights of many centuries of activity, all simply waiting to be put into historical perspective and analyzed for motivation—dogmatic, textual, polemical—which produced them in the first place. The material is there ready to be worked upon; only the surface has been scratched in this kind of approach. Nor would I wish to suggest that this is *all* that can be done with the material, but this does strike me as a particularly profitable line of investigation.

A number of other interrelated textual or masoretic topics have also received some attention, especially in John Wansbrough's *Quranic Studies: Sources and Methods of Scriptural Interpretation*[11] which will

---

[6] New Delhi, 1977.

[7] Rampur, 1980.

[8] See, for example, his *Al-Muqniʿ fī Maʿrifa Marsūm Maṣāḥif Ahl al-Amṣār* (Damascus, 1940).

[9] See. G. Bergsträsser and O. Pretzl, *Geschichte des Qorāns von Theodor Nöldeke: III Die Geschichte des Korantexts* (Leipzig: Dieterich'sche Verlagsbuchhandlung, 1938).

[10] A. Rippin, "Qurʾān 21:95: 'A ban is upon any town'," *Journal of Semitic Studies*, XXIV (1979), 43–53; "Qurʾān 7.40: 'Until the camel passes through the eye of the needle'," *Arabica*, XXVII (1980), 107–13; "Qurʾān 78/24: A Study in Arabic Lexicography," *Journal of Semitic Studies*, XXVIII, ii (1983).

[11] Oxford: Oxford University Press, 1977.

be discussed more fully later in this article. Worthy of being noted now, however, is the work on vocabulary lists such as that of Muhammad Abdus Sattar on the genre of tafsīr known as *wujūh al-Qurʾān,*[12] Paul Nwyia's treatment of the same subject but from quite a different perspective in his *Exégèse coranique et langage mystique*[13] and my own treatment of a list of Qurʾanic "dialect" words.[14] Lothar Kopf's studies on the lexicographical tradition and its relationship to the Qurʾān, all reprinted in his *Studies in Arabic and Hebrew Lexicography,*[15] made very important strides in revealing the hidden tendencies of this tradition and its traps, but also revealed the potential for research in the field. Study in these textual-masoretic fields has been helped immensely by the publication of some very important early texts including those of Ibn Qutayba, *Taʾwīl mushkil al-Qurʾān*[16] and *Tafsīr Gharīb al-Qurʾān*[17] and Abū ʿUbayda's *Majāz al-Qurʾān.*[18] The publication of Muqātil b. Sulaymān, *Al-Ashbāh wa 'l-Naẓāʾir*[19] is also a valuable contribution. Once again there is much material available, ready for analysis, but so far it has raised little concentrated interest except perhaps in Wansbrough's work.

The greatest efforts and steps in the study of tafsīr in recent years seem to have occurred in the field of early commentaries and the development of the exegetical tradition. This was a topic raised at least briefly by Jeffery in his work in the context of his discussion of what still remains the seminal book in the entire field of tafsīr, Ignaz Goldziher's *Die Richtungen der Islamischen Koranauslegung*[20] and of Harris Birkeland's monograph *Old Muslim Opposition against Interpretation of the Koran.*[21] Nabia Abbott picked up this discussion in an excursus in her *Studies in Arabic Literary Papyri: II: Qurʾānic Commentary and Tradition*[22] and argues that both Goldziher and

---

[12] "*Wujuh al-Qurʾan:* A Branch of tafsir Literature," *Islamic Studies,* XVII (1978), 137–52.

[13] Beirut: Dar el-Machreq Editeurs, 1970.

[14] "Ibn ʿAbbās's *al-Lughāt fī 'l-Qurʾān,*" *Bulletin of the School of Oriental and African Studies,* XLIV (1981), 15–25.

[15] Ed. M.H. Goshen-Gottstein (Jerusalem: Magnes Press, 1976). The two most important articles are "Religious Influences on Medieval Arabic Philology," *Studia Islamica,* V (1956), 33–59 and "The Treatment of Foreign Words in Medieval Arabic Lexicography," *Scripta Hierosolymitana,* IX (1961), 191–205.

[16] Cairo, 1973.

[17] Beirut, 1978 (second edition).

[18] Cairo, 1954–1962 (two volumes).

[19] Cairo, 1975.

[20] Leiden: E.J. Brill, 1920.

[21] Oslo: Jacob Dybwad, 1955.

[22] Chicago: University of Chicago Press, 1967.

Birkeland had erred in their understanding of the development of tafsīr. Birkeland's argument, as summarized by Abbott, was to suggest that one, there was no opposition to tafsīr until late in the first century; two, strong opposition arose in the second century; and three, thereafter tafsīr as an activity was brought into and under the sphere of orthodox doctrine and requirements, that is most especially in the addition of strict methods of transmission, and therefore gained total acceptability. To this latter part Abbott asserts there is general agreement; to the other two propositions she objects.[23]

The idea of opposition to early tafsīr was suggested first by Goldziher on the basis of reports concerning ʿUmar I and his punishment of a certain person (variously identified) for interpreting ambiguous passages of the Qurʾān. This Birkeland rejected on the basis of evaluation of traditional biographical information which suggested to him certain contradictions, most especially over the identity of the victim of the flogging and over whether the punishment was in keeping with ʿUmar's character. Abbott then reasserts, once again on the basis of traditional biographical information, that the person in question certainly existed and that flogging was in keeping with ʿUmar's character. These kinds of back and forth discussions reveal nothing if not the extreme flimsiness of all such arguments based around such information in which it is possible to find statements, or at least to interpret them, so as to fit the data to a preconceived theory.

Abbott suggests that ʿUmar was, therefore, opposed to tafsīr in the early period or at least to that involved in the interpretation of the *mutashābihāt*. The basis on which she says this is once again traditional biographical material where the names of those sometimes mentioned (e.g., in al-Ṭabarī) as being opposed to tafsīr are, in fact, found to have transmitted much exegesis. Therefore, for Abbott, the only opposition to tafsīr that ever existed was that connected to the *mutashābihāt*. Now, as Wansbrough first pointed out in his review of Abbott's book[24] and then again in *Quranic Studies*,[25] Abbott seems to have glossed over the most crucial point in the argument (or to have missed the point entirely) which concerns the question what precisely is to be understood by the *mutashābihāt*. As any worker in the field of tafsīr should be able to testify, one person's ambiguous verse is another person's obvious or clear verse. One person's *ẓāhir* is another's *bāṭin*. Such a simplistic use of a term of interpretation (and, potentially, of polemic) must always be guarded against.

---

[23] Ibid., pp. 106–13.

[24] *Bulletin of the School of Oriental and African Studies*, XXXI (1968), 613–16.

[25] P. 158.

One of the other concerns about Abbott's arguments is that, despite the context in which they appear—the discussion of early papyri—her case is not based upon textual evidence at all, but rather upon reports of early opinion as found in later sources. None of the actual texts which she analyzed comes from earlier than the third century and thus are separated from the actual events in question by a century or two.

Volume one of Fuat Sezgin's *Geschichte des Arabischen Schrifttums*[26] may be viewed by some as a source where earlier material may be found in order to provide the documentary evidence needed for Abbott's arguments. Indeed Abbott and Sezgin seem quite close in their overall aims. Sezgin has compiled lists of works—primarily manuscripts—from the first four centuries of Islam. His treatment of tafsīr specifically appears to document the notion of written texts existing and being transmitted from very early on in the Muslim world. This is Sezgin's desired aim: he wants to prove the existence of these early written documents in order to substantiate claims for the validity of *ḥadīth* transmission and the *isnād* mechanism. Examining his listing of tafsīr works reveals, however, a remarkably flimsy basis for his position; author's names proliferate, for example, because a listing in Ibn al-Nadīm's *al-Fihrist* has proven sufficient to justify an entry even though there is no actual evidence today of the text's existence. Less obvious is the tendency to allow a single text to be entered under a multitude of names; an example of this occurs with text entitled *Gharīb al-Qurʾān* (in the MS copy Atif Efendi, 2815/8), that is being entered under the names of three different authors. A text may also be assigned to an earlier figure than is obviously suggested by the text itself; an example of this occurs in the treatment of the tafsir listed by Sezgin under Mūsā b. ʿAbd al-Raḥmān al-Thaqafī al-Sanʿānī (d. 190/805) whereas an examination of the text reveals that Bakr b. Sahl al-Dimyāṭī (d. 289/902) or, at best, ʿAbd al-Ghanī b. Saʿīd al-Thaqafī (d. 229/843) should be isolated as the central figure concerned with the work.[27]

Still, Sezgin's work does draw attention to a substantial body of material coming from at least the second and third centuries which is available to be employed; while Sezgin may not have been able to find the conclusive evidence for which he was searching, the basic bibliographical impetus has truly been uplifting to the discipline of

[26] Leiden: E.J. Brill, 1968; especially relevant here are pp. 3–49.

[27] For further details of these points and some of their implications see my "Al-Zuhrī, *Naskh al-Qurʾān* and the problem of early *tafsīr* texts," *Bulletin of the School of Oriental and African Studies*, XLVII (1984).

tafsīr studies. It is in Wansbrough's work *Quranic Studies* where for the first time some of the benefits of Sezgin's book are reaped. Wansbrough constructs a historical and thematic classification system for the chronological development of tafsīr through a literary analysis of a multitude of early pre- al-Ṭabarī works. His scheme suggests the following historical sequence: narrative (haggadic), legal (halakhic), textual (masoretic), rhetorical and allegorical.[28] All this has been accomplished through analysis of many tafsīrs which remain available only in manuscript form and for which there is a desperate need for proper editions, for example Muqātil b. Sulaymān, *Tafsīr*; Abū ʿUbayd, *Faḍāʾil al-Qurʾān*; ʿAbd al-Razzāq, *Tafsīr*; al-Kisāʾī, *Mushtabihāt al-Qurʾān*. Other works which have appeared in printed editions, such as Mujāhid b. Jabr, *Tafsīr*;[29] Sufyān al-Thawrī, *Tafsīr*;[30] al-Farrāʾ, *Maʿānī al-Qurʾān*;[31] and Muqātil b. Sulaymān, *Tafsīr Khams Mīʾat Āya*[32] and his previously mentioned *Al-Ashbāh wa 'l-Naẓāʾir*,[33] have all added most welcome source material from the early period.

Other scholars have attempted to sketch out the early history of tafsīr but none, in my opinion, have been as successful as Wansbrough in bringing to light new facets and new methods of analysis. Mujāhid al-Ṣawwāf,[34] Musa O.A. Abdul[35] and Rashid Ahmad[36] have all made valiant efforts but, for the most part, their analyses of early tafsīr have been detached from actual analysis of early texts.

In studying the early texts, at least two basic approaches are already well-testified: F. Leemhuis' analysis of Mujāhid,[37] Isaiah Goldfeld on Ibn ʿAbbās[38] and Muqātil[39] and Hamadi Sammoud on Yaḥyā b. Sallām[40] all employ traditional biographical material and traditional

---

[28] Pp. 117–246.

[29] Qaṭar, 1976 (but many other prints also).

[30] Rampur, 1965.

[31] Cairo, 1955–1972 (three volumes).

[32] Shfaram, Israel, 1980.

[33] See note 19.

[34] "Early *tafsīr*: A Survey of Qurʾānic Commentary up to 150 AH," in K. Ahmad, Z.I. Ansari, eds., *Islamic Perspectives: Studies in Honour of Mawlana Sayyid Abul Aʿla Mawdudi* (Leicester: The Islamic Foundation; Jeddah: Saudi Publishing House, 1979), pp. 135–45.

[35] "The Historical Development of Tafsīr," *Islamic Culture*, L (1976), 141–53.

[36] "Qurʾānic Exegesis and Classical Tafsīr," *Islamic Quarterly*, XII (1968), 71–119.

[37] "Ms. 1075 *tafsīr* of the Cairene Dār al-Kutub and Mujāhid's *Tafsīr*," in R. Peters, ed., *Proceedings of the 9th Congress of the Union Européenne des Arabisants et Islamisants* (Leiden: E.J. Brill, 1981), pp. 169–80.

[38] "The *Tafsīr* of Abdallah b. ʿAbbās," *Der Islam*, LVIII (1981), 125–35.

[39] "Muqātil Ibn Sulaymān," *Bar Ilan Arabic and Islamic Studies*, II (1978), xiii–xxx.

[40] "Un exégète oriental en Ifriqiya: Yaḥyâ ibn Sallâm (742–815)," *IBLA*, XXXIII (1977), 227–42.

methods of analysis (for example, that of isnād analysis) to discuss elements in the text. Wansbrough's literary approach, on the other hand, paying attention to content, style and form of presentation and their interrelationships rather than to isnāds and sources, is beginning to open new directions in approaches to texts. My own studies on texts ascribed to Ibn ʿAbbās, *Al-Lughāt fī 'l-Qurʾān*[41] and *Gharīb al-Qurʾān*[42] and a forthcoming analysis with text of al-Zuhrī, *Naskh al-Qurʾān*[43] are attempts to pursue this direction of work a little further. Wansbrough's article on Abū ʿUbayda's *Majāz al-Qurʾān*,[44] more extensive than his comments on that work in *Quranic Studies*,[45] is another example of an extended study. On this latter text, however, attention should also be paid to E. Almagor's article in the Baneth *Festschrift*[46] where the dispute over implications of the terminology is continued. Just in passing it is worthy of note that the technical terminology of tafsīr has once again received very little attention except in Wansbrough's *Quranic Studies* and his earlier article on *tafsīr* as literary figure.

Employing early tafsīr texts in a larger framework or to demonstrate other themes has yet to progress very far; the possibilities are, however, virtually endless. The development of grammar, of theology, of sectarian trends and of mysticism are all potentially traceable through a close analysis of these early works.

Tafsīr from the more classical period of Islam, after al-Ṭabarī, has rather naturally tended to attract more attention, perhaps the prime reason being the easy availability of the texts in printed editions. Major works of tafsīr continue to appear, some in welcome new editions, others in almost as welcome reprint editions. The new edition of al-Ṭabarī, edited by Shākir, reached S. 14 in volume 16 in 1969[47] but since then no further volumes have appeared, although rumors continue to circulate about having the rest printed elsewhere. Many

---

[41] "Ibn ʿAbbās's *al-Lughāt fī 'l-Qurʾān*," *Bulletin of the School of Oriental and African Studies*, XLIV (1981), 15–25.

[42] "Ibn ʿAbbās's *Gharīb al-Qurʾān*," *Bulletin of the School of Oriental and African Studies*, XLVI (1983).

[43] "Al-Zuhrī, *Naskh al-Qurʾān* and the Problem of early *tafsīr* Texts," *Bulletin of the School of Oriental and African Studies*, XLVII (1984).

[44] "*Majāz al-Qurʾān*: periphrastic exegesis," *Bulletin of the School of Oriental and African Studies*, XXXIII (1970), 247–66.

[45] Pp. 219–21 and 228–29.

[46] "The early Meaning of *Majāz* and the nature of Abū ʿUbayda's exegesis," *Studia Orientalia: Memoriae D.H. Baneth Dedicata* (Jerusalem: Magnes Press, 1979), pp. 307–26.

[47] Abū Jaʿfar al-Ṭabarī, *Jāmiʿ al-Bayān ʿan Taʾwīl Āy al-Qurʾān* (Cairo, 1954–1969).

works by Ibn Taymiyya,[48] Ibn al-Anbārī[49] and al-Zajjāj,[50] just to cite very few examples, have all appeared recently.

Various specific works of classical tafsīr have recently also received concentrated attention. Abdus Sattar on al-Ḥīrī,[51] and Roger Arnaldez[52] and Jacques Jomier[53] on al-Rāzī have raised general and specific issues in these works. A number of Arabic works have also been published, among them studies on al-Rummānī,[54] al-Zamakhsharī[55] and al-Wāḥidī.[56] The theological implications of tafsīr have received attention, for example, in the whole series of articles by Lutpi Ibrahim on al-Zamakhsharī and al-Bayḍāwī,[57] and in the contributions by Manfred Götz[58] and Ahmad M.A. Galli[59] on Māturīdī and that by Mazher ud-Din Siddiqi on the general Muʿtazilite approach in Qur'ān interpretation.[60] Interreligious and polemical interest in terms of tafsīr have raised substantial interest, especially in the journal *Islamochristiana* in

---

[48] Many of his works have been printed recently; see for example *Tafsīr Sūrat al-Nūr* (Kuwait, 1977); *Muqaddima fī Uṣūl al-Tafsīr* (Kuwait/Beirut, 1971).

[49] *Al-Bayān fī Gharīb Iʿrāb al-Qur'ān* (Cairo, 1970).

[50] *Iʿrāb al-Qur'ān wa Maʿānīhi* (Cairo, 1963–1965).

[51] "Al-Ḥīrī's Kifāyat al-Qur'ān: a rare MS on exegesis of the Qur'ān," *Islamic Studies*, XVI (1977), 117–30.

[52] "Trouvailles philosophiques dans le commentaire coranique de Fakhr al-Dīn al-Rāzī," *Études philosophiques et littéraires*, III (1968), 11–24.

[53] "Les mafatiḥ al-ghayb de l'imam Fakhr al-Din al-Razi: quelques dates, lieux, manuscripts," *Mélanges de l'Institut Dominicain d'études orientales du Caire*, XIII (1977), 253–90; "Unité de Dieu, Chrétiens et Coran selon Faḫr al-Dīn al-Rāzī," *Islamochristiana*, VI (1980), 149–77; "Qui a commenté l'ensemble des sourates al-ʿankabūt à yāsīn (29–36) dans 'le tafsīr al-kabīr' de l'imām Fakhr al-Dīn al-Rāzī?," *International Journal of Middle East Studies*, XI (1980), 467–85.

[54] Māzin al-Mubārak, *Al-Rummānī al-Naḥwī* (Beirut, 1974).

[55] M.S. Juwaynī, *Minḥaj al-Zamakhsharī fī Tafsīr al-Qur'ān* (Cairo, 1959).

[56] Jawdat M.M. al-Mahdī, *Al-Wāḥidī wa minhajuhu fī 'l-tafsīr* (Cairo, 1978).

[57] "Al-Bayḍāwī's life and works," *Islamic Studies*, XVIII (1979), 311–21; "A comparative Study of the Views of az-Zamakhsharī and al-Bayḍāwī about the Position of the Grave Sinner," *Islamic Studies*, XXI (1982), 55–73; "The Concept of Divine Justice according to al-Zamakhsharī and al-Bayḍāwī," *Hamdard Islamicus*, III (1980), 3–17; "The Concept of *Iḥbāṭ* and *Takfīr* according to az-Zamakhsharī and al-Bayḍāwī," *Die Welt des Orient*, XI (1980), 117–21; "The Place of Intercession in the Theology of al-Zamakhsharī and al-Bayḍāwī," *Hamdard Islamicus*, IV (1981), 3–9; "The Questions of the Superiority of Angels and Prophets between az-Zamakhsharī and al-Bayḍāwī," *Arabica*, XXVIII (1981), 65–75; "The Relation of Reason and Revelation in the Theology of az-Zamakhsharī and al-Bayḍāwī," *Islamic Culture*, LIV (1980), 63–74; "Az-Zamakhsharī: his Life and Works," *Islamic Studies*, XIX (1980), 95–110.

[58] "Māturīdī und sein Kitāb Ta'wīlāt al-Qur'ān," *Der Islam*, XLI (1965), 27–70. One volume of the *tafsīr* has appeared in print, Cairo, 1970.

[59] "Some Aspects of al-Māturīdī's Commentary on the Qur'ān," *Islamic Studies*, XXI (1982), 3–21.

[60] "Some Aspects of the Muʿtazilī Interpretation of the Qur'ān," *Islamic Studies*, II (1963), 95–120.

general, and for example in articles by Khalil Samir[61] and Abdel Majid Charfi[62] on al-Ṭabarī and J.M. Gaudeul, with R. Caspar, on *taḥrīf*.[63] Grammatical studies have been the focus of Michael Schub's dissertation[64] and many articles[65] through the means of al-Zamakhsharī's commentary. Finally, simple presentation of interesting tafsīr material continues to attract, for example in C.E. Bosworth's account of Ibn Taymiyya's treatment of Shuʿayb.[66]

Wider studies employing classical tafsīr are still not frequent in appearance but what has been done indicates the possibilities: Jane Smith's published dissertation *An Historical and Semantic Study of the Term 'Islām' as seen in a Sequence of Qurʾān Commentaries*[67] and her book with Yvonne Y. Haddad, *The Islamic Understanding of Death and Resurrection*[68] are both excellent illustrations. In a more minor way, Uri Rubin's article on Abū Lahab[69] traces the material successfully through commentaries, although the study is marred, in my perception, by its pursuit of the "true meaning" of the verse. John Burton's work, *The Collection of the Qurʾān*,[70] is also at least superficially concerned with a limited number of *naskh* and other legal -tafsīr texts, but the distance between his theories and the actual texts he is using is immense and for the most part his work cannot be considered a study in tafsīr except in the most peripheral way. Finally

---

[61] "Le commentaire de Ṭabarī sur Coran 2/62 et la question du salut des non-musulmans," *Annali Naples Instituto Orientale*, XL (N.S. XXX) (1980), 555–617.

[62] "Christianity in the Qurʾan Commentary of Ṭabarī," *Islamochristiana*, VI (1980), 105–48.

[63] "Textes de la tradition musulmane concernant le *taḥrîf* (falsification) des écritures," *Islamochristiana*, VI (1980), 61–104.

[64] "Linguistic Topics in al-Zamakhsharī's Commentary on the Qurʾān" (Ph.D. dissertation, University of California at Berkeley, 1977).

[65] Many of Schub's articles are also found in his dissertation (which even includes copies of proofs of various published works!); others include "A Sublime Subtlety?" *Zeitschrift für arabische Linguistik*, VI (1981), 72–73 (cf. M.G. Carter in *Zeitschrift für arabische Linguistik*, VII [1982], 79–81)—this article is mainly concerned with al-Rāzī; "It is Easier for a Cable to go through the Eye of a Needle than for a rich Man to enter God's Kingdom," *Arabica*, XXIII (1976), 311–12 (cf. A. Rippin in *Arabica*, XXVII (1980), 107–13); "Three Syntactic Discussions in al-Zamaḫšarī's Commentary," *Al-Andalus*, XLII (1977), 465–69; also several articles in the *Journal of the American Association of Teachers of Arabic*, VII, X, XI (1975, 1977, 1978).

[66] "The Qur'anic Prophet Shu'aib and Ibn Taimiyya's epistle concerning him," *Le Museon*, LXXXVII (1974), 425–40, reprinted in his *Medieval Arabic Culture and Administration* (London: Variorum Reprints, 1982).

[67] Missoula: Scholars Press, 1975.

[68] Albany: State University of New York Press, 1981.

[69] Abū Lahab and Sūra CXI," *Bulletin of the School of Oriental and African Studies*, XLII (1979), 13–28.

[70] Cambridge: Cambridge University Press, 1977.

Mohammed Arkoun's study of S. 18[71] is a stimulating and valuable attempt to construct a new method of reading—that is, of interpreting—the Qur'ān in the modern context, but while doing so he compares and contrasts the methods of the classical exegetes in a most enlightening and revealing manner.

Other specific types of classical tafsīr have drawn attention in varying degrees. *Tajwīd*, the art and practice of recitation, has been treated by Muhammad Abul Quasem in his translation of al-Ghazālī in *The Recitation and Interpretation of the Qur'ān*;[72] the partial translation of Labid as-Said's *The Recited Qur'ān*[73] also provides a traditional opinion on this subject. Fred Denny's article on "Exegesis and recitation: their development as classical forms of Qur'ānic piety" in the Kitagawa *Festschrift*[74] is also a fair summary of the subject. Denny is preparing a translation of al-Nawawī's *al-Tibyān fī Ḥamalat al-Qur'ān* which will be a welcome addition when it arrives. One of the few truly technical studies of tajwīd and its styles is M. Talbi's article on *qirā'a bi 'l-alḥān*.[75] While the related field of *al-waqf wa 'l-ibtidā'* has received attention through the publication of original texts, most valuably that of al-Anbārī,[76] no detailed studies have yet appeared on this important matter. The relationship between exegesis and styles and methods of recitation, which is interlocked with the notion of verse endings, needs careful study and consideration.

One field where a number of researchers are producing results is the *qiṣaṣ al-anbiyā'*. Jan Pauliny has published numerous articles on several texts, including that of al-Kisā'ī;[77] R.G. Khoury has produced

---

[71] "Lecture de la Sourate 18," *Annales: Économies, Sociétés, Civilisations*, XXXV (1980), 418–35; also see his forthcoming *Lectures du Coran* (Paris: Maisonneuve-Larose).

[72] *The Recitation and Interpretation of the Qur'ān: Al-Ghazālī's Theory* (Kuala Lumpur: M.A. Quasem, 1979).

[73] *The Recited Koran: A History of the First Recorded Version* (Princeton: Darwin Press, 1975).

[74] "Exegesis and Recitation: Their Development as Classical Forms of Qur'ānic Piety," in F.E. Reynolds, T.M. Ludwig, *Transitions and Transformations in the History of Religions* (Leiden: E.J. Brill, 1981), pp. 91–123.

[75] "La qirā'a bi-l-alḥān," *Arabica*, V (1958), 183–90.

[76] *Al-Īḍāḥ li 'l-Waqf wa 'l-Ibtidā'* (Damascus, 1971).

[77] "Einige Bemurkungen zu den Werken 'Qiṣaṣ al-Anbiyā' in der Arabischen Literatur," *Graecolatina et Orientalia*, I (1969), 111–23; "Glossen zur Arabischen eschatologischen Volksliteratur," *Graecolatina et Orientalia*, IX–X (1977–8), 209–23; "Kisā'ī und sein Werk Kitāb ʿAǧā'ib al-Malakūt I" and "II," *Graecolatina et Orientalia*, VI (1974), 157–89 and VII–VIII (1978), 217–50; "Kisā'īs Werk *Kitāb Qiṣaṣ al-Anbiyā*," *Graecolatina et Orientalia*, II (1970), 191–282; "Literarisches Charakter des Werkes Kisā'īs *Kitāb Qiṣaṣ al-Anbiyā*," *Graecolatina et Orientalia*, III (1971), 107–25; "Ein Werk '*Qiṣaṣ al-Anbiyā'* von *Abū ʿAbdallāh Muḥammad ibn Saʿīd al-Ḥiǧrī al-Aḫbārī*,"

the edition and study of the text by al-Fārisī[78] and a related article.[79] Finally, M.J. Kister is at work on the previously unknown text by Abū ʿUbayd on the *qiṣaṣ* and hopes that it will appear shortly. Questions concerning the sources of this type of material, much like questions concerning the source of tafsīr material generally, have yet to be raised. While the use of the Bible in tafsīr has been studied by Khoury,[80] Kister,[81] Gerard Lecomte[82] and Gordon Newby,[83] there is much more to be done. The recent translation of al-Kisāʾī's *Qiṣaṣ al-Anbiyāʾ*[84] reveals by the very paucity of its annotations the need for this kind of work. Haim Schwarzbaum's *Biblical and Extra-Biblical Legends in Islamic Folk-Literature*[85] although poorly written provides a wealth of material for future research in this direction. Note should especially be made of his 32 page bibliography.

Aḥkām texts have benefited from the re-editing of Ibn al-ʿArabī's text[86] and the republication of al-Jaṣṣāṣ.[87] Muqātil's work, already mentioned,[88] has filled in a valuable early gap. Little work has been done with the material though. *ʿUlūm al-Qurʾān* likewise have received a boost with the excellent new edition by Muḥammad Faḍl Ibrāhīm of

---

Asian and African Studies (Bratislava), VI (1970), 87–91; "Zur rolle der quṣṣāṣ bei der Entstehung und Überlieferung der populären Prophetenlegenden," *Asian and African Studies* (Bratislava), X (1974), 125–41.

[78] *Les légendes prophétiques dans l'Islam depuis le Ier jusqu'au IIe siècle de l'Hégire* (Wiesbaden: Harrassowitz, 1978).

[79] "Die Bedeutung der Handschrift Badʾ al-ḫalq wa qiṣaṣ al-anbiyāʾ des Abū Rifāʿa ʿUmāra b. Waṯīma b. Mūsā b. al-Furāt al-Fārisī für die Erforschung des Frühislams," *Zeitschrift der Deutschen Morgenländischen Gesellschaft, Supplementa II. XVIII Deutscher Orientalistentag von 1. bis zum 5. Oktober 1972 in Lübeck* (Wiesbaden: Harrassowitz, 1974), pp. 186–91.

[80] "Quelques réflexions sur les citations de la Bible dans les premières générations Islamiques du premier et du deuxième siècles de l'Hégire," *Bulletin d'études Orientales,* XXIX (1977), 269–78.

[81] "*Ḥaddithū ʿan banī isrāʾīla wa-lā ḥaraja,*" *Israel Oriental Studies,* II (1972), 215–39.

[82] "Les citations de l'ancien et du nouveau testament dans l'oeuvre d'Ibn Qutayba," *Arabica,* V (1958), 34–46.

[83] "Tafsir Isra'iliyat," *Journal of the American Academy of Religion,* XLVII (1979), Supplement, 685–97; "Abraha and Sennacherib: A Talmudic Parallel to the *Tafsīr* on *Sūrat al-Fīl,*" *Journal of the American Oriental Society,* XCIV (1974), 431–37. Also David J. Halperin and Gordon D. Newby, "Two Castrated Bulls: A Study in the Haggadah of Kaʿb al-Aḥbar," *Journal of the American Oriental Society,* CII (1982), 631–38.

[84] Translated by W.M. Thackston Jr., *The Tales of the Prophets of al-Kisaʾi* (Boston: Twayne, 1978).

[85] Walldorf-Hessen: Verlag für Orientkunde Dr. H. Vorndran, 1982 (Beiträge zur Sprach- und Kulturgeschichte des Orients, Band 30).

[86] *Aḥkām al-Qurʾān* (Cairo, 1967).

[87] *Aḥkām al-Qurʾān* (Beirut, n.d.).

[88] See above note 32.

al-Suyūṭī's *al-Itqān*[89] and with the publication of al-Zarkashī's *al-Burhān*.[90] These two texts and their interrelationship were the subject of a Hartford dissertation by Kenneth Nolin.[91]

Naskh texts have been the subject of an article by Ahmad Hasan[92] and at least documented in the previously mentioned work of Burton.[93] Muṣṭafā Zayd's Arabic book, *al-Naskh fī 'l-Qur'ān al-Karīm*,[94] while arguing his own peculiar point of view, provides a very valuable compilation of information. As far as naskh texts go, Burton has apparently prepared an edition of Abū ʿUbayd's work while I am at work on the text by al-Baghdādī and also the short work ascribed to al-Zuhrī; the latter will be published shortly.[95] Furthermore, the publication of Makkī al-Qaysī's naskh text[96] means that in the near future this sub-discipline of tafsīr should be well documented in original texts at the very least. *Asbāb al-nuzūl* texts were the focus of my McGill dissertation from which at least the bibliographical sections will probably appear shortly;[97] the re-editing of al-Wāḥidī's text on the subject by Aḥmad Ṣaqr[98] was certainly a valuable service for the study of this material. *Iʿjāz* or stylistics in general, have been looked at by Max Weisweiler in the context of al-Jurjānī[99] and by Heinz Grotzfeld in a more general way.[100]

Sectarian tafsīr continues to receive minimal attention, as does the whole field of the Shīʿa in general. Abdul's work on al-Ṭabarsī along with his dissertation on the same subject (which has been published) is one of the few that have appeared.[101] Two articles which will be

---

89 *Al-Itqān fī ʿUlūm al-Qur'ān* (Cairo, 1967).

90 *Al-Burhān fī ʿUlūm al-Qur'ān* (Cairo, 1957).

91 "The *Itqān* and its Sources: A Study of *Al-Itqān fī ʿUlūm al-Qur'ān* by Jalāl al-Dīn al-Suyūṭī with special Reference to *Al-Burhān fī ʿUlūm al-Qur'ān* by Badr al-Dīn al-Zarkashī" (Ph.D. dissertation, Hartford Seminary, 1968).

92 "The Theory of Naskh," *Islamic Studies*, IV (1965), 181–200.

93 See above note 70.

94 Cairo, 1963.

95 See above note 42.

96 *Al-Īḍāḥ li Nāsikh al-Qur'ān wa Mansūkhihi* (Riyad, 1975). Note, too, that a number of other *tafsīr* works by Makkī have been printed recently, e.g., *Mushkil Iʿrāb al-Qur'ān* (Damascus, 1974) and *Al-Kashf ʿan Wujūh al-Qirā'āt al-Sabʿ wa ʿIlalihā wa Hijājihā* (Damascus, 1974).

97 "The Qur'anic *asbāb al-nuzūl* Material: An Analysis of its Use and Development in Exegesis" (Ph.D. dissertation, McGill University, 1981).

98 Al-Wāhidī, *Kitāb Asbāb Nuzūl al-Qur'ān* (Cairo, 1975).

99 "ʿAbdalqāhir al-Curcānī's Werk über die Unnachahmlichkeit des Korans und seine Syntaktisch-Stilistischen Lehren," *Oriens*, XI (1958), 77–121.

100 "Der Begriff der Unnachahmlichkeit des Korans in seiner Entstehung und Fortbildung," *Archiv fur Begriffsgeschichte*, XIII (1969), 58–72.

101 Musa O.A. Abdul, "The unnoticed *mufassir* Shaykh Ṭabarsī," *Islamic Quarterly*, XV (1971), 96–105; *The Qur'ān: Shaykh Ṭabarsī's Commentary* (Lahore, Ashraf, 1979).

published shortly will perhaps provide a boost to the field: Mahmud Ayoub, "The Speaking Qur'ān and the Silent Qur'ān: A Study of the Principles and Development of Imāmī Shīʿite exegesis" and Azim Nanji, "Towards a Hermeneutic of Qur'ānic and other Narratives in Ismāʿīlī Thought."[102]

Ṣūfī tafsīr, on the other hand, has been the focus of attention for a number of productive scholars, of whom the most outstanding was of course the late Paul Nwyia whose many works, both text editions and studies, added valuable insights.[103] Quasem's article on al-Ghazālī's defense of Ṣūfī interpretation provides some documentation of a crucial subject.[104] Gerhard Böwering's published McGill dissertation on al-Tustarī[105] is a model of both source criticism and thematic analysis of individual tafsīr texts which should serve as an example to all later workers in the field. Böwering continues to work in the field, most especially on al-Sulamī's tafsīr. Rashid Ahmad's general history of tafsīr has a valuable section on Ṣūfī texts especially concerning the person of al-Qushayrī, the subject of his dissertation.[106]

As has frequently been noted by writers in the discipline, the modern Islamic world continues to produce tafsīrs in vast quantities and it seems pointless even to try to list any of them here. They range tremendously in approach, stretching from repetition of traditional information to the introduction of new points of view and methods. Critical studies of modern tafsīr are fairly abundant also; two basic texts have appeared, summarizing trends in interpretation, J.M.S. Baljon covering the years 1880 to 1960[107] and J.J.G. Jansen on specifically the Egyptian situation.[108] Jomier's book on the Manār school[109] was noted by Jeffery but Jomier has continued to work in the

---

[102] Both will appear in Richard C. Martin, ed., *Islam and the History of Religions: Essays in Methodology.*

[103] "Le *tafsīr* mystique attribué à Ǧaʿfar Ṣādiq," *Mélanges de l'Université Saint-Joseph,* XLIII (1967), 179–230; also see above note 13.

[104] M.A. Quasem, "Al-Ghazālī in defence of Ṣūfistic Interpretation of the Qur'ān," *Islamic Culture,* LIII (1979), 63–86.

[105] *The Mystical Vision of Existence in Classical Islam: The Qur'ānic Hermeneutics of the Ṣūfī Sahl al-Tustarī (d. 283/896)* (Berlin: DeGruyter, 1980).

[106] See above note 36; also "Abū al-Qāsim al-Qushairī as a Theologian and Commentator, a Critique of his Age and his Work on the Qur'ānic Exegesis" (Ph.D. dissertation, SOAS London, 1969).

[107] *Modern Muslim Koran Interpretation (1880–1960)* (Leiden: E.J. Brill, 1961).

[108] *The Interpretation of the Koran in Modern Egypt* (Leiden: E.J. Brill, 1974).

[109] Jacques Jomier, *Le commentaire coranique de Manār. Tendances modernes de l'exégèse coranique en Égypte* (Paris: G.-P. Maisonneuve, 1954).

field after that point, producing articles on Amīn al-Khūlī,[110] Ṭanṭāwī Jawharī[111] and Egypt in general.[112] Other persons treated include Mawdūdī by F.K. Abbott,[113] Jawhārī by F. De Jong,[114] Azad by I.H.A. Faruqi,[115] Bint al-Shāti' by Issa Boullata,[116] Quṭb by Yvonne Haddad,[117] and Muṣṭafā Maḥmūd and Aḥmad Khalaf Allāh by Marc Chartier.[118]

One of the surprising elements in tafsīr studies is that we still lack a general introduction to the subject as a whole. Some attempts have been made to provide introductory overviews, for example in sections of Kenneth Cragg's *The Mind of the Qur'ān*[119] and in Ilse Lichtenstadter's article "Quran and Quran exegesis."[120] There still remains, however, a need for a suitable textbook to introduce students and fellow Islamicists to the general field in an appropriately technical manner. Helmut Gätje's work,[121] compiling various pieces of tafsīr at least provides a taste of the material but little else. But one should not complain about this book too loudly, for translations of tafsīr material are sorely lacking with A.F.L. Beeston's translation of al-Bayḍāwī on S. 12, one of the few extended pieces to have been published in recent years.[122] Its presence in paperback now at least provides students of

---

[110] J. Jomier and P. Caspar, "L'exégèse scientifique du Coran d'après le Cheikh Amin al-Khouli," *Mélanges de l'Institut Dominicain d'études orientales du Caire,* IV (1957), 269–80.

[111] "Le Cheikh Tantawi Jawhari (1862–1940) et son commentaire du Coran," *Mélanges de l'Institut Dominicain d'études orientales du Caire,* V (1958), 115–74.

[112] "Quelques positions actuelles de l'exégèse coranique en Egypte revelées par une polémique recente (1947–1951), *Mélanges de l'Institut Dominicain d'études orientales du Caire,* I (1954), 39–72.

[113] "Mawlana Maududi and Quranic Interpretation, *M.W.*, XLVIII (1958), 6–19.

[114] "The Works of Ṭanṭāwī Jawharī (1862–1940). Some Bibliographical and Biographical Notes," *Bibliotheca Orientalis,* XXXIV (1977), 153–61.

[115] *The Tarjuman al-Qur'an: a critical analysis of Maulana Abu'l-Kalam Azad's Approach to the Understanding of the Qur'an* (Delhi: Vikas, 1982).

[116] "Modern Qur'ān Exegesis: A Study of Bint al-Shāṭi's Method," *M.W.*, LXIV (1974), 103–13.

[117] Yvonne Y. Haddad, "The Qur'anic Justification for an Islamic Revolution: the View of Sayyid Quṭb," *The Middle East Journal,* XXXVII (1983), 14–29.

[118] "Muhammad Ahmad Khalaf Allâh et l'exégèse coranique," *IBLA*, XXIX (1976), 1–31; "Un essai récent d'interpretation du Coran: Muṣṭafā Maḥmūd," *Oriente Moderno,* LII (1972), 716–28.

[119] *The Mind of the Qur'ān: Chapters in Reflection* (London: George Allen and Unwin, 1973).

[120] "Quran and Quran Exegesis," *Humaniora Islamica,* II (1974), 3–28.

[121] *Koran und Koranexegese* (Zürich: Artemis Verlag, 1971), translation by Alford T. Welch, *The Qur'ān and its Exegesis* (Berkeley: University of California Press, 1976).

[122] *Baiḍāwī's Commentary on Sūrah 12 of the Qur'ān* (Oxford: Oxford University Press, 1963).

Arabic with a readily accessible text for learning how to read this sometimes obscure material. The translation of al-Kisā'ī[123] mentioned above is the only full-length translation of any classical tafsīr work of which I am aware. Translations of modern tafsīr are not much more frequent than classical ones, with Sayyid Quṭb,[124] Mawdūdī[125] and Azad's[126] works appearing but little else available except works originally written in Western languages.[127]

To conclude, two final points must be raised. One is the desperate need for bibliographical control in our subject. It is increasingly difficult to stay aware of all the tafsīr editions appearing from all over the Islamic world, most especially for those of us who are in universities where for example Arabic, Persian, Urdu, and Indonesian books are acquired infrequently. While *Quarterly Index Islamicus* remains an effective tool for keeping an eye on Western language materials, those of us interested in tafsīr must by some means coordinate bibliographical activities especially for original texts.

The other point which needs attention is the production of a historical synthesis of Islamic exegesis to finally replace Goldziher's *Richtungen*. Through the convening of a conference at the University of Calgary in 1985 with invited papers on various topics, it is my hope that the resultant publication of the papers will at least be a step along the way to this very desirable end.

---

[123] See above note 84.

[124] *In the Shade of the Qur'ān* (London: Muslim World Publishers, 1980).

[125] *The Meaning of the Qur'ān* (Lahore, 1967).

[126] *Tarjumān al-Qur'ān* (Bombay: Asia Publishing House, 1965).

[127] For example, the notes which accompany A. Yusuf Ali, *The Holy Qur'ān* (Beirut, 1968 and many other prints).

XII

Interpreting the Bible through the Qur'ān

It is commonly stated that Muslims approach the Bible with the attitude that when the biblical text agrees with the Qur'ān, the statements may be accepted, but when it disagrees, the Qur'ān is to be preferred.[1] The aim of this paper is to sketch out the ramifications this attitude has had in practice and to put it in historical perspective. This paper is no more than an attempt to outline a field of study and investigate some of its potential directions.[2] Clearly, there is a lot of work to be done here, both conceptually, in discovering new approaches to the material, and constructively, in bringing disparate sources together for analysis. It is significant to note that Muslims themselves have generally not separated out this field of biblical interpretation-allusion within their own intellectual systematizations; this is not a 'genre' of *tafsīr*. From a Muslim perspective, it may well be said that this question cannot be separated from the notion of quranic interpretation in general. Yet, from a modern academic perspective, such a topic seems to have legitimacy by virtue of the way in which it reflects an investigator's own interests and construction of reality. That is, quranic studies as a modern, academic discipline cannot, even must not, stay within the intellectual constraints (as it often does) of what are frequently the medieval Muslim efforts towards the categorization of knowledge (as represented, for example, in the works of al-Suyūṭī). Our intellectual efforts to make sense of the world around us must reflect our own understandings and form our knowledge into meaningful elements of our own world view.

I

There are essentially three areas of literature which need to be covered under the rubric of Muslim interpretation of the Bible: the use of biblical material in the Qur'ān itself, its use in *tafsīr* material especially the *qiṣaṣ al-anbiyā'*, and its use in polemical literature. The modern context provides what might be considered an additional area for study, because of the manner in which it frequently brings all three of these elements together into one unit.

Within itself, the Qur'ān provides Muslims with a view of the Bible. Mention is made of the 'scrolls' of Abraham and Moses, the *Tawrāt* (Torah) of Moses, the *Zabūr* (usually understood as the Psalms) of David and the *Injīl* (Gospel) of Jesus, all conceived as direct revelation from God to the prophet concerned: 'Surely We sent down the Torah, wherein is guidance and light' (Qur'ān 5.48); 'And We sent, following in their footsteps, Jesus son of Mary, confirming the Torah before him; and We gave to him the Gospel, wherein is guidance and light' (Qur'ān 5.50). In this way, all previous scriptures are pictured within the revelatory and compositional image of the Qur'ān itself. Additionally, the Muslim scripture is seen to be a confirmation of these earlier revelations; it also serves to make disputed matters clear: 'We have sent down to thee the Remembrance [i.e. the Qur'ān] that thou mayest make clear to mankind what was sent down to them' (Qur'ān 16.46). The Qur'ān also serves a correcting function: humans have misinterpreted and tampered with the works of Moses and Jesus especially; people have been 'perverting words from their meanings' (Qur'ān 5.45). The Qur'ān thus presents an uncorrupted version of the word of God and all scripture culminates in the Qur'ān, according to Muslim interpretation of these verses.[3]

The Qur'ān retells stories found in the Bible in a recognizable form but the accounts are always shorn of their overall biblical narrative context. Frequently the stories are truncated to such an extent that reference to the biblical tradition is necessary in order to make sense of the narrative elements provided in the Qur'ān. Some of the stories are clearly influenced by the exegetical tradition within Judaism and, to a lesser extent, Christianity.[4] The exact source of the stories – variously suggested to be Arabian Jews or Christians, Samaritans, remnants of the Qumran community, Jewish-Christian groups and so forth – remains a matter of debate,[5] but a great deal of emphasis in contemporary research falls on the oral nature of the transmission of the biblical material into the Arabic context in accounting for the form and the content of the narrative.[6]

Scholarship has not, as yet, it seems to me, paid much attention to the actual issue of the interpretation of the Bible from within the quranic perspective. Of far greater concern up to this point has been the attempt to establish the sources of the basic information itself. A few generalities may be suggested, however. It is clear that the biblical stories are cited not for their narrative or historical significance but for their spiritual and moral guidance, most especially in emphasizing the notion of God's determination of, and involvement in, history. The constant suggestion in the citation of the stories of the prophets of the past (starting with Adam and mentioning Noah, Isaac, Ishmael, Lot, Aaron, Ezra, Zechariah, John and so on, for example) is that God has sent messengers in the past with their message but the people have rejected both the message and the messengers. As a result, punishment has come down upon each community and God has thereby triumphed in the end. This stylized narrative plot line is illustrated by isolated episodes or single details from the life of individual prophets, stories which are familiar from the biblical tradition as a whole. Muḥammad's own career is frequently pictured in terms of this plot. Combined with this constant narrative element in the Qur'ān is a reworking of the Abrahamic tradition in the light of Muḥammad.[7] Abraham becomes the pivotal figure in the quranic picture of salvation history, seen as living before the Judaism of Moses and the Christianity of Jesus. This is the true faith, *hanīfiyya*, which Muḥammad revives in Makka, where Abraham had established the shrine known as the Ka'ba to the glory of God. The sense in which the Qur'ān 'reworks' this biblical material is limited, however; for the most part, the quranic position on Abraham is assumed or hinted at, rather than explicitly detailed and proven on the basis of proof-texts or the like.

II

Because of the truncated and referential style in the quranic citation of biblical material which presupposed knowledge on the part of its audience of the actual details of the narratives,[8] the emergent Muslim community was faced with the problem of how to understand its own scripture once the original Judeo-Christian environment was left behind and Islam was established as the religion of the newly-formed and widespread Arab empire. On the evidence of extant literary sources, this matter became problematic some 150 years after the death of Muḥammad; at this time, we see the emergence of *tafsīr*: written works providing interpretation of the Qur'ān and thus, given the content of the scriptural text itself, providing a view of Muslim interpretation of the Bible.[9]

One of the earliest such works still extant is that ascribed to Muqātil ibn Sulaymān (d. 767), which clearly displays the way in which biblical materials were interpreted and incorporated into the Muslim tradition in order to complete and supplement the bare bones of the Bible as presented in the Qur'ān.[10] The interpretation of the biblical text is generally left on the level of providing the narrative elements which were needed to embellish the Qur'ān text; certainly the Bible never becomes of relevance to legal issues within the Muslim community itself, nor, generally, for any theological judgements.[11]

Many early Muslim writers, including such people as Ibn Isḥāq (d. 767),[12] al-Jāḥiẓ (d. 869)[13] and Ibn Qutayba (d. 889),[14] display a certain measure of acquaintance with the actual text of the Bible itself. The recent publication of the book by Abū 'Ubayd (d. 838), *Kitāb al-khuṭab wa'l-mawā'iẓ*,[15] provides an interesting illustration of this type of knowledge. In recounting various speeches of the ancient prophets, Abū 'Ubayd often indirectly cites biblical passages; sometimes these are cited as being 'quotations' from the 'scrolls of Abraham and Moses'[16] *but on other, more interesting, occasions, the passages provide what might be best termed 'allusions':*

> Abū 'Ubayd told us that Yazīd ibn Hārūn said on the authority of Abū Ma'shar on the authority of Sa'īd ibn Abī Sa'īd al-Maqburī that he said: 'A man came to Jesus, son of Mary, and said "O teacher of good deeds! Teach me something which you know but I do not, which will serve me well but not harm you." Jesus said, "What might that be?" The man said, "How can the servant be faithful to God?" Jesus replied, "That is simple. You should love God truly from your heart, work for God through your exertion and strength as much as you are able, and treat your brothers (*banū jinsika*) compassionately through your mercy and selflessness." The man said, "O teacher of good deeds! Who are my brothers?" Jesus replied, "All of the offspring of Adam. Whatever you consider to be inappropriate for yourself, do not inflict upon others. In this way, you are truly faithful to God."'[17]

This sort of passage cannot be taken simply as imaginative quranic exegesis: its allusion to the New Testament is evident and while it may not prove the case for actual knowledge of the biblical text itself, it does demonstrate that Muslims were, at an early stage, working with more raw material in their elaborations of the Qur'ān than their imaginations. Indeed, one of the purposes of citing the Bible as these authors did, may have been to provide a check on the more imaginative embellishments which were being made in the interpretation of the Qur'ān in general which were often claimed to stem from the Bible or Jewish and Christian sources. These exegetical excesses, at times, went to the extent of creating wholely spurious texts going under the name of *Tawrāt* or *Zabūr*, examples of which still exist.[18]

The tendency to incorporate biblical materials into the Islamic tradition, and to Islamicize them in doing so (and thus, it might be suggested, picking up on the Qur'ān's own way of retelling biblical stories), sees its ultimate manifestations in the genre of literature known as the *dalā'il al-nubuwwa*, the 'proofs of prophecy', and especially the *qiṣaṣ al-anbiyā'*, the 'stories of the prophets'. These latter tales, several of which are available in whole or in part in English translation,[19] display the end result of the exegetical process: a history of the prophets of the past, recounted in an order which for the most part accepts the biblical chronology, focused around passages of the Qur'ān supplemented by the biblical and most especially biblical-exegetical tradition. Much of this material has become known, pejoratively, as the *isrā'īliyyāt*, stories supposedly transmitted in the Islamic world by Jewish (and Christian) converts, although the material included within this term generally encompasses far more than that.[20] Frequently viewed with suspicion by Muslims, the material has provided the basis for the legendary expansion of the picture of the past prophets, but it is always filtered through a Muslim perspective: characteristics of the Islamic conception of prophets, for example their sinlessness, mould every image; the Arabian context becomes the focal point of many stories. The stories themselves must always agree with the quranic version of the events, even if this reconciliation requires a certain amount of interpretational ingenuity.[21] Overall, it may be said that the point of all these *qiṣaṣ al-anbiyā'* books is to demonstrate the continuity of the prophets from the time of Adam down to Muḥammad. In the recounting of the lives of the prophets, there is certainly a tendency to avoid any Christian symbolic prefigurements in the events of the 'Old Testament'. Likewise, there is no emphasis on Israel as a land and Judaism's connection to it. The stories are retold, once again, for their value in enhancing the spiritual and moral guidance implicit in the Qur'ān itself. Their function is always to interpret the Qur'ān by providing an authoritative, Muslim account of earlier history.

The end result of this writing down of the interpretational process – as embodied in the *tafsīr* works, the spurious bibles and the *qiṣaṣ al-anbiyā'* genre – was that it was never necessary for Muslims to consult the Bible itself nor write commentaries upon it, for the necessary material had early on been incorporated into the Muslim exegetical literature. Another aspect of this is reflected in the way in which Muslim elaborations have then re-entered Jewish and Christian circles, especially in the exegetical material of those two religions,[22] but also, according to some, into translations of pseudepigraphical books such as the Ethiopic version of the *Life of Adam and Eve*.[23]

III

There was one specific issue, however, which caused the Muslims to look at the Bible itself and provide a more self-conscious biblical interpretation. The Qur'ān suggests that Muḥammad was spoken of in the Bible ('... the Messenger, the Prophet of the common folk, whom they find written down with them in the Torah and the Gospel', Qur'ān 7.156). The notion arose in Islam, certainly with some support from the Qur'ān itself, that these references had been removed or hidden by the Jews (rarely are the Christians attacked in this manner): 'Why do you confound the truth with vanity, and conceal the truth and that wittingly?' says Qur'ān 3.64. This alteration of the text of scripture was denoted by the term *taḥrīf*. Despite what would seem to be the consequence of this stance that there would thus be no references to Muḥammad found in the Bible, Muslims were quick to try to isolate any evidence of 'fulfilment' of earlier scripture that could be proclaimed by the coming of Muḥammad. The stimulus for this was undoubtedly Christian polemical pressure to provide proof of the validity of Islam. The earliest apologetic treatises – which are some of the earliest pieces of Islamic literature available – speak at some length about the biblical passages which refer to Muḥammad. The most famous of these, *The book of religion and empire*, written by 'Alī al-Ṭabarī probably in the mid-ninth century,[24] details a large number of passages from both Jewish and Christian scriptures which are interpreted in light of Muḥammad. Prominent passages and ones which recur throughout this type of literature down to the modern day include Genesis 17.20: 'I have heard your prayer for Ishmael. I have blessed him and made him fruitful. I will multiply his descendants; he shall be a father of twelve princes and I will raise a great nation from him', (the 'nation' was, of course, the Arabs to whom no greater promise God ever made, according to the author);[25] Deuteronomy 18.15: 'The Lord your God will raise up a prophet from among you like myself'[26] (and similarly in verse 18), interpreted to be a reference to Muḥammad rather than any of the other prophets or Jesus, none of whom, it is suggested, are actually 'from among you like myself'; Deuteronomy 33.2, with its mention of Mount Paran, identified as 'the land which Ishmael inhabited', frequently further glossed (in light of the Qur'ān) as Makka;[27] and John 14.26: 'but your Advocate [Paraclete], the Holy Spirit whom the Father will send in my name, will teach you everything,' glossed as Muḥammad, often connected to Qur'ān 61.6 with its reference to Jesus designating 'Aḥmad' as the one to come after him.[28]

This tendency to find Muḥammad in the Bible, despite its rather obvious apologetic nature, remains a popular topic in contemporary Muslim circles. This is evidenced not only by the recent editing of a series of medieval texts dealing with the topic[29] but also by works from the Muslim world in Arabic[30] and from elsewhere in, for example, English and French. All are really no more than continuations of medieval polemic. A widely circulated pamphlet by the South African Ahmed Deedat entitled 'What the Bible says about Muḥammad (Peace be upon him)' uses Deuteronomy 18.18 as its major discussion point; the prophet 'most like' Moses here is Muḥammad, not because of issues of descent as in 'Alī al-Ṭabarī, but because of such similarities as Moses and Muḥammad having a mother and father and Jesus not; Jesus having a miraculous birth and the other two not; Jesus not marrying as compared to the others, and so on. Emphasis also falls on the latter part of the biblical verse, 'I will put my words into his mouth,' as a reference to the mode of revelation of the Qur'ān to the illiterate Muḥammad. Another instance of this is in the Arabic work by al-Ṭahṭāwī, *Muḥammad nabī'l-Islām fī 'l-Tawrāt wa'l-Injīl wa'l-Qur'ān*. This work contains extensive quotations from the Bible and elaborates them in a straight-forward manner. Al-Ṭahṭāwī has included a number of typical passages in his work, which provide an interesting example of this mode of interpretation. The following details a prophecy in Micah (chapter 4, verses 1–7) :

> It will be in the last days that the mountains of the Lord's house shall be established at the top of other mountains, lifted above the hills.
> Peoples shall come streaming to it and many nations shall come and say:
> 'Come let us go up to the mountain of the Lord and to the house of the God of Jacob.
> He will teach us his ways and we will walk in his paths.'
> Because from Zion comes the law and out of Jerusalem comes the word of the Lord.
> He will be judge between many peoples.

and so on to verse 7:

> And on that day, says the Lord, I will gather the lame, and I will assemble the exiles and those who were forced (to leave).
> I will make the lame a remnant and those driven away a powerful people.
> The Lord shall rule them on Mount Zion now and for ever.

On this, al-Ṭahṭawī comments:

> This is a message that the special temple of the Lord at the end of time shall be revealed on the tops of mountains and this is a precise description of the mountain of 'Arafat and the pathway of the *ḥajj* to the Holy Mosque which Abraham and Ishmael (upon whom may there be peace) built. That message points to the word of the Lord

> that He will gather all the lame, assemble the exiles and those who have been harmed and taken away, so that He may begin to produce a powerful nation of them. Those descriptions can only be connected to Hagar when she and her son Ishmael were sent far away to the land of the Ḥijāz. From his offspring comes the community of Islam.[31]

Another aspect to this polemical debate is found in attacks on the Bible and its veracity, a topic frequently subsumed under the notion *taḥrīf*.[32] Ibn Ḥazm (d. 1064), for example, while responding to supposed Jewish attacks on the Qur'ān[33], retaliates with a collection of attacks on the Bible. Muslim apologists pointed to instances of immorality in the biblical text, logical inconsistencies, absent doctrines (e.g., life after death in the Torah) and anthropomorphisms as evidence of the corrupt character of the scripture. Many of the characteristics that are seized upon by Ibn Ḥazm are precisely those which Christians especially had cast at Muslims in attacks on the latters' own scripture.

The modern world has produced other areas of thought in which the Bible is contemplated by Muslims; all such situations are tinged by polemic and apologetics. Social organization, family structure and science are some of the issues in which the attitude of the Qur'ān and the Bible are compared. Most famous in this regard is certainly Maurice Bucaille, *The Bible, the Qur'ān and science*.[34] Abū'l-A'lā al-Mawdūdī (1903–79), a prominent Pakistani religious and political leader, also uses the text of the Bible in his commentary on the Qur'ān. The purpose is not only to provide explanation of various items in the Muslim scripture but also to illustrate the errors of the Bible and the greater reliability of the quranic text; the criterion used to determine this, it is always asserted, as would be expected, is that where the Bible and the Qur'ān agree, the Bible is right; where the two disagree, the Bible is wrong.[35]

One of the few attempts made by a Muslim to write a commentary on the actual text of the Bible itself was that by Sayyid Aḥmad Khān (d. 1898). Called *The Mohomedan commentary on the Holy Bible*, it was published in 1862 and 1865. Two parts, the first being the 'Preliminary Discourse' (covering the history of the biblical text and questions of dogma) and the second (covering Genesis 1 to 11) were published in Urdu with English summaries. A portion covering Matthew 1 to 5 together with a short history of Christianity was apparently prepared at the same time but was not published until 1887 and is available in Urdu only.[36] Aḥmad Khān's general attitude is that the Bible should have a positive role in Muslim life as long as it is read in light of the quranic message, so that any distortions which have occurred as a result of Jewish and Christian misinterpretation (the only extent to which he considers *taḥrīf* to have occurred) can be corrected. His work is remarkably free of polemic and is aimed at bringing about a common understanding and inspiration through revealed scripture within the Judeo-Christian-Muslim tradition. Such tendencies continue in contemporary works such as that by the Groupe de Recherches Islamo-Chrétien, *The challenge of the scriptures: the Bible and the Qur'ān*.[37]

NOTES

1 The idea clearly stems from the notion of *taḥrīf*, alteration of scripture; see further below.

2 This paper attempts to expand, and expose to a wider, specialist audience, my article called 'Muslim interpretation of the Bible', in R. Coggins, L. Houlden, eds, *Dictionary of biblical interpretation*, London 1990. All translations from the Qur'ān are from A. J. Arberry, *The Koran interpreted*, London 1955; Arberry's verse numbering is also used. Bible translations are from *The new English Bible* (unless translated from the Arabic). I should like to express my appreciation to Professor John Burton, University of St Andrews, for his detailed and helpful response to this paper at the *Colloquium*; his continued interest in, and encouragement of, my work is greatly appreciated.

3 A good treatment of the data related to this issue is to be found in A. Jeffery, 'The Qur'ān as scripture' *The Muslim World*, XL (1950), pp. 41–55, pp. 106–34, pp. 185–206, pp. 257–75; reprinted in book form with a supplement, *The Qur'ān as scripture*, New York 1952.

4 There are, of course, many works which attempt a summary and an analysis of the material. A concise treatment is to be found in J. Jomier, *The Bible and the Koran* (French original: *Bible et Coran*), New York 1964, chapter 10. Noteworthy for its general reflections is Franz Rosenthal, 'The influence of the Biblical tradition on Muslim historiography', in B. Lewis and P. M. Holt, eds, *Historians of the Middle East*, Oxford 1962, pp. 35–45. M. S. Seale, 'How the Qur'ān interprets the Bible: towards a Christian-Muslim dialogue' in his *Qur'ān and Bible: studies in interpretation and dialogue*, London 1978, pp. 71–7, is rather superficial.

5 See the excellent discussion of this subject, with extensive bibliography, in Tryggve Kronholm, 'Dependence and prophetic originality in the Koran,' *Orientalia Suecana*, XXXI-XXXII (1982–1983), pp. 47–70.

6 See e.g. M. R. Waldman, 'New approaches to "Biblical" materials in the Qur'ān', *The Muslim World*, LXXV (1985), pp. 1–13. Also see W. M. Brinner, S. Ricks (eds), *Studies in Islamic and Judaic traditions. Papers presented at the Institute for Islamic-Judaic Studies, Center for Judaic Studies, University of Denver*, Atlanta 1986; Haim Schwarzbaum, *Biblical and extra-biblical legends in Islamic folk-literature*, Beiträge zur Sprach-und Kulturgeschichte des Orients, Bd. 30, Walldorf-Hessen, H. Vorndran 1982; this work has an extensive bibliography.

7 See A. Rippin, *Muslims, their religious beliefs and practices*, volume 1, *The formative period*, London 1990, chapter 3, for a discussion of this in the context of the mythic dimension of the Qur'ān.

8 See the discussion of this in John Wansbrough, *Quranic studies: sources and*

methods of scriptural interpretation, Oxford 1977 and A. Rippin, 'Literary analysis of Qur'ān, *sīra* and *tafsīr*: the methodologies of John Wansbrough', in R. C. Martin (ed.), *Approaches to Islam in religious studies*, Tucson 1985, pp. 151–63.

9 For a recent example of a study displaying this aspect of Muslim exegesis, see Reuven Firestone, 'Abraham's son as the intended sacrifice (*al-Dhabīḥ*, Qur'ān 37.99–113): issues in Qur'ānic exegesis', *Journal of Semitic Studies*, XXXIV (1989), pp. 95–131.

10 *Tafsīr Muqātil ibn Sulaymān*, ed. A. M. Shihāta, Cairo [1969], volume 1 only, volumes 1–5 published Cairo 1979–89.

11 However, the 'biblical' elements of the Qur'ān text are certainly relevant in the overall scheme: see Roger Arnaldez, 'Les éléments bibliques du Coran comme sources de la théologie et de la mystique musulmanes', in *Aspects de la foi de l'Islam*, Brussels 1985, pp. 29–55.

12 See e.g. A. Guillaume, 'The version of the Gospels used in Medina circa 700 A. D.,' *Al-Andalus*, XV (1950), pp. 289–96.

13 See his *Kitāb al-radd 'alā'l-Naṣārā*, ed. J. Finkel, Cairo 1926 (under the title: *Thalāth rasā'il li... al-Jāḥiẓ*), and J. Finkel, 'A Risāla of al-Jāḥiẓ', *Journal of the American Oriental Society*, XLVII (1927), pp. 311–34.

14 See G. Lecomte, 'Les citations de l'ancien et du nouveau testament dans l'oeuvre d'ibn Qutayba', *Arabica*, V (1958), pp. 34–46.

15 Edited by Ramaḍān 'Abd al-Tawwāb, Cairo 1986. On the text see Claude Gilliot, 'Textes arabes anciens édités en Egypte au cours des années 1985 à 1987', *MIDEO*, XIX (1989), pp. 319–21.

16 E.g. *ibid*., p. 125, paragraph 37.

17 *Ibid*., p. 153, paragraph 73; the editor notes that this tradition, as with many others in this book, is found in Ibn Ḥanbal, *Kitāb al-Zuhd*. Cf. Matthew 22.34–40.

18 See J. Sadan, 'Some literary problems concerning Judaism and Jewry in medieval Arabic sources,' in M. Sharon, ed., *Studies in Islamic history and civilization in honour of Professor David Ayalon*, Jerusalem / Leiden 1989, esp. pp. 370ff. and the section entitled 'The "genuine" Pentateuch (*tawrāt*) of Moses, as rediscovered and reshaped by Islamic literature'.

19 See e.g., W. M. Thackston, Jr. (trans.), *The Tales of the Prophets of al-Kisa'i*, Boston 1978 and W. M. Brinner (trans.), *The History of al-Ṭabarī*, volume 2, *Prophets and Patriarchs*, Albany 1986.

20 The rise and employment of this term *isrā'īliyyāt* deserves a special study; my impression is that it comes into wide circulation as a pejorative term in *tafsīr* – material which is not to be accepted as valid in interpretation – only with writers as late as Ibn Taymiyya (d. 1328) and Ibn Kathīr (d. 1373). This fact seems to be ignored in works such as Gordon Newby 'Tafsir Isra'iliyat', *Journal of the American Academy of Religion*, XLVII (1979), supplement, pp. 658–97. On the rise of the term, see A. J. Johns, 'David and Bathsheba. A case study in the exegesis of Qur'anic story-telling', *MIDEO*, XIX (1989), p. 263, and Norman Calder's contribution to this volume.

21 See Norman Calder, 'From Midrash to Scripture: the sacrifice of Abraham in early Islamic tradition', *Le Muséon*, CI (1988), pp. 375–402, who points also to the status of the quranic narrative itself as a link in the centuries old interpretational process.

22 See e.g., the EI 1st ed. articles of J. Heller on various biblical figures for illustrations.

23 See the references provided in J. Charlesworth, *The pseudepigrapha and modern research*, Missoula, MT 1976.

24 *Kitāb al-dīn wa'l-dawla*, ed. A. Mingana, Manchester 1923, English translation, 1922, reprinted Lahore, Law Publishing Co., n. d. Doubts have occasionally been uttered regarding the authenticity of the text but see 'Notes and News', *Bulletin of the John Rylands University Library of Manchester*, LXIX (1986), pp. 1–7.

25 English trans., pp. 77–8.

26 English trans., pp. 85–6.

27 English trans., pp. 86–7.

28 English trans., p. 140.

29 Aḥmad Ḥijāzī'l-Saqqā has been most active in this respect; see the prefaces to those editions and the citations of them in a number of G. Anawati's annual articles 'Textes arabes anciens édités en Egypte', in *MIDEO* (e.g. XVII, pp.188–9, XVIII, pp. 292–5). One example of a text which I have at hand of al-Saqqā's editing is Imām al-Ḥaramayn al-Juwaynī, *Shifā' al-Ghalīl fī bayān mā waqa'a fī'l-Tawrāt wa'l-Injīl min al-tabdīl*, Cairo 1979.

30 See e.g., James Robson, 'Does the Bible speak of Mohammed?', *The Moslem World*, XXV (1935), pp. 17–26.

31 Maḥmūd 'Izzat Ismā'īl al-Ṭahṭāwī, *Muḥammad nabī'l-Islām fī al-Tawrāt wa'l-Injīl wa'l-Qurān*, [Cairo c. 1978], p. 24.

32 See e.g., Jean-Marie Gaudeul, Robert Caspar, 'Textes de la tradition musulmane concernant le *taḥrīf* (falsification) des écritures', *Islamochristiana*, VI (1980), pp. 61–104, which covers aspects of falsification of the text as well as the meaning of scripture. Also see Norman Roth, 'Forgery and abrogation of the Torah: a theme in Muslim and Christian polemic in Spain', *Proceedings of the American Academy for Jewish Research*, LIV (1987), pp. 203–36; Harry Gaylord Dorman Jr, *Towards understanding Islam. Contemporary apologetic of Islam and missionary policy*, Columbia University, New York 1948 for a valuable overview of Muslim treatments.

33 The status of this refutation continues to be a matter of dispute; see Sarah Stroumsa, 'From Muslim heresy to Jewish-Muslim polemics: Ibn al-Rāwandī's *Kitāb al-Dāmigh*', *Journal of the American Oriental Society*, CVII (1987), pp. 767–72. Also see the citations from Ibn Ḥazm's *Kitāb al-fiṣal* in Gaudeul and Caspar, *op. cit.*, pp. 78–82.

34 English translation from French original, American Trust Pub., Indianapolis 1979.

35 See C. J. Adams, 'Abū' l-A'lā Mawdūdī's *Tafhīm al-Qur'ān*', in Andrew Rippin (ed.), *Approaches to the History of the Interpretation of the Qur'ān*, Oxford 1988, esp. pp. 317–20.

36 For some details, see Christian W. Troll, 'Sayyid Ahmad Khan on Matthew 5. 17–20', *Islamochristiana*, III (1970), pp. 99–105.

37 Translated from the French by Stuart E. Brown, Orbis Books, Maryknoll, N. Y., 1989, originally published as *Ces écritures qui nous questionnent: la Bible et le Coran*, Paris 1987.

XIII

IBN 'ABBĀS'S *AL-LUGHĀT FĪ'L-QUR'ĀN*

The study of Muslim lexicology concerned with the Qur'ān has a short but illustrious bibliography, the highlights of which may be summed up for the purposes of the following discussion by mentioning four people: Arthur Jeffery, whose *Foreign vocabulary of the Qur'ān* contains a lengthy introduction concerning various classical Muslim attempts to come to grips with the Qur'ānic lexicon;[1] Chaim Rabin, who in his *Ancient West-Arabian* attempts to use a text which deals with dialect words in the Qur'ān as one of his sources for the reconstruction of 'pre-literary Arabic dialects';[2] Lothar Kopf, who, through his articles and posthumously published dissertation extracts, exposes many of the trends and pitfalls in Arabic dictionaries, most notably those features which result from the influence of the Qur'ān;[3] and John Wansbrough, who via his *Quranic studies* has treated us to his analysis of some of the early texts and has provided some very cogent and persuasive arguments concerning the motivations behind the compilation of such treatises.[4]

The primary works underlying all these studies are texts uniformly ascribed to 'Abd Allāh ibn 'Abbās (d. *c.* 68/687), although for Jeffery and Kopf the actual texts employed were limited to those distilled primarily by al-Suyūṭī (d. 911/1505). Three such texts exist today and are listed by Sezgin under Ibn 'Abbās:[5]

1. *Gharīb al-Qur'ān*, a collection of Qur'ānic words listed by *sūra* order and given brief definitions; the work exists in two manuscripts according to Wansbrough, Atıf Efendi 2815/8, listed by Sezgin, and Esad Efendi 91 under the title *Al-Lughāt fī'l-Qur'ān* but, in fact, containing the text of *Gharīb*. Wansbrough describes the list as being 'similar' to one found in al-Suyūṭī's *al-Itqān*.[6]
2. *Masā'il Nāfi' ibn al-Azraq*, a collection of 189 words from the Qur'ān in seemingly random order given brief definitions and then poetical *shawāhid* supporting (*istashhada* in the text) the use of the word in 'pre-Islamic' poetry. The formula of presentation is often, but not always, that Nāfi', the Khārijī rebel-protagonist, asks what a certain Qur'ānic word means, to which Ibn 'Abbās gives a simple answer. Nāfi' then asks 'Do the Arabs know that?'[7] to which Ibn 'Abbās answers, naturally enough, 'Yes, have you not heard the

[1] Baroda, 1938, 1–41. See the bibliography (pp. xi–xiv) for a full listing of earlier works relevant to the topic.

[2] London, 1951.

[3] 'Religious influences on medieval Arabic philology', *Studia Islamica*, v, 1956, 33–59; 'The treatment of foreign words in medieval Arabic lexicology', in Uriel Heyd (ed.), *Studies in Islamic history and civilization* (Scripta Hierosolymitana, IX), Jerusalem, 1969, 191–205; extracts from: 'Arabic lexicography—its origin, development, sources and problems' [in Hebrew] in his *Studies in Arabic and Hebrew lexicography*, M. H. Goshen-Gottstein (ed.), Jerusalem, 1976, 13–114; the above two articles are reprinted in this latter volume, pp. 19–45 and 247–61 respectively.

[4] *Quranic studies: sources and methods of scriptural interpretation* (hereafter *QS*), Oxford, 1977. Mention should perhaps also be made of Stephan Wild, *Das Kitāb al-'Ain und die arabische Lexikographie*, Wiesbaden, 1965, especially ch. iv.

[5] Sezgin, *GAS*, I, 25–8, works nos. 2, 3, and 4.

[6] *QS*, 218–19; al-Suyūṭī, *al-Itqān fī 'ulūm al-Qur'ān*, Cairo, 1967, II, 6–46; I have been unable to consult the manuscripts of this work and am thus unable to ascertain the degree of similarity between the lists. The ascription of the Atıf Efendi manuscript is multifarious; see *GAS*, I, 27; I, 31 (no. 7); I, 39 (no. 8).

[7] cf. al-Anbārī, *Kitāb īḍāḥ al-waqf wa'l-ibtidā'*, Damascus, 1971, I, 77, and elsewhere where Nāfi''s statement is more explicit: 'Did the Arabs know that before the Qur'ān was revealed?'

line from such-and-such a poet ? ' The text has been published by itself at least twice, once alphabetically by 'Abd al-Bāqī and once with full analysis by 'Ā'isha 'Abd al-Raḥmān.[8] Both of these editions are, however, simply taken from al-Suyūṭī. In fact, al-Suyūṭī is the compiler of the text as we now know it, for he states in his introduction and conclusion to this text [9] that he has selected the passages which comprise it from two sources: Al-Ṭabarānī (d. 360/971), *Mu'jam al-Kabīr* [10] and al-Anbārī (d. 328/940), *Kitab īḍāḥ al-waqf wa'l-ibtidā'*. Al-Anbārī's text is only a portion of al-Suyūṭī's text and is not of the same uniform presentation—al-Anbārī lists fifty words in his section of the text mostly in their Qur'ānic order; only twenty-seven of those are found in al-Suyūṭī and of those twenty-seven, only eighteen give the same definition while only nineteen have the same poetical *shāhid*.[11] An additional source, but one not employed by al-Suyūṭī, is al-Mubarrad (d. 285/898), *al-Kāmil fī'l-lugha* where the confrontation between Nāfi' and Ibn 'Abbās is detailed, but, over and above the episode which witnesses the presence of five Qur'ānic words in pre-Islamic poetry, Nāfi' and Ibn 'Abbās also have a dispute over plain exegesis, not involving the use of poetry. Nāfi' obviously was supposed to have acted as the foil for much of Ibn 'Abbās's demonstration of his intimacy with the Qur'ān.[12] There also exists one old manuscript of twelve folios with the title *Masā'il Nāfi' ibn al-Azraq*: Ẓāhiriyya 3849, dating apparently from the fourth century *hijrī*.[13] A study is needed in order to ascertain the exact contents of this manuscript; a few remarks on it are found in the editor's notes in al-Anbārī's work [14] from which it is at least clear that the text is not merely an extract from al-Anbārī, but its exact status remains, one hopes for the time being only, open to speculation. Finally, it is worth noting that the ascription of *Masā'il* to Ibn 'Abbās has generally been accepted by earlier scholarship, on grounds which, it must be admitted, are not totally evident.[15] Wansbrough, however, has certainly called that into question, arguing, forcefully in my opinion, that the methodological principle underlying the text (i.e. the comparison of scripture with profane literature) represents a position ' considerably posterior to the activity of Ibn 'Abbās '.[16]

[8] 'Abd al-Bāqī, *Mu'jam gharīb al-Qur'ān*, Cairo, 1950, 234–92; 'Ā'isha 'Abd al-Raḥmān, *al-I'jāz al-bayānī li'l-Qur'ān wa Masā'il ibn al-Azraq*, Cairo, 1971, 267–507—references in this article are to this edition.

[9] Al-Suyūṭī, *al-Itqān*, II, 55–88.

[10] Apparently not printed, see Brockelmann, *GAL*, Suppl. I, 279.

[11] Al-Anbārī, *Īḍāḥ*, I, 76–99; note also the ' supplement ' to this, I, 57–75, where poetry is used to define the Qur'ānic lexicon but is not put within the framework of the Ibn 'Abbās/Nāfi' confrontation.

[12] Al-Mubarrad, *al-Kāmil fī'l-lugha*, Leipzig, 1874, I, 566–72. Sezgin, *GAS*, I, 27, also gives Abū 'Ubaid (d. 224/838), *Faḍā'il al-Qur'ān*, as a source for the text. There, two words (*wasaqa* and *sāhira*) are defined and given poetical *shawāhid* by Ibn 'Abbās; *wasaqa* is also found in al-Mubarrad while the *Masā'il* itself treats *ittasaqa*, found in the same Qur'ānic verse, with the same root meaning suggested and basically the same *shāhid* employed. *Sāhira* is not found in either of these other two sources. Most notably, however, Abū 'Ubaid does not mention the figure of Nāfi'; he prefaces these quotations by saying ' Ibn 'Abbās used to be asked about the Qur'ān and he would recite poetry concerning it '. See Staatsbibliothek Preussischer Kulturbesitz, Orientabteilung, Petermann MS 449, fol. 47a, ll. 19–27. For further considerations on the text of *Masā'il* see E. Mittwoch in *A volume of oriental studies*, Cambridge, 1922, 339–44 and *QS*, 216 at note 7.

[13] *GAS*, I, 27; 'Izza Ḥasan (ed.), *Fihris makhṭūṭāt dār al-Kutub al-Ẓāhiriyya*, I: *'ulūm al-Qur'ān*, Damascus, 1962, 425.

[14] Al-Anbārī, *Īḍāḥ*, e.g.: I, 77, n. 1; 80, n. 5; 87, n. 2 citing a word not found in al-Suyūṭī's text; 87, n. 6; 97, n. 4; 98, n. 2.

[15] e.g. W. M. Watt, *Bell's introduction to the Qur'ān*, Edinburgh, 1970, 168: ' It appears to be the case . . . that [Ibn 'Abbās] employed the method of referring to pre-Islamic poetry in order to establish the meaning of obscure words.'

[16] *QS*, 216–17.

3. *Al-Lughāt fī'l-Qur'ān.* As noted above, Wansbrough examined one of the manuscripts under this title (Esad Efendi 91) and discovered it to be the text of *Gharīb*; however, at least three other manuscripts exist of a work with this title and examination of them reveals that indeed there does exist a third, distinct work ascribed to Ibn 'Abbās under this heading and that this is not merely a case of proliferation of titles.

The three manuscript sources for *Lughāt* are:

(*a*) Ẓāhiriyya *ḥadīth* 273/5 (hereafter = Ẓ) 9 fols., dated A.H. 652; the manuscript has been edited and published by Ṣalāḥ al-Dīn al-Munajjid. Wansbrough had not seen this edition when writing *QS*.[17]

(*b*) Chester Beatty 4263 (hereafter = CB) 9 fols., dated A.H. 875.[18]

(*c*) Princeton Yahuda 3167 (hereafter = P) 12 fols., dated A.H. 1292. This manuscript is not listed by Sezgin.[19]

The text itself consists of a collection of some 325 Qur'ānic words (in Ẓ) listed by *sūra* order (with numerous misplacements) which are generally given a brief (usually one word) lexical definition and then identified as to the Arabic tribal dialect (*lugha*) to which they belong or the foreign language with which the word coincides (*wāfaqa/tawāfuq*). Before proceeding any further with an examination of the text, however, it is necessary to establish more closely the sources of the text, their interrelationships and their ascription.

In Munajjid's edition of Ẓ, he had recourse only to a listing of tribal dialect words, listed by dialect rather than by *sūra* order, found in al-Suyūṭī's *al-Itqān*[20] (hereafter this list = S) to help in his editing. This latter list is attributed to one Abū'l-Qāsim, probably to be equated with the Abū'l-Qāsim Muḥammad ibn 'Abd Allāh listed in al-Suyūṭī's bibliographical introduction to *al-Itqān* and who is credited there with a work entitled *Al-Lughāt allatī nazala bihā al-Qur'ān*. This attribution, however, has become complex and confused because this name in al-Suyūṭī's bibliography has been changed in some editions of the text to Abū 'Ubaid al-Qāsim ibn Sallām, the famous philologist/exegete who died in 224/838; this change was apparently made for the first time in the Kastaliyya edition of *al-Itqān* dating from A.H. 1279.[21] The justification for this change is made by reference to *nau'* 47 of *al-Itqān* where Abū 'Ubaid is indeed mentioned. But that is hardly a sound basis for such a change since that chapter of *al-Itqān* deals with *naskh* and thus reference to Abū 'Ubaid in that context is not totally unexpected.[22] Be that as it may, the

[17] *Kitāb al-lughāt fī'l-Qur'ān rawāya ibn Ḥasnūn al-Muqrī bi-isnādihi ilā Ibn 'Abbās*, Cairo, 1946 (repr. Beirut, 1972—this latter is used here); cf. *QS*, 219, n. 4.

[18] A. J. Arberry, *The Chester Beatty Library: a handlist of the Arabic manuscripts*, Dublin, 1962, v, 82.

[19] Rudolf Mach, *Catalogue of Arabic manuscripts* (*Yahuda Section*) *in the Garrett Collection, Princeton University Library*, Princeton, 1977, 15.

[20] II, 91–102.

[21] Al-Suyūṭī, *al-Itqān*, I, 19. Compare the popular, two-volume Ḥalabī edition: I, 7.

[22] Al-Suyūṭī, *al-Itqān*, III, 59; see *QS*, 193–4, 198–9 on *Kitāb al-nāsikh wa'l-mansūkh* by Abū 'Ubaid. The editor of the latest edition of *al-Itqān*, Muḥammad Abū'l-Faḍl Ibrāhīm, has complicated the matter even further. He seems to think that al-Suyūṭī is using two works: 1. *Lughāt al-Qur'ān* by Abū 'l-Qāsim al-Lālakā'ī, i.e. the list found on II, 91–102; a person with this name is found in *GAL*, I, 181; Suppl. I, 308 (d. 418/1027) but there is no particular reason to suppose that our Abū 'l-Qāsim was al-Lālakā'ī; al-Suyūṭī does not state it; 2. *Lughāt al-Qabā'il* by Ibn Sallām (i.e. Abū 'Ubaid) mentioned only in the bibliographical introduction and *ad* one citation (II, 198) which is, indeed, credited to Abū 'Ubaid al-Qāsim ibn Sallām; that quotation deals with foreign words, not dialect words and, regardless, al-Suyūṭī mentions no title from which the quotation is taken. See al-Suyūṭī, *al-Itqān*, Index, IV, 289 and Addendum, IV, 308. The potential for confusion here is almost endless: witness the work by Abū 'Ubaid Aḥmad ibn Muḥammad al-Harawī (d. 401/1011), *Kitāb al-Gharībain: Gharībai al-Qur'ān wa'l-ḥadīth*, Cairo, 1970 (see *GAL*, I, 131–2; Suppl. I, 200). Ibn Sallām is also known by his *nisba*, al-Harawī.

attribution of this list of dialect words to Abū 'Ubaid has become widespread. Under Abū 'Ubaid, Brockelmann lists a text as published on the margin of al-Dirīnī, *al-Taisīr fī 'ilm al-Qur'ān* published in Cairo in A.H. 1310 (hereafter = D).[23] There, in fact we find not the list from al-Suyūṭī, but a text virtually identical with Ẓ, an observation already made by Rabin.[24] How this text had become attributed to Abū 'Ubaid is made clear in the following note by which the editor prefaced the text:

> This is an important treatise because of the brilliance of its merits. It is comprised of that which occurs in the Qur'ān from the languages of the tribes and I think it is by Abū'l-Qāsim Ibn Sallām according to what is related about it by the author of the *Itqān*.[25]

This is the text which was used by Rabin in his studies and the ascription of it to Abū 'Ubaid was there accepted. Rabin noted that the text was also printed on the margin of *Tafsīr al-Jalālain*, Cairo, 1356/1937 (actually several prints: also Cairo, 1342/1923; hereafter = J). In J, the preface found in D is repeated, but left out is the ' I think ', concerning the attribution: the editor seems certain this time.[26]

There is, however, virtually no justification for such an identification. Al-Suyūṭī does not state it, nor does the *isnād* of the work support it. The *isnād* of the text is in fact significant for it reveals that the first five elements are common to all the versions of the work. (See chart on page 19.) Abū 'Ubaid is to be found in no path of the *isnād*. However, what is important is that the very structure of these *isnāds* suggests that we have a single text originating some time just prior to or slightly after the fifth person in the *isnād*, that is some time in the third *hijrī* century, then transmitted through varying sources, being modified slightly along each path. An analysis of the texts demonstrates that this is so. Between D and J the differences are quite minimal; the above mentioned absence of ' I think ' in J and the lack of the final two elements in the *isnād* of J are the only major elements differentiating the texts; they are evidently based on the same (unknown) manuscript and thus for the purposes of the following discussion only D will be referred to. S has been fully compared to Ẓ by Munajjid: S has 20 additional words in its listing [27] but omits 33 others and attributes 34 to different dialects or languages.[28] Of the 20 words added by S to Ẓ, 14 are found in D; when compared to Ẓ, D adds 34 words but omits 23 others (of which three are also omitted in S) and attributes 23 words to different dialects or languages.[29] CB and P are virtually identical and exhibit even less variation from Ẓ than D. All this is out of a total of over 300 words, so the identity of the basic source underlying all the texts seems certain.

It is unfortunate that Munajjid did not avail himself of at least D, if not

[23] *GAL*, Suppl. I, 167.

[24] Rabin, *Ancient West-Arabian*, 7, para. d and the Addenda *ad* p. 7, found on page 211; this information has then been repeated in Michael Zwettler, *The oral tradition of classical Arabic poetry*, Columbus, Ohio, 1978, 113. Rabin stated that he hoped to deal with the various versions of the list in a future publication. As far as I have been able to determine he has never done so.

[25] Al-Dirīnī, *al-Taisīr*, 139 (margin). The editor obviously makes reference to the Kastaliyya edition of *al-Itqān*.

[26] Rabin, *Ancient West-Arabian*, 7; *Tafsīr al-Jalālain*, Cairo, 1342/1923, I, 124.

[27] See pp. 58–9 of Ẓ for full listing.

[28] Information cited by Munajjid in footnotes throughout the text.

[29] The variation in dialect attribution in many cases may well be a copyist's error (dittography especially seems likely, e.g. *ad* Q. 9:39) and misreadings (especially Kināna/Kinda, e.g. *ad* Q. 11:29; 18:60; also Quraish/Fars *ad* Q. 39:63).

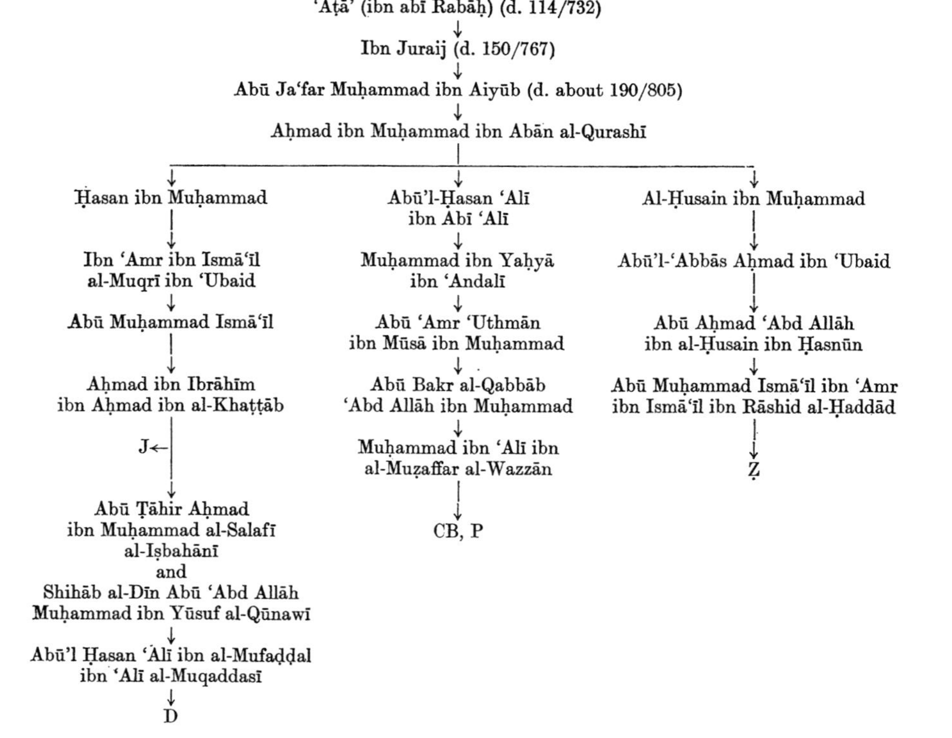
('Abd Allāh) ibn 'Abbās (d. 68/687)
'Aṭā' (ibn abī Rabāḥ) (d. 114/732)
Ibn Juraij (d. 150/767)
Abū Ja'far Muḥammad ibn Aiyūb (d. about 190/805)
Aḥmad ibn Muḥammad ibn Abān al-Qurashī
Ḥasan ibn Muḥammad
Ibn 'Amr ibn Ismā'īl
al-Muqrī ibn 'Ubaid
Abū Muḥammad Ismā'īl
Aḥmad ibn Ibrāhīm
ibn Aḥmad ibn al-Khaṭṭāb
J
Abū Ṭāhir Aḥmad
ibn Muḥammad al-Salafī
al-Iṣbahānī
and
Shihāb al-Dīn Abū 'Abd Allāh
Muḥammad ibn Yūsuf al-Qūnawī
Abū'l Ḥasan 'Alī ibn al-Mufaḍḍal
ibn 'Alī al-Muqaddasī
D
Abū'l-Ḥasan 'Alī
ibn Abī 'Alī
Muḥammad ibn Yaḥyā
ibn 'Andalī
Abū 'Amr 'Uthmān
ibn Mūsā ibn Muḥammad
Abū Bakr al-Qabbāb
'Abd Allāh ibn Muḥammad
Muḥammad ibn 'Alī ibn
al-Muẓaffar al-Wazzān
CB, P
Al-Ḥusain ibn Muḥammad
Abū'l-'Abbās Aḥmad ibn 'Ubaid
Abū Aḥmad 'Abd Allāh
ibn al-Ḥusain ibn Ḥasnūn
Abū Muḥammad Ismā'īl ibn 'Amr
ibn Ismā'īl ibn Rāshid al-Ḥaddād
Ẓ

CB and P, in his editing if, in the first place, it was worth publishing a text which in its essence had been printed previously. Ẓ is certainly a far less than satisfactory manuscript by the evidence of the edition. It has, for example, numerous lacunae in the identification of the dialects and meanings for various words throughout the text, identifications which are made on the other hand in D.[30] The perils of editing from a single manuscript are well demonstrated by a number of errors in the text [31] and a number of places where Munajjid's proposed corrections would appear to be incorrect on the basis of the other texts.[32]

A feature worthy of note concerning the text of *Lughāt*, especially in the light of Wansbrough's analyses, is that the introduction to the text is the same as that published by Wansbrough which he found at the beginning of *Gharīb*. The text of the introduction as printed by Wansbrough runs as follows: [33]

> From Ibn 'Abbās concerning the words of God ' In a (clear) Arabic tongue ' [i.e. Q.16 : 103 ; 26 : 195]. He said : [that is] in the language of Quraish : if there had been other than Arabic in [the Qur'ān], [the Arabs] would not have understood it. God has not revealed a book without it being in Arabic and then Gabriel translated it for each prophet into the language of his people.[34] Therefore God said : ' We do not send a prophet except in the language of his community ' [i.e. Q.14 : 4]. There is no language of a people more comprehensive than the language of the Arabs. There is not in the Qur'ān any language other than Arabic although that language may coincide [*wāfaqat*] with other languages ; [35] however, as for the origin and category [of the language used], it is Arabic and nothing is mixed in with it.

A textual variant to this passage found in Ẓ, CB and P, but not in D, gives a somewhat different perspective to the significance of the introduction. There, rather than stating that God reveals his books in Arabic and then Gabriel translates them, the view is put forth that God reveals his books in Hebrew.[36] A dispute as to the language ' spoken ' by God reflects popular and probably early speculation of a fundamentalist nature : God must speak Hebrew because he spoke to Moses directly ; additionally, if God spoke Arabic, Gabriel would not be needed to translate to Muḥammad ; on the other hand, God must speak Arabic for it is the ' most comprehensive ' (*ausa'*) of languages. The dilemma posed by approaching the Qur'ān with such an attitude is easily understood.

This introductory text, however, does not seem totally appropriate as a prologue to the work as a whole ; that would seem to suggest, then, that the introduction may have had an existence independent of the *Lughāt* text itself (and perhaps *Gharīb* as well). Only later may the introduction have been

[30] e.g. *ad* Q. 3 : 49 ; 11 : 8 ; 19 : 8 ; 56 : 86 ; 61 : 5 ; 72 : 6 ; 79 : 8.

[31] e.g. *ad* Q. 2 : 63 *al-ḥadīth*, read *al-ḥarf* with D, CB, P ; *ad* Q. 11 : 78 where the omission of *ḍidd* ' opposite ', found in D, has resulted in strange definitions ! ; *ad* Q. 11 : 101 *taḥayyur* read *takhsīr* with D, CB, P also *Masā'il*, 380.

[32] e.g. *ad* Q. 12 : 23 ; the original text has as a definition for *haita laka*, according to Munajjid, هى لك which he has corrected to *halumma laka* (in agreement with CB, P as it happens)—the original would seem closer to D and *Masā'il* (pp. 381–2) *tahaiya'tu laka* in basic idea (i.e. ' I am ready for you ! '), cf. 'Abd al-Raḥmān's remarks in *Masā'il*, 382.

[33] *QS*, 218.

[34] Reading *li-kulli nabiy bi-lisān qaumihi* of Ẓ/D/CB contra *QS*/P.

[35] Rather than *wa rubbamā wāfaqat al-lugha al-lughāt* of *QS* and Ẓ or *wa rubbamā wāfaqat ba'ḍu'l-lughāt ba'ḍ^{an}* of D, this phrase reads in CB and P *wa rubbamā al-lughāt*. This may well not be *lapsus calami*, but rather an attempt to make the preface relevant to the argument of the text as a whole (see further below) by giving the meaning ' there is not in the Qur'ān any language other than the language of the Arabs *or perhaps* (*their*) *dialects* '.

[36] Ẓ, p. 16 ; CB, fol. 1b ; P, fol. 2a.

added to the whole text, being brought into conjunction because of the ascription of both items to Ibn 'Abbās and the fact that both texts, in whatever fashion, deal with the principle of the language of the Qur'ān.

As stated above, about 325 words (in Ẓ) are defined and assigned to tribal dialects or foreign languages. In nine instances, no definition is given (each of those occasions being where a Qur'ānic variant reading is adduced; see below) and in seven instances, no language is stated (these cases perhaps being omissions in the manuscript of Ẓ). On one occasion (*ad* Q. 23 : 108), the definition suggested varies with the Qur'ānic variant. However, these exceptions hardly impinge upon the purpose of the text: to define problematic lexica and suggest that the difficulty or the strange appearance of the word is attributable to tribal dialectical origin or foreign language resemblance. Munajjid has provided the following table as a breakdown of dialects;[37] some words, it is to be noted, are attributed to more than one dialect.

Quraish	104 words
Hudhail	45 words
Kināna	36 words
Ḥimyar	23 words
Jurhum	21 words
Tamīm	13 words
Qais 'Ailān	13 words
Ahl 'Umān, Azd Shanū'a, Khath'am	6 words each
Ṭaiy', Madhḥaj, Madyan, Ghassān	5 words each
Banū Ḥanīfa, Ḥaḍramaut, Ash'ar	4 words each
Anmār	3 words
Sab', Ahl al-Yamāma, Muzaina, Thaqīf, Khuzā'a, Banū 'Āmir, Lakhm, Kinda	2 words each
'Amāliqa, Sudūs, Sa'd al-'Ashīra	1 word each

For foreign languages, the following totals have been compiled:

Aramaic (*Nabaṭiyya/nabaṭ* plus once *al-anbaṭ*)	11 words
Syriac (*Suryāniyya, Suryāniyyīn*)	5 words
Ethiopic (*Ḥabashiyya*)	3 words
Persian (*Fars*)	3 words
Hebrew (*'Ibrāniyya*), Coptic (*Qibṭiyya*), Greek/Latin (*Rūm*)	2 words each

In these instances of foreign words, the phrase employed is *wāfaqat bi-lugha* . . . or *bi-lugha tawāfuq* . . ., that is, that the same word occurs in both languages. The omission of this qualifying phrase *ad* Q. 18 : 9 *al-raqīm* [*ya'nī*] *al-kalb bi-lughat al-Rūm* and *ad* Q. 33 : 8 (*'adhāb*) *alīm ya'nī mūji' bi'l-'Ibrāniyya* should probably be considered instances of *lapsus calami* rather than intentional implications of actual borrowed words in the Qur'ān. *Al-Raqīm* may well be a proper name in the view of this text, although the point is hardly made totally clear. Even so, in the only other instance of citing a proper name, *Ibrāhīm ad* Q. 2 : 126, the phrase *bi-lugha tawāfuq al-Suryāniyya* is used.[38]

When confronted with these statistics, the introduction to the text gains a new significance. The introduction makes no reference to dialects, only to Quraish as the language of the Arabs in which the whole Qur'ān was revealed,

[37] Ẓ, p. 7; in the following list, note that D always uses the spellings Qais Ghailān and Madḥaj.

[38] *Ad* Q. 23 : 20 *sainā'* appears, but it is not treated as a proper name (meaning *ḥusn*, coinciding with Aramaic). Cf. the list of 119 foreign words in the Qur'ān in al-Suyūṭī, *al-Itqān*, II, 108–19.

and, as such, it may be thought to provide a theoretical basis for the text of *Gharīb* and also *Masā'il* [39] (although it is not appended to the latter) but it hardly suits *Lughāt*. In the body of *Lughāt* we have the representation of the argument that the Qur'ān was revealed either in seven *aḥruf* (dialects) or in the dialects of all the Arabs in order to make the Qur'ān appeal to all of them.[40] The introduction (along with the texts of *Gharīb* and *Masā'il*) on the other hand, is pursuing the argument of the pure Arabic Qur'ān written in 'classical Arabic', that is Quraish dialect.[41] Thus it would seem quite likely that the introduction found in *Lughāt* was imported from another source and grafted onto the text; such would suggest the likelihood of an earlier existence for the introduction, a notion confirmed and reinforced by the Arabic/Hebrew controversy found in the textual variant to the introduction.

In comparison with the early, fundamentalist ideas promulgated in the introduction, the body of the text, for the most part, represents a somewhat later and more sophisticated point of view. Contrary evidence may, however, be thought to be exhibited by the somewhat confused structure of the work as a whole. In a number of places, for example, it is not the first occurrence of a word in the Qur'ān which is treated; one such instance of this is the defining of *fa lā rafath ad* Q. 2 : 197 but not *al-rafath ilā nisā'ikum ad* Q. 2 : 187, the only two instances of the use of this word in the Qur'ān and where both quite plainly mean the same thing (*al-jimā'*). Furthermore, for the majority of the definitions suggested, no room is allowed for presenting a variety of interpretations; typical is the case where *ad* Q. 12 : 31 *utrujj* 'citrus' (coinciding with Coptic), but not 'reclining', 'cushions', nor any of the other possible meanings, is adduced for the meaning of *muttak'an*.[42] Such a composition, it may be suggested, can be conceived of in one of two ways: either as a tentative working out of rudimentary solutions to these lexical problems or as a distillation of several centuries of scholarly debate.

The latter suggestion is more likely, however, because of the large number of elements contained in the text which presuppose a prolonged and reasonably sophisticated treatment of the Qur'ānic text.[43]

[39] The presence in *Masā'il* of eight instances of identification of tribal dialects or foreign languages can hardly invalidate the contention that this text is arguing for an Arabic Qur'ān (alongside arguing for the use of poetry in clarifying the Qur'ān, see *QS*, 217). See *Masā'il*:

p. 286	*yay'asi*	dialect of Banū Mālik
p. 329	*yaḥūr*	Ethiopic
p. 406	*ḥūb*	Ethiopic
p. 413	*yaftinakum*	dialect of Hawāzin
p. 439	*naqqabū*	dialect of Yaman
p. 449	*būr*	dialect of 'Umān, also in Ẓ *ad* Q. 25 : 18
p. 468	*yalitkum*	dialect of Banū 'Abs, also in Ẓ *ad* Q. 49 : 14 but attributed to Qais 'Ailān
p. 482	*murāgham*	dialect of Hudhail

cf. al-Suyūṭī, *al-Itqān*, II, 90–1, where only five of these are enumerated.

[40] See, among many Arabic sources, Abū 'Ubaid, *Faḍā'il al-Qur'ān*, fols. 46b–47a; al-Ṭabarī (d. 310/923), *Jāmi' al-bayān 'an ta'wīl āy al-Qur'ān* (ed. Shākir), Cairo, 1373/1953, I, 21, 46–8; also Rabin, *Ancient West-Arabian*, 19, paras. e, f.

[41] e.g. al-Zarkashī (d. 793/1390), *al-Burhān fī 'ulūm al-Qur'ān*, Cairo, 1957, I, 218, citing Ibn Qutaiba (d. 276/889). Also see Rabin, *Ancient West-Arabian*, 21–3, paras. n–r; Kopf, 'Religious influences', 46–50; Zwettler, *Classical Arabian poetry*, ch. iii; *QS*, ch. iii.

[42] See *QS*, 138–9.

[43] I can hardly agree with Rabin, *Ancient West-Arabian*, 7, that 'the dialect meanings recorded in the Risāla hardly ever fit the passage they are supposed to elucidate, a circumstance which lends some verisimilitude to the information'. The examples here cited prove, I believe, the exact opposite point. Even definitions which at first sight may seem absurd, for example, *bard* 'cold' meaning *naum* 'sleep' in the dialect of Hudhail *ad* Q. 78 : 24, in fact have long exegetical traditions behind them and were meanings established for good exegetical reasons; for further details of this point, see my forthcoming study: 'Qur'ān 78 : 24: a study in Arabic lexicography.'

Definitions which presuppose legal debate are prominent. Typical are two separate entries *ad* Q. 2 : 282 defining the phrase *safīh^{an} ḍa'īf^{an}*. The problem of this verse centres around those who are unable to enter into written, legal contracts. A legal guardian may undertake a contract on behalf of one who, among other qualifications, is *safīh* or *ḍa'īf*. *Ḍa'īf* is defined as *aḥmaq*, ' stupid ', *safīh* as *jāhil* ' unlettered ', both given as the dialect of Kināna. These two definitions correspond with those given in later *aḥkām* works, for example, the text by Ibn al-'Arabī (d. 543/1148) ; there, however, a choice is given : *ḍa'īf* could mean stupid, mute or foolish ; *safīh* unlettered, a child, women and children, or squanderers of money and corrupters of religion. In each case, however, Ibn al-'Arabī's first mentioned definition is the one proposed in *Lughāt*.[44] Other such examples may be found *ad* Q. 2 : 180 ; 4 : 4 ; 4 : 15 ; 4 : 176 ; 5 : 107 ; 16 : 72 ; 33 : 32.

Textual emendations are several times proposed under the guise of dialect variation. *Ad* Q. 4 : 176 ' God makes (it) clear to you so that you do not err ', the Qur'ānic text actually reads *an taḍillū*, ' that you err ' ; as an example of Quraish dialect, *Lughāt* suggests that this actually means *an lā taḍillū* (as the verse is actually translated above). Such an emendation is also found, for example, in al-Farrā' (d. 207/822), allowing the conclusion there that ' *lā* is permissible in the place of *an* '.[45] Other examples of proposed textual emendation occur in *Lughāt ad* Q. 18 : 74 ; 24 : 13 ; 38 : 3.

Even more prominent a feature is dialect identification made in order to explain Qur'ānic variant readings. I have dealt elsewhere with one of these instances *ad* Q. 21 : 95 where *ḥirm* is identified as Hudhail dialect and *ḥarām* as Quraish.[46] Another thirteen examples spread throughout the text are all similar. Eleven of the readings are found in the scheme of the seven readers, two are listed in *shawādhdh* readings, while one fails to find entry into any classical collection of readings.[47]

Grammatical discussions are also to be noted ; four times, *ad* Q. 54 : 13 ; 69 : 7 ; 78 : 14 ; 88 : 15 is the singular form pointed out for a word which occurs in the Qur'ān in the plural.

Theological motivations are not absent either. *Ad* Q. 6 : 125 *ḥaraj* is defined as *shākk*, ' in doubt ', in the dialect of Quraish ; the passage is ' predestinary ' and refers to making the breast *ḥaraj*, often rendered ' constricted '. The point of the definition proffered in *Lughāt*, however, seems to be to make the individual responsible for his disbelief (resulting from ' doubt ') rather than having God responsible for causing disbelief due to a ' constricted ' heart.[48] Other such examples include perhaps *ad* Q. 7 : 2 (where *ḥaraj* is defined as *shakk* again) ; 63 : 4 ; 83 : 9 ; 98 : 1.

Finally, a feature noted by Rabin, is the definition of *yā-sīn*, the initial letters of *Sūra* 36, as *yā-insān*, ' O mankind ! ' in the dialect of Ṭaiy'.[49] That

[44] Ibn al-'Arabī, *Aḥkām al-Qur'ān*, Cairo, 1967, I, 249.

[45] al-Farrā', *Ma'ānī al-Qur'ān*, Cairo, 1955–66, I, 297 ; see the editor's footnote there for other interpretations of the passage.

[46] Rippin, ' Qur'an 21 : 95 : " A Ban is upon any town " ', *JSS*, XXIV, 1, 1979, 43–53, esp. 51, n. 1.

[47] *ad* Q. 3 : 140 ; 6 : 99 ; 6 : 111 ; 8 : 60 ; 9 : 21 ; 18 : 96 ; 21 : 95 ; 23 : 72 ; 38 : 63 ; 47 : 15 ; 81 : 24 readings are found from the 7 readers ; *ad* Q. 2 : 255 ; 9 : 124 are *shawādhdh* readings ; *ad* Q. 37 : 16 the reading *mitna* or *mutna* (i.e. ' we died '), see Rabin, *Ancient West-Arabian*, 114–15, 159 ; the presence of non-canonical variants would tend to suggest that this text is at best peripheral to the mainstream of masoretic exegesis.

[48] cf. al-Zamakhsharī (d. 538/1144), *al-Kashshāf 'an ḥaqā'iq al-tanzīl*, Calcutta, 1856, I, 424, who proposes a different solution : ' constricting the breast ' is the end result of God ' holding back his grace ' and faith therefore is resisted and refused.

[49] Rabin, *Ancient West-Arabian*, 8–9, para. i.

these initial letters themselves had a meaning was a widespread notion in exegetical literature; al-Farrā', for example, cites *yā-sīn* as meaning *yā rajul* while *ad Ṭā-hā* (*Sūra* 20) he gives the possible meanings of *yā-rajul* or *yā-insān*. The flexibility of such definitions is thereby well demonstrated.[50]

The technical terminology of the treatise and a few methodological considerations are also worthy of attention. In a total of 22 cases, the text cites a second passage from elsewhere in the Qur'ān in which the same word is found with the same definition. These instances are introduced by *wa-kadhālika* (10 times), *wa-kaqaulihi* (4 times), *wa-qauluhu* (4 times), *mithla qaulihi* (2 times) and simply *wa* (2 times). Notably, never is the developed technical term *naẓīr* used. In four passages, *ad* Q. 9 : 2; 33 : 87; 46 : 25; 51 : 9 (the latter repeating information already given *ad* Q. 33 : 87), the definitions given are qualified by the statement that 'every time this word occurs in the Qur'ān it means . . .'.[51] Another method of analysing the lexicon is employed: the Qur'ān is compared to profane speech. This occurs in two places in Ẓ, CB and P although both are, perhaps significantly, omitted in D. *Ad* Q. 11 : 77 *sī'a bihim ya'nī karihahum* is then compared to one saying (*kaqaulika*): *wa-allāh laqad sī'tu bika*—'by God I detest you!' The second instance is found *ad* Q. 51 : 9: *man ufika* is clarified by the statement *yuqālu afaka al-rajal idhā kadhaba* 'one says "*afaka*" when a man tells a lie'. At the very end of Ẓ, CB and P [52] a number of similar instances of comparing the Qur'ān to profane speech are found 'tacked on' to the end of the text. They may well be evidence of editorial intrusion, but the parallel instances in the actual body of the text are not so easily explained away.

The last item of terminology concerns the use of *wāfaqa/tawāfuq*. The view represented by the use of these terms, as revealed by Kopf's studies, is that coincidence of languages is employed to explain the fact that both Arabic and other languages employ the same words in the same meaning; that is, these words were neither borrowed at the time of the Qur'ānic revelation from the other languages, nor are they to be considered naturalized Arabic words borrowed in the centuries before the Qur'ān's appearance. That these two latter views were a powerful influence competing with the theory proposed in the *Lughāt* text has been exposed by Kopf. However, the argument of our text, embodied in the idea of *tawāfuq*, is also argued by al-Ṭabarī, although it did not originate with him.[53] It does seem clear, however, that the earliest idea concerning foreign words in the Qur'ān was to acknowledge their presence; [54] the argument given in *Lughāt* can be seen to stand after the earliest period of debate on these matters.

[50] Al-Farrā', *Ma'ānī*, II, 371 (*ad* Q. 36); II, 174 (*ad* Q. 20); also see Abū 'Ubaida (d. 210/825), *Majāz al-Qur'ān*, Cairo, 1954–1962, II, 15, where *ṭā-hā* in the meaning of *yā insān* is suggested (but rejected). On the whole subject, with the complete range of suggested solutions to the 'mysterious letters' including the one put forth by this text, see M. S. Seale, 'The mysterious letters of the Qur'an' in his *Qur'an and Bible: studies in interpretation and dialogue*, London, 1978, 29–46, which includes a translation of the relevant section from al-Suyūṭī, *al-Itqān* (III, 21–31).

[51] Other early exegetical works are devoted to working these methods out in full, e.g. Muqātil (d. 150/767), *Al-Ashbāh* [*al-Wujūh*] *wa'l-naẓā'ir fī'l-Qur'ān*, Cairo, 1975, also the extract of Muqātil (?) found in al-Malaṭī (d. 377/987), *Kitāb al-tanbīh wa'l-radd 'alā ahl al-ahwā' wa'l-bida'*, Cairo, 1949, 72–80, and al-Kisā'ī (d. 189/805), *Kitāb Mushtabihāt al-Qur'ān*, MS Beyazit 436 (note that another manuscript exists, Princeton, Yahuda 903). On the whole topic see *QS*, esp. pp. 208–16.

[52] Ẓ, pp. 53–4; CB, fols. 8b–9a; P, fol. 12a; 12b is blank and the text is incomplete.

[53] Kopf, 'Religious influences', 40–5; 'Foreign words', 200–4; Jeffery, *Foreign vocabulary*, 4–11; al-Ṭabarī, *Jāmi' al-bayān*, I, 13–20.

[54] See *QS*, 142–3; Kopf, 'Religious influences', 42–3.

The point of this extended summary of tendencies in this text is this: all these factors, the nature of the definitions, the technical terminology and the methodologies, may well not be exceptional in and by themselves; however, to find them all combined in one text is, I would suggest, evidence that we are dealing with a work whose genesis is after each of the individual procedures had become established processes and components within the exegetical canon. It is perhaps a not very surprising conclusion to state that this text, like *Masā'il* and *Gharīb*, although attributed to Ibn 'Abbās, can hardly stem from him. The three works clearly do not even originate from the same pen. The *Masā'il* treats 45 words which are also dealt with in *Lughāt* but in 14 cases the definitions in the two texts do not agree. The attribution to Ibn 'Abbās is clearly a fiction designed to give the texts more credence by assigning them to an early and prominent figure.[55]

[55] I would like to express my thanks to Dr. John Wansbrough, SOAS, for having read and commented on an early draft of this paper. Thanks are also due to the Berlin Staatsbibliothek, the Chester Beatty Library and the Princeton University Library for microfilms of the manuscripts consulted in this study.

XIV

IBN 'ABBĀS'S *GHARĪB AL-QUR'ĀN*

In a previous article discussing the text entitled *al-Lughāt fī'l-Qur'ān* attributed to Ibn 'Abbās, mention was made of two manuscripts of *Gharīb al-Qur'ān* also attributed to Ibn 'Abbās.[1] A recent visit to Istanbul allowed an examination of these works, leading to the discovery that, in fact, these manuscripts contain two additional copies of *al-Lughāt fī'l-Qur'ān* and that an independent text *Gharīb al-Qur'ān* attributed to Ibn 'Abbās does not exist. A proliferation of titles has taken place regarding this text and, most significantly of course, around the figure of Ibn 'Abbās and his role in Qur'ānic lexicography.

The manuscript Esad Efendi 91/3 (ff. 104a–112b) is entitled *al-Lughāt fī'l-Qur'ān* and has been accurately described by Sezgin.[2] The *isnād* of the text is essentially the same as that found in Chester Beatty 4263 and Princeton Yahuda 3167 ; on f. 104a the full *isnād* minus the name of al-Wazzān appears ; the latter name does occur, however, at the end of the work on f. 112b where the quotation given by Sezgin is found. Textually the work varies only a little from the other two manuscripts although the introduction to the text reads such that Arabic is the language of God and describes the language of the Qur'ān as 'nothing but Arabic *wa rubbamā wāfaqat al-lughāt*' which is yet another variation on this phrase, indicating once again, perhaps, a conscious effort to bring the introduction into alignment with the text itself.[3]

The manuscript Atıf Efendi 2815/8 (ff. 102a–107a) is entitled *Gharīb al-Qur'ān* but contains a text in the tradition of *Lughāt*. The manuscript follows most closely the text as printed in al-Dirīnī and Jalālain [4] although it would appear that this copy is not the ultimate source of these printed versions, thus there may well remain, somewhere in the world, yet another manuscript of *Lughāt*. Only the final names of the *isnād* vary from that printed in al-Dirīnī ; Abū'l-Ḥasan al-Muqaddasī is omitted and two names are added : Abū 'Abd Allāh Muḥammad ibn 'Abd al-Ghaffār al-Muqaddasī who received the text from Rashīd al-Dīn Abū Muḥammad ibn 'Abd al-Ṭāhir. Textually there are some differences between the manuscript and the printed versions ; the body of the work has become somewhat shorter, losing a number of its entries, especially towards the beginning. The text of the introduction closely follows that printed in Wansbrough's *Quranic studies* but leaves out, due to homeoteleuton with the word *qaumihi*, the line in which Q. 14:4 is quoted.[5]

The addition of these two manuscripts and the elimination of *Gharīb* from consideration in the works attributed to Ibn 'Abbās does not substantially alter the argument concerning the text of *Lughāt* ; in fact, the manuscripts provide clear evidence of title proliferation which may well be an indication in itself of text compilation well after the time of Ibn 'Abbās. Additionally, the Atıf Efendi manuscript also provides another example of transmission of the basic text through multiple paths. Wansbrough's description of the texts in *Quranic studies* should be understood to imply that in *literary form* the Istanbul manuscripts are similar to al-Suyūṭī's list of difficult words supplied with simple

[1] A. Rippin, 'Ibn 'Abbās's *al-Lughāt fī'l-Qur'ān*', *BSOAS*, XLIV, 1, 1981, 15.
[2] *GAS*, I, 27.
[3] cf. Rippin, 'Ibn 'Abbās', p. 20 and especially n. 35.
[4] See ibid., 18.
[5] J. Wansbrough, *Quranic studies: sources and methods of scriptural interpretation*, Oxford, 1977, 218 and Rippin, 'Ibn 'Abbās', 20.

glosses; as far as the exegetical principle behind the work goes, the text of *Lughāt* is closest to al-Suyūṭī's section on 'dialect' words.[6] Of course, the underlying principle with which all these texts are concerned is giving an honorable pedigree to various approaches in analysing the Qur'ān; it is there that the role of Ibn 'Abbās finds its central place.[7]

[6] See Wansbrough, *Quranic studies*, p. 219 at n. 6; al-Suyūṭī, *al-Itqān fī 'ulūm al-Qur'ān*, Cairo, 1967, II, 6–46 (difficult words), II, 91–102 (dialect words).

[7] Thanks are due to the Director, Süleymaniye Kütüphanesi, Istanbul, and Dr. Ahmed Subhi Furat, Istanbul University, for their assistance. Travel to Istanbul was made possible by a grant from the Social Sciences and Humanities Research Council of Canada.

TAFSĪR IBN ʿABBĀS AND CRITERIA FOR DATING EARLY *TAFSĪR* TEXTS*

I. Introduction

The intention of this paper is twofold. First, it wishes to clear up a degree of confusion which exists concerning the ascription of a very popular text of Qurʾānic commentary, the authorship of which is listed in various authoritative reference books as attributable to persons living at some point between the first and the ninth Muslim centuries; this task is relatively simple, although it does provide a tale with some degree of complication and the sense of being a detective on the trail of a fraud — a case of intrigue, misunderstanding, misascription, and perhaps even wilful misleading. It is a story of medieval book production and its encounter with the modern period, and that period's interest in things of the past, the older the better.

Second, the paper attempts to raise some more critical problems in the history of *tafsīr* and perhaps in other fields also. At stake is how we determine the accuracy of ascription of a given text, especially one that is portrayed as being from the earliest period of Islam — from any time before the third Muslim century, to be more specific. If

* This paper was written while I was on research leave from the University of Calgary (1986-87), with the financial assistance of the Social Sciences and Humanities Research Council of Canada. I benefited greatly during this period from the facilities provided to me by the School of Oriental and African Studies, London. Parts of this paper were given as lectures at the universities of Leeds, Manchester, and Groningen; I am grateful to Adrian Brockett, Norman Calder, and Fred Leemhuis for the possibility of being able to explore some of the issues raised in this paper in their respective universities. I would also like to extend my thanks to the British Library, the Chester Beatty Library, the Princeton University Library, the Berlin Staatsbibliothek, and the University of Leiden Library for access to their manuscript collections and for providing microfilms of the necessary items.

we pose the question, as one of my alternative titles for this paper had it — "Do we have a *tafsīr* of Ibn ʿAbbās?" — we must ask what we actually mean by posing that question. How in fact could one judge such a matter? This involves matters of general principle, as well as specifics on Ibn ʿAbbās alone; any results of this sort of investigation may well prove useful in the analysis of other early *tafsīr* works also. The factors are methodological problems: How do we know if a text is early or not? What sorts of criteria can we set up? What of the employment of traditional criteria? Why does modern scholarship see these as of not much use? This is especially crucial for the ubiquitous figure of Ibn ʿAbbās, who would seem to have a certain political significance and to whom material has been ascribed in many different works, due to his literary role as the storehouse of Qurʾānic knowledge.

II. The Text

The work which this study will examine as a test case for the establishment of criteria for dating, but which also has certain intrinsic interests, has seen a large variety of ascriptions. The text, often known as *Tanwīr al-miqbās min tafsīr Ibn ʿAbbās*, is (1) found listed under Ibn ʿAbbās in both Brockelmann and Sezgin; (2) listed under al-Kalbī in both Brockelmann and Sezgin, and studied as such in Wansbrough's *Quranic Studies*; (3) treated as the *tafsīr* of al-Dīnawarī by myself in an article on al-Zuhrī, where I first raised this issue of ascription and suggested simply that assigning this text to the fourth century made the most sense (a point I now wish to argue more fully and to justify; the relationship between the texts ascribed to al-Dīnawarī and al-Kalbī was also noted in Wansbrough's work); and (4) listed under al-Fīrūzābādī, once again in both Brockelmann and Sezgin.[1]

For convenience I shall refer to the text as *Tafsīr Ibn ʿAbbās* in the context of this paper, but this should be taken as the title of the work and not as an indication of authorship. I have provided a list in Appendix 1, at the end of this paper, of all the editions

---

1 The exact bibliographical details for these references will be found below, in the sections of part II of this paper dealing with these specific ascriptions.

and manuscripts of this text I have been able to consult; in order to facilitate precise reference, the number of the text according to this listing is often referred to.

Within the limits of textual transmission, all these texts, ascribed to these four people who lived between the first and the ninth *hijrī* centuries, are identical; there can be no doubt that we have a case here of proliferation of ascription. The translation provided in Appendix 3, part I, entitled *Tafsīr Ibn ʿAbbās*, is fully documented in respect to textual variation among the various copies existing with different ascriptions, precisely in order to demonstrate the limits of this transmission consistency. Evidence is available, even in the short segment of the *tafsīr* presented here in translation, of the intrusion of later writers into the text; of confusion, expansion, and contraction of the text. Yet the text still remains the same, of that there can be no doubt. Many of these points will be expanded upon in later segments of this paper, but a few observations should be made now. Printers' errors and scribal errors account for most of the textual differences, and the proliferation of these types of variations can be seen within the various printed editions produced in the last century. Three of the lithographs (texts 4, 5, and 6) coming from India would appear to be copies having a certain common element, although their original source remains unclear, each introducing different changes into the text. While the Egyptian editions (texts 1, 7, 10, and 11) display less variation, there too changes resulting from the printing process (*fāʾ* changing to *qāf*; lack of grammatical number concord) are apparent.

The prime fact to keep in mind in the following discussion is very simple: all the texts discussed here are, in essence, identical; only the ascription varies.

II.i. Al-Fīrūzābādī, *Tanwīr al-miqbās min tafsīr Ibn ʿAbbās*

Abū ʾl-Qāhir Muḥammad ibn Yaʿqūb ibn Muḥammad ibn Ibrāhīm Majd al-Dīn al-Shirāzī al-Fīrūzābādī al-Shāfiʿī was born in 729/1329 and died in 817/1414. He is most famous for his dictionary *al-Qāmūs*[2] but is also reported to have written some six works of *tafsīr*

2 For details of his life and works, see Brockelmann, *EI*[1], II, 113-14; Fleisch, *EI*[2], II, 926-27.

on the Qurʾān. One of these works is entitled *Tanwīr al-miqbās*[3] *min tafsīr Ibn ʿAbbās*. Al-Dawūdī (d. 945/1538)[4] and, probably repeating the information from him, Ḥājjī Khalīfa (d. 1068/1658)[5] report that this was a four-volume work. Brockelmann[6] lists this work as printed in Cairo in 1290 and 1316, the latter edition being published along with the *naskh* text of Muḥammad ibn Ḥazm;[7] Fleisch[8] then adds mention of a print in Cairo, 1345/1926. Sezgin in his entry on Ibn ʿAbbās[9] adds the following list of prints of this al-Fīrūzābādī text (under the supposition that it represents a transmission of Ibn ʿAbbās's *tafsīr*): Būlāq, 1863, 1866, 1873, 1885; Cairo, 1302, 1316, 1332, 1937, 1960. This list appears to be a somewhat updated restatement of what is found in Brockelmann under Ibn ʿAbbās,[10] although Sezgin does not make this explicit.

For the purposes of this study I have employed a print of al-Fīrūzābādī, *Tanwīr al-miqbās*, published in Cairo in 1951 and listed as the "second printing" (text 1). It has two texts in the margin: al-Suyūṭī (d. 911/1505), *Lubāb al-nuqūl fī asbāb al-nuzūl*, followed by the previously mentioned Muḥammad ibn Ḥazm, *Kitāb fī maʿrifat al-nāsikh wa ʾl-mansūkh*. This would appear to be an edition that is readily available today. The text, on the title page, is explicit in citing al-Fīrūzābādī as the author and providing the title *Tanwīr al-miqbās*. Other editions are available that provide the title *Tanwīr al-miqbās* but do not cite the author as al-Fīrūzābādī. One such print is available to me and was published in Beirut in 1360/1941 in the margin of the text of the Qurʾān (text 2); this edition is also readily

---

3 *Miqyās* in Flügel's edition of Ḥajjī Khalīfa, *Kashf al-ẓunūn ʿan asāmī al-kutub wa ʾl-funūn* (Leipzig-London, 1835-58), II, 456, no. 3706, but this may well be an error; the Istanbul edition of Ḥajjī Khalīfa, *Kashf al-ẓunūn* (Istanbul, 1941-43), I, 502, has the title as *miqbās*.

4 *Ṭabaqāt al-mufassirīn* (Cairo, 1972), II, 276, no. 601.

5 *Kashf al-ẓunūn* (ed. Flügel), II, 456, no. 3706.

6 *GAL*, Suppl. II, 235, item 11.

7 Which is itself falsely ascribed to Ibn Ḥazm al-Ẓāhirī; see A. Rippin, "al-Zuhrī, *naskh al-Qurʾān*, and the problem of early *tafsīr* texts," *BSOAS* 47 (1984), 26, note 38.

8 *EI*², II, 926-27.

9 *GAS*, I, 27; for more on this ascription, see below, section II.iv.

10 *GAL*, Suppl. I, 331.

available in bookshops. Another is the marginal print in the old six-volume edition of *al-Durr al-manthūr* of al-Suyūṭī, a work that has been reprinted many times and here is used in an undated print from Beirut (text 3); this refers to *Tanwīr al-miqbās*, but not al-Fīrūzābādī, on page 1 of volume 1 (which is preceded by an unnumbered title page). The two Bombay editions, dated 1863 and 1885 (texts 8 and 9), give the title *Tanwīr al-iqtibās min tafsīr ʿAbd Allāh ibn ʿAbbās*, a title otherwise unknown and whose origin has not been traced, unless it is a simple error. The writing of this title should be noted, at least for its oddity: it is essentially written backwards, with Ibn ʿAbbās at the top and *tanwīr al-iqtibās* at the bottom; this is done in order to fit it into a dome-shaped ornament at the top of the page.[11]

Manuscript copies of this text with the title *Tanwīr al-miqbās* and with (or even without) the name al-Fīrūzābādī do not appear to exist, at least as far as my investigation into the matter has led me. Certainly, Brockelmann did not uncover any manuscripts and neither have I. This leads one immediately to wonder whether this text really is al-Fīrūzābādī's *Tanwīr al-miqbās*. That he wrote a book with this title there is no doubt. As already stated, there are reports that the work was in four volumes, and this suggests a fairly large book. However, with *Tafsīr Ibn ʿAbbās* we are dealing with a book that fits into some 300 pages.[12] This could be taken immediately as an indication that the two texts should not be equated. Now, of course, such matters are not that easy to argue: one person's volume could be another's few folios, but we do have some information that may shed light on the issue with regard to al-Fīrūzābādī. Al-Dawūdī reports[13] that al-Fīrūzābādī's *Baṣāʾir dhawīʾl-tamyīz fī laṭāʾif al-kitāb al-ʿazīz* was written as a two-volume work. This intriguing and very valuable commentary-plus-concordance-plus-dictionary is available in a printed edition of six large volumes.[14] It is a well-prepared edition, to be sure, with large type and lots of empty

11 Norman Calder has informed me that this seeming oddity is also found in Persian texts printed in Iran.

12 Most manuscript copies of al-Dīnawarī/al-Kalbī comprise some 300 folios.

13 *Ṭabaqāt al-mufassirīn*, II, 276, no. 601.

14 Edited by Muḥammad ʿAlī al-Najjār, Cairo, 1964-73; reprint Beirut, n.d. [ca. 1985].

space on the page, but it does indicate the unlikelihood that *Tanwīr al-miqbās* as a four-volume manuscript when written could be reduced to 300 folios or printed pages.

There is one particular piece of evidence available to us that militates even more strongly against the text being *Tanwīr al-miqbās*. Remembering that the text of al-Dīnawarī (to be discussed below in section II.ii) is identical to the printed editions of *Tanwīr al-miqbās* ascribed to al-Fīrūzābādī, the date of the manuscript copies ascribed to al-Dīnawarī must be considered; the earliest of these comes from the sixth *hijrī* century,[15] well before al-Fīrūzābādī was even born. This being the case, and if one wishes to suppose that the work in question is indeed the text of al-Fīrūzābādī's *Tanwīr al-miqbās*, then one must suppose that al-Fīrūzābādī took a work that he did not write, foisted it upon an unsuspecting public as his own, and became quite successful with this exploit. Some evidence for this devious ploy may be thought to reside in the fact that the manuscripts of the text which are listed under al-Kalbī in Sezgin[16] (and which generally simply have the title *Tafsīr Ibn ʿAbbās* — I reiterate that no manuscripts have been found which call this al-Fīrūzābādī, *Tanwīr al-miqbās*) date from the ninth *hijrī* century onwards; the fact that there are some fifty of these manuscripts at the very least indicates a tremendous rise in popularity of the text in the post al-Fīrūzābādī era. Perhaps he did have something to do with this work after all!

However, the fame of al-Fīrūzābādī and his quite apparent excellence in scholarship clearly militates against this suggestion. That particular explanation of fraud does not seem a reasonable account of the facts. Far more likely is that in one of the early printed editions, the editor (or more likely, simply the scribe) wanted to be able to provide a full title for the work he had in manuscript copy, perhaps with just the title *Tafsīr Ibn ʿAbbās*; any number of biographical and bibliographical references would have provided him with the fact that al-Fīrūzābādī wrote a text called *Tanwīr al-miqbās min tafsīr Ibn ʿAbbās*, and thus the two works were put together

15 Full details on this will be found below in the discussion of al-Dīnawarī, section II.ii.

16 *GAS*, I, 34-35; these will be discussed below in section II.iii.

with no particular thought as to the accuracy of the supposition. It is interesting to note the process that such ascriptions go through and that this would appear to be a common occurrence; I have noted the case before in the so-called Ibn ʿAbbās text, *al-Lughāt fī ʾl-Qurʾān*.[17] There, an early editor of the text (published in the margin of al-Dirīnī, *al-Taysīr fī ʿilm al-Qurʾān*) suggested that he "thought" this was the work of Abū ʿUbayd (on the basis of a statement already incorrectly changed by another editor in al-Suyūṭī's *al-Itqān*); this supposition became "fact" when the text was reprinted a few years later (in the margin of *Tafsīr al-Jalālayn*), when the later editor left out the words "I think."

That the ascription of *Tafsīr Ibn ʿAbbās* to al-Fīrūzābādī is just a result of ignorance, based on no real substance, is suggested by the *isnād* of the text found at the very beginning of virtually every copy, both printed and manuscript, which ends sometime in the fourth *hijrī* century.[18] No mention whatsoever is found of al-Fīrūzābādī. A similar phenomenon was noted in the *Lughāt* text just mentioned and its ascription to Abū ʿUbayd, who is never mentioned in the *isnād*s of the work, although the lines of transmission extend beyond his death date.

It seems likely that the ascription of *Tafsīr Ibn ʿAbbās* to al-Fīrūzābādī occurred when the text was published. It has not been possible, however, to determine for certain just when the first edition came out. The earliest edition I have seen is that from Bombay published in 1863; that is also the earliest date that Brockelmann gives,[19] in

---

17 "Ibn ʿAbbās's *al-Lughāt fī ʾl-Qurʾān*," *BSOAS* 44 (1981), 15-25, see also the follow-up note, "Ibn ʿAbbās's *Gharīb al-Qurʾān*," *BSOAS* 46 (1983), 332-33. I regret that when writing those articles I had not seen Ismail Cerrahoğlu, "Tefsirde Atâ b. Ebi Rabâh ve Ibn Abbâs'dan rivâyet ettiği Garibu'l-Kur'ani," *Ankara Üniversitesi ilâhiyat fakültesi dergisi* 22 (1978), 17-104, where the texts of the Esad Efendi and the Atif Efendi manuscripts and the so-called Abū ʿUbayd printed text are published in full (in Arabic) and compared. For more on the place of Ibn ʿAbbās in Qurʾānic lexicography, see A. Rippin, "Lexicographical texts and the Qurʾān," in A. Rippin (ed.), *Approaches to the history of the interpretation of the Qurʾān* (Oxford, 1988), pp. 158-74.

18 The exact point in time varies; see below, section II.ii, on al-Dīnawarī.

19 In his listing under Ibn ʿAbbās; see below, section II.iv, on Ibn ʿAbbās.

that case for an edition from Būlāq. That these two editions are independent seems likely, but it also seems probable that they stem from an earlier common, printed source. Even if it became possible to determine the earliest printed copy, that there would necessarily be any indication there that the scribe/editor was the one responsible for this attribution is a matter of speculation.

Finally, if one wished to produce literary and stylistic evidence against this ascription, such would certainly be theoretically possible, if at this point somewhat superfluous. Al-Fīrūzābādī's previously mentioned *Baṣāʾir dhawī ʾl-tamyīz* may be compared to the *Tafsīr Ibn ʿAbbās* in terms of a matter such as style of compression; such a comparison might then suggest if it would at least be possible to conceive that the two texts are related. A parallel could be drawn between two *tafsīr*s of al-Wāḥidī (d. 468/1075),[20] *al-Wajīz fī tafsīr al-Qurʾān* (or *Tafsīr al-Qurʾān al-wajīz*), a very brief work comparable in style to *Tafsīr Ibn ʿAbbās* (the two texts will be compared more fully later in this paper), and his *al-Wasīṭ bayn al-maqbūḍ wa ʾl-basīṭ*, a more expansive type of commentary; al-Wāḥidī also wrote a third, even larger *tafsīr*, *al-Basīṭ*, but this is not available to me, nor do I believe that it would add much to the discussion. The purpose of this parallel would be to act as a control mechanism: to exhibit the methods of compression of information that do in fact take place in works known to stem from one author and then see if comparable methods are exhibited in the case of al-Fīrūzābādī and *Tafsīr Ibn ʿAbbās*.

In his comments on Q. 1/7 ≪The path of those whom You have blessed≫ al-Wāḥidī says the following in *al-Wasīṭ*:[21]

> His saying: ≪The path of those whom You have blessed≫: that is, [blessed] with perseverance and sincerity in faith and guidance to the path. They are the prophet,

---

20 On al-Wāḥidī, see *GAL*, I, 411, Suppl. I, 730, and A. Rippin, "The exegetical genre *asbāb al-nuzūl*: a bibliographical and terminological survey," *BSOAS* 48 (1985), 4-5.

21 Berlin manuscript Sprenger 415, f. 6b; see W. Ahlwardt (ed.), *Die Handschriften-Verzeichnisse der Königlichen Bibliothek zu Berlin* (Berlin, 1887), I, 298-99. This text is now published under the title *Tafsīr al-wasīṭ bayn al-wajīz wa ʾl-basīṭ* in *al-Mawrid*, 17 (1988), 301; there are some differences in wording between the printed text and the Berlin manuscript. This edition, by M.U. Jāsim and N.Ḥ.

> may the peace and blessing of God be upon him, Abū Bakr and ʿUmar, may God be pleased with the two of them. This is the statement of Abū'l-ʿAliya. Al-Suddī and Qatāda said: it means the road to Islam. Ibn ʿAbbās said: they are the people of Moses and Jesus before they turned away from the religion of God [cf. Q. 8/53].

While this is a fairly brief section of *al-Wasīṭ*, compared to other paragraphs of the commentary, it would seem to exhibit most of the characteristics of this work, especially when compared to its author's treatment of the same passage in *al-Wajīz*:[22]

> <<The path of those whom You have blessed>> with guidance; they are the communities of Moses and Jesus before the blessings of God turned against them [cf. Q. 8/53]. It is also said [that it means] those whom God has mentioned in His statement: <<[anyone who obeys God and the messenger] stands by those whom God has favored [such as prophets, loyal persons, martyrs and honorable men]>> [Q. 4/69].

Neither of al-Wāḥidī's commentaries, in this instance, provides a fully explicit explanation of the passage in question. The technique of cross-reference within the Qur'ān and, implicitly at least, within the *tafsīr* itself, marks the concision of *al-Wajīz* as compared to *al-Wasīṭ*. The absence in the latter text of the justification of the gloss concerning Muḥammad, Abū Bakr, and ʿUmar may seem a rather major shortcoming, but perhaps the reference is assumed to be well enough known not to require support of this type. The citation of the authorities of the various statements is absent from *al-Wajīz*, as is the full extent of the range of possible meanings. Likewise, the technical terminology of the science of *tafsīr* — *ay, yaʿnī, qawluhu* — is missing from *al-Wajīz*, where only the word *wa-qīla* — in order to introduce alternative meanings — is in evidence in this passage.

Ṣāliḥ, covers only al-Wāḥidī's introduction and *sūrat al-fātiḥa*; the editors also provide a biographical introduction. I have not been able to consult any issues of *al-Mawrid* past 1988 and do not know if further sections have been published; the editors mention in the introduction that they hope to publish the whole text in the future.

22 British Library, Or. 9485, f. 4a, and printed in the margin of al-Nawawī, *Marāḥ Labīd* (Cairo, 1305), p. 3; my thanks to F. MacKay of Montreal for providing me with a copy of the printed text.

To this procedure may be compared al-Fīrūzābādī and *Tafsīr Ibn ʿAbbās*. The latter states:[23]

> ≪The path of those whom You have blessed≫: the religion of those to whom You have shown favor by means of religion. They are the followers of Moses (before the blessings of God changed against them [cf. Q. 8/53]) when clouds put them in the shadow and manna and quail were sent down to them in the desert [cf. Q. 2/57]; it is also said [that the people who have been blessed are] the prophets.

Al-Fīrūzābādī's *Baṣāʾir dhawīʾl-tamyīz* is not set up as a verse-by-verse commentary in the style of the others, and thus it is more difficult to make immediate comparisons. It is possible for example to look at his treatment of the root *nūn-ʿayn-mīm*[24] as used in Q.1/7, *anʿamta*, ≪You have blessed≫, where a number of facts immediately become clear. His is a very technical discussion, involving variant readings and matters of pronunciation and spelling, all concerned with the entire root and its use in the Qurʾān. There is no relationship between this work and *Tafsīr Ibn ʿAbbās*. The two books are speaking to radically different audiences, and while this would not necessarily rule out the possibility of them being written by the same author, the likelihood is quite small. It is not possible to see any measure of relationship between the two, in terms of those sorts of parallels between the two texts of al-Wāḥidī, for example, and thus the exercise is rather one of futility. Perhaps if a more standard *tafsīr* work of al-Fīrūzābādī were available, a more profitable comparison could be made; but at this point, that does not seem possible.

II.ii. Al-Dīnawarī, *al-Wāḍiḥ fī tafsīr al-Qurʾān*

Abū Muḥammad ʿAbd Allāh ibn Muḥammad ibn Wahb al-Dīnawarī died in 308/920. He is listed in Sezgin[25] as the author of a *tafsīr* entitled *al-Wāḍiḥ fī tafsīr al-Qurʾān*, which is found in three manuscript copies: Leiden 1651 (written 726/1326, 311ff.), Aya Sofya

---

23 For a translation of the full passage, see below, Appendix 3, part 1.

24 Al-Fīrūzābādī, *Baṣāʾir dhawī ʾl-tamyīz*, V, 88-91; see also I, 128-32, for a collection of comments on Sūra 1.

25 *GAS*, I, 42.

221 (written 585/1189, 312ff.) and 222 (written 578/1182, 234ff.),[26] and Hyderabad Āṣafīya *tafsīr* 5.[27] Al-Dawūdī[28] knows the author and this title but knows nothing else, not even the date of death. At an even earlier date, al-Thaʿlabī (d. 427/1035) also knows the author and the work under this title, transmitted by Abū Ḥanīfa al-Qazwīnī to one of al-Thaʿlabī's contemporaries, Abū Bakr Muḥammad ibn Yaʿqūb al-Ustuwāʾī.[29]

Al-Thaʿlabī's *al-Kashf waʾl-bayān fī tafsīr al-Qurʾān*, in which mention of al-Dīnawarī is found in its bibliographical introduction, is a large compendium of *tafsīr* reports taken from a wide variety of sources. If one were able to find in this book any quotes ascribed to al-Dīnawarī, then one would have grounds for deciding whether the work that in the printed editions is ascribed to al-Fīrūzābādī and in these manuscripts is called *al-Wāḍiḥ* were in fact the same as that in the possession of al-Thaʿlabī. Unfortunately, as with so many similar things, this is not so easy. Al-Thaʿlabī does not cite "books" as such, despite the bibliographical introduction. The citations tend to be *isnād*-oriented (that is, giving a full chain back to Muḥammad or his companions) or simply presented in the name of the person

---

26 Sezgin's listing suggests that these two are only partial copies of the text, citing them as parts 1 and 2.

27 *Fihrist-i Kutub-i ʿArabī wa Fārisī wa Urdū makhzūna-i Kutubkhāna-i Aṣafīya-i Sarkār-i ʿAlī* (Hyderabad, 1332), I, 534 — no further information is available to me at this point; this manuscript was also listed by Brockelmann, *GAL*, Suppl. I, 334, in his entry for al-Dīnawarī.

28 *Ṭabaqāt al-mufassirīn*, I, 244, no. 233.

29 See Isaiah Goldfeld, *Qurʾānic commentary in the eastern Islamic tradition of the first four centuries of the hijra: An annotated edition of the preface to al-Thaʿlabī's "Kitāb al-kashf wa ʾl-bayān ʿan tafsīr al-Qurʾān"* (Acre, 1984), p. 52; Goldfeld was unable to identify either of these people. My thanks to Uri Rubin for providing me with a copy of this text. Josef van Ess has also dealt with questions concerning the identity of al-Dīnawarī and the problem of the *tafsīr* in his *Ungenützte Texte zur Karrāmīya. Eine Materialsammlung*, Sitzungsberichte der Heidelberger Akademie der Wissenschaft, Phil.-hist. Klasse, 1980, 6 (Heidelberg: Carl Winter Universitätsverlag, 1980), pp. 50-53; van Ess did not compare the *isnād*s of the printed editions of the text. See also Claude Gilliot, "Les débuts de l'exégèse coranique," *Revue du Monde Musulman et de la Méditerranée*, 58/4 (1990), 87-88.

to whom a given report is ultimately attributed.[30] A properly edited version of the text may help in the search for "reconstructed sources"; but at this point, with the extent of the text available to me and no proper study of the full text having been done, it does not seem possible to verify matters concerning the text of al-Dīnawarī in this way.

Overall, it would be tempting simply to say that the text which is in our possession is, in all of its manifestations, the work of al-Dīnawarī and leave it at that — the work is a late third century, early fourth century text that over the period of transmission lost various features, especially the title page and introduction[31] and simply came to be called *Tafsīr Ibn ʿAbbās* on account of its *isnād*. This is indeed what I had been inclined to do in my article on al-Zuhrī.[32] However, things are not so plain, as a result of a complex series of *isnād*s found attached to the various transmissions of the text, not all of which go through al-Dīnawarī. The *isnād* structure is illustrated in the chart found at the end of this paper in Appendix 2.

How are we to account for the fact that not all the *isnād*s go through al-Dīnawarī? Any logical explanation of the *isnād* structure might suggest that the text perhaps has its origin in the time of ʿAmmār ibn ʿAbd al-Majīd al-Harawī. Strangely enough, however, in the very next generation, al-Dīnawarī is claiming to have written the work. An introduction to the work, found only in the Leiden 1651 manuscript copy (perhaps also in the Aya Sofya copy, but it has not been possible to check this aspect) states the following: "Abū Muḥammad al-Dīnawarī, author (*ṣāḥib*) of this *al-Wāḍiḥ* which he has gathered, extracting it from the sources and abbreviating it for the people of knowledge, says...." It would appear, however, that other people in his generation transmitted the same text without any reference to him. Multiple transmission of the text may well suggest that the material has its ultimate origin in preaching[33] in the time

30 See, e.g., British Library manuscripts of al-Thaʿlabī, *al-Kashf wa ʾl-bayān*: Add. 9478 (no title page), Add. 19926 (part 1), Or. 9060 (part 3); and the Chester Beatty manuscripts 3617 (part 1), 3876 (part 1), 3903 (part 7), 5052 (part 2).

31 On which see below, section II.iii, on al-Kalbī.

32 See "al-Zuhrī," *BSOAS* 47 (1984), 23-24, nn. 15-17.

33 An issue to be considered further in section III, below.

of the generation before al-Dīnawarī; if that preaching was copied down by various students and pious people, the question then is, would al-Dīnawarī claim actual authorship for the work?

The implications of these aspects of the ascription issue are raised in the analysis section of this paper (section III), where an attempt is made to elicit some criteria for determining ways of isolating the date of the text.

II.iii. Al-Kalbī, *Tafsīr al-Kalbī*

In Sezgin[34] a listing is given for the *Tafsīr* of Muḥammad ibn al-Sā'ib al-Kalbī (d. 146/763) comprising a list of some fifty manuscripts, the earliest copy among these being that found in the Şehid Ali Paşa library dated to 885/1480. Wansbrough[35] also used this text (in manuscripts Aya Sofya 118 and Hamidiya 40). He ascribed it to al-Kalbī; however, he exhibits some degree of puzzlement in trying to understand how this text could be so early, and he decides that it must be substantially later than the era suggested by the ascription, at least in the form in which the text now exists. That any of the text itself ever had an "earlier" existence is, to me, questionable, as I hope will become evident in this paper. Neither Wansbrough nor Sezgin mention explicitly that this text is published with a different ascription. Schwally,[36] seeming to want to have it all ways, talks of the Berlin manuscript Sprenger 404[37] listed under Ibn 'Abbās as the *tafsīr* of al-Kalbī and points out that it was published in Bombay in 1302, as Brockelmann[38] had stated in his listing under Ibn 'Abbās. Brockelmann also refers to the *tafsīr* of al-Kalbī[39] with

34 *GAS*, I, 34-35.

35 John Wansbrough, *Quranic studies: Sources and methods of scriptural interpretation* (Oxford, 1977) [hereafter cited as *QS*], esp. pp. 131-37, 140-46.

36 T. Nöldeke and F. Schwally, *Geschichte des Qorans* (Leipzig, 1909-19) [hereafter cited as *GdQ*], II, 171.

37 See W. Ahlwardt, *Handschriften-Verzeichnisse*, I, 290, no. 732.

38 That is, *GAL*, I, 190, in the first edition — this reference was not repeated in the Supplement or in the second edition of the first volume, which of course was not available to Schwally. Of the printed copy, Schwally said: "*Ich nicht habe auftreiben können*."

39 *GAL*, Suppl. I, 331-32.

reference to al-Thaʿlabī's citation of him as a source and also to an article by Levi della Vida, to be discussed in a moment. Many more manuscripts of this work other than those found in Sezgin could be listed, including several additional ones listed under Ibn ʿAbbās in Brockelmann but inexplicably omitted from Sezgin.[40]

The justification for considering this as the *tafsīr* of al-Kalbī would appear to be twofold. One reason obviously enough is the presence of his name in the *isnād*; the second is his fame as a writer of *tafsīr*. That he is traditionally considered to be part of a very unreliable chain of transmission in *tafsīr*[41] is not of much concern

---

40 *GAL*, Suppl. I, 331, lists the following manuscripts not found in *GAS*, I, 34-35: Beyazit 94 (although Sezgin does have Beyazit 563, not listed in *GAL*); Selim Aga 46 (although Sezgin does have Selim Aga 45, not found in *GAL*, so perhaps one of these entries is incorrect); Ḥūr Laila 19, 20 (the identity of this library — presumably in Istanbul — is unknown to me); Cairo, *Fihrist ...Kutubkhānah al-Khidīwīya* (Cairo, 1310, 2nd printing), I, 139-40, a reference that comprises copies 6334, 6335, 6336, 6337; Cairo, *Fihrist al-kutub al-ʿarabīya al-mawjūda bi-Dār al-Kutub li-ghāyat sanat 1921* (Cairo, 1924), I, 37, a reference that comprises six manuscripts: numbers 149 and 1 through 5 *mīm*, along with printed copies, Būlāq, 1290; Fez, Qarawīyīn, 188. *GAL*, I, 190, first edition, also lists the following manuscripts, not listed in *GAS*, I, 34-35, and not repeated in *GAL*, Suppl. I, 331: Ambrosiana, A. 47 (see O. Löfgren and R. Traini, *Catalogue of the Arabic manuscripts in the Biblioteca Ambrosiana: Vol. II Nuovo Fondo: Series A-D* [Venice, 1981], p. 25); Berlin 732 (see W. Ahlwardt, *Handschriften-Verzeichnisse*, I, 290, manuscript Sprenger 404) — which is my text 21. It was a mistake on my part, however, to state in "al-Zuhrī," *BSOAS* 47 (1984), 23-24, n. 15, that the copies missing from *GAS*, I, 34-35 were primarily from European libraries. Further additions to the list of manuscripts are: Istanbul University 4560A, 5039A, and 6904A (see I. Goldfeld, "The *tafsīr* of ʿAbdallāh b. ʿAbbās," *Der Islam* 58 [1981], 129, n. 30), and British Library, Or. 9277. Suliman Bashear of the Hebrew University drew my attention to Princeton Yahuda 2411 (on which see R. Mach, *Catalogue of Arabic manuscripts (Yahuda section) in the Garrett collection, Princeton University Library* [Princeton, 1977], p. 29), which certainly is the same text but exhibits some rather odd *isnād*s at the beginning of each of the first 5 Sūras (especially Sūra 2, which ends "Ibn Jurayj from ʿAṭāʾ from Ibn ʿAbbās," f. 5a). Given the relatively late date of this manuscript (Mach suggests the tenth *hijrī* century), it seems likely that this manuscript is to be viewed as evidence of confusion rather than as evidence of an independent (and uncorroborated) tradition in the text.

41 See, e.g., al-Suyūṭī, *al-Itqān fī ʿulūm al-Qurʾān* (Cairo, 1967), IV, 209.

to this analysis, except insofar as it may have played an almost perverse role in supporting the ascription. After all, the famous report stating that, in al-Shāfiʿī's opinion, at most 100 reports of Ibn ʿAbbās on *tafsīr* are reliable[42] would appear to be immediate evidence, in traditional terms, that this *tafsīr* is unreliable, seeing that it ascribes its entire content to Ibn ʿAbbās; al-Kalbī, having a suspect pedigree to begin with, may well have tried to foist such a thing on his unsuspecting public, or so that sort of logic would seem to go.

Interestingly enough, it would seem to be an Orientalist notion to suggest that this specific text should be ascribed to al-Kalbī; this would appear to have been motivated by a desire to discover material as old as possible, combined with a (healthy) skepticism which would doubt that an ascription to anyone from the very early generations of Muslims (i.e., Ibn ʿAbbās and his ilk) was actually true. The isolation of al-Kalbī out of the *isnād* is arbitrary and based for the most part on that desire to discover early texts.

The ascription is also based, however, on the notion that al-Kalbī is, after all, supposed to have written a *tafsīr* and perhaps this is it. It has already been pointed out by other scholars, however, that quotations which are supposedly taken out of al-Kalbī's *tafsīr* do not to the slightest extent match the material found in *Tafsīr Ibn ʿAbbās*. G. Levi della Vida[43] appears to have noted this first in an article where a contrast is drawn between the quotes ascribed to al-Kalbī by al-Damīrī[44] on the one hand, and passages in the manuscript copies of *Tafsīr al-Kalbī* and the printed edition of *Tanwīr al-miqbās*, on the other, with the conclusion that there is no material connection between them. Al-Damīrī's text, dealing with *faras* (horse), cites the story of Paul's conversion to Christianity (and the image of his ride on a horse) as reported by al-Kalbī's comments on Q. 9/30, «The Christians say the Messiah is the

42 See al-Suyūṭī, *al-Itqān*, IV, 209; for a general assessment of Ibn ʿAbbās, see idem, IV, 205-08, and also the references provided in *GdQ*, II, 163-70.

43 G. Levi della Vida, "al-Kalbī e gli scismi cristiani," *RSO* 13 (1932), 327-31, esp. p. 330, n. 4.

44 *Ḥayāt al-ḥayawān* (Būlāq, 1283), II, 254.

son of God. That is what they say with their mouths>>. The very extensive haggadic narrative in the commentary connected to this verse, reported by al-Damīrī and ascribed to al-Kalbī, would be worth comparing to similar treatments in other *tafsīr*s. What is significant here, however, is that at least a fair portion of the material found in other *tafsīr* works said to stem from al-Kalbī's *tafsīr* is precisely of this haggadic nature, and this contrasts very clearly with the brief, unelaborated, matter-of-fact approach in *Tafsīr Ibn ʿAbbās*. Al-Fīrūzābādī's *Baṣāʾir dhawīʾl-tamyīz* provides a number of examples. He quotes al-Kalbī as the authority for the age of Zakariyā at the birth of John.[45] Another time he is quoted regarding the Qurʾānic use of "Shekhina" (*sakīna*)[46] and finally for the definition of *kanūd* ("grudging") (Q. 100/6), here glossed as "being ungrateful for a blessing."[47] These are the only quotes from al-Kalbī in the entire work; certainly the last instance could be said to have something in common stylistically with *Tafsīr Ibn ʿAbbās*,[48] but the other two are of a more haggadic nature. Obviously the scope of this comparison is not really sufficient for a full judgment, but the point seems reasonably clear.

Al-Dawūdī[49] in his entry on al-Kalbī makes the observation that al-Kalbī wrote two works: *Nāsikh al-Qurʾān wa-mansūkhuhu* and "his famous *tafsīr*," *Tafsīr al-āy alladhī nazala fī aqwām bi-aʿyānihim*.

45 *Baṣāʾir dhawīʾl-tamyīz*, VI, 95; whether al-Fīrūzābādī is actually quoting a book of al-Kalbī is of course still open to question.

46 *Baṣāʾir dhawīʾl-tamyīz*, III, 240.

47 *Baṣāʾir dhawīʾl-tamyīz*, IV, 389.

48 The first gloss in *Tafsīr Ibn ʿAbbās* is: "He is indeed ungrateful for the blessing of his Lord," using the same vocabulary as does al-Fīrūzābādī's quote from al-Kalbī; the word is said to be in the dialect of Kinda (*Tafsīr Ibn ʿAbbās* [Beirut, 1360], p. 517). Essentially the same treatment is found in Ibn Ḥasnūn, *al-Lughāt fī ʾl-Qurʾān* (Beirut, 1946; see Rippin, "Lughāt," p. 17) but is said to be the dialect of Kināna (although the textual tradition of the work is very varied and such divergences could easily have crept into either *Tafsīr* or *Lughāt*). *Tafsīr Ibn ʿAbbās* goes on, however, to provide three alternative glosses for *kanūd*, never expressing an opinion of course as to what "Ibn ʿAbbās" or "al-Kalbī" actually thought the word meant. *Tafsīr al-Jalālayn* provides a similar definition to that provided by al-Kalbī/al-Fīrūzābādī.

49 *Ṭabaqāt al-mufassirīn*, II, 144, no. 491.

The latter sounds as if it may well have been from the *ta'yīn al-mubham* genre, similar to al-Suhaylī (d. 581/1285),[50] *Kitāb al-ta'rīf wa 'l-i'lām fī-mā ubhima min al-Qur'ān*[51] or al-Suyūṭī, *Kitāb al-mufḥamāt al-aqrān fī mubhamāt al-Qur'ān.*[52] Both of these works are fairly brief but provide a glimpse of the haggadic material with which the genre is generally concerned. The point to be noted, however, is that works of this type display a mode of exegesis that would certainly be in keeping with the character of the passages ascribed to al-Kalbī in later works. That this book could be described as "famous" some 500 years ago and all trace of it have disappeared from view by today is rather disheartening but nevertheless apparently true.

Al-Tha'labī also knows of *Tafsīr al-Kalbī*[53] through three different paths, none of which corresponds to that found in the *isnād* of *Tafsīr Ibn 'Abbās*, although all three of his cited versions do end: al-Kalbī → Abū Ṣāliḥ → Ibn 'Abbās; also, the transmission of Yūsuf ibn Bilāl has Muḥammad ibn Marwān as the name preceding that of al-Kalbī. Al-Tha'labī does not give a title other than *Tafsīr al-Kalbī* for this work; only quotes from within the text would have established the actual character of the *tafsīr* cited by al-Tha'labī, but it does not appear possible to document that in any sort of conclusive way, as noted above. Al-Suyūṭī's *al-Durr al-manthūr fī 'l-tafsīr bi 'l-ma'thūr*[54] might have been a better source for this type of analysis; that author, however, does not list al-Kalbī (or al-Dīnawarī or al-Fīrūzābādī) in his *Ṭabaqāt al-mufassirīn*,[55] thus suggesting he does

---

50 See *GAL*, I, 413, Suppl. I, 733-34.

51 Published Cairo, 1938.

52 Published in the bottom margin of volume IV (starting on page 491) of al-Jamal (d. 1204/1798), *al-Futūḥāt al-ilāhīya bi-tawḍīḥ tafsīr al-Jalālayn* (recent Beirut reprint, but a different edition than the one referred to here as text 11; it does not have *Tafsīr Ibn 'Abbās* in the margin but has, in addition to al-Suyūṭī, marginal prints of *Tafsīr al-Jalālayn* and al-'Ukbarī, *Imlā' mā manna bihi al-Raḥmān min wujūh al-i'rāb wa'l-qirā'āt fī jāmi' al-Qur'ān*). Al-Suyūṭī's treatise is now also available separately, edited by Muṣṭafā Dīb al-Bugha, Beirut/Damascus, 1407/1986.

53 See Goldfeld, *Qur'ānic commentary*, pp. 23-26.

54 Tehran, 1377.

55 Beirut, 1983.

not know the works or at least does not value them highly enough to consider citing them. It is not surprising, therefore, that I have been unable to locate a citation of a *tafsīr* of al-Kalbī in *al-Durr al-manthūr*, at least to the extent that I have been able to check it.

The introduction to *al-Wāḍiḥ* of al-Dīnawarī, mentioned above, is known to me only in the Leiden manuscript copy; it most certainly does not appear in the printed versions of *Tafsīr Ibn ʿAbbās*, nor is it found in the Abū Mūsā recension in British Library Or. 9277. Nevertheless, that one version does provide an interesting view on the existence of the *tafsīr* of al-Kalbī and its relationship to the text in question here. The whole text of the introduction reads as follows:[56]

> Abū Muḥammad al-Dīnawarī, author of this *al-Wāḍiḥ* which he has gathered, extracting it from the sources and abbreviating it for the people of knowledge, says:
>
> Know that all of the Qurʾān includes the commanded and the forbidden, the promise and the threat, the abrogator and the abrogated, the permitted and the forbidden, the clear and the ambiguous, the literal and the metaphoric, the specific and the general, information on the present and the future, the urging of good and the censuring of evil, and the description of the Creator and things related to Him and the description of the creation and things related to it.
>
> Wherever God Most High mentions in the Qurʾān <<O you who believe>> [Q., *passim*], He commands them with an order or forbids them from something. Wherever God Most High mentions <<What will make you realize [*mā adrā ka*]>> [Q. 101/3, 10, etc.], He informs His prophet about that (matter); wherever God Most High mentions <<What will make you realize [*mā yudrīka*]>> [Q. 33/63, 42/17, 80/3], He does not inform him about that (matter).
>
> Anything that is difficult for you in this abbreviated (*tafsīr*), look for (the explanation of) that in the *tafsīr* of al-Kalbī in the transmission of Yūsuf [ibn] Bilāl. Praise be to God and may there be prayers for the messenger of God.

It is of course this last paragraph that is significant, for al-Dīnawarī would appear to be suggesting that there is some

56 F. 2b of Leiden manuscript 1651 (Warn. 507); both the beginning and the end of this introduction are printed in the Leiden catalogue, P. de Jong and M.J. de Goeje (eds.), *Catalogus Codicum Orientalium Bibliothecae Acadamiae Lugduno Batavae* (Leiden, 1866), IV, 16.

relationship between this work of his and the *tafsīr* of al-Kalbī but that, most certainly, the two works are not the same. Note that the transmission via Yūsuf ibn Bilāl is one of those versions known and mentioned in al-Thaʿlabī's bibliographical introduction to his *tafsīr*, as mentioned above.

In conclusion, there is no justification for Sezgin or Wansbrough claiming that this *tafsīr* is actually that of al-Kalbī or even that it necessarily belongs to the formative period of Islamic exegesis, at least on the basis of the ascription alone.

II.iv. Ibn ʿAbbās, *Tafsīr Ibn ʿAbbās*

In Brockelmann[57] we find a listing under ʿAbd Allāh ibn ʿAbbās (who is thought to have died in about 68/687) for a *tafsīr* that is said to exist in some 20 manuscript copies and to have been published in Būlāq in 1863, 1866, 1873, and 1885/1290, and in Cairo in 1302/3, 1316 with *Tafsīr al-Jalālayn*, and in the margin of *al-Durr al-manthūr* by al-Suyūṭī in 1314. He also lists a work under the title of *Tanwīr al-Qiyās* (*sic*; it actually reads *iqtibās*) published with *Tafsīr al-Jalālayn* (Meerit [*sic*] 1299), with reference to the Ellis and Ellis/Fulton British Library catalogues of printed Arabic books. He also suggests that the *Tafsīr* of Ibn ʿAbbās is cited by Ibn Qutayba[58] and al-Ghazzālī.[59] Why Brockelmann should

57 *GAL*, Suppl. I, 331.

58 *GAL*, Suppl. I, 331, cites Ibn Qutayba, *ʿUyūn al-akhbār* (2nd ed.) II, 340, line 13; I have not been able to ascertain which edition Brockelmann is referring to here; presumably it is his own, but that reference does not tally with the copy of his work that I have been able to locate. The Egyptian edition (Cairo, 1925, in 4 volumes) indicates in the index that there are 8 citations of Ibn ʿAbbās in the work; only one of those is in reference to the Qurʾān — IV, 123, line 7 — where Q. 46/35 and 79/46 are commented upon by Ibn ʿAbbās; there is no indication there, however, that this is being quoted from a book by him.

59 *GAL*, Suppl. I, 331, refers to al-Ghazzālī, *al-Tibr al-masbūk*, 120/10, 115/15; in the edition of the text available to me (Cairo, 1861) I have not been able to locate any comments of Ibn ʿAbbās with regard to the Qurʾān, although he is quoted in the work as the source of a variety of anecdotes (e.g., p. 116).

have isolated these two particular sources remains unclear to me. There are, of course, many citations of Ibn ʿAbbās in all the major *tafsīr*s, especially, e.g., al-Ṭabarī, although none of these actually suggests they are citing a book of Ibn ʿAbbās, any more than such would appear to be suggested in these works of Ibn Qutayba or al-Ghazzālī. Brockelmann also suggests that a *Tafsīr* of Ibn ʿAbbās exists in a version ascribed to al-Kalbī with reference made to the article of Levi della Vida, cited above in section II.iii.

Sezgin, under Ibn ʿAbbās,[60] speaks of the quotations cited from Ibn ʿAbbās in works such as al-Ṭabarī, *Jāmiʿ al-bayān ʿan taʾwīl āy al-Qurʾān*, and then mentions that the *tafsīr* under the name of Ibn ʿAbbās has been transmitted through al-Kalbī and that it is also available partially in the work of al-Fīrūzābādī in numerous prints, as mentioned above in section II.i.

Other references to a *Tafsīr* of Ibn ʿAbbās abound, all indicating some measure of confusion over the ascription of the text. H. Ritter[61] appears to have known that the manuscripts were the same as the printed text, although he is less than explicit. Goldfeld notes in his article[62] that the *Tafsīr Ibn ʿAbbās* in the Istanbul University manuscripts which he had examined is identical to the *Tanwīr al-miqbās* of 'al-Fīrūzābādī'; he then connects this to the *tafsīr* of al-Kalbī.

---

60 *GAS*, I, 25-28.

61 H. Ritter, "Ayasofya kütüphânesinde tefsir ilmine ait arapça yazmalar," *Türkiyat Mecmuası*, 7/8 (1945), part 2, pp. 6-7. Ritter specifically mentions only Bankipore 1322 (see M.M. Nadwi, *Catalogue of the Arabic and Persian manuscripts in the Oriental Public Library at Bankipore* [Patna, 1932], vol. 18, part 2, pp. 1-3, on manuscripts 1322 and 1323, both *Tafsīr Ibn ʿAbbās*: see *GAL*, Suppl. I, 331, and *GAS*, I, 34-35) as a comparable manuscript but does also cite A.G. Ellis, *Catalogue of Arabic books in the British Museum* (London, 1894-1935), I, 4-5, and its supplement by A.S. Fulton and A.G. Ellis, *Supplementary catalogue of Arabic printed books in the British Museum* (London, 1926), p. 4, suggesting that he was aware that this text was the same as the published one (which, in the British Library catalogues, is ascribed to Ibn ʿAbbās, although it is noted there [for at least one printed copy] that it is also found ascribed to al-Fīrūzābādī — see Ellis, *Catalogue*, II, 278).

62 Goldfeld, "ʿAbdallāh b. ʿAbbās," *Der Islam* 58 (1981), 129, n. 30.

In Ahlwardt's catalogue of the Berlin manuscripts, for a text listed under Ibn ʿAbbās, *Tafsīr al-Qurʾān*,[63] the following comment is made at the end: "Ueber den Commentar hat Elfiruzabadi 817/1414 ein grosses Werk geschrieben, das er [*Tanwīr al-miqbās*] genannt hat." This would appear to be an important statement; it is a logical supposition trying to explain how the various ascriptions may have come about, but I see no proof for it whatsoever.

Finally, Goldziher too notes the *tafsīr* in his discussion of Ibn ʿAbbās[64] but is non-committal about its ascription, deferring the issue to a full study. This attitude is continued by Veccia Vaglieri in her encyclopedia article on ʿAbd Allāh ibn ʿAbbās,[65] where she mentions "a *tafsīr* or *tafsīr*s ascribed" to Ibn ʿAbbās, with reference to Brockelmann and Goldziher, but notes that the material needs studying before its ascription can be confirmed or denied.

All this becomes very confusing as to whether Brockelmann and/or Sezgin at the very least were aware of the identity of all these texts, which they are citing in various places, but such an issue is fortunately not of great concern here. It is apparent, though, that a number of printed editions of the text in question make no mention of al-Fīrūzābādī or the title *Tanwīr al-miqbās* and simply call the work *Tafsīr Ibn ʿAbbās*. I have consulted three editions published in Meerut (India) between 1866 and 1882 (texts 4, 5, and 6), an edition published in the margin of al-Jamal, *al-Futūḥāt al-ilāhīya* (text 11), as well as the Chester Beatty manuscripts 4224 and 5465 (text 14) and British Library manuscript Or. 9277 (text 13); all of these versions are entitled *Tafsīr Ibn ʿAbbās*, with no mention of al-Fīrūzābādī or al-Dīnawarī (all mention al-Kalbī in the *isnād* of course).

Another *tafsīr* attributed to Ibn ʿAbbās is found in folios 65b through 92b, line 11, of India Office manuscript 3795. A short section dealing with *Sūrat al-Wāqiʿa*, it bears no relationship to the *Tafsīr Ibn ʿAbbās* in question here. Most of the anecdotes in the

---

63 W. Ahlwardt, *Handschriften-Verzeichnisse*, I, 290, entry 732.

64 Ignaz Goldziher, *Die Richtungen der islamischen Koranauslegung* (Leiden, 1920), esp. p. 77.

65 L. Veccia Vaglieri, *EI*², I, 40-41.

text that are transmitted in Ibn ʿAbbās's name (and these account for only a small proportion of the whole text) relate to eschatological matters rather than to direct exegesis of the Qurʾān; the exegetical material that is present is not attributed to Ibn ʿAbbās.[66] The text, although perhaps interesting on its own merits, has no bearing on the work in question here.

All this discussion, however, raises two related problems that must be confronted: first, why would it be so commonly assumed that this is the *Tafsīr* of Ibn ʿAbbās, and why would it have been ascribed to him to begin with (in the *isnād* at least); second, how do we know that it is not from Ibn ʿAbbās; or, to put the issue positively, how can we determine the time of origin of the text: what are the criteria that are available to do so? These considerations, then, lead to the "criteria" part of this paper. The detective work of collecting the basic facts is over; the analysis must now commence.

III. Criteria for Dating

At the beginning of the Leiden manuscript (text 12) there is the introduction, translated above, in which al-Dīnawarī claims to have written the text. This, as has already been suggested, is not without its problematic elements, given the existence of the text in recensions that make no mention of al-Dīnawarī. The question that must therefore be faced is whether it is possible for us to elicit other types of information from the text so as to obtain some idea concerning the date of origination of the work and, perhaps, its likely ascription (although I would consider the latter task to be of lesser concern than the former).

Two general approaches immediately suggest themselves; one involves a more detailed analysis of the *isnād* structure, in line with common analyses of *isnād* "trees" in scholarship. The other approach suggests an analysis of the text itself for various literary factors that may give some indication of time of origin; by "literary factors" I mean those elements that may be considered methodological

66 See C.A. Storey, *Catalogue of Arabic manuscripts in the library of the India Office* (Oxford, 1930), vol. II, part 1, pp. 9-10 (catalogue entry number 1075), for some sample extracts from the text.

matters contained within the actual process of interpretation of given exegetes. Other approaches are of course imaginable: intrinsic factors, for example, where the actual meaning of the Qur'ān as elucidated by a commentator is to be considered; such an approach may suggest that a certain element in the text provides a covert reference to a historical period or even an event at the time of the author, or something similar. I have not found any instances in *Tafsīr Ibn ʿAbbās* that would provide such information, however. For example, the gloss of the word *ḥikma* in the common Qur'ānic phrase *al-kitāb wa 'l-ḥikma* could give dating information in some situations.[67] Where the word is glossed as *sunna*, as it is in one tradition in al-Ṭabarī, for example (in his commentary on Q. 2/129),[68] the report must be post-al-Shāfiʿī. *Tafsīr Ibn ʿAbbās* glosses the phrase consistently (e.g., in comments on Q. 2/129, 2/151, 2/231) as *al-ḥalāl wa'l-ḥarām*. This, however, cannot be taken to mean that the *tafsīr* is pre-al-Shāfiʿī; *Tafsīr al-Jalālayn*, for example, glosses the word (at, e.g., Q. 2/129) as *mā fī ['l-kitāb] min al-aḥkām*; and al-Ṭabarī's better-documented gloss (and the interpretation with which he agrees) is *al-maʿrifa bi 'l-dīn wa 'l-fiqh fīhi*.[69] Perhaps a large number of such examples of intrinsic elements that are dateable on external grounds could be gathered together to provide sufficient material for an argument concerning dating, but I do not see that emerging from *Tafsīr Ibn ʿAbbās*; nor does the state of our studies of *tafsīr* in general at this point even allow us to draw up a list of such elements, which would provide convincing material for the argument. For the time being, the *isnād* and literary factors seem to hold the most promise.

III.i. *Isnād* Structure

Appealing to the *isnād* structure of the work on the basis of the people involved — i.e., the *isnād* Muḥammad ibn Marwān → al-Kalbī → Abū Ṣāliḥ → Ibn ʿAbbās — with the result that the *isnād* is

---

67 My thanks to Gautier Juynboll for suggesting this example to me.

68 Al-Ṭabarī, *Jāmiʿ al-bayān fī ta'wīl āy al-Qur'ān* (Cairo, 1954-), III, 86-87, a report attributed to Qatāda.

69 Al-Ṭabarī, III, 87; none of the reports is attributed to Ibn ʿAbbās.

always found to be faulty, or appealing to the statement that very few *tafsīr* reports from Ibn ʿAbbās are valid, is not very helpful in the overall quest for criteria for dating;[70] the problem is that such matters give us no keys for the analysis which would allow placing the *tafsīr* in any specific historical period, be it much later than Ibn ʿAbbās or not. What the question demands is the setting up of some criteria by which all early texts may be judged.

In the above treatment of the ascription of the text of *Tafsīr Ibn ʿAbbās* to al-Dīnawarī, the matter of the *isnād* of the text was raised. The purpose was simply to point out that there did not seem to be full support for a simple ascription of the text to al-Dīnawarī; for there were, in the various *isnād*s, rival claims that seemed to have an equal priority. We know, especially from the work of Joseph Schacht, that *isnād*s tell us a variety of things, while realizing that they do not tell us what they actually claim to tell us.

The single most important element here is to recognize that the *isnād*, as a mechanism, came to be required at a certain point in Islamic history as the element that provided authenticity and validity to reports supposedly stemming from earlier authorities. The presence of *isnād*s automatically dates a report to the second century or later, at least in its final recension: it would always have been possible, after all, for a later editor to add an *isnād* to an earlier text in order to give it validity. That is of course what happened with individual reports as found in all the *ḥadīth* collections; where an opinion is simply ascribed to a prominent scholar in an early text, in a later text an *isnād* is attached to the report, tracing the information back to one of the companions of Muḥammad and finally to Muḥammad himself.

It is, according to the work of Schacht, the convergence of *isnād*s that indicates a crucial element in the understanding of the creation of reports and their authenticating structure. In the case of the *isnād* attached to *Tafsīr Ibn ʿAbbās*, the name of ʿAlī ibn Isḥāq would appear to be the pivotal one. Whether it suggests his authorship of the text is another matter, however. Superficially at least, for the same text to exist in different *isnād* versions, there must be

70 See above, n. 42.

a common source in order to account for the *isnād* always going to ʿAlī ibn Isḥāq. That is, for example, Abū Mūsā and al-Dīnawarī must have had a common source, and they would not have been dishonest in naming their source. Furthermore, the person they both name ʿAlī ibn Isḥaq must be one and the same person. This principle is the presupposition of much of this type of analysis: that once the mechanism of the *isnād* is firmly established, people will have to use it according to the rules of the game. To contemplate that these people were students of a great man, each copying down a dictated text of *tafsīr*, would be possible and would perhaps account for some of the discrepancies in the text, although I would have thought that such transcriptions would have produced greater variation in the text.

The other problem which must be faced is the possibility that the *isnād* has been attached to a text which already existed, one which may have even originated earlier than the convergence of the *isnād*s would suggest. For this reason, analysis of the *isnād* cannot provide a full criterion for dating a text; it may provide some additional evidence in order to substantiate a conclusion based upon other grounds, but as independent evidence it seems to me quite limited.

III.ii. Literary Criteria

The approach to *tafsīr* texts enunciated in Wansbrough's *Quranic Studies* embraces a variety of aspects that could be termed a "literary" approach. These include, in his book, a typology of the material as a whole and a list of twelve of what he terms "procedural devices" that perform explicative functions within each of those types, allowing analysis of the relationship "between element and framework."[71]

To illustrate and explore the possibilities of this approach in relationship to *Tafsīr Ibn ʿAbbās*, I have chosen to examine the exegesis of Sūra 1, al-Fātiḥa, as a test case; a translation of the text is found in Appendix 3, part 1, and reference to the paragraphs of that translation is made below. While the section is short and could always be argued not to be totally representative of the text, it does provide a rather nice illustration of a number of points; an

---

71 *QS*, pp. 119-21.

analysis based on such a short segment could obviously never be fully conclusive, but it does provide a place to start.

The amount of technical terminology used in the explication of Sūra 1 according to *Tafsīr Ibn ʿAbbās* is rather limited; however, even within this brief span of text some interesting facts may be noted. The text is characterized, as Wansbrough[72] has already pointed out in his analysis of "al-Kalbī" on Sūra 12 in *Quranic Studies*, by a lack of separation between commentary and text. Particles are interjected for specific purposes: *yuqālu*, "it is said," in order to introduce alternative explanations; *ay*, "that is" (e.g., in paragraph 11), in order to gloss explanations; *yaqūlu*, "He is saying" (i.e., "that is"), in order to provide a connective between text and gloss. Although an interpretation of the *basmala* does precede the interpretation of Sūra 1, it may well be that this use of *yaqūlu* in its position at the beginning of the text of interpretation (i.e., paragraph 2) should be taken as a connective applying to the entire section of the text. On the other hand, the pointing of the text in the version of Abū Mūsā (text 13) (with the possibility of it being read this way in al-Dīnawarī [text 12] also) as *naqūlu*, "We are saying," in fact makes much more sense and provides an interpretative gloss rather than a connective; that is, the statement "We are saying" is there to indicate that al-Fātiḥa is a Sūra to be recited by the individual, it is a prayer — indeed, is a part of the *ṣalāt* — and that those who recite this are stating these words as a petition to God. One could well argue also that the reading *yaqūlu* could be interpreted along these lines, that the commentator is reminding the reader/listener that the words come from God, even though they are to be recited by individuals as a petition.

Regardless of the use of *yaqūlu/naqūlu*, the point is clear: there is a predominant lack of connectives and, especially, a marked lack of the common words found in other *tafsīr*s, such as *yaʿnī* or *ay*, to provide textual markers. But what are we to make of this? The text of al-Wāḥidī, *al-Wajīz fī tafsīr al-Qurʾān*, provides a somewhat similar case, although *ay* is used there four times in the comments on Sūra 1 as a connective.[73] One suggestion which

72 See ibid, pp. 131-32.

73 See above, section II.i, and below, Appendix 3, part 2.

could be made is that the commentary with no connective indicates that its intended audience is well acquainted with the text of the Qurʾān, so that there is no question of confusing the text and the commentary. It may also indicate an origin of the text in oral delivery, where the separation is marked within the voice of the preacher.

The lines providing the glosses of *al-raḥmān* and *al-raḥīm* (paragraphs 8-9), however, need some special attention in this regard. There is a great deal of confusion among the texts as to how these sections are to be read, a problem that clearly originated in faulty pointing of the text at some time. One definition predominates: *raḥmān* means *raqīq* and *raḥīm* means *rafīq*. However, we find exactly the opposite in at least one text, i.e., *raḥmān* means *rafīq* and *raḥīm* means *raqīq*. We also find the notion that both words mean *raqīq* (as in the translation provided in Appendix 3, part 1, which has been based on a widely available version of the text) and that both mean *rafīq*. All possibilities are, therefore, covered in the suggested definitions![74] That of course is not surprising given the potential difficulties with reading the word in its unpointed form, and such confusion is easily understood. However, the significant matter is the various glosses that are then given to *raqīq* in some of the texts. We do not find further glosses when the meaning is said to be *rafīq*; but that word is found in the Qurʾān itself, and its meaning may even be deduced from the context: Q. 4/69, "The best of company are they," *wa-ḥasuna ūlāʾika rafīqan*; other etymologically related uses include *mirfaq* in Q. 18/16, meaning "pillow," *marāfiq* in Q. 5/6 meaning "elbows," and *murtafaq* in both Q. 18/29 and Q. 18/31 meaning "resting place." *Raqīq*, though, obviously caused some difficulty, at least for some editors/ transmitters/ copyists of the text. I intentionally say "editors/ transmitters/ copyists," for it is totally unclear as to when such confusion may have arisen, although the confusion which the text suggests makes it apparent that it is not the work of the actual author of the text. The root of the word is used once in the Qurʾān itself, at Q. 52/3, in a meaning generally understood to be "parchment" — not a great deal of help in

---

74 See the footnotes to the lines of Appendix 3, part 1 (nn. 113-33) for details of the variations among the texts.

understanding the gloss *raqīq* in this interpretative context. Text 12 provides a straightforward gloss: *al-raḥmān: al-raqīq alladhī yariqqu ʾl-qulūb*. Even this would suggest a certain confusion over what *raqīq* was supposed to mean, such that it was found necessary to add the etymological gloss to the word. Texts 1, 7, and 10 are more explicit in their confusion: *al-raḥmān: al-raqīq, min al-riqqa wa hiya ʾl-raḥma*. In this case not only has the gloss *raqīq* required explanation, but that explanation itself has then been glossed by a word derived from the original word for which we are looking for the meaning. This is a less than satisfactory interpretational method! However, the significant point here is that we clearly see traces of editorial intrusion into the text of the commentary. When the transmission of the text became confused or when the meaning of *raqīq* itself became unclear, it became necessary for an editor to intrude and explain the explanation that was there in the text. This is especially so in the case of a text that might well have been oral in its original presentation; such awkward explanations clearly interrupt the flow of an oral text and are the mark of a literary composition.

The citation of parallel or clarificatory passages from the Qurʾān itself is also to be noted. This is only done indirectly in *Tafsīr Ibn ʿAbbās*, at least in the section that is being examined, where, once again, knowledge of the Qurʾān would appear to be presupposed; examples are the references to Moses, the manna and the quail, and the clouds and the shadow, which within this text can simply be cited (in reverse order from their Qurʾānic origin, indicating that the author is certainly working from memory) and not indicated as being from the scriptural source. In this regard, the *tafsīr*s of Muqātil (d. 150/769) and al-Wāḥidī are far more explicit, generally introducing such glosses by *wa qāla taʿālā* or the like. This occurs, for example, seven times in the *tafsīr* of Muqātil within his commentary on Sūra 1.[75] As the translation of al-Wāḥidī in Appendix 3, part 2, illustrates, on one occasion this author is explicit (introduced by *fī qawlihi* — paragraph 8) and on another, allusive (paragraph 7).

75 See Muqātil ibn Sulaymān, *Tafsīr al-Qurʾān* (Cairo, 1969), pp. 9-12; translated in A. Rippin and J. Knappert, *Textual sources for the study of Islam* (Manchester, 1986; reprint Chicago, 1990), pp. 46-47.

The fact that *Tafsīr Ibn ʿAbbās* segments the Qur'ānic text into very short elements has been noted by Wansbrough.[76] This is the consistent approach in this work, and while it is paralleled in al-Wāḥidī, *al-Wajīz*, for Sūra 1, in that text the segments get substantially longer as the *tafsīr* progresses. It is, however, a technique clearly used in *Tafsīr al-Jalālayn* (see Appendix 3, part 3) and might also be thought to have a parallel in the *tafsīr* of Mujāhid (d. 104/722) (i.e., Warqa [d. 160/776])[77] in its very isolated segmentation of the text (and so paralleled also by the *Tafsīr* of Sufyān al-Thawrī [d. 161/777][78]). The *tafsīr* of Muqātil, on the other hand, contrasts with this type of approach because of that author's concern with narrative continuity, which forces him to attempt to face the overall sense of a given passage; this is of course the essence of the haggadic method and what separates that *tafsīr* from *Tafsīr Ibn ʿAbbās*, as Wansbrough has so masterfully illustrated.[79]

Most remarkable about this section of the *Tafsīr Ibn ʿAbbās* is the lack of superfluous interpretative material. What Wansbrough has termed "haggadic embellishment" is a prominent feature of a *tafsīr* such as that of Muqātil, who in his treatment of this Sūra adduces the *ḥadīth* also found in the Ṣaḥīḥ of Muslim, concerning God's creation of *al-fātiḥa*.[80] Muqātil also adds reports concerning the definition of Sūra 1 as the seven *mathānī*. Al-Wāḥidī's *al-Wajīz* provides another example where a summary of the interpretative stance on the Sūra is provided at the end. *Tafsīr Ibn ʿAbbās* is direct and to the point in comparison to these. This is certainly not a *tafsīr* for edification through entertainment, as may be the case for Muqātil's.

A feature of a work such as *Tafsīr al-Jalālayn*, but one also found in Muqātil, at least in his treatment of this Sūra, is the mention of

---

76 *QS*, p. 131.

77 Edited by al-Ṣūratī: Qatar and Islamabad, 1976. For the identification of *Tafsīr Mujāhid* and *Warqa*, see F. Leemhuis, "Origins and development of the *tafsīr* tradition," in A. Rippin (ed.), *Approaches*, pp. 13-30.

78 Rampur, 1965.

79 *QS*, pp. 122-24, 127: "it was the story that mattered."

80 See, e.g., *QS*, p. 133: "the unhurried, almost chatty style of Muqātil" versus the "terse, humourless, matter-of-fact" manner of *Tafsīr Ibn ʿAbbās*.

variant readings to the text of the Qurʾān. Absence of "canonical" variants in a text of *tafsīr* indicates, perhaps, a redaction of the text prior to the time of their final canonization, a feat attributed to the work of Ibn Mujāhid and given caliphal authority in the year 322/934.[81] This would seem the best way to understand the variability in the citation of this type of information.

Variants are cited in *Tafsīr Ibn ʿAbbās* (although not in Sūra 1), but there would appear to be no system as to whether a variant is cited or not in the text as a whole. In Sūra 1 there is one common variant found in the "canonical" lists, yet it is not cited in *Tafsīr Ibn ʿAbbās*: *malik* versus *mālik* with a written *alif*, read the latter way by ʿĀṣim and al-Kisāʾī. Other uncited possible variants include reading *ṣirāṭ* with a *sīn* instead of a *ṣād* (attributed to Qunbal) and leaving the pronoun *hum* with a *ḍamma* even when preceded by a *kasra* or *yāʾ*, thus reading *alayhum*; the latter is attributed to Ḥamza.[82]

The matter of verse division could also be considered, for it is a related, masoretic activity; a basic dispute exists between the Kufans, who make the *basmala* into verse 1, and the Medinans, who do not but who split the last verse after "those whom You have blessed," such that both versions end up with seven verses in total (probably because of the strong tradition concerning Sūra 1 being the seven *mathānī*).[83] Of this dispute we likewise see no trace in *Tafsīr Ibn ʿAbbās*, although the sense of "canonization" of verse division traditions may well be thought to be slight anyway.

The significance of the absence of this information on variants and verse divisions is perhaps not hard to establish. Adrian Brockett has recently written on the notion that the variants to the text of the Qurʾān are more intellectual treats than items of significance to the individual Muslim.[84] Their presence in a work such as that of *Tafsīr al-Jalālayn* is to be expected therefore, since it is by its very

81 See A. Welch, "Ḳurʾān," *EI*², v, 408-09.

82 Al-Dānī, *Kitāb al-taysīr fīʾl-qirāʾāt al-sabʿ* (Istanbul, 1930), pp. 18-19.

83 Traditions do exist such that the Sūra has six or eight verses, the division still taking place at the same point of the text; see al-Farrāʾ (although this ascription is doubtful), *Kitāb ʿadad al-āy fīʾl-Qurʾān*, Chester Beatty manuscript 4788.

84 A. Brockett, "The Value of the Ḥafṣ and Warsh transmissions for the textual history of the Qurʾān," in A. Rippin (ed.), *Approaches*, pp. 31-45.

character a precise distillation of centuries of intellectual discussion. Wansbrough's inclination to see the variants as intrusive editorial elements in most of the early *tafsīr*s seems a logical explanation.[85] The fact that the *tafsīr* of Muqātil, for example, records variants outside of the canonical systems, however — as for example in Sūra 1, with its citation of Ibn Mas'ūd's reading *arshidnā* rather than *ihdinā* — would seem to be somewhat puzzling; once again, resolution of the issue would require a complete study of the text and its citation of variants. *Tafsīr Ibn 'Abbās* most certainly does cite variants in certain places as well. In fact, Wansbrough sees this fact as a characteristic of the *tafsīr* as a whole, as compared to the more obviously very intrusive nature of the variants in Muqātil. Wansbrough took this as "editorial reformulation" within the *tafsīr*; but that way of expressing it would appear to hinge upon some sense of acceptance of this *tafsīr* as legitimately connected to the name of al-Kalbī. I can see no reason for supposing that whatever variants are cited in *Tafsīr Ibn 'Abbās* are not those of the original author, whoever that person may be. The one point I would wish to raise is whether the very absence of accepted standard variants being cited in the commentary might indicate a date of composition prior to the effective canonization of such lists of variants.

Finally, the text of *Tafsīr Ibn 'Abbās* is notable for its approach in the citation of different resolutions of problems in interpretation. The solution attempted in the work is one of a toleration for defined and limited amounts of disagreement within the framework of consensus. This Wansbrough has rightly termed another major characteristic of the work, one that is evident in the frequent use of the term *yuqālu*, "it is said," used, as was explained above, to introduce alternative meanings. That approach may be contrasted quite readily with the stance of al-Wāḥidī's *al-Wajīz* and *Tafsīr al-Jalālayn*, both of which are very limited in the amount of disagreement they wish to present. Yet to suppose that such an attitude is therefore older than either of those two authors would not seem to be necessarily justified; it could certainly be argued that accepting differences of opinion is a developed trait in a religious community, rather than

---

85 *QS*, pp. 132-33.

an early one, being based upon a desire to unify people in the face of the development of differences of opinion.

The question is, of course, what to make of all of these data in terms of the overall quest for criteria which will help in dating these texts. Literary elements by themselves can provide no historical data. It is only when we put such elements in a framework of comparison with other works of known dating that it is possible to attempt to date such factors. This is of course not easy to do. When using a similar method to deal with the text on *al-nāsikh wa ʾl-mansūkh* ascribed to al-Zuhrī,[86] it was possible, especially in the case of legal terminology and discussions which presupposed certain prior argumentation, to have evidence of the necessary passing of a certain amount of time to allow for such debates to have evolved to a certain point — a type of method referred to above as analysis of "intrinsic" elements. In dealing with a more general *tafsīr* text, however, it is not quite so easy to elicit such criteria. Wansbrough has noted[87] that the variant readings, when presented, are often found in elliptical form, presupposing the workings of masoretic scholars such as al-Farrāʾ and the audience's knowledge of those discussions. A similar point has been made by Crone, in passing, for more basic haggadic material in the text. She has noted that the discussion of a particular point of interpretation in *Tafsīr Ibn ʿAbbās* is only truly intelligible if an entire exegetical discussion as witnessed in texts such as al-Ṭabarī's *Tafsīr* is already known to the audience.[88] Oddly but clearly, the text is not overly technical, which might imply an early, unevolved stage of origin but may say more about the intended audience than about the state of the science of *tafsīr* when it was written. It may well be that identification of the intended audience is a more crucial element in attempts to date the text than is direct speculation on the implications of the other elements.

Observations on the fact that the *Tafsīr Ibn ʿAbbās* presupposes an audience that is fully acquainted with the text of the Qurʾān and conversant with random references to it would seem to be

---

86 See A. Rippin, "al-Zuhrī," *BSOAS* 47 (1984), 37-43.
87 *QS*, p. 133.
88 See P. Crone, "Jāhilī and Jewish law: The *qasāma*," *JSAI* 4 (1984), p. 174, n. 111.

significant, especially when tied in with Wansbrough's discussions of the elliptical presentation of the variant readings. Clearly too, the work is pious and hortative in tone — as compared to *Tafsīr al-Jalālayn*, for example, where the technicalities of *tafsīr* are presented concisely within a system of technical expression and elitist concerns. This is made all the more evident by the existence of supercommentaries on *Tafsīr al-Jalālayn*, which pay precise attention even to the grammatical structure of the base text.[89]

Two types of situations immediately come to mind in the contemplation of the location of any given text of *tafsīr*: an intellectual one, located in an academic setting devoted to study of the Qur'ān in its many aspects; and a popular one, where a preacher uses the Qur'ān for the edification of his audience. Of the former type there are of course many examples, for it is hard to see any of the bulky and/or technical *tafsīr*s with which most of us are acquainted having much use except in that sort of situation. The text of Muqātil, and others such as al-Wāḥidī's *al-Wajīz*, would appear to be aimed at the second situation. *Tafsīr Ibn ʿAbbās* does not fit neatly into either of these stereotyped situations, but rather seems to locate itself somewhere in between. Perhaps we can conceive of another situation, less scholarly but yet semi-learned, one that would work on a fairly local level to produce people sufficiently familiar with the Qur'ān so that they might become respected persons within their own groupings.[90] It may well be this sort of marginally intellectual situation to which this *tafsīr* addresses itself.

But what does all this add up to? We seem to have a *tafsīr* that by its structure presupposes a great deal on the part of its audience, which would tend to suggest that it is a late production, coming at a time when the distillation of knowledge into succinct packages was desirable, even demanded. I believe that the rest of the evidence can be read this way as well, except that there would appear to be a core of material that has been transmitted from earlier times and has simply been taken over without much thought as to its precise implications and its structural compatibility with the rest of the

---

89 See, e.g., al-Jamal, *al-Futūḥāt al-ilāhīya* (e.g., as cited here as text 11).

90 Thanks go to Fred Leemhuis for sharing his reflections on this issue with me.

text. Elements such as the variability in citation of variant readings would seem to be evidence of this. To me, al-Dīnawarī's introduction is likely to be an accurate record of how the *tafsīr* came into being: it is some sort of distillation of knowledge written for the purpose of introducing the complexity of the Qurʾān to budding students, done with reference to al-Kalbī's *tafsīr* yet probably stemming not from al-Dīnawarī himself but from one of his teachers or from within his circle. That we have any way of extracting what would be the opinion of al-Kalbī from the rest of the text is quite plainly not the case; the opinions expressed can be taken only as an expression of the later author's opinion and learning.

IV. The Matter of Ibn ʿAbbās

The question that should arise at this point is, Why is the *isnād* present at the beginning of *Tafsīr Ibn ʿAbbās* if, as has been suggested, the origin of the *tafsīr* lies somewhere in the late third or early fourth century? Surely the *isnād* itself must have some significance and is not just a false and useless appendage.

Indeed, some may wish to suggest that even if the *tafsīr* was written in the third century, it could still represent the opinion of Ibn ʿAbbās. Even if the notion of the backward growth of *isnād*s is accepted, the objection would still be there.

Perhaps the most substantial way to rebut such a position is simply to point out that there is no way of proving the fact that Ibn ʿAbbās is connected to the material found in this *tafsīr*. Indeed, it is very easy to demonstrate the arbitrary nature of ascriptions to Ibn ʿAbbās. In the *tafsīr* of Ibn ʿAṭīya (d. 546/1151),[91] for example, we find that three different opinions are ascribed to Ibn ʿAbbās concerning who is meant by the phrase "Those whom You have blessed" in Sūra 1: "the prophets, the righteous, the martyrs, those who do good," or "the believers," or "the companions of Moses before they were changed." Now while the last definition fits the one in *Tafsīr Ibn ʿAbbās* (although it is different in its precise vocabulary, but that is beside the point) there is no way to determine whether or not that is actually the opinion of Ibn ʿAbbās, as compared to the other

91 Ibn ʿAṭīya, *al-Muḥarrar al-wajīz fī tafsīr al-kitāb al-ʿazīz* (Rabat, 1975), I, 82.

two proposed identifications of the Qur'ānic reference.[92] Al-Ṭabarī's *Tafsīr* likewise provides numerous reports ultimately derived from Ibn ʿAbbās (in Sūra 1 most of these are transmitted via al-Ḍaḥḥāk), but it is impossible to discover any consistent relationship between the information there and that contained in *Tafsīr Ibn ʿAbbās*.[93] These sorts of examples could be duplicated innumerable times in numerous different texts of *tafsīr*. The fact is that arbitrary ascription of data has taken place on so many occasions that it is simply no longer possible to distinguish the false from the true in the matter of opinions ascribed to Ibn ʿAbbās, or indeed any companion of Muḥammad.

But then why Ibn ʿAbbās, and why is this *isnād* present? There can be little doubt, it seems to me, that the presence of the *isnād* in this work serves to fit it within debates over *tafsīr bi 'l-ra'y* and *tafsīr bi 'l-ma'thūr*. The presence of the *isnād* is a signalling device indicating that this *tafsīr* is not to be taken as the "opinion" of its "author" but rather as a distillation of the most honorable material that may be found in tradition. The point must be to recognize that the debate over *ra'y* and *ma'thūr* was really over authority and who had it: the words may only be considered ones of reprobation from one side or the other, just as words indicating political alliance — tory, liberal, socialist, communist — are used today and have always been used from the perspective of the accuser, with no "objective" criteria being substantiated thereby.

There were of course other methods of substantiating one's opinion, as illustrated by the *tafsīr*s of Mujāhid and Sufyān al-Thawrī; there the individual reports are each given an *isnād*, as in the common *ḥadīth* method, an approach that culminated (in the world of *tafsīr*) in al-Ṭabarī's work. In the two earlier works this approach

---

92 *Tafsīr Ibn ʿAbbās* also suggests "the prophets" for "those whom You have blessed," which is partially parallel to Ibn ʿAtīya's first statement; compared to the way al-Wāḥidī provides the identifications, however, I am inclined to see the glosses as different — Ibn ʿAṭīya's reference is in fact the same as al-Wāḥidī's cross-reference to Q. 4/69.

93 See al-Ṭabarī, *Jāmiʿ al-bayān*, I, 129, on *al-raḥmān* and *al-raḥīm* as *al-raqīq* and *al-rafīq*, but this is given further explanation within the report; I, 151-217, all contain reports on Sūra 1 attributed to Ibn ʿAbbās.

is appropriate to the fragmentary nature of the exegetical exercise in both texts; *Tafsīr Ibn ʿAbbās*, in attempting to provide an "interlinear gloss" for the entire text,[94] simply does not need to provide such a framework.

The notion of ascription of this text to Ibn ʿAbbās, however, is also caught up in the whole picture of this person as a pivotal figure in the history of *tafsīr*. In some other studies, I have examined the works *al-Lughāt fī ʾl-Qurʾān* and *Gharīb al-Qurʾān* as well as looking briefly at the *Masāʾil Nāfiʿ ibn al-Azraq*.[95] Amid confusion regarding ascription in these cases also, it became clear that these texts were substantially later than their supposed author, especially in these cases because of the use of poetry as a means of elucidating the Qurʾān, once again a methodological point that took a number of centuries to be firmly established within the field of *tafsīr* and one that these texts tend to assume rather than particularly argue. That the *Tafsīr Ibn ʿAbbās* does not appear to resort very often to citation of this aspect of "Ibn ʿAbbās's" activity is worthy of note:[96] there is no attempt in this citation of earlier authorities to create a consistent picture of the person to whom one is appealing for authority.

It is at this point that one must go beyond the merely textual and embark upon a socio-mythological study such as that done recently by Claude Gilliot.[97] For Gilliot, Ibn ʿAbbās is the symbol of the formative Muslim community, embodying those abilities and understandings most cherished by the generation that cites him as their authority. Ibn ʿAbbās is also the person through whom those people conduct their arguments over legitimate procedures and legal deductions. In the same way that we understand the story of

---

94 I have suggested viewing *Tafsīr Ibn ʿAbbās* as an Arabic translation of the Qurʾān, in "Lexicographical Texts and the Qurʾān," in A. Rippin (ed.), *Approaches*, p. 164.

95 See Rippin, "Lughāt," 15-25, and idem, "Gharīb," 332-33.

96 One instance has been noted above with regard to the word *kanūd*.

97 C. Gilliot, "Portrait ≪mythique≫ d'Ibn ʿAbbās," *Arabica* 33 (1985), 127-84.

Adam and Eve as mythic, a story presenting certain human truths, so too Ibn ʿAbbās is mythic, in that his life is embellished with those elements that are important to the people creating the story. Ibn ʿAbbās is a mythic exemplum for the Muslim community. That is why he is cited within the *isnād* for *Tafsīr Ibn ʿAbbās*.[98]

98 If at this point one wished to ask again, "Why Ibn ʿAbbās?" one would probably want to discuss such issues as his relationship to Muḥammad as developed within the *Sīra* and biographical literature; this may suggest that Ibn ʿAbbās's role in *tafsīr* depends first on the development of the character within this literature and within the propaganda of the ʿAbbasids.

Appendix 1

I. *Copies Consulted*

1. *Tanwīr al-miqbās*, Cairo, 1951, with ascription to al-Fīrūzābādī, with al-Suyūṭī, *Lubāb al-nuqūl*, followed by Muḥammad ibn Ḥazm, *al-Kitāb fī maʿrifat al-nāsikh wa'l-mansūkh*, in the margin.
2. *Tanwīr al-miqbās*, Beirut, 1360, printed in the margin of the Qur'ān text.
3. al-Suyūṭī, *al-Durr al-manthūr fī 'l-tafsīr bi 'l-ma'thūr*, with *Tanwīr al-miqbās* in the margin; there are many prints of this, but all of one edition it would seem, in six volumes, e.g., Cairo, 1314; Tehran, 1377.
4. Qur'ān text with Persian and Hindustani interlinear translation, with *Tafsīr Ibn ʿAbbās* in the margin, [Meerut?], 1866.
5. Qur'ān text with Persian and Hindustani interlinear translation, with *Tafsīr Ibn ʿAbbās* in the margin, also *Tafsīr al-Jalālayn* and other notes, Meerut, 1869.
6. Qur'ān text with Persian and Hindustani interlinear translation, with *Tafsīr Ibn ʿAbbās* in the margin [Meerut], 1299/1882, with *Tafsīr al-Jalālayn* in the margin also [a different lithograph than no. 5].
7. *Tanwīr al-miqbās* ascribed to al-Fīrūzābādī in the bottom margin of six-volume work containing *tafsīr*s of al-Bayḍāwī, al-Khāzin, and al-Nasafī, Cairo, 1317/1899.
8. *Tanwīr al-iqtibās* [*sic*] *min tafsīr ʿAbd Allāh ibn ʿAbbās*, with *Tafsīr al-Jalālayn* in the margin, Bombay, 1280/1863.
9. *Tanwīr al-iqtibās* [*sic*] *min tafsīr ʿAbd Allāh ibn ʿAbbās*, with *Tafsīr al-Jalālayn* in the margin, Bombay, 1302/1885 [a different lithograph than no. 8].
10. *Tanwīr al-miqbās*, Būlāq, 1290/1873, ascribed to al-Fīrūzābādī, with Abū Yaḥyā Zakariyā al-Anṣārī, *al-Maqṣad li-takhlīṣ mā fī 'l-murshid fī 'l-waqf wa 'l-ibtidā'* in the margin.[99]
11. *Tafsīr Ibn ʿAbbās* in the margin of al-Jamal, *al-Futūḥāt al-ilāhīya*, with the text of *Tafsīr al-Jalālayn*, in four volumes, Cairo 1302-3/1885-86.
12. Leiden manuscript 1651, al-Dīnawarī, *al-Wāḍiḥ fī tafsīr al-Qur'ān*;[100] Aya Sofya 221 has been consulted to confirm that it is indeed ascribed to al-Dīnawarī, but no further information is available at present.
13. British Library manuscript Or. 9277, *Tafsīr Ibn ʿAbbās*.
14. Chester Beatty manuscripts 5465 and 4224, *Tafsīr Ibn ʿAbbās*.[101]

---

99 Despite Ellis, *Catalogue*, I, 4 (with the information then repeated in *GAL*, Suppl. I, 331), this print does not have the title *Tanwīr al-miqyās*; the confusion seems to be only in Flügel's edition of Ḥajjī Khalīfa (see above, n. 3).

100 See above, section II.ii and n. 56, for bibliographical references.

101 Both of these copies were written by the same scribe, Ḥusayn Ḥasanī. Manuscript 4224 (dated 1159/1746) is especially beautiful, with a lavish gold folio 1b, a gold margin throughout the text, and the Qur'ān text overlined in gold throughout. The Sūra titles are done in white on a gold band. Manuscript 5465 is almost

II. *Copies with Information Available in Other Sources*

15. Bankipore, *Catalogue*, vol. 18, part 2, manuscript number 1322.[102]
16. Bankipore 1323, but according to the catalogue this text is minus the introduction.
17. Aya Sofya 114.
18. Aya Sofya 115.
19. Aya Sofya 116.
20. Aya Sofya 118 — manuscripts Aya Sofya 114 through 118 are described by H. Ritter, "Ayasofya kütüphânesinde tefsir ilmine alt arapça yazmalar," *Türkiyat Mecmuası*, 7/8, part ii (1945), 7.
21. Berlin 732 (Sprenger 404), Ahlwardt, *Handschriften-Verzeichnisse*, I, 290.

III. *Other Sources*

22. Introduction to al-Thaʿlabī, *al-Kashf wa ʾl-bayān*, ed. Goldfeld, *Qurʾanic commentary*, p. 52.
23. Al-Dhahabī, *al-Tafsīr waʾl-mufassirūn* (Cairo, 1961-62), I, 82.
24. Print of Hindustani translation of *Tafsīr Ibn ʿAbbās*, Agra, 1307/1890, which omits the *isnād*s but repeats much of the Arabic text.

---

as fine; it is dated 1158/1745. The only textual differences between the two copies relate to lines 1, 18, and 21 of the translation and are duly noted there; that such differences should occur in a text written superbly by the same scribe illustrates nicely the way such changes have been introduced into the text.

102 For bibliographical details see above, n. 61.

Appendix 2
Part 1

Tafsīr Ibn ʿAbbās/Tanwīr al-miqbās on Sūrat al-Fātiḥa, as found in the copy ascribed to al-Fīrūzābādī, second printing, Cairo, 1951 (text 1).

1. With its *isnād*[113] from Ibn ʿAbbās,[114] concerning the saying of God, most High,
2. ≪Praise be to God≫: He is saying:[115] "Thanks to God." He it is who made His created beings, so they praise Him.
3. It is also said [that it means]: "Thanks to God" for his abundant blessing on His servants whom He guides[116] to faith.
4. It is also said [that it means]: Thanks and [testifies that] unity and divinity belong to God who has no offspring, partner, supporter or helper.[117]
5. ≪Lord of the worlds≫:[118] Lord of all possessors of spirit (*rūḥ*) moving on the face of the earth and of all the inhabitants of heaven.
6. It is also said [that it means]: Master of the *jinn* and of humanity.
7. It is also said [that it means]: Creator of the created beings for whom He provides the subsistence and whom He takes from one condition [of faith] to another.
8. ≪The Merciful≫: *al-raqīq* (the One who feels mercy),[119] derived from *al-riqqa*, mercy, and that is kindness (*raḥma*).[120]
9. ≪The Compassionate≫: the One who feels mercy (*raqīq*).[121]
10. ≪Ruler of the day of religion≫: Judge on the day of religion (*dīn*)[122] which is the day of reckoning and destiny on which He shall divide up His creatures.
11. That is, the day on which people shall be repaid (*yudānu*)[123] for their deeds. There is no judge other than Him.

---

113 "With its *isnād*" is omitted from text 12.

114 Text 12 and Chester Beatty 4224 (text 14) add: "May God be pleased with him."

115 "He is saying" appears as "We are saying" in text 13; text 12 is not pointed and may be read this way also.

116 "Whom He guides" appears as "and He guides them" in text 12.

117 "Belong to God who has no offspring, partner, supporter or helper" is omitted from text 12.

118 "Lord of the worlds" is added in red above the line in text 12; this is in the same hand as the manuscript — the titles are generally added in red.

119 "*Al-raqīq*" (the One who feels mercy) appears as "*al-rafīq*" (the One who is gracious) in texts 4, 5, 6, 8, 9, 13, 14, 24.

120 "Derived from *al-riqqa* and that is kindness (*raḥma*)" appears as "who makes hearts tender [*yariqqa*]" in text 12; omitted from texts 4, 5, 6, 8, 9, 13, 14, 24.

121 "The One who feels mercy (*raqīq*)" appears as "the One who is gracious (*rafīq*)" in texts 2, 3, 4, 5, 6, 7, 8, 9, 10, 11, 12, 14, 24 (but not 13).

122 "Judge on the day of religion" is omitted from texts 12, 13.

123 Text 2 adds "in it."

12. ≪Only You do we serve≫: to You[124] do we profess our belief in Your oneness and to You[125] do we yield.
13. ≪Only from You do we seek aid≫: with You do we seek aid in our performance of Your worship and from You[126] we receive trust to perform in Your obedience.
14. ≪Guide us along the straight path≫: direct us to the steadfast religion which pleases You which is Islam.
15. It is also said [that this means] strengthen us in it.
16. It is also said [that it means] it is the book of God [such that] He is saying: Guide us in [its categories of] permitted and forbidden and [in] an explication of what is in [the book].
17. ≪The path of those whom You have blessed≫: the religion of those to whom You have shown favor by means of religion.
18. They are[127] the followers of Moses[128] (before[129] the blessings of God changed against them [cf. Q. 8/53]) when clouds put them in the shadow and manna and quail were sent down to them in the desert [cf. Q. 2/57].
19. It is also said [that the people who have been favored are] the prophets.
20. ≪Not those against whom You have sent your wrath≫: other than the religion of the Jews against whom You have been wrathful[130] and have abandoned and have not preserved their hearts in order for them to become [true?] Jews.
21. ≪Nor those who are astray≫: nor the religion of the Christians who err away from Islam.
22. ≪Amen≫: thus, His community≪[131]≫ will come into being.
23. It is also said [that it means]: So be it thus.[132]
24. It is also said [that it means]: O our Lord, do with us as we ask of You.
25. God knows best.[133]

---

124 "To You" (*laka*) appears as "with You" (*bika*) in text 12.
125 "To You" (*laka*) appears as "with You" (*bika*) in text 12.
126 "From You" (*minka*) appears as "with You" (*bika*) in text 12.
127 "They are" appears as "It is also said [that it means]: they are" in text 12.
128 "Moses" appears as "Moses, son of ʿImrān" in text 12; "Moses, upon whom may there be peace" appears in Chester Beatty 4224 (text 14).
129 "Before" (*qabla an*) reads *qabla aw* in text 13.
130 "Against whom You have been wrathful" (*alladhī...ʿalayhim*) reads *alladhīna ...ʿalayhim* in texts 2, 3, 5, 6, 7, 8, 9, 10, 11, 12, 13, 14.
131 "His community" (*ummatuhu*) in text 12 and in Chester Beatty 4224 (text 14) is quite clear and makes the most sense; other texts vary in giving *hamza-mīm-nūn-tāʾ-hāʾ* — as in text 1 — occasionally, without the final *hāʾ*. The texts may be aiming at some sense of "faith," but this does not really produce a viable meaning for me.
132 Text 6 omits "thus" (*kadhālika*); text 4 reads "or (*aw*) it is said [that it means] so be it"; text 13 reads *hākadhā* rather than *kadhālika*.
133 Lines 23 and 24 are omitted from texts 4, 5, 6, 8, 9, 12, 14.

Appendix 2
Part 2

Al-Wāḥidī, *al-Wajīz fī tafsīr al-Qurʾān* on *Sūrat al-fātiḥa.*[134]

1. ≪Praise be to God≫: high praises to God and thanks to Him for His blessings.
2. ≪Lord of the worlds≫: ruler of all created things.
   [≪the Merciful, the Compassionate≫ omitted here, treated in the beginning of the text as part of the *basmala*]
3. ≪Ruler of the day of religion≫:[135] judge on the day of recompense and reckoning because He performs singlehandedly on that day in His judgment.
4. ≪Only You do we serve≫: that is, we are dedicated to You and we strive towards You in our works, which is obedience with submission.
5. ≪Only from You do we seek aid≫: from You does help come forth.[136]
6. ≪Guide us along the straight path≫: that is, indicate it to us and establish us in it and make us travel along it.
7. ≪The path of those whom You have blessed≫: with guidance; they are the communities of Moses and Jesus before the blessings of God turned against them [cf. Q. 8/53].
8. It is also said [that it means] those whom God has mentioned in His statement: ≪[anyone who obeys God and the messenger] stands by those whom God has favored [such as prophets, loyal persons, martyrs, and honorable men]≫ [Q. 4/69].
9. ≪Not those against whom You have sent Your wrath≫: that is, not those to whom God is wrathful who are the Jews; and the meaning of ≪wrath from God≫ is the punishment which He intends (for them).
10. ≪Nor those who are astray≫: that is nor those who went astray[137] who are the Christians.
11. The Muslims had asked God Most High to guide them in the path of those whom He had blessed and not those against whom He had sent His wrath, as He was wrathful against the Jews, nor those who were astray from the truth, just as the Christians were astray.

---

134 British Library Or. 9485, ff. 3b-4a; also published in the margin of al-Nawawī, *Marāḥ Labīd*, p. 3.

135 The printed text adds here: "[*mālik*] ('the one who rules') is derived from *mulk* ('kingship') which is itself derived from *malik* ('king'); that is...." In the printed text, therefore, *ay* is used five times (rather than four) in this section of the *tafsīr*.

136 The printed text reads: "from You do we seek help."

137 Note the theological implications of this and the previous explanation concerning the Jews.

Appendix 2
Part 3

Tafsīr al-Jalālayn on Sūrat al-Fātiḥa.[138]

1. ≪Praise be to God≫: [this is] a predicative sentence which intends thereby praising God such that [the sentence] affirms that the Most High is the possessor of all the praise from His creation. Or, [it is the praise] which He deserves because they should praise Him. *Allāh* ("God") is the personal name of He who is worthy of worship.
2. ≪Lord of the worlds≫: that is, ruler of all creation including humanity, the *jinn*, the angels, the animals and other creatures, all of whom may be said to be endowed with intelligence. It is also said [that it means] those intelligent members of humanity and those intelligent members of the *jinn* and so forth. The plurality [of "worlds" — *ʿālamīn*] with the *yāʾ* and the *nūn* [i.e., the masculine sound plural] indicates the supremacy of those who possess knowledge over all others. [The word *ʿālamīn*, "worlds"] is derived from *ʿalama* [mark, sign or characteristic] because [the world] provides a sign of its Creator.
3. ≪The Merciful, the Compassionate≫: that is, the possessor of mercy, which entails intending good for His people.
4. ≪Ruler of the day of religion≫: that is, [the day of] requital which is the day of the resurrection. [The day] is singled out for mention because there is no ruler in reality for anyone on that day other than God Most High, as indicated by ≪To whom is the rulership of the day? To God!≫ (Q. 40/16). Those who read *mālik* (with an *alif*) understand it to mean the ruler of the entire affair on the day of resurrection; that is, He is characterized in that way ceaselessly, in the same way that He is the One who pardons sin. The occurrence [of *mālik* with *alif*] is sound for [it indicates] a characteristic of knowledge.
5. ≪Only You do we serve; Only from You do we seek aid≫: that is, we devote only to You acts of Islamic [*tawḥīd*] worship and the like. We request help [only from You] in the acts of worship and the like.
6. ≪Guide us along the straight path≫: that is, lead us to [the path], which is [grammatically] substituted by the [following phrase — in the accusative case].
7. ≪The path of those whom You have blessed≫: with guidance. The resumptive pronoun is then substituted by *ghayr* ["not" — which is in the genitive case, being governed by the *ʿalā* of the preceding phrase].

---

138 This is often found at the end of the text of the *tafsīr*, apparently because al-Maḥallī did not do it and it was left to al-Suyūṭī when he finished the rest of the book (from Sūra 18 on). I would like to thank A.A.M. Shereef, SOAS, for helping me understand this passage.

8. ≪Not those against whom You have sent your wrath≫: who are the Jews.
9. ≪Nor≫: and other than [and thus is equivalent to the preceding ***ghayr***].
10. ≪those who are astray≫: and they are the Christians. The subtlety of the substitution is [that it is] an indication that those who are guided are not Jews or Christians.
11. And God knows best what is right.

Appendix 3
ISNĀD STRUCTURE OF
TAFSĪR IBN ʿABBĀS

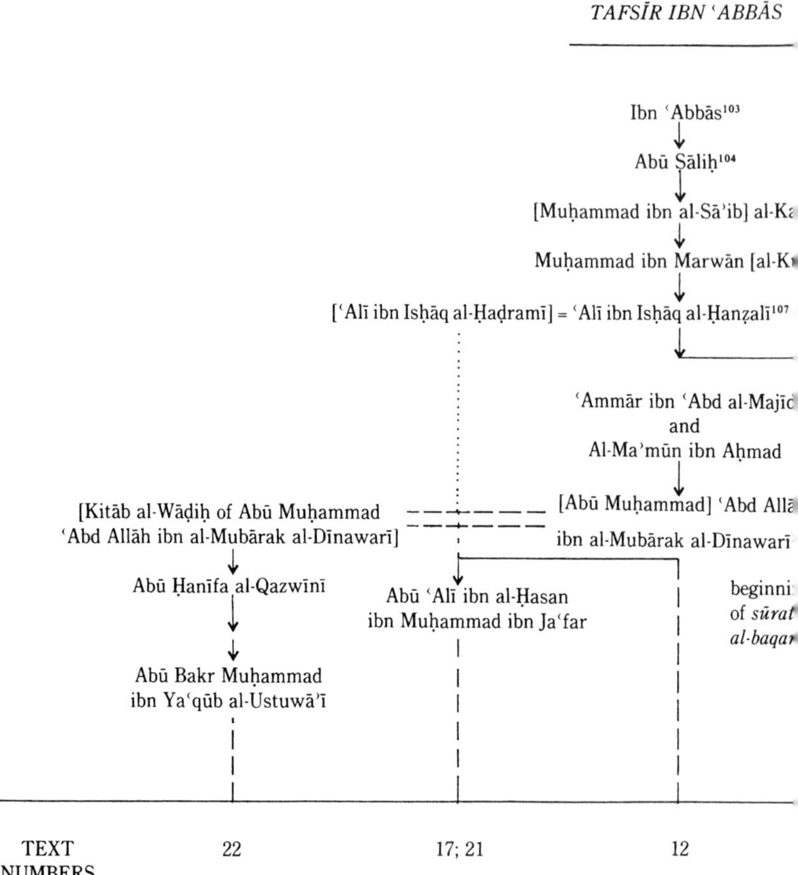

103 Died 68/687; see *GAS*, I, 25, and section II.iv, above.

104 Died 101/719; see *GAS*, I, 790 (in the index); some copies add to his name: Bādhān mawlā of Umm Hānī.

105 Died 146/763. See *GAS*, I, 34-35, and section II.iii, above.

106 Died 189/805. See Ibn al-Jazarī, *Ghāyat al-nihāya fī ṭabaqāt al-qurrāʾ* (Cairo, 1933-35), II, 261, entry 3464, where it is said that he heard the *tafsīr* of al-Kalbī.

107 I consider it most likely that [ʿAlī ibn Isḥāq] al-Ḥanẓalī/ al-Ḥanẓalī al-Samarqandī/ al-Samarqandī/ al-Ḥaḍramī are all the same person, as is indicated here, and that he is to be identified as ʿAlī ibn Isḥāq al-Ḥanẓalī al-Samarqandī, died 237/851; see al-ʿAsqalānī, *Tahdhīb al-tahdhīb* (Hyderabad, 1326), VII, 283. My thanks to Gautier Juynboll for this reference.

108 Abū Muḥammad al-Dīnawarī, according to text 12, title page f. 2b; ʿAbd Allāh ibn

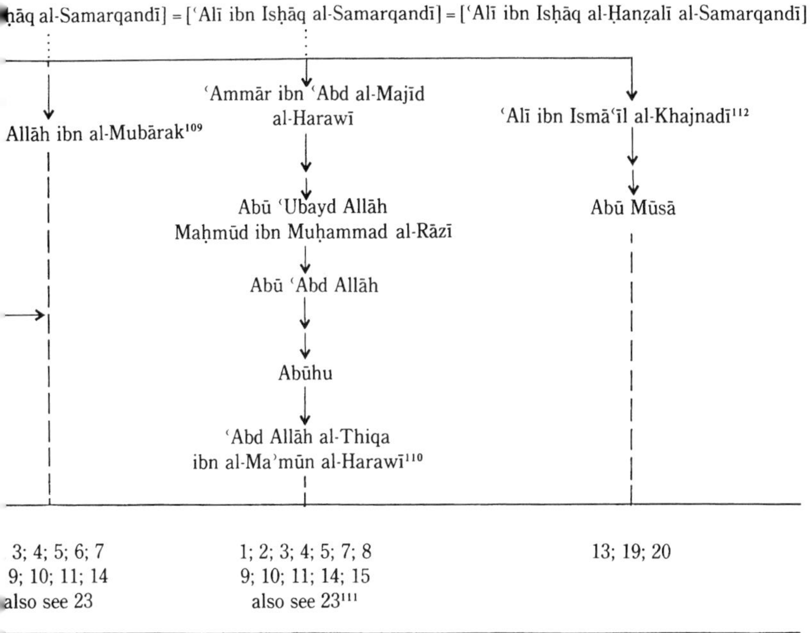

al-Mubārak al-Dīnawarī, according to text 12 in the opening *isnād* f. 3a; Abū Muḥammad ʿAbd Allāh ibn al-Mubārak al-Dīnawarī, according to text 22, p. 52.

109 Note that if this is al-Dīnawarī, a name would appear to be missing in the *isnād*. In text 12, at *sūrat al-baqara*, the statement is simply: *bi-isnād Muḥammad ibn Marwān ʿan al-Kalbī ʿan Abī Ṣāliḥ ʿan Ibn ʿAbbās.*

110 Al-Maʾmūr in text 1.

111 This *isnād* thus represents both the Indian and the Egyptian printed versions; text 6 follows this *isnād* but by haplography started with the name ʿAbd Allāh (only) and then put as the next link Abū ʿUbayd Allāh Maḥmūd ibn Muḥammad al-Rāzī.

112 ʿAlī ibn Ismāʿīl al-Khajnadī is ʿAlī ibn Ismāʿīl in text 20.

XVI

AL-ZUHRĪ, *NASKH AL-QUR'ĀN* AND THE PROBLEM OF EARLY *TAFSĪR* TEXTS

While interest in early exegetical works concerned with the Qur'ān has certainly increased in the last few decades, no clear consensus seems to have emerged concerning how to establish the genesis of a supposedly early text. The basic problem to be faced is whether the texts we have today are compilations extracted from later works and then put in the name of a single, early authority or whether they are genuinely transmitted works from early teachers and writers, albeit with the definite possibility of some reformulation and intrusion from a later date by editors and copyists. The question to be discussed is one of both the date and method of composition.

The rise in interest in early exegetical works and the dramatic increase in the scope of the problem can be traced primarily to the publication of Nabia Abbott's studies on papyri and other early literary documents [1] and, even more importantly, Fuat Sezgin's first volume of *Geschichte des arabischen Schrifttums*.[2] Especially in pages 19 to 49, Sezgin produces an impressive list of early *tafsīr* works. The overall argument to which this mass of data contributes is quite traditional and, upon further investigation, none too subtle. Sezgin desires to prove the existence of early written documents in order to substantiate claims for the validity of *ḥadīth* transmission and the *isnād* mechanism. An examination of his listing of *tafsīr* works which contribute to the evidence reveals, however, a remarkably flimsy basis; names and works proliferate, for example, because a listing in Ibn al-Nadīm *al-Fihrist* or a mention by al-Khaṭīb al-Baghdādī has proven sufficient to justify an entry even though no tangible evidence of the works in question exists.[3] Less obvious is the tendency to allow a single text to be entered under a multitude of names; the example of the text entitled *Gharīb al-Qur'ān* (manuscript Atıf Efendi, 2815/8) is the most flagrant case, that being entered under three different authors.[4] A single text may also be assigned to an earlier figure than is obviously demanded or suggested by the text itself; an example of this occurs in the treatment of the *tafsīr* listed under Mūsā ibn 'Abd al-Raḥmān al-Thaqafī al-San'ānī (d. 190/805) [5] where an examination of the extracts printed by Griffini [6] reveals that Bakr ibn Sahl al-Dimyāṭī (d. 289/902) or, at best, 'Abd al-Ghanī ibn Sa'īd al-Thaqafī (d. 229/843) could be isolated as the central figure concerned in the text just as easily and with more justification.

However, even after the superfluous entries are excised from Sezgin, there is still a sizeable body of significant works remaining and it is concerning these that some understanding of their origin must be reached. Thanks to the work of John Wansbrough, *Quranic studies: sources and methods of scriptural*

[1] Of greatest interest here is her *Studies in Arabic literary papyri*, II: *Qur'ānic commentary and tradition* (University of Chicago Oriental Institute Publications, Vol. LXXVI), Chicago, 1967.

[2] Leiden, 1967.

[3] See, for example, the listings for al-Ḥasan al-Baṣrī, *GAS*, I, 30, and Qatāda, *GAS*, I, 31–2.

[4] See *GAS*, I, 27, 31, 39, and Rippin, 'Ibn 'Abbās's *al-Lughāt fī'l-Qur'ān*', *BSOAS*, XLIV, 1, 1981, 15–25, and 'Ibn 'Abbās's *Gharīb al-Qur'ān*', *BSOAS*, XLVI, 2, 1983, 332–3.

[5] *GAS*, I, 39.

[6] E. Griffini, 'I manoscritti sudarabici di Milano', *RSO*, II, 1908–9, 7–13 (entry number 11, manuscript Milan Ambrosiana A 47). Also see O. Spies, 'Die Bibliotheken des Hidschas', *ZDMG*, XC, 1936, 103 (item number 3).

Reprinted by kind permission of Oxford University Press

interpretation,[7] some definite steps have been made and some criteria have emerged to assist in the overall task of classification of early texts. Wansbrough's approach is a literary one, concerned with extracting information on the basis of considerations of style and function of information as displayed in exegetical texts. The extent to which *historical* information may legitimately be derived from literary criteria has to be of prime concern here and cannot be answered simply one way or the other. The most for which one may hope would seem to be a comparative system of dating based upon a presupposed framework of literary development; this approach is certainly exemplified (for the most part) in Wansbrough's work.[8] Employing the literary approach of Wansbrough should, then, allow for an evaluation of early *tafsīr* works and their composition, at least on a relative scale.

To a certain extent Wansbrough has already accomplished the essential work which needed to be done; for many early exegetical works there can be little left to add to his insights. The *tafsīr* of Muqātil ibn Sulaimān (d. 150/769), for example, has been shown to be so unique and distinctive (not to mention fascinating) that, while editorial intrusion and reshaping will most certainly have taken place as Wansbrough has suggested, the assertion that the text is at the very least representative of a distinct line of interpretation originating in the early (second to third) Islamic centuries seems fairly safe.[9] However, the inter-relationship between Muqātil's *Tafsīr* and his other ascribed works, most especially *Tafsīr khams mi'a āya min al-Qur'ān*[10] and *al-Ashbāh wa'l-naẓā'ir fī'l-Qur'ān*,[11] needs investigation. As Goldfeld points out in his introduction to the edition of *Khams mi'a āya*,[12] there can be little doubt about the close relationship between that book and the larger *Tafsīr*, although to simply state that '*Tafsīr al-khams mi'at āya* is an abstract of *Tafsīr* Muqātil' as Goldfeld does (p. 7) is to gloss over a myriad of literary questions which have yet to be confronted. Recognition of the literary form of these works, as Wansbrough has argued, is as important a consideration as is the actual content. A full analysis of this question with regards to Muqātil, however, must await a properly prepared edition of the *Tafsīr* which it is to be hoped will be produced before too long.

It may be tempting to include consideration of the *tafsīr* ascribed (by some) to al-Kalbī (d. 146/763) along with that of Muqātil. Wansbrough's treatment of the text, however, reveals that it has gone through multiple redactions and that to treat it as the work of al-Kalbī (or, even more absurdly, Ibn 'Abbās [d. 68/687]) is highly questionable.[13] The fact that the text ascribed to al-Kalbī is identical in all respects (within the limits of textual transmission) to that ascribed to al-Dīnawarī (d. 308/920) with the title of *al-Wāḍiḥ fī tafsīr al-Qur'ān*,[14] something not noted in Sezgin's confused listing of these texts[15]

[7] London Oriental Series, Vol. 31, Oxford, 1977. Hereafter cited as *QS*.

[8] See my 'Literary analysis of the Qur'ān, *tafsīr* and *sīra*: the methodologies of John Wansbrough', in Richard C. Martin (ed.), *Islam and the history of religions: essays on the study of a religious tradition*, Phoenix, California, forthcoming, 1984.

[9] *QS*, 122–36, 140–6.

[10] MS British Library OR 6333; edition prepared by Isaiah Goldfeld, Shfaram, 1980.

[11] MS Beyazit 561; edition prepared by 'Abd Allāh Maḥmūd Shiḥātah, Cairo, 1975.

[12] English pp. 3–8.

[13] *QS*, 130–7, 140–6.

[14] See *GAS*, I, 42; I have examined the manuscripts Aya Sofia 221 and Leiden 1651.

[15] Sezgin, *GAS*, I, 27, under Ibn 'Abbās lists the printed edition *Tanwīr al-miqbās min tafsīr Ibn 'Abbās* (often listed under the name of al-Fīrūzābādī [d. 817/1415]) but this, too, is identical to all the manuscripts listed under al-Kalbī, *GAS*, I, 34–5 (and, of course, those of al-Dīnawarī). In listing al-Kalbī's manuscripts, Sezgin left out all those listed in Brockelmann under Ibn 'Abbās (*GAL*, Suppl. I, 331: they are primarily copies held in European libraries), but they

nor noted explicitly by Wansbrough [16] (who states that al-Dīnawarī's work is ' a nearly verbatim reproduction ' of al-Kalbī), would suggest that the fourth century is a preferable era in which to assign this text for the matter of initial investigation at least.[17]

Other early *tafsīr* works have been revealed to be quite technical, and cohesively so, such that acceptance of single authorship by their ascribed authors (always considering the possibility of editorial intrusion and reformulation) also seems to be a safe course. Works such as Abū 'Ubaid (d. 224/834), *Faḍā'il al-Qur'ān*,[18] Abū 'Ubaida (d. 210/825), *Majāz al-Qur'ān*,[19] al-Farrā' (d. 207/822), *Ma'ānī al-Qur'ān*,[20] and al-Kisā'ī (d. 187/803), *Mushtabihāt al-Qur'ān* [21] all fit this category.

There exists, however, a series of texts, little examined by Wansbrough, whose nature is by no means so cohesive and whose fragmentary composition raises grave doubts but yet concerning whose status there is still a need for tools to be developed in order to categorize them. Major texts of this type include Sufyān al-Thaurī (d. 161/778), *Tafsīr al-Qur'ān*,[22] Mujāhid ibn Jabr (d. 104/722), *Tafsīr*, [23] 'Abd al-Razzāq (d. 211/827), *Tafsīr*,[24] Ibn 'Abbās, *al-Lughāt fī'l-Qur'ān*,[25] and al-Zuhrī (d. 124/742), *Naskh al-Qur'ān*. This latter text ascribed to al-Zuhrī [26] is a typical example of these works and is, therefore, a valuable source with which to work through some considerations of the basic problem of composition; this is most especially so because of its brevity and precise technical nature. It is necessary first, however, to establish some basic facts concerning the text since that has become a matter of some confusion; this normally simple issue also interestingly raises some points

too are identical to the other copies. Other MSS also exist, e.g., BL OR 9277, listed under Ibn 'Abbās. There is some variation in *isnād* between these various manuscripts and the various printed versions which, for a matter of form primarily, should probably be compiled and compared.

[16] *QS*, 146.

[17] Wansbrough mentions, *QS*, 146, that al-Dīnawarī's work seems to originate from use in a popular preaching context as compared to the intellectual function of a work such as the *tafsīr* of al-Ṭabarī (d. 311/923); note should also be made in this context of al-Wāḥidī (d. 468/1075), *Tafsīr al-Qur'ān al-Wajīz*, printed on the margin of al-Nawawī, *Marāḥ labīd*, Cairo, 1305, which is virtually identical in form (although not in content) to al-Dīnawarī. The appearance of the work of al-Dīnawarī as late as the fourth *hijrī* century is therefore perhaps not so strange considering the role of the basic form throughout Islamic history (also cf. al-Jalālain, *al-Tafsīr*).

[18] MS Berlin Staatsbibliothek Petermann 449; see *QS*, 203–4.

[19] Ed. F. Sezgin, Cairo, 1954–62; see *QS*, 219–20 and references, also E. Almagor, ' The early meaning of *majāz* and the nature of Abū 'Ubayda's exegesis ', in *Studia Orientalia: memoriae D. H. Baneth dedicata*, Jerusalem, 1979, 307–26.

[20] Cairo, 1955–72; see *QS*, 206–7.

[21] MS Beyazit 436; see *QS*, 212–15.

[22] Rampur, 1965; this text has been dealt with to some extent in *QS*, 137–8 and 140–5.

[23] Ed. 'Abd al-Raḥmān al-Ṭāhir al-Sūratī, Qatar, 1976; this text has been analysed in a traditional manner (i.e. by analysis of the *isnāds* and reports in biographical works) by F. Leemhuis, ' MS. 1075 Tafsīr of the Cairene Dār al-Kutub and Muǧāhid's *Tafsīr* ', in R. Peters (ed.), *Proceedings of the ninth congress of the Union Européenne des Arabisants et Islamisants*, Leiden, 1981, 169–80 (and as Leemhuis notes, p. 176, has also been the subject of a dissertation by G. Stauth, Giessen, 1969). Leemhuis has taken to referring to this text as *Tafsīr Warqā'*: see his ' Qur'ānic *Siǧǧil* and Aramaic *SGYL* ', *JSS*, XXVII, 1, 1982, 47–56.

[24] MS Cairo Dār al-kutub, *tafsīr* 242.

[25] See my ' Ibn 'Abbās's *al-Lughāt fī'l-Qur'ān* ', *BSOAS*, XLIV, 1, 1981, 15–25, for an attempt at a literary analysis of this text.

[26] On the person of al-Zuhrī see *GAS*, I, 280–3; J. Horovitz, ' The earliest biographies of the Prophet and their authors ', *IC*, II, 1928, 33–50, and his synopsis in *EI* (1st ed.),; N. Abbott, *Studies in Arabic literary papyri*, *II*, *passim* but especially 168–84; A. A. al-Duri, ' Al-Zuhrī: a study on the beginnings of history writing in Islam ', *BSOAS*, XIX, 1, 1957, 1–12. These sources provide all the traditional type of information that could possibly be desired; the fruitlessness of this type of approach is indicated by the extent of the material and the artificiality of the resultant analyses.

worthy of attention regarding medieval scribal practices and the extent of errors committed in that context.

Under Abū Bakr Muḥammad ibn Muslim ibn 'Ubaid Allāh ibn 'Abd Allāh ibn Shihāb al-Zuhrī, Sezgin lists the text *al-Nāsikh wa'l-mansūkh fī'l-Qur'ān*[27] as transmitted by the famous Ṣūfī Abū 'Abd al-Raḥmān Muḥammad ibn al-Ḥusain ibn Muḥammad ibn Mūsā al-Azdī al-Sulamī (d. 412/1021), under whose name the text is also listed.[28] As Wansbrough discovered,[29] Sezgin erred in the listing of one of the manuscripts of the text; the manuscript cited, Beyazit 445, is in fact a copy of 'Abd al-Qāhir al-Baghdādī, *al-Nāsikh wa'l-mansūkh*. Sezgin's error probably stems from a miscopying of the *Fihrist makhṭūṭāt al-muṣawwara* of the Cairo (Arab League) Institute of Arabic Manuscripts[30] where the two texts are listed sequentially. The intended entry for al-Zuhrī's text would appear to be Cairo Dār al-kutub, *tafsīr* 1084, for which Sezgin has listed the correct number of folios (16: they are in fact pages) instead of the Beyazit 445's 76 folios. A second manuscript is listed by Sezgin, that of Princeton Yahuda 228/2.[31]

Examination of the manuscripts reveals that Dār al-kutub 1084 is, in fact, a photographed copy of what is now the Princeton text; it was apparently photographed before it passed into Yahuda's hands, given that the photographed copy reveals no trace of Yahuda's possession of it. Muṣṭafā Zaid in his book on *naskh* had already noted that the Cairo manuscript was a photographed copy but he was unable to determine the whereabouts of the original.[32] Zaid also noted that Cairo Dār al-kutub *tafsīr* 1087 was another copy of al-Zuhrī's text; that text was copied in 1350/1931 by a certain Maḥmūd Ḥamdī from the photographed copy. The text was certainly not ' edited ' in any sense by this scribe, whose copy only multiplies the already numerous errors of the original. It is, therefore, of no independent value whatsoever. In sum, there exists only one copy of any value of this text, that contained in the Princeton manuscript Yahuda 228.

The ascription of this text has created as much confusion as the manuscript copies themselves. Not unexpectedly for those who have seriously considered the person of the Ṣūfī al-Sulamī and who have even simply glanced at his *tafsīr*,[33] the connexion of this *naskh* text to him in any degree is totally fallacious. The title page of the work is probably what misled Ṣalāḥ al-Dīn al-Munajjid when he edited one folio from the end of the work under the title *Kitāb al-tanzīl*,[34] and from him comes the confusion in Sezgin and Wansbrough apparently; it may well have been, however, confusion or ignorance on the part of a copyist

[27] *GAS*, I, 283, item no. 4.
[28] *GAS*, I, 674, item no. 18.
[29] *QS*, 199.
[30] Cairo, 1957, I, 48.
[31] See also R. Mach (ed.), *Catalogue of Arabic manuscripts (Yahuda section) in the Garrett collection, Princeton University Library*, Princeton, 1977 (hereafter cited as Mach), 14, item 137, ff. 2a–6b. The manuscript is a *majmū'a*: ff. 1b–14a, on the margin primarily, an anonymous *al-Kalām fī'l-ṣalāt* (not in Mach); ff. 2a–7b, al-Zuhrī, *Kitāb fīhi al-nāsikh wa'l-mansūkh* (including *Kitāb al-tanzīl*, ff. 7a–b); ff. 9a–50a, Muḥammad ibn Barakāt, *Kitāb al-ījāz fī ma'rifa mā fī'l-Qur'ān min mansūkh wa nāsikh* in the same hand as the preceding al-Zuhrī text; the scribe identifies himself as a certain Aḥmad ibn al-Naṣīr and states that he finished the work on the 10th of II Rabī' in the year 753 (A.H.); ff. 52a–111b, al-Jarīrī, *Kitāb tafsīr mushkil i'rāb al-Qur'ān*, written in another very distinct hand.
[32] Muṣṭafā Zaid, *al-Naskh fī'l-Qur'ān al-Karīm*, Cairo, 1963, p. 296, n. 1 and p. 297, n. 2. The Princeton copy contains no clear indication of its previous whereabouts, nor does the Library have any information concerning when, where or how Yahuda acquired it.
[33] *Ḥaqā'iq al-tafsīr*, e.g. MS British Library 9433; see *GAS*, I, 671–2.
[34] Beirut, 1963.

of the text at a certain point in time that created the problem in the first place. The title page (f. 2a) reads as follows (see also pl. I):

كتاب فيه الناسخ والمنسوخ للزهرى
تاليف الشيخ الامام ابى عبد الرحمن الحسين بن محمد السلمى
رواية الشيخ ابى حصين [35] عنه
رواية سفين بن سعيد الثورى عنه
رواية ابى نعيم الفضل بن دكين عنه
رواية ابى اسحق ابرهيم الهمذانى عنه
رواية ابى طلحة احمد بن محمد القرارى عنه
رواية احمد بن محمد الصرصرى عنه
رواية ابى طلحة [36] الحسين بن محمد الثقفى عنه
رواية ابى سعد الحسن بن عثمن عنه
رواية الشيخ الجليل ابى البركات المقرى الشهرزورى عنه
رواية الشيخ الامام زين الدين ابى الحسن [37] بن ابرهيم بن غنايم
ابن نجا الانصارى عنه

Note that the *isnād* itself does not even mention al-Zuhrī but this is not really surprising for it is simply a copy of the first *isnād* of the work appearing on f. 2b which is adduced for a version of the famous tradition concerning ʿAlī ibn Abī Ṭālib, the (Kufan) preacher and his knowledge of the principles of *al-nāsikh wa'l-mansūkh* with which this text, like virtually every other *naskh* text, begins.[38] Several versions of this tradition are to be found in various books on *naskh*, but among them the figure of Abū ʿAbd al-Raḥmān ʿAbd Allāh ibn Ḥabīb ibn Rabīʿa al-Sulamī predominates as the first witness to the event.[39] The first four names of the chain of transmitters as found in the text of al-Zuhrī, Ibn Dukain (d. 219/834)[40] from Sufyān al-Thaurī (d. 161/778)[41] from Abū Ḥuṣayn (d. 132/749 or 127–8/744–5)[42] from al-Sulamī are also witnessed in

[35] Not Ḥafs as per Mach, 14.

[36] Compare f. 2b where this name reads Abī ʿAbd Allāh; this latter is probably correct and the name Abī Ṭalḥa most likely appears due to homoeoteleuton from the previous line in the original which begins with Abī Ṭalḥa Aḥmad ibn Muḥammad.

[37] Illegible on title page; see text folio 2b.

[38] e.g. al-Naḥḥās (d. 338/950), *al-Nāsikh wa'l-mansūkh*, Cairo, 1938, 5–6; Hibat Allāh (d. 410/1019), *al-Nāsikh wa'l-mansūkh*, on the margin of al-Wāḥidī, *Asbāb nuzūl al-Qur'ān*, Cairo, reprint 1400, 5–8; ʿAbd al-Qāhir al-Baghdādī (d. 429/1037), *al-Nāsikh wa'l-mansūkh*, MS Berlin Petermann 555, f. 2a, MS Beyazit 445, f. 1b; Abū ʿAbd Allāh ibn ʿAbd Allāh al-ʿĀmirī al-Isfarā'īnī (d. sixth/twelfth century ?) *al-Nāsikh wa'l-mansūkh*, MS British Library OR 12608, ff. 1b–2a; Abū ʿAbd Allāh Muḥammad ibn Barakāt (d. 520/1126), *Kitāb al-ījāz fī maʿrifa mā fī'l-Qur'ān min mansūkh wa nāsikh*, MS Princeton Yahuda 228, ff. 11a–b; Ibn Khuzaima (d. ?), *Kitab al-mūjaz fī'l-nāsikh wa'l-mansūkh*, printed at the end of al-Naḥḥās, *al-Nāsikh wa'l-mansūkh*, Cairo, 1938, 259; Muḥammad ibn Hazm, *Fī maʿrifat al-nāsikh wa'l-mansūkh*, on the margin of al-Jalālain, *Tafsīr al-Qur'ān al-ʿAẓim*, Cairo, 1924, II, 150–1—this text is most certainly not by Abū Muḥammad ibn Ḥazm al-Ẓāhirī (d. 456/1064) *pace GAL*, I, 400, Suppl. I, 696, nor is its attribution to Abū ʿAbd Allāh Muḥammad ibn Aḥmad ibn Ḥazm (d. 320/932) likely, *pace* M. Zaid, *al-Naskh fī'l-Qur'ān al-Karīm*, 324 and p. 324, n. 3, given the extremely facile nature of the body of the text; the fact that the introduction to this text, II, p. 151, line 27 to II, p. 153, line 26, corresponds word for word to that of Abū Bakr Muḥammad ibn Mūsā ibn ʿUthmān ibn Ḥāzim al-Hamdhānī known as al-Ḥāzimī (d. 584/1188), *al-Iʿtibār fī bayān al-nāsikh wa'l-mansūkh min al-āthār*, Hyderabad, 1359, p. 5, line 21 to p. 7, line 4 may well suggest that this latter writer is responsible for both works. The major exception to the citation of the 'principles of abrogation' report is in Makkī al-Qaisi (d. 437/1045), *al-Īḍāḥ li-nāsikh al-Qur'ān wa-mansūkhihi*, Riyad, 1976, where despite an extensive introduction no such reports are found.

[39] e.g. al-Naḥḥās, *al-Nāsikh wa'l-mansūkh*, 6; on al-Sulamī see Ibn al-Jazarī, *Ghayāt al-nihāya fī ṭabaqāt al-qurrā'*, Cairo, 1932, I, 413–14; Ibn Saʿd, *al-Ṭabaqāt al-Kabīr*, Beirut, 1957, VI, 172–5.

[40] See al-Dāwudī, *Ṭabaqāt al-mufassirīn*, Cairo, 1972, II, 29; al-Suyūtī, *Ṭabaqāt al-ḥuffāẓ*, Cairo, 1973, 159.

[41] See *GAS*, I, 518–19.

[42] See Ibn al-Jazarī, *Ghāyat al-nihāya*, I, 505–6.

other texts.[43] It would seem, then, that at some point a copyist of this text, perhaps knowing the Ṣūfī al-Sulamī, changed 'Abd Allāh ibn Ḥabīb's name to al-Ḥusain ibn Muḥammad.[44] Why he did this and just what his understanding of the situation was is entirely unclear; all that exists is the evidence of the apparently changed name.

That the last copyist of this text at the very least was prone to error and may well have changed the text in various ways is witnessed in a number of other errors also. Whether *all* these errors are necessarily the fault of the last copyist is not clear; some may well have occurred in earlier copies and have then been repeated here. On the other hand, the fact that this copyist did not correct the obvious errors (including the title page) reveals that he was at best a very mechanical copyist, if he was not, in fact, totally responsible for the errors to begin with. Most serious and surprising among these are the instances of the Qur'ān being misquoted in the text; this does, of course, happen in many manuscripts, but that a total of 17 substantial errors should occur [45] in a text that is only four and one-half folios long with nineteen lines per page is significant because of what it reveals of the scribe's qualifications and abilities. Mistakes in the actual discursive text are not infrequent either and there may exist in fact far more errors than indicated in the critical apparatus of the text for, in instances of simply sloppy writing, it was generally felt more fair to give the scribe the benefit of the doubt. One other error arises also in paragraph one of the text in the *isnād*; the date of Abū Isḥāq Ibrāhīm al-Hamdhānī's transmission of the text is given as 378 (988). Since Ibn Dukain may be identified as someone who died in 219/834,[46] either there is a gap in the *isnād* or a mistake has been made in the date. It is possible to identify Abū Isḥāq Ibrāhīm ibn al-Ḥusain ibn 'Alī al-Hamdhānī as someone who died in 281/894 [47] which would perhaps indicate simply that the hundreds digit in the date has been subjected to change or simple error. Just why this should be is also unknown.

In the following text, the punctuation and paragraphs are those of the editor. The *Kitāb al-tanzīl*, while perhaps an integral part of the manuscript and text (ff. 7a–b), is already available in the edition published by al-Munajjid and since it adds nothing to the overall analysis, it has not been reproduced here. (For notes to the Arabic text see p. 36.)

[كتاب نسخ القرآن لابن شهاب الزهرى]

٢ ب بسم الله الرحمن الرحيم

(١) قال الشيخ الامام العالم الأوحد الورع زين الدين واعظ المسلمين

[43] See, e.g., al-Naḥḥās, 6.

[44] Note that the proper name of al-Sulamī the Ṣūfī is actually Muḥammad ibn al-Ḥusain ibn Muḥammad, so, that the copyist/compiler even necessarily intended this person is still not totally evident.

[45] These instances have been noted in the critical apparatus of the text below. I do not consider, of course, that they are of any textual value; rather they are included to illustrate the extent of copyist error. Qur'ānic orthographic variants (which are numerous) have not been noted; the standard Cairo text orthography has been uniformly imposed as has its variant reading version with one exception where the text requires a different reading (see paragraph 9). A short and corrupt text such as this is of little value in the study of Middle Arabic and thus preservation of these discrepancies seems pointless.

[46] See above note 40.

[47] *GAS*, I, 321.

28

ابـو الحسن بـن ابراهيم بن غنايـم بـن نجـا الأنصـاري • قـال : اخبرنا الشيخ الامـام الجلـيل عمـدة الملك ابـو البركات المقـرئ المعروف بالشهرزوري • قال : حدثنـا الشيخ الامـام ابو سـعد الحسن بـن عثمـان بن محـمـد العجلي • قال : حدثنا ابو عبـد اللـه الحسين بن محمـد بن الحسين الثقفـي ، حدثنـا احمـد بن محمـد الصرصري ، حدثنا ابو طلحـة احمـد بن محمـد بن يوسف بن مسعدة الفزاري • قال : حدثنا ابواسحاق ابراهيم بن الحسين بن علـي الهمذاني سنة ثماني وسبعين وثلاثمايـة[1] • قـال : حدثنا ابو نعيم الفضـل بن دكين ، حدثنـا سفيـان بن سعيد الثـوري ، حدثنا ابـو حصين • قال : حدثنا ابو عبد الرحمان الحسين بن محمـد[2] السلمي • قال : مـر علـي بن ابي طالب كرم اللـه وجهـه بقاص يقص علـى الناس فقال لـه : علمت الناسخ مـن المنسوخ ؟ فقـال : لا • فقـال لـه علـي عليه السـلام : هلكت واهلكت !

(٢) وحدثنـا موسـى بن اسماعيـل ، حدثنـا حمـاد عـن عطـاء بن السـائب عـن البختري[3] • قـال : مـر علي عليه السـلام بمسجد الكـوفـة فراى قاصـا يقص على الناس فقال : مـن هذا ؟ فقالوا : رجل يحـدث الناس • فقـال علي عليـه السـلام : هـذا يقـول اعرفـوني اعرفـوني انـا فـلان بـن فـلان • ثـم قـال : اسـالوه هـل يعرف الناسـخ مـن المنسـوخ ؟ فقالـوا لـه : اميـر المؤمنيـن يقـول لك هـل تعـرف الناسـخ مـن المنسوخ ؟ فقـال : لا • فقـال علـي : فـلا يرجـع يحدث حديثـا •

(٣) حـدثنا شعبـة • قال : حدثنا ابو الوليـد • قال : اخبـرني ابو الحصين[4] • قال : سمعت ابا عبـد الرحمـان السلمـي يقـول : قال علـي بـن ابـي طالب كرم اللـه وجهـه لرجـل يقـص علـى الناس : هـل تعـلم الناسـخ مـن المنسـوخ ؟ فقـال : لا • فقـال : هلكـت واهلكـت !

(٤) حدثنـا ابـو نعيـم سـلمـة • قال : حدثنـا ميـط بن شريط ، حدثنـا الضحـاك بن مـزاحـم • قال : مـر ابـن عباس بقـاص يقـص فـوكزه برجلـه ثم قـال لـه : هل تـدري الناسـخ مـن المنسـوخ ؟ فقـال : لا • فقال

٣أ لـه : هلكـت / واهلكـت !

(٥) وبـه حدثنـا مسـدد ، حـدثنا حميـد الجمانـي عـن سلمـة بن نبيـط عـن الضحــاك • قال : ورد فى تفسيـر قولـه تعالـى ﴿ هـو الـذى انـزل عليـك الكـتٰب منـه ءايت محكمٰتٌ هـن ام الكـتٰب ﴾ [٣ / ٧]

ثم قال ﴿ ما ننسخ من ءاية ﴾ [٢ / ١٠٦] ﴿ واخر متشبهٰت ﴾ [٣ / ٧] فقال : هو ما قد نسخ ٠

(٦) وحدثنا مسدد ٠ قال : حدثنا عبد الوارث عن حميد الاعرج عن مجاهد : ﴿ او ننسها[٦] ﴾ [٢ / ١٠٦] قال : نبدل حكمها ونثبت خطها ٠

(٧) اول الناسخ ما رواه محمد بن مسلم الزهرى ٠ حدثنا ابراهيم ، حدثنا ابو يزيد[٧] هو عبد الله بن محمد بن يزيد الهذلى ، حدثنا الوليد ابن محمد الموقرى[٨] الاموى المدينى ٠ قال : حدثني محمد بن مسلم الزهرى ٠ قال : هذا كتاب منسوخ القران ٠ قال الله تعالى ﴿ ما ننسخ من ءاية او ننسها[٩] ﴾ [٢ / ١٠٦] وقال عز وجل ﴿ واذا بدلنا ءاية مكان ءاية ﴾ [١٦ / ١٠١] وقال تعالى ﴿ يمحوا[١٠] الله ما يشاء ويثبت[١١] وعنده أم الكتٰب ﴾ [١٣ / ٣٩] ٠

(٨) وحدثنا ابراهيم ٠ قال : حدثنا ابو يزيد ، حدثنا الوليد بن محمد ٠ قال : حدثني محمد بن مسلم الزهرى ٠ قال : اول ما نسخ من القران من سورة البقرة القبلة كانت نحو بيت المقدس تحولت نحو الكعبة ٠ فقال الله عز وجل ﴿ ولله المشرق والمغرب فاينما تولوا فثم وجه الله ان الله وسع عليم ﴾ [٢ / ١١٥] نسخ بقوله تعالى ﴿ قد نرى تقلب وجهك فى السماء فلنولينك قبلة ترضها فول وجهك شطر المسجد الحرام ﴾ [٢ / ١٤٤] ٠

(٩) وايضا في اية الصوم قال الله تعالى ﴿ فدية طعام مساكين[١٢] ﴾ [٢ / ١٨٤] و مسكين رواية ٠ فكان [في] اول الاسلام من شاء صام ومن شاء افتدى بطعام مسكين وقال فيها ﴿ فمن[١٣] تطوع خيرا فهو خير له وان تصوموا خير لكم ان كنتم تعلمون ﴾ [٢ / ١٨٤] ٠ نسخ منها ﴿ فمن شهد منكم الشهر فليصمه ومن كان مريضا او على سفر فعدة من ايام اخر ﴾ [٢ / ١٨٥] ٠

(١٠) وقال ايضا ﴿ كتب عليكم الصيام[١٤] كما كتب على الذين من قبلكم لعلكم تتقون ﴾ [٢ / ١٨٣] كانوا في اول الصيام اذا صلى الناس العتمة
٣ ب ونام احدهم حرم عليه الطعام والشراب والنساء ، واصلوا[١٥] / الصيام حتى الليلة المقبلة ٠ فاختان رجل نفسه فجامع اهله بعد ما صلى العتمة فنسخ ذلك فقال ﴿ علم الله أنكم كنتم تختانون انفسكم فتاب عليكم وعفا عنكم ﴾ [٢ / ١٨٧] وهو عمر

بن الخطاب رضي الله عنه وامراته الانصارية ام عاصم بن عمر واسمها جميلة [وكان][16] عاصم الذى حماه الدين أن يوخذ راسه وقتلوا يوئذ أبا الجيلان بن هذيل واسروا خبيب بن عدى وزيد بن الدثنة فنسخ شأن الصوم والنساء فقال تعالى ﴿ فالئن[1] بشروهن وابتغوا ما كتب الله لكم وكلوا واشربوا حتى يتبين لكم الخيط الابيض من الخيط الاسود من الفجر ثم اتموا الصيام الى الليل ﴾ [٢ / ١٨٧] والذى انزلت فيه اية الصوم هو صرمة بن ابي اياس غلبته عينه فنام فحرم عليه الطعام والشراب حتى الليلة المقبلة فانزل الله عز وجل الرخصة في الصوم والفرج والنسوة[17] وذلك [قوله تعالى ﴿ احل لكم ليلة الصيام الرفث ﴾ [٢ / ١٨٧]][18]

(١١) [و] قوله تعالى ﴿ ان ترك خيرا الوصية للولدين والاقربين ﴾ [٢ / ١٨٠] فنسخت باية الميراث[19].

(١٢) وقال تعالى ﴿ والمطلقت[1] يتربصن بانفسهن ثلثة قروء ولا يحل لهن ان يكتمن ما خلق الله فى ارحامهن ان كن يؤمن بالله واليوم الاخر وبعولتهن احق بردهن فى ذلك ان ارادوا اصلحا ﴾ [٢ / ٢٢٨] ذلك ان الرجل كان اذا طلق زوجته كان احق بردها ان كان قد طلقها ثلاثا فلما انزل الله عز وجل ﴿ الطلق مرتان فامساك بمعروف او تسريح باحسن ﴾ [٢ / ٢٢٩] فضرب الله حينئذ اجلا لمن مات او لمن طلق .

(١٣) فقال تعالى ﴿ والذين يتوفون منكم ويذرون ازوجا وصية لازوجهم متعا الى الحول غير اخراج ﴾ [٢ / ٢٤٠] فنسخها باية الميراث[20] التى فرض لهن فيها الربع والثمن .

(١٤) وقال تعالى ﴿ ولا تنكحوا المشركت حتى يؤمن ولامة مؤمنة خير
من مشركة ولو اعجبتكم ولا تنكحوا المشركين حتى يؤمنوا ولعبد مؤمن
خير من مشرك ولو اعجبكم ﴾ [٢ / ٢٢١] فنسخ منها / ما احل من ٤أ
المشركات من نساء اهل الكتاب من اليهود والنصارى في النكاح[21].

(١٥) وقال الله عز وجل ﴿ ولا يحل لكم ان تاخذوا مما ءاتيتموهن شيئا الا ان يخافا الا يقيما حدود الله فان خفتم الا يقيما حدود الله فلا جناح عليهما فيما افتدت به ﴾ [٢ / ٢٢٩] .

(١٦) وقال تعالى ﴿ لا يكلف الله نفسا الا وسعها ﴾ [٢ / ٢٨٦]

فيما فرض ان لم يستطع الحج ولا الجهاد او لم يستطع ان يصلى قائما فيصلى جالسا قال تعالى * ان تبدوا ما فى انفسكم او تخفوه يحاسبكم به الله فيغفر لمن يشاء ويعذب من يشاء * [٢ / ٢٨٤] نسخت بقوله تعالى * لا يكلف الله نفسا الا وسعها لها ما كسبت وعليها ما اكتسبت * [٢ / ٢٨٦] اى لا يكتب على احد الا ما فعل وما عمل ٠

(١٧) وقال فى سورة النساء * واذا حضر القسمة اولوا القربى واليتمى والمسكين فارزقوهم منه * [٤ / ٨] نسختها اية الميراث[22] فياخذ كل نفس ما كتب لها من الفرايض وفي اموال اليتامى ٠

(١٨) [و] قال * ومن[23] كان غنيما فليستعفف ومن كان فقيرا فلياكل بالمعروف * [٤ / ٦] نسخت بقوله تعالى * ان الذين[24] ياكلون اموال اليتمى ظلما انما ياكلون فى بطونهم نارا وسيصلون سعيرا * [٤ / ١٠] ٠

(١٩) وقال تعالى * والتى ياتين الفحشة من نسائكم فاستشهدوا عليهن اربعة منكم * الى قوله * سبيلا * [٤ / ١٥] وهذه المراة وحدها ليس معها رجل فقال رجل كلاما فقال الله عز وجل * والذان[25] يأتينها منكم فاذوهما فان تابا واصلحا فاعرضوا عنهما[26] * [٤ / ١٦] اى فاعرضوا عن عذابهما ٠

(٢٠) وقال * ولا يحل لكم أن ترثوا النساء كرها ولا تعضلوهن لتذهبوا ببعض ما ءاتيتموهن الا ان ياتين بفحشة مبينة * [٤ / ١٩] قال ابو يزيد : بلغني ان الرجل كان فى الجاهلية لا يرث[27] امراة ابيه [الذى] لا يورثها من الميراث شيئا حتى تفتدى ببعض ما اعطوها ٠ قال ابن شهاب فوعظ الله سبحانه فى ذلك عباده المؤمنين ونهاهم عنه ٠

ب (٢١) وقال تعالى * والذين عقدت ايمنكم / فاتوهم نصيبهم * [٤ / ٣٣] قيل ان الرجل اول ما نزل رسول الله صلعم المدينة تحالف الرجل : انك ترثني وارثك ٠ فنسخها الله عز وجل بقوله * واولوا الارحام بعضهم أولى ببعض فى كتب الله ان الله بكل شىء عليم * [٨ / ٧٥] ٠

(٢٢) وقال تعالى * يايها الذين ءامنوا لا تقربوا الصلوة وانتم سكرى حتى تعلموا ما تقولون * [٤ / ٤٣] وقال تعالى * يسئلونك[28] عن الخمر والميسر قل فيهما اثم كبير ومنفع للناس واثمهما اكبر من نفعهما * [٢ / ٢١٩] فنسخها الله عز وجل بقوله سبحانه * يايها الذين ءامنوا انما الخمر والميسر والانصاب والازلم رجس من عمل الشيطن فاجتنبوه لعلكم تفلحون * [٥ / ٩٠] ٠

(٢٣) وقال تعالى * الا الذين يصلون الى قوم بينكم وبينهم ميثق او جاءوكم حصرت صدورهم ان يقتلوكم او يقتلوا قومهم ولو شاء الله لسلطهم عليكم فلقتلوكم فان اعتزلوكم فلم يقتلوكم والقوا اليكم السلم * الى قوله * سلطنا مبينا * [٤ / ٩٠ – ٩١] وقال تعالى * لا ينهكم الله عن الذين لم يقتلوكم فى الدين ولم يخرجوكم من ديركم ان تبروهم وتقسطوا اليهم ان الله يحب المقسطين * انما ينهكم الله عن الذين قتلوكم في الدين واخرجوكم من ديركم وظهروا على اخراجكم ان تولوهم ومن يتولهم[٢٩] فاولئك هم الظلمون * [٦٠ / ٨ – ٩] وقال تعالى * الا الذين عهدتم عند المسجد الحرام * [٩ / ٧] وهم بنو ضمرة بن بكر كان قد عاقد عليهم مخشي بن حويل : انا نأمنكم وتأمنوا حتى ندبر وننظر فى الامر. نسخ هولاء الأربعة . فقال تعالى * براءة من الله ورسوله الى الذين عهدتم من المشركين * فسيحوا فى الارض اربعة اشهر واعلموا انكم غير معجزى الله وان الله مخزى الكفرين * [٩ / ١ – ٢] فجعل لهم اجلا اربعة أشهر يسيحون في الأرض * فاذا انسلخ الاشهر الحرم
فاقتلوا المشركين حيث وجدتموهم وخذوهم واحصروهم[٣٠] واقعدوا / لهم كل مرصد ٥أ
فان تابوا واقاموا الصلوة وءاتوا الزكوة فخلوا سبيلهم ان الله غفور / رحيم * [٩ / ٥] وقال عز وجل * وان احد من المشركين استجارك فاجره حتى يسمع كلم الله * [٩ / ٦] .

(٢٤) وقال تعالى * لا تاكلوا اولكم بينكم بالبطل الا ان تكون تجرة عن تراض منكم * [٤ / ٢٩] فنسخ هذا فقال * ولا على انفسكم ان تاكلوا[٣١] من بيوتكم او بيوت ءابائكم او بيوت امهتكم[٣٢] او بيوت اخونكم او بيوت اخوتكم او بيوت اعممكم او بيوت عمتكم او بيوت اخولكم او بيوت خلتكم او ما ملكتم مفاتحه او صديقكم ليس عليكم جناح ان تاكلوا جميعا او اشتاتا * [٢٤ / ٦١] .

(٢٥) وقال الله فى الانفال * ان يكن منكم عشرون صبرون يغلبوا مائتين وان يكن منكم مائة يغلبوا الفا من الذين كفروا بانهم قوم لا يفقهون * [٨ / ٦٥] فضج المسلمون عند ذلك وقالوا : من يطيق ذلك وهل يقدر الرجل الواحد يلقى عشرة رجال ؟ فنسخ الله عز وجل ذلك بقوله * الئٰن خفف الله عنكم وعلم أن فيكم ضعفا فان يكن منكم مائة صابرة يغلبوا مائتين وان يكن منكم الف يغلبوا الفين باذن الله والله مع الصبرين * [٨ / ٦٦] .

(٢٦) وقال تعالى * ان الذين ءامنوا وهاجروا وجهدوا باموالهم وانفسهم
في سبيل الله والذين ءاووا ونصروا اولئك بعضهم اولياء[٣٣] بعض والذين
ءامنوا ولم يهاجروا مالكم من وليتهم من شئ حتى يهاجروا *
[٨ / ٧٢] وقيل ان الاعرابي كان ايرثه المهاجر وكان المهاجر لا
يورثه فنسخ الله عز وجل ذلك بقوله * واولوا الارحام بعضهم اولى
ببعض فى كتب الله ان الله بكل شئ عليم * [٨ / ٧٥] .
(٢٧) وقال تعالى * وان جنحوا للسلم فاجنح لها وتوكل على الله *
[٨ / ٦١] وقال تعالى * قاتلوا[٣٤] الذين لا يؤمنون بالله ولا باليوم
الاخر * [٩ / ٢٩] وقال تعالى * وما كان الله ليعذبهم وانت فيهم
وما كان الله معذبهم وهم يستغفرون * [٨ / ٣٢] فنسخت فقال تعالى / ٥ ب
* وما لهم الا يعذبهم الله وهم يصدون عن المسجد الحرام * الى
* كنتم تكفرون * [٨ / ٣٤ ـ ٣٥] فقاتلوا بمكة فاصابهم خصاصة وجوع .
(٢٨) وقال فى سورة براة * الا تنفروا يعذبكم عذابا اليما * [٩ / ٣٩]
وقال ايضا * وما كان لاهل المدينة ومن حولهم من الاعراب ان
يتخلفوا عن رسول الله ولا يرغبوا بانفسهم عن نفسه ذلك بانهم لا
يصيبهم ظمأ ولا نصب * [٩ / ١٢٠] نسخها قوله تعالى * وما كان
المؤمنون لينفروا كافة فلولا نفر من كل فرقة منهم طائفة
ليفقهوا فى الدين * [٩ / ١٢٢] .
(٢٩) وقال تعالى * لا يستئذنك الذين يؤمنون بالله واليوم الاخر * الى
قوله * يترددون * [٩ / ٤٤ ـ ٤٥] نسخها قوله تعالى * فاذا
استئذنوك لبعض شانهم * الى قوله * غفور رحيم * [٢٤ / ٦٢] .
(٣٠) وقال تعالى * الاعراب اشد كفرا ونفاقا * الى قوله * عليم *
[٩ / ٩٧ ـ ٩٨] نسخها قوله تعالى * ومن الاعراب من يؤمن
بالله واليوم الاخر * الى قوله تعالى * قربة لهم * [٩ / ٩٩] .
(٣١) وقال تعالى فى سورة النحل قوله * من كفر بالله من بعد ايمنه الا
من اكره وقلبه مطمئن بالايمن * الى قوله تعالى * عظيم *
[١٦ / ١٠٦] نسخ منها * ثم ان ربك للذين هاجروا من بعد
ما فتنوا ثم جهدوا وصبروا ان ربك من بعدها لغفور رحيم *
[١٦ / ١١٠] .
(٣٢) وقال تعالى فى سورة بني اسرائيل * وقل رب ارحمهما كما ربياني صغيرا *
[١٧ / ٢٤] فنسخ منها قوله تعالى * ما كان للنبى والذين ءامنوا

34

ان يستغفروا للمشركين ولو كانوا اولى قربى من بعد ما تبين لهم انهم اصحب الجحيم * [٩ / ١١٣] .

(٣٣) وقال عز وجل قائلا[٣٥] * ولا تجهر بصلاتك ولا تخافت بها وابتغ بين ذلك سبيلا * [١٧ / ١١٠] فنسخ بقوله تعالى * واذكر ربك فى نفسك تضرعا وخيفة ودون الجهر من القول بالغدو والاصال * [٧ / ٢٠٥] .

(٣٤) وقال تعالى * فاصدع بما تؤمر واعرض عن المشركين * انا كفينك المستهزءين * [١٥ / ٩٤ ـ ٩٥]

١٦ أ (٣٥) وقال تعالى / فى سورة النور * والذين يرمون المحصنت[١]
ثم لم يأتوا باربعة شهداء * الى قوله تعالى * هم الفسقون * [٢٤ / ٤] نسخ منها * والذين يرمون أزوجهم ولم يكن لهم شهداء الا انفسهم * الاية [٢٤ / ٦] ان كان من الصادقين الى آخر اللعان فان حلف ، فرق عنهما ولم يجلد واحد منهما ، وان لم يحلف ، أقيم عليه الحد .

(٣٦) وقال تعالى * وقل للمؤمنت يغضضن من ابصرهن * الى قوله تعالى * او الطفل الذين لم يظهروا على عورت النساء * [٢٤ / ٣١] نسخ منها * والقوعد من النساء التى لا يرجون نكاحا * الى قوله * سميع عليم *[٣٦] [٢٤ / ٦٠]

(٣٧) وقال تعالى * يايها الذين ءامنوا لا تدخلوا بيوتا غير بيوتكم حتى تستأنسوا وتسلموا على اهلها * الى قوله تعالى * لعلكم تذكرون * [٢٤ / ٢٧] نسخ منها قوله تعالى * ليس عليكم جناح ان تدخلوا بيوتا غير مسكونة فيها متع لكم * [٢٤ / ٢٩] وهى بيوت المتاجرة ومنازل الضيف فقال * والله يعلم ما تبدون وما تكتمون * [٢٤ / ٢٩] .

(٣٨) وفى الشعراء قوله تعالى * والشعراء يتبعهم الغاوون * الى قوله * يفعلون * [٢٤ / ٢٢٤ ـ ٢٢٦] نسختها هذه الاية قوله تعالى * الا الذين ءامنوا وعملوا الصلحت وذكروا الله كثيرا * الى اخر السورة [٢٤ / ٢٢٧] .

(٣٩) وفى حم الاحقاف قوله تعالى * قل ما كنت بدعا من الرسل وما ادرى ما يفعل بى ولا بكم * [٤٦ / ٩] نسختها هذه الاية قوله تعالى * انا فتحنا لك فتحا مبينا * ليغفر لك الله ما تقدم من ذنبك وما تأخر * الى قوله[٣٧] * ويهديك صرطا مستقيما * [٤٨ / ١ ـ ٢]

فعلم سبحانه ما يفعل به من الكرامة فقال رجل من الانصار : قد حدثك ربك ما يفعل بك من الكرامة فهنيئا لك يا رسول الله ! فما يفعل بنا نحن ؟ فقال سبحانه ﴿ وبشر المؤمنين بان لهم من الله فضلا كبيرا ﴾ [٣٣ / ٤٧] وقال تعالى ﴿ ليدخل المؤمنين والمؤمنٰت جنت تجرى من تحتها الانهر ﴾ [٤٨ / ٥] فبين تعالى فى هذه الاية كيف يفعل به وبهم ./ ٦ ب

(٤٠) وقال تعالى فى سورة المجادلة ﴿ يايها الذين ءامنوا اذا نجيتم الرسول فقدموا بين يدى نجواكم صدقة ﴾ الى قوله تعالى ﴿ غفور رحيم ﴾ [٥٨ / ١٢] فنسختها[٣٨] هذه الاية قوله تعالى ﴿ ءاشفقتم ان تقدموا بين يدى نجواكم صدقٰت ﴾ الى قوله تعالى ﴿ وءاتوا الزكوة ﴾ [٥٨ / ١٣] .

(٤١) وقال تعالى فى سورة المزمل ﴿ قم اليل الا قليلا * نصفه او انقص منه قليلا * او زد عليه ورتل القرءان ترتيلا ﴾ [٧٣ / ٢ — ٤] فنسخها قوله تعالى ﴿ علم الن تحصوه فتاب عليكم فاقرءوا ما تيسر من القرءان ﴾ الى قوله تعالى ﴿ وءاتوا الزكوة ﴾ [٧٣ / ٢٠] .

(٤٢) وقال تعالى ﴿ ان ناشئة اليل هى اشد وطأ واقوم قيلا ﴾ [٧٣/٦] وناشئة الليل اوله كانت صلواتهم فى اول الليل . يقول هو : احذر ان تحصوه وما فرضت عليكم قيام الليل . وذلك ان احدهم كان اذا نام ما يدرى متى يستيقظ فقال تعالى ﴿ واقوم قيلا ﴾ [٧٣ / ٦] يعنى القران ومنفعتهم به . يقول : حتى يفهم القران ويتدبر اياته ويفقه ما فيه وقال عز وجل ﴿ ان لك فى النهار سبحا طويلا ﴾ [٧٣ /٧] يقول : فراغا طويلا . يقول : من اول الليل يكون النوم والتهجد يكون فى وسطه وفى اخره ولا يشتغل بالحاجات .

(٤٣) وقال تعالى فى سورة الذاريات ﴿ وذكر فان الذكرى تنفع المؤمنين ﴾ [٥١ / ٥٥] .

(٤٤) وقال فى سورة المائدة ﴿ انما جزاؤا الذين يحاربون الله ورسوله ويسعون فى الارض فسادا ان يقتلوا او يصلبوا او تقطع ايديهم وارجلهم من خلف او ينفوا من الارض ﴾ الى قوله تعالى ﴿ من قبل ان تقدروا عليهم ﴾ [٥ / ٣٣ — ٣٤] يقول : فلا سبيل لكم عليهم بعد التوبة . اراد بذلك الرجل المسلم الذى يكون منه الفساد ثم يتوب من قبل ان يظفر به رب الامر واما الكفار الذين يفسدون فى الارض وهم فى دار

الحرب فهولاء فلا تقبل فانهم لو كانت توبتهم صادقة للحقوا ببـــــلاد
٧ أ المسلميـن ./ .... 7_ كتـاب التنزيل ‾7 ....
[٧ ب] تم كتـاب الناسخ والمنسوخ وللـه الحمـد والمنـة والحمـد للـه وحده وصلواته علـى سيدنـا محمـد نبيـه والـه وسـلم[٣٩].

---

١) ثلاثمـائة : كذا فـى الاصـل ، انظـر ص 27 .

٢) الحسين بـن محمد : كذا فـى الاصـل ، انظـر ص 27 .

٣) البحترى : فـى القرطبى ، الجامع لاحكام القران : البختري وفـى النحاس ، النـاسخ والمنسـوخ : البحتـرى .

٤) ابو الحصين : لعله ابو حصين ، انظـر الفقـرة ١ .

٥) ايت محكمـت هن ام الكتب : ايت محكمـت وقالـه بـه هن ام الكتـــب " وقالـه بـه " زيـادة فـوق الخط .

٦) ننسها : ننساها وهى القراءة المشهورة عن ابن كثيـر وابـى عمــــرو .

٧) فـى Mach : ابو زيـد ، وهو خطـاء .

٨) فـى Mach : الموقـدى . انظر المنجد ، كتاب التنزيل لابن شهاب الزهري.

٩) انظـر الملاحظـة ٦ .

١٠) يمحـوا : يمـح .

١١) ويثبت : سقط من الاصـل .

١٢) مساكين : هى قراءة نـافع وابن عـامر والباقـون : مسـكين .

١٣) فمـن : ومـن .

١٤) الصيام : الصـوم .

١٥) واصلوا : لعله " وصلة " وفـى الاصـل : وصلـوا .

١٦) فـى الاصـل : ؟؟

١٧) النسوة : النسـو ؟

١٨) ما بين [ ] سقط مـن الاصـل ؟ انظـر هبـة الله ، كتـاب الناسخ والمنسوخ ص٥٦ ــ ٦٣ .

١٩) يعنـى القران ٤ / ١١ ــ ١٢ .

٢٠) يعنـى القران ٤ / ١١ ــ ١٢ .

٢١) يعنـى القران ٥/٥ .

٢٢) يعنـى القران ١١/٤ ــ ١٢ .

٢٣) ومـن : فمـن .

٢٤) ان الذيـن : الذيـن .

٢٥) والذان : الذيـن .

٢٦) فاعرضوا عنهما : فاعنهما •

٢٧) يرث : يورث •

٢٨) يسئلونك : ويسئلونك •

٢٩) يتولهم : يتولهم منكم •

٣٠) وخذوهم واحصروهم : واحصروهم •

٣١) فى الاصل : ليس عليكم جناح ان تاكلوا الخ •

٣٢) او بيوت امهتكم : او امهتكم •

٣٣) اولياء : اولى •

٣٤) قاتلوا : وقاتلوا •

٣٥) قائلا : قايل •

٣٦) سميع عليم : حكيم عليم •

٣٧) الى قوله : الاية الى قوله •

٣٨) فنسختها : فنسخت •

٣٩) سلم : سلام •

A literary analysis of a text of this type may take advantage of several lines of approach, each of which will provide material appropriate to establishing a relative dating of the text. The internal structure of the work, the literary style, the legal discussions and the implications thereof and the terminological usages are all appropriate facets to be examined in some detail.

The structure of the text is, of course, what draws our attention to it in the first place and creates the distinctive grouping of texts as classified above. The order of presentation of al-Zuhrī's work is not as random as that of Sufyān al-Thaurī's *tafsīr*, for example, but it does reveal traits which may be explained either as evidence of rushed composition done with little care and perhaps compiled from a variety of disparate sources or as evidence of a rudimentary working out of the problem of *naskh* on the part of an author early on in the Islamic era. In this way the text is much like Ibn 'Abbās's *al-Lughāt*.[48] With the major exception of the final two paragraphs,[49] which by the evidence of their content could well be later additions to the text, the work does follow basic *sūra* order of the abrogated verses (which is the standard approach in most *naskh* texts),[50] but it does not impose a rigorous system of verses in sequence within that order. Neither consideration of the topic being discussed nor the order of the abrogating verses would seem to explain the discrepancies.

In a similar way, the discussions in each paragraph are of an uneven nature. In paragraphs 15, 34, 43 and 44 there is no mention of abrogation at all. Q. 2 : 229 mentioned in paragraph 15 is, according to Hibat Allāh,[51] the abrogator of Q. 2 : 228; Q. 15 : 94–5 in paragraph 34 is partially abrogated by *āyat al-saif*, once again according to Hibat Allāh; [52] Q. 51 : 55 in paragraph

[48] See Rippin, *BSOAS*, XLIV, 1, 1981, 22.

[49] Paragraph 34 is also out of order but is aberrant in other details as well: see below.

[50] The exception here being the work by al-Baghdādī which is divided into chapters according to whether or not there is agreement by most scholars on the matter (see *QS*, 199).

[51] Hibat Allāh, 89–91.

[52] ibid., 206–7.

43 abrogates Q. 51 : 54 [53] while Q. 5 : 33–4 in paragraph 44 is a subject of much debate.[54] Yet none of this is mentioned here. Various explanations for these absences are possible here once again although it does seem quite likely that careless copying could be the culprit. This too may explain the less essential loss at the end of paragraph 10. Yet, at the same time, the variability in the depth of discussion contained in the other paragraph itself may well indicate an *overall* uneven composition; in a total of 15 paragraphs, a simple juxtaposition of abrogated and abrogating verses takes place,[55] whereas in other cases there is at least some discussion of the matter, generally tailored in order to establish clearly the interpretation of the verse in question. Compared to this as well, then, is the very expansive treatment to which the reader is treated in paragraph 10 and, to some extent, also in paragraph 23. Paragraph 10 most especially is marked by a superfluity of information, some of it totally irrelevant to the topic at debate. The passage Q. 2 : 187 deals with night-time activities during the fast of Ramaḍān, abrogating practices generally tied to Q. 2 : 183 where the fast ' as prescribed for those before you ' is enjoined. In virtually every treatment of the verse found in various works and genres of *tafsīr*, the anecdote dealing with 'Umar having intercourse with his wife during a night of Ramaḍān after having previously fallen asleep that evening is among those cited (along with that of [Qais ibn] Ṣirma quite frequently).[56] To find the anecdote in this text, then, is by no means exceptional; that the text should, however, launch into a relatively lengthy explanation concerning 'Āṣim, the son of 'Umar by Jamīla, the wife involved in this scenario (who is, in fact, rarely named in other versions of the story), and 'Āṣim's untimely end shortly after the battle of Uḥud [57] is most peculiar given the strangely haggadic nature of those comments coming in the midst of a serious legal matter.

Similar to the superfluous quality of paragraph 10 is the series of introductory reports concerning 'Alī ibn Abī Ṭālib in paragraphs 1 to 3 and Ibn 'Abbās in paragraph 4, and the knowledge of the principles of Qur'ānic abrogation. All four reports are virtually identical in thrust and intent (that knowing about *naskh* is the prime requirement of someone who wishes to speak about the Qur'ān) and the only remarkable thing about them is their sheer quantity. While most *naskh* texts find it necessary to adduce at least one of these reports (or something similar) in order to provide a traditional underpinning for their enterprise,[58] that this text which is so short and generally direct in its approach should bother to gather four such reports together is to be viewed with a certain degree of curiosity.

While the historical matter of attribution is not of concern in considerations of the literary structure of the text, the matter in paragraph 20 with the comment attributed to Abū Yazīd (d. third century A.H.) and then a return to the name of Ibn Shihāb al-Zuhrī, produces in the reader a disruptive effect similar to a narrator's intrusions into a work of fiction. That it occurs only once in this text, however, leaves its status and significance somewhat in doubt;

[53] ibid., 291–2.

[54] See e.g. ibid., 150–1 and *QS*, 185–8.

[55] This, of course, is the method followed by Muḥammad ibn Ḥazm in his entire text; it is the variability in procedure that is important here, not the procedure *per se*.

[56] Al-Wāḥidī, *Asbāb nuzūl al-Qur'ān*, Cairo, 1400, 33–5; al-Suyūṭī, *Lubāb al-nuqūl fī asbāb al-nuzūl* on the margin of *Tafsīr Jalālain*, Beirut, [1397], 66–71; al-Tabarī, *Jāmi' al-bayān 'an ta'wīl āy al-Qur'ān*, Cairo, 1376, III, 493–503, reports 2935–52; al-Qurṭubī, *al-Jāmi' li-aḥkām al-Qur'ān*, Cairo, 1935–7, II, 315; Muqātil ibn Sulaimān, *Tafsīr*, MS Ahmed III 74, f. 28b; Ibn al-'Arabī, *Aḥkām al-Qur'ān*, Cairo, 1959, 91; Hibat Allāh, 17–18.

[57] See al-Ṭabarī, *Ta'rīkh*, Leiden, 1879–1901, I, 1451.

[58] See above, note 38.

is the effect desired by the author (copyist ?) one of verisimilitude, that is, is it a way of reassuring the reader that al-Zuhrī *really is* the author of the work but that here (at almost the very centre of the book !) someone has found it necessary to add a comment ? On the other hand, perhaps one is justified in suggesting that this ' ascription ' is simply further evidence of careless compilation. In a rather peculiar way, the text has added the confusion of ascription into an already confusing and confused text.

The overall interest of this text is, of course, centred on legal issues but objective criteria for dating legal positions in the early centuries of Islam [59] are extremely difficult to find, precisely because of the vast quantities of *ḥadīth* material contained in later texts making pretence to represent early opinion. Such is well known and has been demonstrated many times. It has to be, therefore, the *type* of discussion that takes place rather than the actual substance of the discussion upon which the focus of a literary study falls.

The presence of various types of presentation of the material in the text has already been noted ; the approach ranges from simple juxtaposition of verses to fairly careful elaboration. Three other facets deserve to be studied : the truncated nature of the discussion occurring in three paragraphs, the treatment and order of presentation for serial abrogation in four paragraphs and the use of additional Qur'ānic verses for explication in one paragraph.

What may only be described as truncated discussion of complex legal issues is present in paragraphs 19, 20 and 35. If the reader of the text is not previously aware of the issues which are at stake in the general discussion of the Qur'ānic verses involved, then the discussion ascribed to al-Zuhrī in these cases is virtually unintelligible. Paragraph 19 deals with the penalty for adultery (without ever mentioning *ḥukm/āyat al-rajm* which is usually seen to abrogate Q. 4 : 16). The interpretation of the passage, it must be admitted, however, is not assisted by the rather odd phrase فقال رجل كلاما which is most certainly how the text reads. Be that as it may, the explanation ' This woman is alone, a man not being with her ', which follows the citation of verse 15, while it may be suggesting that the Qur'ānic reference is to lesbianism (*suḥaqiyya*), an interpretation of the verse entertained by al-Zamakhsharī,[60] it would seem to be best read as suggesting that the verse provides a penalty of banishment for the woman alone, not the man. Abrogation [61] then took place with the revelation of Q. 4 : 16 which gave the provision for a woman to repent and therefore be freed from her punishment (i.e. *'adhābihā*) of banishment. The explanation of the text by the author is cryptic to the point of hindering understanding.

Paragraph 20 is also not without its textual difficulties, ones which are more acute than those in paragraph 19, but the two suggested corrections as indicated in the text above would seem to be demanded. ' Abū Yazīd said : [the report] has reached me that in the Jāhiliyya a man would not inherit the wife of his father (who did not bequeath anything to her) so that she could redeem herself with some of what she had been given.' This is a strange statement especially in light of other *naskh* books in which the treatment of the verse concentrates on the notion of the Jāhilī practice of inheriting women against their will which is here outlawed. The statement, however, does

[59] In later centuries it does, however, seem at least possible to trace development in legal positions ; see, for example, Norman Calder, ' Zakāt in Imāmī Shī'ī jurisprudence, from the tenth to the sixteenth century A.D.', *BSOAS*, XLIV, 3, 1981, 468–80, and ' Khums in Imāmī Shī'ī jurisprudence, from the tenth to the sixteenth century A.D.', *BSOAS*, XLV, 1, 1982, 39–47.

[60] *al-Kashshāf 'an ḥaqā'iq al-tanzīl*, Cairo, 1343, I, 196.

[61] Later theorists would call this an instance of *takhṣīṣ*, specification ; see further below.

receive a full clarification in the rather nice synopsis of the subject provided by al-Qurṭubī:

> According to their custom, when a man died his son [from another woman] or his closest relative would throw his cloak over the woman [i.e. his father's wife] and gain more rights to her than she herself or her children had. If he wished, he would marry her, (giving her) no dowry other than the dowry which the deceased had given her. If he wished, he could marry her off to someone else and he would take her dowry and give her none. And if he wished, he could prevent her from marrying so that she (would have to) free herself from him with what she had inherited from the bequest [i.e. her dowry] or (until) she died and she bequeathed it [i.e. her dowry, to the son in question].[62]

It would seem to be the last of these three possibilities to which al-Zuhrī's text makes reference, yet without the whole body of information into which it may be put in context, there is very little sense to be made of the discussion.

Paragraph 35 deals with the *liʿān*, the ritual swearing of an oath in the accusation of adultery. Q. 24 : 4 prescribes the penalty of flogging for being unable to produce four witnesses to the act of adultery after making such an accusation. Abrogation takes place in Q. 24 : 6 where husbands are stated not to need four witnesses to support them in bringing the accusation against their wives; rather, they simply need to swear four times that they are telling the truth (i.e. swear the *liʿān*). The explanation presented in the text outlines the implications of *one* of the potential outcomes of this swearing: the husband swears but the wife continues to deny the charge and likewise swears the oath. The text explains that in this case the marriage is dissolved and neither party is flogged. Should the husband be unwilling to swear after having raised the accusation then he receives the appropriate penalty (of flogging, according to Q. 24 : 4, as implied in this text). The explanation, note, only explicates one possible situation arising from the legal position implied in the ruling and is totally severed from discussions of the entire, very vast legal topic, without any obvious reason being isolated for why *this* particular situation should especially be worthy of attention.

The phenomenon of abrogation of verses in sequence is famous, most especially in the case of the progressive banning of the drinking of wine. This latter topic is dealt with in the text in paragraph 22 where Q. 4 : 43, then 2 : 219 and finally 5 : 90 are revealed seriatim. The ordering of the verses here is somewhat distinctive; perhaps the most frequently encountered version is to reverse the order of Q. 2 : 219 and 4 : 43 [63] with the latter seen as an intermediate stage when people still had not taken the hint when coming to prayer concerning the injury to man inherent in wine. Other writers add even more verses to the sequence, for example, Hibat Allāh and the citation of Q. 16 : 67.[64]

Paragraph 23 is a rather complex sequence of verses relating to not allowing fighting when such had not been initiated by the polytheists, until the final revelation of *āyat al-saif* (Q. 9 : 5). The sequence itself is undistinguished, *āyat al-saif* normally taking the champion position in the number of verses abrogated; [65] similar comments may be made for paragraphs 27 and 28, also involving sequential *naskh*. The point of relevance here is the implication of

[62] Al-Qurṭubī, *al-Jāmiʿ li-aḥkām al-Qurʾān*, v, 94.
[63] See e.g. Muqātil, *Tafsīr khams miʾa āya*, 141–7.
[64] Hibat Allāh, 73–4.
[65] See *QS*, 197–8.

a reasonably developed working out of legal problems and of abrogation theory. A sustained narrative of a haggadic type, often finding the form of a *sabab al-nuzūl* as so forcefully displayed in Muqātil's *Khams mi'a āya* for example, is likely to have been the prerequisite historically for his theory of sequential abrogation. That the text of al-Zuhrī can, for the most part, dispense with the haggadic framework and simply state the legal position indicates that, as far as the opinion of the author/compiler/copyist goes, the issue is clearly settled and no longer needs any argumentation or support.

Paragraph 39 suggests a related approach to the notion of sequential *naskh*, one in which the latter may have, in fact, found its origin. Here the simple abrogation of Q. 46 : 9 by 48 : 1–2 is clarified by adducing Q. 33 : 47 and 48 : 5 in order to explain ' how He will deal with him [Muḥammad] and with them '. These latter verses certainly establish that the passage Q. 46 : 9 is to be taken in a legal sense and add, at the very least, some specification to the nature of the *ni'ma* promised in Q. 48 : 1–2. These two functions, of legal contextualization and specification, are common to many, if not all, instances of abrogation and in some cases one can conceive of a gradual slide from contextualization by the additional verses to full specification and thus abrogation.

Technical terminology in a text such as this, while by no means an easy matter through which to construct a datable framework, does provide some of the most valuable insights into the work. A selection of the basic fixed exegetical terminology in the Qur'ānic/Arabic tradition is to be found here; the term *tafsīr* (paragraph 5) for ' explication ', the use of *dhālika anna* (paragraphs 12 and 42) and *alladhī anzalat fīhi āya* . . . (paragraph 10) to introduce *asbāb al-nuzūl* information and the adducing of minority opinion with the word *qīla* (paragraphs 21 and 26) are all quite familiar. Similar too are the usages *arāda bi-dhālika* (paragraph 44), *ya'nī* (paragraph 42), *ay* (paragraphs 16 and 19), *yaqūlu* (paragraphs 42 and 44) and no connective word (e.g. paragraphs 16, 23 and 35) between canonical text and commentary. Notable in this connexion is the first use in paragraph 42 of *yaqūlu* with the added pronominal emphasis, *yaqūlu huwa*. The stress here seems to be on accenting the idea that the commentary is functioning to express ' God is saying ' such-and-such a thing, rather than having the word simply standing for a way of saying ' that is ', as it certainly does in other commentaries; in a usage such as this with its very literal intent, may well be found the origin of *yaqūlu* as equivalent to *ya'nī* and *ay*.[66] Another notable usage is *riwāya* for the technical term *qirā'a* in paragraph 9.[67]

It is, of course, the use of the term *naskh* which predominates in the text and which, in fact, gives it its thematic unity. *Naskh* as a technical term meaning ' abrogation ' (although the precise sense of that must be left open) makes its appearance early on in exegesis, for example in Muqātil's *Khams mi'a āya* (and, of course, his *tafsīr*). The text of al-Zuhrī provides three paragraphs (5 to 7) whose intent would seem to be to provide a Qur'ānic basis for a theoretical definition of *naskh*. The significance of these definitions within the varied and rather tumultuous history of the term can be determined by placing them in the context of the information available on the subject in texts such as those by al-Baghdādī[68] and al-Ḥāzimī.[69] Al-Zuhrī's text indicates

[66] For further details on the use of all these terms in other exegetes, see *QS*, 129, 132 and 138.

[67] Also note the use of the verbal formulation of the word *fiqh* in the sense of belief in paragraph 42; this is reminiscent of the use of the word in Abū Ḥanīfa, *Fiqh Akbar*, I.

[68] MSS Berlin Petermann 555, ff. 2b–3b, and Beyazit 445, ff. 2b–3a.

[69] *Kitāb al-i'tibār*, 9–22.

some of the variation in definition but also a measure of confusion. In paragraph 5, by rudimentary exegesis of juxtaposition of Qur'ānic verses, *al-āyāt al-mansūkha* are equated with *al-āyāt al-mutashābiha*, a well known, although not overly popular solution to two grave exegetical problems with the single stroke of the pen. Paragraph 6 would seem to be making reference to what is known as (or became known as) a mode of *naskh: naskh al-ḥukm dūna'l-tilāwa* while, at the same time, equating *naskh* and *badl* (' substitute '), once again a well-known definition, as well as formula for expressing it; it is, for example, precisely the wording found in al-Ṭabarī as ascribed to Mujāhid,[70] with, however, one difference. Al-Zuhrī's text would seem to be suggesting this definition for *nansa'hā*, normally understood as ' postpone ', and thus having little relationship to the proposed definition. That some confusion may have arisen in the mind or the work of the author or the copyist is most certainly a possibility, if not in fact in this case a total likelihood. Paragraph 7, finally, is once again rudimentary exegesis by juxtaposition of phrases, giving the equivalents *naskh*, *badl* and *maḥw* (' erasure '). Here, too, we have reference to a mode of *naskh: naskh al-ḥukm wa'l-tilāwa* through the added notion of erasure. Also raised, at least implicitly, is the question, much debated in some circles, of the relationship between abrogated verses and the *umm al-kitāb*; here the simple statement of the Qur'ān is adduced apparently to suggest that all such verses are preserved in heaven but not in the terrestial *muṣḥaf*.

Most significant as regards the definition of *naskh*, however, is the actual content of the work as a whole. In comparison to other works of *naskh*, this text embraces a wide definition of the phenomenon within the term. Three types of *naskh* are included: one, the ' normal ' (orthodox) mode of replacing the legal ruling of one verse (either present or not in the *muṣḥaf*) with that contained in another; two, the replacement of a ruling from pre-Islamic Arabia (the '*jāhiliyya*') with a Qur'ānic ruling; and three, the possibility of exceptive provisions to a given Qur'ānic ruling. The first type is common enough and needs no further comment.[71] The second mode is at least implicit in many works of *naskh* although rarely is it very prominent; in al-Zuhrī's text it figures only in the somewhat problematic paragraph 20 as detailed above. It is the third type of *naskh* that is so distinctive; what is called *takhṣīṣ* (' specification ') by al-Shāfi'ī (d. 204/820) and most later theorists is here plainly included under the term *naskh*. Alongside this distinctive usage also comes distinctive terminological phrasing; in each case where ' specification ' would be the developed designation of the relationship between two verses, the phrase *nasakha min* [*al-āya*], ' an exception is provided to [the verse] ', is employed. This occurs in seven passages.

Paragraph 9 details the ' abrogation ' of Q. 2 : 184 by 2 : 185. The allowance of feeding a poor person instead of fasting (verse 184) is limited to those who are sick or travelling (verse 185). Those who are otherwise able must either fast at the time or later; that is the exception provided to (*nasakha min*) the verse. Paragraph 14 provides an exception for women of the ' People of the Book ' who may marry Muslims (Q. 5 : 5), a practice implicitly denied legitimacy in Q. 2 : 221. Paragraph 31 denies the right of *taqiyya* (' concealment [of faith] ') to be practised by those who leave their homes to escape persecution (Q. 16 : 110), a practice which in Q. 16 : 106 was allowed for all those ' under compulsion '.

[70] Al-Ṭabarī, II, 473.

[71] Note should be made of the terminological form in this type of *naskh* and how, perhaps, this has been dictated by the order of presentation (or vice versa); for example, *nasakhahā qauluhu* (paragraphs 29, 30, 31) *nasakhahā allāh bi-qaulihi* (paragraphs 21, 22), etc.

Paragraph 32 provides an exception against praying to God on behalf of polytheist parents (Q. 9 : 113), something implicitly required in Q. 17 : 24. In paragraph 35, an exception is made for the husband (Q. 24 : 6) charging his wife with adultery in that he need not produce four witnesses (Q. 24 : 4) but rather need only swear the *li'ān* four times.

In paragraph 36, women past child-bearing age (Q. 24 : 60) are excepted from the general rule requiring that women cover 'their beauty' (*zīna*) contained in Q. 24 : 31. Finally, paragraph 37 provides an exception for unoccupied houses (Q. 24 : 29, here limited even further to specific houses of trade and guest houses) to the rule of requiring permission before occupying them as stated in Q. 24 : 27. In each of these cases, the general rule of the initial verse maintains its validity but the second verse provides an exception to that legal position.

Given this summary of the various literary traits of this work, it is now a matter of trying to assess the overall implications of it in terms of the initial questions posed concerning the composition and dating of the text. This remains, of course, a task that is far from easy and it still may well be impossible to state as definitively as some would wish just what the answer is; this is, of course, a limitation with which the literary critic is prepared to live.

Some of the above analysis would indicate an early date of origin for the text; this would seem to be most obviously the case in the instance of the technical terminology, but also in the actual method of interpretation of the Qur'ān practised at various points (e.g. simple juxtaposition of verses). To this, however, must be opposed the evidence of a situation indicating a developed stage in legal discussions, most especially as revealed in the nature of the truncated discussions in a number of verses. A majority of the rest of the information deduced can, unfortunately perhaps, be interpreted either way: as evidence of careless and late composition or as evidence of a tentative working out of new problems arising in the interpretative task.

Only two truly practical solutions suggest themselves in order to resolve the contradictory nature of these results. One is to postulate the creation of a text in the early centuries of Islam (perhaps even at the time of al-Zuhrī) which has subsequently been transmitted from generation to generation without a great deal of attention and which has also suffered from accretions and deletions. The other is to postulate a late composition extracted from earlier sources which provide data from the first few centuries of Islam. In this case such compilation was obviously not done very carefully. It seems hard to avoid the conclusion that there is in the text at least a remnant of early material; the process by which it reached its final form is still far less than clear and may well remain beyond any form of historical reconstruction. That fact in itself implies that the text cannot be relied upon to provide a source of early material because of the multiplicity of writers involved regardless of which postulate of composition is finally entertained.[72]

[72] Funding for the research and travel for this paper was provided by the Social Sciences and Humanities Research Council of Canada. Thanks are due to all the libraries concerned for access to their manuscript collections and to Princeton University Library for their permission to publish the text of their manuscript Yahuda 228, ff 2 to 7 and for permission to reproduce plate I. Thanks are also due to Dr. John Wansbrough, SOAS, for much assistance and encouragement.

PLATE I

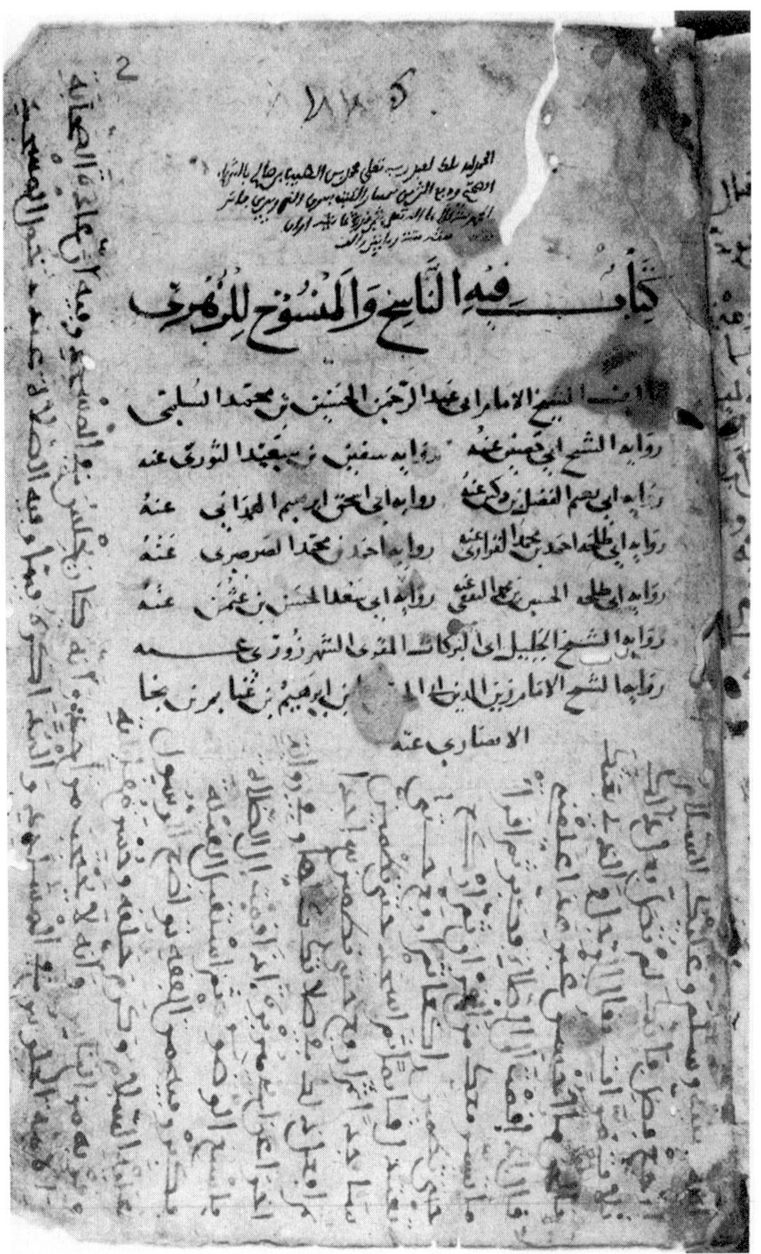

XVII

THE EXEGETICAL GENRE *ASBĀB AL-NUZŪL*: A BIBLIOGRAPHICAL AND TERMINOLOGICAL SURVEY[1]

> *'Ilm asbāb al-nuzūl*, one of the subdivisions of *'ilm al-tafsīr*, deals with the transmission of the *sabab* of the revelation of a *sūra* or verse and the time, place and so forth of its revelation. It is verified by the well-known principles of transmission from the pious ancestors [*salaf*]. Its goal is the precise rendering of these matters.[2]

Thus Ḥājjī Khalīfa, the Ottoman bibliographer of the eleventh/seventeenth century, introduces his listing of books contained within the genre of exegetical literature connected to the Qur'ān entitled *asbāb al-nuzūl*. That account of the genre has barely been exceeded in more recent scholarship. Ignaz Goldziher in his *Die Richtungen der islamischen Koranauslegung* [3] finds occasion only once to mention the ' classic ' work of the type, that by al-Wāḥidī (d. 468/1075),[4] and devotes no further space to consideration of the literature. Régis Blachère in his *Introduction au Coran* [5] deals with the genre in a brief footnote while Bell/Watt's *Introduction to the Qur'ān* [6] confines comment to a dozen or so lines. The standard tome of scholarship, Nöldeke/Schwally, *Geschichte des Qorāns*, *II: Die Sammlung des Qorāns*, gives the longest treatment known, extending for almost two pages of text. The introduction to the section is worthy of quotation :

> Die unter dem Namen Asbāb al-nuzūl gehenden Werke unterscheiden sich von den Kommentaren dadurch, dass sie nur das auf Veranlassung der Offenbarungen bezügliche Material enthalten. Da dieses aber den religionsgeschichtlich wie literargeschichtlich wichtigsten Teil der Kommentare ausmacht und hier, alles störenden Beiwerkes entkleidet, besonders leicht zu übersehen ist, begreift es sich leicht, wie gross der Wert dieser Bücher für die Forschung ist. Die Muslime haben, wie es scheint, weniger Verständnis dafür gehabt, sonst würde die Zahl der einschlägigen Werke, von denen wir Kunde haben, nicht so gering sein.[7]

The only works which Nöldeke cites are the famous ones of al-Wāḥidī and al-Suyūṭī (d. 911/1505) ; [8] a reference is also made to the listing of two texts in Ibn al-Nadīm, *al-Fihrist*,[9] both of which are rightfully doubted to exist.

[1] This paper is a revised version of ch. i and portions of ch. iv of my McGill Ph.D. thesis, ' The Qur'anic *asbāb al-nuzūl* material : an analysis of its use and development in exegesis ' (1981). My gratitude is extended to Dr. C. J. Adams, McGill and Dr. J. Wansbrough, SOAS, for their invaluable assistance and encouragement. This study would not have been possible without the co-operation of many libraries in giving access to their manuscript collections, including the Berlin Staatsbibliothek, the British Library and the Princeton University Library. Financial support during the period of my dissertation was provided by the Government of Quebec; additional later research including travel to Berlin, Cairo and Istanbul was made possible by a grant from the Social Sciences and Humanities Research Council of Canada.

[2] Ḥājjī Khalīfa, *Kashf al-ẓunūn 'an asāmiy al-kutub wa'l-funūn*, ed. G. Flügel, Leipzig, 1835, 267.

[3] Leiden, 1920, 305.

[4] On Abū'l-Ḥasan 'Alī ibn Aḥmad al-Wāḥidī al-Nīsābūrī, see Brockelmann, *GAL*, I, 411, Suppl. I, 730; also see below p. 4.

[5] Paris, 1977, p. 234, n. 334.

[6] W. M. Watt, *Bell's introduction to the Qur'an*, Edinburgh, 1970, 167.

[7] Theodor Nöldeke, Friedrich Schwally, *Geschichte des Qorāns* (hereafter *GdQ*), Leipzig, 1909–1938, II, 182–4.

[8] On Jalāl al-Dīn al-Suyūṭī see *GAL*, II, 143, Suppl. II, 178; *EI* (1st ed.), IV, 573–5; also see below p. 9.

[9] Ed. G. Flügel, Leipzig, 1871, 38, in reference to the texts by 'Ikrima and al-Ḥasan al-Baṣrī, on which see below p. 2.

The limitations of statements such as these made in scholarship up to this point will be immediately apparent to anyone who has looked closely at the texts themselves or even has simply perused the various listings of manuscripts held in the libraries of the world and other bibliographical tools. The genre of *asbāb al-nuzūl* consists of substantially more texts than Nöldeke lists in his treatment, although it must be admitted immediately that the quantity is not as plentiful as for example in *al-nāsikh wa'l-mansūkh.* The following list and discussion of texts has been culled from a variety of sources; undoubtedly more texts do exist, most especially from the twelfth/eighteenth century onwards.[10] So, while this list makes no pretence at completeness, it does more fairly indicate the extent of the genre of literature, while at the same time allowing for some further clarification of the actual subject matter at hand.

1. 'Ikrima (d. 105/723),[11] *Nuzūl al-Qur'ān*, transmitted from Ibn 'Abbās (d. 68/687); [12] noted in *Geschichte des Qorāns* as quoted from *al-Fihrist* by Ibn al-Nadīm (d. *c.* 380/990).[13] As Nöldeke states, there is no reason to suppose that this work, even if it existed, would be truly ascribable to the (semi-) mythical Ibn 'Abbās,[14] or even to 'Ikrima for that matter. No such manuscript has yet been located. The ambiguity of the title *Nuzūl al-Qur'ān* should be noted, too: what exactly does Ibn al-Nadīm mean when he classifies the work under this category? Is he really suggesting that the book recorded accounts of 'occasions' of revelation or were they reports intended to document the process of revelation itself? Ibn al-Nadīm gives no evidence as to what he conceived the contents to be, but the evidence is far from conclusive that he is even trying to suggest that these were books of the (later) *asbāb al-nuzūl* genre.

2. Al-Ḥasan al-Baṣrī (d. 110/728),[15] *Nuzūl al-Qur'ān*; Nöldeke, in *Geschichte des Qorāns*, has this name as al-Ḥusayn ibn abī'l-Ḥusayn perhaps modifying Flügel's edition of Ibn al-Nadīm's *al-Fihrist* where the name is al-Ḥasan ibn abī'l-Ḥusayn.[16] Dodge and Sezgin,[17] having access to another manuscript tradition of *al-Fihrist*,[18] identify this person as al-Ḥasan [al-Basrī] ibn abī'l-Ḥasan. As Nöldeke noted, the handwriting of حسن/حسين is too easily confused to allow positive identification; Sezgin's zeal for identifying early authorities in *tafsīr* may well have led him to what can only be called a questionable judgement—other instances of a similar procedure in his work have been noted elsewhere.[19]

[10] Certainly a large number of modern printed works exist, e.g. Muḥammad M. Khalīfa, *Ma'a nuzūl al-Qur'ān*, Cairo, [1972]; such works are, however, simply culled from readily available classical sources and are of little, if not no independent value. It should also be noted that this study has limited itself to works written in Arabic; I have discovered the existence of only one Persian work; see C. Storey, *Persian literature: a bibliographical survey*, London, 1927–39, I, p. 58, item 10. A modern Turkish text also exists: H. Tahsin Emiroglo, *Esbab-i Nüzūl: Kur'an Āyetlerinin iniş Sebepleri ve Tafsirleri*, Konya, 1965.

[11] On 'Ikrima (mawlā ibn 'Abbās) see Sezgin, *GAS*, I, 23, 24, 26, 81, 91, 243, 285 for brief details; *EI* (2nd ed.), III, 1081–2; Goldziher, *Richtungen*, 75–6.

[12] On 'Abd Allāh ibn 'Abbās see *GAS*, I, 25–8; *EI* (2nd ed.), I, 40–1.

[13] *GdQ*, II, 183; Ibn al-Nadīm, *al-Fihrist*, 38.

[14] On Ibn 'Abbās and his role in exegetical literature see A. Rippin, 'Ibn 'Abbās's *al-Lughāt fi'l-Qur'ān*', *BSOAS*, XLIV, 1, 1981, 15–25. Also see John Wansbrough, *Quranic studies: sources and methods of scriptural interpretation* (hereafter *QS*), Oxford, 1977, ch. iv *passim*. For more traditional interpretations of Ibn 'Abbās's role see *GAS*, I, 25–8; Goldziher, *Richtungen*, 65–81.

[15] On al-Ḥasan ibn Abī'l-Ḥasan al-Baṣrī see *GAS*, I, 30, 591–4; *EI* (2nd ed.), III, 247–8.

[16] *GdQ*, II, 183; Ibn al-Nadīm, *al-Fihrist*, 38.

[17] Bayard Dodge (tr.), *The Fihrist of al-Nadim: a tenth century survey of Muslim culture*, New York, 1970, I, 82; *GAS*, I, 30, 592.

[18] Specifically Chester Beatty 3315 and Shahīd 'Alī Pasha 1934; see introduction to *al-Fihrist* translation, I, xxiii–xxx and *GAS*, I, 388.

[19] See my 'Al-Zuhrī, *naskh al-Qur'ān* and the problem of early *tafsīr* texts', *BSOAS*, XLVII, 1, 1984, 22–43.

No such manuscript has yet been located, so nothing definitive can really be said; the ambiguity of the title of Ibn al-Nadīm's section, *Nuzūl al-Qur'ān* must be noted, as for 'Ikrima above.

3. 'Alī ibn al-Madīnī (d. 234/848),[20] *Kitāb al-tanzīl*; a book by this title is found listed under Ibn al-Madīnī in Ibn al-Nadīm although it is not listed under the (perhaps) appropriate section *Nuzūl al-Qur'ān* but rather under Ibn al-Madīnī's name in the *ḥadīth* section.[21] Once again, Ibn al-Nadīm leaves ambiguous the exact contents of this *Kitāb al-tanzīl*; is it a book of *asbāb* or something else? The connexion of 'Alī ibn al-Madīnī with a work specifically on *asbāb al-nuzūl* appears to start in al-Zarkashī (d. 794/1391),[22] is repeated by al-Suyūṭī (d. 911/1505)[23] and is then entered into Ḥājjī Khalīfa's *Kashf al-ẓunūn*, in which quotations are lifted from al-Suyūṭī *in extenso*.[24] None of these works list a title for Ibn al-Madīnī's book. Whether these listings are guess work derived from the title *Kitāb al-tanzīl* in *al-Fihrist* or derived from another source cannot be answered. No manuscript of the work has been located although 'Alī ibn al-Madīnī certainly does seem to be a historical personage; a *ḥadīth* scholar, he is credited with a long list of works, at least one of which is known and has recently been published and in which a brief account of his life and works may be found.[25]

It is also significant to note that despite the fact that al-Zarkashī and, more importantly, al-Suyūṭī list the book, neither makes use of such a text as a source.[26] It would also seem that al-Wāḥidī does not use a text ascribed to Ibn al-Madīnī in his *Kitāb asbāb al-nuzūl* either; while the name is cited within *isnāds* a few times,[27] that fact is hardly firm evidence of literary dependency, given Ibn al-Madīnī's stature in *ḥadīth* and given the fact that al-Wāḥidī does give, on occasion at least, the literary sources of his information, especially for *ḥadīth* books.[28] The whole notion of Ibn al-Madīnī's authoring a book on *asbāb al-nuzūl* may well rest with al-Zarkashī, or at least with the scholarly tradition which he distils, which ultimately may have derived from Ibn al-Nadīm's ambiguous listing. There seems no particular reason to have faith in the existence of this book.

4. 'Abd al-Raḥmān ibn Muḥammad Abū'l-Muṭarrif al-Andalusī, (d.

[20] On 'Alī ibn 'Abd Allāh ibn Ja'far al-Madīnī see *GAS*, I, 108. Ibn al-Nadīm, *al-Fihrist*, 231, gives 258/871 as the death date. Also note that Ḥājjī Khalīfa, *Kashf al-ẓunūn*, 268, followed by W. Ahlwardt (ed.), *Die Handschriften-Verzeichnisse der Königlichen Bibliothek zu Berlin*, Berlin, 1887, I, 185, gives his name as 'Alī ibn al-Madanī. It should be noted that Ahlwardt provides in his catalogue of Berlin manuscripts, I, 185, a list of titles of works to which he had discovered reference connected to the topic of *asbāb al-nuzūl*; further references will be made to this list below.

[21] *al-Fihrist*, 231, translation I, 556; Dodge gives the title as *Kitāb al-tanzīl al-laṭīf*, 'The gracious revelation'. Ahlwardt, *Handschriften-Verzeichnisse*, I, 185, gives the title as *Asbāb al-nuzūl* but this is probably just given in lieu of anything else.

[22] Al-Zarkashī, *al-Burhān fī 'ulūm al-Qur'ān*, Cairo, 1957, I, 22. On Badr al-Dīn al-Zarkashī see *GAL*, II, 91, Suppl. II, 108.

[23] Al-Suyūṭī, *al-Itqān fī 'ulūm al-Qur'ān*, Cairo, 1951, I, 28; also see *GdQ*, II, 183. The relationship between these works of al-Zarkashī and al-Suyūṭī has been the subject of an exhaustive and very useful study by K. E. Nolin, 'The *Itqān* and its sources: a study of *al-Itqān fī 'ulūm al-Qur'ān* by Jalāl al-Dīn al-Suyūṭī with special reference to *al-Burhān fī 'ulūm al-Qur'ān* by Badr al-Dīn al-Zarkashī', Ph.D. Thesis, Hartford Seminary, 1968.

[24] *Kashf al-ẓunūn*, 268; see also Aḥmad Ṣaqr, introduction to al-Wāḥidī, *Asbāb nuzūl al-Qur'ān*, Cairo, 1969, 23.

[25] *Al-'ilal* [*'ilal al-ḥadīth wa ma'rifat al-rijāl* according to *GAS*, I, 108], Beirut, 1972, 3–34.

[26] See below pp. 9–10 for al-Suyūṭī's list of sources.

[27] e.g. *ad* the report for Q. 21 : 101.

[28] See below nn. 43, 44, 45 for example.

402/1011),[29] *Al-qiṣaṣ wa'l-asbāb allatī nazala min ajlihā al-Qur'ān*; this work, whose author's existence is not acknowledged in *GAL* or *GAS*, is given the simple title *Asbāb al-nuzūl* in Ḥājjī Khalīfa and Ahlwardt's catalogue,[30] but the more descriptive title is given by al-Dāwudī (d. 945/1538)[31] and perhaps from this source comes the description given by Aḥmad Ṣaqr.[32] According to both Ḥājjī Khalīfa and al-Dāwudī, the book was written in one hundred parts.

Most unfortunately, this book has not come down to us. There seems to be no particular reason for disbelieving in its existence, although the fact that neither al-Zarkashī nor al-Suyūṭī seem to know it may be deemed suspicious. A most significant aspect of the work, however, is its title and that for two reasons: first, the conjunction but separation of *qiṣaṣ* and *asbāb*, which was a bone of contention between later contributors to the genre, e.g., al-Wāḥidī and al-Suyūṭī, and second, the notion that the Qur'ān was revealed ' on account of ' or ' because of '—*min ajli*—*asbāb* and *qiṣaṣ*; clearly *asbāb* are not conceived of as ' causes ' or ' reasons ' themselves but rather perhaps as the ' circumstances '. This matter will be explored further below in the discussion of the rise to technical status of the term *sabab*.

5. Ismā'īl ibn Aḥmad ibn 'Abd Allāh al-Ḥīrī al-Nīsābūrī al-Ḍarīr, (d. 430/1038),[33] *Asmā' man nazala fīhim al-Qur'ān*. The work, mentioned in Ahlwardt's catalogue, seems to owe its record of existence to the bibliographical introduction to al-Suyūṭī's *al-Itqān*.[34] Al-Dāwudī lists only a *tafsīr* by this author as does Brockelmann.[35] The work apparently no longer exists. Once again, the relevance of the work to *asbāb al-nuzūl* remains in the realm of speculation; it may relate to the (sub-)genre of *ta'yīn al-mubham*, identification of the unknown,[36] or may be quite similar to other *asbāb* books.

6. Abū'l-Ḥasan 'Alī ibn Aḥmad al-Wāḥidī al-Nīsābūrī (d. 468/1075),[37] *Kitāb asbāb nuzūl al-Qur'ān*. This work is called by al-Zarkashī and those following him ' the most famous of its type '.[38] The modern proliferation of prints of the text witnesses its continued popularity. The only critical edition of the text is that prepared by Aḥmad Ṣaqr and printed in Cairo in 1969 by Dār al-Kitāb al-Jadīd.[39]

Al-Wāḥidī was a student of al-Tha'labī (d. 427/1035),[40] a famous exegete who wrote the magisterial although still unpublished commentary, *al-Kashf wa'l-bayān 'an tafsīr al-Qur'ān*.[41] Al-Wāḥidī himself was a prolific writer of

[29] Abū'l-Muṭarrif's date of death is given as 335/946 in Ahlwardt, *Handschriften-Verzeichnisse*, I, 185. On him see al-Dāwudī, *Ṭabaqāt al-mufassirīn*, Cairo, 1972, I, 285–7.

[30] *Kashf al-ẓunūn*, 268; *Handschriften-Verzeichnisse*, I, 185.

[31] *Ṭabaqāt al-mufassirīn*, I, 285–7.

[32] Introduction to al-Wāḥidī, *Asbāb nuzūl al-Qur'ān*, 23.

[33] On al-Ḥīrī see *GAL*, Suppl. I, 729.

[34] I, p. 8, l. 13.

[35] Al-Dāwudī, *Ṭabaqāt al-mufassirīn*, I, 104–5; *GAL*, Suppl. I, 729. Also of interest is M. Abdus Sattar, ' Al-Ḥīrī's *Kifāyat al-tafsīr*: a rare manuscript on exegesis of the Qur'ān ', *Islamic Studies*, XVI, 1977, 117–30.

[36] See *QS*, 135–6.

[37] See above n. 4.

[38] Al-Zarkashī, *al-Burhān*, I, 22; al-Suyūṭī, *al-Itqān*, I, 28; Ḥājjī Khalīfa, *Kashf al-ẓunūn*, 268.

[39] Also see the basic description of the text given in Ahlwardt, *Handschriften-Verzeichnisse*, I, 180–1 (MSS 463–4).

[40] On Abū Isḥāq Aḥmad ibn Muḥammad al-Tha'labī al-Nīsābūrī see *GAL*, I, 350–1, Suppl. I, 592.

[41] See e.g. British Library Add. 19926 (Vol. I), OR 9060 (Vol. III). It is worthy of note that al-Tha'labī provides at the beginning of Vol. I of his *tafsīr* a bibliography of sources employed by and/or known to him, a list which Sezgin has used in *GAS* extensively; no *asbāb al-nuzūl* text is given in this list.

tafsīrs, authoring at least three.[42] His book on *asbāb al-nuzūl*, according to his own thinking, represents the distillation of the most essential elements of his *tafsīr*. In the book he lists *asbāb* for various verses contained in a total of 83 *sūras* of the Qur'ān, prefacing those reports by a brief introduction, speculation on the first and last pieces of the Qur'ān to be revealed and an account of the revelation of the *basmala*. A vast majority of the reports of the individual *asbāb* which al-Wāḥidī brings forth are in the form of *ḥadīth* reports, complete with full *isnād*, traced back to a companion of Muḥammad or another early authority. Occasionally the literary source of the report is mentioned—al-Bukhārī (d. 256/870),[43] Muslim (d. 261/875) [44] and al-Ḥākim (d. 404/1014) [45] are among the *ḥadīth* texts cited. Frequently, too, one encounters a truncated *isnād*, the report simply being ascribed to Mujāhid (d. 104/722),[46] Muqātil ibn Sulaymān (d. 150/767),[47] al-Kalbī (d. 146/763) [48] or the like; as well, reports are found attributed simply to the *mufassirūn*. At other times, absolutely no ascription is given as in the case of the brief report for *sūra* 105.

7. Muḥammad ibn As'ad al-'Irāqī (d. 567/1171),[49] *Asbāb al-nuzūl wa qiṣaṣ al-furqāniyya* according to the Chester Beatty manuscript 5199, a work of 151 folios, 19 lines to the page which has lost various sections of the text. An apparently complete copy of the manuscript exists in Berlin, Landberg 971 (173 folios, 23 lines to the page, written in 1187/1773) in which the author's name is given as Aḥmad ibn As'ad al-'Irāqī and the title of the work is *Asbāb al-nuzūl bi'l-āyāt al-Qur'āniyya wa qiṣaṣ al-furqāniyya*.[50] Ḥājjī Khalīfa gives the title simply as *Asbāb al-nuzūl*.[51] Confusion also exists concerning the date of the author; al-Dāwudī gives born 484/1091, died 567/1171. Flügel apparently has added this date of death into Ḥājjī Khalīfa in brackets. However Ahlwardt, followed by Brockelmann and Arberry gives born 580/1184, died 667/1268; [52] the origin of the confusion has not been traced, nor has a satisfactory answer been found.

The text itself consists of a listing of *asbāb al-nuzūl* with the traditional material of *qiṣaṣ al-anbiyā'* interspersed. The reports are totally *isnād*-less and are quite clearly not simply taken from al-Wāḥidī but edited independently or, at least, are taken from another, unknown source. Generally only one report is given for any given verse. The stories of the prophets occupy about half of the text and are elaborated at appropriate points though not in systematic fashion: that is, the stories do not necessarily come at the first occurrence of the name of the prophet. The following table of contents of *sūra* 2 in the Chester Beatty manuscript should make the basic outline clear.

[42] His works include *Tafsīr al-Qur'ān al-wajīz*, Cairo, 1305; *al-wasīṭ bayn al-maqbūḍ wa'l-basīṭ*, e.g., Berlin MS Sprenger 415; *al-Basīṭ*, e.g., Nur Osmaniye MSS 236–40.

[43] *Ad* 2 : 143 Abū 'Abd Allāh Muḥammad ibn Ismā'īl al-Bukhārī al-Ju'fī is cited; on him see *GAS*, I, 115–34; *GAL*, I, 157–60, Suppl. I, 260–5; *EI* (2nd ed.), I, 1296–7.

[44] *Ad* 2 : 143 Abū'l-Ḥusayn Muslim ibn al-Ḥajjāj al-Qushayrī al-Nīsābūrī is also cited; on him see *GAS*, I, 136–43; *GAL*, I, 160–71, Suppl. I, 265–6; *EI* (1st ed.), III, 756.

[45] *Ad* 12 : 3 Abū 'Abd Allāh Muḥammad ibn 'Abd Allāh ibn Ḥamdawayh al-Ḥākim al-Nīsābūrī is cited; on him see *GAS*, I, 221–2; *GAL*, I, 166, Suppl. I, 276; *EI* (2nd ed.), III, 82.

[46] On Mujāhid ibn Jabr see *GAS*, I, 29.

[47] On Muqātil ibn Sulaymān see *GAS*, I, 36–7.

[48] On al-Kalbī see *GAS*, I, 34–5 and Rippin, *BSOAS*, XLVII, 1, 1984.

[49] On al-'Irāqī see *GAL*, I, 415.

[50] Ahlwardt, *Handschriften-Verzeichnisse*, I, 182, MS 465.

[51] *Zashf al-ẓunun*, 268.

[52] Al-Dāwudī, *Ṭabaqāt al-mufassirīn*, II, 87–9; Ḥājjī Khalīfa, *Kashf al-ẓunūn*, 268; Ahlwardt, *Handschriften-Verzeichnisse*, I, 182; *GAL*, I, 415; A. J. Arberry, *The Chester Beatty Library: a handlist of the Arabic manuscripts*, Dublin, 1964, VII, 64.

folio	*contents*
1a	title page
1b	3 line introduction; *asbāb* for 2 : 6; 2 : 8; 2 : 14
2a	*sabab* for 2 : 14 continued; *qiṣṣa* of Adam at 2 : 35
2b	*asbāb* for 2 : 109; 2 : 114; 2 : 115; 2 : 154
3a	*asbāb* for 2 : 168; 2 : 187
3b	*asbāb* for 2 : 189a; 2 : 189b
4a	*asbāb* for 2 : 190; 2 : 204; 2 : 207
4b	*asbāb* for 2 : 208; 2 : 215; 2 : 217
5a	*sabab* for 2 : 217 continued
5b	*sabab* for 2 : 220
6a	*asbāb* for 2 : 221; 2 : 222; 2 : 224; 2 : 228; 2 : 229
6b to 8b	*sabab* for 2 : 230; *qiṣṣa* of kings of Israel at 2 : 243; *qiṣṣa* of David and Goliath at 2 : 246
8b	*qiṣṣa* of Nimrod at 2 : 258
9a	*qiṣṣa* of Ezra at 2 : 259
9b	*qiṣṣa* of Abraham at 2 : 260
10a	*sabab* for 2 : 278

Once again note must be taken of al-ʿIrāqī's separation of *qiṣṣa* and *sabab* especially since some of what al-ʿIrāqī includes under *qiṣṣa* al-Wāḥidī has under (implicitly) *sabab* (e.g., *ad* 2 : 260).[53]

8. Abū Jaʿfar Muḥammad ibn ʿAlī ibn Shuʿayb al-Māzandarānī (d. 588/1192),[54] *Kitāb asbāb al-nuzūl.* This work finds mention in Ḥājjī Khalīfa and probably from there in Ahlwardt's catalogue. Al-Dāwudī knows the author but not the work; Brockelmann knows not even the author.[55] No trace has been found of a copy of the work.

9. Abū'l-Faraj ʿAbd al-Raḥmān ibn ʿAlī ibn al-Jawzī al-Baghdādī (d. 597/1200),[56] *Kitāb asbāb al-nuzūl.* Once again, this work is listed in Ḥajjī Khalīfa and Ahlwardt's catalogue,[57] but while the author is, of course, famous and prolific, this title does not seem to be extant or even well-known.

10. Burhān al-Dīn Ibrāhīm ibn ʿUmar al-Jaʿbarī (d. 732/1333).[58] The situation concerning al-Jaʿbari's authorship of a work on *asbāb al-nuzūl* is complicated; two basic works are often listed for him:

(*a*) an abridgement of al-Wāḥidī, described by al-Suyūṭī, who is followed by Ḥājjī Khalīfa, as being simply al-Wāḥidī's text minus the *isnāds* and with nothing added. One problem is whether to accept this statement literally or view it as al-Suyūṭī's cryptic attack upon one of his predecessors, an attack such as he is so prone to make. This text is thought to exist according to Brockelmann; under al-Wāḥidī,[59] rather than al-Jaʿbarī, he lists two manuscripts ascribed to al-Jaʿbarī and described as abridgements of al-Wāḥidī.

The first of these, Berlin 3578, has been described extensively by Wagner in his recent catalogue.[60] Now, even a cursory glance at the Berlin manuscript is

[53] Note that the gaps in the treatment of *sūra* 2 in the MS of al-ʿIrāqī seem intentional (e.g., between verse 39 and 109); there is no evidence of loss of text.

[54] On al-Māzandarānī see al-Dāwudī, *Ṭabaqāt al-mufassirīn*, II, 199–200.

[55] Ḥājjī Khalīfa, *Kashf al-ẓunūn*, 269; Ahlwardt, *Handschriften-Verseichnisse*, I, 185; al-Dāwudī, *Ṭabaqāt al-mufassirīn*, II, 199–200.

[56] On Ibn al-Jawzī see *GAL*, I, 500–6, Suppl. I, 914–20; *EI* (2nd ed.), III, 751–2.

[57] Ḥājjī Khalīfa, *Kashf al-ẓunūn*, 268; Ahlwardt, *Handschriften-Verzeichnisse* I, 185.

[58] On al-Jaʿbarī see *GAL*, II, 109, Suppl. II, 134–5.

[59] *GAL*, Suppl. I, 730.

[60] Ewald Wagner, *Arabische Handschriften Teil I. Verzeichnis der Orientalischen Handschriften in Deutschland, Band XVII, Reihe B*, Wiesbaden, 1976, I, 8–9.

sufficient to raise grave doubts concerning the attribution of this manuscript and that fact can only leave one amazed that Wagner did not question that ascription in writing his catalogue. An obviously different hand has given the work the following title: *Mukhtaṣar asbāb al-nuzūl li'l-Wāḥidī al-Nīsābūrī wa ma'a ziyādat al-nāsikh wa'l-mansūkh ilayhi li'l-shaykh Burhān al-Dīn Ibrāhīm ibn 'Umar al-Ja'barī al-Khalīlī tuwuffiya 732*[*1333*]. The original first few folios of the manuscript are missing and the title page has quite evidently been added later. Additionally, the work does not conform to al-Suyūṭī's description of al-Ja'barī's work at all; elements have been added to the *asbāb* part of the work; for example, toward the beginning of *sūra* 2, at verse 6, an extra *sabab* is added which is not found in al-Wāḥidī, and likewise at verse 14. This is only significant, in a sense, if one is prepared to overlook the more obvious discrepancy that an entire *naskh* work alternates with the *asbāb* text *sūra* by *sūra* throughout the text. The point is somewhat confused, however, due to a reference made in al-Ujhūrī (d. 1190/1776), *Irshād al-raḥmān li-asbāb al-nuzūl*, which makes reference to al-Ja'barī's work with the following sentence: 'Imām Ibrāhīm al-Ja'barī shortened (the work of al-Wāḥidī) and he added to it the science of *al-nāsikh wa'l-mansūkh*.'[61] However, given the late date of al-Ujhūrī it would seem preferable and more reliable to trust the information of al-Suyūṭī rather than the later writer.

Furthermore, in the Berlin text not all the *isnāds* are missing, at least not in the sense that they are in al-'Irāqī's text; the work virtually always supplies the final authority for each report given. Finally, the manuscript was written, according to the last page, in the year 709 (1309),[62] that is, during al-Ja'barī's lifetime. It is, of course, not impossible that the manuscript was written during the lifetime of its supposed author, but one is entitled to wonder why there seems to be no notation of the author's approval of the copy of the text or of some kind of laudatory exclamation concerning the author by the copyist (one Yūsuf ibn 'Abd al-Qādir ibn Yūsuf al-Ḥanbalī al-Kūfī).

The fact that this work is almost certainly not that of al-Ja'barī should not be allowed to affect the estimation of its worth; if anything it probably increases it. One suspects that this Berlin manuscript has been ascribed to al-Ja'barī merely because of the fame of that name due to its mention in al-Suyūṭī.

As described by Wagner, the manuscript covers the whole Qur'ān, treating each *sūra* in two parts: *al-faṣl al-awwal fī musabbibihi* and *al-faṣl al-thānī fī mansūkhihi*. In 27 *sūras*, the statement *laysa fī* (*l-sūra*) *musabbib* is made.

The second of the two manuscripts, Dar al-Kutub al-Miṣriyyah *majāmi'* 221, is a water-damaged collection of works with some loss of text especially at the beginning and on the outer edge. The work has been described by Aḥmad Ṣaqr, in the introduction to his edition of al-Wāḥidī, *Kitāb asbāb nuzūl al-Qur'ān*, as 'an abbreviated work, with no merit to it, due to the destructive tendencies of abbreviation.'[63] An examination of this manuscript certainly confirms Ṣaqr's opinion; this may well be the work of al-Ja'barī, there being no particular reason to suppose that this is not the case, but the work is certainly of little value, with the abbreviation of al-Wāḥidī's work being comprised almost exclusively of omission of the *isnāds*.

[61] Al-Ujhūrī, *Irshād al-raḥmān*, Dār al-Kutub al-Miṣriyyah MS *tafsīr* 42, f. 1b; on this text see below p. 11.

[62] See folio 116b; Wagner, *Arabische Handschriften*, I, 8.

[63] Dār al-Kutub manuscript catalogue, *Fihrist al-kutub* 2nd ed., Cairo, 1952, I, 61; see his introduction to al-Wāḥidī, *Asbāb nuzūl al-Qur'ān*, 28.

(*b*) *Taqrīb al-ma'-mūr fī tartīb al-nuzūl*. This work, listed as an *asbāb al-nuzūl* work in Ahlwardt's catalogue [64] and in Blachère's *Introduction au Coran*,[65] brings a new issue into the question of the definition of this genre of literature. *Taqrīb al-ma'mūr*, whose ascription to al-Ja'barī there is no cause to dispute, has been printed numerous times, at least once as a work by itself at the end of al-Dīrīnī (d. 697/1297), *al-Taysīr fī 'ilm al-Qur'ān*,[66] and, as well, as an integral part of al-Suyūṭī, *al-Itqān*.[67] The work is a poem of 21 lines, listing the *sūras* of the Qur'ān according to their chronological order. This text is not, in fact, a part of the *asbāb al-nuzūl* literature, but belongs to a separate, although perhaps not totally unrelated,[68] genre of lists of *sūras*; such lists exist in numerous places and, it should be noted, in at least four different versions.[69]

11. Hibat Allāh ibn 'Abd al-Raḥīm ibn al-Bārizī (d. 738/1338),[70] *Anwār al-taḥṣīl fī asrār al-tanzīl*. Ahlwardt lists this work under the title *Asrār al-tanzīl* and considers it to be an *asbāb* work; [71] there seems, however, to be no particular justification for this description. The work appears not to exist today, but al-Suyūṭī lists the text in his bibliographical introduction to *al-Itqān* under the section *i'jāz/balāgha*.[72]

12. Ibn Qayyim al-Jawziyya (d. 751/1350),[73] *Raf' al-tanzīl*. Once again, given in only Ahlwardt's list,[74] this work ascribed to Ibn Taymiyya's famous pupil appears in no other listing consulted and appears not to exist today, thus its contents are not really ascertainable.

13. Abū'l-'Abbās Aḥmad ibn 'Alī ibn al-Naqīb al-Ḥanafī (d. 816/1413),[75] *Kitāb al-Muwāfaqāt allatī waqa'at fī'l-Qur'ān al-'aẓīm li-amīr al-mu'mīnīn abī Ḥafṣ 'Umar ibn al-Khaṭṭāb al-'Adawī al-Qurashī*. A manuscript of this work exists in Berlin, We. 1782.[76] It is a short work of 18 folios and consists of a series of reports concerning 20 verses of the Qur'ān (e.g. *sūra* 2:97) which were revealed 'concurring' with the opinion of 'Umar ibn al-Khaṭṭāb. The reports apparently have been culled from the *Faḍā'il al-saḥāḅa* literature. A similar text although shorter and in verse form by al-Suyūṭī is dealt with in more detail below.[77]

[64] *Handschriften-Verzeichnisse*, I, 185.

[65] p. 234, n. 334.

[66] Cairo, 1310, 162–3. 'Izz al-Dīn 'Abd al-'Azīz al-Dīrīnī himself apparently wrote a similar work, see Ahlwardt, *Handschriften-Verzeichnisse*, I, 182, MS 466.

[67] I, 25–6.

[68] See *QS*, 177–80. It seems to me that these lists are crucial to the notion of chronology of the Qur'ān whereas *asbāb* are exegetical; see my 'The Qur'anic *asbāb al-nuzūl* material: an analysis of its use and development in exegesis', Ph.D. thesis, McGill, 1981.

[69] See *QS*, 180; GdQ, I, 59–62; Blachère, *Introduction au Coran*, 245; al-Suyūṭī, *al-Itqān*, I, 8–12; al-Zarkashī, *al-Burhān*, I, 184–94; Ibn al-Nadīm, *al-Fihrist*, 25–6; Abū 'Ubayd, *Faḍā'il al-Qur'ān*, Berlin MS Petermann 451, ff. 51a–52b; al-Zuhrī, *Kitāb al-tanzīl*, Beirut, 1963, 23–32. Other examples are to be found in Abū 'Abd Allāh Muḥammad ibn Ayyūb ibn Yaḥyā ibn al-Ḍurays al-Rāzī (d. 294/906), *Faḍā'il al-Qur'ān wa mā nazala min al-Qur'ān bi-Makka wa mā nazala bi'l-Madīna*, Ẓāhiriyyah MS 3814, ff. 61–83 and 88–121; this work would seem to be quoted in al-Suyūṭī, *al-Itqān* giving a list of *sūra* order. Also see Abū'l-Qāsim al-Ḥasan ibn Muḥammad ibn al-Ḥasan ibn Ḥabīb al-Nīsābūrī (d. 406/1015), *Kitāb al-tanzīl wa tartībihi*, Ẓāhiriyya MS 3763, ff. 221–32.

[70] On Ibn al-Bārizī see *GAL*, II, 86, Suppl. II, 101.

[71] *Handschriften-Verzeichnisse*, I, 185.

[72] I, p. 8, l. 2.

[73] On Ibn Qayyim al-Jawziyya see *GAL*, II, 105–6, Suppl. II, 126–8; *EI* (2nd ed.), II, 821–2.

[74] *Handschriften-Verzeichnisse*, I, 185.

[75] On Ibn al-Naqīb see *GAL*, II, 112, Suppl. II, 138.

[76] MS 468, being folios 142a–159b of We. 1782; see Ahlwardt, *Handschriften-Verzeichnisse*, I, 182–3.

[77] See pp. 10–11.

14. Shihāb al-Dīn Aḥmad ibn 'Alī ibn Ḥajar al-'Asqalānī (d. 852/1449),[78] *Al-i'jāb fī* [or *bi*] *bayān al-asbāb*. This work by the prolific *ḥadīth* scholar is cited by al-Suyūṭī, Ḥājjī Khalīfa and Ahlwardt [79] although, as al-Suyūṭī makes clear, it was never finished by its author and thus is not a work to be reckoned with. Why al-Suyūṭī even bothers to mention it is a reasonable question but one that cannot really be answered.

15. Jalāl al-Dīn Abū'l-Faḍl 'Abd al-Raḥman ibn Abī Bakr al-Suyūṭī (d. 911/1505).[80] The perhaps overly-prolific writer al-Suyūṭī penned at least two works connected with *asbāb al-nuzūl*.

(*a*) *Lubāb al-nuqūl fī asbāb al-nuzūl*. This very popular work has been printed numerous times, although never in a 'critical' edition. The most popular edition today is that found on the bottom of the *Tafsīr al-Jalālayn* although that print has omitted the introduction to the work and deleted the sign (a ك) that al-Suyūṭī apparently put in to denote where he had added new material as compared with al-Wāḥidī.[81] Al-Suyūṭī acknowledges his debt to al-Wāḥidī, although he criticizes the latter on a number of points, most especially on his inclusion of material which did not truly belong; he then proceeds, in a sense, to re-edit al-Wāḥidī's book, clarifying the sources of each report and omitting or adding reports as he conceives it be to necessary. The sources which al-Suyūṭī goes back to, other than al-Wāḥidī himself, are specified by him [82] as the following:

(i) the six books, that is, the *ḥadīth* collections of al-Bukhārī,[83] Muslim,[84] Abū Dāwūd (d. 275/888),[85] al-Tirmidhī (d. 279/892),[86] Ibn Māja, (d. 273/886) [87] and al-Nasā'ī (d. 303/915) [88]
(ii) *Al-mustadrak* (of al-Ḥākim) [89]
(iii) *Ṣaḥīḥ* of Ibn Ḥibbān (d. 354/965) [90]
(iv) *Sunan* of al-Bayhaqī (d. 458/1066) [91]
(v) *Sunan* of al-Daraquṭnī (d. 385/995) [92]
(vi) *Musnad* of Aḥmad (d. 241/855) [93]

[78] On Ibn Ḥajar see *GAL*, II, 67–70, Suppl. II, 72–6; *EI* (2nd ed.), III, 776–8.

[79] Al-Suyūṭī, *al-Itqān*, I, 28; Ḥājjī Khalīfa, *Kashf al-ẓunūn*, 268–9; Ahlwardt, *Handschriften-Verzeichnisse*, I, 185; also see Aḥmad Ṣaqr's introduction to al-Wāḥidī, *Asbāb nuzūl al-Qur'ān*, 23.

[80] On al-Suyūṭī see n. 8.

[81] Reference here is to the edition of *Lubāb al-nuqūl* done in 5 fascicules, Cairo, 1382, which includes the introduction.

[82] *Lubāb al-nuqūl*, 7.

[83] Al-Bukhārī, *al-Jāmi' al-ṣaḥīḥ*; on him see n. 43.

[84] Muslim, *al-Jāmi' al-ṣaḥīḥ*; on him see n. 44.

[85] Abū Dāwūd Sulaymān ibn al-Ash'ath, *Kitāb al-sunan*; on him see *GAS*, I, 149–52; *EI* (2nd ed.), I, 114.

[86] Abū 'Īsā Muḥammad ibn 'Īsā al-Tirmidhī, *al-Jāmi' al-ṣaḥīḥ*; on him see *GAS*, I, 154–9; *EI* (2nd ed.), IV, 796–7.

[87] Abū 'Abd Allāh Muḥammad ibn Yazīd ibn Mājah, *al-Sunan*; on him see *GAS*, I, 147–8; *EI* (2nd ed.), III, 856.

[88] Abū 'Abd al-Raḥmān Aḥmad ibn 'Abd Allāh al-Nasā'ī, *Kitāb al-sunan*; on him see *GAS*, I, 167–69; *SEI*, 439–40.

[89] *al-Mustadrak 'alā'l-ṣaḥīḥayn*; on him see n. 45.

[90] Abū Ḥātim Muhammad ibn Ḥibbān al-Bustī, *al-Musnad al-ṣaḥīḥ 'alā'l-taqsīm wa'l-anwā'*; on him see *GAS* I, 189–91; *EI* (2nd ed.), I, 799. Some editions of *Lubāb al-nuqūl* have Ibn Ḥayyān; cf. below nn. 100, 101.

[91] Abū Bakr Aḥmad ibn al-Ḥusayn al-Bayhaqī, *Kitāb al-sunan al-āthār* [*al-kabīr*]; on him see *GAL*, I, 363, Suppl. I, 618–9; *EI* (2nd ed.), I, 1130.

[92] Abū'l-Ḥasan 'Alī bin 'Uthmān al-Daraquṭnī, *Kitāb al-sunan*; on him see *GAS*, I, 206–9; *EI* (2nd ed.), II, 136.

[93] Abū 'Abd Allāh Aḥmad ibn Muḥammad ibn Ḥanbal, *al-Musnad*; on him see *GAS*, I, 502–9; *EI* (2nd ed.), I, 272–7.

(vii) *Musnad* of al-Bazzār (d. 292/905) [94]
(viii) *Musnad* of Abū Ya'lā (d. 307/919) [95]
(ix) *Ma'ājim* of al-Ṭabarānī (d. 360/971) [96]
(x) *Tafsīr* of Ibn Jarīr (d. 310/923) [97]
(xi) *Tafsīr* of Ibn Abī Ḥātim (d. 327/938) [98]
(xii) *Tafsīr* of Ibn Mardawayh (d. 410/1019) [99]
(xiii) *Tafsīr* of Abū'l-Shaykh (d. 369/979) [100]
(xiv) *Tafsīr* of Ibn Ḥibbān (d. 354/965) [101]
(xv) *Tafsīr* of al-Faryābī (d. 301/913 ?) [102]
(xvi) *Tafsīr* of 'Abd al-Razzāq (d. 211/827) [103]
(xvii) *Tafsīr* of Ibn al-Mundhir (d. 318/930) [104]

He ends his list with the note that ' other works ' were also consulted.

Thus al-Suyūṭī's sources cover the realm of *ḥadīth* and *tafsīr* but, it is to be noted, no other *asbāb* book is cited. Al-Suyūṭī generally cites the reports from these sources, naming only the source (or sources) and the last authority of the *isnād*. In this way, a total of 102 *sūras* is covered in the work.

(*b*) *Qaṭf al-thamar fī muwāfaqa Sayyidinā 'Umar.* This work exists in at least two manuscripts, one consisting of just the 18-line poem itself (Berlin 3967) [105] and the other in a 12-folio work consisting of the poem plus a commentary by a certain Muḥammad Badr al-Dīn al-Baysabānī, the title of the whole work being *Fatḥ al-wahhāb fī muwāfaqāt Sayyidinā 'Umar ibn al-Khaṭṭāb* (Berlin Landberg 290).[106] The poem published as part of al-Suyūṭī's work *al-Ḥāwī li'l-fatāwī* is identical.[107]

These *muwāfaqāt* books are a specialized part of the *asbāb* in that they collect together reports which deal with 'Umar specifically and his special merit in making statements with which the revelation agreed in verbal formulation.

[94] Abū Bakr Aḥmad ibn 'Amr ibn 'Abd al-Khāliq al-Bazzār, *al-Musnad* ; on him see *GAS*, I, 162 ; Nolin, ' The *Itqān* and its sources ', 131, has al-Bazār ; some editions of *Lubāb al-nuqūl* have al-Bazzāz.

[95] Abū Ya'lā Aḥmad ibn 'Alī al-Tamīmī al-Mawṣilī, *al-Musnad* ; on him see *GAS*, I, 170–1.

[96] Abū'l-Qāsim Sulaymān ibn Aḥmad al-Tabarānī, *al-Mu'jam al-kabīr* ; *al-Mu'jam al-awsaṭ* ; *al-Mu'jam al-saghīr* ; on him see *GAS*, I, 195–7.

[97] Abū Ja'far Muḥammad ibn Jarīr al-Ṭabarī, *Jāmi' al-bayān 'an ta'wīl āy al-Qur'ān* ; on him see *GAS*, I, 323–8 ; *EI* (1st ed.), IV, 578–9.

[98] Abū Muḥammad 'Abd al-Raḥmān ibn Abī Ḥātim al-Rāzī, *al-Tafsīr* ; on him see *GAS*, I, 178–9.

[99] Abū Bakr Aḥmad ibn Mūsā ibn Mardawayh al-Iṣfahānī, *al-Tafsīr* (not extant) ; on him see *GAS*, I, 225.

[100] On Abū Muḥammad 'Abd Allāh ibn Muḥammad ibn Ja'far ibn Ḥayyān Abū'l-Shaykh see *GAS*, I, 200–1 ; according to Sezgin, Ibn Ḥajar knew of a *tafsīr* by this author but it is not extant ; cf. below n. 101.

[101] Abū Ḥātim Muḥammad al-Tamīmī al-Hanẓalī al-Bustī ibn Ḥibban, *al-Tafsīr*, extant in part ; on him see *GAS*, I, 189–91 ; Nolin, ' The *Itqān* and its sources ', 141, considers Abū'l-Shaykh (above n. 100) and Ibn Ḥibbān to be the same person and the ' *wa* ' between their names in *al-Itqan* to be a mistake ; he bases this on one manuscript. However, prints of *Lubāb al-nuqūl* are uniform in separating the two. The mistake may actually have crept into Nolin's manuscript since Abū'l-Shaykh is Ibn Ḥayyān (i.e. a confusion between حيان and حبان).

[102] There are two possibilities here : Abū Bakr Ja'far ibn Muḥammad al-Firyābī, b. 207/822, d. 301/913 ; see *GAS*, I, 166 ; no *tafsīr* is listed for this author although a *Faḍā'il al-Qur'ān* text is extant ; less likely is Abū 'Abd Allāh Muḥammad ibn Yūsuf al-Firyābī, b. 120/738, d. 212/827 ; see *GAS*, I, 40 ; his *tafsīr* is cited by al-Ṭabarī and al-Tha'labī.

[103] Abū Bakr 'Abd al-Razzāq ibn Hammām al-Ḥimyārī, *al-Tafsīr* : on him see *GAS*, I, 99.

[104] Abū Bakr Muḥammad ibn Ibrāhīm ibn al-Mundhir al-Nīsābūrī, *Tafsīr al-Qur'ān* ; on him see *GAS*, I, 495–6.

[105] See E. Wagner, *Arabische Handschriften*, I, 9–10.

[106] See Ahlwardt, *Handschriften-Verzeichnisse*, I, 183, MS 469.

[107] Al-Suyūṭī, *al-Ḥāwī li'l-fatāwī*, Cairo, 1352, I, 377–8 ; I hope to deal with the poem and its commentaries more specifically in a future publication.

It is quite possible that these kinds of works celebrating 'Umar are a response to Shī'ite works extolling 'Alī in very similar ways. 'Ubayd Allāh ibn 'Abd Allāh ibn Aḥmad al-Ḥākim al-Ḥaskānī, a Shī'ī who died in the year 470/1077, wrote a book called *Shawāhid al-tanzīl li-qawā'id al-tafḍīl fi'l-āyāt al-nazila fī ahl al-bayt.*[108] This work, as the title explains, is concerned with verses revealed in connexion with 'Alī and his family and is, quite apparently, arguing for the supremacy of 'Alī in all matters.

Two other works are listed in Brockelmann, ascribed to al-Suyūṭī: *Risāla fī nuzūl al-Qur'ān 'alā sab'a aḥruf* (India Office 1217) and *Su'al kayfiyyat al-nuzūl* (Paris 4088, 40) and are listed there as though they were similar to *Lubāb al-nuqūl.*[109] The titles of both of these works, however, indicate that their content matter is more likely to be information taken from or expanded from his *al-Itqān fi 'ulūm al-Qur'ān* and peripheral at best to actual texts of *asbāb al-nuzūl.*

16. Muḥammad ibn Tāj al-'Ārifīn [110] wrote an apparently untitled poem in the year 1094/1682, a manuscript of which is found in Berlin, Petermann 554 (Ahlwardt 471). The work is primarily a versification of al-Wāḥidī's text (although note that Ibn Daqīq al-'Īd [111] is mentioned also in the introduction to the poem); in fact, the brief pieces quoted in Ahlwardt's catalogue indicate that the work follows al-Wāḥidī's work closely and is of little independent value.

17. 'Aṭīya Allāh ibn 'Aṭiya al-Ujhūrī (d. 1190/1776),[112] *Irshād al-raḥmān li-asbāb al-nuzūl wa'l-naskh wa'l-mutashābih wa-tajwīd al-Qur'ān.* A number of manuscript copies exist of this rather voluminous work; it has been possible to examine the copy in Cairo, Dār al Kutub al Miṣriyyah, *tafsīr* 42, a text of 420 folios, 21 lines to the page, written (up to f. 377) in the eighteenth century, with the last folios being a modern addition in order to complete the copy.[113] The book is structured so that each of the topics indicated in the title is interleaved *sūra* by *sūra* with others. The only exception to this is found in the case of the *tajwīd* portion which has been added to the end of the work, ff. 395–420. The treatment of *asbāb* for *sūra* 2, for example, runs from f. 9a through 24a at which point the discussion turns to the 33 verses considered to be abrogated in that *sūra.* The text is a compendium of material drawn, as far as the *asbāb* text goes, from standard earlier sources such as al-Wāḥidī and al-Suyūṭī. Al-Ujhūrī is quite frank about his debt to his predecessors and the text can perhaps best be seen as a forerunner of many modern works on these subjects, compiled with few critical insights from earlier sources.

18. An unknown abridgement of al-Wāḥidī exists in the Princeton Garrett Collection 135 (Yahuda 5143).[114] The work has been given the title, by a hand different from the original scribe [*Kitāb*] *asbāb nuzūl al-āya* [sic] *wa'l-suwar*; the first part of the manuscript, called in the text *Kitāb asbāb nuzūl al-āyāt,* consists of a work much like that ascribed to al-Ja'barī; it is limited totally to reports given by al-Wāḥidī and is minus the *isnāds* (with the exception of the

[108] On al-Ḥaskānī see the introduction to the text, Beirut, 1974, 7–12.
[109] See *GAL,* Suppl. II, 179, items 3a, 3b.
[110] Al-'Ārifīn is apparently not identifiable any further; see *GAL,* II, 327 and cf. Suppl. II, 694, 978; also see Ahlwardt, *Handschriften-Verzeichnisse,* I, 184.
[111] On Tāqī al-Dīn Abū'l-Fatḥ Muḥammad ibn 'Alī ibn Daqīq al-'Īd al-Manfalūṭī (b. 625/1228, d. 702/1302) see *GAL,* II, 63, Suppl. II, 66.
[112] On al-Ujhūrī see *GAL,* II, 328–9, Suppl. II, 456; Ahlwardt, *Handschriften-Verzeichnisse,* I, 185.
[113] Other manuscripts include Selim Aga 35 and Taymūr *tafsīr* 408.
[114] See Rudolph Mach, *Catalogue of Arabic manuscripts (Yahuda Section) in the Garrett Collection, Princeton University Library,* Princeton, 1977, 14.

final authority). On f. 63b a second book begins, with the simple title *Kitāb asbāb al-nuzūl* and consists of selected extracts quoted directly from al-Suyūṭī's *al-Itqān fī 'ulūm al-Qur'ān*. It is certain, therefore, that the work must have been written after al-Suyūṭī, and thus cannot be the work that al-Ja'barī is said to have compiled, for example, and is, therefore, of little independent value except antiquarian.

19. The Berlin catalogue also lists a work by an unknown author, *Tafṣīl li-asbāb al-nuzūl*, manuscript OR 1300.[115] The work consists of only 8 folios and is incomplete. The manuscript was written around the year 900/1494.

The final position arrived at, therefore, is that there are today four basic, important texts available and central to a study of *asbāb al-nuzūl*, each of which has its own special contribution of information to make: al-Wāḥidī; al-'Irāqī; Berlin 3578 (pseudo al-Ja'barī); al-Suyūṭī, *Lubāb al-nuqūl*.

One significant element which may be observed from this bibliographical survey of *asbāb* books is that it is a genre of exegetical literature which appears to emerge late and that, on the evidence of the titles, the technical term *sabab* in reference to the ' cause ' or ' occasion ' of relevation would appear to emerge somewhat after the time of the establishment of the genre.

Further light may be shed on this point by paying attention to the actual term *sabab* and its rise to technical status. An obvious place to look for the meaning of the term and the context of its rise to technical status may be the Qur'ān; other technical terms of exegesis find their place of origin in that book: *ta'wīl*, *mutashābih*, *muḥkam*, *naskh* are all terms whose use in a technical sense may (perhaps) be derived in the first place from their Qur'ānic usage.[116]

The root SBB is used a total of 11 times in the Qur'ān; twice the verb is used in Q. 6:108 where clearly the meaning is ' to curse ': ' Do not curse [*lā tasubbū*] those who call on other than God, or they will curse [*yasubbū*] God in revenge without knowledge.'

The nine other instances of the use of the root—five times as a singular noun *sabab*, four times as a plural *asbāb*—are divided by some classical exegetes[117] into four different meaning groups.

(*a*) *sabab* = gates/doors (*abwāb*)

Q. 38:10: Do they have the kingdom of the heavens and the earth and what is between them? Let them mount *fī'l-asbāb*!

Q. 40:36–37: Pharaoh said: ' Oh Haman! Build me a tower so that I may reach *al-asbāb*!
Al-asbāb of the heavens so I may look upon the God of Moses—for I think he is a liar!'

[115] Ahlwardt, *Handschriften-Verzeichnisse*, I, 183–4, MS 470.

[116] See *QS*, ch. iv, for consideration of these and other examples.

[117] The primary work here is Muqātil ibn Sulaymān, *al-Ashbāh wa'l-naẓā'ir fī'l-Qur'ān al-karīm*, Cairo, 1975; this work is virtually copied totally by al-Dāmaghānī (d. 478/1085; see *GAL*, I, 373), *Iṣlāḥ al-wujūh wa'l-naẓā'ir fī'l-Qur'ān al-karīm*, Beirut, 1970, and the analysis has become almost a standard one within the genre of *wujūh* literature. A methodological note may be appropriate here. The thought may occur that it would be more appropriate to try to ascertain the so-called ' original meaning ' of *sabab/asbāb* in the following Qur'ān passages in order to determine if the technical term is derived from the Qur'ān. This, it may be thought, is especially necessary because the classical *wujūh* literature here employed is (quite obviously) imposing ' later ' ideas on the Qur'ān, e.g. fully developed notions of the afterlife most prominently. It is the imposition of ' later ' ideas, however, which is central here; the question being asked of these passages is have any of these verses ever been read so as to support the use of *sabab* as a technical term? What could have been made of the passages is irrelevant; what was done with them is vital.

These three instances have produced a wide variety of interpretation in modern translations of the Qur'ān—rope, cords, ways and means—as opposed to the ' classical ' explanation that the *asbāb* here are the gates of heaven,[118] in keeping with the common Qur'ānic (and Biblical) imagery of the entrance-way to heaven.[119] Both the unbelievers in 38 : 10 and Pharaoh in 40 : 36–37 are tempted with the vision, the latter, of course, only to be frustrated, and the former given the possibility only in an ironic sense.

(*b*) *sabab* = stations, places, supports (*manāzil*)
Q. 2 : 166 : When those who were followed disown their followers—they would see the punishment and *al-asbāb* are cut off from them.
Q. 18 : 89 : He [Dhū'l-Qarnayn] followed a *sabab*.
The interpretation of the first verse is connected with events in the hereafter concerning the unbelievers; those who have strayed from God's way will assemble on platforms, *manāzil*, *asbāb*, according to their degree of rebellion, but their support/platform will be withdrawn from them.

Q. 18 : 89 is explained by Muqātil as meaning that he followed the stations (*manāzil*, *asbāb*) of the earth and its path (*ṭuruq*). Such an interpretation is ambiguous, lending itself to full mystical overtones. The entire passage is indeed often taken in that way.

(*c*) *sabab* = knowledge (*'ilm*)
Q. 18 : 84 : We established him [Dhū'l-Qarnayn] in the land and we gave him a *sabab* from/of [*min*] all things.
Q. 18 : 85 : So he followed a *sabab*.
To separate these verses about Dhū'l-Qarnayn from the entire exegesis concerned with the passage renders their interpretation extremely difficult. However, *sabab* in verse 84 is taken to mean knowledge simply and in verse 85 as knowledge of the *manāzil* according to the explanation of Muqātil. The precise relationship between this latter verse and verse 89, treated above, is not clear (nor in fact do the texts make clear which passage is being referred to; the Arabic phrase is the same in both cases).

(*d*) *sabab* = rope (*ḥabl*)
Q. 22 : 15 : Whoever thinks God will not help him [Muḥammad ?] in the world now and in the hereafter, let him [the accuser ?] stretch a *sabab* to *al-samā'* and then let him cut (it); then let him see if his plan removes that which annoys him [i.e., gets rid of Muḥammad ?]
A problematic verse for exegetes indeed, especially as to whether this is a reference to a specific event and specific people or is a general statement. *Al-samā'*, normally ' the heavens ', is often understood and translated here as ' the ceiling '; ' let him cut (it) ' is variously explained as ' cutting off his support or rope ' or, as in Lane, ' let him die strangled ' or even ' let him traverse (the heavens) '.[120] All interpretations, however, seem to see *sabab* as the means by which to reach up, and this means is made specific by defining the word as ' rope.'

Now, quite obviously, there is no easy peg in any of these verses in which the term *sabab*/*asbāb* is used that would allow an easy derivation from the Qur'ān

[118] Muqātil, *al-Ashbāh*, 174; al-Dāmaghānī, *Iṣlāḥ*, 225; cf. al-Farrā', (d. 207/822; on him see *GAL*, I, 116), *Ma'ānī al-Qur'ān*, Cairo, 1955–1972, II, 399.
[119] See for example Q. 7 : 40 and E. F. F. Bishop, ' Gates and doors in the New Testament and the Qur'ān ', *Glasgow University Oriental Society Transactions*, XXII, 1967–8, 39–45.
[120] Edward W. Lane, *An Arabic-English lexicon*, London, 1863–93, IV, 1285.

of the technical sense of *sabab* as connected with the process of revelation. None of the verses seem the least bit related to a statement concerning revelatory procedure.[121]

A study of exegetical use of the term *sabab* indicates a late rise in the use of the term. While it would not be unreasonable to expect to find phrases such as ' and the *sabab* of that verse being revealed was ' or ' that was the *sabab* of that verse ' in early exegetical works, in fact such phrases seem not to be found either in early exegetical works—e.g., those of Muqātil,[122] Mujāhid [123] or Sufyān al-Thawrī (d. 161/778) [124] nor in early *sīra* works by Ibn Isḥāq (d. 151/768) [125] or al-Wāqidī (d. 207/823) [126] or in the *Kitāb al-tafsīr* of the major *ḥadīth* collections by al-Bukhārī [127] or Muslim.[128] The phrase used in most of these texts to introduce anecdotes which later become considered *asbāb* is *dhālika anna* ; this has already been pointed out by Wansbrough in his *Quranic studies*.[129] The actual term *sabab* seems to begin to make its appearance in the *tafsīr* of al-Ṭabarī (d. 310/922) and the *naskh* work of al-Naḥḥās (d. 338/950) [130] and in both cases it would seem to be a case of seeing the term actually in the midst of evolving into its technical status. In al-Ṭabarī's discussion of the banishment of the word *rā'inā* in Q. 2:104, he begins his discussion in the following way: *ikhtalafa ahl al-ta'wīl fī'l-sabab min ajlihi nahā allāh* [*dhālika*].[131] The question being asked by this kind of phraseology is not concerned with the reason (*sabab*) for the revelation of the verse (and that is certainly the later technical sense of the term) but rather with the reason (*sabab*) for the prohibition of the word *ra'inā*. The two are, without a doubt, related but there would seem to be a subtle distinction between them with regards to the actual technical status of the word in question. Numerous other instances of this same kind of semi-technical-but-not-quite usage are to be found throughout the *tafsīr*.[132] Yet at the same time, al-Ṭabarī also says *ikhtalafa ahl al-ta'wīl fī 'l-sabab alladhī min ajlihi anzala allāh dhikr hādhihi'l-āya 'alā nabīhi* and other similar statements.[133] Clearly the word is used here in its technical sense but yet the excessive verbiage which has to go along with it once again indicates that the word here is still in search of its true technical status ; the use of *min ajlihi* is consistent throughout all of al-Ṭabarī's usages but is one that would be considered tautologous in later usage. The same thing may be said of the phrase *dhikr hādhihi'l-āya*.

[121] For an analysis of intra-Qur'ānic considerations of the revelatory process see *QS*, 36–8.

[122] Muqātil, *Tafsīr*, MS Ahmet III 74 ; on him see above n. 47.

[123] Mujāhid, *Tafsīr Mujāhid*, Qatar, 1976 ; on him see above n. 46.

[124] Sufyān al-Thawrī, *Tafsīr al-Qur'ān al-karīm*, Rampur, 1965 ; on him see *GAS*, I, 518–9. Other early works such as al-Farrā', *Ma'ānī al-Qur'ān*; Abū 'Ubayda (d. 210/825 ; on him see *GAL*, I, 103), *Majāz al-Qur'ān*, Cairo, 1954, 1962 ; al-Shāfi'ī (d. 204/820 ; on him see *GAS*, I, 484–90), *Al-risāla fī uṣūl al-fiqh*, Cairo, 1940, are also free of the term.

[125] Muḥammad ibn Isḥāq ibn Yasār, *al-Sīrat al-nabawiyya*, Cairo, 1955 ; on him see *GAS* I, 288–90.

[126] Abū 'Abd Allāh Muhammad ibn 'Umar al-Wāqidī, *Kitāb al-maghāzī*, Oxford, 1966 ; on him see *GAS*, I, 294–7.

[127] Al-Bukhārī, *al-Ṣaḥīḥ*, Book LX ; on him see above n. 43.

[128] Muslim, *al-Ṣaḥīḥ*, Book XLI ; on him see above n. 44.

[129] *QS*, 141.

[130] On Abū Ja'far Aḥmad ibn Muḥammad al-Naḥḥās see *GAL*, I, 132 ; on al-Ṭabarī see above n. 97.

[131] *Jāmi' al-bayān 'an ta'wīl āy al-Qur'ān*, Cairo, 1374–88, II, 460.

[132] e.g., *Jāmi' al-bayān*, II, 364, 377 ; IV, 520.

[133] *Jāmi' al-bayān*, III, 267 ; also see IV, 58, 250 ; V, 559. Note should also be taken of al-Māturīdī (d. 333/944 ; on him see *GAS*, I, 604–6) and the absence of the term *sabab* in his *Ta'wīlāt ahl al-sunna* ; see the introduction to the work as printed in Manfred Götz, ' Māturīdī und sein Kitāb Ta'wīlāt al-Qur'ān ', *Der Islam*, XLI, 1965, 32, and the statement *al-amr alladhī nazala fīhi al-Qur'ān*.

Likewise, al-Naḥḥās seems not totally aware of a technical status of the word *sabab*. He does not use the word to any great extent but in at least one instance noted, once again in the treatment of Q. 2:104, he seems more concerned with the pun between *sabb*, ‘ curse ’, (i.e., the Jewish use of the word *rāʿinā*) and *sabab*, ‘ reason ’, than anything else.[134]

It is only with al-Jaṣṣāṣ (d. 370/981) that the term *sabab* would appear to be used with any regularity and to win its fully technical sense and phraseology in introducing reports about the revelation of the Qur'ān.[135] The legal context in which the term itself seems to have gained technical status may well be thought to be a significant fact in light of Wansbrough's analysis of exegetical use of the material [136] although it can be argued that the material itself, as opposed to the term, should be traced to a purely haggadic source and impetus rather than halakhic as Wansbrough (at least in *Quranic studies* [137]) seems to suggest.

Thus it should not be any great surprise that al-Wāḥidī's work is probably the earliest extant work gathering together such reports into one book ; it was perhaps only a century earlier that the term *sabab* became fixed and thus that the existence of a distinct type of exegetical information was marked out. Indeed, al-Wāḥidī's statement that the *asbāb* are the key to all exegesis [138] could perhaps be interpreted in such light, in the sense that he saw himself as a major figure in the isolation and solidification of this material which was ill-defined prior to his time.

After al-Wāḥidī, the term and the genre are, of course, well established. Like other technical terms within the exegetical canon, the term *sabab* has been subjected to a variety of changes and redirections throughout its history.[139] For *sabab*, the main reorientation comes quite late, perhaps first with al-Zarkashī [140] but most significantly, and lastingly, with al-Suyūṭī.[141] Al-Wāḥidī appears to have defined his notion of a *sabab* in a fairly mechanical kind of way ; if an anecdote included the phrase *fa-anzala allāh* (or *wa nazalat al-āya* or other variants on that idea) then the report qualified as a *sabab*. It was that postulated connexion between an event (whether contemporaneous with the revelation, as in most cases, or contemporaneous with the events talked about in the revelation as in Q. 2 : 260 or Q. 105) and the revelation that defined the idea of the *sabab* for al-Wāḥidī. For al-Zarkashī and al-Suyūṭī however, the idea of a *sabab* had to be limited to events contemporaneous with the revelation ; those which were only connected to events mentioned in the Qur'ān were reclassified as *akhbār*. While al-Suyūṭī accuses al-Wāḥidī of ‘ error ’ by having included this ‘ false ’ information in his book and, note, Nöldeke/Schwally uncritically go along with this notion,[142] this is simply a further evolution in the idea of what a *sabab* is and what its importance is. It is necessary to keep this fact in mind in order to avoid anachronistic readings of early *tafsīr* works when they adduce material which fits in the later categories of *asbāb*.

[134] *Kitāb al-nāsikh wa'l-mansūkh*, Cairo, 1938, 26 ; also see p. 91 for a somewhat more technical employment of the word.

[135] Abū Bakr Aḥmad ibn ʿAlī al-Jaṣṣāṣ, *Aḥkām al-Qur'ān*, Istanbul, 1335 ; on him see *GAS*, I, 444–5 ; *QS*, 185–8.

[136] *QS*, 177–8.

[137] cf. John Wansbrough, *The sectarian milieu : content and composition of Islamic salvation history*, Oxford, 1978, ch. i, for a somewhat modified view.

[138] *Asbāb nuzūl al-Qur'ān*, 5–6.

[139] See *QS*, ch. iv for numerous examples (e.g., *tafsīr* and *majāz*).

[140] *al-Burhān*, I, 31–2.

[141] *Lubāb al-nuqul*, 6.

[142] *GdQ*, II, 183–4.

AL-ZARKASHĪ AND AL-SUYUTĪ ON THE "OCCASION OF REVELATION" MATERIAL *

EXTENSIVE discussions on the role on *asbāb al-nuzūl* material in Qur'ānic exegesis are far more infrequent in medieval Muslim literature than one may have hoped or perhaps even have expected. Likely places for such considerations would be introductions to actual exegetical works or within the genre of literature which has become known as *'ulūm al-Qur'ān.* Within the most famous books of that type, al-Suyūṭi (d. 911/1505), *al-Itqān fī 'Ulūm al-Qur'ān*, and al-Zarkashī (d. 794/1391), *al-Burhān fī 'Ulūm al-Qur'ān*, chapters are indeed found on the topic; their late date of composition and the ahistorical approach employed by both authors in their treatment of the subject has led, one suspects, to a blurring of any possible historical development in the conception of the topic and a glossing of contentious points by dogmatic assertion. Thus, to arrive at a comprehensive understanding of the role of the *sabab* in exegesis through a study of theoretical considerations of the topic in Arabic exegetical texts, a series of significant works from various centuries would be the most promising source. Unfortunately, a survey of earlier likely texts reveals that very little consideration of the topic of the *sabab* took place at all in forms other than discussions within the context of limited discussions of the role of the *sabab* in the exegesis of a specific verse.

Probably the earliest work which gathers together any theoretical considerations about the Qur'ān is Abū 'Ubayd (d. 224/838), [1] *Faḍā'il*

---

* This article is a slightly revised version of Chapter 2 of my 1981 McGill University Ph.D. Thesis, "The Quranic *Asbāb al-Nuzūl* Material: An Analysis of Its Use and Development in Exegesis." My thanks are extended to Dr. Charles Adams, McGill, and Prof. John Wansbrough, SOAS, for their encouragement and assistance. An abbreviated version of this paper was presented at the Annual Meeting of the American Academy of Religion in Chicago, December, 1984.

(1) Abū 'Ubayd al-Qāsim ibn Sallām, (A.H. 154-224); see Carl Brockelmann,

al-Qur'ān. Despite its title, the work deals with much more than the merits of recitation of various portions of the Qur'ān, the topic often understood by the rubric *faḍā'il.* While the first half of the text does treat *faḍā'il* topics,[2] the rest of the work deals with such topics as variant readings, collection of the Qur'ān and the language of the Qur'ān. To some extent, this pattern is duplicated in later *faḍā'il* works, such as al-Bukhārī (d. 256/869), *Kitāb Faḍā'il al-Qur'ān,*[3] and the commentary on that work by Ibn al-Kathīr (d. 774/1372),[4] entitled *Faḍā'il al-Qur'ān.*[5] Folios 51a to 52b of the Berlin manuscript of Abū 'Ubayd's work are entitled "Chapter on the revelation of the Qur'ān in Mecca and Medina and the description of the first and the last (to be revealed)" ; dealt with here are all sorts of matters dealing with respective ordering of the passages of the Qur'ān — the first and the last verses to be revealed, the order of Meccan and Medinan *sūrahs* including statements on how one determines that (for example, by the presence of *ayyuhā al-ladhīna āmanū* in Medinan *sūrahs*) and also on the actual process of revelation over a period of some twenty years, but nowhere is the idea of the relevance of an individual *sabab* for a verse broached.

The next similar and promising text would appear to be the introduction to the *tafsīr* by al-Tabarī (d. 310/922) which is comprised of over one hundred pages of text in the Shākir edition. Al-Tabarī even appears to have named the section separately : *Risālat al-Tafsīr.*[6] Al-Tabarī's concerns in this introduction are, however, far from *asbāb*

Geschichte des Arabischen Litteratur [hereafter = *GAL*] (Leiden, 1937-1949), vol. i, pp. 105-107, Supplement [= S], vol. i, 166-67; Fuat Sezgin, *Geschichte des Arabischen Schrifttums* [= *GAS*] (Leiden, 1967), vol. i, p. 48.

(2) Berlin Staatsbibliothek Preussischer Kulturbesitz, Orientabteilung, Petermann 449; the first 35 folios of the 58 folio manuscript are devoted to *faḍā'il.*

(3) *Al-Ṣaḥīḥ* (Cairo, 1978), vol.vi, pp. 473-522.

(4) 'Imād al-Dīn Abū al-Fidā' Ismā'īl ibn al-Kathīr (A.H. 701-774) ; see *GAL,* vol. ii, p. 49 ; S, vol. ii, pp. 48-49.

(5) See pp. 1-58 at the end of volume iv of his *Tafsīr al-Qur'ān al-'Aẓīm* n.d.).

(6) *Jāmi' al-Bayān 'an Ta'wīl Āy al-Qur'ān* (Cairo, A.H. 1374-1388), vol. i, pp. 8-113.

al-nuzūl; most of the space is devoted to a discussion of the language of the Qur'ān, especially the meaning of the seven *aḥruf*, the collection of the Qur'ān and the distinction between *tafsīr* and *ta'wīl*, ending finally with an explication of "the names of the Qur'ān, its *sūrahs* and its verses." That similar topics are covered in the introduction to the work by al-Tabarī's near contemporary, al-Anbārī (d. 328/939),[7] *Kitāb Īḍāḥ al-Waqf wa'l-Ibtidā' fī Kitāb Allāh*,[8] would indicate that these were the topics of controversy during that era and that perhaps *asbāb al-nuzūl* was not of great concern.[9]

In 1954 Arthur Jeffery published two independent works under the title *Muqaddimatān fī 'Ulūm al-Qur'ān*. The first work in the book, and the most extensive, is the introduction to the anonymous *Kitāb al-Mabānī li-Naẓm al-Ma'ānī*.[10] The author devotes considerable space to a listing of the chronological order of *sūrahs* and then to a consideration of the arrangement (*tartīb, naẓm*) of the Qur'ān. Here the process of revelation comes in the documentation, the author stating that the Qur'ān was revealed according to the needs of the situation (*'alā ḥasab al-ḥājah*) but that the arrangement of the Qur'ān as it stands today mirrors in the *lawḥ maḥfūẓ*.[11] The further implications of the "revelation by need" are not explored in any way other than by its naked assertion. The second text in the book, the *muqaddimah* to the *tafsīr* by Ibn 'Aṭīyah (d. 541/1146),[12] *al-Jāmi' al-Muḥarrar*,[13] is similar in its treatment of topics to al-Tabarī's

(7) Abū Bakr Muḥammad ibn al-Qāsim al-Anbārī (A.H. 231-328); see *GAL*, vol. i, p. 119; S, vol. i, pp. 182-83; *GAS*, vol. i, p. 18.

(8) *Īḍāḥ al-Waqf wa'l-Ibtidā'* (Damascus, 1971), vol. i, pp. 4-148.

(9) Within the course of al-Ṭabarī's *tafsīr* there are occasions on which he does deal with the value of the *sabab* but only within a limited context of a single verse.

(10) See pp. 5-250 of Jeffery's text (2nd edition, Cairo, 1972). The full title of the work is found on p. 6 of the text. The work was begun by its author in the year 425 according to the text itself.

(11) See *passim*, *al-faṣl al-thālith*, especially p. 40.

(12) Abū Muḥammad 'Abd al-Ḥaqq ibn 'Aṭīyah al-Gharnāṭī (A. H. 481-541); see *GAL*, vol. i, p. 412; S, vol. i, p. 732, where date of death is given as 542.

(13) See pp. 252-93 of Jeffery's text. At least the first volume of the entire *tafsīr*, including the *muqaddimah*, has been published — Cairo, 1974.

tafsīr, covering the merits (*faḍā'il*) of the Qur'ān, the seven *aḥruf* and the *i'jāz* of the Qur'ān only.

The earliest discussion of the role of the *sabab* which appears to exist today is found in Ibn Taymīyah (d. 728/1327),[14] *Muqaddimah fī Uṣūl al-Tafsīr.*[15] This title, it is to be noted, is that given to the work by the editor. The actual title page of the manuscript calls the work *Qā'idah 'Aẓīmat al-Qadr Sharīfah fī Tabyīn mā Yu'īnu 'alā Fahm al-Qur'ān,*[16] while the introduction to the actual text of the work implies the title to be *Qawā'id Kullīyah Tu'īnu 'alā Fahm al-Qur'ān*[17]; it is thus probably identical to the only work al-Suyūṭī lists in his bibliographic introduction to *al-Itqān* by Ibn Taymīyah : *Qawā'id fī al-Tafsīr.*[18] Regardless the actual title, the work is definitely a source for al-Suyūṭī's discussion and is quoted extensively in *al-Itqān.* Ibn Taymīyah's concern with the *sabab* is brought about by the presence of so much contradictory material within the collections; to explain how the apparent disagreement, *ikhtilāf*, arose among the "pious ancestors" (*salaf*) is the point of the chapter in which discussion of the *sabab* arises.[19]

The earliest extensive discussion of the role of *asbāb al-nuzūl*, as suggested above, would appear to be found in al-Zarkashī, *al-Burhān.* This work is the model after which al-Suyūṭī patterned his whole treatise and certainly after which he patterned most of his discussion on the *asbāb al-nuzūl.*[20] This, in fact, al-Suyūṭī himself makes clear in his introduction to *al-Itqān* : he had first written a book *al-Taḥbīr*

(14) Taqī al-Dīn Aḥmad ibn 'Abd al-Ḥalīm ibn Taymīyah (A.H. 661-728); see *GAL*, vol. ii, pp. 100-105; S, vol. ii, pp. 119-26.

(15) Beirut, 1972; see pp. 44-49.

(16) See *Maqaddimah*, p. [27], facsimile of the manuscript title page.

(17) *Muqaddimah*, p. 33.

(18) *Al-Itqān fī 'Ulūm al-Qur'ān* (Cairo, 1967), vol. i, p. 19 (lines 5-6).

(19) Further details concerning Ibn Taymīyah's ideas on the *sabab* are found below in the course of analysis of al-Suyūṭī's discussion.

(20) See K. E. Nolin, "The *Itqān* and Its Sources," Ph.D. Thesis, Hartford Seminary, 1968, especially pp. 2-31. Note how al-Suyūṭī's text has acted as the source, generally unacknowledged, of most of the modern *'ulūm al-Qur'ān* works; see, for example, Manā' al-Qaṭṭān, *Mabāḥith fī 'Ulūm al-Qur'ān* (Beirut, 1978).

fī 'Ulūm al-Tafsīr[21] but then he discovered *al-Burhān* and wrote, as a result, *al-Itqān*.

Prior to discovering the work of al-Zarkashī, al-Suyūṭī had known only two reasonably comprehensive but unsatisfactory *'ulūm al-Qur'ān* works[22]: one was by Muḥyī al-Dīn al-Kāfiyajī, (d. 879/1474),[23] the other by Jalāl al-Dīn al-Bulqīnī, (d. 824/1421), entitled *Mawāqi' al-'Ulūm min Mawāqi' al-Nujūm*.[24] The fact that both of these authors are relatively late and that these two works are the only ones al-Suyūṭī bothers to mention as being similar to his work confirms what has been suggested above that al-Zarkashī's and al-Suyūṭī's works are the most significant works extant on *'ulūm al-Qur'ān*.

The sources quoted by al-Suyūṭī within his specific chapter on *ma'rifat sabab al-nuzūl* likewise prove to be of little help in finding other statements on the role of the *sabab*. Among those mentioned are, obviously enough, al-Wāḥidī (d. 468/1075) and al-Ja'barī (d. 732/1331), both of whom are connected with actual books on *asbāb*.[25] Another person mentioned is Ibn Daqīq al-'Īd (d. 702/1302), although it may be significant that al-Zarkashī attributes a quotation, credited by al-Suyūṭī[26] to Ibn Daqīq, to a certain unidentified Abū al-Fatḥ al-Qushayrī.[27] Finally, a work by Ibn Ḥabīb al-Nīsābūrī (d. 406/

---

(21) See *al-Itqān*, vol. i, pp. 6-10; copies of *al-Taḥbīr* do exist (for example, Chester Beatty 4655 and 5112) but I have not been able to avail myself of any of them.

(22) *Al-Itqān*, vol. i, p. 4.

(23) Muḥammad ibn Sulaymān al-Muḥyawī Muḥyī al-Dīn al-Kāfiyajī (A.H. 788-879); see *GAL*, vol. ii, pp. 114-15; S, vol. ii, pp. 140-41. A work by him with the title *al-Taysīr fī Qawā'id al-Tafsīr* is known (see *GAL* and Princeton Yahuda 4515 = Mach 118) but I have not seen it; al-Suyūṭī gives no title.

(24) 'Abd al-Raḥmān ibn 'Uthmān ibn Raslān al-Bulqīnī Jalāl al-Dīn (A.H. 762-824); see *GAL*, vol, ii, pp. 112-13; S, vol. ii, p. 139 where this title is not listed although a *tafsīr* by him is extant, for example, British Library OR 1553-1557.

(25) See A. Rippin, "The Exegetical Genre *Asbāb al-Nuzūl*: a Bibliographical and Terminological Survey," *BSOAS*, XLVIII (1985).

(26) See *ibid.* for references to Ibn Daqīq al-'Īd's ambiguous involvement in *asbāb al-nuzūl*.

(27) *Al-Itqān*, vol. i, p. 83; al-Zarkashī, *al-Burhān fī 'Ulūm al-Qur'ān* (Cairo,

1015),[28] *al-Tanbīh 'alā Faḍl 'Ulūm al-Qur'ān*, is quoted by both al-Zarkashī and al-Suyūṭī, but it is used very infrequently[29]; one feels justified in presuming that the work was considered by none of them to be of great significance, despite its promising title, and that, therefore, not too much is being lost by its absence.[30]

Thus the only important, detailed texts are those by al-Suyūṭī and al-Zarkashī. Al-Suyūṭī's work, effectively being an edition and expansion of al-Zarkashī, does serve as a useful basis for the discussion of the role of the *sabab* by bringing together what few sources there were available to him as well as his own opinion on the matter, although the ahistorical nature of his approach, as mentioned above, does leave something to be desired.

Al-Suyūṭī's chapter on *ma'rifat sabab al-nuzūl* takes a prominent position on his treatment of the Qur'ānic sciences. The section is ninth, out of a total of eighty chapters, and follows on chapters devoted to other considerations of the process of revelation, for example, the time and physical place of revelation.[31] The discussion in the chapter itself is composed of answers to a series of five questions, which follows after a brief bibliographic introduction and a quote from al-Ja'barī to the effect that the Qur'ān was revealed in two ways, "spontaneously" (*ibtidā'*) or "as a result of a particular event

---

1957), vol. i, p. 22. For the tendency of al-Suyūṭī to attribute quotes to different authorities than al-Zarkashī, see Nolin, pp. 80-84.

(28) Presumably the same Ibn Ḥabīb al-Nīsābūrī dealt with in A. Rippin, "The Exegetical Genre *Asbāb al-Nuzūl*," although this work is not noted in *GAS*, vol. i, p. 47.

(29) See the index to *al-Itqān*, vol. iv, p. 280; *al-Burhān*, vol. iv, p. 502.

(30) A number of other works with promising-sounding titles have come to my attention but by title only; for example, Abū Bakr al-Udhfawī (d. A.H. 388), *al-Istighnā' fī 'Ulūm al-Qur'ān* (see Ibn al-Jazarī, *Ghāyat al-Nihāyah* [Cairo, 1932], entry number 3240); the above survey of texts, then, can in no way pretend to be a complete inventory of possible texts, merely a view of a few significant texts which are reasonably readily available.

(31) *Cf.* al-Zarkashī's arrangement of *al-Burhān Ma'rifat asbāb al-nuzūl*, *naw'* 1; *ma'rifat al-Makkī wa'l-Madanī*, *naw'* 9 — out of a total of 47 chapters.

(in the life of Muḥammad) or a query (put to Muḥammad)." [32] This, of course, is the theoretical basis of the entire concept of the *sabab*, that the revelation of the Qur'ān responded, at times, to the needs and requirements in the life of Muḥammad, and that those situations and the Qur'ānic response to them are recorded in the *asbāb al-nuzūl* material. The rest of al-Suyūṭī's chapter is then structured in the following way, dealing approximately with these topics :

Question 1 : Of what use is the *sabab* to exegesis ? To this question, six points are delineated in response.[33]

Question 2 : Is a law derived from the generality of the expression (of the verse) or according to the particularity of the *sabab* ? [34]

Question 3 : How does the *sabab* act in considerations of context ? [35]

Question 4 : What criteria make a *sabab* report valid ? [36]

Question 5 : Can one verse have more than one *sabab* ? [37]

In attempting to discern the theoretical position on the function of the *sabab*, al-Suyūṭī's answers to the first three of these questions are of vital importance, the fourth and fifth questions being only marginally related.

The reply to Question 1 comes as a response to a statement of objection to the entire topic : the *sabab* is of no value, it is claimed, because "it is analogous to history." Such an objection may simply be implying that some exegetes felt that they could leave the *sabab* out of consideration because it was of no use in exegesis, since it was "only" history and thus a separate discipline; on the other hand, a more

---

(32) *Al-Itqān*, vol. i, p. 82 ; also see John Wansbrough, *Quranic Studies : Sources and Methods of Scriptural Interpretation* [= *QS*] (Oxford, 1977), p. 178.

(33) *Al-Itqān*, vol.i , pp. 82-85; *cf. al-Burhān*, vol. i, pp. 22-29, a virtually identical survey with a few changes in internal order ; see below for further details of the comparison.

(34) *Al-Itqān*, vol. i, pp. 85-87.

(35) *Ibid.*, pp. 87-88 ; *cf. al-Burhān*, vol. i, p. 32.

(36) *Al-Itqān*, vol. i, pp. 89-91.

(37) *Ibid.*, pp. 91-98 ; *cf. al-Burhān*, vol. i, pp. 29-32.

serious objection is perhaps being raised, that the Qur'ān cannot be treated as historically conditioned in any sense (as the *sabab* may imply), for it is an uncreated work, written on the celestial tablet (*lawḥ maḥfūẓ*). It can hardly be claimed that what follows in al-Suyūṭī constitutes a really effective response to the first interpretation of the objection suggested above, even less so to the second; one may well doubt that the objection was really being taken seriously in al-Suyūṭī's time (or al-Zarkashī's where the exact same phrasing is found), the statement acting more as a convenient point of departure for the following discourse rather than as the basis of serious discussion.

Be that as it may, al-Suyūṭī then lists as part of his response to this, the first question, a series of six points comprising the functions the *sabab* fulfils in relationship to the proper understanding of the Qur'ān, thus demonstrating its functional value. As the first point[38] al-Suyūṭī states that the *sabab* reveals "knowledge of the aspect of divine wisdom which provoked the promulgation of the ruling [contained in the verse]"; that is, the *sabab* reveals God's concern with His creation through His action in providing mankind with laws to guide its life. *Sabab* here is clearly the metaphorical "tent rope" connecting heaven and earth.[39] It might also be suggested that this too is the main emphasis, theologically, of Question 5, where the possibility of multiple revelation of a Qur'ānic passage is endorsed. From a critical standpoint there can be little doubt that al-Suyūṭī is driven to this point because of the existence of vast quantities of contradictory material; that he, however, saw great merit in this feature, because of its emphasis on God's close involvement with His creation, can hardly be doubted.

The second point[40] in response to Question 1 consists of the idea that the *sabab* can reveal "the specification of the ruling by [the *sabab*], according to [the opinion of] those who hold that the precept is connected to the particularity of the *sabab*." A law in the Qur'ān, according to this idea, can be understood as having either a specific

(38) *Al-Itqān*, vol. i, p. 83; also *al-Burhān*, vol. i, p. 22, first point.

(39) On the analysis of the term *sabab* see "The Exegetical Genre *Asbāb al-Nuzūl*."

(40) *Al-Itqān*, vol. i, p. 82; also *al-Burhān*, vol. i, p. 22, second point.

relevance to the inhabitants of Arabia in the 7th century (CE) only or as being limited in its scope of application in later times by the circumstances of history at the time of its revelation. The important *proviso* here, however, is that this is true (for the most part) only according to those who hold that opinion, for it is quite clear that al-Suyūṭī does not agree with this point of view. Indeed, al-Suyūṭī gives no examples of exactly what is meant by this statement, and it is only when one comes to Question 2 in his discussion that the full extent of the implications of the statement becomes clear.

Question 2 deals with the problem of interpreting the Qur'ān: are legal rulings to be derived according to the generality of the wording of the verse or according to a particular situation implied by the *sabab*? Al-Suyūṭī clearly states that the former proposition is the soundest one. Many famous verses with widespread legal ramifications, he points out, were revealed concerning specific people (that is, with a specific *sabab*). For example, *āyat al-ẓihār* (Q. LVIII : 1) was revealed about Salamah ibn Ṣakhr,[41] *āyat al-li'ān* (Q. XXIV : 6) about Hilāl ibn Umayyah,[42] and Q. XXIV : 11-12 about 'Ā'ishah specifically.[43] To interpret these verses not by the generality of their wording would imply that the ruling was limited to the specific situation given in the *sabab*. Quoted in this connection is al-Zamakhsharī's rejection of that position : "It is possible that the *sabab* is specific while the threat (*wa'īd*) is general, for all who rejoice in that

---

(41) For these examples also see Ibn Taymiyah, *Muqaddimah*, p. 44, and *al-Burhān*, vol. i, pp. 24-25 ; the latter includes all those examples in his discussion of the "rejection of the illusion of limitation," see further below. The identification of Salamah as connected to Q. LVIII : 1 is problematic ; *cf.* al-Wāḥidī, *Asbāb Nuzūl al-Qur'ān* (Cairo, 1969), pp. 433-34, and al-Suyūṭī, *Lubāb al-Nuqūl fī Asbāb al-Nuzūl* (Cairo, A.H. 1382), p. 205, neither of whom mention this person. Also see the extensive comments of the editor of Ibn Taymiyah, *Muqaddimah*, pp. 44-45, note 5. The example is probably derived from an unknown traditional source listing the examples "par excellence" for the point taken. Such widespread copying of traditional opinion is a revealing insight into medieval scholarship.

(42) See al-Wāḥidī, *Asbāb*, pp. 328-30 ; al-Suyūṭī, *Lubāb*, p. 124.

(43) See al-Wāḥidī, *Asbāb*, pp. 330-55 ; al-Suyūṭī, *Lubāb*, pp. 125-26 ; al-Suyūṭī also lists a number of other examples in more detail.

evil deed are included (*yatanāwalu*) and that [threat] will certainly follow the same course as intimated." [44] It is on this occasion that al-Suyūṭī quotes Ibn Taymīyah also,[45] the latter putting forth forcefully the point of view that one could not be considered a Muslim if one held that the ruling of a verse was to be limited to the person identified in the *sabab*; this is, of course, the generally accepted notion in Islam and the basis of the elaboration of *fiqh* and not something unique to Ibn Taymīyah's particular polemic. As he states it, a verse is not limited to a person specified by the *sabab*, but it includes (*mutanāwil*) that person along with everyone else in the same situation (*bi-manzilatihī*).[46]

In certain cases, however, al-Suyūṭī acknowledges that specification by the *sabab* does, indeed, take place. His third point in dealing with Question 1 on the value of the *sabab* suggests that "perhaps the wording [of the verse] is general but there exists evidence of specification [of the wording]. If the *sabab* is known, then the specification is limited to what is required by the form [of the *sabab*]. The inclusion of the *sabab* [in the derivation of the law] is the determining factor (*qaṭ'ī*) and exclusion [of the sense of the *sabab*] by *ijtihād* is prohibited." [47] Thus it seems clear that, on certain occasions, verses *are* made specific, but the key would appear to lie in the notion of the "evidence of specification [of the wording] (*al-dalīl 'alā takhṣīṣihī*)." The full implications of this statement arise once more in Question 2, specifically in the *tanbīh* ("additional note") at the end.[48]

---

(44) *Al-Itqān*, vol. i, p. 85; also *al-Burhān*, vol. i, p. 32. See al-Zamakhsharī, *al-Kashshāf 'an Haqā'iq al-Tanzīl* (Calcutta, 1856), vol. ii, p. 1631 (*ad.* Q. CIV: 1); his purpose in the statement seems to be to reconcile the numerous possible different identifications of the protagonist.

(45) *Al-Itqān*, vol. i, pp. 86-87; Ibn Taymīyah, *Muqaddimah*, pp. 44-47.

(46) The reasoning involved here is inference *a minori ad maius*, what applies in a less important case will certainly apply in a more important case, equivalent to *qal wa-homer* in the seven *middot* of Hillel; see D. Daube, "Rabbinic Methods of Interpretation and Hellenistic Rhetoric," *HUCA*, XXII (1949), pp. 239-64, esp. pp. 251-52 and J. Bowker, *The Targums and Rabbinic Literature* (Cambridge, 1969), pp. 315-18. Also *QS*, pp. 166-70.

(47) *Al-Itqān*, vol. i, p.82; *cf. al-Burhān*, vol. i, pp. 22-23, al-Zarkashī's fourth point; al-Zarkashī's wording differs slightly.

(48) *Al-Itqān*, vol. i, p. 87.

There, as Wansbrough has already pointed out, al-Suyūṭī embarks on "a discussion of the elative *al-atqā* in Q. XCII : 17, 'He who is [the] most pious shall be spared.' Desire to restrict that reference to Abū Bakr provoked some very dogmatic observations on the grammatical function of the definite article."[49] The reason is, for al-Suyūṭī at least, that, in theory, a *sabab* does not make a verse specific in and by itself; it can only confirm a specification known by some other means, as in the case above, by the qualities of the definite article. In other instances, it would seem to be the prior existence of a law which then needs Qur'ānic support that acts as the "other means" of specification. But, as point three of Question 1 certainly does indicate, the *sabab* at least in theory overrides *Ijtihād* (and *Ijmā'* in al-Zarkashī it is to be noted)[50] within the discussions of specification. This is not really very surprising in a sense because the *sabab* is generally considered a part of the Prophetic *sunnah*, abiding by its rules and regulations, and thus within the hierarchy of the *uṣūl* to be rated second only to the Qur'ān. Question 4 in al-Suyūṭī's discussion delves into this topic, prefaced by al-Wāḥidī's only statement of his criterion of *asbāb* reports, that they be valid *ḥadīth* reports.[51] For al-Suyūṭī, it is to be noted, this is one method of separating the wheat from the chaff in the voluminous assortment of *asbāb* material; his actual work on the *asbāb* often quotes the judgement of the *isnād* by *ḥadīth* criteria for the individual reports.[52]

A further aspect of the problem of specification is brought up by al-Suyūṭī in his Question 3, where the possibility of a verse which has a specific intent but which has been put within a context of general intent due to the dictates of *naẓm/tartīb* is broached.[53] It is important to note at this time that all the discussions of "generality of the

(49) *QS*, p. 178.

(50) *Al-Burhān*, vol. i, p. 23; note also *al-Itqān*, vol. i, p. 85, the beginning of Question 2 suggests the same: "verses are limited to their *asbāb* by agreement due to an indication which exists suggesting that."

(51) See al-Wāḥidī, *Asbāb*, p. 4; also *QS*, p. 179.

(52) See al-Suyūṭī, *Lubāb*, e.g. p. 16.

(53) See also *al-Burhān*, vol. i, pp. 25-26 which al-Suyūṭī has lifted *in toto* uncredited; al-Zarkashī is however discussing what is actually al-Suyūṭī's point five, see below.

wording" or "specification of the wording" are based on an unenunciated theory of the "plain meaning" of the Qur'ān. The "plain meaning" intended by al-Suyūṭī in these instances is, of course, simply the meaning that he feels to be "authoritative" at that point.[54] There is not, and many would argue that there cannot be, any universally accepted "plain meaning" of any given text; any interpretation varies according to one's own presuppositions and intellectual background. Thus, it may be fairly argued that al-Suyūṭī's problem of a specific verse versus the general context is one that arises only through approaching the Qur'ān with presuppositions and expectations of desired result. The desire is to use a given Qur'ānic passage to support an already existing law; the result is a possible rupture of the context of the Qur'ānic passage in question. Al-Suyūṭī cites only one Qur'ānic example of this phenomenon in action at this point of his discussion, Q. IV : 58, the legal intent of which is separate from the context created by Q. IV : 51 and following. Verse 51 begins "Have you not seen those who were given a portion of the Book... ?," referring, by general consensus in interpretation, to the Jews of 7th century (CE) Arabia and their conspiracy to hide the description of Muḥammad in the Torah; this description of Muḥammad, al-Suyūṭī explains, was their "covenantal obligation" or "trust" (*amānah*). Verse 58 then goes on to state, "God orders you to give the trusts (*amānāt*) to their owners." If one were governed in interpretation by the specific *sabab*, verse 58 would refer to the Jews also; but, in fact, al-Suyūṭī argues, verse 58 is general, in reference to everything given in trust by anyone. Thus, a specific verse (Q. IV : 51) has been joined to a general context (Q. IV : 58).[55]

The whole topic of the "joining together" of verses and the subsequent problems is treated more extensively in a separate chapter in *al-Itqān* and especially in *al-Burhān* where al-Zarkashī devotes the very next chapter after *ma'rifat asbāb al-nuzūl* to *ma'rifat munāsabāt*

---

(54) On the "plain meaning" of Scripture see especially Raphael Loewe, "The 'Plain' Meaning of Scripture in Early Jewish Exegesis," *Papers of the Institute of Jewish Studies London*, vol. i (1964), pp. 140-85.

(55) See also Ibn al-'Arabī, *Aḥkām al-Qur'ān* (Cairo, 1959), vol. i, pp. 449-50, especially "question three."

al-āyāt.[56] It is also to be noted that the relationship between this genre and that of *al-waqf wa'l-ibtidā'* is quite close also ; although the latter is often thought to be connected only to *tajwīd*, it is exegetical in intent and probably in origin.[57]

While it requires leaving the order of points as discussed by al-Suyūṭī, it seems sensible to deal with point five in answer to Question 1 now, for it too deals with the problem of specification and the *sabab* but from the other way around than the previous point. A verse may appear in its "plain meaning" to be specific or limited in its application but, in fact, when the *sabab* is taken into account, the true intent of the verse is revealed ; thus, the *sabab* acts to "reject the illusion of limitation."[58] The prime example of this proposition is a quote from al-Shāfi'ī found in both al-Suyūṭī and al-Zarkashī but not *in extenso* in any other text consulted.[59] The problem here revolves around Q. VI : 145, "Say : I do not find in what is revealed to me anything forbidden to one who eats it, except dead animals, blood poured out, pork — it is an abomination — or impure (meat) hallowed by (a name) other than God's." The difficulty here clearly is that, in fact, foods other than those mentioned in this list are known to be forbidden to people.[60] Abrogation of the verse would seem to be a logical answer but apparently not a popular one, although

(56) *Al-Burhān*, vol. i, pp. 35-52 ; *al-Itqān*, vol. iii, p. 323-38, *naw'* 62.

(57) For an example of this, see al-Anbārī, *Kitāb Īḍāḥ al-Waqf wa'l-Ibtidā'*, vol. ii, p. 778 (*ad.* Q. XXI : 95) and *cf.* A. Rippin "Qur'ān 21:95," *JSS*, XXIV (1979), pp. 43-53.

(58) *Al-Itqān*, vol. i, p. 84 ; also *al-Burhān*, vol. i, pp. 23-26, fifth point, but this includes much material included by al-Suyūṭī elsewhere, for example, see point two above.

(59) For example, al-Jassās, *Aḥkām al-Qur'ān* (Istanbul, A.H. 1335), vol. ii, pp. 16-17 ; al-Qurṭubī, *al-Jāmi' li-Aḥkām al-Qur'ān* (Cairo, 1935-36), vol. vii, p. 116, where the interpretation is credited to al-Shāfi'ī but the *sabab* is quoted in extremely short form.

(60) Makkī al-Qaysī, *al-Īḍāḥ li-Nāsikh al-Qur'ān wa-Mansūkhihī* (Riyad, 1976), pp. 249-50, suggests that meat of domestic donkeys, predatory animals having eyeteeth and birds with claws are forbidden by the Prophetic *sunnah*, thus forming additions to this list. Also see Ibn al-'Arabī, vol. ii, p. 756.

it does find minority mention in the exegetical tradition.[61] Al-Shāfi'ī's answer, however, was to say that the verse was revealed specifically about the unbelievers who "forbade what God permitted and permitted what God forbade"; the specific items listed in this verse were those things the unbelievers permitted of what God had forbidden. Thus the verse listed only the relevant items and "did not intend to permit other things beside them. The intention was to assert the forbidding, not assert the permitting."[62] Thus, while the verse would appear to limit the actual number of things forbidden, that limitation is rejected by consideration of the *sabab* which acts to establish the context of the verse in question.

It is evident that in the above example the *sabab* serves primarily an exegetical function by taking the Qur'ānic phraseology and elaborating it through narrative embellishment in order to remove the apparent intra-Qur'ānic conflict, and that the *sabab* does not simply act as an external verificant of time and place of revelation. This trend is actually developed by al-Suyūṭī's point four in answer to Question 1 where the explanation is given that the *sabab* serves to "explicate the meaning and eliminate ambiguity." Several quotes preface the actual examples of this aspect of the *sabab* function, all of which witness the importance of the *sabab* in explication of the meaning of a verse.[63] The Qur'ānic examples which al-Suyūṭī gives reveal, once again, that it is the "plain meaning" which seems to

(61) See for example, Makkī al-Qaysī, pp. 249-50. The reluctance to admit the verse as abrogated undoubtedly stems from the fact that the additional forbidden foods are found in the *sunnah* only (see note 60) and thus would require abrogation of the Qur'ān by the *sunnah*, a category generally discouraged although employed on numerous occasions in fact: see John Burton, *The Collection of the Qur'ān* (Cambridge, 1977), especially pp. 50-59.

(62) This interpretation is only one of many suggested for the verse in the exegetical sources : chronological considerations play a large part in al-Qurṭubī's discussions, *al-Jāmi'*, vol. vii, pp. 115-19; note also Ibn al-'Arabī, vol. ii, pp. 755-59; al-Jassās, vol. ii, pp. 16-23.

(63) *Al-Itqān*, vol. i, pp. 82-84; see *al-Burhān*, vol. i, pp. 22 and 27-29; al-Zarkashī's third and sixth points combine to form point four in al-Suyūṭī. Al-Suyūṭī quotes al-Wāḥidī, Ibn Daqīq and Ibn Taymīyah (see his *Muqaddimah*, p. 47) as authorities for his quotations.

contradict the generally accepted legal derivation connected with the verse and thus the *sabab* plays a role only slightly different from point five treated above.

An example given by al-Suyūṭī in dealing with this point is what he calls "the most difficult" example, in the case of Q. III : 188 : "Think not that those who rejoice in what they have brought...that they are in a place of security from the punishment."

> Marwān ibn al-Ḥakam used to say: "If everyone who rejoices in what he has brought and likes to be praised for what he has not done will be punished, then all of us will be punished," until Ibn 'Abbās explained that the verse was revealed about the *ahl al-Kitāb* when the Prophet asked them about something and they concealed (the answer) from him and told him something else. It appeared that they had told him what he had asked them and they asked to be praised for that.[64]

Once again, the *sabab* acts to correct misinterpretation, not by extensive historical detail of time and place of revelation but by exegetical explanation through specification of a narrative context.

Finally, point six in answer to Question 1 indicates another function of the *sabab*, "knowledge about whom the verse was revealed and identification of the ambiguous in it."[65] It is the haggadic function of the *sabab* which is alluded to here, the exegetical aspect that fills in the details especially in narrative passages. Only one example is given by al-Suyūṭī, that Marwān thought Q. XLVI : 17 was revealed about 'Abd al-Raḥmān ibn Abī Bakr until 'Ā'ishah corrected him on that score and told him of its correct *sabab* ; thus, 'Ā'ishah is pictured as stating that the *sabab* is the key to identification.[66] The methodological principle established, al-Suyūṭī does not even bother

---

(64) *Al-Itqān*, vol.i, p. 83 ; also *al-Burhān*, vol. i, p. 27 ; similar to reports in al-Bukhārī, *al-Ṣaḥīḥ*, vol. vi, pp. 73-74 ; Muslim, *al-Ṣaḥīḥ* (Cairo, A.H. 1390), vol. v, pp. 648-49, report 7 : also Aḥmad ibn Ḥanbal, *al-Musnad* (Cairo, A.H. 1313), vol. i, p. 298, bottom.

(65) *Al-Itqān*, vol. i, pp. 84-85 ; not in *al-Burhān* as a function of the *sabab*. This perhaps reflects al-Zarkashī's definition of *sabab* over-against al-Suyūṭī.

(66) See also al-Suyūṭī, *Lubāb*, p. 194.

to state the correct identification; he does, however, deal with the topic more extensively in a later chapter of *al-Itqān*.[67]

Considering al-Suyūṭī's presentation as a whole, it should be evident that he sees the halakic or legal function of the *sabab* as primary; specific and general aspects of wording are to be verified through the *sabab*. The *sabab* does, however, have other functions. Exegetical examples have been noted although they seem often to be close to the halakic specification role; the haggadic function of the *sabab* seems minor according to al-Suyūṭī's summary, although it is certainly manifested. Finally, the significance of point one in answer to Question 1 cannot be overlooked; the *sabab* acts in a historical-theological way, acting as the guarantor of the veracity of God's revelation to man and His concern for His creation; there is a polemical and theological value to the *sabab* over and above its exegetical role.

(67) *Al-Itqān*, vol. iv, pp. 58-101 (*naw*ʿ 69-71); also see *al-Burhān*, vol. i, pp. 155-63 (*naw*ʿ 6).

XIX

THE FUNCTION OF *ASBĀB AL-NUZŪL* IN QUR'ĀNIC EXEGESIS

In John Wansbrough's work, *Quranic studies: sources and methods of scriptural interpretation*, several theses are put forth regarding the material known as *asbāb al-nuzūl*, occasions of revelation; the overall view of Wansbrough is one which is derived (critically) from al-Suyūṭī,[1] which is that the *asbāb* material has its primary reference point in works devoted to deriving law from the text of the Qur'ān, that is, halakhic works. He suggests that the presence of *asbāb* material as found in a haggadic or narrative *tafsīr* such as that of Muqātil is 'accidental' because, while the narrative *asbāb* reports serve as anecdotes, they do not fulfil what Wansbrough sees as the 'essential function,' that of establishing 'a chronology of revelation'.[2]

The purpose of this study is to pursue a specialized investigation of this function of the *asbāb* in exegesis: to pose the fairly straightforward question of what are the *asbāb* narratives designed to accomplish? Are they providing history or exegesis? Is that exegesis haggadic or halakhic in character? The question is to be addressed both in terms of direct literary analysis of the narratives themselves and by looking at the use of the material within texts of exegesis. The questions to be posed in this vein are the following: why within the context of a work such as that of al-Ṭabarī is *asbāb al-nuzūl* material adduced? What is the exegete's purpose in doing so? What does he hope to accomplish by doing so? What does he do with the material after adducing it?

The framework of the investigation is limited to that of exegesis of the Qur'ān written by Sunnī authors in Arabic from the early (i.e., pre sixth-century *hijrī*) period primarily (although not exclusively), when the literary techniques of exegesis were fairly uncomplicated and uncluttered. The range of exegetical works surveyed includes the early narrative-haggadic types, those of Muqātil (d. 150/767), pseudo al-Kalbī (d. 146/763),[3] Sufyān al-Thawrī (d. 161/777), Mujāhid (d. 104/772), 'Abd al-Razzāq (d. 211/826), al-Ṭabarī (d. 310/922), and al-Wāḥidī (d. 468/1075), the legal-halakhic *aḥkām* works, those of Muqātil again, al-Jaṣṣāṣ (d. 370/981), Ibn al-'Arabī (d. 543/1148) and al-Qurṭubī (d. 671/1272), and the *naskh*-abrogation texts of al-Naḥḥās (d. 338/949), Hibat Allāh (d. 410/1019), al-Baghdādī (d. 429/1037) and Makkī al-Qaisī (d. 437/1045). The point of employing these three sub-genres of *tafsīr* for the investigation is simply because they have been suggested within the context of previous discussions of the role of *asbāb al-nuzūl* in exegesis primarily as found in both of Wansbrough's recent works, *Quranic studies* and *The sectarian milieu*, but also as indicated within the discussions of the topic by al-Zarkashī (d. 794/1391) and al-Suyūṭī (d. 911/1505). Once again, the purpose of using these texts is to focus on an essentially literary question: why is the *asbāb* material adduced within the context of these works? The results should provide an insight into the exegetical technique or method of literary interpretation employed by these exegetes.

Rather than go through all these texts looking for *asbāb* reports, the study places its primary focus upon another exegetical sub-genre, that called *asbāb al-nuzūl*, which is devoted to compiling these reports. Each time a report is cited in

[1] See Rippin, 'al-Zarkashī', 248–58.

[2] See Wansbrough, *Quranic studies*, 141–2, 177–85.

[3] The text in question here is *Tanwīr al-miqbās min tafsīr Ibn 'Abbas* referred to by Wansbrough as the *tafsīr* of the al-Kalbī and catalogued in that way in *GAL* and *GAS*; for further details and the argument that the text originated in the third or fourth century, see Rippin, 'al-Zuhrī', 23–24.

this literature as a *sabab* for a verse, the exegetical employment of that *sabab* has been checked within the *tafsīr* literature. The study was limited to *sūra* 2 which presented some 107 verses to be treated. *Sūra* 2 was selected because it contains a near ideal mix of Qur'ānic material, with extensive narrative, polemical, exhortative and legal material. Ibn al-ʻArabī, for example, treats over 80 verses out of the 286 in his *aḥkām* text; al-Naḥḥās discusses 30 verses in the context of *naskh*. This kind of representative selection of verses is important because essentially the final result of the study is statistical; the overall aim of the study is to see which purposes behind adducing the *asbāb* material predominate and which are subsidiary. While the precise proportions of the statistical result may well change somewhat if the entire Qur'ān were treated in the same way, *sūra* 2, being a representative cross-section of the whole, should produce fairly accurate results while at the same time not presenting the problem of prejudicing the whole issue by selective citation of verses which happen to be illustrative of certain traits preconceived to be crucial in the role of the *asbāb*.

Four *asbāb al-nuzūl* texts were employed in combination to act as the primary focus. The texts by al-Wāḥidī (d. 468/1075) and al-Suyūṭī (d. 911/1505) are famous and should need no further comment. The third text is by Muḥammad (or Aḥmad) ibn Asʻad al-ʻIrāqī who died in 567/1171 or perhaps 667/1268. Entitled *Asbāb al-nuzūl wa qiṣaṣ al-furqāniyya,* it is contained in the manuscript copy held by the Chester Beatty Library (no. 5199). The fourth text is found in the Berlin Staatsbibliothek, catalogue no. 3578, and is ascribed to al-Jaʻbarī; this ascription has been shown to be incorrect although no other likely writers have arisen to claim authorship. The manuscript itself was written in the year 709.[4]

The actual definition of a *sabab* is a matter which has already been treated in another paper [5] but it is worth emphasizing now that the term has definitely seen a measure of evolution over the years. Indeed, some of the reports studied would often be classified as *akhbār* rather than *asbāb,* as al-Suyūṭī himself argues against al-Wāḥidī. Suffice it to say here that al-Wāḥidī did consider such reports to be *asbāb al-nuzūl* and for this study that is the important point, since the aim is to try to see what the exegetes thought, not whether their categories and understandings conform to our own. Al-Waḥidī's conception of a *sabab* seems to revolve around the phrase *al-āya nazalat fī hādhā,* 'the verse was revealed about such and such' and the like; if a report contained the phrase, then it was *sabab*. Al-Suyūṭī disagreed.

One result of this study points to an essentially theological rather than literary result. On many occasions it seems that the *asbāb* reports are adduced by the commentators for no reason at all; they are cited and then ignored. Of course, for the informed readership of such works, the simple mention of the report may well summon up the related background discussion. But, additionally, such reports are cited in these instances, out of a general desire to historicize the text of the Qur'ān in order to be able to prove constantly that God really did reveal his book to humanity on earth; the material thereby acts as a witness to God's concern for His creation. Indeed al-Suyūṭī cites this as one of his understandings of the function of the *sabab* [6] and it seems to me to be quite true, and is a statement which underpins the entire phenomenon of the *sabab*. The *sabab* is the constant reminder of God and is the 'rope'—that being one of the understood meanings of *sabab* in the Qur'ān [7]—by which human

[4] On all of these *asbāb* texts, see Rippin, 'Exegetical genre', 4–7, 9–10.
[5] See Rippin, 'Exegetical genre', 12–15.
[6] See Rippin, 'al-Zarkashī', 250.
[7] See Rippin, 'Exegetical genre', 12–13.

contemplation of the Qur'ān may ascend to the highest levels even while dealing with mundane aspects of the text.

The major literary exegetical role that the *sabab* plays, however, is what could be called a ' haggadically exegetical ' function; regardless of the genre of exegesis in which the *sabab* is found, its function is to provide a narrative account in which the basic exegesis of the verse may be embodied. The standard interpretational techniques of incorporating glosses, masoretic clarification (e.g., with variants), narrative expansion and, most importantly, contextual definition predominate within the structure of the *sabab*.

Exegetical glosses provided with the narrative context of the *sabab* may be noted to occur quite frequently: as an example the following treatment of Q. 2: 44 may be cited. The verse reads: ' Do you order right conduct for the people but forget yourselves while reciting the scripture? Will you not understand? '

Al-Wāḥidī, al-Suyūṭī, and Berlin 3578, all give the same basic report regarding this verse: ' The verse was revealed about the Jews of Medina. A certain man had said to his son-in-law and to his relatives and to those with him (and among them were some who were in foster relationship with the Muslims): " Be upright in your religion and in what this man—meaning Muḥammad—orders you to do! Indeed his command is true? " So they had ordered the people to do that but they did not do it.' [8]

Embedded here is the gloss of the Qur'ānic *birr*, ' right conduct ' as the *sunna* of Muḥammad. Even the Jews, this *sabab* seems to be arguing, acknowledged the legitimacy of the *sunna*, that is, following the orders of Muḥammad, although, of course, in their hypocrisy they did not follow it. From the Muslim perspective, as reflected in the entire body of *tafsīr*, here was the evidence of the major sin of the Jewish rabbis, summed up in the term *kitmān*: the knowledge of the true status of Muḥammad while concealing that fact in order to mislead the entire community.

Closely aligned to the lexical content of the *sabab* is the concern for more literary matters, as in the resolution of ellipsis in Q. 2: 215: ' They are asking you: " What should they give? " Say: " Whatever you give of good, that is for parents, relatives, orphans, the poor and the followers of the way; whatever you do of good, God knows of it ".'

Al-Wāḥidī cites two reports for this verse, one of which is the following: ' It was revealed about 'Amr ibn al-Jumūḥ al-Anṣārī who was an old man and had a lot of money. He said: " What shall he [*sic*] give as alms [*bi mādhā yataṣaddaqu*] and to whom shall he give (it) [*'alā man yunfiqu*]." So this verse was revealed.' [9] The *sabab*, by employing the keywords of the Qur'ānic phraseology—*mādhā yunfiqūna*—but dividing them into the two parts, serves to make explicit what could be considered as rather elliptical Qur'ānic wording, where the question seems to be *what* to give but the reply more relevant to the question of to *whom* to give it.[10]

Disputes over masoretic matters such as variant readings have also left their

[8] Al-Wāḥidī, *Asbāb*, 22, report from al-Kalbī, also *Wajīz*, 12; al-Suyūṭī, *Lubāb*, 19; Berlin 3578, f. 5b, is slightly different: ' The Jews said to those from their families who had converted to Islām secretly: " Be upright in what you are in and do what he [Muḥammad] says, for it is the truth." So the verse was revealed.' Also see al-Qurṭubī, I, 365, who adds other reports, found nowhere else, concerning precisely what the Jewish rabbis said.

[9] Al-Wāḥidī, *Asbāb*, 60 and *Wajīz*, 57; Berlin 3578, f. 12b; al-'Irāqī, f. 4b, 'Amr asks about gifts for *jihād* and obedience; also al-Suyūṭī, *Lubāb*, 42, second report, 'Amr asks: ' What shall we give from our possession and where shall we put it? ' Al-Qurṭubī, III, 36, with 'Amr's words in the first person. Muqātil, *Tafsīr*, f. 24a, ' How much shall we give and to whom shall we give it? '

[10] That there appears to be no halakhic input in the *sabab* is apparent from Ibn al-'Arabī, I, 145–46, and al-Jaṣṣāṣ, I, 319–21, who do not cite the *sabab* but rather use only the appeal to the *sunna* to elaborate the non-compulsory nature of this alms-giving.

trace in the *asbāb* material. Q. 2: 119 provides a vivid example of this: 'Indeed we sent you with the truth as a bringer of good tidings and as a warner. You will not be questioned [*or* Do not ask] about the inhabitants of hell!'

As the translation indicates, two radically different interpretations of this verse can be suggested depending upon the reading of the text. The word in question تسئل is read according to the *qirā'āt* literature either in the first form passive *tus'alu* or in the first form imperative *tas'al.*[11] Accompanying these two readings are different *asbāb*, each apparently designed to explicate the appropriate meaning and thereby confirm a choice of textual reading.

In explanation of the reading *tus'alu*, the following *sabab* is cited: 'The prophet said: "If God would reveal his strength to the Jews, they would believe." So God revealed: "You will not be questioned about the inhabitants of hell!"', i.e., they are not your responsibility.[12] Second, to support *tas'al*, the following report is adduced: 'The prophet said one day: "If only I knew what happened to my parents!" So this verse was revealed "Do not ask about the inhabitants of hell!"'[13] Al-Wāḥidī and Berlin 3578 give both of these *asbāb.*[14]

Narrative expansion of a Qur'ānic verse is a more frequent feature in the *sabab*, ranging from the most simple setting of the scene to a full elaboration, spinning an entire narrative structure around a Qur'ānic verse. Often such elaborations revolve around polemical motifs—disputation over sectarian emblems, over the respective values of each religious tradition, over merits of prophets and scriptures, over *taḥrīf*, *kitmān* and hypocrisy. All these motifs, and many more, are familiar from Wansbrough's analysis of the *Sīra* literature[15] and may be illustrated here by the treatment of Q. 2: 130: 'Who could turn away from the religion of Abraham without his soul being foolish? Indeed, We choose him in the world, and in the hereafter he will be among the righteous.'

Al-Suyūṭī and Berlin 3578 quote a *sabab* for this verse, derived from Muqātil's *Tafsīr* (according to Berlin 3578). ''Abd Allāh ibn Salām called his brother's two sons, Salama and Muhājir, to Islam. He said to them: "You know that God said in the Torah: 'I am sending from among the children of Ishmael a prophet named Aḥmad. He who believes in him will be rightly guided and a true believer; he who does not believe in him will be cursed'." So Salama converted but Muhājir turned away. So God revealed . . . [2: 130].'[16]

Exegesis of the verse is provided here with Muhājir obviously representing the foolish one, and Salama the one who sticks with 'the religion of Abraham.' More important in the *sabab*, it would seem, is the continual motif of Jewish rejection of the alleged prognosis of Muḥammad/Aḥmad in the Torah—that being the Qur'ānic 'turning away' made equivalent here to *taḥrīf*/*kitmān*. The verse is elaborated in a narrative form constructed around standard polemical motifs. It might also be noted that we seem to have an aetiological narrative here: Salama, the one who is safe and Muhājir, the one who has left.

Other elaborations are not so much polemical as illustrative of the desire to create a good yarn: nowhere is this more apparent than in Q. 2: 260 and Abraham's questioning. This verse states: 'Indeed, Abraham said: "Lord show me how you gave life to the dead!" He said: "Do you not believe?" (Abraham)

[11] See e.g., al-Dānī, *al-Taisīr*, 76, *tas'al* is the reading of Nāfi', *tus'alu*, of all the others.

[12] Al-Qurṭubī, II, 92; also see al-Wāḥidī, *Wajīz*, 32, the only *sabab* there adduced.

[13] Al-Qurṭubī, II, 92–3; also al-Ṭabarī, II, 558–9, reports 1875–7; in report 1876, Muḥammad repeats the formula: 'If only I knew what happened to my parents', *layta shi'rī mā fa'ala abawai*, three times.

[14] Al-Wāḥidī, *Asbāb*, 36–7; Berlin 3578, f. 8a; al-Suyūṭī, *Lubāb*, 28, who gives only the one version about Muḥammad's parents, in two renditions, equalling al-Ṭabarī's reports 1876 and 1877; both reports al-Suyūṭī considers *mursal*, incomplete in *isnād*.

[15] See Wansbrough, *Sectarian milieu*, ch. i.

[16] Al-Suyūṭī, *Lubāb*, 29; Berlin 3578, ff. 8a–8b; Muqātil, *Tafsīr*, f. 22a.

said: " Why yes, but to satisfy my heart . . . ! " He said: " Take four birds, then turn them to you. Then put a part of them in each hill and call them and they will come to you swiftly. Know that God is powerful and wise! " '

For the curious mind, a reading of this verse will raise many questions; it certainly did for the classical exegetes. One major question was what was Abraham supposed to do with the birds? Was he supposed to kill them and cut them up and scatter them around? This is certainly the most popular explanation, although the verse says nothing about killing the birds. Perhaps he was just supposed to take whole birds to the various hills and they would fly back. But wherein is the test in that interpretation? Another question revolves around God's statement, ' Do you not believe? ' Did God not know whether Abraham believed? Another question, the one that the *asbāb al-nuzūl* information tries to answer, is why did Abraham ask the question to begin with? Why does Abraham need his heart to be satisfied? It is this situation to which God responds, sending down (*nuzūl!*) the instructions, because of Abraham's need or stimulus (*sabab!*).

A majority of the reports concerning Abraham's question revolves around his contemplation of the processes of nature; this situation brought the question to his mind.

> Qatāda said . . . Abraham came upon a dead animal which the sea and land creatures were distributing among themselves. So he said: ' Lord, show me how you bring life to the dead.' Al-Ḥasan, 'Aṭā' al-Khurasānī, al-Ḍaḥḥāk and Ibn Juraij said that it was a corpse of a donkey on the shore of the sea; 'Aṭā' said: the lake of Tiberias (i.e., the Sea of Galilee). They all said: (Abraham) saw it, the land and sea creatures devouring it. When the tide came in, the fish and the sea animals came and ate from it; what fell off it became a part of the water. When the tide went out, the beasts of prey came and ate it; what fell off it became a part of the land. When the beasts of prey left, the birds came and ate from it; what was dropped became part of the wind. When he saw that, Abraham was amazed at it and he said: 'Oh Lord, You know that it amazes us. Show me how You will bring life to it so I may see it with my own eyes.' [17]

Abraham's amazement leads him to question God, and God's response to him is as indicated in the Qur'ānic verse. Another version of the same basic report has Satan put the evil question into Abraham's mind after witnessing the same events: ' How can God gather together all these parts from all these bellies? ' This question apparently troubled Abraham's heart, so he asked God.[18]

The second major theme relates to Abraham's adventures with Nimrod; the account in al-Wāḥidī, credited to Ibn Isḥāq, is also found in similar form in al-Kisā'ī's *Qiṣaṣ al-anbiyā'*.

> When Abraham argued with Nimrod he said: ' (It is) my Lord who gives life and brings death.' (Q. 2: 258) So Nimrod said: ' I give life and bring death.' (Q. 2: 258) He then killed a man and set a man free and said: ' I brought death to the former and gave life to the latter.' Abraham said to him: ' God gives life by restoring the soul to a dead body.' So Nimrod said to him: ' Have you witnessed that of which you speak? ' He was not able to reply, ' Yes, I have seen it,' so he turned to a different proof. Then he asked

[17] Al-Wāḥidī, *Asbāb*, 79, first report; Berlin 3578, ff. 14b–15a, third report (another possible version: a dead man); Muqātil, *Tafsīr*, f. 44b, (donkey corpse); al-Ṭabarī, v, 485–6; al-Qurṭubī, III, 300, third report.

[18] Al-Wāḥidī, *Asbāb*, 79–80, second report; al-Wāḥidī's third report, p. 80, is a comment of 'Ikrima on the same subject but with no reference to Abraham.

> his Lord to show him giving life to the dead in order to settle his heart about the argument. So he (Abraham) informed him (Nimrod) of the witnessing and viewing (of the act of God).[19]

The reference in this story to the 'different proof' may well be Abraham's demand of Nimrod to make the sun rise from the west if he is so powerful (i.e., Q. 2: 258); this is an intermediate argument for the power of God which, according to this *sabab*, interrupts the flow of the overall argument between Nimrod and Abraham over life and death. The special quality of this *sabab* is its ability to continue the context of the Nimrod encounter from verse 258 onwards; while the first *sabab* develops in a minor way the theme of the donkey which God 'clothes with flesh' in verse 259, the overall Nimrod context is lost in that version. The Nimrod *sabab* is clearly an effort at continual haggadic narrative.

A third option also disregards the context of the passage but tries to explain Abraham's question:

> When God took Abraham as a friend, the messenger of death asked permission of his Lord to go to Abraham and tell him the good news of that. So he went and said: 'I come to you bringing you good news that God has taken you as a friend.' So he praised God and said: 'What is the sign of that?' He said: 'That God will answer your call and give life to the dead at your request.' Then he proceeded on his way and left. So Abraham said: 'Lord, show me how you gave life to the dead.' He said: 'Do you not believe?' He said: 'Why yes, but in order to set my heart at ease by knowledge that you answer when I call and give me what I ask for and that you have taken me as a friend.'[20]

This *sabab*, rather cleverly, turns the focus to God: that it was God who put the whole matter to Abraham to begin with. This *sabab* illustrates clearly what is implicit in all the other accounts as well: that Abraham could not possibly have had any doubts in his faith and that the reason for his question was totally innocent. Theological motivation colours the *asbāb* material in this, as in other instances, but the main concern is for a good story and, in some cases, the narrative context.

The notion of *ta'yīn al-mubham*, identification of the unknown, is, of course, closely related to narrative expansion as well, and is most obviously seen in examples where identification is made of the Qur'ānic 'they' which is so frequently left ambiguous in the text, as in, for example, Q. 2: 116: 'They say: "God has taken a son; glory be to him!" Rather, to Him is what is in the heavens and the earth, each obeying Him.'

Al-Wāḥidī and Berlin 3578 each provide reports for this verse which function to explicate who the 'they' of 'they say' are: 'It was revealed concerning the Jews when they said 'Uzair is the son of God and concerning the Christians of Najrān when they said the Messiah is the son of God and concerning the polytheists among the Arabs who said the angels are the daughters of God.'[21] As Blachère has stated, the 'horror of the uncertain' is the prime motivation in haggadic exegesis,[22] and the *sabab* seems to be a particu-

[19] Al-Wāḥidī, *Asbāb*, 80, fourth report; al-Kisā'ī, 134–5; Berlin 3578, f. 14b, second report; al-Ṭabarī, v, 487; al-Qurṭubī, III, 300, second report.

[20] Al-Wāḥidī, *Asbāb*, 80–1, fifth report; Berlin 3578, f. 14b, first report, the angel named as 'Izrā'īl; al-Qurṭubī, III, 300, first report; al-Ṭabarī, v, 487–9.

[21] Al-Wāḥidī, *Asbāb*, 36 and *Wajīz*, 31; Berlin 3578, f. 8a.

[22] R. Blachère, *Introduction au Coran* (2nd ed., Paris, 1977), 233, cited in Nwyia, 61–4.

larly favoured and appropriate literary form in which to incorporate such information and thereby quiet restless minds.

It is this kind of interpretation of the motivation behind the citation of the *sabab* which would also seem to explain best the resolution of metaphorical language by means of the *sabab*, which is displayed most clearly in Q. 2: 19–20: 'Or (it is) like rain from the sky in which is darkness and thunder and lightning. They put their fingers in their ears because of the thunder-claps as protection from death. But God encircles the unbelievers. The lightning almost takes away their sight; whenever it gives them light, they walk in it. But when it darkens on them, they stand still. If God wished He would take away their hearing and their sight. Indeed God has power over everything.'

Al-Suyūṭī is alone among *asbāb* authors in bringing forth a *sabab* for this verse, and a very extensive one at that; the report is derived from al-Ṭabarī's *Tafsīr*.

> Two men of the Medinan hypocrites were fleeing from the prophet to the polytheists when this rain [*maṭar*] which God mentioned befell them, and in it was loud thunder and thunder-claps and lighting. Every time the thunder-claps befell them, it made both of them put their fingers in their ears out of fear [*faraq*] that the thunder-clap would enter their ears [*masāmi'*] and kill them [*taqtuluhumā*]. When the lightning flashed they walked in its light and when it did not they stood in their place, not walking. They began saying: 'If only we had begun by going to Muḥammad and putting our hands in his [i.e., converting].' So they arose and went out and converted to Islam, putting their hands in his. Their conversion was good. So God made the affair of these two fleeing hypocrites into an extended simile [*mathal*] applicable to the hypocrites of Medina.

From here the report goes on to explain the application of this story as a simile:

> When the hypocrites were present at the assembly of the prophet, they put their fingers in their ears out of fear of the speech of the prophet concerning something that was revealed about them or they were reminded of something; so they were killed. (That is) just like those two fleeing hypocrites who put their fingers in their ears. And (the Qur'ānic statement) 'Whenever it gives them light, they walk in it,' when their property and children increase and they gain booty or win battles. They walk in it and they say: 'Indeed Muḥammad's religion is true for this time' and they stick to it, just as those two hypocrites walked when the lightning gave them light. And (the Qur'ānic statement) 'But when it darkens, they stand still,' when their property and children are destroyed and misfortune befalls them, they say: 'This is because of the religion of Muḥammad' and they fall back into their disbelief, just as those two hypocrites stood when the lightning darkened for them.[23]

Now this *sabab* accomplishes a number of things, very prominently the function of incorporating glosses. But probably most significantly, the *sabab* acts to concretize the simile in human events. As the second half of al-Suyūṭī's report explains, the verse is normally taken as a simile, the second one in a row after the explicit mention of *mathal* in verse 17, with the resolution of the

[23] Al-Suyūṭī, *Lubāb*, 18; also al-Ṭabarī, I, 347–8, report 452 although there are minor differences between the two accounts especially towards the end; there would also appear to be a number of editing or typographical errors in al-Suyūṭī's report which I have corrected by reference to al-Ṭabarī.

vocabulary being rain = the Qur'ān, darkness = the disbelievers and so forth. But the *sabab* provides an intermediary stage in the interpretation of the terms of the simile. In fact the *sabab* would seem to suggest that an exemplum may be extracted directly from the wording of the text rather than being taken on a symbolic level. The underlying desire is to read the text as literally as possible. This *sabab* then would seem to be grounded in the basic haggadic notion of removing any ambiguity and at the same time of generating a story for repetition and (edifying) entertainment.

Creating a story not only satisfies a haggadic impulse (along with providing opportunities for lexical and masoretic elaboration) but also performs a basic exegetical function of providing an authoritative interpretational context and determining the limits of each narrative pericope. It has often been remarked that the Qur'ān lacks an overall cohesive structure (albeit that in that very fact may well lie the text's special literary power) and does not provide within itself many keys for interpretation. One of the very basic problems is that it is often impossible to tell where one theme or pericope ends and the next one begins. This has been noted above with regards to Q. 2: 260 but it is most clearly indicated in the exegetical flurries in the form of *asbāb* reports that alight around Q. 2: 113–121. The questions posed by the exegetes are: is this one section? Does the one section have the same referent (be it Jews, Christians or pagans)? Those who wish to make legal deductions from Q. 2: 115 are forced to break up the section and see the referent of the passage as varying; others, from the opposing camp, attempt to maintain one narrative context throughout and downplay any legal implications (or see such as an additional 'level' in the reading). The *sabab* plays a central role in supporting exegetical decisions regarding the establishment of context; note, however, the *asbāb* information is frequently far too varied and flexible to allow decisions to be based primarily upon it—rather, the exegete clearly makes the decision on the interpretation and supports it *ex post facto* with the appropriate *sabab*. What does occur, however, is that narratives are adduced, for example, concerning Jewish–Christian disputation in front of Muḥammad, and each verse from Q. 2: 113 through 121 is seen as a response to this disputation by means of the *sabab*.

The reverse situation to this establishing of a context may occur, where a *sabab* is cited in order to defeat the seeming context. An example occurs in Q. 2: 280: 'If he [the debtor] is in difficulty, then (grant him) a delay until (it is) easy (for him). If you give charity, (it is) better for you, if only you knew.'

Only one *sabab* is found for this verse; the report continues the saga of Banū 'Amr and Banū'l-Mughīra as related in the *asbāb* material for verse 278.[24] It is Muqātil who makes the matter clear:[25] verses 278 and 279 are the response which Muḥammad sent to 'Attāb concerning the situation of the usury. As a result, the following *sabab* arises for verse 280. 'Banū 'Amr ibn 'Umair said to Banū'l-Mughīra: "Give us the principal and we will give you the interest." Banū'l-Mughīra said: "We are in difficulty today; let us delay until the dates ripen." They refused to postpone (it) for them. So God revealed . . . [2: 280]'[26]

So Banū 'Amr, it would seem, agreed to forget the interest (in response to verse 278) but still wanted their principal (*ru'ūs amwālihim*) which now Banū'l-Mughīra decided they could not repay.

Implicit in this *sabab*, and that would seem to be the point, is that the verse

[24] Al-Suyūṭī, *Lubāb*, 50, first report; similar reports are found in al-Wāḥidī, *Asbāb*, 87, first report; Berlin 3578, f. 16a, third report; al-Qurṭubī, III, 363.

[25] Muqātil, *Tafsīr*, ff. 47a–47b.

[26] Al-Wāḥidī, *Asbāb*, 88; Berlin 3578, f. 16a; al-Qurṭubī, III, 371; also see Ibn al-'Arabī, I, 245; al-Jaṣṣāṣ, I, 473.

refers not to the repayment of usury—which after all, would appear to have been the topic of the pericope—but rather, to the repayment of all debts. The contrary view was argued by some; several reports are found in al-Ṭabarī to the effect that the verse was revealed specifically about usury.[27] But, as al-Naḥḥās points out,[28] that makes little sense since usury has already been forbidden; a gloss in al-Ṭabarī of ' until (it is) easy ' as ' death ' is probably an attempt at maintaining the usury interpretation while recognizing the illegality of the situation to begin with.[29]

An extension of this haggadic notion in the role of the *sabab* is to be detected in a seeming halakhic context as well, that of providing the Jāhilī background to verses of apparent legal intent. Such *asbāb* reports do not, in general at least, function to provide a context from which legal deductions can be made; rather they answer the naturally curious (haggadic) question of why does the Qur'ān say to do (or not to do) such-and-such a thing? Why would anyone have done it (e.g., enter their houses from the rear as in Q. 2: 189b) anyway? Numerous examples of this occur, as for example in the just cited Q. 2: 189b: ' It is not piety to enter houses from their rear. But piety is the fear of God and entering houses by their doors. Fear God, perhaps you will prosper.'

There is a total agreement among the exegetes, in one sense at least, that this verse was revealed about people who did not enter their houses through the door but rather through the rear when they were in the state of *iḥrām*. Several of the *asbāb* reports state precisely no more than that and then imply that this verse was revealed in order to remove any sanction for the necessity of such a practice.[30]

A larger series of *asbāb* reports concerned with this verse, however, is found concerning the practices of the pre-Islamic group, the Ḥums. It has been pointed out especially by Wansbrough[31] that the type of information found concerning the Ḥums (and other similar pre-Islamic groups) is totally exegetical: what has been ' preserved ' is only what is relevant to understanding the Qur'ān and *ḥadīth*. This is certainly true for any details concerning the Ḥums and entering houses in *iḥrām*, and it is a notion which is only emphasized by the discovery that, in fact, contradictory information is preserved concerning the Ḥums and this activity: they either did or did not enter their houses from the rear, depending on the report. A typical narrative is the following from al-Suyūṭī: ' The Quraysh were called the Ḥums and they used to enter their houses in *iḥrām* while the Anṣār and the rest of the Arabs did not enter by the door in *iḥrām*. While the prophet was in a garden, he went out of the door and Quṭba ibn 'Āmir al-Anṣārī went out with him. They said: " Oh prophet, Quṭba is an immoral man; he has gone out of the door with you." (The prophet) said to him: " What prompted you to do this? " He said: " I saw you doing it, so I did as you did." (The prophet) said: " I am of the Ḥums," to which he responded: " My religion is your religion! " So God revealed . . . [2: 189b] '[32]

But precisely the opposite point is made in some sources; one such report is found in al-'Irāqī, al-Ṭabarī and, most explicitly, al-Azraqī (d. about 220/835) as found in Guillaume's translation of the *Sīra:* ' If one of (the Ḥums) before

[27] e.g., al-Ṭabarī, VI, 30, reports 6277, 6279.
[28] Al-Naḥḥās, 83–4; also al-Jaṣṣāṣ, I, 473.
[29] Al-Ṭabarī, VI, 32, report 6288.
[30] Al-Bukhārī, *Al-ṣaḥiḥ, kitāb al-tafsīr*, VI, 30; al-Wāḥidī, *Asbāb*, 48, first report and *Wajīz*, 50; al-Suyūṭī, *Lubāb*, 36, first report and third report; Berlin 3578, f. 10b, first report; al-Ṭabarī, III, 556–60, reports 3075, 3076, 3080, 3084, 3088; Ibn al-'Arabī, I, 100–1 but somewhat more extensive; al-Jaṣṣāṣ, I, 256.
[31] See *Quranic studies*, 16–17.
[32] Al-Suyūṭī, *Lubāb*, 36, second report; al-Wāḥidī, *Asbāb*, 48, second report; Berlin 3478, f. 10b, second report; al-Ṭabarī, III, 559–60, report 3087; Muqātil, *Tafsīr*, ff. 29a–29b; al-Qurṭubī, II, 345.

and at the beginning of Islām was in *iḥrām* and was one of the house dwellers, i.e., living in houses or villages, he would dig a hole at the back of his house and go in and out by it and not enter by the door . . . The year of Ḥudaibiya the prophet entered his house. One of the Anṣār was with him and he stopped at the door, explaining that he was one of the Ḥums. The prophet said: " I am one of the Ḥums too. My religion and your religion are the same," so the Anṣārī went into the house by the door as he saw the prophet do.' [33]

Exegetically, whether the Ḥums did or did not enter the doors matters very little of course; the point of the *sabab* is clearly to answer that perpetual question of why: why does the Qur'ān mention such a thing as how to enter one's house, a notion probably quite foreign to those involved in the development of the exegetical tradition? The *sabab*, once again, responds to the basic haggadic impulse.

This adducing of the Jāhilī ' foil ' or background is, in my estimation, one of the most significant element of the *asbāb* reports. Provided in these reports is an implicit evaluation of the Islamic dispensation; it is saying: ' this is how things were before Islam but now Islam has arrived and things have improved substantially.' It is to be noted that it is through the complementary notion of the Abrahamic legacy of Islam that this hermeneutical device is able to function almost perfectly. What is carried over from the pagan age is then to be contrasted either positively (in the case of the Abrahamic legacy) or negatively (in the case of the Jāhilī foil) with the provisions of the Islamic dispensation.

There is implicit in this adducing of the Jāhilī foil another at least potential function; this is made most explicit, as it happens, by Maimonides in his treatment of the Jewish law. One reason which Maimonides brings forth to provide an explanation of the legal regulations in Judaism (over and above their rational worth) is that they serve to protect the Jews from foreign (i.e., pagan) influence and thereby produce a positive group identity; ' You will know from texts of the *Torah* figuring in a number of passages that the first intention of the Law as a whole is to put an end to idolatry, to wipe out its traces and all that is bound up with it, even its memory as well as all that leads to any of its works—as, for instance, *familiar spirits,* or as a *wizard . . .*'.[34]

Only by detailing pagan practice can the accomplishment and the protection implicit in Jewish law by rationally perceived. ' As for the prohibition against eating *meat* [*boiled*] *in milk,* it is in my opinion not improbable that in addition to this being undoubtedly very gross food and very filling—*idolatry* had something to do with it. Perhaps such food was eaten at one of the ceremonies of their cult or at one of their festivals. . . . According to me this is the most probable view regarding the reason for this prohibition.' [35]

Maimonides, of course, faced problems when he had to deal with an obvious continuation of pagan practice in Judaism, most especially with sacrifice; his only rationale was that sacrifice as a religious rite was too popular to be immediately abolished although eventually it too would be declared a part of the pagan heritage (as indeed it became with the destruction of the Temple). Maimonides did not have available to him the exegetical tool with which Muslims were able to approach their legal structure, that of the Islamic–Abrahamic heritage that could be postulated for a continued pagan practice under the new dispensation. Muslims did then face the problem of determining

[33] A. Guillaume, *The life of Muhammad,* 89, somewhat modified; al-'Irāqī, f. 3b; al-Ṭabarī, III, 559, report 3085; also see W. M. Watt, ' Ḥums ', *EI* (2nd ed.), III, 576–7.

[34] Maimonides, *Guide,* III, 29, p. 517; the basic point was made in pre-Islamic times as well, e.g., in the *Letter of Aristeas.*

[35] Maimonides, *Guide,* III, 48, p. 599; also see Menahem Haran, ' Seething a kid in its mother's milk ', *Journal of Jewish Studies,* XXX, 1979, 23–5.

exactly what was Abrahamic and what was not, however, and this problem is nowhere more clearly illustrated than in the various traces of totally opposing opinions which are recorded in the *asbāb* information, as, for example, in Q. 2: 158.[36] Still, the basic point remains that the production of a Jāhilī background provides a measure by which Islam is evaluated and provides evidence of the protection and of the sense of identity which Islam entails.

Within this notion of the Jāhilī background it is to be observed quite frequently that there is a flexibility in the identity of the Jāhilī opponents; both Jews and pagans may perform the function, for example, as in Q. 2: 26. This would seem to indicate a mixing of apologetical (i.e., as implied in the 'evolution' of Islam away from paganism in the Jāhiliyya) and polemical (i.e., *taḥrīf* on the part of the Jews in haggadic-narrative expansion) concerns and in no way can this really be seen to affect the understanding of the basic purpose of such exegesis. Q. 2: 26 states: 'Indeed God is not ashamed to form a simile from the gnat or something higher. Those who believe, they know that it is the truth from their Lord; but those who disbelieve say: 'What does God mean by this parable?"'

A number of *asbāb* reports are found for this verse in al-Suyūṭī, al-Wāḥidī and Berlin 3578, all of which basically tell the same story: extended similes included in the Qur'ān were ridiculed by Muḥammad's opponents and this verse was revealed as a rebuttal. There is, however, debate over exactly which parables were being ridiculed and exactly who the ridiculing opponents were.

Two choices are presented for which similes are intended; the first makes reference to the two examples previously cited in the *sūra:* the man who kindled the fire in 2: 17 and the rain from the sky in 2: 19. This solution pays attention to the context and canonical order of the scripture.[37] The alternate choice seems more concerned to do justice to the Qur'ānic phrase *mā ba'ūḍa fa mā fauqahā,* 'from the gnat or something higher'; cited are the extended similes of the *dhubāb 'fly',* in Q. 22: 73 and the *'ankabūt* 'spider', in Q. 29: 41.[38] *Ba'ūḍa* is frequently glossed by exegetes as simply something weak or small;[39] *dhubāb* as 'fly' certainly fits that category, just as *'ankabūt,* spider, fits *fauqahā,* the fly being the favourite food of the spider. The intention of this choice of similes seems exegetical.

The question of which opponents of Muḥammad ridiculed him about these extended similes is, it seems, related to the choice of similes as well. One possible opponent group was the Jews and they are always pictured as ridiculing the fly and spider similes by laughing and saying that such talk 'does not resemble the speech of God' or asking rhetorically, 'Is this supposed to resemble the speech of God?', a gloss of the Qur'ānic 'What does God mean by this simile?' The dispute is plainly polemical, over the respective merits of Jewish and Muslim revelation, and does not touch on the meaning of the simile.[40] The other group of opponents to Muḥammad, the polytheists, makes exactly the same accusation against the Qur'ān and these extended similes in other versions of the

[36] See al-Wāḥidī, *Asbāb,* 42, fourth report and in basic thrust, *Wajīz,* 41, but cf. al-Wāḥidī, *Asbāb,* 41, second report; Muqātil, *Khams mi'at āya,* 90, where the tradition is connected to the practice of the Ḥums.

[37] Al-Wāḥidī, *Asbāb,* 21, first report; al-Suyūṭī, *Lubāb,* 18–19, first report; Berlin 3578, f. 5b., second report; al-Ṭabarī, I, 398, the same as al-Wāḥidī's report.

[38] Al-Wāḥidī, *Asbāb,* 21–2, second and third report; al-Suyūṭī, *Lubāb,* 19, second, third and fourth reports (from 'Abd al-Razzāq in whose *tafsīr* the report would seem not to be found, although there are numerous large water-stains at the beginning of the manuscript making reading difficult); Berlin 3578, f. 5b., first report; al-Ṭabarī, I, 400; Muqātil, *Tafsīr,* f. 7a.

[39] e.g., al-Ṭabarī, I, 401, 402.

[40] Al-Wāḥidī, *Asbāb,* 21, second report; Berlin 3578, f. 5b., first report; Muqātil, *Tafsīr,* f. 7a; al-Qurṭubī, I, 242.

sabab; this once again demonstrates the interchangeability of these two groups in the accounts of the life of Muḥammad.[41]

That considerations of Qur'ānic context play a role in selecting the examples of similes as being 2: 17 and 2: 19 is confirmed by the fact that it is always the 'hypocrites' who are pictured as confronting Muḥammad about these specific similes and verses. 'God is above making such similes,' the hypocrites are given to say.[42] This would seem to go back to an understanding that verses 7 to 21 of *sūra* 2 were revealed specifically about the hypocrites. Reading scripture in its canonical order and giving consideration to the connexion between various pericopes—that is, paying attention to the context—provides the exegetical impulse for the citation of such *asbāb* reports. It is to be noted that al-Ṭabarī, and following him al-Suyūṭī, argues precisely this point, thus giving support to this version of the *sabab.*[43] As well, al-Suyūṭī considers the mention of the polytheists inappropriate in connexion with this verse 'because it is Medinan' (!);[44] the introduction of the Jews into al-Wāḥidī's text he seems to consider a textual error, for he modifies the report which he cites from al-Wāḥidī to make it read 'polytheists' and seems to be able conveniently to ignore the multiplicity of reports in other works which leave little doubt that al-Wāḥidī did intend to cite the Jews in the passage.[45]

Now all the above cited functions of the *sabab* are interrelated in their basic haggadic nature and, indeed, this, I would argue, seems to be the predominant aspect in all *asbāb* reports. It would, however, be totally incorrect to gloss over the situations where quite clearly the *asbāb* do have halakhic value as argued by Wansbrough and by Muslim scholars although, even there, whether the chronological aspect is primary in the material here studied, as has been the general assumption, would seem to be quite doubtful.

Halakhic *asbāb* material can function in a number of ways. Frequently a *sabab* will provide an appropriate context in which a halakhic meaning may be extracted from the verse: this happens most prominently in Q. 2: 115 where the incredible multiplicity of material illustrates the point well that the legal meaning to be taken from the verse can be created or destroyed by the *asbāb* material. Q. 2: 115 reads: 'To God belong the east and the west; wherever you turn, the face of God is there. Indeed, God is omnipresent, all-knowing.'

One thing unites all the *asbāb* reports adduced for this verse; virtually all of the material is constructed such that the verse is *not* to be included as a part of the *qibla* controversy. Approximately ten different major themes are found in the *asbāb* material each of which suggests a totally different intention behind the verse. Some leave the verse halakhically relevant only in a partial way; this is found in a report which suggests this verse is a continuation of Q. 2: 114 which concerns the destruction of mosques and thus that this verse, 115, intends that the destruction of mosques does not mean that one can no longer face a *qibla.*[46] Here, narrative context is the important factor, as suggested previously.

[41] Al-Wāḥidī, *Asbāb*, 21–2, third report; al-Suyūṭī, *Lubāb*, 19, second and third reports; al-Ṭabarī, I, 400; al-Qurṭubi, I, 235.

[42] Al-Wāḥidī, *Asbāb*, 21, first report; al-Suyūṭī, *Lubāb*, 18, first report; Berlin 3578, f. 5b, second report; al-Ṭabarī, I, 398; al-Qurṭubi, I, 241–2.

[43] Al-Ṭabarī, I, 400; al-Suyūṭī, *Lubāb*, 19. On the 13 verses of *sūra* 2 as revealed about the hypocrites, see e.g. al-Wāḥidī, *Asbāb*, 19; al-Suyūṭī, *Lubāb*, 17; Berlin 3578, f. 5a; Sufyān al-Thawrī, 41.

[44] *Lubāb*, 19.

[45] *Lubāb*, 19; compare al-Wāḥidī, *Wasīṭ*, f. 17b and *Wajīz*, 8, where the Jewish report concerning the parables of the fly and spider is cited. Note that in the order of presentation this is al-Wāḥidī's second report of three in *Asbāb*, yet apparently it is his preferred one; see also Muqātil, *Tafsīr*, f. 7a and note that pseudo al-Kalbī, 5, glosses the party as the Jews.

[46] Al-Qurṭubī, II, 83.

Another series of reports concerns the Najāshī, named Aṣḥama or Aḍḥama ibn Abḥar and Muḥammad's call for a prayer for him. The simplest report is found always attributed to Qatāda: 'The prophet said: " Indeed our brother the Najāshī has died, so pray for him! " They said: " Should we pray for a man who was not a Muslim?! " So, " Among the people of the book are some who believe in God and what has been revealed to you and what has been revealed to them, humbling themselves to God " [Q. 3: 199] was revealed. So they said: " But he did not pray toward the *qibla*." So God revealed . . . [2: 115].'[47]

A variant on this, found only in al-Wāḥidī and Berlin 3578 [48] and attributed to 'Aṭā', adds the idea of Gabriel communicating the death to Muḥammad, removes the revelation of 3: 199 and makes explicit that the Najāshī had prayed always to Jerusalem and had not been informed of the change of *qibla* to the Ka'ba.[49]

Significant in these reports is the use of *qibla* as a sectarian emblem. The Najāshī is not a Muslim, the claim is, purely because he did not pray to the correct *qibla*. The overall impact of this report could perhaps be best classified as haggadic elaboration of a polemical motif.

But most important without a doubt are two series of reports which give the verse a definite legal content, but, interestingly enough, make two radically different legal points, each justified by its own *asbāb* material. One series of reports is structured with the following elements: (1) travelling either with or without the prophet; (2) the travellers stop at the time for prayer; (3) it is cloudy, dark or foggy and the *qibla* cannot be determined; (4) everyone prays towards the direction he thinks best; (5) next morning the error becomes clear; (6) the prophet is asked about it, the verse is revealed.[50]

The elaborations evidenced in these reports all make more plain the halakhic point of the anecdote: that prayer was legally valid, if, out of ignorance, the *qibla* was not faced. This was the generally accepted ruling among the *madhāhib*, according to al-Qurṭubī, the exceptions being al-Shāfi'ī and al-Mughīra who considered the *qibla* a *sharṭ*, i.e., a part of the obligation of prayer.[51] Thus this *sabab* is halakhically relevant and, by establishing the appropriate context for interpretation, it serves to pose the halakhic problem for which the answer is given by scripture; that is, the problem of an undeterminable *qibla* is posed and, through the interpretational means of a *sabab*, a passage of the Qur'ān is seen to be relevant.

This being the case, one can only express a certain amount of surprise at finding an alternate series of *asbāb* for the verse with its own halakhic point to make, the legal implications of which are generally accepted in combination with those of the previous *sabab*. The basic *sabab* is terse but manages to pose

[47] Al-Ṭabarī, II, 532–3. Also see al-Qurṭubī, II, 81; Ibn al-'Arabī, I, 35; al-Suyūṭī, *Lubāb*, 27, seventh report taken from al-Ṭabarī. The report is also found in *ḥadīth* literature, but not connected to the scriptural verse: see A. J. Wensinck, *A handbook of early muhammadan tradition* (Leiden, 1960), 175, ' Nadjāshī '. Also see Ibn Isḥāq, *Sīra*, I, 341.

[48] Al-Wāḥidī, *Asbāb*, pp. 35–36, fourth report; Berlin 3578, , ff. 7b–8a, second report. Cf. al-Ṭabarī's understanding, II, 532 that the Najāshī had not known a *qibla* at all.

[49] Cf. al-Ṭabarī, *Annales* (Leiden, 1879–1901), I, 1473 (as cited in A. Guillaume, *The life of Muhammad*, 658–9) for the death of Khusro and Muḥammad's knowledge of it at the same time as that king's death; also Ibn Sa'd, *Ṭabaqāt*, II, 24–5, the king dies at the same time that a delegation from Persia arrives.

[50] Al-Jaṣṣāṣ, I, 62, four parallel reports; Ibn al-'Arabī, I, 34, his fourth opinion; al-Qurṭubī, II, 79–80, first opinion, two reports; al-Ṭabarī, II, 531–2, reports 1841–43, the most frequent reports from Ibn Rabī'a rejected as weak; al-Wāḥidī, *Asbāb*, 34–5, first two reports and *Wajīz*, 31; al-Suyūṭī, *Lubāb*, 26–7, fourth, fifth and sixth reports, the sixth report is attributed to al-Kalbī but is much more elaborate than that found in the printed pseudo al-Kalbī text; Berlin 3578, f. 7b, first report.

[51] Al-Qurṭubī, II, 80; cf. Ibn al-'Arabī, I, 35, who gives the dissenting opinions as the Mu'tazila and al-Shāfi'ī.

the problem of what to do if one is riding a camel at prayer-time—is it necessary to dismount or may one ride and pray in the direction the camel is facing?

Many different variant reports are found but the following from *al-Ṣaḥīḥ* of Muslim [52] are typical:

(*a*) from Ibn 'Umar: 'The prophet used to pray the *witr* prayer on his camel.'

(*b*) from Sa'īd ibn Yasār: 'I was travelling with Ibn 'Umar on the road to Mecca. When I feared morning (was approaching), I dismounted and prayed the *witr* prayer and then caught up with him. Ibn 'Umar said to me: "Where have you been?" I said to him: "I feared dawn (was approaching) so I dismounted and prayed the *witr* prayer." So 'Abd Allāh (ibn 'Umar) said: "Is there not in the prophet an example [*uswa*] for you?" I said: "Indeed, there is by God!" He said: "Indeed, the prophet prayed the *witr* prayer on his camel."'

(*c*) from Sālim ibn 'Abd Allāh: 'The prophet used to pray supererogatory prayers on his camel toward whichever direction it faced and he prayed the *witr* prayer on it, although he did not pray the prescribed prayers on it.'

(*d*) from Ibn 'Umar: 'The prophet used to pray while going from Mecca to Medina on his camel in whatever direction it pointed. He said "Concerning this was revealed . . ." [Q. 2: 115].'

The *sabab* is used to support the notion that supererogatory prayers may be said while riding, regardless of the direction faced.[53] Al-Qurṭubī also uses the verse as an occasion to deal with an analogous situation of those who are sick and being carried.[54] Al-Ṭabarī also considers this verse as related to the 'prayer of fear', normally attached to Q. 2: 239 and 4: 101–4.[55]

A second way in which the *asbāb* material functions to produce halakhic relevance for the verse is by providing an example of the application of a law as found within the Qur'ān; an example here is Q. 2: 232: 'When you divorce the women and they reach their term, do not prevent them from marrying their husbands if they come to terms between themselves honourably. That is the preaching to those among you who believe in God and the last day. That is cleaner and purer for you. God knows and you do not know.'

The *asbāb* material for this verse divides between specification of two people who tried to prevent the marriage of a woman under their care. The most popular identification is presented in three different versions by al-Wāḥidī as well as being cited by al-Suyūṭī and Berlin 3578. 'Ma'qil ibn Yasār narrated: I had given my sister in marriage to a man. He divorced her, then, when her waiting-period was over, he came to propose to her. I said to him: "I let you marry, I supported you and honoured you, then you divorced her. Now you come to propose to her. No, by God, you may never return!" He narrated: The man had no objection and the woman wished to return to him. So God revealed

[52] Muslim, *Al-ṣaḥīḥ*, II, 350–3, reports 26–34. This topic of the 'travel prayer' is a complex one, extensively treated in Muslim legal literature. Many different types of 'travel prayer' are known, each varying according to the conditions in which it is performed. The selections given here from Muslim does not even scratch the surface of the available material. I would like to thank Dr. J. Burton for drawing this fact to my attention.

[53] Al-Qurṭubī, II, 80; Ibn al-'Arabī, I, 35, his third opinion, 'sound'; al-Jaṣṣāṣ, I, 63, sixth opinion, little legal derivation; al-Ṭabarī, II, 530, two reports from Ibn 'Umar. The *sabab* also appears in: al-Wāḥidī, *Asbāb*, 35, third report attributed specifically to *madhhab Ibn 'Umar;* al-Suyūṭī, *Lubāb*, 26, first report; briefly, Berlin 3578, f. 8a, third report. It is to be noted that not all schools of law agreed on the exact restrictions on the practice. See e.g., al-Qurṭubī, II, 81.

[54] Al-Qurṭubī, II, 80–1; see Wansbrough, *Quranic studies*, 167–9, on *'illa/qiyās* as halakhic deduction.

[55] Al-Ṭabarī, II, 530; also al-Qurṭubī, II, 80. See e.g., Muslim, *Al-ṣaḥiḥ*, II, 489–94, reports 297–305, for 'prayer of fear' (i.e., when in fear of being attacked) but note no Qur'ānic prop. Note that al-Wāḥidī, *Asbāb*, quotes no occasion for Q. 2:239.

this verse. I then said: "Now I will do it, oh prophet!" So I married her to him.'[56]

A clearly less popular although fairly widely circulated report is the following: 'Jābir ibn 'Abd Allāh al-Anṣārī had care of the daughter of his uncle, whose spouse divorced her. She completed her waiting period, then he returned wanting her to return to him. Jābir refused. He said: "You divorced a daughter of our uncle; now you wish to marry her again?" The woman wanted her spouse (again) because she was pleased with him. So this verse was revealed.'[57]

Once again, these reports provide the background information of the fact that an act contrary to the Qur'ānic regulation took place but the Qur'ān then corrected the situation. The *sabab* also includes a gloss of the Qur'ānic *'aḍala* as *mana'a*, 'to prevent.' But the importance of the reports is much greater than that, and it would seem that they have been tailored to their purpose. Both al-Qurṭubī[58] and Ibn al-'Arabī[59] cite the *sabab* of Ma'qil in order to support their position that marriage is not permitted without a guardian to give permission. As al-Qurṭubī states: 'Marriage is not permitted without a guardian because the sister of Ma'qil was a divorcee and if she had been able to marry by herself, then there would have been no need for Ma'qil.'[60] Quite explicitly, the *sabab* establishes the truth of this position for al-Qurṭubī. It would thus seem significant that in both versions of the *sabab* a reference is made to the fact that the woman in question wanted to re-marry but could not because of the lack of permission. Such a reference, unnatural to the narrative flow of both reports, is undoubtedly a reference made in the story so that the specific halakhic point can be made.

As is acknowledged by al-Qurṭubī, the followers of the legal school of Abū Ḥanīfa do not agree with this ruling; basing themselves on Q. 2: 230, 'If he divorces her, she is not permitted to him after that, until she marries a different spouse and he divorces her', in which there is no mention of a guardian, they reject the entire notion. Al-Jaṣṣāṣ,[61] being a Ḥanafite, represents this position. Towards the end of his multi-page argument he mentions the *sabab* of Ma'qil, in two versions, and rejects it on the grounds of its *isnād*.[62] *Isnād* criticism is obviously a tool which can be employed when needed and disregarded when not. The fact that the report is found in al-Bukhārī makes no difference to al-Jaṣṣāṣ who is quite apparently in the position of having to reject the *sabab*.

A *sabab* may also act to deflect exegetically an apparent halakhic content of a verse such as in Q. 2: 79: 'Woe to those who write the book with their own hands and then say: "This is from God" in order to sell it at a small price. Woe to them for what their hands write and woe to them for what they gain.'

Various *asbāb* reports are found for this verse, virtually all of which centre on the notion of the malicious alteration of Jewish scripture. Al-Wāḥidī provides the most extensive report: '(The Jews) changed the description of the prophet in their book and made him a man with long hair and of medium brown (colouring). They said to their companions and followers: "Look at the description of the prophet who is to appear at the end of time; it does not

[56] Al-Wāḥidī, *Asbāb*, 73–4, first report, also see his second and third reports, 74–5 and *Wajīz*, 65; al-Suyūṭī, *Lubāb*, 46, first report; Berlin 3578, f. 14a, first report; al-Bukhārī, *Al-ṣaḥīḥ, kitāb al-tafsīr*, VI, 39–40; al-Ṭabarī, V, 17–21, reports 4927–4938; Mujāhid, 109; pseudo al-Kalbī, 26; Muqātil, *Tafsīr*, ff. 37b–38a and *Khams mi'at āya*, 186, with full identification of all the actors.

[57] Al-Wāḥidī, *Asbāb*, 75–6, fourth report; al-Suyūṭī, *Lubāb*, 46, second report; Berlin 3578, ff. 14a–14b, second report; al-Ṭabarī, V, 21–2, report 4939.

[58] Al-Qurṭubī, III, 158, in five different versions.

[59] Ibn al-'Arabī, I, 201.

[60] Al-Qurṭubī, III, 158–9.

[61] Al-Jaṣṣāṣ, I, 399–403.

[62] Al-Jaṣṣāṣ, I, 402.

resemble the description of this (man)." The Rabbis and the learned ones used to receive provisions from the rest of the Jews and they feared that they would not receive it if they revealed the (true) description; therefore they changed it.'[63]

While similar reports of scriptural falsification are found in al-Suyūṭī and Berlin 3578 and while the latter adds that the Jews did this out of 'distaste' and 'envy' (of the Arabs being chosen to receive the final prophet), al-Wāḥidī's report is unique in that it combines a gloss on the monetary aspect of the Qur'ānic verse with the standard *taḥrīf* charge; that is, the Jewish leaders 'sold', figuratively at least, the description of Muḥammad for a small price, their free food-supply.

Notable within various reports given by al-Ṭabarī are some traditions which suggest that what is involved in this verse is not *taḥrīf*, alteration, of the Torah but rather the writing of entire books and claiming that they are from God (Mishna? Talmud? variations on that polemical theme have certainly been common within the Christian world) which would suggest that the polemic over scripture between Jews and Muslims may have gone further than the charge of alteration and faulty transmission.[64] An isolated report also in al-Ṭabarī pictures the Gentiles (*ummiyyūn*) as upset because they had no prophet nor a book, so they wrote a scripture themselves and proceeded to tell a group of 'lowly ignoramuses' that the book was from God, in order to be able to sell it to them.[65]

Finally, al-Ṭabarī (followed by al-Qurṭubī) has his perpetually impertinent questioner ask: 'What is the meaning of "Woe to those who write the book with their own hands?" How can one write without the hand?'[66] One should not overlook the distinct possiblity that al-Ṭabarī was endowed with a certain sense of humour, but the point does lead him to a discussion of the difference between author and writer and to state that the verse most certainly intends a stricture upon the Jews and that it does not necessarily imply a restriction upon writing, buying or selling books. Indeed, the *sabab* in this case serves to remove possible 'misinterpretation' with serious legal implications.

On the other hand, *asbāb* reports which seem to have halakhic content are on occasion apparently not employed in exegesis in that way, for example in Q. 2: 230: 'If he divorces her, she is not permitted to him after then until she marries a different spouse and he divorces her. There is no sin on the two of them if they return, if they think that they can maintain the rules of God. These are the rules of God (which) he explains to a people who understands.'

Al-Suyūṭī and al-'Irāqī stand alone among the *asbāb* books and almost all the exegetical works consulted in citing a *sabab* for this verse. '(The verse) was revealed about 'Ā'isha bint 'Abd al-Raḥmān ibn 'Atīk, who was living with Rifā'a ibn Wahb ibn 'Atīk (he was the son of her uncle). He divorced her with the final divorce and she married 'Abd al-Raḥmān ibn al-Zubair al-Quraẓī after him. He then divorced her. She then went to the prophet and said: "He divorced me before having slept with me. May I return to (my) first (husband)?" So ... [Q. 2: 230] ... was revealed. So he slept with her and divorced her after that; thus there was no sin on the two of them when they rejoined.'[67]

[63] Al-Wāḥidī, *Asbāb*, 24, and *Wajīz*, 21, in more general terms; al-Suyūṭī, *Lubāb*, 20, second report (the first report merely says the verse was revealed about *ahl al-kitāb*); Berlin 3578, f. 6a; al-Qurṭubī, II, 9, from al-Kalbī and Ibn Isḥāq although I have not located a similar report in the *Sīra*. Also see Mujāhid, 81.

[64] Al-Ṭabarī, II, 270–1, reports 1388, 1393.

[65] Al-Ṭabarī, II, 270, report 1389.

[66] Al-Ṭabarī, II, 272–3; al-Qurṭubī, II, 9.

[67] Al-Suyūṭī, *Lubāb*, 45–6; al-'Irāqī, f. 6b, somewhat shortened.

The same identification of the protagonists is made in al-Kalbī and al-Ṭabarī,[68] and a shortened version of the report is found in Muqātil,[69] although the report is absent from explicit mention in the *aḥkām* texts, despite its halakhic relevance. Much debate is conducted in the *aḥkām* works concerning whether intercourse is necessary to confirm the legal status of the intervening marriage, the precise point with which this *sabab* is concerned; [70] the appeal to *ijmā'* is made by al-Ṭabari [71] in order to prove the need for intercourse to legalize the marriage. It would seem that a *sabab* may well be halakhic in application or even in origin, but that fact does not necessarily mean that it will actually be advanced for such purposes.

It is within discussions of *naskh* that one intuitively expects to find the majority of the discussions about chronology and one also expects that such discussions will centre around *asbāb* reports; indeed, this was an emphasized point within most previous scholarly discourses on *asbāb*. In very few cases, however, is that discussion about chronology and *asbāb* ever carried on in the verses that were examined in this study, at least on an overt level. An example of where it does happen to some extent at least occurs in Q. 2: 104: ' O you who believe! Do not say *rā'inā!* For those who disbelieve, there will be a great punishment.'

The numerous *asbāb* reports which are connected to this verse all attempt to answer the many questions that arise about this prohibition: Why should it not be said? Why was it said in any case?

The prohibition contained in the verse was seen, quite obviously, as applying to Muslims, so it must have been Muslims who were saying the word at one time; this assumption is reflected in all the reports. Just where, why and how the Muslims used this word is a matter of some debate, with three original contexts being suggested by the *asbāb* reports:

(*a*) the word was Jewish—perhaps used mockingly—which the Muslims misunderstood and adopted into their speech. Al-Suyūṭī presents the following report in this vein: ' When two Jewish men, Mālik ibn al-Saif and Rifā' ibn Zaid, met and talked to the prophet they would say: *rā'inā sam'aka wa-sma' ghair musma'* [compare Q. 4: 46]. The Muslims thought that this was something that the people of the book (said) to honour their prophets. So they said that to the prophet. So God revealed . . . [2: 104].' [72]

Just why it was necessary for the word to be banned is not made clear in this report; another report of al-Suyūṭī suggests simply that God ' detested ' the phrase.[73] Al-Ṭabarī's reports, however, state that the Jews said it ' to mock ' Muḥammad and thus it was banned; [74] the Muslims apparently did not realize that this was mockery, an observation which leads al-Ṭabarī to reject the reports since the *aṣḥāb* would not have been so careless or foolish as such an oversight would suggest.[75]

(*b*) the word, in the ' Jewish language ' was a curse, although it was an innocent word in Arabic.

Al-Wāḥidī, among others, gives an extensive account of this matter: ' The

[68] Pseudo al-Kalbī, 26; al-Ṭabarī, IV, 588–96, especially report 4893.

[69] Muqātil, *Tafsīr*, f. 37b.

[70] e.g., Ibn al-'Arabī, I, 198; al-Qurṭubī, III, 147–8. The report is cited in the works of Mālik and al-Shāfi'ī; these later works may well be assuming that their readers are aware of the background to the discussions and thus do not feel there is a need to cite the *sabab*.

[71] Al-Ṭabarī, IV, 588–9.

[72] Al-Suyūṭī, *Lubāb*, 24; also al-Ṭabarī, II, 460–1, reports 1728–1731, and II, 462–3, report 1738.

[73] Al-Suyūṭī, *Lubāb*, 24, fourth report.

[74] Al-Ṭabarī, II, 460–1, reports 1728–1731; also al-Jaṣṣāṣ, I, 58.

[75] Al-Ṭabarī, II, 465–6.

Arabs used to say (*rā'inā*) and when the Jews heard (the Muslims) saying it to the prophet they were amazed at that. *Rā'inā* was a severe curse in their language. They said: "We used to curse Muḥammad secretly but now they know the curse of Muḥammad because it is (also) in their speech." They used to come to the prophet and say: "Oh Muḥammad, *rā'inā*," and then they would laugh. One of the *anṣār*, Sa'd ibn 'Ubāda who knew the Jewish language, noticed it and said: "Oh enemies of God! May God's curse be on you! By Him who has the soul of Muḥammad in His hand, if I hear it from anyone of you, I will break his neck!!" They said: "Have you not said it to him (yourself)?!" So God revealed . . . [2: 104].'[76]

The notion of an inter-lingual play, perhaps رأى / רע , 'see' and 'evil', is seen to be the reason for the prohibition.

(*c*) the word was a part of Arab-Jāhilī speech. Al-Suyūṭī, among others, has the simple report that the Arabs used to say this word in the Jāhiliyya and that God then prohibited its use.[77] No further explanation is given; the report is one more of the numerous instances of the flexibility of the motif of opposition to Muḥammad.

All these *asbāb* reports fulfil a basic haggadic function of providing answers for matters left unstated in the Qur'ān. But the importance of the verse goes somewhat beyond the haggadic level; for one thing, the verse is considered to be a case of abrogation by al-Naḥḥās, on the basis of the *sabab*.[78] The *sabab* implies for al-Naḥḥās that at one time it was permitted (*mubāḥ*) to say the word, then that permission was removed or abrogated. This seems significant because many other laws with the Qur'ān are not considered by al-Naḥḥās as abrogators (food laws for example); rather the assumption seems to be these rulings confirm past practice; but here, on the basis of the *sabab*, prior usage is established and thus the verse enters the realm of *naskh*.

Even more important here is the halakhic significance of the *sabab*. Al-Jaṣṣāṣ sees the legal significance of the verse as going beyond merely not saying *ra'inā;* the Jews (or the Arabs) said the word to mock others, according to *sabab*—therefore mockery is not permitted; nor are *double-entendres* permitted (or at least, maliciously intended ones).[79] The wording of the verse is extended in legal application through application of the *sabab*.

While it cannot really be doubted that there is an implicit assumption of the chronological-progressive order of the Qur'ān in the *naskh* texts, it is notable that the discussions themselves do not generally make this point explicit; *naskh*, be it with regards to wine or direction of prayer, always assumes that the present law is known (that is, no wine and facing Mecca), and the verses which agree with that fact are necessarily the valid ones. Any verses which contradict this are necessarily invalid, and thus can be logically arranged according to a basic notion of 'progressive revelation.' The arguments found in the *naskh* texts are, in short, based on logic not chronology. Where that logic needs backing up in terms of specifics, appeal is generally made to the ordering of *sūras* and, once again, not *asbāb* information. Of course, the two notions of ordering *sūras* and

[76] Al-Wāḥidī, *Asbāb*, 31 and *Wajīz*, 28; also al-Suyūṭī, *Lubāb*, 24, second report; Berlin 3578, f. 7a; al-Qurṭubī, II, 57; Muqātil, *Tafsīr*, f. 19a; also al-Naḥḥās, 26; Ibn al-'Arabī, I, 32.

[77] Al-Suyūṭī, *Lubāb*, 24, reports six and seven and perhaps three; al-Ṭabarī, II, 461–2, reports 1733–7; al-Jaṣṣāṣ, I, 58 makes the transferral Jews-Jāhiliyya complete by having the expression as one of mockery to the pagan Arabs. Al-Suyūṭī, *Lubāb*, 24, report five, indicates a combination of reports also: the expression was Arabic, the Jews picked it up, so God prohibited its usage; no explanation is given. On this verse, see David Kunstlinger, '"Rā'inā"', *BSOAS*, v, 4, 1930, 877–82 and Arthur Jeffery, 'The Qur'ān as scripture', *Muslim World*, XL, 1950, 260.

[78] Al-Naḥḥās, 26; also see Makkī, 107.

[79] Al-Jaṣṣāṣ, I, 58; also Ibn al-'Arabī, I, 32; al-Qurṭubī, II, 57–60.

the *asbāb* interact through the adducing of the *sabab* regarding the *qiyāsī* method of *sūra* ordering at Q. 2: 21.[80] Even there, however, the connexion is deflected by al-Wāḥidī at least who suggests that this *sabab* refers to the people who are addressed (that is, the Meccans or the Medinans) and not the place (and therefore the time!) of revelation.[81] To emphasize the point once more: the bringing forth of the *asbāb* as explicit proof of 'progressive revelation' within these texts is simply not done very frequently.[82]

A matter which appears not to have arisen in the examination of *sūra* 2 is the explicit question of prophecy; is prophecy in the Qur'ān not closely interrelated with chronology and therefore, one may assume, *asbāb?* In the polemical text of Ibn Kammūna, a list of ten verses from the Qur'ān which are traditionally claimed to be prophecies is adduced; cited in it is Q. 2: 61, which states in reference to the Jews, 'Struck upon them was humiliation and poverty', about which the argument runs: '[the truth of] this became clear from the fact that after this word no forceful power appeared among the Jews.'[83] Now the precise 'prophetic' sense of this passage is admittedly vague, but it is worthy of note that no *sabab* is found in the *asbāb* texts to support the necessary chronology and interpretation of the assertion. Once again, as far as the verse-prophecy is concerned, the fact is known and not in need of proof. In addition, two instances may be noted in *sūra* 2 (Q. 2: 142, 189a) where the *sabab* appears to deflect exegetically possible prophetic qualities in the verses concerned.[84]

In conclusion, then, in comparison to Wansbrough's statements, the following may be asserted:

(*a*) the primary (i.e., predominant) function of the *sabab* in the exegetical texts is not halakhic.

(*b*) the essential role of the material is found in haggadic exegesis; that is, the *sabab* functions to provide an interpretation of a verse within a basic narrative framework. I would tentatively trace the origins of this material to the context of the *quṣṣāṣ*, the wandering story-tellers, and pious preachers and to a basically popular religious worship situation where such stories would prove both enjoyable and edifying.[85]

[80] Al-Wāḥidī, *Asbāb*, 20–1; Berlin 3578, f. 5a.

[81] Al-Wāḥidī, *Asbāb*, 21; note that Berlin 3578, f. 5a, presents some alternative identifications for verse 21 as well: the unbelievers (according to al-Suddī) or the hypocrites (according to Muqātil; see his *Tafsīr*, f. 6b).

[82] Dr. J. Burton has pointed out to me that this apparent lack of halakhic discussion is reflective of the nature of the sources employed in this study; these sources, he suggests, present only a distillation of discussions going on elsewhere, in this case primarily in *fiqh* literature. This would indicate that there is another entire study to be done, beyond the context of the traditional *'ulūm al-Qur'ān* to which this study has directed its attention, in order to discover the complete picture of the *sabab* in the Islamic religious sciences, especially as that material relates to halakhic matters.

[83] Ibn Kammūna, *Examination of the three faiths*, text, p. 87, transl., p. 127.

[84] In 2:142 the reference *sa-yaqūlu*, 'they will say,' is not elaborated in the *asbāb* material; in 2: 189a, the idea of 'they will ask you' is likewise not seen as prophetic.

[85] This paper is a distillation of ch. iii, part d, of my 1981 McGill dissertation 'The Quranic *asbāb al-nuzūl* material: an analysis of its use and development in exegesis'. Thanks are extended to Professor J. Wansbrough, SOAS, and Dr. C. J. Adams, McGill, for their help and encouragement. This paper was read at the Colloquium on Qur'ān and Ḥadīth held at University of Cambridge, September, 1985. M. Hinds, P. Crone and G. Juynboll must be thanked for inviting me to the colloquium; the participants at that meeting, especially Dr. J. Burton, were most helpful with their comments.

References

'Abd al-Razzāq. *Tafsīr*. Cairo MS *tafsīr* 242.
Al-Baghdādī. *Kitāb al-nāsikh wa'l-mansūkh*. Beyazit MS 445 (also Berlin MS Petermann 555).
Al-Bukhārī. *al-Ṣaḥīḥ*. Cairo, 1378/1958.
Al-Dānī. *al-Taisīr fī'l-qirā'āt al-sab'*. Istanbul, 1930.
Guillaume, Alfred (tr.). *The life of Muhammad: A translation of [Ibn] Isḥāq's Sīrat rasūl Allāh*. London, 1955.
Hibat Allāh. *al-Nāsikh wa'l-mansūkh*. Cairo, 1960.
Ibn al-'Arabī. *Aḥkām al-Qur'ān*. Cairo, 1959.
Ibn Isḥāq. *al-Sīrat al-nabawiyya*. Cairo, 1955.
Ibn Kammūna. *Ibn Kammuna's examination of the three faiths*. M. Perlmann (tr.). Berkeley, 1971; Arabic text, M. Perlmann (ed.), Berkeley, 1967.
Ibn Sa'd. *Kitāb al-ṭabaqāt al-kabīr*. E. Sachau et al. (ed.). Leiden, 1905–1940.
Al-Jaṣṣāṣ. *Aḥkām al-Qur'ān*. Istanbul, 1935.
Pseudo al-Kalbī. *Tafsīr;* printed as al-Fīrūzābādī, *Tanwīr al-miqbās min tafsīr Ibn 'Abbās*. Cairo, 1951.
Al-Kisā'ī. *Qiṣaṣ al-anbiyā'*. Leiden, 1922.
Maimonides, Moses. *The guide of the perplexed*. S. Pines (tr.). Chicago, 1963.
Makkī al-Qausī. *al-Īḍāḥ li-nāsikh al-Qur'ān wa-mansūkhihi*. Riyad, 1976.
Mujāhid. *Tafsīr*. Qatar, 1976.
Muqātil b. Sulaymān. *Tafsīr*. Ahmed III MS 74.
Muqātil b. Sulaymān. *Tafsīr khams mi'at āya min al-Qur'ān*. I. Goldfeld (ed.). Shefaram, 1982.
Muslim. *Ṣaḥīḥ Muslim ... bi sharḥ al-Nawawī*. Cairo, 1390/1970.
Al-Naḥḥāṣ. *al-Nāsikh wa'l-mansūkh*. Cairo, 1938.
Nwyia, Paul. *Exégèse Coranique et langage mystique: nouvel essai sur le lexique technique des mystiques musulmans*. Beirut, 1970.
Al-Qurṭubī. *al-Jāmi' li-aḥkām al-Qur'ān*. Cairo, 1935–1936.
Rippin, Andrew. 'The exegetical genre *asbāb al-nuzūl:* a bibliographical and terminological survey,' *BSOAS*, XLVIII, 1, 1985, 1–15.
Rippin, Andrew. 'al-Zarkashī and al-Suyūṭī on the function of the occasion of revelation material,' *Islamic Culture*, LIX, 1985, 243–58.
Rippin, Andrew. 'al-Zuhrī, *naskh al-Qur'ān* and the problem of early *tafsīr* texts,' *BSOAS*, XLVIII, 1, 1984, 22–43.
Sufyān al-Thawrī. *Tafsīr*. Rampur, 1965.
Al-Suyūṭī. *al-Itqān fī 'ulūm al-Qur'ān*. Beirut, 1983 (4th printing).
Al-Suyūṭī. *Lubāb al-nuqūl fī asbāb al-nuzūl*. Cairo, 1382/1962.
Al-Ṭabarī. *Jāmi' al-bayān 'an ta'wīl āy al-Qur'ān*. Cairo, 1374–1388/1954–1968.
Al-Wāḥidī. *Asbāb nuzūl al-Qur'ān*. A. Ṣaqr (ed.), Cairo, 1969.
Al-Wāḥidī. *Tafsīr al-wajīz*, on the margin of al-Nawawī, *Marāḥ Labīd: Tafsīr al-Nawawī*. Cairo, 1972, reprint.
Al-Wāḥidī. *al-Wasīṭ bain al-maqbūd wa'l-basīṭ*. Berlin Staatsbibliothek MS Sprenger 415.
Wansbrough, John. *Quranic studies: sources and methods of scriptural interpretation*. Oxford, 1977.
Wansbrough, John. *The sectarian milieu: content and composition of Islamic salvation history*. Oxford, 1978.
Al-Zarkashī. *al-Burhān fī 'ulūm al-Qur'ān*. Cairo, 1957.

XX

Lexicographical Texts and the Qur'ān

I. LEXICOGRAPHY AND LEXICOLOGY

Lexicography has been classically understood to be the art of dictionary-making. In modern times, this art has become a more fully conscious science (according to some people, at least) under the influence of linguistic theory; in fact, it would now be argued that underlying every dictionary can be said to be some sense of a theory of language. European dictionaries of the nineteenth century, for example, often reflect the emphasis of unusual detail and explanation tied to history, and generally encompass the whole language and provide a normative slant while emphasizing the part played by the written language. All this reflects an understanding of language which is normative in its written form and is supposed to be unchanging in its character; such dictionaries are, in sum, the result of Romantic linguistics with its historical emphasis. The Oxford masterpiece, *A New English Dictionary on Historical Principles*, is, of course, a prime example of the type.

Recent scholarly activity has manifested itself both in the emergence of the study of dictionaries—in itself a historical study—and in the creation of other forms of dictionaries—dictionaries of usage (a linguistic description of language), conceptual dictionaries (synchronic rather than historical or universal), and notional dictionaries (as opposed to alphabetical). As a result, comprehensive works are being supplemented today by inventories of vocabulary used by 'a particular author or field or technique in relation to a precise historical or geographical situation or event'.[1]

Just how the notion of a dictionary is to be defined is somewhat problematic. Some would want to define it stringently such that it is equal to a former sense of 'lexicon', so that the word 'dictionary' becomes reserved for a total inventory of language, however that

[1] Bernard Quedama, 'Lexicology and Lexicography', *Current Trends in Linguistics*, 9 (1972), 436–7.

concept be defined and limited; opposed to dictionaries, therefore, would be things such as 'concordances', 'glossaries', 'vocabularies', and 'word books'.[2] Others[3] see the idea of a dictionary as more inclusive, being defined more simply as a work dealing with lexical meaning. It is in this sense that the word will be used in this paper.

Lexicology has only recently been distinguished as a field of study separate from lexicography. It is the field which attempts to look at the morphological structure and the semantic function of lexical units and to analyse the use of vocabulary.[4] It is, therefore, the science underlying lexicography. One of the crucial questions faced by lexicology revolves around the definition of the lexical unit; some consensus has been reached such that the term is to be identified with 'a complete linguistic sign for which the "consubstantiality" of the name (*significant*) and the sense (*signifié*) will not be questioned, even if determination appears delicate'.[5]

2. APPROACHES TO QURANIC VOCABULARY

In analysing the vocabulary of the Qur'ān, the Arabs of the classical period developed several approaches. The literary genres resulting from this activity have already been outlined in masterful form by John Wansbrough in his *Quranic Studies: Sources and Methods of Scriptural Interpretation.*[6] The aim of this paper, therefore, is fairly modest; what I hope to do here is to clarify and expand the treatment of Wansbrough, adding a little to the scope of his

[2] Allen Walker Read, 'Approaches to Lexicography and Semantics', *Current Trends in Linguistics*, 10 (1973), 166.

[3] Ladislav Zgusta, *Manual of Lexicography* (The Hague and Paris, 1971); also Yakov Malkiel, 'A Typological Classification of Dictionaries on the Basis of Distinctive Features', in Fred W. Householder and Sol Saporta, eds., *Problems in Lexicography: Report of the Conference on Lexicography held at Indiana University, November 11–12, 1960* (Bloomington, 1960), 23.

[4] For a good introductory treatment see Sydney M. Lam, 'Lexicology and Semantics', in Archibald A. Hill, *Linguistics Today* (New York, 1969), 40–9.

[5] Quedama, p. 401.

[6] See pp. 202–27; see also his *The Sectarian Milieu: Content and Composition of Islamic Salvation History* (Oxford, 1978), ch 1. The recent publication of Sezgin's *GAS* viii: *Lexikographie bis ca. 430 H.* (Leiden, 1982) has added immensely to the material available on this topic. Basic works on Arabic lexicography include F. Rundgren, 'La lexicographie Arabe', in P. Fronzaroli, ed., *Studies on Semitic Lexicography* (Firenze, 1973); S. Wild, *Das Kitāb al-'Ain und die Arabische Lexikographie* (Wiesbaden, 1965); J. A. Haywood, *Arabic Lexicography* (Leiden, 1965).

observations, and, most importantly, indicating possibilities for further areas of exploration and attention.

Three kinds of texts are to be examined. The *gharīb* works are the most prominent. These texts are the closest to the modern sense of lexicography; they are dictionaries of 'difficult words'. Note that there is implicit in that statement a comparative sense; included in these dictionaries are words which later authors found difficult to understand in terms of the language usage of their day. Of course, this lexicographical insight of the notion of what difficulty is all about is modified by observations which hold just as true for medieval Arabic works as they do for modern English dictionaries; such dictionaries are constrained by a number of factors including convenience and especially convention, as well as, in modern times, commercial viability. As a result of these factors, certain words simply entered the stock of 'difficult words' and were passed down through the generations as such. Dictionaries of this type work on the level of synonymity, whether that be expressed by a single lexeme or by a phrase. Vocabulary studies such as these go back to the earliest studies of language in many cultures; direct parallels are to be seen in the Greek works from the fifth to the first centuries BC cataloguing 'difficult words' in Homer.[7]

Employing a typology of dictionaries such as that proposed by Yakov Malkiel[8] could provide a number of useful criteria for classifying these *gharīb* works. Malkiel provides a three-fold categorization with ten subdivisions:

i. Range

(*a*) Density of entries in relation to total lexical stock. In theory, there would be no problem of a changing lexicon for the *gharīb* works, since they are based upon a fixed corpus of scriptural text, so the density will only vary according to the author's perception of the task; all will be severely limited compared to the entire stock of Arabic lexemes, but will vary in the proportion of the vocabulary of the Qur'ān treated. The only other variable factor here may be the treatment of variant readings to the text of scripture.

(*b*) Number of languages involved. While no bilingual dictionaries

[7] R. L. Collison, *A History of Foreign-language Dictionaries* (London, 1982), ch. 1.

[8] Malkiel, pp. 3–24. See also Ali M. al-Kasimi, *Linguistics and Bilingual Dictionaries* (Leiden, 1977), ch. 1.

as such have been uncovered in this research, the role of the interlinear translation, because of its very special character, may need to be considered here. The recent review article concerned with Janos Eckmann's *Middle Turkic Glosses of the Rylands Interlinear Koran Translation*[9] by A. J. E. Bodrogligeti brings up this aspect very clearly: 'In dealing with the primary source one must remember that "The Rylands interlinear Koran translation" is not what Turcologists have up to now taken it for: it is not the Qur'ān in three—Arabic, Persian and Turkic—languages. It is the Qur'ān in Arabic with Persian and Turkic interlinear glosses. The glosses translate words or phrases mostly in isolation, irrespective of their grammatical, and often even semantic context.'[10]

(*c*) Extent of concentration on purely lexical data. Here one will have to consider infiltration of commentary (the encyclopedic approach) and excessive verbiage in definition. Itemization of proper names would also be a factor.

ii. Perspective

(*a*) The fundamental dimension, that is, synchronic versus diachronic. Such an issue is of little concern, for the medieval Arab lexicographers seem to have had few qualms over having a mixed historical perspective in their works; dictionaries of the Qur'ān are ahistorical but not synchronic, if by that is meant the absence of archaism. Note, too, that such Quranic dictionaries are not etymological (or diachronic) for the most part, although a text such as *Al-lughāt fī'l-Qur'ān* ascribed to Ibn 'Abbās (d. 68/687)[11] may well be argued to be of some relevance to this category with its identification of tribal dialects, a clear and thorough-going backwards-looking perspective.

(*b*) Arrangement of entries. Possibilities here are conventional (that is, alphabetic, popularly seen as a defining character of a dictionary), semantic, or arbitrary. *Gharīb* works display variation as to whether they are arranged according to the words as actually employed in the Qur'ān or according to the root of the word. They

[9] Budapest, 1976.

[10] A. J. E. Bodrogligeti, 'Ghosts, Copulating Friends and Pedestrian Locusts in Some Reviews of Eckmann's "Middle Turkic glosses" ', *JAOS* 104 (1984), 455.

[11] Printed in numerous versions, e.g., as Ibn Ḥasnūn, *al-Lughāt fī'l-Qur'ān* (Beirut, 1972). On this text see A. Rippin, 'Ibn 'Abbās's *Al-lughāt fī'-Qur'ān*', *BSOAS* 44 (1981), 15–25, and id., 'Ibn 'Abbās's *Gharīb al-Qur'ān*', *BSOAS* 46 (1983), 332–3.

also vary in following alphabetical order or the order of occurrence in the text of scripture.

(*c*) The tone of the work. Possibilities here range from detached through preceptive, normative, didactic, to facetious. The normative (that is, a Muslim theological perspective) is universal in the *gharīb* works.[12]

iii. Presentation

(*a*) Definition. The glosses provided in most *gharīb* works are generally very specific as compared to being fully comprehensive for the language or for the text as a whole.

(*b*) Verbal documentation. Two elements enter here. Is the full passage of the text cited in order to provide the context, or are shorter segments or simple bare references given? Is there any indication of frequency of usage? Secondly, what other type of material is adduced to provide a context: literary or oral (living) examples; historical or contemporary material?

(*c*) Graphic illustration. Of this I am not aware of any applicability to Quranic vocabulary texts.

(*d*) Special features. This would include the use of abbreviations, linking words (especially prominent in some texts), indications of pronunciation (perhaps crucial when considering variants), and designation of the social plane of the lexeme (perhaps a phenomenon parallel to the citation of dialects in the aforementioned *lughāt* text).

In the second category of texts to be examined are the works known as *al-wujūh wa'l-naẓā'ir*, which would seem to fall under the modern classification of semantic lexicology. The works deal with homonyms (two words which are spelt in the same manner but which are perceived—either by native speakers and/or etymology[13]—to have different roots because of the inability to determine any connection between two senses of the word) and polysemy (where words have different senses of meaning and can

[12] For the normative character of Arab lexicography, see the work of Lothar Kopf, especially 'Religious Influences on Medieval Arabic Philology', *SI* 5 (1956), 33–59, and 'The Treatment of Foreign Words in Medieval Arabic Lexicology', *Scripta Hierosolymitana*, 9 (1961), 191–205; both articles are reprinted in his *Studies in Arabic and Hebrew Lexicography* ed. M. H. Goshen-Gottstein (Jerusalem, 1976), 19–45 and 247–61 respectively.

[13] See Zugusta, pp. 74 and 77.

be classified according to those different senses). Whether this is taken at a root level or on the level of the form of the word is one matter which needs to be noted. Since these texts deal with the written text of the Qur'ān, as studied by scholars (a significant clarification in light of Wansbrough's understandings of the function of these texts[14]), the question of homophones (words which are spelt differently but sound the same) does not generally arise. Homographs (where words are written in the same way but are pronounced differently) are a phenomenon that exists (most especially as revealed in discussion over variant readings—this may, one should note, provide some material related to homophones also), but that does not appear to enter into the consideration of the *wujūh* texts—another factor impinging on Wansbrough's understanding of the function of these works. In general, one may say that the *wujūh* texts analyse the semantic diversity on the level of context and not by syntax or any other such means. It should be noted that polysemy was studied by the ancient Greeks as a part of their investigations into language; they appear to have desired to develop principles in order to distinguish nuances of senses of words.[15] The Arab use of this mode of vocabulary classification, therefore, has a long heritage prior to the development of Quranic exegesis.

Finally, the phenomenon of the texts known as *mushtabihāt* does not seem to fall easily under any modern scholarly category. Perhaps the best one can do is call the mode of analysis 'phraseological lexicology'.[16] On the other hand, these texts do follow an ancient tradition, like the *gharīb* and the *wujūh* texts, in this case one of 'enumeration of scriptural examples', and therefore it could be argued, on these grounds, that the category lies outside lexicology altogether and that, as such, it performs a totally different function, such as that of homelitic indexation.

[14] See *QS* 202–27.

[15] See Gene B. Gragg, 'Redundancy and Polysemy: Reflections on a Point of Departure for Lexicology', in Donka Farkas, Wesley M. Jacobsen, Karol W. Todrys, eds., *Papers from the Parasession on the Lexicon, Chicago Linguistic Society, April 14–15, 1978* (Chicago, 1978), 174–83.

[16] Cf. Wansbrough's characterization, *Sectarian Milieu*, 61: 'phraseological commocation'.

3. BEGINNINGS OF QURANIC LEXICOGRAPHICAL INTEREST

There are two areas of related lexicographical interest which, while standing somewhat outside the genres of literature being treated in this paper, may well provide the background material from which the lexicographical tradition developed. The first type of material which must be considered, though it is not necessarily historically first, is formed from lexicographical intrusions into the text of the Qur'ān. These consist of simple glosses to the text, and were first isolated by Goldziher and subsequently analysed by Bergsträsser.[17] This material is evidenced in variant readings, and, in fact, lexicographical synonymity is one of the traditional ways of disposing of any supposed significance to the existence of variants within the Quranic textual tradition.[18] Just how the interaction between this kind of material and the lexicographical tradition might have worked is difficult to assert, primarily because of the lack of hard historical data for the ordering of the emergence of the variants; the influence could have worked either way.

Even more significant, perhaps, is the existence of early works of *tafsīr*; examples of commentaries on the Qur'ān which are essentially 'Arabic translations' of the scripture are worthy of note. Most significant in this regard would be the work known as *Tanwīr al-miqbās min tafsīr Ibn 'Abbās*, the work ascribed variously to al-Kalbī (d. 146/763),[19] Ibn 'Abbās,[20] and al-Fīrūzābādī (d. 817/1415),[21] but which has its most likely origins in the third or fourth Muslim centuries.[22] The approach is continued in a work such as *Tafsīr al-Jalālayn* of Jalāl al-Dīn al-Maḥallī (d. 864/1459) and Jalāl al-Dīn al-Suyūṭī (d. 911/1505).[23] Perhaps early lexicographical works should be seen as extracts of such texts, putting into some more readily accessible form the crucial and most

[17] Goldziher, *Richtungen*, 3–32; *GdQ* iii. 57–115, as assessments of extra-canonical readings especially; *QS* 203–4.

[18] See, e.g., Ahmad von Denffer, *'Ulūm al-Qur'ān. An Introduction to the Sciences of the Qur'ān* (Leicester, 1983), 115–16.

[19] *GAS* i. 34–5; *QS* 130–7, 140–6.

[20] *GAS* i. 27.

[21] *GAL* S ii. 235.

[22] See A. Rippin, 'Al-Zuhrī, *naskh al-Qur'ān* and the Problem of Early *tafsīr* Texts', *BSOAS* 47 (1984), 23–4.

[23] In many prints, e.g., Beirut, 1978, with a marginal print of al-Suyūṭī, *Lubāb al-nuqūl fī asbāb al-nuzūl*.

'difficult' pieces of information. The style of commentary found in *Tanwīr al-miqbās*, because it is devoid of most textual and grammatical analysis,[24] many well have lent itself to such lexicographical extraction. Still, the lack of historical evidence makes it hard to argue the matter one way or the other.

4. *GHARĪB* WORKS

'Difficulty', as manifested in the variety of Arabic writings which go under this title, is conceived in a variety of ways: foreign words, dialect words, bedouin words, or lexical oddities (in the tradition of *hapax legomenon*). While some works devoted to Quranic vocabulary tend to isolate one aspect of this 'difficult' tradition, others tend to be more all-inclusive. A few examples will prove illustrative.

The work of Ibn Qutayba (d. 276/889), *Tafsīr gharīb al-Qur'ān*,[25] is a straightforward work presenting the lexical difficulties of the Qur'ān in *sūra* order and providing glosses to each entry generally connected simply by *ay*, with a moderate amount of poetry and proverbial material adduced to support the suggestions. The book is preceded by a treatment of the names of God (a total of 26)[26] and by a list of meanings of words which occur frequently in the Qur'ān and are, for the most part, prominent theological terms.[27] Forty such words are presented in this way.

Al-Sijistānī's (d. 330/942) *Nuzhat al-qulūb fī gharīb al-Qur'ān*[28] is perhaps the most famous book of its type; there are few other books of *tafsīr* listed in Sezgin[29] which have such a large number of manuscript copies still in existence. Al-Sijistānī created a dictionary composed on an alphabetic principle of the first letter of the word as it appears in the text of the Qur'ān,[30] further subdivided according to whether the first vowel of the word is a *fatḥa*, *kasra*, or

[24] See *QS* 130–37, 140–6.

[25] Ed. A. Ṣaqr (Beirut, 1978).

[26] pp. 6–20.

[27] pp. 21–37.

[28] Available in many editions, here Beirut, 1983 ('third printing'). A. Jeffery, *Foreign Vocabulary of the Qur'ān* (Baroda, 1938), 8 n. 3, makes reference to al-Sijistānī's view on the language of the Qur'ān, but I have not been able to find Jeffery's reference in the edition of al-Sijistānī available to me. On al-Sijistānī's work, see Josef Feilchenfeld, *Ein einleitender Beitrag zum ġarîb al-ḳur'ân nebst einer Probe aus dem Lexikon des Seġestâni* (Wien, 1892).

[29] *GAS* i. 43–4.

[30] See J. A. Haywood, pp. 96–7, for the historical significance of this.

ḍamma.[31] Within that basic order, the text would appear to follow the sequence of the words as they occur in the Qur'ān. For the most part, the author provides simple glosses bridged by *ay*; intra-Quranic proofs are used frequently, applying the principle of definition by context. Occasionally poetry is adduced and, more frequently, comparisons are made to profane speech (introduced by *yuqālu*, 'one says'). On occasion, also, explanatory exegetical remarks are added, including items such as occasion of revelation reports. On some occasions, the author seems to be led into conceptually related passages.[32] On other occasions, he will cite the number of meaning-aspects (*wajh*) for a given word.[33]

Al-Rāghib al-Iṣfahānī's (d. 502/1108) *al-Mufradāt fī gharīb al-Qur'ān*[34] is a far more complete work and is virtually a complete inventory of Quranic vocabulary rather than a simple dictionary of 'difficult' words. Checking the entries under the letter *thā'*, for example, shows that all words beginning with that letter are included, with the apparent omission of the root *thā'-rā'-yā'*.[35] The author has pursued a rigorous application of alphabetic ordering according to roots, as compared to al-Sijistānī's alphabetic treatment on the word level.[36]

There are a large number of other works in this genre,[37] but these three books are typical ones, dealing with 'difficult' vocabulary on an intuitive, ill-defined level. This is well illustrated by the tremendous variation in the number of words treated in the various texts; there are, as one would indeed expect, no criteria for determining what is a 'difficult' word. At the same time, it is in these kinds of texts that the conventional nature of the enterprise will be most clearly revealed, in that certain words are always considered a part of the stock of *gharīb* lexemes.

There are, however, other works to be included within the consideration of this genre, composed of texts which use different criteria or different lexicological principles than the general type of books in order to isolate words for attention or to provide a

[31] See al-Sijistānī, p. 2, for his explanation of this.

[32] See, e.g., ibid. 126–7.

[33] See, e.g., ibid. 111 on *al-ṣāmid*.

[34] Cairo, n.d.

[35] See ibid. 76–82.

[36] Cf. the treatment by al-Sijistānī of words beginning with *thā'*: pp. 64–7.

[37] See, e.g., *GAS* i. 557 (Zayd ibn 'Alī); *GAS* viii. 24, 173, 225 (the famous work of Abū 'Ubayd al-Harawī), 230; see also al-Zarkashī, *al-Burhān fī 'ulūm al-Qur'ān*, ed. Muḥammad Abū'l-Faḍl Ibrāhīm (Cairo, 1957), i. 291–6, for a brief review of the genre.

unifying approach to the topic of 'difficult words'. Foreign words are listed by al-Suyūṭī, for example, in his famous *al-Mutawakkilī.*[38] Elsewhere I have given extensive attention to a text dealing with dialect words attributed to Ibn 'Abbās;[39] this classification is then followed in texts found in al-Suyūṭī and al-Zarkashī (d. 794/1391)[40] (foreign words also find their place in the text). The *Masā'il Nāfi' ibn al-Azraq*[41] is a listing of words whose meanings are known best by the Bedouin, as is proven by the citation of poetry in every instance; while the words treated in such a text may not substantially differ from the collective *gharīb* tradition, the external criterion by which words found their entry into the text is at least specified (be it fictious historically, and spurious in terms of poetical *shawāhid*). There do not appear to be any texts which isolate *hapax legomenon* as such, however.[42]

5. WUJŪH

Muqātil ibn Sulaymān (d. 150/767) is universally designated as the first author in this genre. His work goes under a variety of names, *Kitāb al-wujūh wa'l-naẓā'ir* and *al-Ashbāh wa'l-naẓā'ir* being two popular titles.[43] The work contains 186 words presented in some sort of conceptual order, although that is certainly unclear. The initial words treated, *hudā*, *kufr*, and *shirk*, indicate the theological import which the author considered of utmost importance in his treatment of the subject. The analysis provides the number of meanings or aspects (*wujūh*) of each word and a gloss for each meaning, and then provides the parallel passages or analogues (*naẓā'ir*) in which the word is used in that sense. By no means are all

[38] Cairo, 1926, ed. and trans. W. Bell; see also al-Suyūṭī, *al-Itqān fī 'ulūm al-Qur'ān* (2 vol. Ḥalabī edn., Cairo, 1951), i. 135–41, and cf. his *al-Muhadhdhab fīmā waqa'a fī'l-Qur'ān min al-mu'arrab*, published in *al-Mawrid*, i (1971), 101–24.

[39] See n. 11, above.

[40] Al-Zarkashī, i. 282–90; al-Suyūṭī, *al-Itqān*, i. 133–5.

[41] See Rippin, 'Lughāt', 15–16.

[42] Cf., however, Sa'adyā Gaon, *Tafsīr al-sab'īna lafẓat al-farīda*. The very existence of this text raises questions as to whether or not something similar is not to be found somewhere for the Qur'ān. For general considerations, see F. E. Greenspahn, *Hapax Legomena in Biblical Hebrew* (Chico, 1984).

[43] See *QS* 208. The work is published (Cairo, 1975). See also P. Nwyia, *Exégèse coranique et langage mystique* (Beirut, 1970), 25–61, and N. Abbott, *Studies in Arabic Literary Papyri, ii: Qur'anic Commentary and Tradition* (Chicago, 1967), 92–106.

the verses provided in the analysis (that is, the concordance function of the text is incomplete), and the analysis of the number of *wujūh* would seem to be primarily dictated by the context of employment rather than clearly distinguishable meanings. The words treated are, for the most part, religiously significant terms, but a few particles are also included for analysis. Wansbrough's conclusion concerning the text is that its function was to elucidate scriptural imagery, and is therefore exegetical,[44] rather than to provide a neutral index of vocabulary.[45]

Ibn Qutayba's *Ta'wīl mushkil al-Qur'ān*[46] is a text of a different character both from his own contribution to the *gharīb* genre and from many other works in the *wujūh* category. Lexicography is never a straightforward art; the problem of the metaphorical versus literal usage of words, for example, depends upon the reader's perspective and, in the case of the Qur'ān, is very much dependent upon theological presuppositions. Ibn Qutayba appears to recognize the importance of such factors and he acts to get them straightened out first in *Mushkil*, before entering into semantic classifications.[47] The author appears to go through the Qur'ān according to *sūra*s selected in a random order, isolating figures of speech for attention. In this respect, the book is a rhetorical analysis of the Qur'ān along the lines of that of Abū 'Ubayda (d. 210/825), *Majāz al-Qur'ān*,[48] a book which, it could be argued, is of the *gharīb* type.[49] But part of Ibn Qutayba's book is also of the *wujūh* type. He has a chapter which covers both technical and theological words which covers single words with multiple meanings,[50] and also a chapter on words which substitute one for another in certain places, for example, *fī makān 'alā*.[51]

[44] *QS* 211.

[45] A similar approach in the inverse is found in Muqātil *apud* al-Malaṭī, *al-Tanbīh wa'l-radd 'alā ahl al-ahwā' wa'l-bida'* (Istanbul, 1949), 72–80; see *QS* 210–11.

[46] Ed. A. Ṣaqr (2nd printing, Cairo, 1973). On the work see Gérard Lecomte, *Ibn Qutayba (mort en 276/889): L'Homme, son oeuvre, ses idées* (Damscus, 1965), 295–9.

[47] See W. Heinrich, 'On the Genesis of the *ḥaqīqa–majāz* dichotomy', *SI* 59 (1984), 130–2.

[48] Cairo, 1954–62.

[49] See Wansbrough's analysis, '*Majāz al-Qur'ān*: Periphrastic Exegesis', *BSOAS* 33 (1970), 247–66; E. Almagor, 'The Early Meaning of *majāz* and the Nature of Abu 'Ubayda's Exegesis', in *Studia Orientalia Memoriae D. H. Baneth* (Jerusalem, 1979), 307–26; W. Heinrichs, n. 47, above. Note that al-Zarkashī, *al-Burhān*, i. 291, lists this work as one of the *gharīb* genre.

[50] *Mushkil*, 439–563.

[51] Ibid. 565–78.

The work by al-Damaghānī (d. 478/1085), *Iṣlāḥ al-wujūh wa'l-naẓā'ir fī'l-Qur'ān al-karīm*,[52] is very similar to that of Muqātil's, although slightly more expansive. The author states in his introduction that he has examined the work of Muqātil and 'others' but has found them to be lacking because of the omission of too many words. Al-Damaghānī then provides an alphabetic listing of the words, enumerating the different meanings of a given word which are provided by glosses introduced by *ay* after a given verse is cited in support. He then gives the *naẓā'ir* for each meaning, those verses being introduced by *kaqawlihi* or *mithlahā*. The actual analysis provided is frequently the same as that in Muqātil (see, for example, the word *sabab*[53]), but the material has been expanded. Under the letter *alif*, al-Damaghānī provides thirty-eight entries while Muqātil scatters entries for only twenty of these lexemes throughout his book. Both texts treat particles (and here are parallel to Ibn Qutayba, *Ta'wīl mushkil al-Qur'ān*), as well as substantives.

Ibn al-Jawzī's (d. 597/1200) work on *wujūh* is available in two printed versions, *Nuzhat al-a'yun al-nawāẓir fī 'ilm al-wujūh wa'l-naẓā'ir*[54] and *Muntakhab qurrat al-'uyūn al-nawāẓir fī'l-wujūh wa'l-naẓā'ir*.[55] The latter of these is an abbreviated version, prepared according to the author for ready reference, while the former is an expansive treatment ordered alphabetically and numbered according to the number of *wujūh*. The work does not provide any evidence of a reworking of the genre, but rather is a restatement of earlier works. Ibn al-Jawzī's exegetical statements are perhaps the prime contribution. Even then, many of the analyses are preceeded by the statement that: 'Many of the exegetes say that [this word] appears in the Qur'ān with [a certain number] of *wajh*', once again reflecting this conservative and conventional nature of the lexicographical enterprise.

There are a number of other books available on the subject of *wujūh*, for the topic itself seems to have become one of theological importance; al-Zarkashī is explicit in stating that the notion of

52 See *GAL* i. 373; Beirut, 1970.

53 See A. Rippin, 'The Exegetical Genre *asbāb al-nuzūl*: A Bibliographical and Terminological Survey', *BSOAS* 48 (1985), 12–14.

54 Ed. Sayyida Mihr al-Nisā' (Hyderabad, 1974). On the text in general see A. J. Arberry, 'Synonyms and Homonyms in the Qur'ān', *IQ* 13 (1939), 135–9, and Ḥātim Ṣāliḥ al-Ḍāmin, review in *al-Mawrid*, 15 (1986), 169–80.

55 Ed. Fu'ād 'Abd al-Munajjim (Alexandria, *c.*1979).

wujūh is a part of the miraculous character of the Qur'ān,[56] and looking at a work such as al-Rummānī's (d. 386/996) *al-Nukat fī i'jāz al-Qur'ān*[57] indicates the way this was conceived. While al-Rummānī does not use the *wujūh/naẓā'ir* terminology, his category of *tajānus*[58] is conceived as a very similar phenomenon, although it is not elaborated in any systematic way as found in the *wujūh* texts. Al-Rummānī argues that a part of the aesthetic effectiveness of the Qur'ān is to be found in this notion which he defines as being of two kinds: totally resemblant, where the words are identical but have different meanings, and resemblant as such, where only the same root is employed with the words having different meanings. Notable in al-Rummānī's treatment of the topic is the impact of theology and the *sharī'a* on the analysis. For example, in his treatment of the case of a totally resemblant word-employment in Q. 2/194: *fa-man i'tadā 'alaykum, fa-i'tadā 'alayhi*, 'Whoever commits aggression against you, commit aggression against him', al-Rummānī glosses the phrase as 'that is, repay that person with that which is deserved in a just way, except that God used for the sense of "that which is deserved" the word "commit aggression" in order to confirm the notion of equality in quantity'. For al-Rummānī, there is a difference between the use of the verb *i'tadā* in the first and second cases, the first being used as 'outright aggression', the second being used as 'appropriate force'.[59]

Al-Zarkashī and al-Suyūṭī, as has previously been pointed out by Abdus Sattar,[60] seem to have a slightly different sense of *wujūh* and *naẓā'ir* than some of the earlier writers. *Wujūh* and *naẓā'ir* are seen by these two writers to be different topics, homonyms and synonyms respectively, rather than interrelated subjects. That is, the term *naẓā'ir*, for al-Zarkashī and al-Suyūṭī,[61] is reserved for the study of words with only one *wajh*, while *wujūh* treats those who

[56] Al-Zarkashī, i. 102; also see al-Suyūṭī, *al-Itqān*, i. 141.

[57] Published in *Thalāth rasā'il fī i'jāz al-Qur'ān*, ed. M. Zaghlūl Salām and M. Khalaf Allāh (Cairo, 1956), 75–113.

[58] Al-Rummānī, pp. 99–100.

[59] Ibid. 99.

[60] Muhammad Abdus Sattar, '*Wujūh al-Qur'ān*: A Branch of *tafsīr* Literature', *IS* 17 (1978), 138–40; this article also contains references to other works in the *wujūh* genre, as does *GAS* viii. Especially noteworthy is the text by al-Mubarrad, *Mā ittafaqa lafẓuhu wa-ikhtalafa ma'nāhu* (Cairo, 1931), see *GAS* viii. 98; I have not been able to locate a copy of this book. See also Yaḥyā ibn Sallām, *al-Taṣārif: al-tafsīr al-Qur'ān mimmā ishtabahat asmā'hu wa taṣarrafat ma'ānihi* (Tunis, 1979), especially the editor's introduction.

[61] Al-Zarkashī, i. 102; al-Suyūṭī, *al-Itqān*, i. 141–2.

have many. Note that al-Zarkashī's presentation of *wujūh* is fairly limited; he gives the outline of *hudā* in seventeen *wujūh* and then goes on to quote a few examples of multiple aspects of words on the authority of Ibn Fāris.[62]

Finally, it should be noted that none of the texts examined seems to distinguish either explicitly or implicitly between homonymity and polysemy. That topic probably deserves a fuller and broader-based study.

Wansbrough has argued that lexicographical/phraseological analyses or 'semantic collation'—as found in texts entitled *wujūh*—were constructed for the purpose of asserting the conceptual unity of the Qur'ān in the same way in which the hermeneutic of analogy and the separation into *muḥkam* ('clear verses') and *mutashābih* ('ambiguous verses') functions.[63] Indeed, it is hard to see what other purpose these texts could serve; they certainly have no particular functional attributes, not being designed for easy reference or the like. They may reflect simply an impulse to collect, but underneath that lies a view of the text of the Qur'ān, as indeed Wansbrough has argued. Whether such motivation was actually conscious on the part of the compilers of these texts I would tend to doubt; it is more a case of an underlying assumption being given conceptualization.

6. *MUSHTABIHĀT*

'Alī ibn Ḥamza al-Kisā'ī is famed as a Qur'ān reciter and transmitter of a *qirā'a* of the Qur'ān (one of the 'seven'). He is said to have died somewhere between 179/795 and 192/807. A work known under two titles is ascribed to him: *Kitāb al-mutashābih fī'l-Qur'ān* (manuscript Paris 665/4) and *Kitāb al-mushtabihāt* (manuscript Beyazit 436).[64] As compared to later books with this same title (or at least, that of the Paris manuscript) which deal with the obscurities of the Qur'ān (that is, as a result of Q. 3/7) and often see this term as equivalent to metaphorical expressions, al-Kisā'ī takes the word in the more literal sense of the 'resemblances' in the

[62] Al-Zarkashī, i. 103–4 on *hudā* (from Muqātil); i. 105–11 provides a rather random list of lexemes from Ibn Fāris, *al-Afrād* (see *GAS* viii. 214).

[63] *QS* 215.

[64] See *QS* 212 n. 8; the Beyazit MS is given the title *Kitāb al-mutashābihāt* at the end.

Qur'ān.[65] The text is ordered by the number of occurrences of a given phrase—once, twice, three to ten times, fifteen times, and twenty times—and within each of those a *sūra* order is followed for citing examples. For the most part, verse order is followed within the *sūra* listings, but this is not consistent. When dealing with examples of what are considered unique phraseologies in the Qur'ān, the text selects a certain phrase of Quranic diction and contrasts it to the rest of the Qur'ān either by displaying how that text states something elsewhere or by stating that there is nothing in the Qur'ān like the phrase in question. When the phraseology is not unique (that is, the phrase occurs between two and twenty times), the text cites the examples of identical scriptural statements where they are found in the text.

The text raises two issues. First, on what basis are phrases selected for comparison—lexical, grammatical, theological, word order, inflectional, and/or orthographical? Second, what is the ultimate purpose of the text?

To question one it seems that the text works on all levels, but with the least amount of emphasis on the semantic value of the phrase. For example, a comparison is made between Q. 2/21: 'O people, serve your Lord', and the rest of the Qur'ān where it is stated: 'Fear your Lord.' The point is not that these two sentences mean the same thing but use different words (that is, are working on the semantic–synonym level), but rather it is that the construction is supposedly unique (although Wansbrough points out that the basis on which this uniqueness is asserted is still unclear).[66]

Although there do not appear to be any books which treat the text of the Qur'ān in quite the same way, a similar listing of material is found in al-Zarkashī.[67] Especially significant here is the treatment of the unique instances, where an attempt is made to classify the instances according to their differences (for example, particles present/absent). Al-Zarkashī has thereby attempted to add some sort of system to al-Kisā'ī's beginning exploration of the genre.[68]

[65] See *QS* 212 ff.—Wansbrough terms this 'distributional analysis of Quranic diction'; see also *GAL* S i. 178.

[66] *QS* 213–14.

[67] Al-Zarkashī, i. 112–54, covering unique expressions and then expressions which occur the following number of times: 2 (i. 133), 3 (i. 137), 4 (i. 140), 5 (i. 144), 6 (i. 145), 7 (i. 146), 8 (i. 147), 9 (i. 147), 10 (i. 148), 11 (i. 149), 15 (i. 151), 18 (i. 151), 20 (i. 152), 23 (i. 153).

[68] Al-Zarkashī, i. 112–32; al-Suyūṭī, *al-Itqān*, ii. 114–16, and refs. given there to other works.

Wansbrough has suggested that, one, this mode of analysis is a short step on from the *wujūh* texts—that is, it is a move from semantic distribution to phraseological distribution—and that, two, there is some connection between this approach and later ones under the same title, which differ because of the impact of rhetorical exegesis and the doctrine of *i'jāz*.[69] It could also be suggested, especially in the light of the way al-Zarkashī formulates the 'unique instances', that there is a connection between Abū 'Ubayda's 'periphrastic exegesis' and the *mushtabihāt*.

Sidney Towner's book *Rabbinic 'Enumeration of scriptural examples'*[70] may be of some help in determining the ultimate purpose of these listings of Quranic phrases. Towner states that 'listing' is an ancient phenomenon which was used 'for systematizing observations about nature, geography and man and as pedagogical and mnemonic tools for conveying information to students and posterity'.[71] This kind of listing trend can easily be identified in a book such as the *Sīra* of Ibn Isḥāq (d. 151/768).[72] However, there is, for Towner, a difference between enumeration of proverbial examples, as just defined, and the enumeration of scriptural examples which, while the latter may have evolved from the former, seems to have an exegetical function, at least within the context of Rabbinic literature. Within the Quranic context, this function may be termed a 'hermeneutical tool', acting just as do other terminological devices (*nāsikh/mansūkh*, *muḥkam/mutashābih*, *tafsīr/ta'wīl*) to demonstrate the unity of the scriptural text, be that on a conceptual, phraseological, or semantic level.

7. CONCLUSIONS

With interest increasing in lexicography and lexicology in general, attention to Arabic, and specifically Quranic, data will undoubtedly prove popular and rewarding in the coming years. One area which will repay a full and broad investigation is the historical development of profane and religious lexicography in relationship to the use of poetry as resource material for definitional analyses. The connection of this to the emergence of the arguments concerning

[69] *QS* 215. [70] Leiden, 1973.
[71] Towner, p. 4.
[72] See *Sectarian Milieu*, ch. 1.

the inimitability of the Qur'ān as compared to the human compositions found in poetry will prove crucial.

The citation of the figure of Ibn 'Abbās in the context of much of this lexicographical material must be viewed in terms of the overall picture of the establishment of a fixed religious system called 'Islam';[73] lexicography provides one element, small yet important, in the overall context, most especially the notions related to the status of the Arabic language, but also as connected to the establishment of the Qur'ān as an authoritative source within the emergent Muslim community.

[73] See C. Gilliot, 'Portrait "mythique" d'Ibn 'Abbās', *Arabica*, 31 (1984), 127–84.

XXI

EPIGRAPHICAL SOUTH ARABIAN AND QUR'ĀNIC EXEGESIS*

In contemplating the historical transition from the so-called period of Jāhiliyya to the age of Islam, the continuing memory of the ancient civilization of Southern Arabia would seem to be a prime candidate for attention. Once a flourishing society, marked by extensive irrigation works, numerous religious buildings, artisan crafts and a well-developed writing system, the South Arabian civilization appears to have entered into its final period of decline just prior to the 7th c. CE, crumbling totally with the rise of the Central Arabian tribes and Islam. The reasons for the initial decline seem evident enough. The imposition of Christianity as the official religion of the Roman empire in the 4th c. CE led to the banning of all pagan rituals, including those employing incense. At the same time, a weakening Roman economy brought in its wake a loss of Roman power and influence throughout the Mediterranean world.[1] The South Arabian economy, which depended to a large extent upon the incense trade with the Roman world, no doubt felt the crunch of the fall of Rome and the consequences of its change in religious persuasion. Nigel Groom also speculates that over-cropping of the incense trees at an earlier period of prosperity may well have led to their depletion;[2] this, added to wholesale destruction of the incense trees for fuel and fodder, along with the loss of foreign markets for the product, would appear to have

---

* My visit to Jerusalem to participate in the third colloquium "From Jāhiliyya to Islam" was made possible by a grant from the Social Sciences and Humanities Research Council of Canada, to whom I express my thanks.

1 Nigel Groom, *Frankincense and Myrrh. A Study of the Arabian Incense Trade* (London, 1981), p. 162. Also see Christian Robin, "La civilisation de l'Arabie méridionale avant l'Islam," in Joseph Chelhod (ed.), *L'Arabie du Sud: histoire et civilisation. 1: le peuple yéménite et ses racines* (Paris, 1984), pp. 195-223.

2 Groom, p. 163; see also Patricia Crone, *Meccan Trade and the rise of Islam* (Princeton, 1987).

spelt an end to South Arabian economic prosperity as it had developed in the centuries prior to Islam. The political division of the area into a number of separate states, aggravated by the various incursions of Ethiopian, Persian and Roman troops in the fifth and sixth centuries will also have wreaked havoc on the region's stability.[3] The final collapse of the South Arabian civilization is witnessed by the failure to keep such monuments as the Mārib dam in proper repair. As is well known, the last inscription referring to repair of the dam dates from the time of Abraha in about the year 540 CE.[4] The loss of the dam is plausibly attributable to its neglect after the rise of Islam, and the emergence of other interests at that time playing a more major part in people's lives, combined with an exodus of Yemenites from the area at that time, their places being taken by Arabs.[5]

We have a great deal of material which would seem to attest to some memory of the history of pre-Islamic South Arabia among Muslims. Just how much of this can be deemed authentic "historical memory" and how much of it is merely embellished folktale and the like has yet to be determined.[6] M.J. Kister's article on the campaign of

---

3 See Sidney Smith, "Events in Arabia in the 6th century A.D.," *BSOAS*, 16 (1954), 425–468.

4 Smith, pp. 437–441; J.M. Solá Solé, *Las dos grandes inscripciones sudarábigas del dique de Mârib* (Barcelona - Tübingen, 1960); inscription number 541 of *Corpus Inscriptionum Semiticarum, Pars quarta. Inscriptiones himyariticas et sabaeas continens* (Paris, 1889–1929) (= CIH).

5 R.B. Serjeant's article, "Some Irrigation Systems in Hadramawt," *BSOAS*, 27 (1964), 33–76, is worth noting in this connection, on account of its elaborate survey of floods and other disasters which severely damaged various areas at different historical periods (pp. 67–72). Serjeant states, and this is the point to which I would like to draw attention, that: "It is surprising to discover that after so many destructive floods there is no evidence quoted of cultivated areas being abandoned and the same localities appear to continue in cultivation." That this would appear not to be true of the Mārib in the 6/7th c. would suggest to me that the destruction of the dam came about gradually due to neglect and disinterest after the rise of Islam.

6 Smith, pp. 463–468, gives a coherent survey of the issues involved but cf. J.M.B. Jones - "The chronology of the Maghāzī - a textual survey," *BSOAS*, 19 (1957), 245–280 and "Ibn Isḥāq and al-Wāqidī: the dream of ʿĀtika and the raid to Nak͟hla in relation to the charge of plagiarism," *BSOAS*, 22

Ḥulubān,[7] while far more positive in its attitude towards the historical sources than I would tend to be, illustrates well the problematic nature of utilizing Arabic–Muslim sources for historical information regarding an important topic as the "Expedition of the Elephant." The same could be said for the memory of the summer and winter caravans in which Quraysh were supposed to be involved.[8] That both of these contentious issues have their focal point in Qur'ānic interpretation renders the issues even more complex and, in my opinion, less likely ever to be firmly resolved.

Rather than examine these historical issues directly, my interest here will be more in the field of language. The question I wish to attempt to explore is: "To what extent did knowledge of the South Arabian language(s) as evidenced in the inscriptions continue into Islamic times?" The question, as we shall see, is difficult to answer because of the uncertainties surrounding the notion of "historical memory". Greater precision can perhaps be attained by formulating the question more concretely thus: "To what extent was knowledge of Epigraphical South Arabian [= ESA] *functional* for Muslims in the centuries following the rise of Islam?" The wider question will not be evaded, I hope, but the more limited approach is where we must start from.

There are three major sources which I wish to examine in order to attempt an assessment of the answer to my question: (i) texts in ESA script dating from Islamic times; (2) Islamic authors who transmit information on ESA language and script; and (3) the

---

(1959), 41–51 –, who shows a far greater awareness of the chronological problems of the early sources, this being just one aspect of the entire source dilemma. See also Lawrence I. Conrad, "Abraha and Muḥammad: Some Observations apropos of chronology and literary *topoi* in the early Arabic historical tradition," *BSOAS*, 50 (1987), 225–40.

7 M. J. Kister, "The campaign of Ḥulubān: a new light on the expedition of Abraha," *Le Muséon*, 78 (1965), 425–436.

8 See M. Cook, *Muḥammad* (Oxford, 1983), pp. 71–73; cf. A. Brockett, "An illustration of the misuse of Qur'ān 'Variant Readings' [viz. *īlāf*]," unpublished paper, based upon a presentation given at the Oxford Colloquium on *ḥadīth*, 1982; U. Rubin, "The *īlāf* of Quraysh. A Study of sūra CVI," *Arabica*, 31 (1984), 165–188 (I can hardly agree with Rubin's positive historical conclusions, however).

traditional exegesis of an apparent ESA word found in the Qur'ān. It is upon the last of these three sources which I shall concentrate, for we are here dealing with a domain in which philological knowledge can be applied and where the practical implications (as opposed to antiquarian interests, especially of those found in the second type of source) of any functional knowledge of ESA should be revealed.

In 1971, David Cohen drew attention to a manuscript of an Arabic letter, written under the name of Muḥammad, addressed to the Yemenites and transliterated into ESA script.[9] Muḥammad Hamidullah has more recently drawn attention to the text again, indicating the sources of the letter and comparing it to other letters of its type written to various world leaders at the time of Muḥammad;[10] the aim of all the letters, including the one in ESA script, is, of course, to invite conversion to Islam. Hamidullah considers the letter a transcript of an original sent by Muḥammad, edited by a Jewish scribe of the Yemen and transliterated by him into ESA script in the year 12 AH.

Jacqueline Pirenne, quoted in Cohen's article,[11] states that the document is, of course, a forgery, done probably in the 20th c., after knowledge of the ESA script became known via scholarly works in the Arab world. Hamidullah does not seem to respond to this suggestion although he may well have objected that the reason for the letter being edited in just the way it is (such that it leaves out references to Jews and Christians and their taxation, among other things) would not seem to be explainable in any particularly convincing way. Still, the errors in the script which Pirenne and Cohen isolate suggest quite clearly that knowledge of ESA on the part of the

---

9 D. Cohen, "Un manuscrit en caractères sudarabiques d'une lettre de Muḥammad," *Comptes rendus du Groupe Linguistique d'Etudes Chamito-Semitiques*, 15 (1970-71), 103-109.

10 Muḥammad Hamidullah, "A letter of the Prophet in the *Musnad* - Script addressed to the Yemenite chieftains," *Hamdard Islamicus*, 5 (1982), 3-20.

11 Cohen, pp. 103-104. The oddities of the transcription seem to have prevented Cohen from simply adopting Pirenne's view and forgetting the whole document; his conclusion, apparently also supported by Pirenne, is that the manuscript is more likely to have originated in the 19th c., in the wake of J. Halevy's explorations.

scribe was rudimentary at best. Without a great deal more evidence, I find the more skeptical explanation - the recent forgery of the document - far more convincing. The suspect nature of all the letters of this type of "invitation to Islam" only makes the likelihood of forgery that much greater.

A second, perhaps more crucial, piece of textual evidence from the Islamic period in the ESA script is found in the two inscriptions discovered and described by Christian Robin - Robin/Umm Laylà 2 and 3.[12] These inscriptions are written in the ESA script but, in fact, contain an Arabic text clearly from the Islamic period. The names, the verb, the definite article and the writing of *ibn* all reflect Arabic rather than Sabaic and, especially as far as the names go, attest to a lexical stratum not otherwise known from the pre-Islamic period.[13] According to Robin - and Simon Hopkins would appear to agree [14] - these inscriptions witness the latest attestation of ESA script in an inscription as well as its use within the first few centuries of Islam.

Crucial questions still remain concerning the infiltration of Arabic into South Arabia, and early evidences of this; in fact, the whole topic is worthy of a careful, detailed study of its own. Walter Müller[15] has provided a good overview of the extent to which Arabic

---

12 Christian Robin, "Résultats épigraphiques et archéologiques de deux brefs séjours en République Arabe du Yémen," *Semitica*, 26 (1976), 188-192. An overall photograph of the Umm-Laylà 1 through 3 inscriptions is found in Christian Robin, *Les Hautes-Terres du Nord-Yemen avant l'Islam, II: Nouvelles Inscriptions* (Louvain, 1982), plate 2.

13 Robin/Umm-Laylà 2 reads: "Written by Muḥammad ibn ʿAbd Allāh ibn ʿAlī ibn al-[ḤRYN]". Robin/Umm-Laylà 3 reads: "Written by ʿAlī ibn ʿAbd al-Raḥmān." While the name ʿAlī is attested in a number of pre-Islamic inscriptions, and Muḥammad is known to have been employed, at least occasionally; the theophoric names are not otherwise attested; see G.L. Harding, *An Index and concordance of pre-Islamic Arabian names and inscriptions* (Toronto, 1971).

14 Simon Hopkins, *Studies in the grammar of early Arabic based upon papyri datable to before 300 A.H./912 A.D.* (Oxford, 1984), p. 2, note 4: "the recently found specimens of Arabic in South Arabian characters probably do fall within the period studied here."

15 Walter W. Müller, "Das Frühnordarabische: Nordarabisches in altsüdarabischen Inschriften" and "Das Altarabische der Inschriften aus

elements – especially names – are prevalent in ESA inscriptions, including the late infiltration of lexical and grammatical items from Arabic, even to the point of the Arabic definite article being used in names quite frequently. However, all this occurs in pre-Islamic times and essentially bears witness to a process occurring the other way around than the one under consideration here: these are not native speakers of Arabic using the ESA script but ESA writers (speakers?) using Arabic words. As far as Robin-Umm Laylà 2 and 3 go, all the evidence would point to the fact that the inscriptions are genuine and are to be dated from a late period in ESA chronology, according to the form of their script. Just how late a period they represent and how much significance should be attributed to these isolated graffiti is unclear.

There are two main authors from Muslim times whose writings would seem to suggest some knowledge of ESA script at least: Ibn al-Nadīm (d. 380/990) and al-Hamdānī (d. 334/945). Both authors present information on ESA but modern scholarship is unanimous in denying any real linguistic knowledge on the part of either author concerning the pre-Islamic South Arabian language.

Ibn al-Nadīm presents a chart of the ESA script towards the beginning of his *Al-Fihrist.* While the transmission of manuscript copies of Ibn al-Nadīm's text will have introduced all sorts of problems without a doubt, it is clear that the list of the ESA alphabet is full of errors and fictitious entries and that the understanding of the correspondences between ESA and Arabic are woefully ill-informed.[16] That Ibn al-Nadīm is able to compile his chart, however, with a certain amount of accuracy, certainly suggests an antiquarian interest on the part of the author or his sources; someone must have actually

---

vorislamischer Zeit," in Wolfdietrich Fischer (ed.), *Grundriss der Arabischen Philologie* (Wiesbaden, 1982), pp. 26–28, 32–35.

16 See Adolf Grohmann, "The problem of dating early Qur'āns," *Der Islam*, 33 (1957), 221 and his reference to Arthur Jeffery's review of Nabia Abbott, *The rise of the North Arabic script and its Kur'ānic development* in *Moslem World*, 30 (1940), 193. Bayard Dodge, *The Fihrist of al-Nadīm* (New York, 1970) I, p. 10, provides a reproduction of the ESA chart.

looked at some of the inscriptions. The lack of accuracy, on the other hand, suggests speculation and a lack of real knowledge.

The situation with al-Hamdānī is more complex and, to some extent, more inconclusive because of the absence of the volume of his *Al-Iklīl* that is said to deal with the "Himyaritic" language. A.F.L. Beeston's position is representative of modern scholarly views: "It is further significant that Hamdānī, though able to read South Arabian script and hence to identify proper names, cites allegedly ancient inscriptions which are so unlike, in their style and content, to any authentic ancient texts, that we must conclude that all knowledge of genuine Sabaic had vanished by his time; yet he certainly knew something that his contemporaries called Himyaritic."[17] It is on this latter point that we have some difficulties perhaps. Chaim Rabin, in his *Ancient West-Arabian*, raises some significant issues concerning the relationship between this Himyaritic and ESA.[18] Certainly the two are not identical, but Himyaritic may perhaps represent an intermediate stage of linguistic evolution between ESA and Arabic. Certain lexical items cited by al-Hamdānī as Himyaritic, which are found in ESA but not in Arabic, would seem to suggest this conclusion. Rabin theorizes that al-Hamdānī took this Himyaritic colloquial language of his time as being identical to the language of the inscriptions. Now, the parallels obtaining between the two do, to some extent, bear out al-Hamdānī, but we are still faced with the final inevitable conclusion that the author's failure to see the difference between Himyaritic and ESA means that he could not deal with the latter in any meaningful way.

Beeston argues that the linguistic evidence of the ESA inscriptions suggests to him that by even as early as the 5th c. CE,

---

17 A.F.L. Beeston, "Languages of pre-Islamic Arabia," *Arabica*, 18 (1981), 179; on al-Hamdānī, also see J. Fück, *Arabiyya* (Paris, 1955), pp. 131-136; O. Löfgren, "al-Hamdānī", *EI*[2]. Christian Robin has also raised this issue in his chapter on al-Hamdānī in *Les Hautes-Terres du Nord-Yemen avant l'Islam*, volume 1, pp. 117-119; Robin affirms, as does Beeston, al-Hamdānī's ability to read the script and thus produce renderings of ESA names, but denies al-Hamdānī's knowledge of the language itself.

18 Chaim Rabin, *Ancient West Arabian* (London, 1951), pp. 42-53, the section on Ḥimyar.

Sabaic, in the Mārib area at least, existed as a learned language rather than as anyone's mother tongue. [19] This transition from ESA to "Himyaritic" may, therefore, have been developing over the preceeding four or five centuries up to the time of al-Hamdānī. That he should not be knowledgeable concerning ESA, then, is perhaps not surprising. The same problem of distinguishing between ESA and a Himyaritic dialect of Arabic also arises with writers as early as Ibn Isḥāq (d. 151/768) and Ibn Hishām (d. 218/834). In the *Sīra*, a reference is made to South Arabian linguistic usage in the context of the account of Dhū Nuwās.[20] While the passage is considered garbled by the editor, the word استرطبان could well represent the Sabaic verb form *sʾtfʿl* ; the word is, at any rate, identified as *kalām Ḥimyār* by Ibn Hishām. It is unclear, however, whether this can really be treated as knowledge of ESA or whether it represents odd pieces of knowledge of the Himyaritic dialect. It most certainly does not indicate, however, a genuine ability to communicate in ESA.[21]

Sūra 34 of the Qurʾān is, like so many others, a composite of apparently disparate passages. Stories of David and Solomon and of the community of Sabaʾ in the Yemen are quickly rehearsed and

---

19 Beeston, pp. 179–180.

20 Ibn Hishām, *al-Sīrat al-Nabawiyya* (Cairo, 1955), I, 30–31. I am indebted to Dr. Moīn Halloun, University of Bethlehem, for drawing this material to my attention. The whole subject of Arabic writers' perceptions of "Himyaritic" needs attention.

21 There are, of course, many other Muslim authors whose writings may need to be taken into account in a full treatment of this question. For example, M.J. Kister has drawn attention to al-Fākihī and his ability, or perhaps that of one of his informants, to read an inscription on the *maqām Ibrāhīm* (*Le Muséon*, 84 [1971], 486). Likewise, in his translation of al-Hamdānī, N.A. Faris indicates four Muslim historians – al-Jurhumī, Wahb ibn Munabbih, al-Kalbī and Nashwān al-Ḥimyarī – the works of whom are, in his opinion, too full of legendary material to be of any historical interest, but nonetheless yield useful information on pre-Islamic inscriptions and the like (see *The Antiquities of South Arabia* [Princeton, 1938], pp. 2–4).

are followed by polemical sections emphasizing God's mercy and power. The town of Saba' is mentioned by name in only one other place in the Qur'ān, *sūra* 27, verse 22, where it is simply cited in passing in connection with Solomon and his first acquaintance with the Queen of Sheba, that is, Saba'. In *sūra* 34, then, we read the most extensive treatment of that fabled community, but the account is limited to some seven verses outlining in vague fashion the community's salvation history. The first two verses of this section are of central concern here:

> [v. 15] There was for Saba', in their homes, a sign:
> two gardens, to the right and the left.
> Eat of the sustenance of your Lord and be
> grateful to Him.
> A good country and a forgiving Lord.
> [v. 16] They turned away so We sent against them the
> flood of the *'arim* and We changed for them their
> two gardens: two gardens producing bitter
> fruit, tamarisk bushes and a few small lote-trees.

Western scholarship has, for about a century, suggested that the occurrence of the word *'arim* here reflects a South Arabian expression meaning "dam."[22] The word is also attested in a number of ESA inscriptions, most strikingly in two very famous texts found near the northern sluice of the remains of the Mārib dam. One of the inscriptions dates from around the year 450 C.E. and the other from 540; the later inscription of the two tells of the South Arabian ruler Abraha, various battles which were fought and the rebuilding of the dam, its ramp, basin and frontal work. The word used in the inscription in reference to the dam is derived from the root *'ayn-rā'-mīm*: Arabic *'arim*. The root is used a total of six times in

---

22 See the bibliography cited in Rudi Paret, *Der Koran: Kommentar und Konkordanz* (Stuttgart, 1980), ad Q. 34/16; also Hubert Grimme, "Über einige Klassen südarabischer Lehnwörter im Koran," *Zeitschrift für Assyriologie und verwandte Gebiete*, 26 (1912), 159. The connection is, however, not commented upon in A. Jeffery, *The Foreign Vocabulary of the Qur'ān* (Baroda, 1938).

this inscription,[23] eight times in its earlier companion inscription[24] and is also attested in at least three other inscriptions,[25] including one case in which it shows up in the plural.[26]

While other Semitic languages are known to employ the root *ʿayn-rāʾ-mīm*, it would seem to be primarily in ESA that the specific technical sense of "dam" predominates.[27] The Arabic root is chiefly associated with the meanings "ill-natured, strong, corrupt" or "stripping the flesh off the bone" (and from there apparently, "to suckle").[28] In Biblical Hebrew usage, the meanings range from "crafty, prudent" to "heaped up."[29] It is in this latter sense that a connection between the ESA and Hebrew meanings is sometimes indicated. Of eleven Biblical occurrences of this root which are often translated as "heap" or "to become heaped up," nine refer simply to piles of things: corn, wheat, garbage or tithes. The two additional usages are somewhat more interesting when seen in the Qurʾānic perspective, however. In Exodus 15/8, the single verbal usage of the *niphʿal* occurs in the middle of Moses' song of triumph, the Children of Israel having passed through the parted waters of the sea:

---

23 CIH 541, lines 43, 60, 68, 81, 111 and 118. See Maria Höfner, *Beleg-Wörterbuch zum Corpus inscriptionum semiticarum, par IV* (SBAW, phil.-hist. Kl., 363, 1980), p. 113; texts of CIH 540 and 541 newly edited in J.M. Solá Solé, *Las dos grandes inscripciones sudarábigas*, pp. 9-12, 23-27.

24 CIH 540, lines 6, 20, 24, 40 (restored reading), 62, 64, 67, and 72.

25 Ja 671: see A. Jamme, *Sabaean Inscriptions from Maḥram Bilqis (Mârib)* (Baltimore, 1962), p. 177; Ja 547: see A. Jamme, "Inscriptions des alentours de Mareb (Yemen)," *Cahiers de Byrsa*, 5 (1955), 278.

26 ʾʿRM in CIH 432, line 4.

27 See A.F.L. Beeston, *et. al.*, *Sabaic Dictionary* (Beirut/Louvain, 1982) *ad loc.* ; J.C. Biella, *Dictionary of Old South Arabic, Sabaean Dialect* (Chico, CA., 1982), *ad loc.*

28 See E.W. Lane, *An Arabic-English Lexicon* (London/Edinburgh, 1863-93) *ad loc.* This sense is apparently also attested in ESA: see A. F. L. Beeston, "Notes on Old South Arabian Lexicography XII," *Le Muséon*, 94 (1981), 59-60.

29 F. Brown, S.R. Driver, C.A. Briggs, *A Hebrew and English Lexicon of the Old Testament* (Oxford, 1972), *ad loc.* The notion "heaped-up" in ESA is also found in the meaning "boundary cairns," i.e. of heaped- up stones: see A.F.L. Beeston, "The 'Ta'lab Lord of Pastures' text," *BSOAS* 17 (1955), 155.

And with the blast of Thy nostrils the waters were piled up (*ne'ermū*) - the floods stood upright in a heap (*nēd*); the deeps congealed in the heart of the sea.

Certainly the imagery of holding back water is clear here in the use of the root. The second passage of interest is an apocalyptic vision found in Jeremiah 50/26:

[v. 25: The Lord hath opened his armoury] Come against her from every quarter, open her granaries, cast her up as heaps (*'arēmīm*) and destroy her utterly; let nothing of her be left.

Aramaic too dispays the word; here the root is used in the sense of "heap"; Accadian has *arimmu* which is generally understood in the specific sense of "dam", and thus provides the only close parallel to the ESA usage.[30]

Thus, by and large, it seems at least likely that the word *'arim* as used in the Qur'ān is an ESA loan-word, especially considering the general context in which it occurs. The usage in the Hebrew Bible cannot be overlooked, however, especially given the destructive contents of all three passages in Exodus, Jeremiah and the Qur'ān.

'Arim is not the only term in the Qur'ān suspected of being an ESA loan, though a number of specific words in this class have recently been questioned by Chaim Rabin,[31] Arthur Jeffery cites in *The Foreign Vocabulary of the Qur'ān* a number of possible cases of apparent ESA loan words (or, at least, loan meanings) including the following: *ḥizb* (party, sect), *tubba'* (title of the King of Himyar), *saṭara* (to write), *wathn* (idol), *ṣūra* (form, picture) *shirk* (association) and *ṣuḥuf* (pages).[32]

However, for the Qur'ānic exegetes, it is clear from the outset that *'arim* was a problematic word to deal with; its difficulty was aggravated by the fact that it was a *hapax legomenon* in the text of the Qur'ān, a situation which, as compared to some of these other apparent ESA loan words, was critical. But, being conscientious exegetes, they felt that, regardless of the word's problematic nature, a solution to its meaning *had* to be provided. In

30 See L. Koehler, W. Baumgartner, *Lexicon in veteris Testamenti Libras* (Leiden, 1958), p. 737.

31 Chaim Rabin, "On the probability of South-Arabian influence on the Arabic vocabulary," *JSAI*, 4 (1984), 125-134.

32 See Jeffery, pp. 108-9, 89, 169-70, 286-7, 201, 185-6, 192-4 respectively.

fact, the solutions proposed by the commentators exhibit the variety of methods by which an interpreter, both ancient and modern, may attempt to assign a meaning to a given, unknown word.

Some Muslim commentators turned to the dictionary meaning of the root of the word and tried to employ an etymological interpretation of the word. The root *ʿayn-rāʾ-mīm* was seen to mean "difficult" or "vicious" and thus the meaning of the phrase *sayl al-ʿarim* was taken to be an extra-specially severe flood.[33] This answer created its own problems in that *ʿarim* was in this case being taken as an adjective of *sayl* whereas grammatically the two words are, of course, in a genitive relationship. Those who cite this meaning, however, generally simply state that this *is* a possible construction in Arabic and thus needs no particular excuse.[34] At least one text suggests, however, that this construction is intended as a hyperbole,[35] thus citing what is commonly asserted to be a frequent Qurʾānic rhetorical device, and which, in many additional instances over and above this one, serves as a means whereby grammatical "difficulties" may be glossed over.[36]

Other commentators seem inclined towards what one may perhaps characterize – for lack of a better term – as "common

---

33 Al-Ṭabarī, *Jāmiʿ al-bayān fī tafsīr al-Qurʾān* (Cairo, 1323-1329), XXII, 54-55; Ibn Kathīr, *Tafsīr al-Qurʾān al-ʿaẓīm* (Cairo, n.d.), III, 532; al-Bayḍāwī, *Anwār al-tanzīl wa-asrār al-taʾwīl* (Cairo, 1344), p. 431; al-Thaʿālibī, *Jawāhir al-ḥisān fī tafsīr al-Qurʾān* (reprint Beirut, n.d.) III, 244; also see Lane, p. 2025.

34 Al-Thaʿālibī, III, 244; Ibn Kathīr, III, 532, *iḍāfa* of the noun to its *ṣifa* like *masjid al-jāmiʿ*.

35 Al-Thaʿālibī, III, 244, *mubālagha*, an opinion attributed to Ibn ʿAbbās.

36 See J. Wansbrough, "*Majāz al-Qurʾān*: periphrastic exegesis," *BSOAS*, 33 (1970), 247-266, for the example of Abū ʿUbayda; the arguments of E. Almagor, "The early meaning of *majāz* and the nature of Abū ʿUbayda's exegesis," in *Studia Orientalia: Memoriae D. H. Baneth Dedicata* (Jerusalem, 1979), pp. 307-326, or W. Heinrichs, "On the genesis of the *haqîqa – majâz* dichotomy," *Studia Islamica*, 59 (1984), 111-140, do not affect this point regarding exegetical procedure. Note should also be made of al-Rummānī, *Al-Nukat fī iʿjāz al-Qurʾān* in M. Khalaf Allāh and M. Zaghlūl Salām, *Thalāth rasāʾil fī iʿjāz al-Qurʾān* (Cairo, 1956), pp. 73-113 for numerous other such examples at work. Ultimately, one could well claim that the entire literary aspect of the *iʿjāz* argument is based upon this premise.

sense." *Sayl* was known to refer to floods – of that there was no doubt – so *ʿarim* could be defined as whatever was suitably seen to be descriptive of floods; this produced phrases such as "the flood of the water,"[37] "the flood of the heavy rains"[38] or "the flood of the *wādī*."[39] All three of these definitions depend upon a concept of a closely defined context that allows deductions to be made for semantic meaning. The question was posed: how would one qualify a "flood"? The answers provided were "water," "heavy rains" or "the *wādī*" which must have seemed like adequate, simple answers.

Another method related to what may be termed the "common sense" approach but is really not an interpretation at all, was for the commentator to opt for *ʿarim* being a proper name; in this case, it could either be a specific name of the *wādī* through which the *sayl* came,[40] or, more loosely, simply the source of the flood waters.[41] This kind of use of proper names as definitions – and the inverse, of providing definitions for words which are thought by some to be proper names – is a fairly common exegetical tool but perhaps one that should be viewed as a last-ditch effort to provide an explanation of an unknown word.

---

37 Ibn Kathīr, III, 532; Mujāhid ibn Jabr, *Tafsīr al-Qurʾān* (Qatar, 1976) pp. 524–525 (= al-Bukhārī, *al-Ṣaḥīḥ, Kitāb al-tafsīr*, ad Q. 34/16), specifically red (i.e. sandy) water; I wonder, though, if there is not a sense of a reflex of the Mosaic Egyptian plagues here in the specification of "red" water.

38 Al-Bayḍāwī, p. 431.

39 Ibn Kathīr, III, 532; al-Bukhārī, *al-Ṣaḥīḥ, k. al-tafsīr* (Ankara, 1976; bilingual edition) VI, 305; "Ibn ʿAbbās", *Tanwīr al-miqbās ʿan tafsīr Ibn ʿAbbās* (reprint, Beirut, 1360), p. 360 – on the attribution of this text see my "Al-Zuhrī, *naskh al-Qurʾān* and the problem of early *tafsīr* texts", *BSOAS*, 47 (1984), 23–24 and note 15. On the *tafsīr* of Ibn ʿAbbās, see my "*Tafsīr Ibn ʿAbbās* criteria for dating early *tafsīr* texts," paper read at the Fourth colloquium, "From Jahiliyya to Islam," Jerusalem, 1987, forthcoming in *JSAI*.

40 Al-Bayḍāwi, p. 431; al-Thaʿālibī, III, 244; al-Ṭabarī, XXII, 54–55; "Ibn ʿAbbās", p. 360 although the sense is vague here as to whether this is really conceived as a proper name; also see Lane, p. 2025.

41 Al-Kisāʾī, *Qiṣaṣ al-anbiyāʾ* (Leiden, 1922–23), p. 286, but due to an obvious textual error the word is printed *gharim* and stands uncorrected in W.M. Thackston Jr., *The Tales of the Prophets of al-Kisāʾī* (Boston, 1978), p. 310.

Another definition of *'arim* fairly frequently encountered seems to go beyond common sense and become more imaginative; the word is glossed as a special kind of red rat.[42] While at first sight this seems quite absurd, it is quite easy to discover the background to it. A story occurs in a number of places[43] concerning the destruction of the people of Yemen by a flood caused by the collapse of a dam which was brought about by the rats (or in another version, moles) burrowing into it. These rats were, of course, sent by God in order to bring about this catastrophe. The best efforts of the people – tying cats to the dam to eat the rats, covering the dam with fishing nets – were of no avail. There can be little doubt that this typical colourful story-teller tale has provided the source of the notion that the *'arim* sent by God signifies these rats; the story finds far greater circulation than that implied in it simply being a means of indicating this gloss, which suggests that the background to the story is to be located outside the narrow field of Qur'ānic lexicography, probably among the *quṣṣāṣ* or story-tellers.

Indeed stories similar to this one also found connected to what is undoubtedly the most popular definition of the word (one that is to be related to our "common sense" category, perhaps) and that is, of course, that it means "dams." [44] Apparently, the story just

---

42 Ibn Kathīr, III, 532; al-Bayḍāwī, p. 431; al-Tha'ālibī, III, 244 (*blind* rats); al-Sijistānī, *Gharīb al-Qur'ān* (Beirut, n.d.), p. 141; also see Lane, p. 2025; the gloss *juradh*, rat, is used consistently.

43 Al-Ṭabarī, XXII, 55; Ibn Kathīr, III, 532; al-Kisā'ī, p. 286, a story ultimately connected to the gloss of *'arim* as a proper name; Ibn Hishām, *Al-sīrat al-nabawiyya*, I, 13-14.

44 Al-Farrā', *Ma'ānī al-Qur'ān* (Cairo, 1966), II, 358, *musannāh*, with a complete explanation of the workings of the dam; Abū 'Ubayda, *Majāz al-Qur'ān* (Cairo, 1962), II, 146, *mashār* (= dike); Ibn Hishām, I, 13, citing Abū 'Ubayda after giving the tradition of the rats, *sadd* ; al-Bayḍāwī, p. 431, *musannāh* ; Ibn Qutayba, *Tafsīr gharīb al-Qur'ān* (Beirut, 1978), p. 355, *mussannāh* quoting the unattributed line of poetry: "From Saba' who dwelt in Mārib when/they built dams (*'arim*) against its flood"; the same poem and gloss is found in al-Ṭabarī, XXII, 54, and in Ibn Hishām, I, 14, where it is attributed to Umayya ibn Abī'l- Ṣalt or al-Nābigha al-Ja'dī; al-Sijistānī,

mentioned was quite flexible enough in the minds of the commentators to support both the meanings "dams" and "rats"; the exegete provides the chosen gloss and then recounts the same story, regardless of whether the initial gloss is "rats" or "dams". Thus the suggestion that the story itself may well have had an existence probably prior to and most certainly independent of its lexical use would seem to gain further credence. In discussing the meaning "dams", a number of commentators emphasize the point that they consider *'arim* to be a plural[45] and thus they suggest that God planned a wholesale destruction of the entire land of the Yemen through a mass inundation caused by breaking all the dams. At least one text also suggests that the water which flooded the dam was not released from the dam as such but was rather a punishment sent by God from wherever he wished.[46]

Other exegetes, however, are quite explicit in naming the Mārib dam specifically as the one being referred to in the Qur'ān as being destroyed.[47]

There is one observation to make immediately concerning all of the commentators and their discussion of *'arim*: as perhaps would be expected, none of them makes any reference to finding the word in *musnad* inscriptions or the like. The solution that *'arim* means "dam" is certainly not based upon direct philological knowledge. Even those commentators who tell us that *'arim* is a Yemenite or Himyaritic[48] word cannot really be assumed to be

---

p. 141.

45 Abū 'Ubayda, II, 146, singular *'arima* ; Ibn Qutayba, p. 355; al-Bayḍāwī, p. 431; al-Suyūṭī, *Tafsīr al-Jalālayn* (Beirut, n.d.), p. 568. Note also Ibn Khalawayh, *Mukhtaṣar fī shawādhdh al-Qur'ān min kitāb al-badī'* (Cairo, 1934), p. 121, who records a variant, *'arm*, perhaps in an attempt to produce an acceptable plural form?

46 Mujāhid, p. 525: "The red water was not from the dam itself but was a punishment sent by God from wherever He pleased", although this is connected to the gloss *'arim* = water.

47 Implicit in the poem cited in Abū 'Ubayda, II, 146-147; Ibn Hishām, I, 13-14.

48 Al-Bukhārī, VI, 305, *laḥn ahl al-Yaman* ; this is not paralleled in Mujāhid, *Tafsīr* ; al-Ṭabarī, XXII, 54, *kalām Ḥimyar* or *laḥn al-Yaman*. Cf. al-Farrā',

providing linguistic knowledge; the commentators' treatment of the category of "foreign words" was flexible enough to allow any word which was "difficult" to be classed as foreign, with the language of the textual context providing the identification needed. Arthur Jeffery and Lothar Kopf[49] have provided plentiful information to support these skeptical conclusions.

The broader question still remains, however, of whether the commentators are in touch with some sort of "historical memory" concerning the breaking of a dam (the Mārib dam specifically perhaps) or of a multitude of dams which provides them with the gloss of *'arim* meaning "dam".

One thing which argues against such implications of the presence of a historical kernel of truth being taken is that there is a great variance on the part of the commentators in the dating of when this destruction is supposed to have taken place. Each of the suggested dates can be explained by reference to some over-riding concern on the part of the commentators which made them then suggest a given historical period. It should be noted that methodologically, once again, this is a process of looking at the exegetical data and ascertaining what process the exegete goes through to arrive at a given solution.

II, 357, who discusses the readings *maskan*, *maskin* and *masākin* (in Q. 34/15) where the first is said to be in the dialect of the Yemen. Abū 'Ubayda, II, 146–147, who declares *'arim* a "foreign word" and cites the poetry of al-A'sha: "Herein is a moral for whoever looks for it / the dams (*'arim*) that destroyed Mārib / Ḥimyar had built them of marble for them / when the floods rose high they stood fast." Also see Ibn Hishām, I, 13–14.

49 A. Jeffery, *The Foreign Vocabulary of the Qur'ān*, introduction; Lothar Kopf, "Religious influences on medieval Arabic philology," *Studia Islamica*, 5 (1956), 33–59; id., "The treatment of foreign words in medieval Arabic lexicology," in Uriel Heyd (ed.), *Studies in Islamic history and civilization*, Scripta Hierosolymitana, ix (Jerusalem, 1969), pp. 191–205; id., extracts from: "Arabic lexicography – its origin, development, sources and problems" [in Hebrew] in his *Studies in Arabic and Hebrew lexicography*, ed. M.H. Goshen-Gottstein (Jerusalem, 1976), 13–114; the above two articles by Kopf are reprinted in this latter volume, pp. 19–45 and 247–61 respectively. Also see my "Ibn 'Abbās's *Al-Lughāt fī'l-Qur'ān*," *BSOAS*, 44 (1981), 15–25.

Three eras are suggested by the commentators: one, that the destruction occurred well before the reign of Bilqis, the Queen of Sheba; two, that it happened a little while after the famous queen's rule; three, that it took place sometime between the eras of Jesus and Muḥammad.

The second of these solutions, that the destruction occurred after the reign of Bilqis[50] is derived from consideration of the overall context of the Qur'ānic passage. The story of Saba' follows directly after that of David and Solomon and since Solomon and the Queen of Sheba are understood to have met, this destruction must have taken place shortly after that era due to the general flow of the narrative. To Bilqis, also, is often ascribed the actual deed of construction of most of the famous monuments remaining in the Yemen,[51] and the Mārib dam, at least in some people's opinion, was no exception. Therefore, the destruction of the dam must be after Bilqis. Once again, it is primarily the Qur'ānic context which seems to rule out this interpretation.

That the dam was destroyed after the time of Jesus may seem historically more congenial to us in terms of linking it to the Mārib dam but actually the tradition to that effect would seem to owe its origins to rather complicated accounts of Arab genealogical history found in works such as the *Sīra* of Muḥammad. Within Ibn Hishām's version of the text, there is a story concerning the rats and the destruction of the dam, very similar to the one already mentioned.[52] In it, 'Amr ibn Umayra flees out of the Yemen along with the entire tribe of 'Azd. This tribe splits up into various family groups and they become the ancestors of the various

50 Al-Ṭabarī, XXII, 54.

51 Al-Tha'ālibī, III, 244; also see W.M. Watt, "The Queen of Sheba in Islamic Tradition" in J.B. Pritchard (ed.), *Solomon and Sheba* (London, 1974), p. 101.

52 Ibn Hishām, I, 13-14; al-Bayḍāwī, p. 431 (era only briefly noted). Also see al-Suyūṭī, *Lubāb al-nuqūl fī asbāb al-nuzūl* (Beirut, 1983), p. 180 and Ibn Kathīr, III, 531, for a tradition which would seem to be related to this theme, concerning the fear that Sabaic nationalism will rise again and the statement of Muḥammad that the appropriate penalty (viz. as in Q. 34/16) has already been imposed upon them.

Arabian tribes of Central Arabia. So, the historical period suggested may well have been stimulated by various genealogical traditions with their potential political ramifications in early Islam rather than historical memory.

My only suggestion for the first tradition that the destruction occurred well before Bilqis[53] is to say that theological motivations may have coloured the picture here. There may well have been the consideration at play that, since Bilqis was converted from sun-worship to the belief in one God by Solomon, the period after her should have been flourishing due to her right faith. That leaves open only the distant past for the period of the destruction, if the exegete wanted to take into account the full implications of the Qur'ānic story.

As was to be expected, some commentators suggest that there was more than one destruction;[54] conflict can always be resolved by entertaining the possibility of multiple occurrences.

As one final point concerning the exegetical treatment of *'arim*, it is interesting to observe a modern treatment in the context of Western scholarship.

Much of modern scholarship has actually gone much further than simply to identify the word *'arim* as "dam." It has become almost a part of the canon of interpretation to see in this word as used in *sūra* 34/16 a specific reference to the Mārib dam being destroyed sometime after 540 CE but before 610 CE. One prominent study which cites this idea is Richard Baron Jr.'s *Archaeological Discoveries in South Arabia*. The chapter in this book dealing with irrigation systems in ancient Qataban reveals that there is no independent evidence for situating the destruction of the Mārib dam before the rise of Muḥammad; the only concrete evidence for that is the aforementioned Qur'ān reference and a fairly detailed reconstruction-cum-exegesis of the dam by al-Hamdānī.[55] Note that the Qur'ān is also the source for

---

53 Al-Kisā'ī, pp. 286-287.

54 See the account related in G. Weil, *The Bible, the Koran, and the Talmud, or Biblical Legends of the Mussulmans* (London, 1846), pp. 191-194.

55 Richard Baron Jr., *Archaeological Discoveries in South Arabia* (Baltimore, 1958), pp. 70-76; N.A. Faris, *The Antiquities of South Arabia*, p. 34.

the belief that the dam irrigated two fields, as is shown in the sketch map provided in the book, where the "left and right gardens" are irrigated by two sluices. But all this is mere speculation, and assumes that the identification of the Mārib dam with the contents of Qur'ān 34/16 is correct! There is, in other words, no certain evidence involved here. The destruction of dams must have been a common event in pre-Islamic South Arabia and may in time have become vested with a proverbial character in the popular imagination.

In fact, the main thrust of the Qur'ānic passage is, if anything, to emphasize this proverbial character. This Qur'ānic passage referring to Saba' is a stereotyped literary form found throughout the Qur'ān, and is often referred to as the "punishment story" form. The themes, structure, and often the phraseology, of these stories are generally closely contiguous within the form. While the story of Saba' omits mention of the prophet's name and his ultimate fate, the general pattern of the story emerges with clarity. John Wansbrough, in his *Quranic Studies*, advances the idea of the literary motif of the *umam khāliya*, the "lost nations," as part of one of the "four characteristic examples found in the imagery appropriate to the theodicy", that is, the theme of "retribution";[56] this story of Saba' clearly fits into that literary mold.

Additionally, the use of the image of the "two gardens" is not restricted to this one passage concerning Saba'. It is found in the elaborate afterlife picture in *sūra* 55, verses 46–77, and also *sūra* 18, verses 32–33 with its parable of the two gardens. The use of gardens – although not in the dual – is, of course, also common in the Bible, and the Qur'ānic usage may quite simply reflect continued use of the motif. Consequently, the notion that the Qur'ān specifically refers to the Mārib dam seems as implausible as it is unnecessary. Furthermore, the use of an unsubstantiated Qur'ānic interpretation as the basis of archaeological speculation is extremely tenuous; that would seem to be a very basic methodological point.

Some attempt may now be made at drawing some conclusions. It seems plain that any sense of linguistic/philological knowledge of ESA

---

56 J. Wansbrough, *Quranic Studies: Sources and Methods of Scriptural Interpretation* (Oxford, 1977), p. 2 and cf. pp. 3ff.

did not carry over into Islam. This would confirm Beeston's suggestion that the language was already well into a state of decline by the 5th c. CE.

On the more vexed question of "historical memory", it is harder to draw firm conclusions beyond saying that the memory was vague at best. The various historical periods which the exegetes suggest for the destruction of the *'arim*, each of which, I would argue, can be explained by other overriding considerations, does not yield much material in which we may have confidence.[57] This is, perhaps, a situation in which we can reduce the material down to a historical kernel of "truth" – that is the tradition that *'arim* does mean "dam" – which the exegetes are transmitting in various fictitious narratives. That we may only conclude this, however, on the basis of external, philological knowledge which we bring to the narratives is significant; it would still suggest that, as historians, we have no bases for deciding on the "historical kernel" unless we have some other sort of external and neutral verificatory information.

---

57 In reference to the same material, cf. the far more positive statements of Watt, in Pritchard, pp. 89, 100–101.

INDEX OF QURʾĀN CITATIONS

note: Egyptian verse numbering only except Flügel numbering in article IV

INDEX OF ARABIC AUTHORS

INDEX OF ARABIC EXEGETICAL TERMINOLOGY